AMERICAN LITERARY ALMANAC

★★★★★★★★★★★★★★★★★★★★★★★★

AMERICAN LITERARY ALMANAC

FROM 1608 TO THE PRESENT

An Original Compendium Of
Facts And Anecdotes About
Literary Life In
The United States of America

EDITED BY KAREN L. ROOD

A Bruccoli Clark Layman Book

Facts On File
New York ● Oxford

AMERICAN LITERARY ALMANAC

American Literary Almanac

Copyright © 1988 by Bruccoli Clark Layman, Inc.

Library of Congress Cataloging-in-Publication Data

American literary almanac.

"A Bruccoli Clark Layman book."
Bibliography: p.
Includes index.
1. American literature—History and criticism.
2. United States—Intellectual life. 3. Authors, American
—Biography. I. Rood, Karen Lane.
PS92.A38   1988   810'.9   88-3689
ISBN 0-8160-1245-8 hc
ISBN 0-8160-1575-9 pb

British CIP data available on request

Printed in the United States of America

10 9 8 7 6 5 4 3 2 1

For R. M. R. and J. M. R.

CONTENTS

Foreword

This almanac for readers departs from the format of current almanacs—which are almost entirely given over to lists—and returns to the spirit of earlier American almanacs. The history of the genre that follows this foreword demonstrates that the colonial almanacs provided interesting reading matter as well as useful facts.

The *American Literary Almanac* presents an overview of our literature organized by topics. Dr. Johnson declared, "Sir, the biographical part of literature is what I love most." Despite the efforts of schools of modern criticism to isolate the work from its creator, literary biography always multiplies the pleasures and rewards of literature. Literary history is literary biography. Accordingly, this almanac devotes most of its space to aspects of writers' lives.

Written and compiled by literary specialists, the *American Literary Almanac* draws on more than 500 sources to bring together in one volume the most reliable information available: a few myths are shattered in these pages, but more than a few true stories arise in their place. The focus is on major writers, but—realizing that a knowledge of lesser literary figures adds color and texture to our understanding of great authors and their times—we have covered interesting minor writers as well. Though it puts a slightly greater emphasis on the twentieth century, this almanac does not neglect the beginnings of our literature in the seventeenth century, its maturation over the next two centuries into a unique expression of our national identity, and its growth in this century to truly international scope and stature. In striving to record the facts that lie behind the history of American literature we have endeavored to be instructive but not dull, entertaining but not trivial.

This volume will be updated, supplemented, and revised at suitable intervals.

–K.L.R.

Acknowledgments

This book was produced by Bruccoli Clark Layman, Inc.

Production coordinator is Kimberly Casey. Copyediting supervisor is Patricia Coate. Typesetting supervisor is Kathleen M. Flanagan. The production staff includes Rowena Betts, Charles Brower, Cheryl Crombie, Mary S. Dye, Charles Egleston, Gabrielle Elliot, Sarah A. Estes, Cynthia Hallman, Pamela Haynes, Judith K. Ingle, Laura Ingram, Maria Ling, Judith E. McCray, Warren McInnis, Kathy S. Merlette, Sheri Neal, Joycelyn R. Smith, and Virginia Smith. Jean W. Ross is permissions editor. Joseph Caldwell, photography editor, and Joseph Matthew Bruccoli did photographic copy work for the volume.

Jean Rhyne and Judith K. Ingle assisted with the research for the "Schooldays" chapter. Eddie Yeghiayan kindly provided the editor with a copy of his unpublished bibliography of works relating to the Vietnam War. Virginia DeLancey and Roberta Faigle helped with illustrations.

Authors of short sections within chapters are identified by initials:

D. C.	Dennis Camp
J. K. I.	Judith K. Ingle
V. H. J.	Victor H. Jones
S. E. M.	Sanford E. Marovitz
J. R.	Jean Rhyne
K. L. R.	Karen L. Rood

AMERICAN LITERARY ALMANAC

Introduction:
The Origins of
American Almanacs

by BENJAMIN FRANKLIN V

Etymologists have suggested that the word *almanac* evolved from one or more of these languages: Arabic, Greek, Dutch, German, Hebrew, Saxon. No one knows for certain the derivation of the word. What it means is decidedly less ambiguous, although its meaning has changed since Roger Bacon first used it in the thirteenth century. To him, it was a source of astronomical information, a concept that antedates him by millennia. In fact, his sense of the word might be used to argue that the Egyptian pyramids were among the first almanacs, since they served as gnomons, the vertical parts of sundials, and therefore permitted the ancients to tell time. Eventually an almanac became a publication that includes annual information; now the word means a book containing facts that are often, but not always, annual in nature. The *World Almanac,* the *Information Please Almanac,* the *Reader's Digest Almanac,* and other such tomes include data ranging from Academy Award winners to toll-free telephone numbers to the names and dates of famous people to notable athletic accomplishments. Astronomical information is still present, but the section devoted to it is no longer the most lengthy in an almanac. A recent *World Almanac,* for example, devotes 30 of approximately 1,000 pages to astronomical data, or three percent. Times have changed: people do not need to use almanacs for such information, as once they did.

Most books are read; almanacs are used, consulted to find the answer to a specific question—such as Greece's per capita income. Once that information is located, the reader might often ignore the rest of the book, interesting and valuable though the other facts might be, although browsing invariably brings serendipitous delights. Almanacs are therefore the ultimate practical literature. And indeed, practicality is the reason why the Puritans in colonial America so valued them.

While almanacs did not originate in colonial America, from the beginning of printing in Cambridge, in the Massachusetts Bay Colony, almanacs have been of considerable importance in this country. In fact, the second item believed to have been produced by the Cambridge press, the first American press, was an almanac compiled by the mariner William Peirce. If so, an almanac came off the Puritans' press before their first religious publication, *The Whole Booke of Psalmes* (1640), better known as the *Bay Psalm Book,* the first full-length American book. This group of dedicated people, the Puritans, immigrated to the New World to worship as they pleased–religion was their major concern–but they also needed to survive in a new environment. The psalter assisted them with the one; the almanac, with the other. They needed both books.

The Peirce almanac (1639?), of which there are no known copies, was but the first of many seventeenth-century American almanacs. The earliest extant almanac is Samuel Danforth's, which the Cambridge press printed in 1646. And if it is typical of the few American almanacs that apparently preceded it, as

3

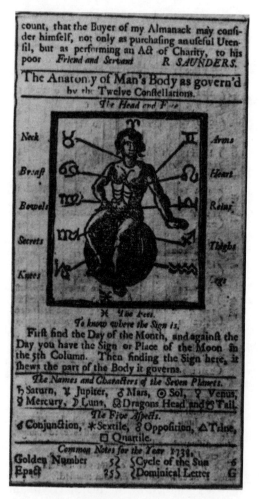

Page from Benjamin Franklin's
first almanac

seems likely, one may conclude that each page in the early almanacs contained information about one month (beginning with March and concluding with February, following the Julian calendar), began with the name of the month and the number of days in it ("The third month called *May* hath xxxi dayes"), told when the sun would rise and set on the first, tenth, and twentieth day of each month, allotted a separate line to each day with approximately every other day having an astrological sign and many days having an occasional comment, and concludes with part of a short essay on the history of calendars ("But wee under the New Testament acknowledge no holy-dayes, ex-

cept the first day of the week only"; 25 December therefore has no special notation). The daily comments in the Danforth almanac range from, in January, "Sun in Aquarius. Full moon the 10 day, 11 *min.* past 5 at night" to, on 6 May, "The Court of ELECTION at Boston. A Fair at Dorchester." In helping the Puritans with their farming and reminding them of significant community events, such publications were invaluable.

The almanac soon became more than just a reference book. The next year the 1647 Danforth almanac included a poem for each month of the year. The poem for March: "A Coal-white Bird appears this spring/That neither cares to sigh or sing./This when the merry Birds espy,/They take her for some enemy./Why so, when as she humbly stands/Only to shake you by your hands?" Other almanac makers began using verse. And as the century progressed, they began adding astronomical essays, lists of England's monarchs, full-page illustrations, advice to farmers, weather forecasts, medical advice, book advertisements, and other features that would appeal to a wide audience.

The 1700 Daniel Leeds almanac is typical of what the almanacs had become by the end of the century. It presents astronomical information, but it has poetry on the title page, a Leeds preface, and an advertisement (for pills "famous for the Cure of *Agues, Feavers, Scurvey, . . . Griping in the Guts, Worms* of all sorts"). Further, it has an essay on the two lunar eclipses of 1700, a two-page list of memorable events and dates, and a list of dates when courts will be held in "West-Jarsey" and Pennsylvania.

Leeds's almanac does not contain the Man of Signs, a feature that first appeared in American almanacs in 1678 (in John Foster's almanac) and soon became popular. The Man of Signs is a naked man with astrological signs attached to or associated with various parts of his body. By consulting this figure and determining when the moon would pass through a certain part of the sky, a reader could determine, ostensibly, which part of his body the moon would influence at a given time.

Almanacs became increasingly comprehensive during the eighteenth century. For example, the *Farmer's Almanac* for 1800 includes all of the categories of information present in the Danforth and Leeds almanacs, but it has an illustrated title page and lists of Friends' meetings, mail stages to and from Boston, and vacations at various colleges (Harvard, Dartmouth, Providence, and Williamstown). It also has two pages devoted to each month (with December as the last month), an expanded coverage of courts, and an agricultural essay ("Of the Plaster of Paris as a Manure"). Further, it includes a letter to the editor, postage rates, currency information, poems, receipts ("To Make Onion Sauce"), mileage from Boston to other towns, advertisements, and anecdotes. An example of the last: "An old lady beholding herself in a looking-glass, espying the wrinkles in her face, threw down the glass in a rage, saying, *it was strange to see the difference of glasses; for,* says she, *I have not looked in a true one these fifteen years.*" Clearly, almanac compilers wished to provide an abundance of useful and entertaining information, which their age required.

While poetry had appeared early in American almanacs, it became a major feature in the eighteenth century. Not inhibited by a copyright, almanac compilers borrowed freely from the best available literature—that is to say, from the esteemed English writers. As a result, almanac readers had access to such recent or current authors as Pope, Dryden, and Addison, and to such earlier poets as Shakespeare and Milton. And since almanac compilers and publishers (often the two were the same person) wanted to sell as many copies of their books as possible, they included material that they thought would attract buyers. Such a strategy indicates that the eighteenth-century American readers' literary tastes were of a high order.

But not all of the almanac verse was of superior quality, nor was all of it imported. Much of it was native. Unfortunately, prerevolutionary America had no bards, although it had an abundance of Pope-inspired poetasters. And aside from Philip Freneau, some of the Connecticut Wits, and possibly one or two others, late-eighteenth-century American poets were also mediocre, at best. These hacks' doggerel appears in the almanacs as frequently as does the good and often great verse. Typical are the opening lines of "An Essay upon the Microscope" in Nathanael Ames's 1741 *Astronomical Diary, or an Almanack:* "Artificer go make a Watch,/In which no seeming imperfection lurks/Whose Wheels with Time exact do onward roll,/And one small Spring maintains the Motion of the whole,/'Tis all an Artless homely Botch/Compared with the least of Natures Works." Too much should therefore not be made of the readers' erudition, although they apparently enjoyed reading poetry.

The Peirce and Danforth almanacs are important because of when they were published. Other early American almanacs are significant for more substantial reasons. The most popular eighteenth-century almanac was—and is— Benjamin Franklin's *Poor Richard's Almanack,* published from 1732, when Franklin was twenty-six, until 1758. As many commentators have noted, Franklin was not a great almanac innovator. Many of his famous aphorisms were borrowed. But one creation accounts for his almanac's immediate and lasting success. In using as his spokesman the unsophisticated yet wise Richard Saunders, Franklin was able to impart his own ideas through a character—a persona— who was one with the readers. Never is there a sense of Franklin preaching to the multitudes, since he is not present in his own voice. His feeling for the common man was as sensitive and accurate as Samuel Clemens's a century and a half later. Both of these authors knew that the vernacular plus basic values plus humor equals literary success. Richard Saunders speaks to the ages, as compilers of literary anthologies regularly attest.

Poor Richard was not the only popular eighteenth-century American almanac. The almanacs created by the two Nathaniel Ameses (*The Astronomical Diary*) were in some ways the equal of Franklin's. Other significant almanacs include those by Benjamin West, in Providence and, as Isaac Bickerstaff, in Boston; Benjamin Banneker, in Philadelphia; and Daniel, Titan, and Felix Leeds, in Philadelphia. Isaiah Thomas, leading publisher and bibliophile, printed and published an almanac in Worcester, Massachusetts, and Boston from 1772 until 1803.

Almanacs have always been and will likely always be a significant genre in America's literature. Those published during the seventeenth and eighteenth centuries, immensely popular reading material that they were, provide substantial information about the nature of the people who compiled and used them, namely their interests and tastes. But one of these almanacs has a special significance. In 1792, during Washington's first term as president, Robert B. Thomas had published, in Boston, the *Farmer's Almanac* for the year 1793. It is still being published as the *Old Farmer's Almanac*, as Thomas retitled it in 1832. Therefore, an almanac is not only probably the second publication in what is now the United States (Peirce's almanac), but another one, Robert Thomas's, is, in all likelihood, the longest-running publication in our history. These facts alone suggest the importance of the almanac in our culture.

First Things First: Milestones in American Literary Culture

by KAREN L. ROOD

1638: FIRST AMERICAN PRESS

The first printing press in the English colonies in North America was established in Cambridge, Massachusetts, in 1638, in one of two houses belonging to Elizabeth Harris Glover, the widow of the Rev. Jose Glover, a dissenting preacher who had died on the voyage from England. Though this first press belonged to Mrs. Glover, the actual running of the press was left to Steven Day, whom the Reverend Glover had hired in England.

The first document printed on this press was the *Oath of a Free-man* (1639), required of all men over twenty who had been householders for at least six months.

Until recently no one believed that any printed copies of this one-page oath existed (the original draft, in the handwriting of John Winthrop, the first governor of the Massachusetts Bay Colony, is at the Boston Public Library). On 2 November 1985 the *New York Times* announced that Mark Hofmann, a rare-manuscript dealer in Salt Lake City, believed that he had bought–for a few dollars in a New York bookshop– one of the copies of the oath printed on Day's press. Although the Library of Congress "found nothing inconsistent with a mid-17th-century attribution" and the American Antiquarian Society agreed that there were "no anomalies," both institutions refused to authenticate the document until they saw the results of tests that would analyze the ink and

provide a computer comparison of the type to that in other documents from the Day press. According to David Hewett, in a two-part article for *Maine Antique Digest* (June-July 1986), Hofmann also claimed to have found a second copy of the oath "in much better shape than the first," but Hewett also reported the statements of expert documents examiners who testified that Hofmann had counterfeited various other documents that he had sold as rare originals. In January 1987 Hofmann pleaded guilty to murder and forgery in connection with the sale of what he had claimed were two rare Mormon church documents.

The next product of Day's press is reported to have been an almanac for 1639 by Capt. William Peirce (or Pierce; in typical seventeenth-century fashion, no one, including the captain himself, worried about consistency in spelling). Though there are no known copies of this almanac, various scholars have estimated its length at anywhere from one to sixteen pages. There has even been some speculation that the almanac contained just maritime calculations, rather than those that would have been useful to farmers.

The first *full-length* book printed in what is now the United States is *The Whole Booke of Psalmes Faithfully Translated into English Metre* (usually called the *Bay Psalm Book*), printed in 1640. Since type had to be made to print the few words of Hebrew in the preface, the *Bay Psalm Book* is also the first book

7

PSALM xxii, xxiii.

25 Concerning thee shall be my prayse
in the great assembly:
before them that him reverence
performe my vowes will I.
26 The meek shall eat & be fatisfi'd:
Iehovah prayse shall they
that doe him seek: your heart shall live
unto perpetuall aye.
27 All ends of th'earth remember shall
and turne unto the Lord:
and thee all heathen-families
to worship shall accord.
28 Becaufe unto Iehovah doth
the kingdome appertaine:
and he among the nations
is ruler Soveraigne.
29 Earths-fat-ones, eat & worship shall:
all who to dust descend,
(though none can make alive his soule)
before his face shall bend.
30 With service a posterity
him shall attend upon:
to God it shall accounted bee
a generation.
31 Come shall they, & his righteousnes
by them declar'd shall bee,
unto a people yet unborne,
that done this thing hath hee.

23 A Pfalme of David.
THe Lord to mee a shepheard is,
want therefore shall not I,

2 Hee

PSALME xxiii, xxiiii.

2 Hee in the folds of tender-grasse,
doth caufe mee downe to lie:
To waters calme me gently leads
3 Restore my soule doth hee:
he doth in paths of righteousnes:
for his names sake leade mee.
4 Yea though in valley of deaths shade
I walk, none ill I'le feare:
becaufe thou art with mee, thy rod,
and staffe my comfort are.
5 For mee a table thou hast spread,
in presence of my foes:
thou dost annoynt my head with oyle,
my cup it over-flowes.
6 Goodnes & mercy surely shall
all my dayes follow mee:
and in the Lords house I shall dwell
so long as dayes shall bee.

Pfalme 24
A pfalme of david.
THe earth Iehovahs is,
and the fulnesse of it:
the habitable world, & they
that there upon doe sit.
2 Becaufe upon the seas,
hee hath it firmly layd:
and it upon the water-floods
most follidly hath stayd.
3 The mountaine of the Lord,
who shall thereto ascend?
and in his place of holynes,

E 2

who

Pages from the
Bay Psalm Book

printed in part from American-made type. It was also the first printed in what is now the United States to include words in a language other than English.

That the first major publishing project the Puritans undertook in the New World was a book of psalms to be sung in church (the near equivalent of a modern hymnbook without the music) seems somewhat surprising. Orthodox Puritans frowned on music in general, and instrumental music was banned from religious services because no justification for such practice could be found in the scriptures. Much of the book's preface (probably written by John Cotton) is devoted to establishing a scriptural basis for the singing of psalms. Recognizing the value of including the congregation in the service through their singing, the Puritan fathers disapproved, however, of the psalter then in general use by the Anglican church because its versions of the psalms were too loosely based on the original Hebrew. Thus, Thomas Welde, John Eliot, and Richard Mather—with the help of such other eminent Puritan divines as John Cotton, Nathaniel Ward, Peter Bulkley, Thomas Shepard, John Norton, and perhaps English poet Francis Quarles—set out to produce their own translation, as close to the Hebrew as they could make it.

As Cotton explained in the preface, "God's altar need not our pollishings." Thus, he added, "wee have respected rather a plaine translation, then to smooth our verses with the sweetness of any paraphrase, and soe have attended Conscience rather than Elegance, fidelity rather than poetry." Modern readers are almost unanimous in agreeing that in their Puritan zeal for accuracy the translators were able to avoid all traces of poetry; though Zoltán Haraszti, whose *The Enigma of the Bay Psalm Book* (1956) is the most comprehensive source of information about our first book, is a strong dissenting voice—arguing that the Puritans' translations in general are not less poetic than those in other seventeenth-century psalters and are sometimes more felicitous.

Whatever its literary merits, the *Bay Psalm Book* was immensely popular, and in various revised and enlarged versions it went through some twenty-five editions (editions published after 1651 are generally called the *New England Psalm Book*). By the mid-eighteenth century the Puritans' psalm book had largely been replaced by the hymnbook of

Isaac Watts, whose verses, and the tunes to which they were sung, were more in keeping with eighteenth-century taste.

1662: FIRST BOOK OF AMERICAN POETRY AND FIRST AMERICAN POETRY BEST-SELLER

The Reverend Michael Wigglesworth's *The Day of Doom*, printed in 1662 by Cambridge printer Samuel Green, is both the first book of original poetry and the first book of poetry by an American to be published in the New World. (Wigglesworth was born in England in 1631 but immigrated to New England with his parents when he was seven and remained there for the rest of his life.)

Like the translators of the *Bay Psalm Book*, Wigglesworth mistrusted fanciful poetic language, writing his epic poem about the Last Judgment in the charac-teristically Puritan "plain style." He began his poem with a prayer to "Christ the Judge of the World," rather than the traditional invocation to the Muses, because, he said, "I do much abominate/ To call the *Muses* to mine aid:/Which is th'Unchristian use, and trade/Of some that Christians would be thought." Indeed, he laments the "deal of Blasphemy, /And Heathenish Impiety" in the works of so-called Christian poets.

If this criticism of fellow poets sounds harsh and narrow-minded, Wigglesworth's serious, didactic poem, in which the reader is not only warned to prepare for the last day but urged to accept the rightness of Calvinist doctrine, found a large and responsive audience. (While it is now hard to believe anyone would willingly read such dreary poetry, it is also true that Wigglesworth's religious fervor does, at times, lend his

WHO PRINTED THE *BAY PSALM BOOK*?

Some historians have insisted that because Steven Day was a locksmith, he was incapable of operating a printing press. He may have put together the press when it arrived in Cambridge and managed the printing business, they say, but the printing was probably done by his son Matthew, who, though only about seventeen in 1638, had had some printing experience in England. Other historians insist that Steven was certainly capable of printing. After all, Samuel Green, who took over the press on Matthew's death in 1649, was largely self-taught except for a few lessons from Matthew, and Steven, if he did know nothing about printing before he was hired to run the press, had access to the same resources.

At any rate, the *Bay Psalm Book* looks as though it could have been printed by either a locksmith or a teenage boy. There are many typographical errors; word breaks at the ends of lines are erratic, and the printer seems to have thought commas and periods were interchangeable and used whichever he picked up first. He does not seem to have realized the necessity of cleaning dried ink off the type, so frequently used letters start to look fuzzy in later pages; he did not ink the type properly, so some pages ended up too light and others too dark. Strangest of all, even given erratic seventeenth-century practices, is the fact that *psalm* is spelled with an *e* on the end at the heads of right-hand pages and without an *e* at the heads of facing pages.

verse an intensity approaching eloquence.)

Often called the first native American "best-seller," *The Day of Doom,* with its descriptions of sinners damned to Hell and saints delighting in God's embrace, was read and reread throughout the colonies and in the Mother Country. Wigglesworth recorded that all 1,800 copies of the first edition were sold within a year of printing. The book was reprinted regularly until 1800. It has been suggested that the reason no copies of the first three, relatively large, editions of the book are in existence is that the poem was so popular, so often read and reread, that the books simply wore out.

1663: FIRST AMERICAN BIBLE

The first Bible printed in what is now the United States was not in English but in the language of the Algonquian Indians. Printed in Cambridge by Samuel Green and Marmaduke Johnson in 1663, it was called *Mamusse wunneetupanatamve Up-Biblum God Naneewe Nukkone Testament Kah Wonk Wusku Testament* (literal translation: "The Whole Holy His-Bible God Both Old Testament and Also New Testament").

Etching based on a portrait by William Whiting

Behold, ye Americans, the greatest honor that ever you were partakers of. The Bible was printed here at our Cambridge, and it is the only Bible that ever was printed in all America, from the very foundation of the world. . . .
    —Cotton Mather on John Eliot's Bible, Magnalia Christi Americana, *1702*

The translation was the work of John Eliot, who had worked on the *Bay Psalm Book* and had begun studying the Algonquian language in the late 1630s so that he could go as a missionary to the tribes of Massachusetts. By 1646 he had learned the language well enough

to preach in it, and he gained an impressive number of converts. But he also believed that true Christians must read the Bible, and here he faced a formidable obstacle: the Algonquians had no written language.

Undismayed, Eliot set out to invent one for them and to teach them how to read it. Beginning in 1654 he had various primers, catechisms, grammars, sermons, and parts of the Bible printed for use of the Indians, but his major work is his 1663 translation of the whole Bible and the revised translation he had printed in 1685. All existing copies of both editions appear to have been much read.

In preparing his translation, as we see in the title, Eliot felt free to substitute English words if he could find no Algonquian equivalents. He also had to deal with cultural differences, having discovered, for example, that people who have never herded animals of any kind did not understand the concept of the Good Shepherd. More flexible and tolerant than some of his fellow Puritans, Eliot, for all his belief in the plain style, sometimes departed from the strictly literal translation that was the norm for the *Bay Psalm Book*. For example, the parable of the Ten Virgins became the parable of the Ten Chaste Young Men because the Algonquians considered male chastity a virtue and female chastity fairly unimportant.

JAMES PRINTER

The son of Naoas, one of John Eliot's Christian Indians, James was born in one of the towns Eliot helped his "Praying Indians" to establish. (The town is now Grafton, Massachusetts.) Educated at the Indian charity school in Cambridge, James had no surname until sometime after 1659, when he became an apprentice to Cambridge printer Samuel Green. People began to call him James the Printer, and he eventually took Printer as his last name. Beginning with the first Algonquian Bible, James Printer, as the only printer who could read the language in which the type had to be set, proved himself indispensable. He took one break from printing in 1675, when he went to fight against the colonists in King Philip's War, but after his side lost he took advantage of an offer for amnesty and in July 1676 returned to work at the Cambridge press. After Samuel Green retired in 1692, Printer went to work with Green's son Bartholomew in Boston. His name appears on only one book, a bilingual edition of the *Massachusetts Psalter* that he and Green printed in 1709.

1665: FIRST AMERICAN PLAY

So many plays from the colonial period were never published and colonial records are so sketchy that it is now impossible to determine the first performance of a play by an American. Puritan New England frowned on playacting, but residents of other colonies sometimes entertained themselves with amateur dramatics. One of the main candidates for the first play by a citizen of what is now the United States is *Ye Bare and Ye Cubb,* probably by William Darby, a citizen of Accomac County, Virginia. No one has ever found the script for this play; its existence is known only because it is mentioned in the colony's legal records. After Darby and two friends performed it on 27 August 1665, they were arrested for their efforts and brought to court several times before they were found "not guilty of fault." Unfortunately the records do not say in what way the court had thought the play might have been objectionable, nor does it give any hints about the subject of *Ye Bare and Ye Cubb.*

1669: FIRST AMERICAN HISTORY BOOK

The first American history book printed in America was Nathaniel Morton's history of the Plymouth Colony, *New England's Memoriall,* printed at Cambridge by Samuel Green and Marmaduke Johnson in 1669. Morton's history was predated by several other histories of colonies in the New World, all printed in London. The most notable of these are John Smith's various books about Virginia and New England (the first of which appeared in 1608), Edward Winslow and William Bradford's 1622 history of the Plymouth Colony, *Mourt's Relations* (so-called because George Morton arranged for its 1622 publication), and Edward Johnson's history of the Massachusetts Bay Colony, *Wonder-*

Working Providence of Sion's Saviour in New England (published in 1654).

While *New England's Memoriall* is often called the first important book of a nonreligious nature (that is, excluding almanacs, primers, and the like) to be published in the American colonies, this history, which served as a standard textbook well into the nineteenth century, had as its motivation the defense of the Plymouth Colony's much-attacked religious separatism.

MARMADUKE JOHNSON

Not all New Englanders were as puritanical and God-fearing as a perusal of these first publications might suggest. A case in point is Marmaduke Johnson. Initially brought over from England to assist Samuel Green in printing the Algonquian Bible, Johnson was the first colonial printer who might actually be called a skilled typographer; but by the standards of some of his neighbors—especially, it seems, Samuel Green—he was also something of a profligate. He was accused of drinking, skipping work, getting into debt, and—the last straw for Green—attempting to seduce Green's daughter with proposals of marriage, despite the fact that he had a wife in London.

Such behavior did not endear Johnson to the authorities. In fact, the first censorship law passed in the colonies was aimed directly at keeping tabs on this one man. In 1665, after Johnson had bought his own press and wanted to set it up in Boston, the Massachusetts General Court passed a law restricting the operation of printing presses to Cambridge (where they could supervise Johnson more closely) and setting up a board of censors to prevent the publication of such "worldly" books as Johnson might try to print. He did try to slip one by the censors in 1668, when he printed without their permission a new edition of Henry Neville's *The Isle of Pines*, a British adventure story that modern scholars have called variously "quasi-erotic" and "innocuous." Johnson's attempt to get around the authorities was unsuccessful, and otherwise he seems to have toed the line well enough. In fact, some historians have suggested that Johnson did not deserve the reputation he gained from his disputes with Green and the censors, pointing out that one of Johnson's most enthusiastic supporters was that purest of Puritans John Eliot. At any rate by 1674 Johnson had sufficiently convinced the authorities of his reliability that they allowed him to set up his press in Boston. He died the same year, and his press and types were sold to John Foster.

1670: FIRST ILLUSTRATED AMERICAN BOOK

The first illustration to appear in an American book was John Foster's woodcut portrait of the first-generation Puritan divine Richard Mather, who had been Foster's pastor. It appeared as the frontispiece to *The Life and Death of That Reverend Man of God, Mr. Richard Mather*, a biography by Richard's son Increase that was printed in 1670 by Cambridge printers Samuel Green and Marmaduke Johnson.

While the portrait is primitive and unflattering—Mather looks rather like a ferret—Foster was considered a good engraver, and, judging by more sophisticated portraits of Increase and his son Cotton, who both had similar noses, Foster's likeness of the first American Mather may well have been true to life.

Foster's knowledge of engraving served him in good stead when in 1674, with little or no experience at the art of printing, he bought the press of the recently deceased Marmaduke Johnson and proceeded to make himself not only the first American engraver but the first Boston printer. His first efforts are considered at least as good as the amateurish productions of Steven and Matthew Day, and his later work as good as anything that had been printed at Cambridge.

Foster scored several other firsts in the history of American book publishing before his death from tuberculosis at the age of thirty-two in 1681.

John Foster's woodcut portrait of
Richard Mather

1677: FIRST AMERICAN MAP

The first map produced in the American colonies was also engraved by John Foster, to illustrate William Hubbard's *A Narrative of the Troubles with the Indians in New-England, from the first planting thereof in the year 1607, to this present year 1677,* printed by Foster in 1677. Foster had trouble reading Hubbard's notoriously bad handwriting and labeled the White Hills the "Wine Hills."

The error was corrected for the London edition, but Hubbard's handwriting continued to be problematic. In 1682 the General Court of Massachusetts refused to pay for the history of New England that they had commissioned until Hubbard presented them with a manuscript they could read. He recopied his history, but even then *A General History of New England from the Discovery to MDCLXXX* remained unpublished until 1815, when the Massachusetts Historical Society took on the task.

In the same year that he completed Hubbard's history of the Indian wars, Foster also printed a broadside that is considered the first medical treatise to be produced in British North America, Thomas Thacher's instruction on treatment for "Small Pocks, or Measles."

In 1678 Foster included in his almanac for that year the first human anatomical chart to be published in what is now the United States. But Foster's most historically interesting production is the first book by a woman printed in America.

1678: FIRST AMERICAN BOOK
BY A WOMAN

John Foster's printing of *Several Poems Compiled with Great Variety of Wit and Learning* is a revised and enlarged edition of Anne Bradstreet's *The Tenth Muse Lately Sprung Up in America,* published in London in 1650. Mrs. Bradstreet had died in 1672 but her beloved husband, Simon, for whom she had written some of her finest poems, was still alive, an influential and respected citizen (he was deputy governor and became governor in 1679).

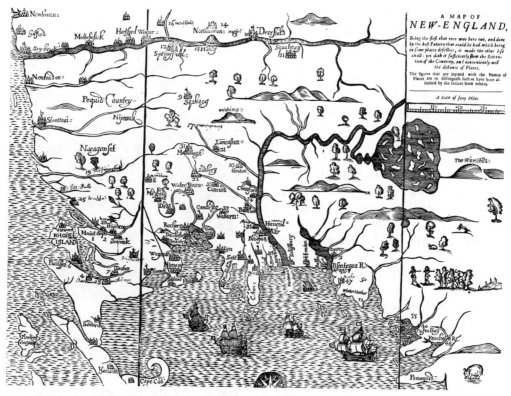

John Foster's map of New England, on which he labeled the White Hills the "Wine Hills" because he had trouble reading William Hubbard's handwriting (courtesy of the John Carter Brown Library at Brown University)

It is worth noting that the poems of Anne Bradstreet are the first by an American that modern readers can be induced to read of their own free will. A somewhat younger colonial poet, Edward Taylor (whose work remained largely unknown until the twentieth century), also has, deservedly, a fair-sized following. Scholars of colonial literature point to two other important seventeenth-century poets, Michael Wigglesworth and Benjamin Tompson, and a number of minor poets, including Nathaniel Ward, John Wilson, Urian Oakes, John James, Philip Pain, Richard Steere, and Joseph Capen. George Sandys, a Virginia Company stockholder who lived in Virginia from 1621 to 1625, could be considered an important American poet, but he is probably more properly considered a British poet because most of his poems were written there and all were published there. While in Virginia he did complete most of his translation of Ovid's *Metamorphoses* (published in 1626), which is considered a major English Renaissance translation.

1682: FIRST WORK BY THE MOST PROLIFIC AMERICAN WRITER

While there are other American authors who have written profusely, including Cotton Mather's father, Increase, who had some 102 separate works published during his lifetime, Cotton Mather, with 444, is probably the most published American writer of all time. (Many of both Mathers' publications are relatively brief pamphlets.)

Cotton Mather's career as an author began in 1682, when John Ratcliff of Boston printed his *A Poem Dedicated to the Memory of the Reverend and Excellent Mr. Urian Oakes,* an elegy for his former teacher, the great Puritan Latin scholar and president of Harvard College. Like most of his writings (and his sermons as well), Mather's poem is long-winded, far longer than most Puritan elegies, and it is clotted with esoteric allusions and rhetorical devices, full of awkward phrasings, ill-chosen rhymes, and rough meters. One of Increase Mather's friends, to whom the proud father had sent the poem, responded that he hoped Cotton was well suited for the ministry because "he will never win the laurel for his poesy."

One thing threatened the younger Mather's success as a religious leader: he stuttered. In fact, he alluded to this speech defect in the first line of his poem—"I the *dumb* son of *Croesus*" (suggesting too his sense of inferiority to his influential and highly respected father). Paradoxically, he himself saw a sort of connection between his difficulty in speaking and his long-windedness: "there is nothing more frequent, than for *stammerers* to speak Ten times more than they need to." His biographer Kenneth Silverman suggests that his extremely prolific writing grew out of a desire to master on the page the language he could not always command orally.

Mather did find success in the pulpit, for the most part overcoming his stutter, though his speech was always extremely slow and deliberate. Never much of a poet, he did develop an eloquent prose style. It was rather "elaborate" for some older Puritans, but Silverman says the first sentence of Mather's magnum opus, *Magnalia Christi Americana: Or the Ecclesiastical History of New-England* (1702), has the epic quality of Virgil. Yet he always went on at length. His *Magnalia Christi Americana* has some 800 pages.

1682: FIRST AMERICAN PROSE BEST-SELLER

The Sovereignty & Goodness of God, Together with the Faithfulness of his Promises Displayed: Being a Narrative of the Captivity and Restauration of Mrs. Mary Rowlandson . . . (the title goes on in characteristic seventeenth-century fashion) is the first example in English (as well as the first printed in North America) of the captivity narrative, which would become a popular and uniquely American genre. First printed by Cambridge printer Samuel Green in 1682, Mrs. Rowlandson's account of her capture by a Wampanoag war party on 20 February 1676 and her two and a half months in captivity has been republished some thirty times.

While all such narratives, including Mary Rowlandson's, appealed to readers hungry for adventure stories, Mrs. Rowlandson, the wife of Puritan pastor Joseph Rowlandson, displayed the usual Puritan talent for turning a good story into a religious tract. Subscribing to a widely held Calvinist precept that her captors were instruments of Satan put on earth to test God's chosen people (i.e., the Puritans), she turned her ordeal (for one thing, her sixteen-year-old daughter died in captivity) into a morally instructive and spiritually satisfying experience. In approximately seventy pages of text she quoted from the Bible more than sixty-five times.

1690: FIRST AMERICAN NEWSPAPER

Authorities in the various colonies were more sensitive to criticism and more wary of rebellion than they were concerned with the people's right to know. Samuel Green was licensed to print a broadside that looked like a newspaper in 1689, but *The Present State of the New-England Affairs* is really just Increase Mather's report on his negotiations in England to secure a new charter for Massachusetts Bay.

Boston bookseller Benjamin Harris did not bother to get a license when he brought out his newspaper, *Publick Occurrences both Foreign and Domestick*, on 25 September 1690. Printed by Richard Pierce, the paper consisted of three printed pages and one blank page and contained the announcement: "It is designed, that the countrey shall be furnished once a moneth (or if any Glut of Occurrences happen, oftener,) with an account of such considerable things as have arrived unto our notice." The governor and his council had different plans for Harris's paper. They were annoyed enough with just the fact that Harris had not gotten a license, and, when they actually read it, they were really angry. For one thing, they said, Harris had printed some "Reflections of a very high nature" (probably the gossip about the morals of the King of France), as well as "sundry doubtful and uncertain Reports." They were especially displeased with a story that accused the Narragansetts, whom they needed as allies, of barbarous treatment of their French captives after a recent battle in King William's War, the first of the French and Indian Wars. As a result, they expressed their "high Resentment and Disallowance of said Pamphlet" and ordered "that the same be suppressed and called in."

Another troublesome item may in fact have been written by Cotton Mather, who, though he was very much a friend of the authorities, felt that the Indian allies had failed to provide all the forces and canoes they had promised. He later denied any involvement with the paper, except, as he wrote ingeniously to his uncle John Cotton, "the publisher had not one line of it from me, only as accidentally meeting him in the highway, on his request, I showed him how to contract and express the report of the expedition."

No more issues of *Publick Occurrences* were published, and Harris came up with another publishing scheme, the first American edition of the uncontroversial and enormously successful textbook *The New England Primer*. His London Coffee House, which he established in his Boston bookshop in 1689, was also a popular meeting place for both sexes, partly because it provided a respectable public place where women and men could socialize (women were not allowed in Boston taverns), and providing coffee, tea, and chocolate also served to boost the sale of Harris's books.

Harris eventually ended up back in England, where he sold "Angelic Pills against all Vapours, Hysterick and Melancholy Fits" and other equally questionable patent medicines. In fact, there was something of the snake-oil salesman in Harris throughout his life, during which he supported a number of unsavory causes. Though Harris made important contributions to the nascence of American literature, historian Frank Luther Mott hit the mark when he noted, "The too frequent occurrence of the ridiculous in the career of Ben Harris prevents our making a hero of him. . . ."

Portrait of Robert Hunter, attributed to Sir Godfrey Kneller (courtesy of the New-York Historical Society)

The first continuing newspaper in the colonies did not appear until 24 April 1704, when Boston's postmaster, John Campbell, brought out the first issue of his *Boston News-Letter*. Campbell had started out by circulating handwritten newsletters, with the help of his brother Duncan as copyist, before he got more ambitious and hired Bartholomew Green to print it. Unlike Harris, Campbell got a license for his paper, and he managed to avoid any serious problems with the authorities. But despite the fact that the *News-Letter* was "Published by Authority," meaning that the governor or his secretary had approved its contents, he did have some minor skirmishes with them. The paper continued under various owners until 1776.

An interesting commentary on the changing connotation of the word *news* is Campbell's reporting of foreign events. The news was two months old before it reached Boston from England anyway, and Campbell was less interested in printing the latest than in getting everything in, in chronological order. With limited space (the *News-Letter* was printed on both sides of a single leaf of paper, maybe five by nine inches) and two suspensions of publication, he had gotten more than a year behind current events by 1718 and noted, in a classic understatement: "After near upon Fourteen years experience, The Undertaker knows that's Impossible with half a Sheet in the week to carry on all the Publick News of Europe." His solution was to add four more pages every other week so that "in a little time, all will become New that u'ed formerly to seem Old."

1714: FIRST PUBLISHED AMERICAN PLAY

Robert Hunter, royal governor of New York and New Jersey from 1710 to 1719, wrote his satirical farce *Androboros* ("Man eater") to sway public

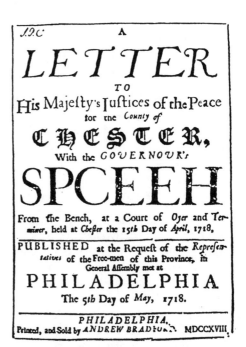

The title page for the first American book printed in color demonstrates that Andrew Bradford could print better than he could spell

opinion in his favor during a dispute which pitted him against not only the legislative assembly and the Anglican church but also the Royal Commissioner of Accounts, General Francis Nicholson, a man noted for his generally vile temper who disliked Hunter. Hunter's play, set in an asylum where the Keeper (Hunter) has uneasy charge over inmates that include Androboros (Nicholson) and various other difficult characters, employed humor to expose his enemies' corruption, and it was an important factor in his restoration of political harmony. Yet, though Hunter's play has some literary and theatrical merit, the true beginning of American drama should probably be considered the professional production of Thomas Godfrey's tragedy *The Prince of Parthia* in 1767.

1718: FIRST AMERICAN BOOK PRINTED IN COLOR

Color printing started off modestly, in 1718, when Andrew Bradford of Philadelphia printed a title page in red and black. Unfortunately for Bradford, he insured his place in history as a bad proofreader as well by making an obvious typo in the largest line of type on the title page for *A Letter to His Majesty's Justices of the Peace for the County of Chester, With the Governor's Spceeh From the Bench.*

1735: FIRST AMERICAN BOOK PRINTED BY A WOMAN

During the colonial period, when the household was usually close to, if not attached to, the family's place of business, it was fairly typical for wives to work with their husbands and to run the business in widowhood.

Though Elizabeth Glover of Cambridge owned the first American press, she had little to do with the actual running of it. Dinah Nuthead, the widow of William Nuthead, the first printer in both Virginia and Maryland, carried on the business after his death in late 1694 or early 1695, an act that says much about her bravery in facing the fact that she had two small children and virtually no inheritance–especially since she could not read or write (though she did know the alphabet). Not surprisingly, her work was crude, and she is not known to have printed any books or pamphlets.

Ann Smith Franklin was a far more accomplished printer. The widow of Benjamin Franklin's older brother James, she helped her husband with the printing, especially during the last years of his life, when he was in ill health. After James Franklin's death in February 1735, Ann Franklin took over the business, in which, according to Isaiah Thomas, the first historian of American printing, she "was aided in her printing by her two daughters, and afterward by her son when he attained to a competent age. Her daughters were correct and quick composers," and, he adds, "sensible and amiable young women."

Ann Franklin's first production was a poem called *A Brief Essay on the Number Seven* (1735), which, despite its intriguing title, no one bothered to save. She became Rhode Island's official printer in 1736, and, though most of the things she printed were fairly short, she proved herself capable of bigger jobs in 1744 when she printed a 308-page volume of Rhode Island acts and laws. She also continued to print the *Poor Robin's Almanac* that James Franklin had started in 1728, and, after the first one she printed, she wrote the almanacs as well.

Whatever reservations she may have had at first about the propriety of putting a woman's name on a title page– she used her husband's name until 1738 and then called herself "Widow Franklin"–in 1758, when she formed a partnership with her son, they listed their names on title pages as "Ann & James Franklin." After her son's death in 1762 she took her son-in-law, Samuel Hall, as a partner and continued in business until her death on 19 April 1763.

1741: FIRST AMERICAN MAGAZINE

The idea for the first American magazine was Benjamin Franklin's, but John Webbe, with whom he had made a preliminary agreement for the editorship, took Franklin's idea to Franklin's rival, Philadelphia printer Andrew Bradford, and asked for better terms. The result of their discussions was Bradford's *American Magazine, or a Monthly View of the Political State of the British Colonies,* edited by Webbe. The *American Magazine* appeared on 13 February 1741, three days before Franklin's *General Magazine, and Historical Chronicle for all the British Plantation in America,* though both monthlies were dated January 1741.

Both magazines were inspired by such successful British magazines as the *Gentleman's Magazine* and the *London Magazine,* though Franklin's imitated them more successfully. The *American Magazine* devoted a major portion of its space to the proceedings of the Pennsyl-

Benjamin Franklin, circa 1738-1746; portrait attributed to Robert Feke (courtesy of The Harvard University Portrait Collection, Bequest of John Collins Warren, 1856)

vania, New Jersey, New York, and Maryland assemblies, and most of the other pages contained rather dry articles on basically noncontroversial political, economic, and religious topics.

Franklin's *General Magazine* also contained proceedings of colonial assemblies (and Parliamentary proceedings), as well as articles on economics and religion, but it devoted less space to them. More prominent were two monthly sections, extracts from books and pamphlets published in the colonies and "Pieces of Poetry" reprinted from American and English newspapers. The magazine also published articles and letters presenting both sides of the paper-currency question (Franklin was for it) and both pro- and anti- views of the religious revivalism of George Whitefield (Franklin liked the man but disagreed with his theology).

Both magazines were short-lived. Bradford's died after three issues; Franklin's lasted through July 1741. The perennial problem–lack of a paying readership–was complicated by another that was to plague American magazines for years–a widely scattered population, bad roads, and an unsympathetic postal system. Postal riders were not required to carry newspapers and magazines, and, as Philadelphia postmaster, Franklin could have refused to accept Bradford's magazines while sending out his own (there is no evidence that he did, however). Even one other of Franklin's advantages, the postmaster's privilege of sending his mail free, could not balance out the problem of revenues that did not meet printing costs.

1743: FIRST AMERICAN BIBLE IN A EUROPEAN LANGUAGE

Printing a book as long as the Bible was an expensive and time-consuming job for the colonial printer, who typically had such a small supply of type that he could print only a few pages at a time. After Samuel Green printed the second edition of the Algonquian Bible in 1685, no other printer attempted the task until the 1740s. Christophe Sauer (he also spelled his name Christoph Saur and later Anglicized it to Christopher Sower), began printing for the Dunkers, or German Baptists, at the press they had established in Germantown, Pennsylvania, in 1738. It took him three years to print the 1,200-copy edition of his Bible, which he finished in 1843. A massive book of 1,286 pages that measure 7¼ by 9¾ inches, it has an elaborate title page printed in red and black.

Sower's son, Christopher Sower II, printed a second edition of 2,000 copies in 1763. British artillerymen seized most of the sheets for his third edition, which he intended to be 3,000 copies, in 1776. They used some sheets for gun wadding, and the rest were later found hid-

BENJAMIN FRANKLIN AND THE *SATURDAY EVENING POST*

If Franklin's one attempt at a magazine occurred in 1741 and was such a disaster that Franklin did not even bother to mention it in his *Autobiography*, why does the *Saturday Evening Post* claim on its front cover and its masthead that it was "Founded A.° D.ⁱ 1728 by Benj. Franklin"? The *Post* draws the line of descent not from the *General Magazine* but from Franklin's newspaper, the *Pennsylvania Gazette*. Even here the magazine is on shaky ground. The *Gazette* was founded in 1728, but by Samuel Keimer, not Benjamin Franklin. After a newspaper war from which Franklin emerged victorious, Keimer sold out to Franklin and his partner Hugh Meredith in 1729. Meredith left the printing business in 1732, and Franklin ran the paper alone until 1748, when he took David Hall as a partner. The Hall family and various partners published the paper until it was discontinued in 1815. Even then David Hall, the grandson of the first David Hall, continued to run his printing business in the paper's printing plant and formed a partnership with Samuel C. Atkinson. Not long after Hall's death in 1821 Atkinson entered into business with Charles Alexander for the purpose of founding the *Saturday Evening Post*. Since Atkinson never had anything to do with the publishing of the *Gazette*, and there is no record of his having worked as a printer for the newspaper (though there is conjecture that he may have) the *Post's* connection to Benjamin Franklin is tenuous.

The whole story dates back to 1884 when two careless historians misread the statement that Hall and Atkinson "carried on the printing business" at the *Gazette's* plant as meaning that the two men were printing the *Gazette*. Of course, if they were, the *Post* would have a legitimate connection with Franklin, but they were not.

Even after this misinformation was published, it was some time before the *Saturday Evening Post* picked it up. An 1891 advertisement mentioned the Franklin story but said the magazine appeared "in its present character in 1821," and the *Post* continued to print "Founded, A. D. 1821" on the first page into 1898. But once the inveterate advertiser Cyrus H. K. Curtis, who had taken over the moribund *Post* in late 1897, heard the Franklin story, he knew that he had found a ready-made tradition. Between 22 January and 29 January in 1898 the weekly magazine aged ninety-three years (Curtis even added ninety-three to the volume number). For about a year the magazine included a note under "Founded A. D. 1728" explaining that Franklin had bought the *Gazette* in 1729, but a year later this cumbersome method was dropped and "Founded A.° D.ⁱ 1728 by Benj. Franklin" (complete with old-fashioned abbreviations to lend further antiquity) was instituted as the official version.

The error of the *Post's* ways has been pointed out many times, and its current publishers can hardly be unaware of the true story. It may be that the words of a few scholars are still outweighed by the publicity value of the Franklin myth.

den in a barn. The only copies of this edition known to exist are the ten saved by Sower's daughter Catharine. Christopher Sower II had no better luck with the other side during the Revolution. Because he was a conscientious objector, a group of patriots descended on his printing plant, destroyed his stock of books, and spread his type over the surrounding countryside.

1760: FIRST PUBLICATION BY AN AFRO-AMERICAN WRITER

Literacy among black slaves during the colonial period was unusual, and the education of slaves was generally frowned upon except in cases where the slave's ability to read, write, and cipher was considered of use to the master. Jupiter Hammon, who was born in 1711 on the estate of the wealthy Lloyd family in Oyster Bay, Long Island, grew up with the two Lloyd sons, his near contemporaries, and learned from their private tutors. It is also thought that he was allowed to study under the teachers sent by the Society for the Propagation of the Gospel, a missionary branch of the Church of England, who arrived in Oyster Bay in 1726.

When he was older Hammon was trusted with the Lloyd's savings and worked as a clerk in the family's business. During the 1730s he found religion and began to preach to his fellow slaves and, some time later, to write poetry. In 1760 he had a poem published after overcoming the obstacles that faced any slave who wanted to have his work printed; he gained the permission of his master and the support of a group of prominent white citizens, who were required to attest to his authorship. *An Evening Thought. Salvation by Christ, with Penetential Cries,* a poem of 88 lines, was published as a broadside on Christmas Day. Written in the jingling meter of hymns and spirituals, the poem is not great literature, but it compares favorably with the religious poetry of the period.

Lewis Hallam, the actor who played the lead in Thomas Godfrey's play

Most of the authenticators of Hammon's work were Oyster Bay Quakers, who were active abolitionists. Though Hammon, who preached only with the acquiescence of his master, stressed that true salvation lay in heaven, his sermons also contained veiled allusions to his opposition to the earthly institution of slavery.

The Lloyd family spent the Revolutionary War years in Hartford, Connecticut, where Hammon had a number of his sermons and poems published as pamphlets or broadsides, including a poem dedicated to his fellow black American poet Phillis Wheatley.

Back in Oyster Bay after the war he disappeared from history after 1790, when he signed a bill of sale. He died some time between then and 1806 when the Quakers included a memorial to him in a reprint of one of his sermons.

1767: FIRST PROFESSIONALLY PRODUCED AMERICAN PLAY

Thomas Godfrey had been dead for nearly four years when his verse tragedy *The Prince of Parthia* was performed by David Douglass's acting company at

Philadelphia's Southwark Theatre on 24 April 1767, making it the first play by an American to receive a professional production.

Though the play does have a political message, it manages to warn against the dangers of allowing a monarch unlimited power without becoming didactic or merely allegorical. While *The Prince of Parthia* is considered a promising play by a promising writer, Godfrey did not live long enough to fulfill that promise, and his play sank into obscurity. Modern dramatists and script writers, who tend to believe that actors get too much of the glory (and the proceeds), may be interested to note that there are no known portraits of Godfrey, but there is one of Lewis Hallam, the actor who played the lead in Godfrey's play.

1770: FIRST PUBLICATION BY AN AFRO-AMERICAN WOMAN WRITER

Unlike Jupiter Hammon, who spent most of his life in obscurity and did not have his first poem published until he was nearly fifty, Phillis Wheatley was lionized in both New England and England and had her first poem published when she was a teenager.

Her early life was inauspicious. She was seized in West Africa and transported to Boston, where Susanna Wheatley, wife of John Wheatley, a well-to-do Boston tailor, bought her for "a trifle" because the slave-ship captain thought she was about to die. Since the child had lost her two front baby teeth, she was judged to be about seven years old.

Nursed back to health by the Wheatleys, Phillis Wheatley lived what by slave standards might be called a pampered existence. She was never entirely excused from domestic work, but once Susanna Wheatley and her children, Nathaniel and Mary, discovered Phillis's extreme intelligence they taught her to read and write. Before long she was reading not only the Bible but works on as-

tronomy, geography, and history, as well as a variety of literature including works by Milton, Pope, Virgil, Ovid, Terence, and Homer.

Her poetry showed the influence of all her reading, as well as her Puritan environment–and she started writing early. When she was about thirteen she had a poem published in a Newport, Rhode Island, newspaper. She achieved larger renown in 1770 (at about sixteen) when her elegy for the well-known evangelist George Whitefield was published as a pamphlet in Boston. It appeared the next year in London, in a volume with Ebenezer Pemberton's funeral sermons for Whitefield.

Through this publication she came to the attention of Selina Hastings, Countess of Huntington, a wealthy abolitionist whom Whitefield had served as chaplain. She made arrangements for the publication of a collection of Wheatley's poems, and on 8 May 1771 the still-frail teenage poet sailed with her mistress's son for London, where she was introduced to British dignitaries as proof that black people could be artistic and intellectual. She also met a fellow American, Benjamin Franklin. Her book, the first by an American black, was printed in London in 1773 for booksellers in London and Boston. More sophisticated than Hammon's poetry, *Poems on Various Subjects, Religious and Moral* is notable for poems that employ classical and neoclassical themes and techniques, as well as those more typically Puritan poems with biblical symbolism. In one of her biblical poems she exhorts her readers, "Remember *Christians, Negroes,* black as *Cain,*/May be refin'd and join th' angelic train."

One result of the appearance of Wheatley's book was her correspondence with George Washington, but the remainder of her life proved unhappy. She was freed three months before Susanna Wheatley's death in March 1774. Though the fact of her slavery had been hateful to her and the Wheatleys had been criticized for not freeing her earlier, they had in fact shielded the poet from the harsh existence that faced free blacks in the hard economic times during and after the Revolution. Mary and John Wheatley died in 1778, and Nathaniel Wheatley went to live in England, leaving Phillis Wheatley without dependable supporters in the white community. In 1778 she married John Peters, an intelligent and ambitious man, whose color made it difficult for him to compete with whites in a tight job market. They slipped farther and farther into poverty; two of their three children died; and the always-frail poet died alone, while her husband was in debtor's prison, on 5 December 1784. Her only surviving child died in time to be buried with her.

1771: FIRST POEM ON THE RISING GLORY OF AMERICA

Early American colonial writing was pretty much like what was being published in seventeenth-century England—but usually not as good. As time went

on though, American speech became noticeably different from British English and by the 1750s inhabitants of the thirteen separate colonies were starting to see themselves, and even the entire North American continent, as a place apart from the Mother Country: A New World free from the Old World's corruptions. Writers began to sing the praises of America, believing that here they could create a utopian society, where the sciences, the arts, and commerce would set standards for the rest of the world.

In 1771 Hugh Henry Brackenridge and Philip Freneau wrote a poem proclaiming that such a utopia could not exist "Till foreign crowns have vanish'd from our view." Not only the first full expression of the American Empire theme, *A Poem, on the Rising Glory of America,* which was delivered at the 1771 commencement exercises at Princeton, gave the whole American genre its name, and marked the end of colonial verse in America.

They were not the only poets to predict that, in a future America, "Paradise anew/Shall flourish, by no second Adam lost," and other writers said it better. Though Freneau went on to write memorable poems and Brackenridge later wrote the ambitious and eccentric prose epic *Modern Chivalry* (1792-1805), their Rising Glory poem is far less memorable than *The Prospect of Peace,* the Rising Glory poem Joel Barlow delivered at Yale in 1778.

1782: FIRST AMERICAN BIBLE IN ENGLISH

The long gap between the establishment of printing in the colonies and the first American edition of the Bible in English was not just the result of the time and money involved in printing it. By British law authorized versions of the Bible could be printed only by a handful of printers (all in England) who were licensed by the king (though this monopoly was sometimes challenged, even by other English printers).

In 1688 William Bradford, who had already gotten into trouble for printing things he was not supposed to and who would continue to do so, printed a proposal for an edition of the Bible. Nothing came of this venture because he could not interest enough people in paying for their copies in advance of publication.

In 1710 Cotton Mather had Bartholomew Green of Boston print a pamphlet called *A New Offer to the Lovers of Religion and Learning,* a prospectus for his massive *Biblia Americana,* his own translation from the original Greek and Hebrew, with extensive annotation and commentary, which he had begun work on in 1695. Because the work was his own translation and included scholarly exegesis, it fell outside the limits of the law. No one in Boston was much interested, and he also failed to find subscribers in England three years later.

About 1752, according to Isaiah Thomas, Samuel Kneeland and Timothy Green, Jr., of Boston printed an edition of the Bible for bookseller Daniel Henchman and ingeniously slipped by the law by putting the name of a London printer on the title page. No copy of this Bible has ever been found (though a forgery was almost passed off as the real thing in 1902), and most historians now believe that it never existed. Thomas, who began his printing apprenticeship in 1756 at the age of six, reported hearing older printers talk of working on it; yet he never saw a copy. Henchman, who had his own book bindery, often saved money by importing sheets of the Bible from England and having them bound in Boston. The misunderstanding could have resulted from this procedure, but one historian has even suggested that the whole story arose as a yarn to impress a young apprentice.

John Fleming of Boston tried, but failed, to interest subscribers in an Amer-

ican edition of the Bible in 1770, but it was not until the outbreak of the Revolution cut off the flow of Bibles from England that there was much interest in an American Bible. During the war Robert Aitken of Philadelphia took advantage of the shortage by printing four editions of the New Testament (in 1777, 1778, 1779, and 1781), and, after they were well received, he petitioned Congress for an official endorsement, which he received, for the whole Bible. He put it together in 1782 by printing copies of the Old Testament and binding them with some copies of his 1781 edition of the New Testament. Despite the Congressional endorsement, the only one the

---

Resolved, That the United States in Congress assembled, highly approve the pious and laudable undertaking of Mr. Aitken, as subservient to the interest of religion, as well as an instance of the progress of arts in this country, and being satisfied from the above report of his care and accuracy in the execution of the work, we recommend this edition of the Bible to the inhabitants of the United States, and hereby authorize him to publish this recommendation in the manner he shall think proper.

—Resolution of the U.S. Congress, 12 September 1782

U.S. Congress ever gave for a Bible, Aitken's Bible did not sell well because, as soon as the Revolution had ended, cheaper imports from England had come back on the American market. Sales did get a boost in 1783, when the Presbyterians of Philadelphia decided to buy only Aitken's Bibles for distribution to the poor.

Three other early American Bibles are worthy of mention. In 1790 Mathew Carey of Philadelphia printed the first American edition of the Catholic Douay Bible. While he was a Catholic himself, he was also an astute businessman and printed several editions of the King James version as well. Another astute businessman, Isaiah Thomas, produced more Bibles than any other eighteenth-century printer, beginning with a popular 1791 edition. In 1790 he made a tremendous financial investment: he hired a London printer to set type for the whole Bible and to ship it to America, where Thomas could keep it standing and ready to print an edition of the Bible whenever he needed one. The shipment of the type proceeded slowly, and Thomas could not complete the first printing of his "Standing Bible" until 1797, but, attractive and priced to sell, it was immediately popular and more than paid back Thomas's investment. Philadelphia's Thomas Dobson produced *Biblia Hebraica,* the first Hebrew Bible printed in the United States, in 1914.

1787: FIRST PROFESSIONALLY PRODUCED AMERICAN COMEDY

Royall Tyler's *The Contrast,* which opened at New York's John Street Theatre on 16 April 1787, was both the first comedy by an American and the first play on a native subject to be performed by a professional company. The play, which is often called the beginning of the American tradition of social comedy, was well received by late-eighteenth-century audiences. They laughed at Colonel Henry Manly, an honorable Revolutionary War veteran given to excessive Fourth of July rhetoric, and his backwoods Yankee servant, Jonathan. But they cheered when Billy Dimple, the dissolute young fop who had been scheming to make Manly's sister his mistress, got his comeuppance, and the virtuous Colonel Manly won the hand and fortune of the equally virtuous, if exceedingly sentimental, Maria Van Rough. The characters in Tyler's play became patterns for American character types that persisted in American comedy well into the twentieth century.

Tyler had no further success in drama, though he achieved some ac-

An 1870 engraving by Samuel Holyer, copied from a miniature on ivory made during Tyler's lifetime

claim for his novel *The Algerian Captive* (1797), the first American novel to be reprinted in England, and became a respected jurist.

1789: FIRST PLAY BY A PROFESSIONAL AMERICAN PLAYWRIGHT

The first American dramatist to make a living (more or less) as a professional playwright was William Dunlap, usually considered the Father of American Drama. Dunlap's first attempt at a long play, which was never produced, was inspired by Tyler's *The Contrast,* and he continued to follow Tyler's lead in employing American characters and settings in many of his later plays.

Dunlap's *The Father; or, American Shandyism,* the second comedy by an American to receive a professional production, was well received when it opened at the John Street Theatre in New York. Though, as its title suggests, the play is written in the spirit of Laurence Sterne's novel *Tristram Shandy*

The Artist Showing a Picture from Hamlet *to His Parents,* painting by William Dunlap, circa 1788 (courtesy of the New-York Historical Society)

(1759-1767), the characters and setting are American, and there are references to issues of the day, including the new Constitution. A play of entangled plots having to do with the various love intrigues of master, mistress, and friends—as well as similar situations among the servants—and with the master's discovery of his long-lost son, *The Father* ends with the reconciliation of master and mistress, and a tongue-in-cheek epilogue warning the audience that public approval of a play by an American will make them appear uncultured.

1789: FIRST AMERICAN NOVEL

The first novel set in America, printed in America, and written by an American is William Hill Brown's *The Power of Sympathy,* printed in 1789 by Isaiah Thomas and Company of Boston, still a bastion of Puritanism, where more than a few of its citizens equated fiction with lies. Brown attempted to forestall this charge by stating on the title page that his story was "Founded in Truth," and he excused his subject—seduction and incest—by claiming that his novel "exposed the dangerous Consequences of SEDUCTION" and proved "the Advantages of FEMALE EDUCATION."

Part of *The Power of Sympathy* was *too*

true in the eyes of two of Boston's most prominent families. The heroine of Brown's novel discovers, before consummation of their love, that she is the illegitimate daughter of her suitor's father, but the novel also contains another incest story, based on an incident in Boston's Apthorp and Morton families, where such a union actually took place.

As a neighbor, Brown had certainly heard stories of how Frances Theodora (Fanny) Apthorp was seduced by Perez Morton, a distinguished citizen who was married to Fanny's sister, the noted poet Sarah Wentworth Morton. After Fanny gave birth to Perez's child, her father scheduled a meeting of all concerned parties, planning to insist on a settlement, but Fanny poisoned herself and died to avoid the confrontation.

Brown's account, in letters 21-23 of his epistolary novel, calls Fanny "Ophelia" and renames the other characters as well, but most Bostonians of the Apthorps' social class must certainly have recognized the story. In fact, the publisher must have counted on it because he included an engraving of the death of Ophelia as the frontispiece, rather than illustrating an episode from the main plot. The Apthorps and Mortons were upset enough to try to suppress the book, but their actions were ineffective, and many copies of the first edition survive today.

Brown wisely chose to have his novel published anonymously (though the Apthorps are said to have discovered his authorship), and during the nineteenth century *The Power of Sympathy* was often attributed to Sarah Wentworth Morton, who, having chosen to remain with her husband and weather out the scandal, would seem to be the last person to spread the story of her husband's philandering.

OTHER CANDIDATES FOR THE FIRST AMERICAN NOVEL

The Power of Sympathy is the first novel that can be considered wholly American: not only is its author an American who set his tale in his native land, but his novel was written and published in America as well.

There were at least two novels by writers born in America published before *The Power of Sympathy*: Charlotte Ramsay Lennox's *The Life of Harriet Stuart*, published in London in 1751, and Thomas Atwood Digges's *Adventures of Alonso*, published in 1775, also in London.

Though Lennox was born in what is now New York State and her novel contains some scenes set in America, she was not strictly speaking a citizen of the colonies. Her father was a British army officer, who took her back to England when she was fifteen, and she never returned to the land of her birth.

Thomas Digges's novel probably has a greater claim to be identified as the first American novel. Yet Digges, a native of Maryland (and a friend of George Washington's) wrote his novel while he was living in Portugal, and none of it is set in America.

1794: FIRST BEST-SELLING AMERICAN NOVEL

Susanna Haswell Rowson's *Charlotte. A Tale of Truth* was little noticed when it appeared in London in 1791, but when Philadelphia publisher Mathew Carey brought out a new edition in 1794 it was a runaway success. Better known as *Charlotte Temple*, the title it was given in later editions, the novel had gone through more than two hundred editions and reprintings by the middle of the nineteenth century.

In many ways a typical sentimental tale of seduction and betrayal, the novel may, at least in part, owe its greater popularity in the United States to the fact that its villain is Lieutenant Montraville, a British soldier who comes to the New World to fight in the American Revolution, bringing with him a fifteen-year-old girl whom he has persuaded to elope with him. Montraville abandons Charlotte in New York, and she dies in childbirth, but only after a tearful deathbed reunion with her father, who forgives her. He also refuses to take revenge on Montraville, and, pointing to her grave, he exclaims, "Look on that little heap of earth, there hast thou buried the only joy of a fond father."

Appealing to the rather maudlin popular tastes of the first half of the nineteenth century, *Charlotte* is believed to be a roman à clef (literally, novel with a key) based on the story of Charlotte Stanley, who eloped with John Montrésor, Rowson's cousin. Pilgrimages to Charlotte Stanley's grave in the graveyard of New York's Trinity Church became popular with many of the novel's readers. Forming a sort of "Charlotte cult," they were so moved by the fictional Charlotte's death that they felt compelled to visit what they considered the final resting place of that "only joy of a fond father."

Rowson drew on the divided loyalties to England and America that she had experienced in her own youth. Born in En-

Susanna Haswell Rowson

gland, she was brought to America when she was five. Because her father, who was a revenue collector for the Royal Navy, remained a Loyalist after the outbreak of the Revolution, the family was interned and deported to England in 1778, when Susanna was eighteen. By the time she and her husband William Rowson, joined Philadelphia's New Theatre Company as actors in 1793, she had published six novels and two volumes of poetry. Back in America she had soon completed *Slaves in Algiers, or A Struggle for Freedom*, a popular play that expressed her patriotic devotion to the New Republic—a sentiment that is combined in *Charlotte* with nostalgia for the Old World.

Rowson continued to write, but in 1797 she left the stage to establish The Young Girl's Academy in Boston, where she was soon educating the daughters of that city's best families. In addition to writing fiction and poetry, she published textbooks for the use of her young ladies, was an editor of the *Boston*

Weekly Magazine, and contributed essays to the *New England Galaxy*. Though she later came to be regarded—perhaps unjustly—as just another "female scribbler," at her death in 1824 she was highly regarded as a member of Boston's literary establishment.

1798: FIRST AMERICAN GOTHIC NOVEL

At a time when the New Republic's literati were calling for a new national literature with American themes and settings, but English Gothic novels were much in vogue with the country's reading public, Charles Brockden Brown, America's first professional man of letters, transferred the horror and violence of the Gothic genre, with its reliance on supernatural effects, from the ruins and subterranean passageways of medieval European castles to a suburb of his native Philadelphia, a pleasant country estate on the Schuylkill River.

Filled with mysterious voices, only some of which are explained by the presence of an ambiguously sinister ventriloquist, and climaxed by a violent mass murder, Brown's novel warns against extremism of any stripe—from rationalism to religious fanaticism. Still readable and hair-raising today, *Wieland* is the beginning of a long American Gothic tradition, which extends through Edgar Allan Poe and Nathaniel Hawthorne on up to Joyce Carol Oates and beyond. In recent years the term *Gothic* has been applied to romances that bear little resemblance to the original Gothic form.

1827: FIRST AMERICAN SCIENCE-FICTION NOVEL

Edgar Allan Poe's "The Unparalleled Adventure of One Hans Pfaall," published in the June 1835 issue of the *Southern Literary Messenger*, is often called the beginning of American science fiction, but is is actually preceded by another story of interplanetary travel, *A Voyage to the Moon*, published in 1827 under the pseudonym Joseph Atterley, by Poe's fellow Virginian George Tucker, Professor of Moral Philosophy at the University of Virginia. Poe refers disparagingly to Tucker's novel in one of his notes to "Hans Pfaall"; yet, like some literary critics since his day, he had read the review but not the book.

Like "Hans Pfaall," Tucker's novel is a satire, and *A Voyage to the Moon* has more in common with *Gulliver's Travels* than with modern science fiction, as Tucker's descriptions of moon life allow him to make known his attitudes on political and economic issues, social, scientific, and religious fads and fanaticisms, and even women's fashions. Yet Tucker went to some effort to create the *sense* of reality in his narrator's discovery of a Hindu holy man and their trip to the moon in a flying machine propelled by a rare metal that, once purified, flies off the earth and is attracted to the moon. And at other points in his novel he employs a number of the scientific theories of his day. In fact the anonymous au-

thor of one of the novel's two reviews wished that the book had footnotes to identify some of the objects of its satire, but he loved the sci-fi aspects of the book.

1841: FIRST AMERICAN DETECTIVE STORY

Edgar Allan Poe's short story "The Murders in the Rue Morgue," first published in the April 1841 issue of *Graham's Magazine* and later collected in *The Prose Romances of Edgar A. Poe* (Philadelphia, 1843), is not only the first detective story published in the United States but the first published anywhere in the world.

Poe set his tale in Paris (he had read some passages from the memoir of the French Minister of Police in *Burton's Gentleman's Magazine* the year before), and for years since, American tourists in Paris have been disappointed to discover that there is no rue Morgue in Paris and never has been.

Poe's story established the archetype that detective stories still imitate today. Among its most copied elements are: 1) the brilliant amateur detective who notices and analyzes every little detail of the crime; 2) his naive friend who has to have everything explained to him (a device that is helpful to the reader as well); 3) incompetent policemen; and 4) the use of a sealed room for the scene of the crime.

1858: FIRST PUBLICATION OF AN AFRO-AMERICAN PLAY

The first published play by a black American is William Wells Brown's *The Escape; or, A Leap for Freedom,* published by the Boston company R. F. Wallcut in 1858. Brown, who had escaped slavery at nineteen and become a prominent Abolitionist, employed both comedy and satire in his melodrama about two slaves who secretly marry and eventually, after much suffering under their master's bondage, escape to Canada. The second

Portrait by James Sharples, circa January 1798 (courtesy of the Worcester Art Museum, Worcester, Massachusetts)

scene in act two is one of the most point-edly satiric: A sanctimonious preacher traveling south by riverboat to hold a revival meeting in Natchez meets a slave trader and asks him "What kind of niggers sells best. . . ?" because, he explains, "it's a long way down to Natchez, and I thought I'd just buy five or six niggers, and take 'em down and sell 'em to pay my travellin' expenses. . . ." At the heart of the play is the warning that slaves are not the contented, light-hearted people their masters would have them seem: "there is a volcano pent up in the heart of the slaves of these Southern States that will burst forth ere long."

Brown had learned young about the black's status as a nonperson. In the narrative of his slavery that he had published in 1847 he recounted not only the various abuses and separations heaped upon himself and his family, but an event that affected him even more deeply, the loss of his only possession, his name. The son of a slave

Very truly your friend,
Wm. Wells Brown.

named Elizabeth and his master's first cousin, John W. Higgins, he was given the name William (slaves did not have surnames). Later, however, his master and mistress adopted a nephew named William and to avoid confusion (William the slave was not only light complected but his master's first-cousin-once-removed) they decided to call their slave Sanford instead.

Brown later retook his original name, and after his escape added "Wells Brown" to it in honor of the Quaker who had sheltered him during his escape. He also learned to use the black's nonperson status to his own advantage and to treat it with considerable wit in his life as well as in his writings. On a lecture tour in Ohio in the summer of 1844 Brown was told he could not ride in the passenger cars with the white train passengers and ended up riding in an open freight car instead. When the conductor asked him to pay the coach fare of $1.25, Brown refused and asked the shipping charge for freight. The conductor said that it was 25¢ per 100 pounds, and Brown, who weighed 150 pounds, gave him 37½¢.

1859: FIRST AMERICAN PUBLICATION OF AN AFRO-AMERICAN NOVEL

The first novel by a black American to be published in the United States is *Our Nig; or, Sketches from the Life of a free Black, in a Two-Story White House, North. Showing That Slavery's Shadows Fall Even There,* published under the pseudonym "Our Nig" by Harriet E. Wilson, who paid the Boston firm of G. C. Rand & Avery to print it for her in 1859. Suffering from continuing ill-health that had prevented her from working and caring for her seven-year-old son, Mrs. Wilson expressed in her preface the hope that the novel would make enough money to "aid me in maintaining myself and child without extinguishing this feeble life," and she appealed "to my colored bretheren universally for patronage, hoping they will not condemn this attempt of their sister to be erudite. . . ."

The cause for her illness was said to be the harsh treatment she received when, after the death of her black father, her white mother abandoned her at the house of a family who took in the seven-year-old as a sort of indentured servant and overworked her until she reached eighteen. The novel is a fictionalized version of her childhood, and Wilson is clearly embittered, but she lovingly portrays the family members who had been kind to her and had tried to protect her from the cruel mistress of the household. Fearing that she might "palliate slavery at the South, by disclosures of its appurtenances North," she insisted, "My mistress was wholly imbued with *Southern* principles." But she also subtly criticized well-intentioned but ineffectual Abolitionists when she commented, "I have purposely omitted what would most provoke shame in our good anti-slavery friends at home."

Wilson's novel reveals her to be widely read and especially familiar with the nineteenth-century sentimental novel, of which her own book is a well-written example. Yet, like most privately published books, it received little notice. Henry Louis Gates, Jr., who discovered the novel and edited it for republication in 1983, suggests another reason as well: miscegenation. In depicting the marriage of her heroine's white mother and black father (and, especially, one suspects, in making the father close to saintly and the mother a weak woman who, after her husband's death, slides closer and closer to depravity), Wilson treated a subject that both proslavery and antislavery forces viewed with extreme discomfort. Yet the subject had been treated before and in another novel by a black American.

While Wilson was the first black to have a novel published in the United States, and the first black American woman to have a novel published anywhere, William Wells Brown, rightfully called the first Afro-American novelist,

had a novel published in 1853 in England, where he was then living at least somewhat against his will.

When he sailed for England to preach his Abolitionist's message in 1849, Brown had been living as a freeman in the North since 1833, but he was still legally the property of his Southern master, who had learned he was living in Boston and sent a letter, offering to sell him his freedom. In 1850 the passage of the Fugitive Slave Law, which made it legal for an escaped slave to be captured anywhere in the United States and returned to his owner, made Brown's presence in the United States seem precarious to his freedom, and he decided to extend his stay in England. He remained until July 1854, when, as the result of extended negotiation, the by-then famous Abolitionist was finally able to buy his "freedom" for $300.

Despite the reason for his five-year-stay, Brown's years in England had been fruitful. Not only had he sent his daughters to school in France and England and traveled about meeting influential people in England and on the Continent, but he had published two books: *Three Years in Europe* (1852), a well-received travel book composed of letters to his friends, and the book for which he is now remembered, *Clotel; or, The President's Daughter: A Narrative of Slave Life in the United States* (1853). The novel did not appear in the United States until 1860 when a revised and retitled version was serialized as *Miralda*. Two further revisions, both published under the title *Clotelle*, appeared in 1864 and 1867.

Like Wilson's later novel, *Clotel* faces miscegenation head on and in an even more controversial manner. In making his heroine, Clotel, the daughter of Thomas Jefferson and a black mistress, Brown may have helped to perpetuate a story that modern historians still argue over. Whether or not Brown's story is literally true, its suggestion that the greatest symbols of this nation's values are

31

tainted by the fact of slavery has metaphorical validity.

Brown intended his novel "to show that the present system of chattel slavery in America undermines the entire social condition of man," and he drew extensively upon his own experiences. Indeed, he has been accused of trying to fit too much into one novel. Overshadowed by Harriet Beecher Stowe's *Uncle Tom's Cabin* (1852) and probably too melodramatic for the tastes of most twentieth-century readers, *Clotel* is still a ground-breaking novel, all the more effective for its basis in firsthand experience.

1860: FIRST AMERICAN PAPERBACK

Scholars have disagreed on what to identify as the first published paperback book. Throughout the colonial period books were sold either bound or in paper wrappers (with the expectation that the purchaser would have them bound to complement the other books in his library). Not all these books in wrappers were bound, of course, and such items as almanacs, political, religious, and educational pamphlets, and tracts were always sold unbound, sometimes with stiffer paper covers. Perhaps the best candidate for the first full-length paperback book in America was the first Dime Novel, published on 9 June 1860 by Irwin P. Beadle and his brother Erastus. They started their Dime Novels series by publishing 10,000 copies of *Maleska: The Indian Wife of the White Hunter,* by the then-famous novelist Ann S. Stephens. The novel had been popular when it had been serialized in the February-April 1839 issues of the *Ladies' Companion,* but now, advertised as "The Best Story of the Day" by the "Star of American Authors," its success was phenomenal. The first 10,000 copies sold immediately; 20,000 more were printed and sold just as quickly. Something in the neighborhood of 300,000 copies of this ten-cent edition

eventually sold and after the Beadles reprinted the novel in several more-expensive editions sales reached close to half a million.

Popular in America and England, Ann Sophia Stephens was called "the best novelist of America." One writer even claimed that "no writer, since Sir Walter Scott, has excelled her." Today's reader would be more likely to agree with Poe, who noted, "Her style is what the critics usually term 'powerful,' but . . . is in fact generally turgid." Her style–strong sensationalism combined with a decorous moral tone–and her subject matter–experience on the American frontier–were, the Beadles correctly recognized, exactly what the American public wanted to read and *Maleska* set the tone for the rest of the Dime Novel series.

This series and its imitators looked more like newspaper supplements than modern paperbacks. Printed on the cheapest paper available, they did not have stiff covers and had fewer and larger pages than today's paperbound books. In fact they were closer to the size of modern comic books.

1867: FIRST AMERICAN DETECTIVE NOVEL

The Leavenworth Case (1878), by Anna Katharine Green, has long been called not only the first full-length detective novel by an American but also the first detective novel by a woman. Ebenezer Gryce, the detective introduced in *The Leavenworth Case*, continues to be well-known among mystery readers, but another, more obscure book is actually ahead on both counts. *The Dead Letter*, published in 1867 under the pseudonym Seeley Regester, has been overlooked because no one knew that Seeley Regester was both an American and a woman: Metta Victoria Fuller Victor.

1895: FIRST AMERICAN BEST-SELLER LIST

When the new American periodical the *Bookman* published its first issue in February 1895 the term *best-seller* was yet to be coined, but the magazine published what is now considered the first best-sellers list. It was actually a series of lists included in an "Eastern Letter" from New York, in a "Western Letter" from Chicago, and in "English Notes," each reporting the books that had sold well in local stores the previous month. These reports were also followed by twenty shorter lists reporting the top six sellers in various larger American cities during the same period. All the lists were quite similar. On the New York list for January 1895 were:

George Du Maurier, *Trilby*
Anthony Hope, *The Prisoner of Zenda*
Hall Caine, *The Manxman*
Anthony Hope, *The Dolly Dialogues*
H. W. Nevinson, *Slum Stories of London*
Ian Maclaren, *Beside the Bonnie Brier Bush*

W. Clark Russell, *The Good Ship Mohock*
F. Marion Crawford, *The Ralstons*
James Bryce, *The American Commonwealth*, revised edition
George Du Maurier, *Peter Ibbetson*
Marie Corelli, *Barabbas*
A. Conan Doyle, *The Adventures of Sherlock Holmes*
John Kendrick Bangs, *Coffee and Repartee*
Robert S. Hichens, *The Green Carnation*
Henry Drummond, *The Ascent of Man*
Benjamin Kidd, *Social Evolution*, revised edition

Like the New York list, the Chicago list was dominated by fiction, though the Chicagoans' tastes seemed to tend slightly more toward American authors:

George DuMaurier, *Trilby*
Hall Caine, *The Manxman*
A. Conan Doyle, *Round the Red Lamp*
Clara Louise Burnham, *Sweet Clover*
Captain Charles King, *Under Fire*
Mary Wilkins Freeman, *Pembroke*
John Kendrick Bangs, *Coffee and Repartee* and *Three Weeks in Politics*
James Lane Allen, *A Kentucky Cardinal*
William Dean Howells, *Traveller from Altruia*
Ian Maclaren, *Beside the Bonnie Brier Bush*
Anthony Hope, *The Prisoner of Zenda* and *Indiscretions of the Duchess*
Elizabeth Wormley Latimer, *England in the Nineteenth-Century*
Constance Carey Harrison, *A Bachelor Maid*
Christine Terhune Herrick, *The Chafing Dish Supper*
Baron Meneval, *Memoirs of Napoleon I*

Hamilton W. Mabie, *My Study Fire,* second series

1911: FIRST MODERN-AMERICAN SCIENCE-FICTION NOVEL

Though the claim has been disputed, Hugo Gernsback–inventor of the first home radio set and the first usable walkie-talkie–has often been credited with writing the first modern science-fiction novel: in the sense that the technology employed in the novel operates according to principles known to modern science. Gernsback's novel *Ralph 124C 41+* (one to foresee for one plus), which was serialized in his magazine *Modern Electrics* from April 1911 through March 1912, predicted a large number of then-uninvented technical advances, including microfilm, tape recorders, radar, jukeboxes, and telephones with television screens. In fact, many readers have noted that, while Gernsback billed his novel as "A Romance of the Year 2660," what there is of the novel's plot–a rather conventional and insipid love story–is totally eclipsed by Gernsback's descriptions and explanations of a vast number of gadgets. While some readers have bemoaned this emphasis on technology, Gernsback did begin the trend toward scientific accuracy, a characteristic that established science fiction as a genre apart from the more general category of fantasy fiction.

Gernsback also started the first magazine devoted solely to science fiction, *Amazing Stories,* in 1926, and in 1929 he named the genre his magazine published *science fiction* (until then he had called it *scientifiction*).

1915: FIRST AMERICAN PULP DETECTIVE MAGAZINE

The first pulp magazine that published exclusively detective fiction was launched on 5 October 1915, when Street and Smith converted their nickel weekly series, *Nick Carter Stories,* into the semimonthly magazine *Detective Story Magazine* (by the time it folded, after 1,057 issues, in summer 1949, the magazine was a quarterly).

A relative of the old-fashioned dime novel, the nickel weekly was a pamphlet of sixteen or thirty-two pages (about 8½ x 11 inches), which, unlike a magazine, contained only one 30,000-to-50,000-word story (though by the 1910s the nickel weekly often included fillers and an episode of a serial as well as the lead story). The popular detective Nick Carter had appeared in pulp fiction by several authors using various pen names since 1880, and his adventures started appearing as nickel weeklies in 1915. By that time, however, Street and Smith saw that their nickel weeklies were becoming less popular and decided to convert them into magazines whose more diverse contents would have broader appeal.

Detective Story Magazine still published stories about Nick Carter. In fact, it held onto Nick Carter fans by carrying over a serial begun in the last issue of

Hugo Gernsback

Nick Carter Stories, and for some time it maintained the fiction that the magazine was edited by "Nicholas Carter," who also wrote some of the stories. But Nick Carter gradually became more sophisticated than he had been in the nickel weeklies aimed at a juvenile audience. Longer than a nickel weekly (the first issue was 128 pages), *Detective Story Weekly* from the start included stories about other detectives as well. In the course of its long life it published the work of many well-known American and British detective writers, including Carolyn Wells, Sax Rohmer, Agatha Christie, Dorothy L. Sayers, Carroll John Daly, and Cornell Woolrich.

1923: FIRST AMERICAN HARD-BOILED DETECTIVE FICTION

Just as Poe invented detective fiction, another American, Carroll John Daly, discarded the gentleman investigator in favor of the tough, cynical wise guy, as often at odds with the law as the criminals and willing to take the law into his own hands. Daly introduced the hard-boiled detective in "Three Gun Terry," published in the 15 May 1923 issue of *Black Mask* magazine. His tough-talking Terry Mack lays out his basic philosophy in the first sentence: "My life is my own, and the opinions of others don't interest me; so don't form any, or if you do, keep them to yourself."

Later in 1923 Daly invented another hard-boiled detective, Race Williams, who was the hero of the first hard-boiled detective novel, Daly's *The Snarl of the Beast,* published by Edward J. Clode, Inc., of New York in 1927. Like Terry Mack, Race Williams operates in a gray area between legality and illegality: "My position is not exactly a healthy one. The police don't like me. The crooks don't like me. I'm just a halfway house between the law and crime. . . . My ethics are my own . . . and I'll shoot it out with any gun in the city–any time, any place."

While Daly is worthy of recognition for his invention of the hard-boiled genre, his writing is artificial and melodramatic, his characters wooden, and his dialogue stilted–and his female characters, when he tried to introduce them, were laughable. Dashiell Hammett's and Raymond Chandler's hard-boiled fiction is read with pleasure today–and assigned reading in college literature classes–but Daly slid into an obscurity that is likely to last. During the 1950s Daly considered it ironic that Mickey Spillane, who acknowledged that Race Williams was the model for his Mike Hammer, was making a fortune "writing about *my* detective." Yet he overlooked the fact that Spillane had successfully introduced the element of raw sex into the old formula.

1926: FIRST MODERN BOOK CLUB

Harry Scherman learned a valuable lesson from his success with the Little Leather Library (cheap editions of the classics sold by mail, as well as in drugstores and Woolworth stores): Americans would buy more books, and would in fact be repeat customers, if they could be reached by mail. In 1926 he founded the Book-of-the-Month Club, with the express purpose of reaching the market that the bookstores were missing.

I turned out to be particularly good at selling books by mail. . . . I had always noticed how people could be influenced to read books by what is said about them.

–Harry Scherman

Two elements in his plan were responsible for his success. The first was the unique, negative-option distribution system that Scherman invented. As the original prospectus describes it, each subscriber is sent a description of the book selected for the month, and, if it is

Painting by Joseph Hirsch of the Book-of-the-Month Club's original officers and selection committee: *(left to right)* Robert K. Haas, Harry Scherman, Christopher Morley, William Allen White, Heywood Broun, Dorothy Canfield Fisher, Henry Seidel Canby (courtesy of the Book-of-the-Month Club)

BOOK-OF-THE-MONTH CLUB
SELECTIONS FOR 1926

April: Sylvia Townsend Warner, *Lolly Willowes*

May: T. S. Stribling, *Teeftallow*

June: Esther Forbes, *O Genteel Lady*

July: Walter Noble Burns, *The Saga of Billy the Kid*

August: John Galsworthy, *The Silver Spoon*

September: Edna Ferber, *Show Boat*

October: Elizabeth Madox Roberts, *The Time of Man*

November: Ellen Glasgow, *The Romantic Comedians*

December: Elinor Wylie, *The Orphaned Angel*

"a book he would probably like," he "does nothing." On the other hand a subscriber who does not want the book must respond, and if he forgets, the book arrives anyway. The first bulletin also offered five "supplementary books" that subscribers could order in addition to, or instead of, the main selection. This list was the precursor of the larger catalogue of alternative books now offered in each month's *BOMC News.*

Scherman also wanted "to provide an authority" that would convince the public that the selections he sent out each month "were going to be books that good readers wouldn't want to miss," and he concluded that a selection committee comprised of literary people would lend his enterprise some cultural class. The first committee, later called the board of judges, was chosen by Scherman's business associate, publisher Robert K. Haas, who served as the company's first president. The five-member committee included two of the founders of the *Saturday Review*, critic Henry Seidel Canby and man of letters Christopher Morley, whose "The Bowling Green" column was one of the magazine's most popular features; Heywood Broun, whose books, columns, and articles had established him as both a drama critic and a champion of social justice; William Allen White, famous author and crusading editor of the *Emporia Gazette;* and New England novelist Dorothy Canfield Fisher, whose literary reputation was nearing its highest point. One critic, Richard Rovere, suggested that the group, informally chaired by Canby, "carried the stamp of culture without being too frighteningly highbrow" and suggested "literature with a strong dash of journalism: bookish taste with the homely Emporia touch. . . ."

The committee was afraid at first that they would be merely figureheads, but their independence was established with their first choice, Sylvia Townsend Warner's novel *Lolly Willowes*, which Fisher later called "delightful" despite "a mystical and almost incomprehensible treatment." Scherman accepted their choice without question and sent the book to the 4,750 charter subscribers. It "came back in droves," he said later. The next month Haas came to the committee's defense when a woman complained that there were thirteen indecent scenes in the May selection, T. S. Stribling's *Teeftallow.* "There were only twelve," he responded. "I don't care what a subscriber says about one of our books, but it should be accurate." A 1927 selection, *The Heart of Emerson's Journals,* edited by Bliss Perry, topped *Lolly Willowes* for subscriber indifference. "It took us years to get rid of that one," Scherman said later.

Other early selections were more popular: by the end of 1926 the club had 45,000 subscribers; by the end of 1927 there were 60,000. In fact, during the BOMC's first decade 93 of the 143 choices became best-sellers—including

---

CLIFTON FADIMAN'S LIST OF THE BEST BOMC SELECTIONS SINCE 1966

Edmund Morris, *The Rise of Theodore Roosevelt* (1979)

William Styron, *Sophie's Choice* (1979)

Robert Stone, *A Flag for Sunrise* (1981)

Isaac Bashevis Singer, *The Collected Stories* (1982)

Robert A. Caro, *The Path to Power,* volume 1 of *The Years of Lyndon Johnson* (1982)

Morris L. West, *The World Is Made of Glass* (1983)

Daniel J. Boorstin, *The Discoverers* (1983)

Frederick Forsyth, *The Day of the Jackal* (1971)

Gore Vidal, *Burr* (1973)

Annie Dillard, *Pilgrim at Tinker Creek* (1974)

George F, Kennan, *Memoirs: 1925-1950* (1967)

Mary Renault, *Fire from Heaven* (1969)

Lewis Mumford, *The Myth of the Machine* (1967)

E. L. Doctorow, *Ragtime* (1975)

Saul Bellow, *Humboldt's Gift* (1975)

John Fowles, *Daniel Martin* (1977)

Aleksandr Solzhenitsyn, *The First Circle* (1968)

—reported in A Family of Readers *(1986), by William Zinsser*

Elmer Gantry by Sinclair Lewis, *Grand Hotel* by Vicki Baum, *The Good Earth* by Pearl Buck, *Mutiny on the Bounty* by Charles Nordhoff and James Norman Hall, and *Anthony Adverse* by Hervey Allen. And by its sixtieth anniversary in 1986 BOMC had distributed 440 million books. Its all-time most popular book has been William L. Shirer's *The Rise and Fall of the Third Reich.* Since the book was offered as a Main Selection in 1960, BOMC has distributed more than 1.5 million copies.

One 1951 selection, J. D. Salinger's *The Catcher in the Rye,* proved to be a "sleeper," and, in fact, many members turned it down. Fearing that club members would not want the book, Scherman and other BOMC officials asked Salinger to give it a less ambiguous title. "Holden Caulfield wouldn't like that," Salinger responded.

1932: FIRST AFRO-AMERICAN DETECTIVE NOVEL

The first detective novel by a black American writer is *The Conjure-Man Dies: A Mystery Tale of Dark Harlem* (Covici-Friede, 1932) by Rudolf Fisher, a young New York doctor whose first novel, *The Walls of Jericho* (Knopf, 1928), had been widely praised for its depiction of life in Harlem during what is now recognized as the Harlem Renaissance. Returning to the same locale for *The Conjure-Man Dies* and focusing on two of the black working-class characters from *The Walls of Jericho,* Jinx Jones and Bubber Brown, Fisher wrote a complexly plotted novel that combines the conventions of detective fiction with descriptions of street life and night life in Harlem. When Jinx Jones is framed for the conjure man's murder, Dr. John Archer, a persona for Fisher himself, solves the case with the help of his friend detective Perry Dart. Fisher planned to write at least two more Archer-Dart detective novels, but at the time of his death in 1934 at the age of thirty-seven he had completed only "John Archer's Nose," a novelette that appeared in the January 1935 issue of *Metropolitan* magazine, and a stage adaptation of *The Conjure-Man Dies,* which proved extremely popular when it opened in Harlem in 1936.

1939: FIRST MODERN-AMERICAN MASS-MARKET PAPERBACK PUBLISHER

Though other publishers had dabbled,

largely unsuccessfully, in paperback publishing, the first major American company established solely for the purpose of publishing paperbacks was Pocket Books, modeled after the popular British Penguin Books founded in 1935. The brain child of Robert Fair DeGraff, the company was formed with three directors of the hardcover publishing company Simon and Schuster: Richard L. Simon, M. Lincoln Schuster, and Leon Shimkin. Unlike earlier twentieth-century paperbacks, which were about the size of *Reader's Digest* (and employed a similar two-column page format), Pocket Books were small enough to fit in a man's pocket or a woman's purse, and, as DeGraff explained, "We stressed the desirability of a portable book and went against tradition by using the lightest possible paper rather than a bulky paper which heretofore had been common practice."

In September 1938 DeGraff tested the market by publishing a 2,000-copy edition of Pearl Buck's *The Good Earth.* Sales for the twenty-five-cent book were encouraging, and in June 1939 Pocket Books published its first ten books, in editions of 10,000 copies of each book (except for Dorothy Parker's *Enough*

THE FIRST TEN POCKET BOOKS

James Hilton, *Lost Horizon*
Dorothea Brand, *Wake Up and Live*
William Shakespeare, *Five Great Tragedies*
Thorne Smith, *Topper*
Agatha Christie, *The Murder of Roger Ackroyd*
Dorothy Parker, *Enough Rope*
Emily Brontë, *Wuthering Heights*
Samuel Butler, *The Way of All Flesh*
Thornton Wilder, *The Bridge of San Luis Rey*
Felix Salten, *Bambi*

The evolution of Gertrude (courtesy of Pocket Books)

Rope, published in an edition of 7,600 copies).

At first the books were distributed by the American News Company, but finding this arrangement unsatisfactory, DeGraff contracted with independent distributors. By 1941 there were 600 all over the country, insuring that the books appeared in even the smallest and most rural towns.

Pocket Books survived the paper shortages of World War II and proved to be enormously successful. Dr. Benjamin Spock's *Pocket Book of Baby and Child Care* (1946) is the all-time paperback bestseller. By the end of 1982 it had sold thirty-two million copies.

The first Pocket Book logo was a bespectacled kangaroo named Gertrude, who is reading one book and carrying another in her pouch. (Her designer, Frank H. Leiberman, named her after his mother-in-law.) Gertrude has been redesigned over the years. In 1942-1943 she was dropped, but she reappeared in 1943, still wearing her eyeglasses and carrying in her pouch a baby who holds her book for her. Legend has it that some readers thought this situation was "unhygienic," so in 1945 Gertrude's baby was replaced by the original book, and not only is she reduced to holding her reading material herself, but she is forced to do so without her glasses because someone decided that her spectacles might suggest that reading Pocket Books caused eyestrain. In 1977 her books were taken away as well, but in August 1986 they were returned to her.

Though paperback companies at first reprinted books that had already been successful in hardcover, they eventually began publishing original works as well. Fawcett's Gold Medal Books were the first successful original paperbacks. Novelists whose work has been published as Gold Medal Books include Kurt Vonnegut, W. R. Burnett, Taylor Caldwell, Mackinlay Kantor, John D. MacDonald, and Louis L'Amour.

1982: FIRST AMERICAN COMPUTER NOVEL

In late 1982 The Source, a subsidiary of Reader's Digest Association located in McLean, Virginia, announced that in addition to the variety of other data bases it had available for computer users, the company's 24,000 subscribers could read a novel on their television or home-computer screens simply by placing a telephone call to The Source.

Canadian Burke Campbell wrote his novel in less than three days on an Apple III personal computer, finishing it at 11:07 A.M. on 17 November 1982, and The Source made it available to subscribers at 8:30 P.M. on the same day. Only 20,000 words–really a long short story–*Blind Pharaoh* shows the effects of its hasty composition.

E. B. and Katharine White (courtesy of Cornell University Library)

William Faulkner (back row, center) with his younger brothers Murry (left), John (right), and Dean (front), circa 1911-1912

Henry and William James, circa 1901

All in the Family: Writers Related to Writers

by MORRIS P. COLDEN

Whether as a result of environment or heredity, America has produced writing families. Among the most noteworthy are the Mathers, Irvings, Lowells, and Lardners.

The Mathers were a dynasty of Puritan divines, all of whom wrote theological treatises, history, and even verse. The most famous and prolific Mather, Cotton (1663-1728), was the son of Increase Mather and the grandson of Richard Mather. Cotton's son Samuel continued the family tradition.

Washington Irving (1783-1859) was the most successful member of another writing clan. His brother William wrote verse; brother Peter was a journalist and wrote romances. Pierre M. Irving, the son of William, wrote his uncle's biography and edited his posthumously published work. Washington's nephew John Treat Irving wrote sketches about the frontier and the Dutch settlers.

James Russell Lowell (1819-1891) and novelist-poet Robert Traill Spence Lowell were brothers; and James was married to poet Maria White Lowell. Poet Amy Lowell (1874-1925) was the sister of Abbott Lawrence Lowell, political scientist and president of Harvard. Poet Robert Lowell (1917-1977), Amy's cousin and the grandson of R. T. S. Lowell, brought two more writers into the flock by marrying Jean Stafford and Elizabeth Hardwick.

The four sons of Ring Lardner (1885-1933) became writers. James and David were journalists killed in war; John was a prominent columnist; and Ring, Jr., is an Academy Award winning screenwriter. Ring Lardner's grandchildren are also writing.

Ring Lardner and sons, 1923: Ring, Jr.; James; David; and John (courtesy of Ring Lardner, Jr.)

BROTHERS AND SISTERS

Journalist Samuel Ward and Julia Ward Howe ("The Battle Hymn of the Republic")

Novelists Susan B. Warner and Anna B. Warner

Editor-story writer N. P. Willis and story writer Sara Payson Willis (Fanny Fern); she married biographer James Parton.

Yiddish novelists Isaac Bashevis Singer and I. J. Singer

Novelist Henry James and philosopher William James; their father, Henry James, Sr., wrote religious works; their sister, Alice James, is now well known for the diary she kept during the last years of her life.

Poet and novelist Wallace Irwin and journalist Will Irwin

Samuel Longfellow wrote books of hymns and a biography of his brother Henry Wadsworth Longfellow.

William Faulkner's brother John was a novelist; they were the great-grandsons of Col. William C. Falkner (*The White Rose of Memphis*, 1880).

Frank Norris's younger brother Charles was a novelist and was married to popular novelist Kathleen Norris.

Critic Gilbert Seldes and journalist George Seldes

Poets Alice and Phoebe Cary

Journalists Hutchins and Norman Hapgood

Edward Everett Hale ("The Man Without a Country," 1863) was the brother of Lucretia Peabody Hale (*The Peterkin Papers*, 1880). His granddaughter is novelist Nancy Hale. Edward Everett, Edward Everett Hale's uncle, was an editor, orator, and president of Harvard—as well as governor of Massachusetts, Secretary of State, and U.S. Senator.

Ernest Hemingway's brother Leicester published a novel.

Poet Stephen Vincent Benét and editor William Rose Benét

Harriet Beecher Stowe and preacher Henry Ward Beecher.

Novelists Alexander and Paul Theroux

SONS AND DAUGHTERS

Novelist Owen Johnson (*Stover at Yale*, 1911) was the son of editor and poet Robert Underwood Johnson.

Joseph Kirkland (*Zury*, 1887) was the son of Caroline Kirkland, who wrote books about frontier life.

Novelist Susan Fenimore Cooper was the daughter of James Fenimore Cooper.

Novelist Julian Hawthorne was Nathaniel Hawthorne's son.

Novelist John Phillips (John Phillips Marquand, Jr.) is John P. Marquand's son.

Novelist Nathaniel Benchley was the son of humorist Robert Benchley; novelist Peter Benchley (*Jaws*) is Nathaniel's son.

Vladimir Nabokov's son Dmitri is his father's translator.

Dog-story writer Albert Payson Terhune was the son of novelist Mary Virginia Terhune (Marion Harland).

Louisa May Alcott was the daughter of transcendentalist Bronson Alcott.

Novelist Nathaniel Beverley Tucker was the son of poet and jurist St. George Tucker. They were related to novelist and historian George Tucker.

Poet Peter Viereck is the son of poet and novelist George Sylvester Viereck.

Novelist Wells Lewis was the son of Sinclair Lewis.

Novelist Elizabeth Stuart Phelps Ward was the daughter of novelist Elizabeth Stuart Phelps.

Richard Henry Dana, Jr. (*Two Years Before the Mast*, 1840) was the son of poet and editor Richard Henry Dana, Sr.

IN-LAWS

S. J. Perelman married Nathanael West's sister; West married novelist Ruth McKenney's sister, the heroine of *My Sister Eileen*.

Nathaniel Hawthorne was the brother-in-law of educators Horace Mann and Elizabeth Palmer Peabody.

WEDLOCK

Given their communion of interests and social opportunities, it is not surprising that writers marry each other. The record of two literary careers in one family has been mixed.

Ernest Hemingway's third wife was novelist Martha Gellhorn (divorced).

Novelist Jean Stafford married poet Robert Lowell (divorced) and reporter A. J. Liebling.

Novelists Gordon Hall Gerould and Katherine Fullerton Gerould

Caroline Gordon and Allen Tate at the University of North Carolina at Greensboro, 1938 (courtesy of Princeton University Library)

Mystery writers Ross Macdonald and Margaret Millar

Robert Penn Warren and novelist Eleanor Clark

Critics Diana Trilling and Lionel Trilling

Fiction writer Shirley Jackson and critic Stanley Edgar Hyman

Novelist Mary McCarthy and critic Edmund Wilson (divorced)

Dashiell Hammett and Lillian Hellman did not marry but were long-time companions. (She had been married to humorist Arthur Kober.)

Playwrights Albert Hackett and Frances Goodrich were husband and wife as well as collaborators.

Editors E. B. White and Katharine White of the *New Yorker*

Sinclair Lewis and political writer Dorothy Thompson (divorced)

Critic William Rose Benét and poet Elinor Wylie

Novelists Jane Bowles and Paul Bowles

Novelists Joan Didion and John Gregory Dunne

Poet Allen Tate and novelist Caroline Gordon were married, divorced, remarried, and redivorced.

Poet H. D. (Hilda Doolittle) and English novelist Richard Aldington; novelist Robert McAlmon and English novelist Bryher (Winifred Ellerman). After their divorces H. D. and Bryher became long-term companions.

Novelist Kay Boyle had a child out of wedlock by editor-poet Ernest Walsh. She subsequently married poet Laurence Vail.

Poets Sylvia Plath and Ted Hughes (divorced).

HAMMETT'S TIPS FOR MYSTERY WRITERS

As a reviewer of mystery fiction for the *New York Evening Post* in 1930 Dashiell Hammett was frequently dismayed by the blunders he encountered. He was moved to publish these "suggestions that might be of value to somebody" in the 7 June and 3 July issues.

(1) There was an automatic revolver, the Webley-Fosbery, made in England some years ago. The ordinary automatic pistol, however, is not a revolver. A pistol, to be a revolver, must have something on it that revolves.

(2) The Colt's .45 automatic pistol has no chambers. The cartridges are put in a magazine.

(3) A silencer may be attached to a revolver, but the effect will be altogether negligible. I have never seen a silencer used on an automatic pistol, but am told it would still make quite a bit of noise. "Silencer" is a rather optimistic name for this device which has generally fallen into disuse.

(4) When a bullet from a Colt's .45, or any firearm of approximately the same size and power, hits you, even if not in a fatal spot, it usually knocks you over. It is quite upsetting at any reasonable range.

(5) A shot or stab wound is simply felt as a blow or push at first. It is some little time before any burning or other painful sensation begins.

(6) When you are knocked unconscious you do not feel the blow that does it.

(7) A wound made after death of the wounded is usually recognizable as such.

(8) Fingerprints of any value to the police are seldom found on anybody's skin.

(9) The pupils of many drug-addicts' eyes are apparently normal.

(10) It is impossible to see anything by the flash of an ordinary gun, though it is easy to imagine you have seen things.

(11) Not nearly so much can be seen by moonlight as you imagine. This is especially true of colors.

(12) All Federal snoopers are not members of the Secret Service. That branch is chiefly occupied with pursuing counterfeiters and guarding Presidents and prominent visitors to our shores.

(13) A sheriff is a county officer who usually has no official connection with city, town or state police.

(14) Federal prisoners convicted in Washington, D.C., are usually sent to the Atlanta prison and not to Leavenworth.

(15) The California State prison at San Quentin is used for convicts serving first terms. Two-time losers are usually sent to Folsom.

(16) Ventriloquists do not actually "throw" their voices and such doubtful illusions as they manage depend on their gestures. Nothing at all could be done by a ventriloquist standing behind his audience.

(17) Even detectives who drop their final g's should not be made to say "anythin' "–an oddity that calls for vocal acrobatics.

(18) "Youse" is the plural of "you."

(19) A trained detective shadowing a subject does not ordinarily leap from doorway to doorway and does not hide behind trees and poles. He knows no harm is done if the subject sees him now and then.

(20) The current practice in most places in the United States is to make the coroner's inquest an empty formality in which nothing much is brought out except that somebody has died.

(21) Fingerprints are fragile affairs. Wrapping a pistol or other small object up in a handkerchief is much more likely to obliterate than to preserve any prints it may have.

(22) When an automatic pistol is fired the empty cartridge-shell flies out the right-hand side. The empty cartridge-case remains in a revolver until ejected by hand.

(23) A lawyer cannot impeach his own witness.

(24) The length of time a corpse has been a corpse can be approximated by an experienced physician, but only approximated, and the longer it has been a corpse, the less accurate the approximation is likely to be.

Schooldays

by KAREN L. ROOD

OLD BOYS AND GIRLS: WHO WENT TO COLLEGE AND WHERE

This section includes lists of writers (and a few notable editors) who attended more than two hundred colleges and universities in the United States and, in some cases, brief articles about writers' activities inside and outside of the classroom. It is arranged in alphabetical order by school, with each school listed under the name by which it is now known. For example, Philip Freneau, who studied at Princeton when it was called the College of New Jersey, is listed with later alumni under Princeton University; Radcliffe alumnae are listed under Harvard University. Dates for degrees are the years in which writers actually received them, not necessarily the dates that appear on their diplomas. For example, Allen Tate was in the class of 1922 at Vanderbilt, but illness prevented him from completing his course work in time to graduate with his class. His diploma, awarded in 1923, was dated 1922. In cases where a writer attended a school but did not receive a degree there, dates of attendance are included. These listings do not necessarily imply that the writer was a full-time student, only that the author was enrolled in at least one course during each calendar year that follows his or her name.

ALFRED UNIVERSITY

Marvin Bell, 1958*

AMERICAN UNIVERSITY

Alice B. Sheldon (James Tiptree, Jr.), 1959
Ann Beattie, 1969

AMHERST COLLEGE

Richard Wilbur, 1942
James Merrill, 1947

ANTIOCH UNIVERSITY

Mark Strand, 1957

ATLANTA JUNIOR COLLEGE

Boyd B. Upchurch (John Boyd), attended 1938-1940

*Unless otherwise stated, the year following an author's name is the date for his or her bachelor's degree.

ATLANTA UNIVERSITY

James Weldon Johnson, 1894
Walter White, 1916

BALDWIN-WALLACE COLLEGE

Lee Pennington, attended 1958

BARD COLLEGE

Anthony Hecht, 1944
Joan Williams, 1950

BARNARD COLLEGE

Babette Deutsch, 1917
Léonie Adams, 1922
Zora Neale Hurston, 1928
Hortense Calisher, 1932
Janet Burroway, 1958
Erica Jong, 1963
Paulette Williams (Ntozake Shange), 1970
Mary Gordon, 1971

BATES COLLEGE

Gladys Hasty Carroll, 1925
John Ciardi, attended 1934-1936

BELOIT
COLLEGE

Lorine Niedecker, attended 1922-1924

BENNINGTON
COLLEGE

Sandra Hochman, 1957

BEREA
COLLEGE

Lee Pennington, 1962

BETHANY
COLLEGE
(Bethany, West Virginia)

Caroline Gordon, 1916

BLACK
MOUNTAIN
COLLEGE

James Leo Herlihy, attended 1947-1948
Joel Oppenheimer, attended 1950-1953
Edward Dorn, 1954
Robert Creeley, 1955
Michael Rumaker, 1955
John Wieners, attended 1955-1956

The Black Mountain Poets

Can writing be taught? Certainly many of the finest American writers never set foot in college classrooms or left college before graduating. Many of them, and many of their college-educated fellows, would probably say they became writers in spite of, not because of, whatever they were taught about writing and literature in school—in fact many writers have said exactly that. Yet whenever creative minds come together exciting and innovative things are likely to happen, and more than once the locations of such events have been college classrooms.

On the surface at least, Black Mountain College, a tiny unaccredited school in a tiny North Carolina town, seems an unlikely birthplace for a literary movement. Yet in the 1950s it gave its name to one of the most important groups of post-World War II poets, and the college's entire twenty-three-year history could be viewed as a preparation for that event.

Always controversial from the time it opened its doors in the autumn of 1933 until it closed down twenty-three years later, Black Mountain College was, appropriately enough, born of the controversy that followed the firing of Professor John Andrew Rice by Rollins College, whose president, Hamilton Holt, called the classics professor "disruptive of that school's peace and harmony." Rice's appeal to the American Association of University Professors resulted in a public hearing before two representatives of the AAUP–Arthur O. Lovejoy, the highly respected professor of philosophy, and Austin S. Edwards, a psychology professor–at which Holt specified for the first time the charges against Rice. They included allegations that he had called a chisel one of the most beautiful objects in the world, had suggested saving time in the courting process by pairing off male and female students as soon as they enrolled for freshman year, had called public debate "a pernicious form of intellectual perversion," had hung "obscene" pictures in his classroom, had convinced one coed to quit her sorority, had an "indolent" walk, had left fish scales in the sink at the college's beach cottage, and had worn a jockstrap on the beach.

Lovejoy dismissed the first charge, explaining to President Holt that Plato had once said something similar about an ashcan (both represent "perfect mating of form and function"), and Rice answered the last by vehemently declaring "I have never worn a jockstrap in my life." He dealt with the other charges as well, denying some and explaining his conduct on others. While Rice was clearly iconoclastic–and, as he admitted later, arrogant, outspoken, and sarcastic–the investigators eventually found that

Dan Rice and Robert Creeley at Black Mountain College, 1955 (photograph by Jonathan Williams)

Holt had not shown sufficient cause to deprive Rice, a tenured professor, of his position. When that decision was announced, Holt, rather than accepting it gracefully, embarked on a campaign against Rice supporters. By mid June 1933 eight more faculty members had been fired, had their resignations requested, or quit in disgust, and Rice, along with three of these eight professors, had decided to start their own college, taking with them quite a few Rollins students.

Opening their new school in a group of rented buildings near the town of Black Mountain, North Carolina (the school moved to its own campus on nearby Lake Eden in 1941), the rebels conceived of Black Mountain College as both smaller and more democratic than other schools, a community in which teachers and students would live and work together, breaking down the barriers between classroom instruction and extracurricular activities.

Founded by individualists, the school quickly attracted more of them to both its faculty and its student body, and in its small closed environment there were, over the years, constant disagreements about the precise definition of the college's goals and how they should be achieved, ending more than once in sizeable exoduses of students and teachers forced out by the winning faction. Yet despite prevailing controversy beneath the surface, frequent shortages of funds, and Black Mountain's failure to receive accreditation (faculty salaries were too low; the library was too small; there was not enough science equipment), Black Mountain College did win respect for its programs. Within a few years many schools followed Harvard in accepting Black Mountain students for graduate study and gave transfer students from Black Mountain credit for courses taken there.

Though the college is now best known as the birthplace of the so-called Black Mountain School of Poets (some of the poets usually included in the group never set foot in Black Mountain), it was known primarily in the 1930s and 1940s for its art curriculum, developed by Bauhaus artist Joseph Albers, whose hiring by Rice in 1933 allowed him to escape Nazi Germany and who managed to be a dominant force at the college despite his virtual inability to speak English. (Kenneth Noland and Robert Rauschenberg are probably the best-known artists to come out of Black Mountain College.) Some noted writers and critics, including Edward Dahlberg, Fielding Dawson, and Alfred Kazin, taught at the college in the 1940s (one writer who attended the school in the late 1940s was James Leo Herlihy), but it was not until Charles Olson, who had first taught there for the 1948-1949 academic year, became rector in 1951 that writing dominated the curriculum.

A highly unorthodox teacher, whom Dahlberg once referred to disparagingly as the "Stuffed Cyclops of Gloucester," Olson had detractors among the student population as well. Francine du Plessix Gray, who spent the summers of 1951 and 1952 at one of Black Mountain's well-known summer institutes, found that Olson's emphasis on self-expression encouraged narcissism in his young students and resulted in poetry that she characterized as "pure messy noise" (or, as another student put it, "There's not enough character here and too much personality"). Even Olson's admirers found his charismatic, domineering presence and the power of his poetry somewhat daunting. Poet Jonathan Williams, who calls Olson "an extremely enkindling man, marvelously quick and responsive," also says, "It took me a long time to get out from under Leviathan J. Olson."

Yet, despite the charges that Olson was primarily interested in gaining disciples and that his students were merely Olson imitators, he emphasized the necessity for finding one's own poetic voice, stressing to his students that "writing traditional forms makes for rhetoric.

The alternative is to write as you breathe. Either one is good if it is done well in its way. Form is then the skin or the how of the art. Your rut is much more important. And this is arrived at by the sharp influx of things . . . ." As an example of what he meant by this "sharp influx of things"–he also stated that "the cleanness of the going out increases the sharpness of the coming in. And vice versa"–Olson quoted William Carlos Williams's famous "Red Wheel Barrow" poem so often that it became a sort of unofficial school motto. Joel Oppenheimer echoed this concept of the perceiving mind seeing its surrounding in new ways when he explained that from Olson he had learned an important definition of the poet as "the man who finds the juxtapositions that make sense–for him and possibly for society."

Another well-known Black Mountain poet is Robert Creeley, who spent a few days at the college in 1944 visiting a female student who would become his first wife. They were married during Creeley's junior year at Harvard, and near the end of his senior year Creeley dropped out of college. By 1954 the Creeleys were living in Majorca, where they had started the Divers Press, which had published among other books, two by Olson, with whom Creeley had been corresponding since the late 1940s. In 1953, when the college decided that publishing a literary magazine would be a good way to increase its visibility and bring in more students to bolster its declining enrollment, Olson invited Creeley, who had already been asked to join the faculty, to edit the *Black Mountain Review*. Creeley did not rush to Black Mountain, and actually put together the first, Spring 1954, issue in Majorca. (Even after Creeley arrived at the school in March 1954 he had the magazine printed in Spain because of lower printing costs.)

Creeley not only taught at the college but also completed his B.A. there. The outside examiner for his oral exams was San Francisco poet Robert Duncan, who visited in 1955 and joined the faculty in 1956. Though Duncan, unlike Creeley and Olson, had close ties to the San Francisco beat poets, these three writers are now considered the preeminent Black Mountain poets–a group which also includes students Ed Dorn, Joel Oppenheimer, Jonathan Williams, Michael Rumaker, John Weiners, and Dan Rice –all of whom were at the college in the 1950s. To confuse matters slightly, some people–following the lead of Donald M. Allen who named the group in his important anthology, *The New American Poetry* (1960)–include in "The Black Mountain School of Poetry" poets such as Denise Levertov, Paul Blackburn, Larry Eigner, and Paul Carroll, none of whom ever attended or taught at the college but whose work Creeley published in the *Black Mountain Review*.

The *Black Mountain Review* did attract attention in the literary community, but it did not bring in new students. While Olson's predecessors as rector had advocated innovation in the classroom, they had also realized the value of such traditional administrative tasks as fundraising and recruitment. Olson seemed to lack talent for either (as his one plan for generating publicity–an avant-garde poetry magazine–undoubtedly proves), and from 1952 to 1956 the total number of regularly enrolled students averaged twenty (down from ninety in 1947). Black Mountain had become more of a community than a school. There were few if any distinctions between students and staff, and more-or-less permanent visitors such as Jonathan Williams and Dan Rice were neither. In fall 1956 the school was closed, and the influential *Black Mountain Review*, after only seven issues, died with it.

In 1967 Black Mountain's first rector, John Andrew Rice, told the school's historian Martin Duberman that "colleges should be in tents, and when they fold, they fold." Yet, Duberman points out, Black Mountain's reputation "grows in magnitude down to the present day,"

Sylvia Plath (photograph by Rollie McKenna)

and, as Olson said, "there's no end to the story" because "her flag still flies."

BOSTON COLLEGE

John Wieners, 1954
George V. Higgins, 1961, J. D. 1967
David Plante, 1961

BOSTON UNIVERSITY

Harry Clement Stubbs, (Hal Clement), M.Ed. 1947
William Ellery Leonard, 1898
Sylvia Plath, attended 1959
Anne Sexton, attended 1959
George Starbuck, attended 1959

A Brief Conjunction of Poets

In spring 1959, while poet Robert Lowell was teaching at Boston University, three younger poets audited his poetry-writing seminar–Sylvia Plath, Anne Sexton, and George Starbuck–and this brief conjunction of poets closed the final link in time and space among a group of poets who have been called by critics (though not by themselves) the Confessional School. Though the membership of this school varies according to who is defining "confessional," the poets most often mentioned are Lowell, Randall Jarrell, John Berryman, W. D. Snodgrass, Anne Sexton, and Sylvia Plath.

Lowell had formed a lifelong friendship with Jarrell when he shared a room with the young instructor in John Crowe Ransom's house during the 1937-1938 academic year at Kenyon College. Berryman and Lowell met and became friends in 1944, and in 1946 Berryman had written a glowing review for Lowell's first book, *Lord Weary's Castle*, in which he called Lowell "a talent whose ceiling is invisible." Both poets were visiting professors in the Writers' Workshop at the University of Iowa in 1953. One of their students there, W. D. Snodgrass, was just beginning to write what he called "domestic" poetry. (In fact one critic, Steven Gould Axelrod, locates the birth of confessional poetry on the evening of 18 November 1973, when Snodgrass began writing the poem "Heart's Needle.") Lowell had at first found Snodgrass's "domestic" poems too personal, but by 1957, when he started work on the autobiographical poems in *Life Studies* (1959), he became convinced that the younger poet had influenced him "though people have suggested the opposite."

Sexton had already studied with Snodgrass at the 1958 Antioch Writers' Conference and had begun writing confessional poetry of her own by the time she showed up in Lowell's classroom. For Plath, however, this sort of poetry was new–it did not employ metaphors that disguised its relationship to painful events in the poet's life, but created a dialectic between these personal matters and public affairs, in a confiding, unpretentious style. Though she had not yet fully developed her own style, and the poems she wrote for the class were only a start in that direction, she later said that Sexton and Lowell (along with Theodore Roethke) had influenced her work.

Though they did not hesitate to criticize one another's poems, Sexton, Plath, and Starbuck did not often speak in Lowell's seminar. As Sexton put it later, "Silence was wiser, when we could command it. We tried, each one in his own manner; sometimes letting our own poems come up, as for a butcher, as for a lover." After class the three used to drive in Sexton's car to the Ritz Hotel bar, where they drank martinis and ate free potato chips. (According to Sexton she always parked in the loading-only zone and told Plath and Starbuck, "It's okay, because we are only going to get loaded!") Some time later they would walk unsteadily to the nearby Waldorf Cafeteria, where they could buy lunch for 70¢.

[Sylvia Plath] gave me credit . . . as an influence upon her work. She gave me and Robert Lowell (both in a rather lump, Sylvia!) credit for our breakthrough into the personal in poetry. I suppose we might have shown her something about daring–daring to tell it true. W. D. Snodgrass showed me in the first place. . . . Maybe I did give her a sort of daring, but that's all she should have said. That's all that's similar about our work. Except for death–yes, we have that in common (and there must be enough other poets with that theme to fill an entire library).
　　–Anne Sexton, "The Barfly Ought to Sing," in The Art of Sylvia Plath *(1970), edited by Charles Newman*

In one of his poems from this period Starbuck wrote, "I weave with two sweet ladies out of The Ritz," but what these "two sweet ladies" talked about more often than not was their suicide attempts. According to Sexton's account at least, the conversation was not depressing, even to Starbuck; in fact "we three were stimulated by it. . . , as if death made each of us a little more real at the moment." Yet death considered abstractly, became real. After Plath's suicide in 1963, Sexton wrote a poem for her, in which she asked,

Thief!–
how did you crawl into,

crawl down alone
into the death I wanted so badly
and for so long.

....

the death we drank to,
the motives and then the quiet
deed?

Anne Sexton took her own life in 1974.

BOWDOIN COLLEGE

Nathaniel Hawthorne, 1825
Henry Wadsworth Longfellow, 1825
Robert P. Tristram Coffin, 1915
Vance Bourjaily, 1947

Two Literary Classmates

Though the coincidence that two of
the greatest American writers of the
nineteenth century graduated in the
same class from a small, backwoods college is remarkable, Nathaniel Hawthorne and Henry Wadsworth
Longfellow–both Bowdoin College,
Class of 1825–did not spend their college years reading each other's work
and fostering each other's literary ambitions. The two were acquainted, but, differing in interests and temperament,
they traveled in separate social circles.

Longfellow, who entered Bowdoin as
a sophomore in 1822 at the age of fifteen, was a serious student and ended
up fourth in a class of thirty-nine. Hawthorne, two years older, had entered
the previous year after protesting to his
mother that "four years of the best part
of my life is a great deal to throw
away." Later he described his "natural re-
pugnance" for schoolwork and explained that he was "negligent of
college rules and the Procrustian details
of academic life, rather choosing to
nurse my own fancies than to dig into
Greek roots and be numbered among
the learned Thebans." He graduated
eighteenth.

Longfellow joined the most prestigious and conservative literary club, the

An 1840 portrait of Henry Wadsworth Long-
fellow, by C. G. Thompson (courtesy of the
National Park Service, Longfellow National
Historic Site)

Peucinian Society, whose members–
including Hawthorne's roommate, Alfred Mason, and Calvin Stowe (now best
known as the husband of Harriet Beecher Stowe, author of *Uncle Tom's Cabin*,
1852)–supported John Quincy Adams
in the 1824 presidential election. Hawthorne belonged to the Democratic and
more social Athenians, who supported
Adams's opponent, Andrew Jackson.
Members of the Athenians included
Longfellow's older brother, Stephen
Longfellow, and the three young men
who were Hawthorne's closest college
friends: Jonathan Cilley (later a U.S.
Congressman), Franklin Pierce (a future
President of the United States), and
Horatio Bridge (who became a naval officer and was subsequently appointed
paymaster general of the U.S.
Navy Department). Hawthorne edited
Bridge's *Journal of an African Cruiser*
(anonymously published in 1845), probably doing a good bit of ghostwriting as
well. When Pierce was nominated for
the presidency in 1852, Hawthorne

wrote his official campaign biography and was rewarded by the successful candidate with the American Consulship in Liverpool.

Though Hawthorne shared Longfellow's love of reading and later earned a somewhat exaggerated reputation as a recluse, he was in fact the more sociable of the two. Both Longfellow and Hawthorne joined the Bowdoin Cadets, a quasi-military group that paraded and drilled on campus. Longfellow preferred the company of his more bookish friends to the group's physical activities and quit just at the point that the Cadets started to turn into a social club. Hawthorne also belonged to the Pot-8-O Club, which met every week at a nearby tavern, where each member recited a poem or dissertation on a set topic. The club seems to have ignored the provision in its constitution forbidding the consumption of alcoholic beverages at its meetings.

Unlike his older brother, Henry Longfellow was never fined for violating college rules, which included prohibitions against drinking and playing cards. In May 1822 Hawthorne was fined 50¢ by Bowdoin's president, the Reverend William Allen, for playing cards, but his quick thinking actually saved him from a larger fine. As he explained to his mother, "when the President asked me what we played for, I thought proper to inform him it was 50 cts., although it happened to be a Quart of Wine, but if I had told him that he would probably have fined me for having a blow." He went on to assure his mother that he hadn't really lied, because "the wine cost 50cts." (One thing he and Longfellow seem to have agreed upon was their dislike of the stern, Calvinistic President Allen who was as dogmatic in his teaching of literature and as unyielding in his enforcement of discipline as he was strict in his adherence to conservative old-line religious doctrines.)

By the time he was a senior Longfellow had had poems published in national magazines. Hawthorne had

An 1840 portrait of Nathaniel Hawthorne, by Charles Osgood (courtesy of Essex Institute, Salem, Massachusetts)

written some short stories, most of which he later burned, and he was working on a novel, which may have been *Fanshawe* (1828), the novel he set at Bowdoin, but which may also have been among the pile of manuscripts he burned a few years later. He kept his ambitions largely to himself.

The sociable Hawthorne was more reticent in another way as well. While he did not mind discoursing in front of his friends at the Pot-8-O Club, he hated public speaking and often paid fines rather than delivering the weekly declamation required of each student. Longfellow did well at such occasions and seemed to enjoy them. Shortly before graduation, President Allen told Hawthorne that because he had cut so many declamations he would not be allowed to give one of the many commencement speeches. Hawthorne considered the so-called punishment "a sufficient testimony of my scholarship, while it saves me the mortification of making my appearance in public at commencement."

Longfellow—who had been improving his idle hours by reading American writers such as Charles Brockden Brown,

James Fenimore Cooper, and Washington Irving–spoke third and called on his audience to nurture those American writers who made their own land their subject matter and associated "whatever is noble and attractive in our national character . . . with the sweet magic of poetry."

After graduation, the eighteen-year-old Longfellow went to Europe to prepare himself for his new position as Bowdoin's first professor of modern languages, and twenty-one-year-old Hawthorne went home to his mother's house in Salem, Massachusetts, to begin his long apprenticeship as a writer. Twelve years later, deferentially referring to their slight acquaintance at Bowdoin, he sent the successful scholar Longfellow (by then at Harvard) a copy of his first collection of short stories, *Twice-told Tales* (1837)–and Longfellow discovered in his classmate the sort of "Native Writer" he had described in his commencement address. The enduring friendship between the two writers dates from this discovery.

The First American College Novel

By setting his first novel at "Harley College," clearly recognizable as his alma mater Bowdoin, Nathaniel Hawthorne became the author of the first American college novel, *Fanshawe* (1828). But while some scholars have seen aspects of his college friends Jonathan Cilley and Horatio Bridge in one of the novel's heroes, Edward Walcott (and characteristics of Hawthorne himself in both Walcott and the titular hero, Fanshawe), the novel has little to do with American college life. Instead its romance-adventure plot demonstrates its author's reading of Sir Walter Scott, and the only member of the faculty portrayed, the president, Dr. Melmoth, is a kind, fatherly man and a good teacher. This portrait is in such marked contrast to Hawthorne's perceptions of Bowdoin's stern, dogmatic Calvinist president, the Reverend William Allen, that

it seems almost like wishful thinking on the young writer's part.

Though the anonymously published novel pales beside Hawthorne's later fiction, some early reviewers liked it, with Sarah Josepha Hale, now best known as the reputed author of "Mary Had a Little Lamb," proclaiming it "worth placing . . . in your library." An unfavorable anonymous review, however, seems to have summarized the novel best, calling it "a love story" that "has, like ten thousand others, a mystery, an elopement, a villain, a father, a tavern, almost a duel, a horrible death, and–heaven save the mark! an end."

Hawthorne soon agreed with this assessment, regretting the $100 he had paid to have the book published. He took back his sister Louisa's copy–probably burning it–and asked his friend Bridge to burn his. He also swore his family to secrecy and refused, for the rest of his life, to acknowledge his authorship. (In 1851, after the publication of his greatest novel, *The Scarlet Letter*, the previous year, Hawthorne wrote to his publisher, who had asked about *Fanshawe*: "I cannot be sworn to make current answers as to all the literary or other follies of my nonage.") His suppression of the novel was aided when, three years after *Fanshawe's* publication, the remainder of the only printing was destroyed in a fire at the publisher's bookstore.

Not surprisingly then, Hawthorne's novel did not inspire a host of imitators, and the models for the popular American college novels that appeared later in the nineteenth century were such enormously successful British college novels as *Tom Brown at Oxford* (1861), by Thomas Hughes, and the *Mr. Verdant Green* series (1853, 1854, 1857) by Cuthbert Bede (Edward Bradley).

BOWLING GREEN STATE
UNIVERSITY

Carolyn Forché, M.F.A. 1975

▼▼▼▼▼▼▼▼▼▼▼▼

CHECKERED CAREER #1

Having failed to graduate from DeWitt Clinton High School, Nathan Weinstein (who had not yet changed his name to Nathanael West) altered his high-school transcript and gained admission to Tufts College. He enrolled at Tufts in September 1921 and by 25 November, failing every course, he was advised to withdraw. (Probably thinking a single *F* an insufficient indication of West's lack of achievement, his French instructor gave him a double *F*.)

Since these were midterm grades, they were not recorded on his transcript, and West could have gotten into another school with a record showing only that he had enrolled at Tufts but had left before the end of the semester. When he went to request a copy of the transcript that attested to the fact, however, he was given the transcript of another Nathan Weinstein, who had earned fifty-seven credits at Tufts. Having never completed a single college course, West used this transcript to gain admission to Brown University in spring 1922 as a second-semester sophomore. His academic career at Brown, where one of his friends was S. J. Perelman (who later married West's sister), was largely undistinguished, and he started his senior year under academic warning. At the end of his last semester his failure in modern drama would have prevented him from graduating, but his soft-hearted professor, after West cried in his office, changed the grade to a *D*, even though West had not completed all the assignments.

▲▲▲▲▲▲▲▲▲▲▲▲

BRADLEY UNIVERSITY

Philip José Farmer, 1950

BRANDEIS UNIVERSITY

Linda Pastan, M.A. 1957

BROOKLYN COLLEGE, CITY UNIVERSITY OF NEW YORK

Irwin Shaw, 1934
Wallace Markfield, 1947
Howard Sackler, 1950
Gilbert Sorrentino, attended 1950-1951, 1955-1957

BROWN UNIVERSITY

John Hay, 1858
Rudolph Fisher, 1919, M.A. 1920
Nathan Weinstein (Nathanael West), 1924
S. J. Perelman, 1925
Susan Cheever, 1965
Steven Millhauser, graduate study 1968-1971

BRYN MAWR COLLEGE

Hilda Doolittle (H.D.), attended 1905-1906
Marianne Moore, 1909
Katharine Sargeant White, 1914

Two Bryn Mawr Poets

As "H.D., Imagiste" (a name given her in 1913 by her friend and former fiancé Ezra Pound) Hilda Doolittle earned a reputation with many as the perfect imagist poet, writing verse that Pound characterized as "Objective—no slither; direct—no excessive use of adjectives, no metaphors that won't permit examination. It's straight talk, straight as the Greek!" Her student prose writing earned no such praise at Bryn Mawr, where she had matriculated in 1905. When she left school in the middle of the next year she had received poor grades in math and English. In fact, she remembered later her essays were used as examples "of the very worst description."

Another major modernist poet, Mari-

Members of the Bryn Mawr Class of 1909: Hilda Doolittle is third from left (partially obscured); Marianne Moore is second from right (courtesy of the Bryn Mawr College Archives)

anne Moore, graduated from Bryn Mawr in 1909. Having majored in biology and histology, Moore told a *Paris Review* interviewer in 1960 that these studies had helped to shape her poetry, for "Precision, economy of statement, logic employed to ends that are disinterested, drawing and identifying, liberate— at least have some bearing on–the imagination, it seems to me." Although she had several poems published in the school's literary magazine and served on its board for three years, she said later that she had not been mature enough for English courses, whenever possible taking biology courses instead because the professors, though "exacting," were "very humane." She also managed to take a class in torts from a professor who "was compassion itself," and she got by in Latin; but, when she took Italian with the ambition of reading Dante in the original, she failed the course— not once, but twice. The only English course she liked was one in which students were asked to imitate in their own writing the prose styles of such sixteenth- and seventeenth-century masters as Lancelot Andrewes, Francis Bacon, Jeremy Taylor, and John Milton. She later said that such prose writers, as well

as Samuel Johnson, Edmund Burke, and Henry James had influenced her more than any poet (she also cited Ezra Pound's 1910 prose work *The Spirit of the Romance* as an influence, rather than his poetry). This amalgamation of poetry and prose, old and new, is a quality as apparent in her poetry as its scientific precision and detachment. When she later called poet Elizabeth Bishop "archaically new," Moore could have been describing herself.

Though Moore was acquainted with Doolittle at Bryn Mawr, she did not know that she was interested in writing poetry. In 1916, after Doolittle had made a name for herself as H.D. the imagist poet, the two poets began corresponding, and in 1920 H.D., who had been living in England, and her friend Bryher (Winifred Ellerman) visited Moore in New York. Thinking to help Moore, whose poems had been appearing in magazines but had not been collected in a book, H.D., Bryher, and Bryher's husband, Robert McAlmon, decided to find a publisher for her. Without Moore's knowledge they selected and arranged twenty-four of her poems and took them to London, where they persuaded Harriet Weaver at the Egoist

Press to publish them. When the book appeared as *Poems* in 1921, Moore was furious. She hated the selection, the arrangement, and even the title. She had not tried to publish a book herself because, as she said in her 1960 *Paris Review* interview, she considered her work still "conspicuously tentative"—and she added, "I disliked the term 'poetry' for any but Chaucer's or Shakespeare's or Dante's." (Throughout her life she insisted repeatedly that her writing "could only be called poetry because there is no other category in which to put it.") The friendship between Moore and H.D. survived, however, and Moore later said she was grateful for "the chivalry of the undertaking."

BUCKNELL UNIVERSITY

Philip Roth, 1954

CALIFORNIA INSTITUTE OF TECHNOLOGY

L. Sprague de Camp, 1930
Larry Niven, attended 1956-1958

CALIFORNIA STATE UNIVERSITY, CHICO

Raymond Carver, attended 1958-1960

CALVIN COLLEGE

Peter DeVries, 1931
Frederick (Feike) Feikema (Frederick Manfred), 1934

CARNEGIE-MELLON UNIVERSITY

Kurt Vonnegut, attended 1943
Richard France, M.F.A. 1970, Ph.D. 1973

CASE WESTERN RESERVE UNIVERSITY

Alice Mary (André) Norton, attended 1930-1932
Roger Zelazny, 1959
Charles Boer, 1961

CATHOLIC UNIVERSITY OF AMERICA

Mart Crowley, 1957
Jason Miller, graduate study 1962-1963
Michael Cristofer, attended 1962-1965
Joseph A. Walker, M.F.A. 1963

CHEVY CHASE JUNIOR COLLEGE

Joan Williams, attended 1947-1948

THE CITADEL

Calder Willingham, attended 1940-1941
Pat Conroy, 1967

CITY COLLEGE, CITY UNIVERSITY OF NEW YORK

Upton Sinclair, 1897
George Sylvester Viereck, 1906
Henry Miller, attended 1909
Jean Toomer, attended 1917
Daniel Fuchs, 1930
William Gibson, attended 1930-1932
Bernard Malamud, 1936
Paddy Chayefsky, 1943
Jerome Rothenberg, 1952
Judith Rossner, attended 1952-1955
Robert Kelly, 1955
Samuel R. Delany, attended 1961
Edgar White, attended 1964-1965
Toni Cade Bambara, M.A. 1965
Israel Horowitz, 1977

CITY COLLEGES OF CHICAGO

Don L. Lee (Haki R. Madhubuti), A.A. 1966

CLARK UNIVERSITY

S. N. Behrman, attended 1912-1914

CLEMSON UNIVERSITY

James Dickey, attended 1942
Mark Harris, attended 1943

COE COLLEGE

Paul Engle, 1931

John Logan, 1943

COLLEGE OF CHARLESTON

William Gilmore Simms, attended 1816-1818
Ludwig Lewisohn, 1901, M.A. 1901
Josephine Pinckney, attended 1910s

COLUMBIA UNIVERSITY

John Kendrick Bangs, 1883, attended law school 1883-1884
Albert Payson Terhune, 1893
Upton Sinclair, graduate study 1897-1900
John Erskine, 1900, M.A. 1901, Ph.D. 1903
Stark Young, M.A. 1902
Ludwig Lewisohn, M.A. 1903
Dorothy Canfield Fisher, Ph.D. 1904
William Ellery Leonard, Ph.D. 1904
Joyce Kilmer, 1908
Josephine Pinckney, attended 1910s
Carl Van Doren, Ph.D. 1911
Charles Reznikoff, graduate study 1916
Kenneth Burke, attended 1917-1918
S. N. Behrman, M.A. 1918
Louis Bromfield, 1919
Matthew Josephson, 1920
Mark Van Doren, Ph.D. 1920
Paul Gallico, 1921
Langston Hughes, attended 1921-1922
Louis Zukofsky, M.A. 1924
Stanley Burnshaw, attended 1924
Edward Dahlberg, 1925
Lionel Trilling, 1925, M.A. 1926, Ph.D. 1938
Lillian Hellman, attended 1924
S. Randolph Edmonds, M.A. 1931
Muriel Rukeyser, attended 1931-1932
Paul Engle, graduate study 1932-1933
Herman Wouk, 1934
Zora Neale Hurston, graduate study 1934-1935
Carson McCullers, attended 1935-1936
John Berryman, 1936
Thomas Merton, 1938, M.A. 1939
Isaac Asimov, 1939, M.A. 1941, Ph.D. 1948
J. D. Salinger, attended 1939
Elizabeth Hardwick, graduate study 1939-1941

Theodore Weiss, M.A. 1940, further graduate study 1940-1941
Jack Kerouac, attended 1940-1942
Walker Percy, M.D. 1941
Bernard Malamud, M.A. 1942
John Clellon Holmes, attended 1943, 1945-1946
James Blish, graduate study 1945-1946
Herbert Gold, 1946, M.A. 1948
Howard Moss, graduate study 1946
William Jay Smith, graduate study 1946-1947
Daniel Hoffman, 1947, M.A. 1949, Ph.D. 1956
Ossie Davis, 1948
Allen Ginsberg, 1948
Louis Simpson, 1948, M.A. 1950, Ph.D. 1959
Lawrence Ferlinghetti, M.A. 1948
Philip Booth, M.A. 1949
Joseph Heller, M.A. 1949
Mario Puzo, attended 1950s
John Hollander, 1950, M.A. 1952
Anthony Hecht, M.A. 1950
Thomas Berger, graduate study 1950-1951
Joseph Charles Kennedy (X. J. Kennedy), M.A. 1951
Richard Howard, 1951, M.A. 1952
Ursula K. Le Guin, M.A. 1952
E. L. Doctorow, graduate study 1952-1953
Kenneth Koch, M.A. 1953, Ph.D. 1959
Robert Pack, M.A. 1953
Robert Kelly, graduate study 1955-1958
Robert Silverberg, 1956
Jack Richardson, 1957
David Slavitt, M.A. 1957
LeRoi Jones (Amiri Baraka), graduate study 1958-1962
Jerzy Kosinski, graduate study 1958-1964
Jerome Charyn, 1959
John Kennedy Toole, M.A. 1959
Terrence McNally, 1960
Michael Benedikt, M.A. 1961
Anne Tyler, graduate study 1961-1962
Roger Zelazny, M.A. 1962
D. Keith Mano, 1963
Louise Glück, graduate study 1963-1965
Ron Padgett, 1964

Steven Millhauser, 1965
Erica Jong, M.A. 1965
Nicholas Delbanco, M.A. 1966
Peter Straub, M.A. 1966
Nikki Giovanni, graduate study 1968
Michael Rumaker, M.F.A. 1970

The "Great Books" Professors Meet The Beats (and A Few Other Eccentrics)

Columbia University has been noted throughout the twentieth century for its distinguished literature professors, among them two who also made names for themselves as fiction writers–John Erskine and Lionel Trilling– and a poet–Mark Van Doren.

Erskine, who earned his B.A., M.A., and Ph.D. at Columbia and taught at his alma mater from 1909 until his death in 1951, had an overnight popular success with his first novel, *The Pri-*

CHECKERED CAREER # 2

Jack Kerouac entered Columbia University on a football scholarship in fall 1940, but, after suffering a broken leg in a game, he took little interest in any of his studies except for Mark Van Doren's Shakespeare course, where he earned an *A.* Convinced that the football coach was making insufficient use of his talents, he dropped out in fall 1941 and worked as a gas-station attendant in New Haven, a sports reporter for the *Lowell* [Massachusetts] *Sun*, a construction worker at the Pentagon, and a seaman in the U. S. Merchant Marine (while also writing a novel). He returned to Columbia in fall 1942, but he quit the football team after he was not allowed to play in the opening game and left school at the end of the semester, enlisting in the U. S. Navy in February 1943.

---

vate Life of Helen of Troy, published in 1925 when Erskine was in his mid forties. His later novels met with less acclaim, though his *Bachelor of Arts* (1934), the story of a Columbia undergraduate, is interesting for Erskine's perceptions of his students. He is now better known for his literary scholarship and his teaching, especially for the Great Books course that he instituted at Columbia. Some of his students became important literary critics, including Carl and Mark Van Doren, Matthew Josephson, Kenneth Burke, Raymond Weaver, Mortimer Adler, and Clifton Fadiman.

After earning his Ph.D. from Columbia in 1911, Carl Van Doren (Mark's older brother) stayed on to teach for five years, numbering among his students not only his brother but his brother's best friend, Joseph Wood Krutch, who also had a distinguished career as a teacher and literary critic. Though he enjoyed scholarship (for example, he worked with Erskine and two other Columbia professors, W.P. Trent and Stuart Sherman, on *The Cambridge History of American Literature,* published 1917-1921), the older Van Doren brother considered teaching "only a trade for me, not a passion," and eventually found more congenial work as a literary editor, first for the *Nation* and then for *Century* magazine.

Mark Van Doren, whom Carl called "the most gifted and charming" of the five Van Doren brothers, earned his Ph.D. from Columbia in 1920 and taught there until 1959. Though he also earned a reputation as a literary critic and scholar (serving for a time, like his brother, as literary editor at the *Nation*) and though he won a Pulitzer Prize in 1940 for his *Collected Poems, 1922-1938* (1939), he made his greatest mark on American literature as a teacher. Now eclipsed by Carl Van Doren as a critic and largely forgotten as a writer of what even friends such as Allen Tate had to admit was second-rate poetry, Mark Van Doren not only taught such

Hal Chase, Jack Kerouac, Allen Ginsberg, and William S. Burroughs in New York, 1946– "playacting as Budapest degenerates, 1933" (photograph by Ginsberg)

important literary critics as Fadiman, Trilling, John Gassner, and Maxwell Geismar (as well as publisher Robert Giroux and Donald Dike, later Joyce Carol Oates's writing teacher), but he had a major influence on American poetry. A conservative, traditional poet himself, Van Doren recognized talent in poetry that was different from his own, providing encouragement and sound advice to poets such as Louis Zukofsky, John Berryman, Thomas Merton, Louis Simpson, and Allen Ginsberg (as well as to another of his students, novelist Jack Kerouac).

In *The Autobiography of Mark Van Doren* (1958) the poet-teacher called Zukofsky "a subtle poet" who had an "inarticulate soul" and explained how, when Merton came to announce that he had become a Catholic and entered a monastery, his decisions "seemed right to me because they did to him"; but Van Doren was surprised to learn "that he thought of me as having helped him to make up his mind."

While Van Doren's influence on Merton's thinking was greater than he himself imagined, his importance to John Berryman was probably greater still. In his autobiography he called the younger poet "first and last a literary youth: all of his thought sank into poet-

ry, which he studied and wrote as if there were no other exercise for the human brain." Berryman returned the compliment, characterizing Van Doren's teaching as "strongly structured, lit by wit, leaving ample play for grace and charm," and concluding, "If during my stay at Columbia I had met only Mark Van Doren and his work, it would have been worth the trouble. It was the force of his example, for instance, that made me a poet." Throughout Berryman's life Van Doren provided valuable advice on his poetry, as well as helping him to find publishers and teaching jobs, on at least one occasion giving him money, and serving as best man at his first wedding.

Van Doren also encouraged Jack Kerouac, recommending his first novel, *The Town and the City* (1950), to Robert Giroux, who accepted it for his employer, Harcourt, Brace and helped Kerouac to cut it. Kerouac was later disappointed that the mentor toward whom he felt an almost filial devotion found his *Doctor Sax* (1959) dull and incomprehensible.

Van Doren was less successful in promoting Ginsberg. Though he had Ginsberg put together a collection of poems for submission to Giroux at about the same time Giroux accepted Kerouac's novel, Giroux was unimpressed and rejected "The Book of Doldrums," which remains unpublished in that form.

Lionel Trilling, who earned his B.A., M.A., and Ph.D. at Columbia and taught there from 1932 until his death in 1975, shared with Van Doren the role of mentor to Ginsberg, which involved not only giving literary advice to the Beat poet, but intervening with angry Columbia authorities. Trilling himself had had to call on Van Doren's good will when in 1936, very much an outsider as a Jew on Columbia's waspish faculty, he had nearly been dismissed "as a Freudian, a Marxist, and a Jew." The support of senior faculty members, including Van Doren, Raymond Weaver, and Emery Neff–as well as completing his doctoral dissertation two years later– had convinced the department chairman to keep him on. (In 1939 his published dissertation, *Matthew Arnold*, met with great success and assured him of acceptance and respect at Columbia.)

In the spring of 1945 Ginsberg needed the support of both Trilling and Van Doren. The previous August Lucien Carr, whom Ginsberg had met in Trilling's Great Books course for freshmen, had been arrested for the murder of a man who had made sexual advances toward him; Kerouac had helped to dispose of the evidence and been arrested as a material witness. During the next school year Carr, who had been expelled, and Kerouac, who was no longer enrolled at Columbia, were discovered to be living with Ginsberg in his dormitory room, a fact that did not endear him to the school's administration. The proverbial last straw came that spring when a cleaning woman told the dean of students that Ginsberg had traced "Fuck the Jews" and "Nicholas Murray Butler [the president of Columbia] has no balls" in the dust on his window. In some but not all of the various versions of this complicated story, the dean burst into the room and found Ginsberg in bed with Kerouac. Regardless of what happened, the dean was so

angry he was ready to expel Ginsberg, and, when Trilling and Van Doren came to speak to the dean on Ginsberg's behalf, he was still so appalled by what Ginsberg had written that he had to write the words on a piece of paper rather than speak them aloud. Unlikely to have approved of Ginsberg's actions, the two professors nevertheless convinced the dean to soften his penalty to a one-year suspension, after which Ginsberg would be allowed to re-enroll if he produced a letter from a psychiatrist who pronounced him mentally stable enough to resume studies. Ginsberg returned to Columbia in 1947 and graduated in 1948, but the next year, when his friendship with a group of petty thieves was about to land him in jail, he called on Trilling again; and, after the dean of Columbia College interceded with the district attorney, Ginsberg was allowed to enter Columbia Psychiatric Institute rather than face charges.

The photograph of E. B. White that appeared in the 1921 *Cornellian* (courtesy of the Department of Manuscripts and University Archives, Cornell University Library)

COMMONWEALTH COLLEGE

Kenneth Patchen, attended 1930

CORNELL UNIVERSITY

Jessie Redmon Fauset, 1905
Kenneth Roberts, 1908
Frank Sullivan, 1914
Louis Bromfield, attended 1914-1916
Laura Reichenthal Gottschalk (Laura Riding), attended 1918-1921
Skipwith Cannell, attended 1919
E. B. White, 1921
Paul Green, graduate study 1922-1923
Sidney Kingsley, 1928
Kurt Vonnegut, attended 1940-1942
William Gass, Ph.D. 1954
Toni Morrison, M.A. 1955
Thomas Pynchon, 1958
Peter Klappert, 1964

Andy White and Professor Strunk's "Little Book"

Elwyn Brooks White—who got his nickname from the Cornell tradition of calling students named White "Andy" after Andrew D. White, the school's first president—arrived at Cornell in fall 1917. He made the board of the *Cornell Daily Sun* during his freshman year, and at the end of his junior year he became editor in chief, writing most of the editorials that appeared in the paper between 5 April 1920 and 5 April 1921 —including one that earned first prize in a contest sponsored by the Convention of Eastern College Newspapers.

While his experience as a journalist must have helped to form White's style, he found a greater influence in William Strunk, Jr., whose English 8 composition course White took in 1919. The textbook was *The Elements of Style*, which Strunk had written and had privately printed for his students. What White later called "a forty-three-page summation of the case for cleanliness, accuracy, and brevity in the use of English," the book was known to Cornell students as "the *little* book," a tag Strunk himself

had given it, "sardonically and with secret pride."

Professor Strunk—and his little book—approached writing with vigor, commanding writers to follow his composition rules. He especially "put his heart and soul" into rule seventeen: "Omit needless words!" In fact, said White, "when I was sitting in his class, he omitted so many needless words, and omitted them so forcibly and with such eagerness and obvious relish, that he often seemed in the position of having shortchanged himself—a man left with nothing more to say yet with time to fill, a radio prophet who had outdistanced the clock. Will Strunk got out of this predicament by a simple trick: he uttered every sentence three times. . . .'Rule Seventeen. Omit needless words! Omit needless words! Omit needless words!' "

The Elements of Style, when I re-examined it in 1957, seemed to me to contain rich deposits of gold. It was Will Strunk's parvum opus, *his attempt to cut the vast tangle of English rhetoric down to size and write its rules and principles on the head of a pin. . . . Even after I got through tampering with it, it was still a tiny thing, a barely tarnished gem.*

—E.B. White, Introduction to The Elements of Style *(third revised edition, 1979)*

White graduated in 1921 and continued his lifelong attempt to follow Strunk's commandments. In 1957, when Macmillan commissioned White to revise *The Elements of Style*, he did not try to soften or change Strunk's amusing and friendly, but decidedly dictatorial, tone. He added a chapter called " An Approach to Style," which is "addressed to those who think that English prose composition is not only a necessary skill but a sensible pursuit as well—a way to spend one's days." White's first revision was published in 1959, and he revised the book twice more, in 1972 and 1979, adding new misused words and expressions, adding new examples under rules and principles, deleting "bewhiskered entries"–but remaining true to Strunk's original. *The Elements of Style* is still a little book (only eighty-five pages in the 1979 edition), but it is a giant among influential American textbooks, and it is probably the only book on English composition that may be read only for the pleasure of savoring its wit and style.

Fiction and Real Life

Vladimir Nabokov and Alison Lurie have placed Cornell in the background of greater *fiction*, but student life at Cornell comes to the foreground in three novels by three friends who attended Cornell in the late 1940s and early 1950s. Clifford Irving (now better-known for his bogus "autobiography" of Howard Hughes), Charles Thompson, and Robert Gutwillig portray a group of students at Cornell whose prime concerns are sex and various forms of intoxication.

Another of the authors' friends appears in all three books: Ken Hutchinson, who seems to have been noted for his drinking, sexual excesses, and fast driving. Hutchinson entered Cornell after an undesirable discharge from the U.S. Air Force and attended from 1948 until 1953, when on 1 August he was killed in a car accident.

In Thompson's *Halfway Down the Stairs* (1957) the Hutchinson character, Hugh Masters, drowns during a drunken midnight swim, and in Gutwillig's *After Long Silence* (1958) Hutchinson is portrayed as Chris Hunt, who, like his real-life counterpart, is killed in an automobile accident. Irving's more ambitious and somewhat less autobiographical novel, *On a Darkling Plain* (1956), portrays Hutchinson as Joe MacFarlane, a young socialist who at the end of the novel is alive and well in New York City, though his girlfriend has been killed after crashing her car. Despite the various dissimilarities in the three portraits, William G. Andrews,

who reviewed Gutwillig's book for the *Ithaca Journal* (24 May 1958), had no trouble recognizing Ken Hutchinson in all three novels.

DARTMOUTH COLLEGE

Joel Barlow, attended 1773
Richard Hovey, 1885
Robert Frost, attended 1892
Richard Eberhart, 1926
Budd Schulberg, 1936
Philip Booth, 1948
Frank D. Gilroy, 1950
Robert Pack, 1951

A Case of Mistaken Identities and Fortuitous Coincidences

Although he had originally hoped to attend his father's alma mater, Harvard, Robert Frost was persuaded to enroll at Dartmouth in 1882, in part because one of his high-school teachers stressed the school's literary associations: poet Richard Hovey had been in the class of 1885, and novelist Arthur Sherburne Hardy was a professor of mathematics there. Frost thought that he should read some of Professor Hardy's work before he got to Dartmouth, but by the time he reached the public library, he could remember only the professor's last name. He ended up with two of the lesser-known novels of Thomas Hardy, *A Pair of Blue Eyes* and *Two on a Tower*. Frost left Dartmouth before the end of his first semester, having never met the minor writer he had confused with a major novelist, but one discovery he made in the Dartmouth College library had an important influence on his career. Browsing in the library he found a magazine he had not noticed before, the *Independent*, whose 17 November 1892 issue had devoted its whole front page to an elegy by Richard Hovey, which an *Independent* editorial compared favorably to Milton's "Lycidas," Shelley's "Adonais," and Arnold's "Thyrsis."

In 1894, probably on the strength of this discovery, Frost submitted his first adult poem, "My Butterfly: An Elegy,"

Robert Frost, 1892 (courtesy of the Jones Library, Amherst, Massachusetts)

to the *Independent*, which paid him $15 and printed it on the first page of the 8 November issue. Even more important than this auspicious beginning were the contacts it afforded him. The *Independent*'s editor, William Hayes Ward, and his sister, Susan Hayes Ward, who served as a sort of in-house poetry editor, admired Frost's poem greatly, and Frost began a long correspondence with Miss Ward. Despite the Wards' conservative taste in poetry (the magazine had championed Sidney Lanier), against which Frost progressively rebelled, Susan Hayes Ward's encouragement sustained the poet during the long years between the 1894 appearance of "My Butterfly" in the *Independent* and the publication of his first book, *A Boy's Will*, nearly twenty years later, in 1913.

Moreover, as he wrote Miss Ward early in their correspondence, "Thomas Hardy has taught me the good use of a few words. . . . "

DAVIDSON COLLEGE

William Styron, attended 1942-1943

DELTA STATE UNIVERSITY

Wirt Williams, 1940

DE PAUL UNIVERSITY

James T. Farrell, attended 1924

DEPAUW UNIVERSITY

David Graham Phillips, attended 1882-1885

John Gardner, attended 1951-1953
John Jakes, 1953

DUKE UNIVERSITY

William Styron, 1947
Reynolds Price, 1955
Fred Chappell, 1961, M.A. 1964
Anne Tyler, 1961

EMORY UNIVERSITY

Mark Steadman, 1951

EMPORIA STATE UNIVERSITY

William Allen White, attended 1884-1886

ERSKINE COLLEGE

Erskine Caldwell, attended 1920-1922

FISK UNIVERSITY

George Marion McClellan, 1885, M.A. 1890
W. E. B. Du Bois, 1888
Joseph Seamon Cotter, Jr., attended 1911-1913
Melvin B. Tolson, attended 1918-1919
Nikki Giovanni, 1967

FLORIDA STATE UNIVERSITY

Mark Steadman, M.A. 1956, Ph.D. 1963

●●●●●●●●●●●●●●●●●●●●

┌─────────────────────────────┐
│   CHECKERED CAREER # 3   │
│   │
│ After attending Fresno State (now │
│ Fresno City College) in 1931, William │
│ Everson (who became Brother Antoni- │
│ nus in 1950) worked in a cannery │
│ and for the Civilian Conservation │
│ Corps before returning to school in │
│ 1934. Discovering the poetry of Robin- │
│ son Jeffers, he became, he said later, │
│ "a pantheist and a poet. At the same │
│ instant." In 1935 he left school for │
│ good "to go back to the land and be- │
│ come a poet in my own right, to │
│ plant a vineyard, commune with na- │
│ ture, and marry my high school │
│ sweetheart." │
└─────────────────────────────┘

●●●●●●●●●●●●●●●●●●●●

FRESNO CITY COLLEGE

William Everson (Brother Antoni-
nus), attended 1931, 1934-1935

GARLAND JUNIOR COLLEGE

Anne Sexton, attended 1947-1948

GENEVA COLLEGE

William D. Snodgrass, attended 1943-
1944, 1946-1947

GEORGE PEABODY COLLEGE

Jesse Stuart, attended 1930, 1931,
1936
William Inge, M.A. 1938

GEORGE WASHINGTON UNIVERSITY

Paul Myron Anthony Linebarger
(Cordwainer Smith), 1933
Dee Brown, 1937
Alice B. Sheldon (James Tiptree, Jr.),
Ph.D. 1967

GEORGIA COLLEGE AT MILLEDGEVILLE

Flannery O'Connor, 1945

GODDARD COLLEGE

Piers Anthony Dillingham Jacob
(Piers Anthony), 1956
David Mamet, 1969
Tom Dent, M.A. 1974

HAMILTON COLLEGE

Ezra Pound, 1905
Alexander Woollcott, 1909
Peter Meinke, 1955

HARVARD UNIVERSITY

William Hubbard, 1642
Benjamin Woodbridge, 1642
Michael Wigglesworth, 1651, A.M. 1653
Increase Mather, 1656
Benjamin Tompson, 1662
Edward Taylor, 1671
Cotton Mather, 1678, A.M. 1681
Royall Tyler, 1776, A.M. 1779
Ralph Waldo Emerson, 1821
Oliver Wendell Holmes, 1829, M.D.
1836
Jones Very, 1836, attended divinity
school 1836-1838
Richard Henry Dana, Jr., 1837, at-
tended law school 1837-1840
Henry David Thoreau, 1837
James Russell Lowell, 1838, LL.B. 1840
Edward Everett Hale, 1839
Horatio Alger, Jr., 1852, B.D. 1860
Henry Adams, 1858
Henry James, attended 1862-1863
Owen Wister, 1882, LL.B. 1888
George Santayana, 1886, Ph.D. 1889
W. E. B. Du Bois, 1890, A.M. 1891,
Ph.D. 1896
Robert Herrick, 1890
Edwin Arlington Robinson, attended
1891-1893
William Vaughn Moody, 1893, A.M.
1894
Frank Norris, attended 1894-1895
George Cabot Lodge, 1895
Joseph Trumbull Stickney, 1895
Percy MacKaye, 1897
Robert Frost, attended 1897-1899

Wallace Stevens, attended 1897-1900
Gertrude Stein, 1898
William Ellery Leonard, A.M. 1899
Witter Bynner, 1902
Leslie Pinckney Hill, 1903, A.M. 1904
John Gould Fletcher, attended 1903-1907
Arthur Davison Ficke, 1904
Angelina Weld Grimké, attended intermittently 1904-1910
Van Wyck Brooks, 1907
Alain Locke, 1907, Ph.D. 1918
Maxwell Perkins, 1907
Edward Sheldon, 1907, A.M. 1908
John Hall Wheelock, 1908
T. S. Eliot, 1909, A.M. 1910, Ph.D. dissertation accepted 1916
Charles Nordhoff, 1909
Haniel Long, 1910
Alan Seeger, 1910
Josephine Pinckney, attended 1910s
Conrad Aiken, 1912
Robert Nathan, attended 1912-1915
Robert Benchley, 1913
S. Foster Damon, 1914
Edward Streeter, 1914
Irwin Granich (Michael Gold), attended 1914
Eugene O'Neill, attended 1914-1915
E. E. Cummings, 1915, A.M. 1916
John P. Marquand, 1915
Sidney Howard, graduate study 1915-1916
S. N. Behrman, 1916
John Dos Passos, 1916
John Brooks Wheelwright, attended 1916-1920
Robert Hillyer, 1917
Robert Sherwood, 1918
Archibald MacLeish, LL.B. 1919
Philip Barry, graduate study 1919-1921
Malcolm Cowley, 1920
Bernard DeVoto, 1920
Ogden Nash, attended 1920-1921
Harry Crosby, 1921
Thomas Wolfe, A.M. 1922, further graduate study 1923
James Gould Cozzens, attended 1922-1924
Marita Bonner Occomy, 1922
Sterling Brown, A.M. 1923
Oliver La Farge, 1924, A.M. 1929

Walter D. Edmonds, 1926
Stanley Kunitz, 1926, A.M. 1927
Countee Cullen, A.M. 1926
Theodore Roethke, graduate study 1930-1931
William Maxwell, A.M. 1931
James Agee, 1932
Richard Eberhart, graduate study 1932-1933
Robert Fitzgerald, 1933
Robert Lowell, attended 1935-1937
Delmore Schwartz, graduate study 1935-1937
Charles Olson, graduate study 1936-1938

I went to Harvard just as students in the twelfth century went to Paris because, for me also, Abelard was there; for I knew I was a writer born,—I seemed always to have known this,—and I supposed that Harvard was the college for writers. It was intensely literary, as it had been for three hundred years,—it was even more literary in my time than ever. . . . While I did not know what I wanted to write, I knew that write I must and even the kind of writing that I was fit for; and for my purpose Harvard was the greenest of pastures.

—Van Wyck Brooks, Scenes and Portraits: Memories of Childhood and Youth *(1954)*

Peter Viereck, 1937, A.M. 1939, Ph.D. 1942
Robert Anderson, 1939, A.M. 1940
James Laughlin, 1939
John D. MacDonald, M.B.A. 1939
Howard Nemerov, 1941
John Malcolm Brinnin, graduate study 1941-1942
Howard Moss, attended 1942
Norman Mailer, 1943
Harry Clement Stubbs (Hal Clement), 1943
Robert Creeley, attended 1943-1946
A. B. Guthrie, Jr., graduate study 1944-1945
Maxine Kumin, 1946, A.M. 1948
Alison Lurie, 1947
Anne McCaffrey, 1947
Richard Wilbur, A.M. 1947

Kenneth Koch, 1948
Peter Davison, 1949
John Hawkes, 1949
Robert Bly, 1950
Frank O'Hara, 1950
Donald Hall, 1951
Ursula K. Le Guin, 1951
Adrienne Rich, 1951
Edward Hoagland, 1954
Linda Pastan, 1954
John Updike, 1954
Susan Sontag, A.M. (English) 1954, A.M. (Philosophy) 1955, further graduate study 1955-1957
William Dickey, A.M. 1955
Jean-Claude van Itallie, 1958
Arthur Kopit, 1959
Israel Horowitz, attended late 1950s
Nicholas Delbanco, 1963
Michael Crichton, 1964, M.D. 1969
John Balaban, A.M. 1967
James Alan McPherson, LL.B. 1968
Mark Helprin, 1969, A.M. 1972

Harvard and the American Renaissance

Harvard's very first class of only nine scholars—the class of 1644—included both poet Benjamin Woodbridge and his-

Ralph Waldo Emerson

torian William Hubbard, and, as Van Wyck Brooks noted much later, it has been a writer's school from that time forward. In fact, it was often remarked in the nineteenth century that the history of American literature was the history of Harvard.

Thus it seems fitting that its contribution to the American Renaissance, the first great flowering of American literature that took place around 1850, should be Ralph Waldo Emerson and Henry David Thoreau, two of the "big five" writers of that period—a group that also includes Nathaniel Hawthorne (a Bowdoin graduate), and Herman Melville and Walt Whitman (neither of whom went to college).

Ironically, Emerson and Thoreau, who were to become well known for their challenges to the status quo, studied a curriculum that had changed little since the colonial period. As in other American colleges of the day the emphasis was on Greek and Latin; modern languages were taught, but they were still academically suspect, and a student who elected to study them got only half the credit he would earn for a nonelective course. Science too had little place in the curriculum. It was not until after the Civil War that American college curricula began to resemble those we have today, and Charles W. Eliot, who became president of Harvard in 1869, is credited with making Harvard the model for the modern American university and establishing the reputation it enjoys today. During Emerson and Thoreau's years at Harvard, instruction was based largely on memorization and recitation, a regimen neither enjoyed. Yet, though both preferred reading books of their own choosing, each employed himself studiously enough to graduate above the middle of his class and to be awarded a speaking part at commencement.

The early history of American colleges is filled with stories of student rebellions, which were usually put down with such stern authority that further dissent was provoked. Emerson, who entered Harvard in 1817 at the age of fourteen, was younger than most of his classmates and remained somewhat aloof from their activities; yet he became a minor figure in a major controversy during his sophomore year. After some of the sophomores staged a food riot in the commons, the faculty suspended the ringleaders for three months. Protests from the class led to further punishments, and about a week later many sophomores left school in anger. The remaining sophomores, including Emerson, agreed to continue the protest by refusing to attend chapel, and they too were sent home by school officials. A little less than half the class, probably including Emerson, was reinstated about a week later. Emerson did well enough and was well known enough to be elected poet for the Class of 1821. Though he was not overly proud of the honor (six others had turned it down before him), he came up with a conventionally appropriate poem that warned "Gambol and song and jubilee are done,/Life's motley pilgrimage must be begun." At the formal commencement exercise he delivered an oration on John Knox, an assigned topic that interested him so little he was unable to memorize it as was expected and relied heavily on the prompter.

Thoreau, who entered Harvard in 1833, was also something of an outsider. He took no part in the Dunkin Rebellion of 1834, the last major student revolt to take place at Harvard, but a month or two later he testified on behalf of a student whom he felt had been unjustly suspended for allegedly having made offensive noises during chapel—an action that led his biographer Walter Harding to conclude that "though he was unwilling to commit civil (or collegiate) disobedience himself, he was not unwilling to come to the rescue of one whom he felt unjustly charged."

Thoreau was forced to leave college

An 1839 portrait of Henry David Thoreau, by his sister Sophia

twice—once because of illness and once to teach school so that he could earn enough money to continue at Harvard— and these absences counted against him in the complicated grading system (which, along with grades for classwork, figured in points for attendance in class and at chapel and deducted points for misconduct). Yet Thoreau did well enough to be asked to deliver with two other students a "conference" on "The Commercial Spirit of Modern Times" at commencement on 30 August 1837. When his turn came, he startled his audience by attributing the spirit to "a blind and unmanly love of wealth" and proclaiming, "The order of things should be somewhat reversed; the seventh should be man's day of toil, wherein to earn his living by the sweat of his brow; and the other six his Sabbath of the affections and the soul,—in which to range this widespread garden, and drink in the soft influences and sublime revelations of nature."

On the next day his Concord neighbor, Emerson, delivered before the Phi Beta Kappa Society the address that has been called America's intellectual declaration of independence: "The American Scholar." While many of the ideas he expressed were in the air, this statement of them seemed both shocking and inspiring. Insisting, "Our day of dependence, our long apprenticeship to the learning of other lands, draws to a close," he called on the scholar to be "Man Thinking," not "the parrot of other men's thinking," and colleges "not to drill, but to create." The scholar should study nature and learn from experience, saving reading for his "idle hours" when "we repair to the lamps," for: "Meek young men grow up in libraries, believing it their duty to accept the views which Cicero, which Locke, which Bacon, have given; forgetful that Cicero, Locke, and Bacon were only young men in libraries when they wrote these books." Ironically, Thoreau, the very sort of scholar for whom Emerson called, was probably absent, already on his way home to Concord.

Though much that he learned at Harvard influenced him profoundly, Thoreau tended to disparage the value of his academic background. Years later, when Emerson commented that most branches of learning were represented at Harvard, Thoreau replied, "Yes, indeed, all the branches and none of the roots."

A Harvard Crusader

The son of a founder of the prestigious *North American Review*, Richard Henry Dana, Jr., entered Harvard in 1831 and within less than a year managed to find himself caught in a campus controversy. In February 1832 Harvard president Josiah Quincy, much loathed by the students (who called him "Old Quinn"), expelled a charity scholar who had refused to testify against a friend accused of a minor infraction. In the manner of other Harvard classes before and after them, Dana's class organized a mass protest, which in this case consisted of hissing, groaning, and scraping their feet on the floor during assemblies. Dana

was not one of the organizers, and college authorities suggested to his father that if his son would simply cease participation and avoid the other protestors, they would overlook his disobedience. Young Dana insisted, however, that he was honor bound to support his class in their protest against injustice, and his father found himself agreeing. On 2 March the son was suspended for six months, which he spent in Andover being tutored by the brilliant scholar Leonard Woods, Jr. Woods's tutoring was, in fact, much more agreeable and of much higher quality than what Dana had received at Harvard, and he was loath to return to Cambridge when his suspension was ended in September 1832. Thanks to his work under Woods he rose to seventh in his class and started his junior year hoping to rise still higher, but the measles he had contracted during summer vacation had damaged his sight. Finding himself unable to read without pain to his eyes he was soon forced to withdraw. After spending almost a year at home, bemoaning his fate as "a useless, pitied & dissatisfied creature," he signed on as a common seaman aboard the *Pilgrim*, and on 14 August 1834 he began the adventures he would later record in *Two Years Before the Mast* (1840). His eyesight much improved, Dana was back in Boston in September 1836, reentered Harvard in December, and graduated with the Class of 1837. Once again he proved himself a brilliant student. He was elected to Phi Beta Kappa and should have been valedictorian of his class, but his irregular record prevented it. Having had his hatred of injustice reinforced by his observations of the common seaman's lot, Dana went on to law school and became known for his work on maritime law and his attacks on the Fugitive Slave Law.

The Harvard Poets—and One Outsider

The first literary school to wear the Harvard label was a group of young poets who attended Harvard in the

Edwin Arlington Robinson, 1888

1880s and 1890s—most notably George Santayana, William Vaughn Moody, George Cabot Lodge, Hugh McCulloch, and Trumbull Stickney. With the exception of Santayana, all these poets died young and are now remembered—when they are remembered at all—as a minor, neotraditionalist poetic movement that immediately preceded the advent of modernist poets such as T. S. Eliot, Ezra Pound, Robert Frost, William Carlos Williams, Wallace Stevens, Hilda Doolittle (H. D.), and Conrad Aiken (three of whom, in fact, attended Harvard as well).

The oldest of the Harvard poets, Santayana had helped in 1885 to found the *Harvard Monthly*, intended as a more avant-garde rival to the established literary magazine, the *Harvard Advocate*, founded in 1866. Santayana earned his A.B. the following year, but after studying in Germany he returned to Harvard in 1888 for graduate study under William James, earning his doctorate and joining the Harvard faculty, where he remained until 1912. Until 1903 he continued to contribute to the *Monthly*, actively associating with and also teaching some of its editors and regular contributors, which included during the 1880s and 1890s not only Moody, Lodge, McCulloch, and Stickney, but George Pierce Baker, Robert Morss Lovett, Bliss Carman, Bernard Berenson, and Norman and Hutchins Hapgood. Though some of these writers also published work in the *Advocate*, their closer association with the *Monthly* made it the more vital of the two journals during those years.

Santayana is still remembered for his work as a philosopher, and Moody, who graduated from Harvard in 1893, is often mentioned in the classroom as a pioneer of realism on the American stage with his play *The Great Divide* (1906); but the truly great poet to come out of Harvard in the years immediately preceding the arrival of the first generation of American modernists was an outsider: Edwin Arlington Robinson. One of Moody's contemporaries, Robinson attended Harvard as a special student from 1890 to 1893, dropping out after the death of his father left the family in straitened circumstances. Robinson wrote much later that he had realized in 1889 that he was "doomed, or elected, or sentenced for life, to the writing of poetry," but, diffident and shy, he was overshadowed by poets who would prove lesser talents. As a freshman, he submitted some poems to the *Monthly*, which rejected them. Though editor Lovett visited him to explain that the *Monthly* rarely took the work of first-year students and to ask him to try again, Robinson never had any of his work published there. He was more successful with the *Advocate*, which took three of his poems during his freshman year; but when the editors invited him to meet them, he found himself too shy to enter into their conversation. He had only two more poems published in the *Advocate* during his three years at Harvard. Ten years later he told a friend, "I expected to cut quite a shine as a poet. But Moody was in the field ahead of me and I just wasn't in it." Robinson was to remain in obscurity until 1905, when President Theodore Roosevelt discovered his *The Children of the Night* (1897). Today Robinson, not Moody, is taught in high-school and college classrooms as one of the last great realist poets.

William James and Gertrude Stein

Like Santayana, Moody, and Robinson, Gertrude Stein, who entered Radcliffe in 1893, studied under and was influenced by William James; yet she applied that influence in a markedly different manner. Under James, she and a graduate student, Leon M. Solomons, conducted experiments in automatic writing using each other as subjects, and Stein then went on to conduct further experiments on her own with a much larger sample–fifty Radcliffe students and forty-one Harvard students. Stein was later to say that the results of her study, published as "Cultivated Motor Automatism" in the May 1898 issue of *Psychological Review*, were "interesting to read because the method of writing to be afterwards developed in Three Lives and Making of Americans already shows itself." Indeed, in the earlier study Solomons had noted a "marked tendency to repetition" in some of Stein's writing–a tendency that became a major stylistic feature of her later work. Yet she always denied that any of her work was automatic writing and said that she and Solomons had not really "been doing automatic writing, we always knew what we were doing."

The tendency for repetition that Solomons noted during their experiments was already apparent in her assignments for other courses. William Vaughn Moody, who had become an instructor at Harvard, referred to this characteristic when he wrote on one of her themes for a sophomore English course, "Your work has shown at times considerable emotional intensity and a somewhat unusual power of abstract thought. It has frequently been lacking in organiza-

---

CHECKERED CAREER # 4

Heedless of the future literary significance of the young poet's extracurricular endeavor, Harvard officials put dean's list student Conrad Aiken on probation during his senior year because he had become so engrossed in translating Theophile Gautier's novel *La Morte Amoreuse* that he cut too many classes. (He later employed the novel's female-vampire theme in his long poem *The Jig of Forslin*, published in 1916.) Even though he had been elected class poet for the Class of 1911, Aiken, feeling his punishment unjust, resigned from Harvard and went to Europe, where he visited his friend T. S. Eliot. (He probably did not regret forfeiting the honor that his classmates had conferred on him because he hated public speaking.) In fall 1911 he returned to school, graduating in the Class of 1912.

---

tion, in fertility of resources, and artfulness of literary method." Moody, who died in 1910, might well have had similar reactions to Stein's later works.

James, however, was overwhelmingly positive about Stein, following her career with interest and even visiting her in Paris in 1908. Yet his reaction to *Three Lives* (1909) seems to have been mixed. A few months before his death in August 1910 he wrote to her from Germany: "You know how hard it is for me to read novels. Well I read 30 or 40 pages, and said 'this is a fine new kind of realism–Gertrude Stein is great! I will go at it carefully when just the right mood comes.' But apparently the right mood never came. I thought I had put the book in my trunk, to finish over here, but I don't find it on unpacking." James never finished the book he left behind, for he was gravely ill and died soon after his return to the United States.

Stein's enthusiasm for James, however, was unqualified and lifelong. In her sophomore year at Radcliffe, beginning with the title of one of James's best-known essays, she wrote an assignment for Moody in a tone of enraptured homage: "Is life worth living? Yes, a thousand times yes when the world still holds such spirits as Prof. James. He is truly a man among men. . . ." Some of the schoolgirl hero worship may have faded, but it was replaced by a mature appreciation of her mentor's influence. Not long before her death, commenting on her method of writing, she said, "Everything must come into your scheme; otherwise you cannot achieve real simplicity. A great deal of this I owe to a great teacher, William James. He said 'Never reject anything. Nothing has been proved. If you reject anything, that is the beginning of the end as an intellectual.' He was my big influence when I was at college. He was the man who always said, 'complicate your life as much as you please, it has got to simplify.' "

Some Harvard Modernists

Between the Harvard Poets and the next cohesive literary group at Harvard, the members of the Harvard Poetry Soci-

ety, four major modernist poets–Robert Frost, Wallace Stevens, T. S. Eliot, and Conrad Aiken–attended the university. They studied under many of the same professors as the Harvard Poets–for example, Frost, Eliot, and Aiken all took courses from Santayana, while Stevens met him early in his Harvard career and visited him frequently. Yet they would eventually develop poetic aesthetics that differed from those of their predecessors in questioning established assumptions about how we know reality. More important, despite some early cross-influence between Eliot and Aiken, each of these poets developed his aesthetic by himself, and the results are as different as they are similar. Ezra Pound's statement that Eliot made himself a modern poet "*on his own*" might be applied to others as well. None found his mature voice at Harvard, and each might have found it without having been there.

Robert Frost, who attended Harvard for eighteen months in 1897-1899, never met Wallace Stevens, who was there as a special student from 1897 to 1900. Stevens was very much a part of the literary inner circle, contributing to both the *Advocate* and the *Monthly*. He was appointed to the *Advocate* staff in 1899 and served as its president during his last semester. Frost lived off campus with his wife and child and did not have time to participate in extracurricular activities. His English composition teacher, Alfred Dwight Sheffield, always gave him better grades for his prose assignments than for his poetry, even though he turned in one of his best early poems, "The Tuft of Flowers," to Sheffield. Though Stevens maintained a lifelong admiration for Santayana, he later rejected much of the older poet's philosophy. Frost, on the other hand, found Santayana's thinking uncongenial from the start and was more interested in the philosophy of William James, under whom he had been eager to study. James, however, was on leave and Frost

---

Looking back on it forty years later I find myself remembering the time I spent at Harvard as a period of afterglow. At nineteen and twenty I was mighty impatient with that afterglow. . . . William James was dead. . . . Graduate students were still retelling awed anecdotes of Santayana. There had been a young poet named Tom Eliot, an explosive journalist named Jack Reed. They had moved out into the great world of hell-roaring and confusion. I felt I'd come too late. . . .
It took me twenty years to discover that I did learn something at Harvard after all. Cambridge wasn't such a backwater as I'd thought.

—John Dos Passos, "P.S. to Dean Briggs," in College in a Yard *(1957)*

The *Harvard Advocate* staff for 1910: T. S. Eliot is seated third from the left in the first row; Conrad Aiken is standing fourth from the left in the second (courtesy of the Houghton Library, Harvard University)

had to settle for using James's psychology textbook in a course taught by another professor.

Santayana's influence upon the youngest of the Harvard modernists was probably the greatest. Aiken, who entered Harvard in 1907–a year after Eliot–later told a *Paris Review* interviewer that Santayana "fixed my view of what poetry would ultimately be. . . . That it really had to begin by *understanding*, or trying to understand."

Aiken later said that his first clear memory of T. S. Eliot, whom he met at the end of his freshman year, was one evening the following year, when Eliot staggered drunkenly out of the *Lampoon* office, where a party was in progress, and embraced Aiken, who was on his way in (causing another friend to comment, "And that, if Tom remembers it tomorrow, will cause him to suffer agonies of silence"). Both poets served on the board of the *Advocate* and their friendship, based on their shared love

of poetry, proved to be lifelong. Eliot did not understand Aiken's admiration of Santayana, however, and Santayana himself tended to dismiss Eliot's "thought," once remarking about Eliot's admiration for Dante, for example: "We can understand why Mr. Eliot feels this to be a 'superior' philosophy; but how can he fail to see that it is false?" Eliot was far more influenced by Harvard professors Irving Babbitt and Josiah Royce, under whom he wrote his Ph.D. dissertation on the philosopher F. H. Bradley.

George Pierce Baker and the Harvard Playwrights

Admitted to English 47. Please report to Upper Dane 4, the opening Friday of the term, at 3:30. How shall I return your manuscript?" George Pierce Baker, affectionately known at Harvard as G. P. B., sent this message to students whose manuscripts showed enough potential to gain them admittance to the advanced course in playwriting at

Harvard. Among those who received Baker's summonses were a number of aspiring playwrights who would make a major impact on the American theater—including Eugene O'Neill; Edward Sheldon, who became one of the first university-trained dramatists to achieve popular success when the well-known actress Mrs. Minnie Maddern Fiske took his play *Salvation Nell* (1908) to Broadway; Sidney Howard, who won a Pulitzer Prize for his long-running play *They Knew What They Wanted* (1924); S. N. Behrman, who achieved popular success with his comedies *The Second Man* (1927) and *Biography* (1932); and Philip Barry, who had a Broadway success with *You and I* (1923), a play he wrote in Baker's class, and who went on to write such enduring favorites as *Holiday* (1928), *Here Come the Clowns* (1938), and *The Philadelphia Story* (1939). Another of Baker's students was dramatist Dorothy Heyward, who with her husband,

DuBose Heyward, had a Broadway success in 1927 with their dramatization of his novel *Porgy* (later to be the basis for the opera *Porgy and Bess*). Other future theater people to study with Baker included drama critics Heywood Broun and John Mason Brown, as well as writer-directors Leonard Hatch, Allan Davis, and Kenneth McGowan. Though not all of Baker's students became playwrights, some went on to literary success in other genres, most notably novelist Thomas Wolfe, humorist Robert Benchley, literary historian Van Wyck Brooks, and novelist Rachel Field.

A member of Harvard's Class of 1888, G. P. B. began his thirty-seven-year teaching career at Harvard the following fall. He began teaching a playwrighting course at Radcliffe in 1903, and in 1905 he offered English 47 for the first time. In English 47 Baker and his students sat at a large round oak table while Baker—without

The *Harvard Advocate* staff for 1907: Van Wyck Brooks is standing second from left in the third row; Edward Sheldon (in light suit) is standing in the center; Maxwell Perkins is seated second from right (courtesy of the Houghton Library, Harvard University)

CHECKERED CAREER # 5

Well known at Harvard as his class's humorist, Robert Benchley failed to graduate with the Class of 1912 because in the final exam for his international-law course he discussed the Newfoundland fisheries dispute between the United States and Great Britain from the point of view of the fish. He graduated in 1913 (though his diploma was dated 1912) and later made a list of what he had actually learned at Harvard, including: "1. Charlemagne either died or was born or did something with the Holy Roman Empire in 800. 2. By putting one paper bag inside another paper bag you can carry home a milkshake in it. 3. There is a double l in the middle of 'parallel'. . . ."

---

identifying the author—would read a student's play and invite the class to comment and make suggestions. English 47 became popular early on, in part because of the publicity generated when Sheldon, a member of the first class, took *Salvation Nell* to Broadway.

The genesis of English 47 was actually the informal meetings with aspiring dramatists that Baker began holding in his home on Friday or Saturday evenings. Even after the course was formally established, Baker continued to invite groups of students, who became known as "Baker's Dozen," to his evening meetings, and he also used his theater connections to bring well-known visitors to the group. Between 1901 and 1913 Baker's Dozen was visited by such leading dramatists as William Archer, translator of Ibsen; Henry Arthur Jones, a pioneer of modern British drama; Edward Knoblock, author of the popular play *Kismet* (and a student of Baker's at Harvard in the 1890s); Clyde Fitch, well known for his efforts to bring realism to the American stage; and Somerset Maugham.

In 1912 Baker established the 47 Workshop because he felt that the students in English 47 needed to see their plays "adequately acted before an audience, sympathetic yet genuinely critical." Hoping to give his playwrights experience in the realities of the theater for which they must write, he also encouraged them to devise their own scenery and lighting and to experiment with new ideas about setting—to become involved in the total art of the theater. He attempted to give the playwright as much freedom as possible in the production of his play so that the "individuality of the artist may have its best expression." The 47 Workshop was a cooperative enterprise, an association of actors, scenic artists, critics, authors, production personnel, and intelligent audiences, who, instead of paying admission, agreed to provide written criticism to be used by the author as a basis for revision. A "rebellious experimentation," the workshop was the logical extension of English 47.

Yet while Harvard provided the physical setting, the 47 Workshop had no official relationship with the university, and Baker's decision to leave Harvard in 1924 was based primarily on Harvard's lack of support for the 47 Workshop. After a fire in spring 1924 caused extensive damage to the roof of Massachusetts Hall, the home of the workshop, the Harvard administration decided to restore the building to its original use as a dormitory, leaving the 47 Workshop homeless. Yale offered not only to build the theater Baker wanted but to make him head of a newly established and generously endowed department of drama and theater (the beginning of the prestigious Yale School of Drama). The offer was too good to refuse. As Heywood Broun put it, "Yale: 47; Harvard: 0." The theater was built, the drama department established, and Baker spent eight years at Yale. (Among his students at Yale was director Elia Kazan.)

Baker was sometimes wrong in his initial judgments–he told O'Neill in 1914 that *Bound East for Cardiff* was not a play– but he could acknowledge his errors, in this case by opening the 1931-1932 season at Yale with that play. Not all his students accepted his comments and criticism gracefully. Thomas Wolfe was particularly reluctant to take Baker's advice and portrayed him unflatteringly as Professor Hatcher (hatcher of playwrights) in his novel *Of Time and the River* (1935), but later, when asked why he had written so bitterly of 47 Workshop, he replied, "I'll have to admit it was a case of sour grapes–I wasn't much good in that class."

O'Neill, who came to appreciate the intelligent encouragement he had received from Baker, wrote to the *New York Times* after Baker's death in 1935, of the "profound influence Professor Baker . . . exerted toward the encouragement and birth of modern drama."

–J. K. I.

Charles Townsend Copeland, an unfinished portrait by William James, son of the philosopher

"Copey" of Harvard

Charles Townsend Copeland (1860-1952), known to most of his students as Copey, may well have taught writing to more preeminent American men of letters (as well as a few women) than any other American college professor. (Le Baron Russell Briggs Copeland's somewhat older contemporary at Harvard, is probably a close second; many of Copeland's students in English 12 went on to take Briggs's more advanced writing course, English 5.)

Poets abounded at Harvard, and would-be poets, when I went there in the fall of 1915.
—Malcolm Cowley,—And I Worked at the Writer's Trade (1978)

A selective list (roughly chronological) of his writing students suggests the solidity of Copeland's reputation: Earl Derr Biggers, Van Wyck Brooks, Maxwell Perkins, Edward Sheldon, Conrad Aiken, Norman Foerster, Haniel Long, Heywood Broun, T. S. Eliot, Kenneth Macgowan, John Reed, Robert Benchley, Harold Stearns, J. Donald Adams, George Seldes, Gilbert Seldes, S. N. Behrman, John Dos Passos, Brooks Atkinson, Malcolm Cowley, Bernard DeVoto, Stanley Kunitz, Oliver La Farge, Robert E. Sherwood, and Walter D. Edmonds. Copeland also taught writing at Radcliffe, where his students included Helen Keller and Rachel Field, and other future literary figures were enrolled in his large lecture courses on eighteenth- and nineteenth-century English literature.

One of the few notable Harvard writers who did not study under Copeland was James Gould Cozzens. After Copeland read Cozzens's first novel, *Confusion* (1924), published during the spring of the young writer's sophomore year, he "virtually ordered" Cozzens to take English 12 the next year, but Cozzens left Harvard at the end of the

---

CHECKERED CAREER #6

Though he eventually graduated from Harvard in 1918, Robert E. Sherwood was nearly kicked out for academic deficiencies three times before he left to join the Canadian army (the U.S. Army and Navy both rejected him because at 6'7" he was too tall). Despite his total lack of interest in scholarship Sherwood had a brilliant literary career at Harvard. He was editor of the freshman-class magazine, *Redbook* (though he failed freshman English), wrote two plays for the Hasty Pudding Club (though his name was deleted from the program for the first because of his poor grades), and contributed regularly to the *Harvard Lampoon*, serving as its editor during his senior year.

---

spring 1924 semester.

Wallace Stevens, who attended Harvard before Copeland took over English 12, was enrolled in the freshman English A course for which Copeland was then one of the instructors. In spring 1899 Stevens took a literature course from Copeland, and the two became good friends. Yet, according to one of Stevens's Harvard contemporaries, when Stevens announced in spring 1900 that he was leaving school to become a poet, Copeland exclaimed, "Jesus Christ!" (Judging by the poems Stevens was then publishing in the *Harvard Advocate*, Copeland's reaction seems appropriate.)

A Harvard classmate of novelist Owen Wister and the eminent Shakespeare scholar George Lyman Kittredge, Copeland had graduated in 1882 and returned to his alma mater, after a period as a newspaper drama critic, as a freshman English instructor in 1893. Never much of a scholar, he be-

came widely known for his literary readings and, after he took over English 12 in 1905, for his then-unorthodox teaching methods.

Limiting the enrollment of English 12 to thirty students per semester, Copeland required a student to write one piece of fiction, nonfiction, or poetry each week and to read it aloud for him in his quarters, Hollis 15 on Harvard Yard (once the rooms of Ralph Waldo Emerson, whom Copeland had seen at Longfellow's funeral in 1882).

He had too deep a reverence for the art of writing to encourage the dull and the hopeless, to praise bad work however well-intentioned, or to tolerate the mischievous superficiality and mere cleverness that are the worst vices of college writers. Praise came rarely from his lips. . . .
The same honesty withheld him from promising us success. Few of us would ever write well, and those who did must serve an apprenticeship much longer and more painful than he could make clear. He prophesied achievement for none of us—he never told a man, I believe, that he would be a writer.
—Bernard DeVoto, Harvard
Crimson, *Copey 75th Birthday Issue,*
27 April 1935

Noted for feigning sleep and snoring loudly during reading of mediocre compositions, Copeland was also known for his tendency to "awaken" in time to deliver wickedly humorous remarks. Once, after Earl Derr Biggers had struggled—to the accompaniment of Copeland's snores—through the reading of a short story about a man in love with his best friend's wife, Copeland "woke up" just as the husband, discovering his wife in his friend's arms, "immediately" understood what was happening. "What a brain!" Copeland remarked. Malcolm Cowley later remembered reading him "a sententious article written for the *Advocate*, in which one wondered how the country knew who . . . he shook his head and groaned, 'Malcolm, when are you going to stop using those knewwhoings and one-wonderings?' " Cowley never did it again.

Copeland's position as a Harvard legend was acknowledged as early as 1901, when he was portrayed as the lovable eccentric Mr. Fleetwood in Charles Macomb Flandrau's *The Diary of a Freshman*, and by 1906 Copeland was so well loved that a large group of his former students formed the Charles Townsend Copeland Alumni Association, which invited him to the Harvard Club in New York for a birthday dinner and reading annually, with only a few breaks, until he was seventy-seven. The association eventually included in its membership a number of admirers who never studied under Copeland or even attended Harvard—among them Alexander Woollcott, Hervey Allen, John Barrymore, Stephen Vincent Benét, Henry Seidel Canby, Finley Peter Dunne, John Farrar, Walter de la Mare, Laurence Stallings, E. B. White, and Thornton Wilder. Copeland's appearance on the cover of the 17 January 1927 issue of

Time magazine established him as a national figure. He retired in 1928 but stayed on in his rooms on the top floor of Hollis Hall–continuing to meet with students–until summer 1932.

A gruesome uproar fills the void
Of Progress, deafening frenetic
Our sons and daughters take to Freud
And gin, that's equally synthetic,
The world's a movietone, that yells
And curvets like a drunken Hopi–
And yet, despite ten thousand hells
There's always Copey!
–Robert E. Sherwood, from lines
written for Copey's seventieth
birthday, 27 April 1930

Not all Copeland's students were unqualified in their admiration for his teaching methods. T. S. Eliot was never more than respectful in his assessments of any of his undergraduate teachers, including Copeland, and both Conrad Aiken and John Dos Passos preferred Briggs's less flamboyant approach to writing. While Maxwell Perkins–who later,

A FEW (FOUR) SUGGESTIONS FOR MAKING UP THE
UNIVERSITY DEFICIT

A Harvard Lampoon cartoon by Robert Benchley

▼▼▼▼▼▼▼▼▼▼▼▼▼▼▼

CHECKERED CAREER # 7

John Wheelwright, one of the Harvard Aesthetes whose poems were published in *Eight More Harvard Poets* (1923), spent most of his academic career on some sort of academic probation and was finally forced to withdraw in June 1920. Though he made up some of the deficit in his grades in summer school and enrolled for the fall semester, he soon found himself in more trouble. After he copied another student's chemistry notebook openly in front of the instructor (to protest the fact that other students copied one another's lab work secretly), he was warned not to miss any more chemistry classes. He soon did so and on 26 October sent the dean a note explaining that "Acute Nausia [*sic*]" from watching the movie *Way Down East* had made him "sick one hour." The dean was enraged by the note and on 14 November 1920, Wheelwright was required to withdraw from school, earning a reputation as the only person ever to be expelled from Harvard for misspelling a word.

▲▲▲▲▲▲▲▲▲▲▲▲▲▲▲

as chief editor at Scribners, published anthologies of Copeland's readings and encouraged him to write his memoirs—was one of his greatest admirers, Van Wyck Brooks was less enthusiastic, writing later that Copeland had called him "wilful and stubborn" because "I did not wish to write in the manner that pleased him. . . ."

Yet the majority of Copeland's students felt indebted to him. One of his favorite students, John Reed, dedicated his book *Insurgent Mex*— would never have seen what I did had it not been for your teaching me." Copeland came to deplore Reed's Bolshevik politics, but after Reed's death he spoke to his English 12 class stressing "the need of respecting and praising an honest man who made great sacrifices for a cause, no matter how strong our own feeling might be against it." Perhaps Heywood Broun summed up Copeland's essential quality as a teacher when he wrote for the 10 May 1924 issue of *Collier's*, "He made us know that writing is honorable and alive. Hundreds of men left Cambridge and Harvard eager to sit down and write the great American novel. None of them has done it yet, but they feel, after knowing him, that about the most important thing anybody could do in the world would be to create something fine in words."

*Dean Briggs and the
Harvard Poetry Society*

While Copeland is undeniably the best-known Harvard writing teacher, some of the more-literary types preferred Dean Le Baron Russell Briggs, who—by the time E. E. Cummings and John Dos Passos got to Harvard—was not only Boylston Professor of Rhetoric and Ora-

S. Foster Damon and E. E. Cummings during their Harvard years (photograph by Moses Photo Studio, Boston)

tory (the English department's most prestigious chair) but also chief assistant to President Abbott L. Lowell and head of Radcliffe College. Despite his heavy administrative duties Briggs met his classes conscientiously, graded all his students' papers himself, and made himself accessible to his students.

Less flamboyant than Copeland, the kindly, modest, and slightly built Briggs had what John Dos Passos later called "an old-fashioned schoolmaster's concern for the neatness of language, a Yankee zest for the shipshape phrase, an old-fashioned gentleman's concern for purity of morals, to use a properly old-fashioned expression, and a sharp nose for sham and pretense. . . ." His taste in literature was also old-fashioned, and sometimes his reactions to his students' work seemed priggish to them. In spring 1916 when E. E. Cummings was in his poetry-writing class—which also included poets S. Foster Damon and Robert Hillyer, future playwright S. N. Behrman, and the future managing editor of the *Dial*, Stewart Mitchell—Briggs was uneasy not only about Cummings's experiments with irregular meters and line lengths but also with his diction and subject matter. After Cummings complied with the assignment for a poem in heroic couplets with one about drunken brawling and prostitutes in a beer hall (in which he used words such as "whore," "bitch," "croak," and "soused"), Briggs acknowledged that Cummings had fulfilled the assignment, but, he appealed, "Please don't forget that a clean subject is never harmful."

Whatever their reservations about Briggs's conservative taste, when some of the *Harvard Monthly* editorial board decided to form the Harvard Poetry Society, they chose Briggs as their adviser. Founded to provide these young poets with a forum for reading and discussing one another's poetry, the society usually kept its meetings closed. Though they sometimes invited prospective members to attend as guests, they wanted to avoid both the criticisms of more-established poets and the petty chitchat of less serious writers. Of the original society members only Robert Hillyer was a conservative. Cummings, Dos Passos, Damon, and Mitchell were modernists, sharing diverse interests in Gertrude Stein, Pound and the imagists, and such modern-art movements as Cubism and Vorticism.

During the first year of the Poetry Society's existence, Mitchell decided that they should compile a volume of poems by some of their members. With its publication costs guaranteed by Dos Passos's father, *Eight Harvard Poets* was published by Lawrence Gomme of New York in fall 1916. Containing poems by Cummings, Dos Passos, Damon, Hillyer, Mitchell Dudley Poore, Cuthbert Wright, and William Norris (a friend of Hillyer's who was actually a member of

---

CHECKERED CAREER #8

James Gould Cozzens did surprisingly well at Harvard considering the amount of time he spent avoiding his studies to read books that interested him, carousing with various friends, and writing—his first novel, *Confusion*, was published on 11 April 1924, during the second semester of his sophomore year. By then, he was on academic probation, and—suffering damaged health from the excessive drinking and lack of sleep that resulted from the celebration surrounding the acceptance and publication of his novel—he was allowed to withdraw from school "in view of his physical condition." Though he was free to return to Harvard, Cozzens never went back. In 1977 he explained, "I did not want to return to Cambridge unable to support myself financially on the scale I felt my 'fame' as a published writer required."

Signet, another literary society), the book is now a collector's item. In 1923 Hillyer and Damon, both instructors at Harvard, edited *Eight More Harvard Poets*, containing poems by some of the younger members: Malcolm Cowley, John Wheelwright, Norman Cabot, Grant Code, Jack Merton, Joel Rogers, R. Cameron Rogers, and Royall Snow.

HAVERFORD COLLEGE

Christopher Morley, 1910
Frederic Prokosch, 1926, M.A. 1928

HIRAM COLLEGE

Harold Bell Wright, attended 1894-1896
Vachel Lindsay, attended 1897-1899

HOLLINS COLLEGE

Annie Dillard, 1967, M.A. 1968
Lee Smith, 1967
Ben Greer, M.A. 1973

HOWARD UNIVERSITY

Zora Neale Hurston, attended 1919-1924
Rudolph Fisher, M.D. 1924
Ossie Davis, attended 1935-1938
Toni Morrison, 1953
Ted Shine, 1953
LeRoi Jones (Amiri Baraka), 1954

Joseph A. Walker, 1956
A. B. Spellman, 1958
Richard Wesley, 1967

HUMBOLDT STATE UNIVERSITY

Raymond Carver, 1963

HUNTER COLLEGE, CITY UNIVERSITY OF NEW YORK

Wilsonia Driver (Sonia Sanchez), 1955
Elaine Kraf, 1965

HUNTINGDON COLLEGE
(Montgomery, Alabama)

Harper Lee, attended 1944-1945

INDIANA UNIVERSITY AT BLOOMINGTON

Theodore Dreiser, attended 1889-1890
Ross Lockridge, Jr., 1935
David Wagoner, M.A. 1949
Gary Snyder, graduate study 1952-1953
Robert Coover, 1953
George Cuomo, M.A. 1955
Clayton Eshleman, 1953, M.A.T. 1961
John Hollander, Ph.D. 1959

IOWA STATE UNIVERSITY OF SCIENCE AND TECHNOLOGY

Philip Klass (William Tenn), 1941

An Indiana University cave-exploring group, 1889-1890: Theodore Dreiser is seated second from right in the rear (courtesy of the Theodore Dreiser Collection, Special Collections, Van Pelt Library, University of Pennsylvania)

CHECKERED CAREER # 9

A member of a large family that repeatedly fled from one poverty-stricken environment to another that was even poorer, Theodore Dreiser was given a respite from that downward spiral of poverty when his high-school English teacher, Miss Mildred Fielding, helped him to spend a year at Indiana University (1889-1890). Unable to finance further study, Dreiser may have learned little in the classroom, but his observations of his fellow collegians fostered in him a desire for upward mobility. In summer 1892 he took a poorly paying job with the *Chicago Globe* and progressed through a series of increasingly better positions in journalism. After publishing his first and most controversial novel, *Sister Carrie*, in 1900, he became an editor of the popular New York-based *Smith's Magazine* in 1905 and an editor of the even more popular Butterick's magazine *Delineator* in 1907.

JOHNS HOPKINS UNIVERSITY

Richard Harding Davis, attended 1885-1886

Gertrude Stein, attended medical school 1897-1901

Paul Myron Anthony Linebarger (Cordwainer Smith), M.A. 1935, Ph.D. 1936

Karl Shapiro, attended 1937-1939

John Barth, 1951, M.A. 1952, further graduate study 1952-1953

Gil Scott-Heron, M.A. 1972

THE JUILLIARD SCHOOL

John Barth, attended 1947

KANSAS STATE UNIVERSITY

Claude McKay, attended 1913-1914

KENT STATE UNIVERSITY

Paul Zimmer, 1968

KENYON COLLEGE

Robert Lowell, 1940

Peter Taylor, 1940

Anthony Hecht, graduate study late 1940s

William Gass, 1947

E. L. Doctorow, 1952

James Wright, 1952

A Boston Brahmin Discovers the Fugitives

As a Harvard freshman looking for a poetic mentor in 1935-1936, Robert Lowell was encouraged by both Ford Madox Ford (whom he met at a cocktail party) and Dr. Merrill Moore (his psychiatrist, who had been a member of the Fugitive poets' group at Vanderbilt) to seek out another Fugitive poet, Allen Tate. Lowell took their advice and in April 1957 set out with a suitcase "heavy with poetry" to visit Tate and his wife, the novelist Caroline Gordon, at Benfolly, their run-down antebellum house in Clarksville, Tennessee, near Nashville.

Lowell's first act upon arrival was to mash "the Tates' frail agrarian mail box post" with the bumper of his car, but he managed to disguise the damage, and he and Tate liked each other immediately. As Lowell put it later, "I had crashed the civilization of the South." He ended up spending the summer in a tent pitched on the Tates' front lawn, with their calf, Uncle Andrew, "sagged against my tent sides." During that time Tate introduced Lowell to John Crowe Ransom and convinced his young protégé that he should transfer to Vanderbilt University so that he could study under Ransom. But late that summer Ransom accepted a new position at Kenyon College, and Lowell transferred there instead.

During his first year at Kenyon Lowell shared a room in the Ransoms' house with Randall Jarrell, then a young instructor and tennis coach who had followed Ransom to Kenyon, and the next year he roomed in Douglass

Randall Jarrell, Robert Lowell, and Peter Taylor (courtesy of Mary Jarrell and the University of North Carolina at Greensboro)

It was not the classes, but the conversations that mattered. We used to memorize and repeat and mimic Ransom sentences. We learned something from that. Somehow one left him with something inside us moving toward articulation, logic, directness, and complexity. . . .

—Robert Lowell, "John Ransom's Conversation," Sewanee Review *(1948)*

House on campus with the future novelist Peter Taylor, another undergraduate who had followed Ransom from Vanderbilt.

Taylor recalled later how Ransom would stop and call for Lowell to go on afternoon walks with him. Indeed, though he was valedictorian of his class and graduated summa cum laude and Phi Beta Kappa, Lowell said more than once that he learned much more from his conversations with Ransom and Jarrell—either together or separately—than he learned in the classroom. Despite their common grounds, Ransom and Jarrell had their differences as well, and they loved dispute. In 1967 Lowell still recalled one argument, over Shakespeare's sonnets, that was characterized by "each expounding to the oth-er's deaf ears his own inspired and irreconcilable interpretation."

Even as an undergraduate Lowell had poems published in the *Kenyon Review*, which Ransom had founded in 1939. Yet Ransom was not impressed with all of Lowell's student poems, especially one that he called "oppressive": a still unpublished anti-British mock epic in which Satan appears as a character witness for John Bull.

KNOX COLLEGE

George Fitch, 1897

Old Siwash

George Fitch protested in the preface to his novel *At Good Old Siwash* (1911) that the school he was satirizing in this book and in his earlier collection of short stories was not his alma mater, Knox College, in Galesburg, Illinois. Yet many readers found his disclaimer unconvincing.

Regardless of Siwash's actual location, Fitch's novel is still considered one of the all-time great satires on the sort of college that puts fraternity life and football above academics (one football player has to be led around on a rope, and the professors "mar the joy of college" by their attempts to educate the students).

Fitch died the year before his last book about Old Siwash, another collection of short stories, was published; but for years afterward the name of that small, private college lived on as a generic term for any hick-town school.

LAFAYETTE COLLEGE

Stephen Crane, attended 1890

LA SALLE COLLEGE

Charles Fuller, attended 1965-1968

LEHIGH UNIVERSITY

Richard Harding Davis, attended 1882-1885
Skipwith Cannell, attended 1905

LEWIS INSTITUTE

Janet Lewis, A.A. 1918

LINCOLN MEMORIAL UNIVERSITY

James Still, 1929
Jesse Stuart, 1929

LINCOLN UNIVERSITY
(Lincoln University, Pennsylvania)

Melvin B. Tolson, 1923
Langston Hughes, 1929
Larry Neal, 1961
Gil Scott-Heron, attended 1967-1970

The Harlem Renaissance on Campus
When Langston Hughes arrived on the campus of Lincoln University in Pennsylvania in February 1926, he had just turned twenty-four, and Alfred A. Knopf had just published his first book of poetry, *The Weary Blues* (1926), which would solidify his position as one of the leading young writers of the Harlem, or New Negro, Renaissance. Older than most of his classmates—one of whom was future U.S. Supreme Court Justice Thurgood Marshall—Hughes had attended Columbia University for the 1921-1922 academic year and then

worked at a variety of jobs in and around New York before he shipped out on a freighter to Africa in 1923 and in 1924 to Europe, where he jumped ship and worked in Paris, with side trips to Italy. Though he was more worldly than the other students at the all-male black college and though he frequently took advantage of the fact that the school was within commuting distance by train from Manhattan, where he frequently spent weekends keeping up literary contacts, the somewhat shy young poet was popular with the other students and joined a fraternity. "Lincoln is more like what home ought to be than any place I've ever seen," Hughes wrote to novelist Carl Van Vechten, who had helped him find a publisher for his first book.

Hughes's literary reputation continued to grow during his student years. In early 1928 Knopf published his second book of poetry, *Fine Clothes to the Jew*, which his biographer Arnold Rampersad calls "one of the most astonishing books of verse ever published in the United States—comparable in the black world to *Leaves of Grass* in the white, "and he was working on a novel, *Not Without Laughter* (1930), which he completed a few months after his graduation from Lincoln in June 1929. But the piece of writing for which he was probably best known on campus was a paper about Lincoln University that he wrote for a sociology class during his last semester.

Examining all aspects of the university, Hughes criticized the students' attitudes and immaturity as well as the faculty and curriculum, but the most controversial part of the paper was the report of a survey of the student body's attitude toward their being taught by Lincoln's white faculty (a few Lincoln graduates had sometimes been employed as temporary instructors, but all the professors were white). About sixty-four percent of the students said that they did not want black teachers at Lincoln. Part of the survey was posted on

Langston Hughes at Lincoln University, 1928 (courtesy of the Schomburg Center for Research in Black Culture, New York Public Library, Astor, Lenox and Tilden Foundations)

the sociology bulletin board, and someone sent it to the *Baltimore Afro-American*, which on 27 April 1929 published a front-page headline that read "LINCOLN VOTED 81-46 AGAINST MIXED FACULTY." The survey provoked considerable controversy, with many Lincoln alumni angrily attacking or defending the majority opinion. Hughes stuck by what he had written. As black educator Alain Locke, who visited Hughes during the controversy, wrote to a friend, the faculty was "scared stiff," but Hughes's criticism seems to have brought no repercussions. He was chosen to write the "Ivy Day Toast," and the university's president, William Hallock Johnson, not only gave him a free dorm room for the summer so that he could continue work on his novel, but he also wrote the foreword for *Four Lincoln University Poets* (1930), which includes poems by Hughes, Waring Cuney, William Allyn Hill, and Edward Silvera.

LOMBARD COLLEGE

Carl Sandburg, attended 1898-1902

LORAS COLLEGE

David Rabe, 1962

LOS ANGELES CITY COLLEGE

Charles Bukowski, attended 1939-1941
William F. Nolan, attended 1953
Ed Bullins, attended intermittently 1958-1963
Quincy Troupe, A.A. 1967

LOUISIANA STATE UNIVERSITY AT BATON ROUGE

Robert Lowell, graduate study 1940-1941
Peter Taylor, graduate study 1940-1941
Wirt Williams, M.A. 1941

MACALESTER COLLEGE

Tim O'Brien, 1968

MASSACHUSETTS INSTITUTE OF TECHNOLOGY

Gelett Burgess, 1887
L. Sprague de Camp, graduate study 1932

MEDICAL UNIVERSITY OF SOUTH CAROLINA

O. B. Mayer, M.D. 1840

MIAMI UNIVERSITY

Ridgely Torrence, attended 1893-1895

MICHIGAN STATE UNIVERSITY

Jim Harrison, 1960, M.A. 1964
Tom McGuane, 1962
Carolyn Forché, 1972

MIDDLEBURY COLLEGE

Bread Loaf Writers' Conference
Usually associated in the public mind
with Robert Frost, who served on the
staff in 1929 and in the late 1930s and
the 1940s, the Bread Loaf Writers' Conference is the most prestigious summer
writers' conference in the country and
the prototype for the many other such
conferences that have sprung up since it
was founded in 1926.

Part of Bread Loaf's longevity must
be attributed to its setting. Not far from
the Middlebury campus, at the foot of
Bread Loaf Mountain just past the village of Ripton, Vermont, the conference
is housed in the former Bread Loaf Inn—
and some twenty cottages and barns, including a large dairy barn that has been
converted into a recreation center—all
constructed in the same shingled,
gingerbread-Victorian style and painted
yellow with dark green trim. The fur-
nishings are rustic but suitably antique.

Built by Joseph Battell (1839-1915),
an eccentric man of means who bought
the land in 1865 because he liked the
view, the inn was a rural retreat for genteel ladies and gentlemen who liked to
hunt, fish, hike, and ride without having to spend their nights in leaky tents
or to eat food under- or overcooked on
the campfire.

After Battell left the inn and all the
surrounding lands to Middlebury in
1915, the college spent several years trying to decide what to do with the property and nearly sold it, but in 1921
several faculty members convinced the
administration to let them start a summer school of English at Bread Loaf.
The Bread Loaf School of English is
still in operation, granting masters' degrees to students who have completed
four intensive summer sessions.

In 1926 Middlebury added a two-
week creative-writing session after the
regular summer session. For the first
three years of its existence, the Bread
Loaf Writers' Conference was directed
by John Farrar, editor of the American
Bookman and later one of the founders
of the publishing house Farrar and
Rinehart. Frost, who often gave readings and lectures at the School of English, was on the writers' conference
staff in 1929, but he grew to dislike Farrar, whom he accused of using the conference as a "Two Week Manuscript
Sales Fair," and he did not return until
summer 1936.

▼▼▼▼▼▼▼▼▼▼▼▼

AMERICAN WRITERS WHO WERE
RHODES SCHOLARS

At his death in 1902 Cecil Rhodes,
the wealthy diamond magnate and former prime minister of South Africa,
left $10 million to endow 170 scholar-
ships at Oxford University for young
men from the United States, Germany, and the countries that were
then British colonies. In 1976 these
prestigious scholarships were made
available to women as well. The following American writers studied at Oxford as Rhodes Scholars:

Alain Locke
Christopher Morley
John Crowe Ransom
Robert P. Tristram Coffin
Robert Penn Warren
Cleanth Brooks
Paul Engle
William Jay Smith
Eugene Burdick
Reynolds Price
Willie Morris
John Edgar Wideman

▲▲▲▲▲▲▲▲▲▲▲▲▲

By that time Frost's friend Theodore Morrison, a poet and Harvard professor, was running the conference, having been appointed director in late 1932. Morrison developed for the conference the national reputation that it still enjoys, bringing to the staff not only Frost but novelists Bernard DeVoto and Wallace Stegner, poets Edith Mirrielees and Louis Untermeyer, biographer Catherine Drinker Bowen, and drama critic John Mason Brown. He also attracted such guest lecturers as Sinclair Lewis, Archibald MacLeish, James T. Farrell, W. H. Auden, William Carlos Williams, Richard Wright, and Katherine Anne Porter. Morrison's most significant accomplishment, however, was the establishment of the Bread Loaf Scholarships for promising new writers. Novelist Howard Fast was given a scholarship for the 1935 session, and in 1940 John Ciardi, Carson McCullers, and Eudora Welty were all granted scholarships. Other notable Bread Loaf Scholarship recipients during Morrison's directorship were Theodore Roethke (1941) and novelist A. B. Guthrie (1945).

The scholarship program expanded under John Ciardi, who took over the directorship in 1956. Among the recipients were May Swenson (1957), Anne Sexton (1959), and Joan Didion (1963).

Since the poet Robert Pack became director in 1973, the staff has included novelists John Gardner, John Irving, Tim O'Brien, Jerome Charyn, and Robert Stone; and poets Howard Nemerov, Marvin Bell, Galway Kinnell, William Matthews, Nancy Willard, Linda Pastan, and Carolyn Forché. By 1983 the conference was granting more than fifty full and partial scholarships, including one in memory of longtime staff member John Gardner, who died in 1982.

MISSISSIPPI COLLEGE

Barry Hannah, 1964

MOREHOUSE COLLEGE

Tom Dent, 1952

MORGAN STATE COLLEGE

James Alan McPherson, attended 1963-1964

MORRIS BROWN COLLEGE

James Alan McPherson, attended 1961-1963, 1964-1965, B.A. 1965

MOUNT SAN ANTONIO COLLEGE

Sam Shepard, attended 1960-1961

MUHLENBERG COLLEGE

Theodore Weiss, 1938

NEW SCHOOL FOR SOCIAL RESEARCH

Robert Anderson, attended 1945-1946

William Styron, attended 1947

John Clellon Holmes, attended 1949-1950

Edgar Lewis Wallant, attended early 1950s

Mario Puzo, attended 1950s

William Price Fox, attended 1961

Jerzy Kosinski, attended 1962-1966

Elaine Kraf, attended 1964

NEW YORK LAW SCHOOL

Wallace Stevens, LL.B. 1903

Elmer Rice, LL.B. 1912

NEW YORK UNIVERSITY

Irwin Granich (Michael Gold), attended 1912-1913

Charles Reznikoff, LL.B. 1915

Lillian Hellman, attended 1922-1924

Countee Cullen, 1925

Delmore Schwartz, 1935

Carson McCullers, attended 1935

J. D. Salinger, attended 1937

Neil Simon, attended 1944-1945

James Jones, attended 1945

Paul Blackburn, attended 1945-1949

Wallace Markfield, graduate study 1947-1949

Joseph Heller, 1948
Cynthia Ozick, 1949
M. L. Rosenthal, Ph.D. 1949
Michael Benedikt, 1956
Wilsonia Driver (Sonia Sanchez), graduate study 1955-1956
Jean-Claude van Itallie, graduate study 1958-1959
Ed Saunders, 1963

NORTH TEXAS STATE UNIVERSITY

Larry McMurtry, 1958

NORTHWESTERN UNIVERSITY

Albert Halper, attended 1924-1925
Peter DeVries, attended 1931
Saul Bellow, 1937
Terry Southern, 1948
John Jakes, attended 1949-1950

NOTRE DAME UNIVERSITY

John Frederick Nims, 1937, M.A. 1939

OBERLIN COLLEGE

Thornton Wilder, attended 1915-1917
S. Randolph Edmonds, 1926

OCCIDENTAL COLLEGE

Robinson Jeffers, 1905

OHIO STATE UNIVERSITY

Dorothy Canfield Fisher, 1899
James Thurber, attended 1913-1918
Kenneth Burke, attended 1916-1917
Elliott Nugent, 1919
W. R. Burnett, attended 1919-1920
Chester Himes, attended 1926-1927
Harlan Ellison, attended 1953-1954
Cynthia Ozick, M.A. 1950
John Jakes, M.A. 1954

A Campus Humorist

Though novelist Dorothy Canfield Fisher, whose father was president of Ohio State University, runs a close second, James Thurber is OSU's best-known literary alumnus. Thurber had mixed feelings about the school. He loved to quote his favorite professor, Dean Joseph Villiers Denney, who accused the administration of spending "millions for manure but not one cent for literature." Yet after an inauspicious start, he became very much caught up in campus social life and in later years was noted for singing college and fraternity songs with his cronies.

Thurber never graduated from Ohio State, in part because, having lost an eye in a childhood accident and having no talent whatsoever for athletics, he failed to complete the two years of military drill required of every male undergraduate who was capable of walking—even though he enrolled in the course every semester for the five years he was in school (1913-1918). His poor eyesight also caused him trouble in botany, a course he needed to fulfill the science requirement. Students were expected to examine plant cells under the microscope and draw what they saw, but Thurber never saw anything, much to the exasperation of his incredulous professor, who tried, Thurber remembered later, "every adjustment of the microscope known to man."

A Columbus, Ohio, native who lived at home, Thurber was pretty much a nonentity during his first years of college. In his freshman year, he was blackballed by the one fraternity that had expressed any interest in him (a fate that his biographer Burton Bernstein has called "akin to a terminal case of leprosy" at a school like Ohio State), and his best friend from high school, who had made the fraternity, dropped him. It took Thurber three years to complete his sophomore year—largely because, though he signed up for courses every semester, for three of those six semesters he never attended a class, probably spending his time at the library or the movies—a fact that acquaintances and even family members somehow failed to notice.

During fall 1916 (the first semester of his third sophomore year), however, he had the good fortune to meet Elliott Nugent, after their American literature instructor read aloud one of Thurber's themes, "My Literary Enthusiasms," a humorous critique of dime novels. Also a budding writer, the popular Nugent enjoyed Thurber's sense of humor and took him under his wing, getting him a haircut and a new suit and convincing the other brothers in his prestigious fraternity, Phi Kappa Psi, to admit Thurber even though most of them considered him an oddball.

Nugent also got Thurber involved in extracurricular activities. They were both reporters for the *Ohio State Lantern* in 1916-1917, and in 1917-1918 each was editor for one issue each week. That same year Thurber was made editor of the *Sundial*, the monthly humor and literary magazine, and appointed Nugent assistant editor. Nugent also got Thurber involved with other groups, and the two friends made both Sigma Delta Chi, the journalism honorary society, and Sphinx, an elite senior men's society.

Despite his good academic standing (largely because he did well in English courses and took as many as he could), Thurber decided in May 1918 to drop out, taking advantage of a provision that allowed him to leave school for war

work without penalty to his academic standing. After service as a code clerk in Washington (where he met Stephen Vincent Benét) and France, Thurber returned to Columbus in early 1920. While he wrote or helped to write librettos for six shows produced by the university's Scarlet Mask Club (which specialized in all-male revues, in the tradition of Harvard's Hasty Pudding Club or Princeton's Triangle Club), he never enrolled for classes, probably because he was convinced that he could never satisfy not only the drill requirements but others in science, foreign language, and physical education.

One of the Scarlet Mask shows, *Tell Me Not*, contains the germ for the plot of *The Male Animal*, Thurber and Nugent's 1940 hit Broadway play. Set on the campus of a state university easily recognizable as Ohio State, *The Male Animal* is a comedy about the confrontation between academic freedom and the moneyed, anti-intellectual, and conformist forces of vested powers and interests. (Dean Frederick Damon, the true spirit of academe, is based on Thurber's English professor Dean Joseph Denney.)

OHIO UNIVERSITY

William Heyen, M.A. 1963, Ph.D. 1967

OREGON STATE UNIVERSITY

George Oppen, attended 1926

PACIFIC UNION COLLEGE

Arna Bontemps, 1923

PEACE COLLEGE

Gail Godwin, attended 1955-1957

PENNSYLVANIA STATE UNIVERSITY

A. Lincoln Gillespie, 1916
Vance Packard, 1936
David Wagoner, 1947
John Balaban, 1966
David Morrell, M.A. 1967, Ph.D. 1970

CHECKERED CAREER #10

The end of Chester Himes's academic career came in 1927, when he was thrown out of Ohio State University for taking part in a speakeasy brawl. Two years later he was sent to prison for armed robbery, and it was there, rather than in college, that he got his start as a writer.

POMONA COLLEGE

Wright Morris, attended 1930-1933
Andrew Hoyem, 1957

PRATT INSTITUTE

Jules Feiffer, attended 1947-1951
Edgar Lewis Wallant, 1950

PRINCETON UNIVERSITY

Hugh Henry Brackenridge, 1771, M.A.
  1774
Philip Freneau, 1771
David Graham Phillips, 1887
Booth Tarkington, attended 1891-1893
Ridgely Torrence, attended 1895-1896
Ernest Poole, 1902
Eugene O'Neill, attended 1906-1907
Harold Loeb, 1913
F. Scott Fitzgerald, attended 1913-1917
Edmund Wilson, 1916
Robert P. Tristram Coffin, M.A. 1916
John Peale Bishop, 1917
Elliott White Springs, 1917
George R. Stewart, 1917
Thornton Wilder, M.A. 1926
Louis Coxe, 1940
William Meredith, 1940
Edgar Bowers, attended 1943
Reed Whittemore, graduate study 1945-
  1946
W. S. Merwin, 1947
Frederick Buechner, 1948
Galway Kinnell, 1948
George Garrett, 1952, M.A. 1956
John Gregory Dunne, 1954

*Booth Tarkington and the Birth
of the Triangle Club*

Though Booth Tarkington attended Princeton for only two years (in 1891-1893), he became a campus legend. As his biographer, James Woodress, discovered, "No one who knew Tarkington during his two years at Princeton ever forgot him." When F. Scott Fitzgerald got to Princeton in 1913, Tarkington, who was just then embarking on the most productive period of his career, was still a topic of conversation. In his first novel, *This Side of Para-*

dise (1920), Fitzgerald recorded one Tarkington legend: the story of how Tarkington used to enjoy "standing in mid-campus in the small hours and singing tenor songs to the stars. . . . " The story seems to have become somewhat garbled in the course of twenty years (for one thing, Tarkington, who was a popular soloist in the Princeton Glee Club, sang bass), but he did serenade the campus late at night at least once. He sang "Danny Deever" outside his dormitory, and, according to his audience, thunder sounded in the distance just as he finished singing the last deep notes.

Princeton University was founded in 1746 as a Presbyterian college and is now one of the most desired and desirable places in America in which to loiter through four years of one's youth.
—John Peale Bishop, "Princeton,"
Smart Set *(November 1921)*

Tarkington's success in the Glee Club (where one of his solos—the show-stopping "It's All Over Now"—was his own composition) was more than matched by his literary accomplishments. He was editor of three campus publications: the *Nassau Literary Magazine* (better known as the *Lit*), the *Tiger* (the campus humor magazine), and the *Bric-a-Brac* (the yearbook). For the *Lit* and the *Tiger* he wrote mediocre verse and mostly forgettable short stories and sketches in the various manners of Bret Harte, Edgar Allan Poe, Mark Twain, and George Ade. Yet he secured his place in Princeton history during his senior year by writing *The Honorable Julius Caesar* for the Dramatic Association, of which he was president.

Tarkington not only wrote the book for this burlesque musical comedy, but he also took care of casting, coaching the chorus, and designing the costumes. He even helped build the scenery and played one of the major parts, Cassius, whom the program (which he also wrote) called "an old-time villain, wily

Booth Tarkington (left) as Cassius in *The Honorable Julius Caesar*, 1893

and tricky, with an unappeasable appetite for crime."

Some time later in Tarkington's last year at Princeton the Dramatic Association changed its name to the Triangle Club. The next year they restaged Tarkington's play, establishing the club's tradition of producing a musical comedy by one or more of its members annually. By the time Fitzgerald got to Princeton, the Triangle Club was famous for its Christmastime tour of major cities, but during its early years, the faculty limited performances to Princeton and Trenton because they feared the shows would give the school a frivolous, theatrical image that might be offensive to the nation's churchgoers.

Tarkington had transferred from Purdue to Princeton as a special student because—on the advice of his successful and practical-minded uncle Newton Booth, a former governor of California—he had not taken Latin and Greek and therefore could not satisfy the classical-

language entrance requirement. While his course work was mostly satisfactory and occasionally brilliant (even though he seldom studied), he was ineligible for a degree, a fact he regretted only once—on graduation day in 1893. He always looked back fondly on Princeton, and years later he said that in his memories the town was filled with flowers, "it never rained! It was always sunshine then."

F. Scott Fitzgerald—And Friends

Tarkington may have been a Princeton legend during Fitzgerald's undergraduate days, but Fitzgerald, who entered Princeton in the class of 1917, is now the writer whose name is most frequently associated with Princeton—in part because of the phenomenal success of *This Side of Paradise*, which devotes somewhat more than forty percent of its pages to the young protagonist's Princeton years. During his own student years, Fitzgerald shared the literary limelight with a few other young writers, most notably John Peale Bishop (Class of 1917) and Edmund Wilson (Class of 1916). Wilson, who made the editorial board of the *Nassau Lit* in his sophomore year and served as its chairman during his senior year, was credited by Christian Gauss, the only one of their literature professors for whom Fitzgerald and Wilson, seemed to have any respect, as a major force in bringing a new vitality to the *Lit*: "Red-haired, eager, tireless, he bubbled with ideas and threw them out by the handful. He would discuss any *Lit* problem with anyone . . . until four a.m. Neither then nor later could he ever resist an idea that tempted him and he had what an editor should have, ideas to give away. He welcomed any kind of writing except the pretentious and the shoddy."

Gauss identified the *Lit*'s inner circle during those years as consisting of Wilson, Bishop, Fitzgerald, and a fourth young man named Stanley Dell; and, he said, though the group never formed a literary school, they "enjoyed carrying the literary war into the country of the Philistines." That the general student population found their literary tastes too advanced is suggested by the fact that Wilson's "philistine" classmates elected him "the worst poet" (their favorite poets were Tennyson, Robert Service, Kipling, and Ella Wheeler Wilcox). Despite the lack of respect it was afforded in some quarters, the *Lit* was successful, and Wilson later remembered that it made a profit.

Princeton drew him most, with its atmosphere of bright colors and its alluring reputation as the pleasantest country club in America.
—F. Scott Fitzgerald, This Side of Paradise *(1920)*

Bishop, who had started at Princeton late because of childhood illness, was three and a half years older than his classmate Fitzgerald, and his maturity was evident in his poetry and his carriage. Gauss later recalled that Bishop "came to Princeton with a more carefully thought out and more accomplished mastery of the technique of English verse than any other undergraduate in that talented group. Even as a freshman John had a self possession and self mastery which gave him the poise and bearing of a young English lord." This manner, as well as Bishop's love for the decadent poets of the 1890s—Wilde, Swinburne, Dowson, to name a few—is reflected in the name Fitzgerald gave him in *This Side of Paradise*: Thomas Park D'Invilliers. Yet Fitzgerald and Wilson saw another side to the young West Virginian who was acutely aware of his Southern heritage. When he wrote the introduction for the posthumous collection of Bishop's essays (1948), Wilson remembered that Bishop was "sometimes shy and sometimes crude amid the monied proprieties of Princeton. . . . What was not at all *fin de Siècle* was the touch of eighteenth-century coarseness that was still country-bred and Southern and

that was not in the least inimical to his fastidious taste and intellect but the soil out of which they grew. . . . " Fitzgerald, like Amory Blaine in his novel, sought to educate his poetic friend about the social and sartorial nuances necessary for campus popularity, and in the novel at least there is some progress. Yet, "it was for poetry" Wilson remembered, that Bishop "chiefly lived," and Bishop, who succeeded Wilson as chairman of the *Lit*'s editorial board, taught Fitzgerald far more about poetry than Fitzgerald taught him about the Princeton social scene. As Fitzgerald wrote his daughter about Bishop in 1940: "I had always dabbled in 'verse' but he made me see, in the course of a couple of months, the difference between poetry and nonpoetry." In fact, Fitzgerald learned more

CHECKERED CAREER #11

In June 1907, near the end of his freshman year at Princeton, Eugene O'Neill received a four-week suspension (effective at the beginning of his sophomore year) for breaking a window in a railroad stationmaster's house; he left without taking his final exams and never returned to Princeton. Later, with the assistance of critic George Jean Nathan, the story of O'Neill's exit from Princeton became more colorful. Nathan reported in his *The Intimate Notebooks* (1932) that O'Neill had been kicked out of Princeton for throwing a beer bottle through a window at university president Woodrow Wilson's house. Once this story had become widely circulated, O'Neill felt compelled to refute it, telling Hamilton Basso of the *New Yorker*: "I liked Woodrow Wilson. I would not have done a thing like that if I had been swimming around in a lake of vodka."

The *Nassau Literary Magazine* board for 1916: John Peale Bishop and Edmund Wilson are seated second and third from the left (photograph from *The Princeton Bric-a-Brac 1917*)

from Bishop than he learned in the college classroom.

Bishop, who was class poet and helped to write the class ode for graduation, never entirely fulfilled his youthful promise; perhaps, as Wilson believed, his "weakness was in allowing himself to be influenced by the idioms of others." Wilson became well known for his literary criticism, essays, and memoirs rather than for his poetry, fiction, and drama. Fitzgerald was less scholarly and less self-consciously literary than Bishop and Wilson, but, though he was not as well read as they, he enjoyed their literary discussions. Gauss remembered later that he "was deeply interested in the problems of art and their techniques and often illuminated discussions with flashes of cre-

ative insight." He also reminded Gauss of "Dostoyevski's *The Brother's Karamozov* for there were in him oddly uncoordinated elements of all three of the brothers," a description that suggests (perhaps unwittingly) the nucleus of Fitzgerald's ability in his mature writing to present and balance various points of view. As he wrote in 1936, "the test of a first-rate intelligence is the ability to hold two opposed ideas in the mind at the same time, and still retain the ability to function." It was Fitzgerald who would become the finest writer of his Princeton generation.

Though he took it upon himself to educate Bishop about Princeton society, Fitzgerald was actually more an outsider than either Bishop or Wilson. Wilson, from a long line of Princeton alumni, had prepped at the prestigious Hill School, and Bishop's prep school, Mercersburg, was better known than Fitzgerald's, the Newman School in Hackensack, New Jersey. As a Catholic attending an Ivy League School, Fitzgerald was part of a decided minority. Wilson later called him "the first educated Catholic I had ever known," and he could not remember meeting any other Catholics at Princeton during that period.

Fitzgerald's concern with achieving literary and social success on a campus

In that most carefree of all colleges, where Apollo lies slumbrous and lazy, we occasionally caught from the lips of the god an oracle muttered in sleep and though we conducted ourselves in such a way as not to be publicly stoned by our fellows, we really succeeded, none the less, in breathing with a certain freedom. It was only after we left Princeton that our thoughts were turned away from life. . . . It was when we both found ourselves in the army and were sent to France.
—Edmund Wilson, Preface
    to The Undertaker's Garland
    (1922), by Wilson and John Peale Bishop

where students from the prestigious Eastern prep schools had the inside track is apparent in his choice of campus activities. In *This Side of Paradise* Amory finds that "writing for the *Nassau Literary Magazine* would get him nothing, but that being on the board of the *Daily Princetonian* would get anyone a good deal. His vague desire to do immortal acting with the English Dramatic Association faded out when he found that the most ingenious brains and talents were concentrated upon the Triangle Club. . . ." Fitzgerald, who had already decided by the time he started college that he would somehow earn a living by writing, never wrote for the campus newspaper; instead during his freshman year he began contributing to the *Tiger* and concentrating much effort on the Triangle Club. His book and lyrics for *Fie! Fie! Fi! Fi!* won the competition for the 1914-1915 Triangle Club show, but Walker Ellis, the club's president, revised the script with Fitzgerald and ended up taking credit for dialogue and characters while crediting Fitzgerald for only plot and lyrics. Fitzgerald's glory was further dimmed when, by the time the show went on tour the following Christmas, his grades were so poor that he was ruled academically ineligible to participate in the show. One reviewer did single out the lyrics, however, saying that he "could take his place right now with the brightest writers of witty lyrics in America." Yet his grades prevented him from achieving the Triangle success he wanted. Though he was elected secretary of the club in February of his sophomore year (the secretary usually succeeded to the presidency), his poor grades for the rest of his academic career made him ineligible for any campus office and to perform in Triangle Club shows. He contributed lyrics to the 1915-1916 show, *The Evil Eye*, and he posed as a showgirl in a publicity photo for the show (part of the humor of all Triangle Club shows was that all the female roles were played by males)—but by the

time *The Evil Eye* began its Christmas tour, he had dropped out of school for the rest of the year because of illness (if he had not done so, he would have been required to leave because of his grades). When he returned the following fall he contributed the lyrics for that year's show, *Safety First*, by John Biggs, Jr., and J. F. Bohmfalk, but ineligible to take part in campus activities from then until he left school without graduating to enter the army in fall 1917, he devoted most of his energy to writing for the *Lit* (he continued to contribute to the *Tiger* as well; shortly before he left for the army he and editor John Biggs, Jr., wrote an entire issue).

While the Triangle Club was, after athletics, the major route to campus prestige and the *Lit*, as Bishop wryly put it, suffered "from its pretentious title, although literature is admitted in the curriculum," many students wrote for both. Fitzgerald began contributing to the *Lit* during the spring of his sophomore year. Wilson wrote the book for *The Evil Eye*, the 1915-1916 show for which

F. Scott Fitzgerald as a chorus girl, publicity photograph for *The Evil Eye*

Fitzgerald provided lyrics, and Bishop, who belonged to the club as well, was in the cast. Though Gauss later claimed to have suspected at the time that Wilson had written *The Evil Eye* "with his tongue in his cheek" and though some of its audience found it rather literary, it seems to have been pretty much like all the other Triangle Club shows. The *Daily Princetonian* for 7 January 1916 reported that in Chicago "three hundred young ladies occupied the front rows of the house and following the show, gave the Princeton locomotive and tossed their bouquets at the cast and chorus."

All Triangle shows started by being "something different—not just a regular musical comedy," but when the several authors, the president, the coach and the faculty committee finished with it, there remained just the old reliable Triangle show with the old reliable jokes and the star comedian who got expelled or sick or something just before the trip, and the dark-whiskered man in the pony ballet who "absolutely won't shave twice a day, doggone it!"

—F. Scott Fitzgerald,
This Side of Paradise
(1920)

Though Fitzgerald's concentration on writing for the *Lit* may not have brought immediate popularity on campus, it contributed—in more ways than one—to the overnight celebrity he achieved in 1920 on the publication of *This Side of Paradise*. Not only did his undergraduate writing for the *Lit* serve as apprenticeship for later writing, but he managed to work some of it into his novel. In fact the unidentified *New Republic* reviewer (whom Bishop suspected to be one of their contemporaries at Princeton) called it "the collected works of F. Scott Fitzgerald."

Princeton Writers, Class of 1917

While Fitzgerald and Bishop's class was not the literary match to those of some of their contemporaries and near-contemporaries at Harvard and Yale, three of their classmates also found some success as writers: Elliott White Springs was a World War I flying ace and wrote about his experiences in *War Birds, Nocturne Militaire*, and *Leave Me with a Smile*, but he had his greatest success with his Spring Maid sheet ads; George R. Stewart found popular success with books such as *Storm* and also wrote scholarly books; Townsend Martin became a screenwriter, and his play *A Most Immoral Lady* was a Broadway hit.

PURDUE UNIVERSITY

George Ade, 1887
Booth Tarkington, attended 1890-1891

The Purdue Circle

Between 1883 and 1895 George Ade, George Barr McCutcheon, and McCutcheon's brothers John T. and Ben F. attended Purdue University. George Barr McCutcheon (1866-1928) was the first of the group to leave Purdue and the last to move to Chicago, the jumping-off point for the other three. McCutcheon dropped out of Purdue after his sophomore year (1884) and went to work in Lafayette, Indiana, first as a photographer and then as a reporter for the *Lafayette Journal*. He spent much of his spare time writing plays, short stories, and novels—none of which were published.

After George Ade (1866-1944) was graduated from Purdue in 1887, he took a job as a reporter on *Lafayette Morning Call*. He and George McCutcheon, who shared interests in vaudeville, local drama and literary events, and social activities at Purdue and in Lafayette, became particularly interested in the vaudevillian Willis P. Sweatnam, who professed to be a member of the Truckmuck family, about which he told humorous stories in dialect. Both Ade and McCutcheon would go on to write dialect stories of their own, Ade's *Fables in Slang* (1900) becoming famous. After the *Call* folded in 1889, Ade took a job selling patent medicine for the Humane

George Ade and John T. McCutcheon during their years at Purdue

Remedy Company. He was also writing on the side, working on short stories and skits with his fraternity brothers at Purdue, just two miles from Lafayette.

John T. McCutcheon (1870-1949) was graduated from Purdue in the Class of 1889, famous because, according to McCutcheon and Ade, it contributed the first songs that "really belonged to the school" and because it published the first issue of the Purdue annual, the *De-bris*. Instead of taking work in Lafayette, like Ade and his older brother, John went to Chicago and took a job in the art department of the *Chicago News*. On trips home and in letters John urged George Ade to join him in Chicago. When Ade realized that his job selling patent medicine might soon end, he joined John in Chicago and went to work as a reporter for the *News*.

Initially Ade's job was to write a daily column about the weather, but one evening when he was the only reporter available he was assigned the task of reporting on an explosion aboard the lake steamer *Tioga*. Ade's story on the disaster (nineteen people were killed and

many were injured) was the best account published in Chicago, and from then on he was given more important assignments.

In addition to newspaper work Ade wrote stories about Chicago, which John McCutcheon illustrated. These stories were published in the *Record* (which had succeeded the *News*) and then were collected in a book as *The Chicago Record's "Stories of the Streets and Town"* (1894). The stories proved so popular that seven more volumes were published between 1894 and 1900. John McCutcheon would eventually publish some fifteen collections of cartoons and illustrated stories. Ade published more than sixty separate works (plays, collections of short stories, sketches, and articles) during his career. By 1895 they were immense successes—at least by Lafayette standards.

The fourth member of the Purdue circle was Ben Frederick McCutcheon (1875-1936), who graduated from Purdue in 1894 and went immediately to Chicago, where he too worked on the *Record*. Though he had published "A Check for Twenty Dollars," a short story, in the *Lafayette Courier*, he was not as interested in writing as were his brothers.

Though his entire family (including his mother, Clara, and his sister, Jessie) had moved to Chicago, George Barr McCutcheon remained in Lafayette, where he had become city editor of the *Lafayette Courier*. He published *Several Short Ones* (a collection of verse privately printed circa 1886-1890), "The Waddleton Mall" (a series of dialect letters in the *Lafayette Sunday Leader*), and "The Wired End" (a serialized novel in the *Lafayette Courier*), but his novels and short stories were going nowhere with major publishers, even though John had tried to interest publisher Herbert Stone of Chicago in George's work. He seemed destined for "failure" in Lafayette. Then literary lightning struck. In 1901 Stone published *Graustark: The Story of*

Love Behind a Throne, a novel that depicts the efforts of the young American Grenfall Lorry to save the kingdom of Graustark for Princess Yetive. The American reading audience loved such romantic adventure stories and McCutcheon's "first" novel was high on the best-seller list for 1901.

Even with the popularity of *Graustark,* McCutcheon remained in Lafayette for several more years. Because McCutcheon had taken Ade's advice to sell all rights to the novel, it earned him only $500, although it made a great deal more for its publisher. Ade had told him that the crucial thing was to get his first novel published. That done, his other work would be easier to sell. In fact, McCutcheon's next novel, *Castle Craneycrow* (1902), was quickly accepted by Stone. Then Dodd and Mead advanced him $15,000 for *The Sherrods* (1903); and Stone wanted still another novel. Using the pseudonym Richard Greaves to avoid offending Dodd and Mead, McCutcheon wrote *Brewster's Millions* (1902) for Stone. Because the plot had been suggested to him by his brother Ben, George shared royalties with him for fifteen years. By 1903, with his finances secure and his reputation as a novelist established, he moved to Chicago.

Ben was the last of the McCutcheon brothers to publish. Under the pseudonym Benjamin Brace, he brought out *Sunrise Acres* in 1905 and *The Seventh Person* in 1906. Although Ben was never to become as well-known as his brothers, he too could count himself among the group of former Purdue students who had gone to Chicago and published novels.

The account of this Purdue circle would be incomplete without mentioning Booth Tarkington. Tarkington went to Purdue in 1891 to learn how to draw and (so the story goes) to follow a young lady. On their trips home from Chicago to Purdue football games and Sigma Chi dances, John T. McCutcheon and George Ade met Tarkington. Recog-

nizing his talent, they often talked with him about literary matters. Ade was particularly impressed and encouraged Tarkington to write. Some years later, John McCutcheon wryly observed that Tarkington could "have made a great name for himself" as an artist had he not gotten "sidetracked" by writing.

Tarkington left Purdue after only a year to pursue his studies at Princeton as a special student. When he returned to Indianapolis, his hometown, he wrote in obscurity for the remainder of the 1890s. In the end his efforts prevailed, for in 1899 *The Gentleman from Indiana* was published. With *Monsieur Beaucaire* in 1900 Tarkington's reputation was assured, and he went on to write some sixty novels, plays, and collections of short stories over the rest of his career.

Though the Purdue Circle was broken up when George McCutcheon moved to New York in 1910, all the friends maintained ties to one another and to the school. Ade and Dave Ross, a Purdue trustee, bought the land for the Purdue football stadium and matched the funds contributed by Purdue alumni for the construction of the stadium. Ross-Ade Stadium, dedicated in 1924, is named for them.

–V. H. J.

QUEENS COLLEGE,
CITY UNIVERSITY
OF NEW YORK

Toni Cade Bambara, 1959
Elaine Kraf, M.A. 1978

REED COLLEGE

William Dickey, 1951
Gary Snyder, 1951
Philip Whalen, 1951

RHODES COLLEGE
(Formerly Southwestern
College at Memphis)

Peter Taylor, attended 1935-1936
Joan Williams, attended 1946-1947

RICE UNIVERSITY

William Goyen, 1932, M.A. 1939
Larry McMurtry, M.A. 1960
Joyce Carol Oates, graduate study 1961

ROANOKE COLLEGE

R. H. W. Dillard, 1958

ROOSEVELT UNIVERSITY

Don L. Lee (Haki R. Madhubuti), attended 1966-1967

RUTGERS UNIVERSITY, NEW BRUNSWICK

Joyce Kilmer, attended 1904-1906
James Blish, 1942
Alan E. Nourse, 1951

RUTGERS UNIVERSITY, NEWARK

Philip Roth, attended 1950-1951
LeRoi Jones (Amiri Baraka), attended 1951-1952

ST. ANDREW ON HUDSON

Daniel Berrigan, 1946

ST. OLAF COLLEGE

O. E. Rölvaag, 1905
Robert Bly, attended 1946-1947

ST. LAWRENCE UNIVERSITY

Irving Bacheller, 1882

SAN DIEGO STATE UNIVERSITY

William F. Nolan, attended 1947-1948
Lanford Wilson, attended 1955-1956
Lee Pennington, attended 1961

SAN FRANCISCO STATE UNIVERSITY

Michael McClure, 1955
Ernest J. Gaines, 1957
Ed Bullins, attended intermittently 1964-1967

SAN JOSE STATE UNIVERSITY

Edwin Markham, diploma 1872

SARAH LAWRENCE COLLEGE

Anne Roiphe, 1957
Louise Gluck, 1962
Alice Walker, 1965

SETON HALL UNIVERSITY

Joseph Charles Kennedy (X. J. Kennedy), 1950

SIMMONS COLLEGE

Linda Pastan, M.L.S. 1955
Harry Clement Stubbs (Hal Clement), M.S. 1963

SMITH COLLEGE

Sylvia Plath, 1955

SOUTHERN ILLINOIS UNIVERSITY AT CARBONDALE

Robert Coover, attended 1949-1951
Eugene B. Redmond, 1964

SOUTHWEST MISSOURI STATE UNIVERSITY

Lanford Wilson, attended 1954-1955

SPELMAN COLLEGE

Alice Walker, attended 1961-1963

STANFORD UNIVERSITY

Maxwell Anderson, M.A. 1914
John Steinbeck, attended 1919-1920, 1922-1925
J. V. Cunningham, 1934, Ph.D. 1945
Yvor Winters, Ph.D. 1934
James Broughton, 1936
Ann Stanford, 1938
Donald Justice, graduate study 1948-1949
Edgar Bowers, M.A. 1949, Ph.D. 1953
Donald Hall, graduate study 1953-1954
Wendell Berry, graduate study 1958-1959

Ken Kesey, graduate study 1958-1959

Nancy Willard, M.A. 1960

Peter S. Beagle, graduate study 1960-1961

Larry McMurtry, graduate study 1960-1961

George V. Higgins, M.A. 1965

Mark Medoff, M.A. 1966

Tom McGuane, graduate study 1966-1967

Raymond Carver, graduate study 1973-1974

Wallace Stegner on the Stanford Writing Program

The Stanford Writing Program developed out of the excitement and opportunity of the years following World War II, when students of unprecedented maturity, experience, and seriousness returned to the campuses to make up for the lost war years.

I arrived at Stanford in the fall of 1945, just when the first GI students were beginning to appear. The first thing I read in my first writing class was "Rest Camp on Maui," a jolting, powerful story by a just-mustered-out navy lieutenant named Eugene Burdick. Shortly he published it in *Harper's*; later it won second prize in the O. Henry Memorial Awards. Burdick went on to a Houghton Mifflin Fellowship, a Rhodes Scholarship, and a short, highly visible career that will probably be best remembered for *The Ugly American* (1958), which he wrote in collaboration with William Lederer, another ex-navy officer.

That was in the future. While he was on the campus, and eight or ten like him nearly or quite as good, it was clear that the university had to provide for them something more than the routine writing course designed for eighteen year olds. Especially since the university was suburban, forty miles from a major city that was itself on the West Coast, nearly three thousand miles from the headquarters of publishing and the literary life, something had to be created that would make a literary career visible

and credible and help young writers prepare for it.

In the spring of 1947 I laid out a program in the form of a proposal. Because young writers need support, it suggested one-year fellowships, six of them, in fiction, poetry, and drama. Because they need instruction, or at least guidance, it proposed a ladder of courses of increasing sophistication, leading to the B.A. and the M.A. To avoid any suggestion that writing degrees were soft, especially as graduate study, the requirements for the M.A. in writing were identical with those for the regular M.A. in English, and demanded in addition an acceptable thesis of stories, poems, or a novel.

All writing courses would be taught by writers. To compensate for our distance from literary centers, the plan also provided for visiting writers, both as lecturers and as teachers for a term or year. Because beginners need to see their work in print, it provided for publication of periodic volumes of poems and stories. It also, borrowing an idea from the Hopwood awards at Michigan, set up annual prizes of one thousand dollars each for the best story, novel, drama, and group of poems.

Before I showed this outline to the general secretary to see if he could raise funds for it, I showed it to the head of the English department, R. F. Jones. Professor Jones showed it to his brother Dr. E. H. Jones, an M.D. who liked literature better than medicine, and who owned Texas oil wells. Dr. Jones asked me to lunch and offered to fund the program for a five-year trial, with the possibility of renewal if it worked.

It worked, because gifted students kept arriving, many drawn by the fellowships and other encouragements; and because, though a long way from the Mermaid Taverns and Hotel Algonquins of the literary world, we were able to create an environment stimulating to literary effort. After three years, Dr. Jones renewed us for another five. Before the five were up, he had begun set-

A Stanford writing seminar, 1950s: (seated, beginning fourth from left) Hannah Green, Bernard Taper, and Wallace Stegner; Hughes Rudd and Stu Miller are standing second and third from left (courtesy of Wallace Stegner)

ting up a permanent endowment. Though both he and his wife died before the endowment was completed, the Jones family loyally fulfilled his intentions. Thanks to them, the Stanford Writing Program has had money since before it was a program.

The original outline has been modified by experience. The prizes, for example, though they generated intense competition, also generated some bad feeling, and not everybody was satisfied with the decisions of the outside judges, who were anyway hard to recruit. After four years we dropped the prizes entirely. Also, the drama fellowships were unsatisfactory from the beginning because the stage apparatus as well as the courses in dramatic writing were over in Speech and Drama, while the rest of us were in English. Drama fellows had a choice between going where their proper facilities were, and losing contact with their colleagues in fiction and poetry, or of staying with their colleagues

and becoming closet dramatists. When we dropped the prizes, we dropped the drama fellowships too.

The basic patterns of support, instruction, and stimulation remain, with periodic adjustments in the number and stipend of fellowships. Fellows need not be regularly matriculated students or candidates for degrees. Their obligation is simply to write as well as they know how and participate in the advanced seminars in poetry or fiction. But many graduate students interested in writing want the M.A. as a teaching credential. By now, in addition to the eight Stegner Fellowships, there are eight others designed strictly for the support of M.A. candidates. Some of the money for that addition was the bequest of the late Edith Mirrielees, the legendary teacher of John Steinbeck, and the only person at Stanford that Steinbeck wholeheartedly respected.

Beginning small, the program has had to grow to accommodate demand.

In the beginning, Yvor Winters in poetry and Richard Scowcroft and I in fiction, all of us part-time, could handle it with a little help from teaching assistants. Now three poets–Denise Levertov, W. S. Di Piero, and Kenneth Fields–and three fiction writers–John L'Heureux, Nancy Packer, and Gilbert Sorrentino–are required, and in addition there are five Jones Lecturers, young writers drawn from the ranks of recent fellows and given half-time appointments for three years while they write their way out of a job.

As for visitors, the years have seen a stream of them: Katherine Anne Porter, Frank O'Connor, Malcolm Cowley, Elizabeth Bowen, C. P. Snow, Hortense Calisher, May Sarton, Walter Van Tilburg Clark, Catherine Drinker Bowen, Bernard DeVoto, Robert Frost, Stephen Spender, W. H. Auden, Jessamyn West, J. Frank Dobie, Erika Mann, George R. Stewart, Anaïs Nin, Wright Morris, and many more, some for a few days, some for whole terms, some more than once.

Good players not only make the coach look good, they make him feel good. Though not all the years have been equally productive and exciting, there have been times when I thought I was seeing the American literature of the future taking shape in my classroom; and I am sure that Yvor Winters, Donald Davie, and others who have dealt with the poets have felt the same way. Every class sees a certain amount, sometimes a large amount, of publication by its members, and by now, former participants in the program have published many hundreds of poems and stories, and at least two hundred novels.

Some of those writings, the literary lottery being what it is, have dropped without a sound into the void. Some have won prizes, some have been best-sellers, some have made their authors into cult figures. But successful or not, distinguished or notorious or unnoticed, they make up a solid fraction of the American writing of the past thirty-eight years. Reading the novels of a recent year as a juror for the National Book Awards, I found that twenty, better than one in ten of those judged worth a reading, were by people I had known in a Stanford class.

Not all the visible ones have been ex-fellows. Donald Justice, a Pulitzer Prize winner in poetry, was not, nor was Ken Kesey, author of *One Flew Over the Cuckoo's Nest* (1962), nor were the Canadian writers Jane Rule and G. D. Godfrey, nor was Evan Connell, the author of the highly regarded novel *Mrs. Bridge*

A group of Stanford writers, 1960s: (standing, from left) Tom McGuane, Richard Scowcroft (in coat and tie), Al Young (far right); seated at right is Mary Jane Moffat (courtesy of Wallace Stegner)

(1959), and of the recent biography of General Custer, *Son of the Morning Star* (1984). But by and large it has been the fellows who have justified the program as a training ground for literary careers. There is space only for a sampling:

In poetry, Donald Hall, now an elder statesman, and Philip Levine, Scott Momaday, Robert Mezey, Thom Gunn, Kenneth Fields, Robert Pinsky, William Penn Root, Robert Hass, John Daniel—active, productive, and influential poets of great range and diversity. Most of them are also teachers, demonstrating the truth of Samuel Butler's remark that poverty and poetry are twin-born brats. In America, poetry is not a career; it is only the best part of one.

In fiction, Cecil Dawkins, Tillie Olsen, William Abrahams, Dan Jacobson, Robin White, Edward Abbey, Donald Moser, Wendell Berry, Ernest Gaines, Nancy Packer, Peter Beagle, Larry McMurtry, Hugh Nissensen, Charlotte Painter, Ed McClanahan, Merrill Joan Gerber, Robert Stone, Stephen Dixon, Sylvia Wilkinson, James Houston, Thomas McGuane, Raymond Carver, Robert Roper, William Kittredge, Harriet Doerr—the list could go on much longer without dropping off much in quality.

Early in the program most fiction writers wrote short stories, for which there was still a market and which are easier to write within the constriction of academic schedules, and easier to deal with in class, than novels. *Stanford Short Stories* was published nearly every year for twenty years, but then dropped because too few stories were being produced. Nevertheless some of our students have built solid reputations on short stories alone. Tillie Olsen, in *Tell Me a Riddle* (1961), established herself as a writer of powerful feeling and a lapidary precision and finish. Raymond Carver, in *Will You Please Be Quiet, Please?* (1976) and *What We Talk About When We Talk About Love* (1981), focused on the bleak and banal moments of uninflected lives

with such a sad sensitivity to the hopelessly unsaid vibrations that he was acknowledged almost overnight to be one of the few real masters of the short-story form. Others among the Stanford writers, notably Nancy Packer, Merrill Joan Gerber, William Kittredge, and Stephen Dixon, have handled the short story with superb control and effect.

Some writers have changed direction since their time at Stanford. Edward Abbey, who came as a fiction writer and worked on *The Monkey Wrench Gang* (1975) while in residence, has become better known for his vehement essays in defense of the environment—*Desert Solitaire* (1968), *Abbey's Road* (1979), *The Journey Home* (1977). In somewhat the same way, but with a more philosophical and less pugnacious emphasis, Wendell Berry has diverged from fiction into poetry that grows as naturally as flowers out of his rural life, and essays on the land, especially *The Unsettling of America* (1977), that have led some people to compare him, in all seriousness, to Thoreau.

Literary prizes and the making of novels into films are both indexes, though by no means infallible ones, of reputation, perhaps even of excellence. Scott Momaday's first novel, *House Made of Dawn* (1968), won the Pulitzer Prize, Robin White's *Elephant Hill* (1959) the Harper Prize. Robert Stone's first novel, *Hall of Mirrors* (1967), won the Faulkner Prize and his second, *Dog Soldiers* (1974), the National Book Award. His third, *A Flag for Sunrise* (1981), an apocalyptic vision of Central American violence, established him as one of the finest and most disturbing writers in English. And Harriet Doerr, who became a writing fellow at an age when most people have retired, astonished everybody except her teachers by producing, in her first effort at fiction, *Stones for Ibarra* (1984), beautifully controlled, economical, and very moving. It won both the American Book Award and the Kirsh Prize of the *Los Angeles Times*, and barely missed the Pulitzer.

A PARTIAL LIST OF STEGNER FELLOWS, 1948-1986*

1948: William Abrahams
Edgar Bowers
1951: Leonard Casper
1952: Turner Cassity
Bernard Taper
1953: Donald Hall
1954: Thom Gunn
1955: Tillie Olsen
William Wiegand
1956: Hannah Green
Dan Jacobson
1957: Edward Abbey
Philip Levine
1958: Wendell Berry
Ernest Gaines
1959: N. Scott Momaday
1960: Peter Beagle
James B. Hall
Larry McMurtry
Robert Mezey
1961: Charlotte Painter
1962: Robert Stone
1964: Robert Pinsky
1965: Sylvia Wilkinson
1966: Thomas McGuane
Al Young
1967: Mary Jane Moffat
1968: Belle Randall
Judith Rascoe
1971: William Joseph Harris
1972: Raymond Carver
Robert Roper
1973-1974: B. Russell Brandon
Alice Hoffman
William Kittredge
Gareth Reeves
Jan Short
Scott Turow
Robert Weston
Peter Whaley
1974-1975: Terrence Davis
Deborah Homsher
Lee McCarthy
John O'Brien
Stephen Ratcliffe
1975-1976: Kathleen Finn
Allan Gurganus
Nahid Rachlin
Doug Terry
1976-1977: Don Bredes
Vicky Hearne
Frances Madoo
Joanne Meschery

Jonathan Polansky
1977-1978: Mary Butler
Tom McNeal
Vikram Seth
James Thomas
Susan Welch
1978-1979: Thomas Beresford
James William Brown
Michael Koch
Thomas Simmons
Stephanie Vaughn
1979-1980: Harriet Doerr
Charles Jenkins
David Leedy
David Low
Sara Vogan
Steven Winn
1980-1981: Katharine Andres
Jonathan Cohen
Gerald Flaherty
Michael Ramsey-Perez
Linda Svendson
Barbara Thomsen
1981-1982: Barbara Anderson
Dennis McFarland
Neil McMahon
Mindy Pennybacker
Gail Perez
Sheila Schwartz
1982-1983: John Daniel
Jody Gladding
Charlotte Holmes
Ralph Lombreglia
Mary Elizabeth Ryan
Rhon Shafner
1983-1984: Andrew Hudgins
Polly Koch
Laura Marello
Ruth Olson
Kent Nussey
Carol Slechta
1984-1985: Leslee Becker
Marilyn Chin
Ehud Havazelet
Charles Hopkins
Patricia MacInnes
James Paul
Greg Smith
1985-1986: Peter Behrens
Fidelito Cortes
Jeffrey Harrison
Fenton Johnson
C. L. Rawlins
Julia Symington

incomplete through 1973-1974

Of movies there have been quite a number, some of them notable. Besides Kesey's *One Flew Over the Cuckoo's Nest* (1975) there have been three by Larry McMurtry: *Hud* (1963; made from his *Horseman Pass By,* 1961), *The Last Picture Show* (1971), and *Terms of Endearment* (1983). Ernest Gaines's *Autobiography of Miss Jane Pittman* (1974), the life of an ex-slave, was a notable television special, as was *Farewell to Manzanar* (1976), by James and Jean Houston. Colin Higgins, a graduate of the Stanford program, has made a series of films, beginning with *Harold and Maude* (1971) and going on to *Silver Streak* (1976) and *Nine to Five* (1980). Tom McGuane, one of the cleverest writers alive, has alternated between novels like *The Bushwhacked Piano* (1971) and *The Sporting Club* (1969), and the writing of films such as *The Missouri Breaks* (1976).

A long list, and growing longer. The best thing about it seems to me to be that only the support and encouragement come from the university. The content and the achievement are from the young writers who for a while find a working-place there. For some, obviously, the program has not worked. For others it just as clearly has. And for others it has worked in indirect ways, leading them not to writing careers but to careers in related fields. We have produced enough editors, publishers, newspaper and television correspondents, and teachers of writing to create, if they were all brought together with the practicing writers, a healthy literary climate. Even dispersed, they contribute to the literary climate of the nation.

STATE UNIVERSITY OF NEW YORK COLLEGE AT BROCKPORT

William Heyen, 1961

STATE UNIVERSITY OF NEW YORK COLLEGE AT BUFFALO

Ishmael Reed, attended 1956-1960

John Wieners, attended 1965-1969
Charles Boer, Ph.D. 1967

STEPHENS COLLEGE

Diane Johnson, attended 1951-1953

STEVENS INSTITUTE OF TECHNOLOGY

L. Sprague de Camp, M.S. 1933

SWARTHMORE COLLEGE

James Michener, 1929
Diane Di Prima, attended 1951-1953

SWEET BRIAR COLLEGE

Hildegarde Flanner, attended 1917-1918
Mary Lee Settle, attended 1936-1938

SYRACUSE UNIVERSITY

Stephen Crane, attended 1891
John D. MacDonald, 1938
Shirley Jackson, 1940
John A. Williams, 1950, graduate study 1950-1951
Marvin Bell, graduate study 1958
Barry N. Malzberg, 1960, graduate study 1964-1965
Joyce Carol Oates, 1960
Paul Theroux, graduate study 1963
Mary Gordon, M.A. 1973
Jay McInerney, M.A. 1984

A Realist Confronts Academe

One of the most notoriously unsuccessful academic careers in the history of American literature must surely be that of Stephen Crane, who, after one academic year at two different colleges, completed only one course. Enrolling at Lafayette College in fall 1890, he spent most of his time reading (he decided that Tolstoy was the world's greatest writer, while Flaubert's *Salammbo* was too long and Henry James's *The Reverberator* was too boring). When the semester ended, he had done none of the work for his courses and was advised to withdraw.

At Syracuse University in spring 1891 he managed to earn an *A* in English literature, but his fascination for playing baseball and other diversions kept him from his studies. Taking a part-time reporting job with the *Syracuse Tribune*, he set out to learn in the police courts and slums lessons about "humanity" that he could not learn in the "cut and dried" classroom. He also decided that he was meant to be a writer and began writing fiction and sketches in his room at the Delta Upsilon fraternity house, including a story about a prostitute, based on his observations in the Syracuse slums—perhaps an early version of his first novel, *Maggie: A Girl of the Streets* (1893), in which the setting is New York City. Crane already demonstrated a talent for shocking people. When reformer Emma Willard came to visit the campus, he refused to meet her because, he said, she was a fool, and one of his professors at the then-very-Methodist school (a training ground for missionaries) was taken aback when Crane announced that he disagreed with Saint Paul. By the end of the year Crane had decided to quit school, and he set out to support himself as a journalist while he worked at writing fiction that met his criteria for realism.

The Syracuse Writing Program

If, as Vance Bourjailly said of Iowa's Writers' Workshop, the proof of a successful creative-writing program is its ability to turn out one notable writer a decade, then Syracuse, which got a fairly late start compared to Iowa or Stanford, is well on its way.

Even before the graduate writing program was established in 1962, Syracuse had produced three notable contemporary fiction writers: Shirley Jackson, Class of 1940; John A. Williams, who graduated in 1950 and wrote his first novel in 1960; and Joyce Carol Oates, valedictorian of the Class of 1960, who took undergraduate writing courses from Donald A. Dike, whom she credits with introducing her to William Faulkner's novels, an important influence on her writing.

Two products of the graduate writing

The Syracuse University baseball team, 1891: Stephen Crane is seated, second row (courtesy of Syracuse University Libraries)

The Phi Mu Sorority at Syracuse University (photograph from the 1960 *Onondagan*); Joyce Carol Oates is standing seventh from left in the second row

program are Mary Gordon, who emerged as a writer in the 1970s, and Jay McInerney, whose master's thesis at Syracuse became his highly acclaimed first novel, *Bright Lights, Big City* (1984).

The graduate writing program is highly selective, accepting only about fifteen students each year. Among the distinguished writers who have taught in the program are poets Philip Booth, Hayden Carruth, Stephen Dunn (a former student in the program), Donald Justice, and W. D. Snodgrass, poet and novelist George P. Elliott, and fiction writers Raymond Carver, Tobias Wolff, and Douglas Unger. McInerney credits Carver and Wolff with teaching him "a hell of a lot about writing, about the basic craft . . . that has to be mastered before you can do original work." "We can't teach them to write," Wolff has explained, "but we can make them aware of how to rewrite, how to make their weaknesses into strengths, and how to use their strengths more efficiently."

TRANSYLVANIA STATE UNIVERSITY

Thomas Holley Chivers, M.D. 1830

TRENTON STATE COLLEGE

Lonne Elder, attended 1949-1950

TRINITY COLLEGE
(Hartford, Connecticut)

Edward Albee, attended 1946-1947

TRINITY UNIVERSITY

Preston Jones, M.A. 1966

TUFTS UNIVERSITY

Nathan Weinstein (Nathanael West), attended 1921
John Ciardi, 1938
Cid Corman, 1945
George Cuomo, 1952

TULANE UNIVERSITY

Shirley Ann Grau, 1950
John Kennedy Toole, 1958, graduate study mid 1960s

TUSKEGEE INSTITUTE

Claude McKay, attended 1912
Ralph Ellison, attended 1933-1936

UNION COLLEGE
(Schenectady, New York)

Edward Bellamy, attended 1867-1868

UNION THEOLOGICAL SEMINARY

Frederick Buechner, B.D. 1958

UNITED STATES
MILITARY ACADEMY

Edgar Allan Poe, attended 1830-1831

UNITED STATES
NAVAL ACADEMY

Hervey Allen, attended 1909-1911
Robert A. Heinlein, 1929

UNIVERSITY OF ALABAMA

T. S. Stribling, LL.B. 1905
William Edward Campbell (William March), attended 1915-1916
Harper Lee, attended 1945-1949
Borden Deal, 1949

UNIVERSITY OF ARIZONA

Michael McClure, attended 1953-1954
Janet Burroway, attended 1954-1955
Peter Wild, 1962, M.A. 1967

UNIVERSITY OF ARKANSAS

Charles Portis, 1958
Barry Hannah, M.A. 1969, M.F.A. 1869

UNIVERSITY OF BRIDGEPORT

Jonathan Penner, 1964

UNIVERSITY OF
CALIFORNIA, BERKELEY

Frank Norris, attended 1890-1894
Charles G. Norris, 1903
Sidney Howard, 1915
Josephine Herbst, 1918
Hildegarde Flanner, attended 1919-1920, 1922-1923
Genevieve Taggard, 1920
Edward Dahlberg, attended 1921-1923
Robert Penn Warren, M.A. 1927
Wallace Stegner, graduate study 1932-1933

Josephine Miles, M.A. 1934, Ph.D. 1938
Robert Duncan, attended 1936-1938, 1948-1950
Jack Vance, 1942
Barbara Guest, 1943
Jack Spicer, 1947, M.A. 1950, further graduate study 1952-1955
Philip Lamantia, attended 1947-1949
Susan Sontag, attended 1948-1949
Philip K. Dick, attended 1950
A. R. Ammons, graduate study 1951-1952
Gary Snyder, graduate study 1953-1956
Joan Didion, 1956
Diane Wakoski, 1960
Coleman Barks, M.A. 1961
Maxine Hong Kingston, 1962, teaching certificate 1965

UNIVERSITY OF
CALIFORNIA, IRVINE

Peter Wild, M.F.A. 1969

UNIVERSITY OF CALIFORNIA,
LOS ANGELES

Josephine Miles, 1932
Robert A. Heinlein, graduate study 1934-1935
Ann Stanford, M.A. (Journalism) 1958, M.A. (English) 1961, Ph.D. 1962
Chad Oliver, Ph.D. 1961
Larry Niven, graduate study 1962-1963
Diane Johnson, M.A. 1966, Ph.D. 1968

UNIVERSITY OF CHICAGO

Carl Van Vechten, 1903
Will Cuppy, 1907, M.A. 1914
Janet Flanner, attended 1913-1914
Jean Toomer, attended 1916
Glenway Wescott, attended 1917-1918
Yvor Winters, attended 1917-1918
Janet Lewis, 1920
Elizabeth Madox Roberts, 1921
Vardis Fisher, M.A. 1922, Ph.D. 1925
Meyer Levin, 1924
James T. Farrell, attended 1925-1929
Leo Rosten, 1930, Ph.D. 1937
Saul Bellow, attended 1933-1935
Elder Olson, 1934, M.A. 1935, Ph.D. 1938

Paul Myron Anthony Linebarger (Cordwainer Smith), graduate study 1935
M. L. Rosenthal, 1937, M.A. 1938
James Purdy, attended 1941, 1946
Arna Bontemps, M.A. 1943
John Frederick Nims, Ph.D. 1945
Kurt Vonnegut, attended 1945-1947, M.A. 1971
Susan Sontag, 1951
David Ray, 1952, M.A. 1957
Philip Roth, M.A. 1955, further graduate study 1956-1957
Lanford Wilson, attended 1957-1958
Marvin Bell, M.A. 1961
Robert Coover, M.A. 1965

UNIVERSITY OF CINCINNATI

Thomas Berger, 1948

UNIVERSITY OF COLORADO

Yvor Winters, 1925, A.M. 1925
Jean Stafford, 1936, A.M. 1936

UNIVERSITY OF CONNECTICUT

Edgar Lewis Wallant, attended 1944
Ann Beattie, M.A. 1970, further graduate study 1970-1972

UNIVERSITY OF DENVER

Neil Simon, attended 1945-1946
Mark Harris, 1950, M.A. 1951

UNIVERSITY OF FLORIDA

Jesse Hill Ford, M.A. 1955
Harry Crews, 1960, M.S. Ed. 1962

UNIVERSITY OF GEORGIA

Henry Timrod, attended 1845-1846

UNIVERSITY OF HAWAII AT MANOA

James Jones, attended 1942

UNIVERSITY OF ILLINOIS AT URBANA-CHAMPAIGN

Carl Van Doren, 1907
Mark Van Doren, 1914, M.A. 1915
William Maxwell, 1930

Nelson Algren, 1931
James Still, 1931
Edward Dorn, attended 1949-1950
Stanley Elkin, 1952, M.A. 1953, Ph.D. 1961
Dee Brown, M.S. 1952
Jack Gelber, 1953
Larry Woiwode, A.A. 1964
Gail Godwin, postdoctoral study 1971-1972

UNIVERSITY OF IOWA

Emerson Hough, 1880
Arthur Davison Ficke, LL.B. 1907
Ruth Lechlitner, M.A. 1926
Paul Engle, M.A. 1932
Wallace Stegner, M.A. 1932, Ph.D. 1935
Thomas Lanier (Tennessee) Williams, 1938
R. V. Cassill, 1939, M.A. 1947
Mona Van Duyn, M.A. 1943
Flannery O'Connor, M.F.A. 1947, further graduate study 1947-1948
W. D. Snodgrass, 1949, M.A. 1951, M.F.A. 1953
John Logan, M.A. 1949
Wirt Williams, Ph.D. 1953
Donald Justice, Ph.D. 1954
William Stafford, Ph.D. 1954
Robert Bly, M.A. 1956
William Dickey, M.F.A. 1956
John Gardner, M.A. 1956, Ph.D. 1958
Philip Levine, M.F.A. 1957
Ted Shine, M.A. 1958
Mark Strand, M.A. 1962
Marvin Bell, M.F.A. 1963
Raymond Carver, graduate study 1963-1964
Lee Pennington, M.A. 1965
Jonathan Penner, M.F.A. 1966, Ph.D. 1975
John Edgar Wideman, graduate study 1966-1967
John Irving, M.F.A 1967
Peter Klappert, M.A. 1967, M.F.A. 1968
James Tate, M.F.A. 1967
Gail Godwin, M.A. 1968, Ph.D. 1971
James Alan McPherson, M.F.A. 1971
Jayne Anne Phillips, M.A. 1978
Don L. Lee (Haki R. Madhubuti), M.F.A. 1984

An Iowa Writers' Workshop fiction seminar led by Frederick Busch (left), May 1977; Jayne Anne Phillips is on Busch's left (photograph by Dennis Mathis)

The Iowa Writers' Workshop

College writers' workshops in general and the University of Iowa's in particular—since it is the oldest, the most respected, and probably the best—have been criticized more than once. In 1973 Nelson Algren, several years after he held a visiting professorship at the Iowa Writers' Workshop, expanded on the usual criticism that great writers cannot be made in the college classroom by charging that the workshop "provides sanctuary from those very pressures in which creativity is forged," and asking "Why has the Iowa Writers' Workshop, in its 35 years of existence, not produced a single novel, poem or short story worth rereading?" Yet novelist Vance Bourjaily, a professor in the workshop from 1957 to 1981, while agreeing that "excellence is unteachable in whatever field," argued that, by bringing young writers together, college writing programs can be the same sort of breeding grounds for literary talent as Paris in the 1920s or Greenwich Village in the 1950s. Moreover, he said, good writing teachers can provide the same sort of intelligent commentary, criticism, and editorial assistance as now-legendary editors, such as Maxwell Perkins at Scribners, used to give their authors. Indeed, the Iowa Writers' Workshop attracts good student-writers because it hires established writers to teach them (conversely, of course, these older writers

are attracted to Iowa both for the pleasure of teaching talented students and for the prestige attached to having taught there).

Though the Iowa Writers' Workshop got its official start in 1939, the University of Iowa began offering creative writing courses in 1897. In fact, the first course was taught by George Cram Cook, who eventually ended up in Provincetown, Massachusetts, where he and Susan Glaspell, another Iowa writer, founded the Provincetown Players. In 1922 Iowa became one of the first institutions of higher learning in the country to allow students to submit works of art, literature, and music in lieu of traditional masters' thesis, and nine years later, it added the same provisions to the Ph.D. requirements.

No one in English submitted a creative master's thesis until 1931, but the next year there were five, including theses by Wallace Stegner and Paul Engle. Engle, whose thesis won the Yale Series of Younger Poets Award for 1932 and was published by Yale University Press, took charge of the Writers' Workshop in 1942. Stegner, who went on to write critically acclaimed and award-winning novels—including *Angle of Repose* (1971; Pulitzer Prize, 1972) and *The Spectator Bird* (1976; National Book Award, 1977) founded the prestigious writing program at Stanford University in 1945. Another well-known writer who studied writing at Iowa in the 1930s was Tennessee Williams, who earned a B.A. in 1938.

Initially encouraged to write by novelist Vardis Fisher, one of his teachers at the University of Utah, Stegner has said that, only when he began to work under Norman Foerster at Iowa, did he begin to write fiction seriously. Director of the School of Letters from 1930 to 1944, Foerster successfully publicized Iowa's creative-writing curriculum by organizing conferences with prominent participants and by inviting other well-known writers to give readings on campus. Among visitors to Iowa between 1931 and 1941 were novelists Zona Gale, Floyd Dell, Louis Adamic, and Wallace Stegner; and poets Stephen Vincent Benét, Archibald MacLeish, Donald Davidson, Robert Frost, and Robert Penn Warren (who was also a visiting lecturer in spring 1941).

In 1939 what everyone had informally called the Writers' Workshop for several years became officially known as such, and Wilbur Schramm, then recognized for his popular Windwagon Smith stories in the *Saturday Evening Post*, was named the first director. Now better known for his later, widely respected writings on the theory of communications, Schramm was a dynamic teacher with what one student called "a missionary zeal about writing."

Yet Paul Engle, who became acting director when Schramm left in 1942 and director in 1943, was responsible for putting the workshop on the national literary map, drawing students and faculty from all over the country and establishing the reputation that it still enjoys today. He was succeeded by George Starbuck in 1965. The workshop's current head, John Leggett, became acting director in 1970 and director in 1971.

In addition to the writers already mentioned, permanent and visiting professors at the workshop have included Andrew Lytle, R. V. Cassill, Ray B. West, Jr., Robert Lowell, John Berryman, Walter Van Tilburg Clark, Donald Justice, Harvey Swados, Hortense Calisher, Marvin Bell, James Tate, Ted Berrigan, George P. Elliott, Philip Roth, Mark Strand, Richard Yates, Kurt Vonnegut, Paul Carroll, Anselm Hollo, John Silkin, William Price Fox, Robert Coover, C. D. B. Bryan, David Ray, Galway Kinnell, Richard Hugo, Dan Wakefield, Gail Godwin, John Irving, Raymond Carver, John Cheever, Stanley Elkin, Stanley Plumly, Mary Lee Settle, Frederick Busch, Frank Conroy, and Nicholas Delbanco—many of them former workshop students themselves.

Bourjaily once said that, if one good writer comes out of a writing program each decade, then "the program is worthwhile." From the 1930s on, even before the official beginning of the Writers' Workshop, at least one Iowa-trained writer has emerged on the national scene during each ten-year period. For example, consider this list:

1930s—Wallace Stegner
1940s—Tennessee Williams
1950s—Flannery O'Connor
1960s—John Gardner
1970s—John Irving

The Crocodile "Was Real Good": Flannery O'Connor at Iowa

By her last academic year at Iowa (1947-1948), Flannery O'Connor was the workshop's star. She had already received her master's degree and had had some of her stories published, but, thanks to Paul Engle, she had been given a grant to spend another year there working on *Wise Blood*, which earned her national recognition when it was published in 1950.

Yet, as Jean Wylder, one of her contemporaries at Iowa, remembered, O'Connor never entered into the sometimes vituperative discussions of her classmates' work and never even defended her own stories when they were attacked in class. Once during the spring 1948 semester, when Andrew

Flannery O'Connor at the time of *Wise Blood*

Lytle was filling in for Engle, Lytle asked her directly what she thought of someone's story. "I'd say the description of the crocodile in there was real good," she responded, neglecting to add that it was the *only* good thing and totally extraneous to the rest of the story.

▼▼▼▼▼▼▼▼▼▼▼▼▼▼▼

Reflecting on the fact that no writer—regardless of talent—can matriculate in the Iowa Writers' Workshop without a bachelor's degree, Saul Maloff, one of Flannery O'Connor's contemporaries at Iowa, commented recently: "Herman Melville may have supposed that 'a whale ship was my Yale College and my Harvard,' but to the dean of any respectable graduate college, including Iowa's, that's just another fish story and not nearly the equivalent of an acceptable degree in icthyology."

▲▲▲▲▲▲▲▲▲▲▲▲▲▲

UNIVERSITY OF KANSAS

William Allen White, attended 1886-1890
William Inge, 1935
William Stafford, 1937, M.A. 1946
James Tate, 1965

UNIVERSITY OF KENTUCKY

Elizabeth Madox Roberts, attended 1900
Elizabeth Hardwick, 1938, M.A. 1939
Wendell Berry, 1956, M.A. 1957
Lee Pennington, graduate study 1966

UNIVERSITY OF MAINE AT ORONO

Elliot Paul, attended 1908-1909
Paul Theroux, attended 1959-1960
Stephen King, 1970

UNIVERSITY OF MARYLAND AT COLLEGE PARK

Michael Mewshaw, 1965

UNIVERSITY OF MASSACHUSETTS–AMHERST

Paul Theroux, 1963

UNIVERSITY OF MIAMI

Donald Justice, 1945
Mark Medoff, 1962

UNIVERSITY OF MICHIGAN

Theodore Roethke, 1929, attended law school 1929, M.A. 1936
Arthur Miller, 1938
Paul Myron Anthony Linebarger (Cordwainer Smith), postdoctoral study 1937, 1939
John Ciardi, M.A. 1939
Howard Moss, attended 1939-1940
Harvey Swados, 1940
John Malcolm Brinnin, 1941
Robert Hayden, graduate study 1941-1946
Cid Corman, graduate study 1946-1947
Douglas Turner Ward, attended 1947-1948
Frank O'Hara, M.A. 1951

Kenneth Millar (Ross Macdonald), Ph.D.
1951
Jerome Rothenberg, M.A. 1953
Lloyd Biggle, Jr., Ph.D. 1953
Joseph Charles Kennedy (X. J. Kennedy), graduate study 1956-1962
Nancy Willard, 1958, Ph.D. 1963
Peter Meinke, M.A. 1961, Ph.D. 1965

UNIVERSITY OF MINNESOTA AT MINNEAPOLIS-ST. PAUL

Robert McAlmon, attended 1916
Richard Eberhart, attended 1922-1923
Ruth Lechlitner, 1923
Max Shulman, 1942
Frederick (Feike) Feikema (Frederick Manfred), graduate study 1944-1945
Poul Anderson, 1948
Gordon R. Dickson, 1948, graduate study 1948-1950
Mark Harris, Ph.D. 1956
Bob Dylan, attended 1960-1961

UNIVERSITY OF MISSISSIPPI

Stark Young, 1901
William Faulkner, attended 1919-1920

Count No 'Count

After leaving high school midway through his final year (he went briefly for a football season, in 1915, and played first-string quarterback), Oxford, Mississippi, native William Faulkner began hanging around the University of Mississippi campus in 1916. Though he was not a student, some of his drawings appeared in the 1916-1917 and 1917-1918 yearbooks.

In 1919, after returning to Oxford from a brief stint in the Canadian RAF, Faulkner enrolled at the University of Mississippi as a special student. Though he joined a fraternity, contributed to student periodicals, and made friends with other literary types, his almost foppish dress and what some nonliterary students considered arrogance earned him the nickname "Count No 'Count." Apparently more interested in writing than school work, Faulkner enrolled again in fall 1920 but stopped attending classes after a few weeks and withdrew officially in November. He continued to contribute to student publications, however, and in spring 1921 his one-act play *Marionettes* was produced by a dramatic club that he and some friends had started while he was still a student.

The Sigma Alpha Epsilon fraternity at the University of Mississippi, fall 1919; William Faulkner is standing on the far right in the second row.

UNIVERSITY OF MISSOURI

Charles Reznikoff, attended 1910-1911

Jack Conroy, attended 1920-1921

Robert A. Heinlein, attended 1924-1925

Thomas Lanier (Tennessee) Williams, attended 1929-1931

Philip A. José Farmer, attended 1936-1937, 1942

Bruce Jay Freidman, 1951

James Tate, attended 1963-1964

UNIVERSITY OF MONTANA

A. B. Gutherie, Jr., 1923

UNIVERSITY OF NEBRASKA AT LINCOLN

Willa Cather, 1895

Mari Sandoz, attended intermittently 1923-1931

UNIVERSITY OF NEVADA AT RENO

Walter Van Tilburg Clark, 1931, M.A. 1932

UNIVERSITY OF NEW HAMPSHIRE

John Irving, 1965

UNIVERSITY OF NEW MEXICO

Preston Jones, 1958

Robert Creeley, M.A. 1960

UNIVERSITY OF NORTH CAROLINA AT CHAPEL HILL

Thomas Wolfe, 1920

Paul Green, 1921, graduate study 1921-1922

Shelby Foote, attended 1935-1937

Walker Percy, 1937

Lawrence Ferlinghetti, 1941

Edgar Bowers, 1947

Guy Owen, 1947, M.A. 1949, Ph.D. 1955

Donald Justice, M.A. 1947

Cid Corman, graduate study 1947

Doris Betts, attended 1954

Coleman Barks, 1959, Ph.D. 1968

Gail Godwin, 1959

William Matthews, M.A. 1966

"Proff" Koch and the Carolina Playmakers

Frederick H. Koch, known to his students as "Proff," arrived in Chapel Hill, North Carolina, in 1918, having studied with the legendary drama teacher George Pierce Baker at Harvard and having taught the future Pulitzer-Prize-winning dramatist Maxwell Anderson at the University of North Dakota. Koch's interest in the academics of theater was slight; he was not concerned with scholarly activities and historical research. It was, rather, his ability to stimulate creativity in those students and colleagues who became known as the Carolina Playmakers and to instill in them an almost evangelistic fervor to write and to perform that resulted in two and a half decades of inspired theater, an era that ended with Koch's death in 1944. Among his students at Chapel Hill were Thomas Wolfe and many other talented writers, including playwright Paul Green (whose Broadway play *In Abraham's Bosom* won a 1927 Pulitzer Prize), Betty Smith (author of *A Tree Grows in Brooklyn*), Frances Gray Patton (author of *Good Morning, Miss Dove*), Jonathan Daniels (editor of the *Raleigh News and Observer* and author of more than a dozen books). Also closely associated with the group was Archibald Henderson, author of the only biography of George Bernard Shaw that was written with Shaw's approval and assistance.

The Playmakers became best known for their expertise in two areas—the folk play and the outdoor drama. Koch had worked with both forms in North Dakota, but it was in Chapel Hill that he developed them to their full dramatic potential. For Koch the folk play dealt "with the legends, superstitions, customs, environmental differences, and the vernacular of the common people," and its underlying concern was "man's

Thomas Wolfe as Buck Gavin in *The Return of Buck Gavin*

plays in 1922. In the beginning they toured only in the Carolinas and Georgia, but, as they became increasingly well known, they performed in the major cities of the Eastern seaboard as well.

Theater historian Arthur Hobson Quinn has associated the Playmakers' growing popularity with the vogue on Broadway in the 1920s for folk plays. Not only did Playmaker Paul Green have a Broadway hit with his play *In Abraham's Bosom*, but other folk plays by non-Playmakers were Broadway successes in the 1920s and 1930s as well—including Dorothy and DuBose Heyward's *Porgy* (1927), Jack Kirkland's adaptation of Erskine Caldwell's *Tobacco Road* (1933), and Lynn Rigg's *Green Grow the Lilacs* (1931–the basis for the even-more-successful musical *Oklahoma!*).

Just as Koch defined the folk play as drama for and about common people, he saw the outdoor drama as a means of combining local history with music, dance, and spectacle to create a popular

conflict with the forces of nature and his simple pleasure in being alive." One of the first such folk plays Koch produced in Chapel Hill was by a member of his first playwriting class, Thomas Wolfe. When no actor could be found to play the title character in Wolfe's play *The Return of Buck Gavin*, set in early Asheville, Koch insisted that Wolfe play the part—over Wolfe's protest that he could not act. "You're a born actor," he told Wolfe, "and you *are* Buck Gavin." Koch later insisted that there was indeed "something uncanny" in Wolfe's performance of the part of a hunted outlaw who returned home to visit his mother and sisters and to lay some flowering arbutus on the grave of a friend killed by revenuers—"something of the pent-up fury of his highland forebears."

The Playmakers took their folk plays on the road for the first time in 1920, and New York publisher Henry Holt published the first collection of their

I am not sure I know what a great teacher is. I think Koch was one. He was no great shakes as a scholar. In that theatre, as in his own life, he was often as corny as North Dakota in August. . . . Sometimes his students in acting and writing learned more from each other than from Koch but only because Koch was the kind of man who could transmit enthusiasm and set it stirring all around him.

—Jonathan Daniels

Proff was then in the business of raising flowers, flowers of the imagination. His warm personality helped them to take root. And always the timid, outreaching tendril-twined student tended to unfold and grow in the sunlight of his favor.

—Paul Green

people's theater. Koch's "pageant-drama" *Raleigh, the Shepherd of the Ocean*, produced in Raleigh, North Carolina, in 1920, was an early success for the Playmakers, but Paul Green proved the master of this genre. *The Lost Colony*, first produced on Roanoke Island on 4 July 1937, near the site of the first English settlement in North America, presents Green's interpretation of the settlers' struggles to survive and how the colony disappeared without a trace (Green accepted the theory that they left with friendly Indians and married into the tribe). The play was so popular that—except for a five-year interruption during World War II—it has been produced on Roanoke Island every summer since its opening season.

The Lost Colony's success also prompted a number of communities all over the country to invite Green and other Playmakers to write and direct outdoor dramas for them. In 1963 the Institute of Outdoor Drama was established at the University of North Carolina to provide information and advice and to promote further developments in the field.

In 1943 Arthur Hobson Quinn effectively summarized the Playmaker's influence: "The best way to estimate the significance of the movement known as the Carolina Playmakers is to try to imagine what American playmaking would have been for the last twenty-five years without them."

–J. R.

UNIVERSITY OF NORTH CAROLINA AT GREENSBORO

Doris Betts, attended 1950-1953

UNIVERSITY OF NORTH DAKOTA

Maxwell Anderson, 1911

UNIVERSITY OF NORTHERN COLORADO

James Michener, A.M. 1936

UNIVERSITY OF NORTHERN IOWA

Mona Van Duyn, 1942

UNIVERSITY OF OREGON

Ken Kesey, 1957

UNIVERSITY OF PENNSYLVANIA

Zane Grey, 1896
A. S. W. Rosenbach, 1898, Ph.D. 1901
Ezra Pound, attended 1901-1903, M.A. 1906; further graduate study 1907-1908
William Carlos Williams, M.D. 1906
Jessie Redmon Fauset, M.A. 1919
Erskine Caldwell, attended 1924
Frederic Prokosch, graduate study 1929
John D. MacDonald, attended 1934-1935
Alfred Bester, 1935
Alan E. Nourse, M.D. 1955
C. K. Williams, 1959
John Edgar Wideman, 1963
Larry Neal, M.A. 1963
Nikki Giovanni, graduate study 1967

Poet Meets Poet

On Tuesday, 30 September 1902, in Room 303 of Brooks Dormitory at the University of Pennsylvania, a freshman dentistry student was introduced to a sophomore "Arts and Sciences" student. Though neither could remember exactly what they talked about at what they later realized was an historic occasion, William Carlos Williams (the freshman, who changed his major to medicine the next year) recalled that he and Ezra Pound (the sophomore, who at seventeen was two years Williams's junior) spent most of their first meeting warily checking each other out. While Williams was shy and earnest, Pound made an effort to appear sophisticated and already seemed sure of his destiny as a great poet. Despite the contrast between Pound's characteristic pose as a decadent poet of the 1890s and Williams's "All-American" high-minded earnestness about his studies, the two

Ezra Pound, 1905

William Carlos Williams, 1906

began a friendship that endured adversities and differences until Williams's death in 1963.

In the 1950s, Pound wrote Williams, remembering the first year of their friendship: "My early rekolektn is you in a room on the South side of the triangle, and me sayin come on nowt, and you deciding on gawd an righteousness and the pursuit of labor in the form of Dr. Gumbo's treatise on the lesions of the bugbone ... " (the odd phonetic spelling is characteristic of Pound). While Williams may not have read Pound any of his early poetic effusions, he did have to endure Pound's recitations of his, made unbearable by the fact that Pound often became so emotional about his poems that his voice became inaudible. Williams listened politely, for the most part in silence, but occasionally, he wrote in his *Autobiography* (1951), he felt compelled "to explode with the comment that unless I could *hear* the lines how could he expect me to have an opinion of them."

Pound transferred to Hamilton College in fall 1903, returning to the University of Pennsylvania for graduate study in fall 1905, but during his two years at Hamilton he saw Williams during his visits to his parents' home in a Philadelphia suburb. In April 1905 he introduced Williams to Hilda Doolittle, the daughter of a professor of astronomy at Penn. Though Pound was interested in the future imagist poet, Williams became infatuated with her too, and began seeing her. For her nineteenth birthday on 13 January 1906 he wrote a sonnet in which each line begins with a letter of her name. Beginning "Hark Hilda! heptachordian hymns," it demonstrates much enthusiasm, but little evidence of the mature, original style that characterizes Williams's mature verse. Though Pound never openly accused Williams of trying to take Doolittle away from him (they were both seeing other young women as well), that March he engaged Williams in a supposedly mock duel with canes and nearly put out Williams's eye.

Between 1905 and 1907 Pound wrote poems for Doolittle, whom he had re-christened Dryad, for his poetic muse (he had a penchant for renaming her—in 1913 he would give her her famous nom de plume, H.D., Imagiste). He handbound twenty-four of these early poems and presented the volume (which was published in 1979 as *Hilda's Book*) to her in 1907. In the same year they became engaged and, though they never married, they remained friends.

The Williams-Pound friendship survived their common interest in Doolittle. In fact, their loyalty to each other continued despite far greater differences of opinion over poetry and politics. During World War II, Williams recorded in his *Autobiography*, he was dismayed to learn that Pound had mentioned his name in one of his pro-fascist broadcasts from Italy. Yet he helped in efforts to gain Pound's release from St. Elizabeths Hospital, where he had been confined after having been judged incompetent to stand trial for treason in 1945, and visited him in the hospital. Still appalled by Pound's politics, he nonetheless posed for photographs with his old friend when Pound was allowed to leave the hospital in 1958.

UNIVERSITY OF PITTSBURGH

Robinson Jeffers, attended 1902-1903
George S. Kaufman, attended 1907
Hervey Allen, 1915
Stanley Burnshaw, 1925
Peter S. Beagle, 1959
John Irving, attended 1961-1962

UNIVERSITY OF REDLANDS

Jack Spicer, attended 1943-1944

UNIVERSITY OF ROCHESTER

Albion W. Tourgée, 1862
Shirley Jackson, attended 1935-1936
Galway Kinnell, M.A. 1949

UNIVERSITY OF SCRANTON

Jason Miller, 1961

UNIVERSITY OF SOUTH CAROLINA

O. B. Mayer, 1837
William Price Fox, 1950
Ben Greer, 1971

UNIVERSITY OF SOUTH FLORIDA

Piers Anthony Dillingham Jacob (Piers Anthony), teaching certificate 1964

Edgar Allan Poe's room, 13 West Range, University of Virginia (photograph by Rebecca Arrington)

UNIVERSITY OF SOUTHERN CALIFORNIA

Robinson Jeffers, graduate study 1905-191

Robert McAlmon, attended sporadically 1917-1920

Wallace Thurman, attended 1922-1923

Joseph Heller, attended 1945

Boyd B. Upchurch (John Boyd), 1947

Frederick Exley, 1953

Paulette Williams (Ntozake Shange), M.A. 1971

UNIVERSITY OF TENNESSEE AT KNOXVILLE

Cormac McCarthy, attended 1951-1952, 1957-1960

UNIVERSITY OF TEXAS AT AUSTIN

Chad Oliver, 1951, M.A. 1952

Willie Morris, 1956

UNIVERSITY OF TULSA

Ted Berrigan, 1959, M.A. 1962

UNIVERSITY OF UTAH

Bernard DeVoto, attended 1914-1915

Wallace Thurman, attended 1919

Vardis Fisher, 1920

Phyllis McGinley, 1927

Wallace Stegner, 1930

Diane Johnson, 1957

UNIVERSITY OF VERMONT

Walter Van Tilburg Clark, M.A. 1934

UNIVERSITY OF VIRGINIA

Edgar Allan Poe, attended 1826

Thomas Nelson Page, LL.B. 1874

Skipwith Cannell, attended 1906-1909

Erskine Caldwell, attended 1923-1925

Ben Belitt, 1932, M.A. 1934, further graduate study 1934-1936

Karl Shapiro, attended 1932-1933

Calder Willingham, attended 1941-1943

R. H. W. Dillard, M.A. 1959, Ph.D. 1965

Michael Mewshaw, M.A. 1966, Ph. D. 1970

Stephen Goodwin, M.A. 1969

CHECKERED CAREER #12

While he did well in his classes during his year (1826) at the University of Virginia, Edgar Allan Poe ran up a staggering $2,000 in debts to local merchants and gambling losses–a fact that led his foster father, John Allan, to refuse to send him back to school.

On 1 July 1830, after having published two books of poetry (*Tamerlane and Other Poems* in 1827 and *Al Aaraaf, Tamerlane, and Minor Poems* in 1829), the twenty-one-year-old Poe entered West Point. At first he did well in his courses, but he ran up debts again, and, after Allan refused to send him money, he began drinking in his room. Despite Poe's request, Allan also failed to send the formal permission that Poe needed to resign from West Point, and Poe set out deliberately to get himself court-martialed, skipping roll call, classes, and church. Though the story is now impossible to substantiate, tradition has it that he once showed up on the parade ground wearing nothing but the crossbuck straps to his uniform. At any rate, he succeeded somehow in making his misconduct conspicuous; his court-martial took place on 27-28 January 1831, and he was formally dismissed on 6 March.

UNIVERSITY OF WASHINGTON

Robinson Jeffers, graduate study 1910-1911

A. B. Gutherie, Jr., attended 1919-1920

Frank Herbert, attended 1946-1947

Richard Hugo, 1948, M.A. 1952

James Wright, M.A. 1954, Ph.D. 1959

Tom Robbins, attended circa 1960

UNIVERSITY OF WISCONSIN-MADISON

Jean Toomer, attended 1914

Horace Gregory, 1923

Kenneth Fearing, 1924

Clifford D. Simak, attended late 1920s

Kenneth Patchen, attended 1929-1930

August Derleth, 1930

Delmore Schwartz, attended 1931

Saul Bellow, graduate study 1937

Edwin Honig, 1941, M.A. 1947

Howard Moss, 1943

Lorraine Hansberry, attended 1948-1950

Paul Blackburn, 1950

David Starkweather, 1957

Joyce Carol Oates, M.A. 1961

Peter Straub, 1965

URSINUS COLLEGE

J. D. Salinger, attended 1938

UTAH STATE UNIVERSITY

May Swenson, 1939

VALPARAISO UNIVERSITY

William Edward Campbell (William March), attended 1913-1914

VANDERBILT UNIVERSITY

John Crowe Ransom, 1909

Donald Davidson, 1917, M.A. 1922

Allen Tate, 1923

Merrill Moore, 1924, M.D. 1928

Andrew Lytle, 1925

Robert Penn Warren, 1925

James Still, M.A. 1930

Jesse Stuart, graduate study 1931-1932

Randall Jarrell, 1936, M.A. 1939

Peter Taylor, attended 1937-1938

James Dickey, 1949, M.A. 1950

Jessie Hill Ford, 1951

The Fugitive Poets

When the Nashville group that would eventually call itself the Fugitives came together in 1915 there was little indication that it would have a major influence not only on how poetry (and to some extent fiction) has been written but also on how literature has been read for more than a quarter of this century.

The birth of the Fugitives is usually located in spring 1915, when John Crowe Ransom, a Vanderbilt graduate and Rhodes Scholar who had returned to teach at his alma mater the previous fall, was invited by a group of his students, including Donald Davidson, to join them on visits to Sidney Mttron Hirsch, the eccentric older half-brother of another student, Nathaniel (Nat) Hirsch, to take part in their discussions of philosophy and religion. Sidney Hirsch was something of an expert on mysticism (his middle name—pronounced Me-tát-tron—comes from the Cabala, where Mttron, as the Angel Prince, is the visible manifestation of the deity) and his interests tended to dominate the discussions during the early years of the group's existence. Other early group members in addition to Ransom, Davidson and the two Hirsches, were William Yandell Elliott, Alec B. Stevenson, and Stanley Johnson—all Vanderbilt students, and Walter Clyde Curry, a brilliant young philosophy professor, who would later become well known for his studies of Chaucer and Shakespeare.

The meetings were discontinued during World War I, while various members—including Ransom and Davidson—served in the armed forces. It drifted back together after the war, adding James Frank and William Frierson to its numbers, and—most important—an undergraduate named John Orly Allen Tate, whom Davidson brought to his first meeting in November 1921. While Sidney Hirsch still presided over the group, Davidson and Tate, at least, recognized Ransom as the true leader. The group's focus soon turned from philosophy to literature, as various members began to read aloud their own poetry and to invite group discussion.

In March 1922 Sidney Hirsch suggested that they had written so many good poems they ought to start their own magazine, and Johnson suggested that they call it the *Fugitive*, after one of Hirsch's poems (by choosing the title they were attempting to present the poet as a wandering outcast, whom Tate called later "the man who carries the secret wisdom around the world").

The magazine became well known and admired in literary circles at home and abroad, but the response in Nashville was ambivalent—the local papers publicized the group and their magazine, but at the same time many Nashville citizens found the enterprise peculiar and "intellectual." When Tate attempted to sell Vanderbilt's chancellor, J. H. Kirkland, a subscription to the new magazine, Kirkland refused, and in fact never offered any sort of support to the group that is now so closely associated with Vanderbilt's history.

The *Fugitive* flourished, however, and new members came to the group, including Merrill Moore, then an undergraduate; Laura Riding, who lived in Louisville and participated by mail; and—most notably—Robert Penn Warren, who joined the group in 1923.

Two other writers, Andrew Lytle and Cleanth Brooks, are sometimes associated with the group. Both were invited to some of the meetings, and Lytle had a poem published in the *Fugitive* (Brooks showed up at Vanderbilt after it had ceased publication), but since neither was listed as a group member on the masthead of the *Fugitive*, purists tend not to discuss them as members, though their careers have been closely linked with the major Fugitives.

The magazine folded after the Decem-

PERIODICALS FOUNDED AND/OR EDITED BY THE FUGITIVES

The Fugitive, April 1922-December 1925 (first issues jointly edited; various editors thereafter)
The Southern Review, 1935-1942, 1965- (founded and edited by Cleanth Brooks, Robert Penn Warren, and Charles W. Pipkin; revived in 1965 by Donald Stanford and Lewis Simpson)
The Kenyon Review, 1937- (founded by John Crowe Ransom, edited by Ransom until 1958)
The Sewanee Review, 1892- (edited by Allen Tate, 1944-1945)

---

ber 1925 issue, not from lack of financial support, but because the poets who had emerged as the four major Fugitives—Ransom, Davidson, Tate, and Warren—had lost interest. Tate and Warren were no longer in Nashville, and Ransom and Davidson, who were still there, had new interests. Davidson wanted to write longer, narrative poems rather than the shorter ones that were better suited for publication in the *Fugitive*. Ransom, whose career as a poet was virtually over and who had written nearly all the poems on which his reputation still rests, was more interested in writing literary criticism.

Indeed, though the Fugitives' poetry was an important contribution to the revival of Southern literature, it was through their teaching, the journals they edited, and their critical writings, as well as their textbooks and the anthol-

Newspaper feature on the Fugitives

ogies they edited, that the major Fugitives (and Brooks) influenced the course of American poetry and criticism. By the mid 1930s, as the Fugitives spread out, with Brooks and Warren at Louisiana State University and Tate taking various visiting professorships, while Davidson and Ransom remained at Vanderbilt, they began to establish a loyal following of students. In 1935-1936, while Tate was serving as a visiting professor at Southwestern at Memphis (now Rhodes College), he convinced Peter Taylor to transfer to Vanderbilt to study under Ransom. Taylor did so in fall 1936 and was warmly welcomed by both Ransom and Davidson, but in fall 1937 Ransom left for Kenyon College, followed by Randall Jarrell (as well as Robert Lowell, who had planned to transfer

from Harvard to Vanderbilt to study under Ransom, but went to Kenyon instead) and David McDowell. Taylor went to Kenyon the next year and after graduating in 1940, he and Lowell went to Louisiana State University for graduate school so they could study under Brooks and Warren. Jarrell, who had finished all the requirements for his M.A. but his thesis at Vanderbilt and gone to Kenyon as an instructor, told Taylor, "You think you like the rest of them—Ransom, Davidson, Tate, Lytle—but wait 'til you meet Brooks and Warren."

Fugitive Pseudonyms

For the first two issues of the *Fugitive* all the contributors employed humorous pseudonyms. Some provide clues to the individual poet's sense of his own person-

THE FUGITIVES' TEXTBOOKS AND ANTHOLOGIES

1935: Topics for Freshman Writing: Twenty Topics for Writing with Appropriate Materials for Study, edited by Ransom.

1936: An Approach to Literature, by Brooks, Warren, and John Thibaut Purser.

1937: A Southern Harvest: Short Stories by Southern Writers, edited by Warren.

1938: America through the Essay: An Anthology for English Courses, edited by Tate and A. Theodore Johnson.

1938: Understanding Poetry: An Anthology for College Students, edited by Brooks and Warren.

1939: American Composition and Rhetoric, by Davidson.

1942: Readings for Composition from Prose Models, edited by Donaldson and Sidney Erwin Glenn.

1942: American Harvest, edited by Tate and John Peale Bishop.

1943: Understanding Fiction, edited by Brooks and Warren.

1949: Modern Rhetoric, by Brooks and Warren.

1950: Fundamentals of Good Writing: A Handbook of Modern Rhetoric, by Brooks and Warren.

1950: The House of Fiction: An Anthology of the Short Story with Commentary, edited by Tate and Caroline Gordon.

1953: An Anthology of Stories from the Southern Review, edited by Brooks and Warren.

1954: Short Story Masterpieces, edited by Warren and Albert Erskine.

1955: Six Centuries of Great Poetry: From Chaucer to Yeats, edited by Warren and Erskine.

1955: Twenty Lessons in Reading and Writing Prose, by Davidson.

1957: A New Southern Harvest, edited by Warren and Erskine.

1958: Modern Verse in English, 1900-1950, edited by Tate and David Cecil.

1960: The Arts of Reading, edited by Tate, Ralph Ross, and John Berryman.

1960: The Scope of Fiction, by Brooks and Warren.

1961: Conversations on the Craft of Poetry, by Brooks, Warren, and others.

1969: Six American Poets from Emily Dickinson to the Present: An Introduction, edited by Tate.

1973: American Literature: The Masters and the Making, edited by Brooks, Warren and R. W. B. Lewis.

A Fugitive reunion, 1956: (first row) Allen Tate, John Crowe Ransom, Donald Davidson; (second row) Alfred Starr, Alec Stevenson, Robert Penn Warren; (third row) William Yandell Elliott, Merrill Moore, Jesse Wills, Sidney Mttron Hirsch (courtesy of the Photographic Archives, Vanderbilt University)

ality; others may have had meaning for the creators but draw a blank with everyone else. The contributors to the first two issues and their pseudonyms are as follows:

John Crowe Ransom–Roger Prim
Donald Davidson–Robin Gallivant
Allen Tate–Henry Feathertop
Alec B. Stevenson–Drimlonigher (first issue), King Badger (second issue)
Stanley Johnson–Jonathan David
Walter Clyde Curry–Marpha
Sidney Mttron Hirsch–L. Oafer
Merrill Moore–Dendric
James Frank–Philora

Tate said that the decision to use pseudonyms was based more on their sense of "romance" than on a desire to conceal their authorship. Ransom seems to have chosen his to poke fun at his own formal, rather aloof nature. Davidson's evocation of a wanderer is historically interesting since he was to wander considerably less than some of his fellow Fugitives, spending his whole life at Vanderbilt. Tate's comes from Nathaniel Hawthorne's "Feathertop," the story of a scarecrow that is brought to life and passes for a fine gentleman. Drim-

lonigher, Stevenson's first pseudonym, is the name of his father's birthplace, a county in Ireland, while King Badger comes from the fact that Brock, his middle name, is the Celtic word for *badger*. Louise Cowan, in her book on the Fugitives, suggests that Johnson chose the names of two famous Old Testament friends to suggest "that he was his own best friend." Curry's choice seems to have baffled everyone but Curry, while Hirsch's obvious pun is a surprise considering his interest in esoteric mystical philosophy. Cowan suggests that Moore, a premed student, probably took his from the *dendrite*, the part of the neuron that conducts impulses toward the main body of the cell; though Tate, in pointing out that Dendric derives from the Greek for tree and thus means *treelike*, suggested later that the gangly young Moore may have been describing his own appearance. Philora could be translated as "loving mouths," and though no one is sure what Stevens had in mind, Cowan suggests it could refer to his interest in philology.

The pseudonyms were discarded for several reasons. The main one, however, was the allegation that the first two issues had been entirely Ransom's work, which came after two critics

Southern verse, making it, as Ransom wrote in the first issue, no longer the preserve of "the high-caste Brahmins of the Old South," but the shared property of all educated people. Over its long history, the *Fugitive* group included not only Ransom, Davidson, Tate, and Warren, but also Merrill Moore, Jesse Wills, Alec B. Stevenson, Walter Clyde Curry, Stanley Johnson, Sidney Mttron Hirsch, James Frank, William Yandell Elliott, William Frierson, Ridley Wills, Alfred Starr, and Laura Riding.

While the Fugitives were all Southern poets, the Agrarians were twelve Southerners from various disciplines, though—along with Ransom, Davidson, Tate, Warren, and Lytle—the group also included novelist Stark Young and poet

---

CHECKERED CAREER #13

During the summer after his 1943 graduation from Phillips Exeter Academy, Gore Vidal joined the Enlisted Reserve Corps of the U.S. Army, which sent him to study engineering at Virginia Military Institute. Instead of doing his course work, Vidal spent most of his time writing a novel, and at the end of one term the army sent him as a private to clerk at Peterson Field in Colorado, thus ending his brief exposure to higher education.

---

learned that he had written the introductory editorials for both numbers. As a note in issue number three explained, the group differed "so widely and so cordially from each other on matters poetical that all were about equally chagrined" to hear that anyone could construe their writings as the work of one individual.

The Fugitives amd the Agrarians; Two Different Groups

Because John Crowe Ransom, Donald Davidson, Allen Tate, and Robert Penn Warren—the four major writers to emerge from the Fugitives—were also Agrarians, the names Fugitives and Agrarians have often been applied interchangeably to the writers who contributed to the magazine the *Fugitive* (1922-1925) and to *I'll Take My Stand* (1930), a collection of essays stating the Agrarians' position. In fact, the two groups are quite different.

The Fugitives, who met frequently between 1915 and 1928 and who published their periodical between April 1922 and December 1925, were a diverse group with no common convictions except a general desire to revive

---

CHECKERED CAREER #14

The author of science fiction that demonstrates his knowledge of technology, Larry Niven failed to make the same impression on his professors at the California Institute of Technology, which he left with failing grades. Attributing his poor showing to "having discovered a used book store jammed with used science-fiction magazines," Niven apparently applied himself more conscientiously at Washburn University, where he earned a B.A. in 1962 with a major in mathematics and a minor in psychology. After one year (1962-1963) of graduate work in math at UCLA, he decided to devote himself full-time to science-fiction writing.

John Gould Fletcher (the others were Frank Lawrence Owsley, Lyle Lanier, H.C. Nixon, John Donald Wade, and Henry Blue Kline). While reference books sometimes describe the group as advocates of replacing industrialism in the New South with the old agriculturally based economy—a view that is then attacked as not only conservative but incredibly naive—the views of the twelve, while they are not entirely homogenous, might better be stated thus: the industrialist's belief that mankind will be perfected through secular progress must be replaced by the moral and religious values of the old agricultural South.

VASSAR COLLEGE

Adelaide Crapsey, 1901
Alice Jane Chandler (Jean) Webster, 1901
Edna St. Vincent Millay, 1917
Muriel Rukeyser, attended 1930-1931
Mary McCarthy, 1933
Elizabeth Bishop, 1934
Eleanor Clark, 1934

VILLANOVA UNIVERSITY

Charles Fuller, attended 1956-1958
David Rabe, M.A. 1968, further graduate study 1970-1972

VIRGINIA MILITARY INSTITUTE

Gore Vidal, attended 1943

WAGNER COLLEGE

Paul Zindel, 1953, M.Sc. 1959

WAKE FOREST UNIVERSITY

Laurence Stallings, 1916
A. R. Ammons, 1949

WASHBURN UNIVERSITY

Larry Niven, 1962

WASHINGTON AND LEE UNIVERSITY

Thomas Nelson Page, attended 1869-1872
Tom Robbins, attended 1950-1952

WASHINGTON UNIVERSITY

Thomas Lanier (Tennessee) Williams, attended 1935-1937
William Jay Smith, 1939, M.A. 1941
John Gardner, 1955
Eugene B. Redmond, M.A. 1966

WAYNE STATE COLLEGE
(Wayne, Nebraska)

John G. Neihardt, 1897

WAYNE STATE UNIVERSITY
(Detroit, Michigan)

Robert Hayden, 1935
Lloyd Biggle, Jr., 1947
Philip Levine, 1950, A.M. 1954

WESLEYAN UNIVERSITY

Thomas Bangs Thorpe, attended 1834-1836
Charles Olson, 1932, M.A. 1933
Robert Ludlum, 1951

Adelaide Crapsey (center), manager of Vassar's Class of 1901 basketball team (photograph from the 1899 *Vassarian*)

WEST VIRGINIA UNIVERSITY

Jayne Anne Phillips, 1974

WESTERN COLLEGE

Margaret Anderson, attended 1903-1906

WHITTIER COLLEGE

Jessamyn West, 1923

WICHITA STATE UNIVERSITY

Michael McClure, attended 1951-1953

WILBERFORCE UNIVERSITY

Douglas Turner Ward, attended 1946-1947

WILLIAM AND MARY COLLEGE

James Branch Cabell, 1898

WILLIAMS COLLEGE

William Cullen Bryant, attended 1809-1810
Sterling Brown, 1922
Jay McInerney, 1976

WILSON JUNIOR COLLEGE

Gwendolyn Brooks, A.A. 1936

WOODSTOCK COLLEGE

Daniel Berrigan, M.A. 1952

YALE UNIVERSITY

Jonathan Edwards, 1720
John Trumbull, 1767, M.A. 1770
Timothy Dwight, 1769, M.A. 1772
David Humphreys, M.A. 1774
Joel Barlow, 1778, M.A. 1781
Noah Webster, 1778
Elihu Hubbard Smith, 1786
James Fenimore Cooper, attended 1803-1805
Augustus Baldwin Longstreet, 1813
Clarence Day, 1896
Henry Seidel Canby, 1899
William Rose Benét, 1907
Sinclair Lewis, 1908

Waldo Frank, 1911, M.A. 1911
Archibald MacLeish, 1915
Donald Ogden Stewart, 1916
Philip Barry, 1919
Stephen Vincent Benét, 1919, M.A. 1920
Robert Coates, 1919
Thornton Wilder, 1920
Andrew Lytle, graduate study 1925-1928
Robert Penn Warren, graduate study 1927-1928
Frederic Prokosch, Ph.D. 1932
John Hersey, 1936
Reed Whittemore, 1941
John Knowles, 1949
William F. Buckley, Jr., 1950
Peter Matthiessen, 1950
Frank D. Gilroy, graduate study 1950-1951
David Slavitt, 1956
Mark Strand, 1959
Janet Burroway, graduate study 1960-1961
Richard France, 1965
William Matthews, 1965
Tom McGuane, M.F.A. 1965
Lonne Elder, attended 1966-1967

Yale and the Connecticut Wits
One of Yale's contributions to the new American Republic was its first literary group, the Connecticut Wits (also known as the Hartford Wits), which included six Yale graduates–John Trumbull (1750-1831), Timothy Dwight (1752-1817), David Humphries (1752-1818), Joel Barlow (1754-1812), Mason Fitch Cogswell (1761-1830), and Elihu Hubbard Smith (1771-1798)–plus Richard Alsop (1761-1815), who studied briefly with a tutor at Yale but never enrolled, and two others who never matriculated at Yale–Lemuel Hopkins (1750-1801) and Theodore Dwight (1764-1846), Timothy's younger brother and the husband of Alsop's sister. Known for the collaborative satires (usually published serially in newspapers) that they wrote throughout the second half of the eighteenth century, the

group is often divided into the Major Wits–Trumbull, Timothy Dwight, Humphreys, and Barlow–all of whom became significant literary figures (Dwight also served as president of Yale from 1795 to 1817) and the Minor Wits–Alsop, Cogswell, Theodore Dwight, Hopkins, and Smith–who, with the exception of Smith, are remembered by literary historians solely for their contributions to the Wits' satires.

Trumbull and Timothy Dwight established the collaborative tradition with two series of essays that they sent to Boston and New Haven newspapers in 1769-1773, during which time the two friends were earning their masters' degrees and then tutoring at Yale. Trumbull, who tutored there in 1772-1773, and Dwight, who began tutoring there in 1771 and stayed on until 1777, are credited with helping to introduce contemporary English literature into the Yale curriculum and with encouraging the literary ambitions of Humphreys and Barlow, who started off his career

as a published poet with a broadside satire on the food at Yale–suggesting that some things never change. (Later, in

---

THE LITERARY COLLABORATIONS
OF THE CONNECTICUT WITS

The Meddler (1769-1770), by John Trumbull and Timothy Dwight.

The Correspondent (1770-1773), by John Trumbull and Timothy Dwight.

The Anarchiad (1786-1787), by Joel Barlow, David Humphreys, John Trumbull, and Lemuel Hopkins.

The Echo (1791-1798), by Richard Alsop, Theodore Dwight, Lemuel Hopkins, and Elihu Hubbard Smith.

The Political Green-house for the Year 1798 (1799), by Richard Alsop, Lemuel Hopkins, and Theodore Dwight.

Joel Barlow in 1807, portrait by Charles Willson Peale; and John Trumbull, portrait of the author by the artist who bore the same name (courtesy of Yale University Art Gallery)

James Fenimore Cooper

quo"–a characteristic as apparent in his administration of Yale as it is in his poetry. Though some scholars, including Parrington, make a case for Trumbull, he is known primarily for one long poem, *M'Fingal* (1776-1782), an anti-Tory satire most often rated as a solid but minor achievement. Barlow, who went beyond the provincialism of the other Connecticut Wits, wrote poetry that–despite the vast change in poetic taste–modern readers can still enjoy.

Yale's Literary Renaissance

As Yale historian Brooks Mather Kelley points out, "Yale had never been a literary place–except for a brief period with the Connecticut Wits"–until the 1890s when a glimmer of literary interest emerged with the appearance on campus of Clarence Day, later to become well known for humorous autobiographical sketches such as *Life with Father* (1935), and Henry Seidel Canby, one of the founders, in 1924 of the *Saturday Review of Literature*. In the next decade future Nobel Prize winner Sinclair Lewis and William Rose Benét, poet and another of the *Saturday Review*'s founders, attended Yale, but it was not until the 1910s that Yale's true literary renaissance began with the arrival on campus

1787, at his own academy in Greenfield Hill, Dwight also taught the youngest of the Wits, Elihu Hubbard Smith, who had entered Yale at eleven and, on receiving his B.A. in 1786, had become the youngest Yale graduate to that date.)

Though Trumbull and Dwight's essays of 1769-1773 set things rolling, the later collaborations were all in poetry and far more political than the earlier essays, which focused their satire on such things as threats to religious orthodoxy. Voicing their support of the Federalist movement for a strong national government, the Wits' conservative salvoes took on various issues and politicians such as law and order, paper money, Thomas Jefferson (a favorite target), and even–after he went to France and adopted political views far more liberal than theirs–Joel Barlow.

Of the so-called Major Wits Barlow alone could be considered a major poet. Humphreys is most often remembered for his biography of Revolutionary War General Israel Putnam, while Timothy Dwight's poetry is so orthodox and didactic that most modern readers find it hopelessly dull. Historian Vernon Louis Parrington once called Dwight "a walking repository of the venerable *status*

CHECKERED CAREER #15

Said by one biographer to have spent his entire career at Yale working on getting expelled, James Fenimore Cooper finally succeeded in his junior year (1805), when he is reputed to have used gunpowder to blast open the door to another student's room. Though reliable information about his college years is scant, according to legend at least, he also put a donkey in a professor's chair.

Sinclair Lewis

of such literary types as future actor-writer Edgar Montillion (Monty) Woolley, Cole Porter, Archibald MacLeish, Donald Ogden Stewart, Philip Barry, future editor and publisher John C. Farrar, Stephen Vincent Benét, Thornton Wilder, and the future founders of *Time* magazine, Britton Hadden and Henry Luce.

Sinclair Lewis, the first great modern Yale writer, arrived in New Haven in September 1903, having described himself accurately several months earlier as "Tall, ugly, thin, red-hair." Affected with a severe case of acne as well as a Midwestern ignorance of Yale customs, he seemed destined to be an outsider. Though he was the first member of his class to have work published in the *Yale Literary Magazine* and the *Yale Courant*, he was virtually friendless in his first year at Yale, and the condition was relieved only slightly during his sophomore year, when he made one friend, Allan Updegraff. Hoping to gain friends through literary associations and to make the *Lit*'s editorial board he bombarded the magazine with submissions. Though the *Lit*'s board accepted many

of his poems and short stories, they rejected many more. By his junior year Lewis had earned the nickname "God-Forbid," which seems to have had several meanings, including "God forbid that Lewis should ever make the *Lit*." Yet selection of the board each spring was based entirely on the number of publications each junior had had in the *Lit*, with the five contributors who had published the most automatically making the board. When the list was posted in February 1906, Lewis was listed third; yet his pleasure was dampened when both the *Yale News* and the issue of the *Lit* that announced the awards called him E. H. Lewis of Syracuse, New York, rather than H. S. Lewis of Sauk Centre, Minnesota.

Whatever his lack of personal popularity, Harry Lewis, as he was called then—had established his literary reputation. During his junior year, he was also invited to join the editorial staff of the new *Yale Monthly Magazine* and elected to the editorship of the *Yale Courant*. (He declined both offices, and his runner-up in the second race, William Rose Benét, with whom he was to develop a close friendship, became editor of the *Courant*.)

Rather than enjoying the *Lit* position he had coveted for so long, Lewis left Yale in October of his senior year, going with Updegraff to live and work at Helicon Hall, Upton Sinclair's experiment in communal living near Englewood, New Jersey. Disillusioned after a month, they went to New York, where Lewis supported himself by working as a clerk and as a translator and writer for various humor and pulp magazines. Before returning to Yale in December 1907, Lewis also traveled to Panama, where he tried unsuccessfully to find employment with companies building the Panama Canal. Back at Yale Lewis managed to finish a year's work in one semester, and, despite some distrust of his socialist views, he was considered for an instructorship (for which Lewis himself recommended someone else).

The editorial board for the *Yale Literary Magazine,* 1919: Stephen Vincent Benét is seated at center; standing are Robert M. Coates (at left) and Thornton Wilder (at right)

Though he later said that his true education began after he entered Harvard Law School in fall 1915, Archibald MacLeish had the sort of success at Yale for which the freshman Lewis had only hoped. Entering Yale in fall 1911, MacLeish made both the football and swimming teams, and had a poem published in the *Yale Lit.*

The high point of MacLeish's undistinguished gridiron career came that same year when, after the Yale freshman had held a supposedly superior Harvard freshman team to a nothing-nothing tie, the Harvard coach walked up to MacLeish and some of his friends and, MacLeish wrote later, "announced in the voice of an indignant beagle sighting a fox that I was, without question, the dirtiest little sonofabitch of a center ever to visit Cambridge, Massachusetts." He added, however, that he "didn't deserve that honor": at five-foot-ten and one-sixty-five he was "little but not *that* little."

MacLeish later said that he managed to make friends among both Yale's athletes and its poets because "The football squad didn't read the *Yale Literary Magazine* and those who did never went to the games." (One exception, however, was humor writer Donald Ogden Stewart. When he tried out for freshman football in 1912, the coach's sophomore assistant was MacLeish.)

MacLeish not only contributed poems and stories to the *Lit* and served as editor, but he also made Phi Beta Kappa in

his junior year, was elected class poet, and won the Yale University Prize for Poetry for his *Songs for a Summer's Day,* which Yale University Press published in 1915.

Thornton Wilder, who entered Yale as a sophomore in fall 1917, after two years at Oberlin had a less distinguished academic career than MacLeish, who had graduated in June 1916. More interested in writing plays than studying, he contributed short plays and essays to the *Lit* and was elected to its editorial board. His major literary triumph during his time at Yale was winning Yale's Bradford Brinton Award in 1918 for his four-act play *The Trumpet Shall Sound.* The play was published serially in the *Lit* and in 1926 it was the first of his plays to be staged professionally. (New York audiences were unimpressed.)

Whatever success lay ahead of Wilder with his novel *The Bridge of San Luis Rey* (1927) and plays such as *Our Town* (1938) and *The Skin of Our Teeth* (1942), he and MacLeish—even with his brilliant career in and out of the classroom—were overshadowed at Yale by a precocious young poet who arrived there at the start of MacLeish's senior year and graduated a year ahead of Wilder.

Stephen Vincent Benét entered Yale in September 1915 having already had a poem published in a national magazine (the *New Republic*) and about to have a book published. That his older brother, William Rose Benét, by then an editor at *Century* magazine and a pub-

CHECKERED CAREER #16

Extremely myopic, but determined not to remain at Yale while his friends went off to war, Stephen Vincent Benét managed to get into the U.S. Army in spring 1918 by memorizing the army's eye chart. The next day his sergeant watched the new recruit peeling potatoes in KP and realized "the way he was carving the things he was likely to nick his nose." He was given a new eye test, with a different chart, and recommended for immediate discharge. His army career having lasted a total of three days, Benét settled for a clerk's job with the U.S. State Department in Washington, where he went in summer 1918. Later that year he took a job as a code clerk for military intelligence, where he found the company especially congenial–James Thurber was a fellow clerk and newspaper columnist Franklin P. Adams was the captain in charge of personnel. Yet cryptography bothered Benét's eyes, and he went back to a job at the state department. (One measure of the extremity of Benét's myopia might be the fact that Thurber, who had lost one eye and had impaired vision in the one that remained, worked as a code clerk for about a year and a half.) By January 1919 Benét was back at Yale.

. . . a Yale class, like most real and historic democracies, begins with a hereditary aristocracy, grows tired of it and knocks out its underpinnings so that its members slide gently back into the general mass.

–Stephen Vincent Benét,
The Beginning of Wisdom *(1921)*

The elder Benét brother also prepared his younger brother's way at Yale by writing to his college friend Henry Canby (then an assistant professor at Yale) about his brother's presence on campus. As a result of the letter, a group of literary sophomores, including John Farrar, was sent to welcome the younger Benét. What they found has been aptly described by Benét's biographer, Charles A. Fenton: "they observed that he needed a haircut, was using language coarse beyond the limits of Yale's muscular Christianity, and was pitching pennies on the stone floor with unsuitable companions. He was taken in hand." One of Benét's friends later explained Benét's tendency to choose "wrong" friends as well as "right" ones by saying that he was "congenial with all sorts of people. . . .genuinely interested in people and people as individuals." (His attention to his appearance never improved either. He later became notorious for stuffing the pockets of his Brooks Brothers suits with numerous scraps of papers and small packages.)

Like the young protagonist in his autobiographical novel, *The Beginning of Wisdom* (1921), Benét showed up at Yale with a sheaf of poems he had written over the previous summer and shoved them "cautiously, three or four a month, through the letter-slit in the door of the *Lit* office" creating the impression, one of his contemporaries noted later, that he "spent his time in a sort of garret, often with a bottle beside him, scribbling furiously." His success with the *Lit* was phenomenal. Though the magazine tended to publish very little work by freshmen, Benét had at

lished poet himself, arranged the subsidized winter 1915 publication of his younger brother's *Five Men and Pompey* by Boston's Four Seas Company, did not diminish the fact that the publisher chose to include the book in a uniform series that also included the work of the well-known verse dramatist Gordon Bottomley and one of the new imagist poets, Richard Aldington.

least one poem in each of the year's eight issues. He also contributed large quantities of material to the *Yale Record*, the humor magazine, and continued to place poems in national magazines as well. In 1917 his long poem *The Drug Shop* won Yale's Albert Stanburrough Cook Prize and was published by New Haven's Brick Row Book Shop.

When Wilder arrived at Yale in fall 1917 he quickly learned that Benét, who was not yet a member of the *Lit*'s editorial board, wielded considerable power over what appeared between its covers. "Without exerting any leadership, or ever being acknowledged as the leader," another friend said later, "Steve was the center and the hub.... Steve was not merely a poet, he was poetry. We did not think of him as a great man. He was not forbidding. He was just everybody's favorite companion."

His renown had spread to other Ivy League campuses as well, in part because the staffs of the various literary magazines kept track of what their counterparts were publishing. At the same time Wilder was writing a friend about Benét's influence on campus, F. Scott Fitzgerald was writing to Edmund Wilson that he was afraid Benét's poetry would "obscure" John Peale Bishop's because Benét's "subjects are less precious and decadent." A Harvard contemporary, Malcolm Cowley, later remembered that Benét "was the bright star not only of Yale but of all the Eastern colleges."

In 1918, the year Benét, who was just twenty, was elected chairman of the *Lit*'s editorial board and became a member of the *Record*'s board, he had his third book, *Young Adventure*, published by Yale University Press in its Yale Series of Younger Poets.

Despite time out for war work, Benét managed to graduate with his class and stayed on for a year of graduate school. In Canby's writing class he began work on *The Beginning of Wisdom*, and in June 1920 he submitted a collection of poems as an M.A. thesis that was published later that year by Henry Holt of New York as *Heavens and Earth*.

Yet, "The bright star . . . of all the Eastern colleges" never achieved the greatness that had been predicted for him. While his best work—which includes his long Civil War poem, *John Brown's Body* (1928) and his short story "The Devil and Daniel Webster" (1936)—deserves its continuing popular acclaim, much of his writing was second rate. "The Devil and Daniel Webster" and a few of his poems still show up in high-school textbooks, but it is the more-innovative MacLeish whose poems (especially the justifiably praised "Ars Poetica," "You, Andrew Marvell," and "The End of the World") are more-often discussed in the college classroom.

Benét has also been eclipsed by Wilder, whose success he predicted in 1919 when he told Wilder's father that Wilder was "the surest candidate for secure fame of anybody who has ever eaten at Mory's." The strength of Benét's best work lies in his personal sense of his nation's history. In 1954, MacLeish told Benét's biographer, "Steve was more conscious of being an American than any other man I ever knew."

WRITERS WHO DIDN'T GO TO COLLEGE
AND WHAT THEY DID INSTEAD

That education is not a prerequisite for literary talent is evident from the long list of American writers who never enrolled in college and in some cases never finished, or even attended, high school. At their inception in the seventeenth century, the first American universities, like their British counterparts, were intended to train young men for the clergy (though not all graduates entered the ministry). Even though their curricula broadened throughout the eighteenth and nineteenth centuries, especially after the Civil War, American colleges and universities remained the preserves of an elite few until well into the twentieth century. In 1890 only slightly more than three percent of the American population between eighteen and twenty-one was enrolled in college. By 1900 the figure had risen to slightly more than four percent, and it continued to rise—to 4.48% in 1910, to 8.14% in 1920, and to 12.37% in 1930. Yet it was not until after World War II that the average, middle-class adolescent began to see college as the main path to success. Many future writers, from Charles Brockden Brown and Washington Irving on through Edgar Lee Masters, chose to read law with established attorneys instead of attending college, a time-honored practice that continued even after law entered college curricula and that was prevalent well into the twentieth century. For most of America's history even a high-school education was reserved for a relatively small number of individuals, and many future writers never saw such education as a path to success, in many cases finding their way into journalism and eventually belles lettres through the printing trade.

While a few colleges began admitting women in the nineteenth century (the first three women *in the world* to receive B. A. degrees graduated from Antioch in 1841), college education for women was rare until after World War II. While the best of the deservedly much-maligned nineteenth-century female seminaries offered the equivalent of a junior-college education, families typically considered them places where daughters might learn proper dress and deportment, acquire useful knowledge for running a household, and maybe develop some sort of cultural "attainment" such as playing the piano or skill in painting miniatures. Typically, a young woman was removed from seminary before she had completed the curriculum. Margaret Fuller (1810-1850), who like many women of her generation was educated at home, was unusual and lucky to have a father who taught her the same subjects he would have wanted a son to study, thus giving her an excellent education. Educator Bronson Alcott (1799-1888) also provided his daughter Louisa May (1832-1888) with an exceptional, if sporadic education. Harriet Beecher Stowe (1811-1896), the product of another family of educators, attended Hartford Female Seminary, run by her sister Catharine Beecher (1800-1878), one of the pioneers in education for women. Emily Dickinson (1830-1886) briefly attended Mount Holyoke Female Seminary in 1847-1848. Though this school was also in the forefront of the movement for improving women's education, the school did not develop the full curriculum that allowed it to be chartered as Mount Holyoke College until 1893.

Later in the nineteenth century Edith Wharton (1862-1937) and Ellen Glasgow (1873-1945) were largely educated by their own reading, having been taught sporadically at home by tutors hired by their well-to-do families. In fact it was more unusual that Gertrude Stein (1874-1946) did go to college. Entering Radcliffe in 1893 and graduating in 1898, she was in one of the first classes of women to earn an actual degree. Until 1893 a woman who attended Harvard Annex (as Radcliffe was called between 1879 and 1893) received only a certificate stating that she had "pursued a course of study equivalent in amount and quality to that for which the Bachelor of Arts is conferred in Harvard College, and had passed in a satisfactory manner examinations on that course, corresponding to the college examinations." The "Annex" became Radcliffe College in 1893 and was empowered to grant degrees in 1894. The following selected list of writers who did not go to college and the jobs they took instead omits women born before 1890. It also omits writers who read law, on the grounds that in the early years of American colleges especially, a young man might well have attained a more valuable education studying with a good attorney than he would have in a college classroom. Perhaps the most interesting fact that can be gleaned from this list is that even now, when college education has become more the rule than the exception, there are still successful and talented writers who have never gone to college.

SHERWOOD ANDERSON (1876-1941), beginning in 1892, worked at odd jobs in Clyde, Ohio, including groom at a race track and farm hand. Around 1894 he became an assembler at the Elmore Bicycle Works in Clyde, and at one point he hopped a freight to Cleveland and Erie, Pennsylvania, where he was a dock hand for two or three weeks before returning home. He went to Chicago in 1896 and worked as a laborer for $2 an hour. Serving with the Ohio National Guard in 1898-1899, he reached Cuba after the armistice that ended the Spanish-American War. He finally completed high school at Wittenberg Academy in Springfield, Ohio (1899-1900), and became an advertising copywriter in Chicago. In 1904 he started a manufacturing business in Elyria, Ohio, and began writing fiction in about 1910, completing drafts of his first two novels before he suffered a nervous breakdown in late 1912. After his recovery he returned to advertising work in Chicago and finally had his first novel, *Windy McPherson's Son*, published in 1916. Though he was later to call his breakdown the catalyst for his decision to leave business forever and to be a writer, he supported himself mainly by advertising work until the early 1920s.

One who like myself could not, because of circumstances, spend the years of his youth in schools must of necessity turn to books and to the men and women directly about him; upon these he must depend for his knowledge of life and to these I turned. What a life the people of books led! They were for the most part such respectable people, with problems I did not have at all or they were such keen and brainy villains as I could never hope to become. . . . In the first place I never could shoot very well, I hadn't the courage to kill people I did not like and to steal on any grand scale involved the risk of prison—or at least I then thought it did. . . .
—Sherwood Anderson, A Story Teller's Story *(1924)*

JAMES BALDWIN (1924-1987) renounced his position as a Holy Roller preacher and, graduating from high school, became a railroad worker in New Jersey, 1942. After odd jobs including freelance book reviewing and after receiving two fellowships to write books that were never published, he left for Paris in 1948. He published *Go Tell It on the Mountain* in 1953.

AMBROSE BIERCE (1842-1914?) enlisted in the Ninth Indiana Infantry Regiment, U.S. Army, 1861; served until January 1865, rising to first lieutenant and fighting in some of the Civil War's bloodiest battles. He suffered a near-fatal head wound at Kennesaw Mountain, and he was later brevetted major for his valor in combat, but his view of humanity was permanently colored by his battlefield experiences. Following the end of the war; he worked as a U.S. Treasury agent in Alabama for several months, and in 1866 he joined an army mapping expedition that went from Omaha to the West Coast, resigning from the army when they reached San Francisco. In 1867, while working at a minor job in the U.S. Sub-Treasury, he began writing for various newspapers, and in December 1868 he became editor of the *San Francisco News Letter and California Advertiser*. Here, in his "Town Crier" column, and in the "Grizzly Papers" he contributed to Bret Harte's *Overland Monthly* in

Sherwood Anderson, 1898 (courtesy of Eleanor Anderson and The Newberry Library)

When I was fourteen I became a preacher, and when I was seventeen I stopped. Very shortly thereafter I left home. For God knows how long I struggled with the world of commerce and industry—I guess they would say they struggled with me—and when I was about twenty-one I had enough done of a novel to get a Saxon Fellowship. When I was twenty-two the fellowship was over, the novel turned out to be unsalable, and I started waiting on tables in a Village restaurant and writing book reviews—mostly as it turned out about the Negro problem, concerning which the color of my skin made me automatically an expert. Did another book. . . . [which] met exactly the same fate as my first—fellowship, but no sale. (It was a Rosenwald Fellowship.) By the time I was twenty-four I had decided to stop reviewing books about the Negro problem—which, by this time, was only slightly less horrible in print than it was in life—and I packed my bags and went to France, where I finished, God knows how, Go Tell It on the Mountain.

—James Baldwin,
Notes of a Native Son *(1955)*

1871, he developed the bitterly humorous commentary for which he was to become well known. Later in 1871, his first short story, "The Haunted Valley," appeared in the *Overland*.

Those who are horrified at Mr. Darwin's theory, may comfort themselves with the assurance that, if we are descended from the ape, we have not descended so far as to preclude all hope of return.

—Ambrose Bierce,
The Fiend's Delight *(1873)*

R. P. BLACKMUR (1904-1965) was expelled from Cambridge High and Latin School in 1918 for arguing with the headmaster and lived at home—earning pocket money by working as a soda jerk and as a clerk in Cambridge bookstores and at Harvard's Widener Library—until 1925 when he opened a bookstore with a friend (he eventually ended up teaching at Princeton).

KAY BOYLE (1902-   ) prepared to study architecture at Cincinnati's Ohio Mechanics Institute in 1918-1920, but after she completed her secondary-school education her father decided that she should work in his office and go to secretarial school at night instead. In 1922 she went to New York with a briefcase full of poems and found work at the American office of the literary magazine *Broom*. By the end of the year she had had a poem published in *Poetry* magazine. Having married a Frenchman earlier that year, she went with him to France in June 1923 and began writing fiction as well. After leaving her husband, having a child by *This Quarter* editor Ernest Walsh (who died before their daughter was born), returning to her husband in April 1927, and leaving him again about a year later, she settled in Paris, where her first book, *Short Stories*, was published in 1929.

RAY BRADBURY (1920-   ), after graduation from Los Angeles High School in June 1938, lived at home, sold newspapers on street corners, and wrote until 1945. Having had his first short story, "Hollerbochen's Dilemma," published in the January 1938 issue of *Imagination!*, a privately printed sci-fi magazine, or "fanzine," he continued to contribute to these nonpaying outlets and started his own mimeographed "fanzine," *Futura Fantasia*, in June 1939 (it lasted for four issues). In July 1941 he sold a story for the first time, receiving $27.50 for "Pendulum," written with his friend Henry Hasse. It appeared in the August issue of *Super Science Stories*, which hit the newsstands in Los Angeles on his twenty-first birthday. By 1943 he had found his style with "The Wind" (*Weird Tales*, March 1943) and "King of the Gray Spaces" (*Famous Fantastic Mysteries*, December 1943), and he had begun to establish the reputation in sci-fi and fantasy circles that led to the publication of his first book, *Dark Carnival*, in 1947.

Science fiction was one among half a dozen . . . grand affairs I had with life. And I wrote it amongst 4,000 students at Los Angeles High School who neither knew nor cared whether or not one damned rocket was ever built or pointed toward the Moon, Mars, or the Universe.

Worse still, I loved and would later write stories for Weird Tales. *So, from the beginning, I was headed wrong in two fields that would never prove out. Yet, I plunged ahead, feeling that if I were wrong I would be the best creative wrong that ever was.*

—Ray Bradbury, Introduction to The
Bradbury Companion (1975),
by William F. Nolan

Ray Bradbury, 1938

CHARLES FARRAR BROWNE (1834-1867) was apprenticed to John M. Rix as a printer for the *Lancaster* [New Hampshire] *Weekly Democrat* in 1847, and —while still in his teens—started printing and writing for the *Carpet-Bag*, a Boston weekly humor magazine, in 1851. Continuing as a journalist, he invented his comic persona, Artemus Ward, in January 1858 for his column in the *Cleveland Plain Dealer*. The first "Letter" from Ward, a flamboyant, semiliterate traveling showman, was reprinted in newspapers all over the country, and Browne obligingly produced more, becoming editor of the New York humor magazine *Vanity Fair* in 1861 and producing *Artemus Ward, His Book* the following year.

EDGAR RICE BURROUGHS (1875-1950) enlisted in the Seventh Cavalry, U.S. Army, in 1896. After a long series of unsuccessful attempts at trying to make a living in everything from panning for gold to working for Sears and Roebuck, he had his first story published in 1912, and his first book, *Tarzan of the Apes*, appeared in 1914.

GEORGE WASHINGTON CABLE (1844-1925), after the death of his father in 1859, went to work stamping boxes in a New Orleans customs warehouse to support his mother and sisters. After service in the Confederate Cavalry, while he was working as a bookkeeper for a cotton-commission merchant, he spent his free time walking about New Orleans observing Creole culture. He began writing a column for the *New Orleans Picayune* in 1870 and was soon writing and publishing short stories as well, becoming a popular regional writer even before his stories were collected in his first book, *Old Creole Days*, in 1879. With the appearance of his first and best-known novel, *The Grandissimes*, in the following year, his literary reputation–and his literary abilities, many critics have added–reached its highest point.

TRUMAN CAPOTE (1924-1984) got a job as a sort of errand boy in the art department at the *New Yorker* in 1942, just after graduating from high school, and stayed about two years, performing tasks such as sorting cartoons and cutting out items from newspapers. He left the only job, other than writing, that he ever held and went to Alabama to finish

his unpublished (and now lost) first novel, "Summer Crossings." His earlier stories had been largely unnoticed, but his short story "Miriam," which appeared in the June 1945 issue of *Mademoiselle*, won a place in the O. Henry Memorial Award collection of the best short stories of that year and led to a contract for his first book, *Other Voices, Other Rooms* (1948), a best-seller that brought him fame and notoriety–probably as much for the photograph of Capote on the dust jacket as for its homosexual theme.

I was determined never to set foot inside a college classroom. I felt that either one was or wasn't a writer, and no combination of professors could influence the outcome. . . . however, I now realize that most young writers have more to gain than not by attending college, if only because their teachers and classroom comrades provide a captive audience for their work; nothing is lonelier than to be an aspiring artist without some semblance of a sounding board.

–Truman Capote,
The Dogs Bark *(1973)*

RAYMOND CHANDLER (1888-1959), though he was born in Chicago and spent much of his early childhood in Nebraska, was taken by his divorced mother to live in England when he was seven. From autumn 1900 until April 1905 he attended Dulwich College Preparatory School; but, intending not to seek a university education, he left the school without graduating and was sent by his family to spend a year in France and Germany to study the languages in preparation for the civil-service exams. By early 1908 he had a clerical job in the Admiralty, which he left after six months and began a generally fruitless attempt to make a living as a writer. Between 1908 and 1912 magazines accepted poems (which he later characterized as mostly "deplorable"), satirical sketches ("the sort of thing that

The photograph of Truman Capote that appeared on the dust jacket for his first book

Saki did so infinitely better"), literary essays ("of an intolerable preciousness of style, but already quite nasty in tone"), and book reviews (in which he "found it very easy to be clever and snotty, very hard to praise without being ingenuous"). In 1912 he gave up the career at which he had "made only a very bare living" and went to California, where working at various odd jobs—picking apricots, stringing tennis racquets—he studied bookkeeping at night school and by 1913 had a job as a bookkeeper at the Los Angeles Creamery. In August 1917 he joined the Canadian army and served in France, where in June 1918 he was the only man in his platoon to survive bombardment by German artillery (he wrote about this war experience only once in an unpublished sketch called "Trench Raid"). Transferring to the Royal Air Force, he began aviation training, which was cut short by the end of the war. After his discharge in February 1919 he returned to Los Angeles.

By 1922 he was working for the Dabney Oil Syndicate, and on 6 February 1924 he married Pearl Hurlburt ("Cissy") Pascal. Chandler rose to an executive position in the oil business, but after heavy drinking began to affect his work he was fired in 1932, at the age of

When the evening sun is slanting
When the crickets raise their chanting,

As I climb the pathway slowly,
With a mien half proud, half lowly,
O'er the ground your feet have trod I
gentle pass

—from Raymond Chandler's "The
Unknown Love" (1908), his first
published poem

At school I displayed no marked literary ability. My first poem was composed at the age of nineteen, on a Sunday, in the bathroom, and was published in Chambers' Journal. *I am fortunate in not possessing a copy. I had, to be frank, the qualifications to become a pretty good second-rate poet, but that means nothing because I have the type of mind that can become a pretty good second-rate anything, and without much effort.*
—Raymond Chandler, Note for
Twentieth Century
Authors, Supplement

forty-four. With a small allowance from friends he took up the literary career he had abandoned twenty years before, finding new models for his work in the hardboiled detective fiction in *Black Mask* magazine. Chandler's first detective story, "Blackmailers Don't Shoot," appeared in the December 1933 issue of *Black Mask*.

JOHN CHEEVER (1912-1982) was expelled from Thayer Academy at seventeen for smoking, wrote an article about it for the *New Republic*, went on a walking tour of Germany, and then settled in New York, where he lived for much of the 1930s on bread and buttermilk and worked at writing. He won an O. Henry Memorial Award in 1941 for his short story "I'm Going to Asia," and his first collection of stories, *The Way Some People Live*, was published in 1943.

It is strange to be so very young and to have no place to report to at nine o'clock. That is what education has always been. It has been laced curtseys and perfumed punctualities.
    —John Cheever, "Expelled,"
    New Republic *(1 October 1930)*

SAMUEL CLEMENS (1835-1910) was apprenticed to John P. Ament as a printer for the *Missouri Courier*, a weekly in Hannibal, Missouri, in 1848. He set type and wrote for various newspapers until 1857, when he began training as a steamboat pilot, earning his license in 1859. He continued work as a pilot until the Civil War closed Mississippi River traffic. For about two weeks he was part of a group of Confederate irregulars who played at soldiering in the vicinity of Hannibal, but when his older brother Orion was appointed secretary to the governor of the Nevada Territory and lacked the funds to get there, Sam Clemens, who had saved money from his years on the river, paid the stage passage for both to Carson City, Nevada, arriving in August 1861. A year later, after unsuccessful speculation in silver, he joined the staff of the *Virginia City Territorial Enterprise*, and on 2 February 1863 he used his famous pseudonym, Mark Twain, for the first time, on one of his contributions to the paper.

Printer's devil Sam Clemens at age fifteen (courtesy of the Mark Twain Project, The Bancroft Library)

The self-taught man seldom knows anything accurately, and he does not know a tenth as much as he could have known if he had worked under teachers; and, besides, he brags, and is the means of fooling other thoughtless people into going and doing as he himself has done. There are those who imagine that the unlucky accidents of life—life's "experiences"—are in some ways useful to us. I wish I could find out how. I never knew one of them to happen twice. They always change off and swap around and catch you on your inexperienced side.
    —Samuel Clemens, What Is Man?
    and Other Essays *(1917)*

IRVIN S. COBB (1876-1944) became a cub reporter at $1.75 a week for the *Paducah* [Kentucky] *Evening News* in 1892 and was managing editor by the time he was nineteen and at twenty was making $12 a week (a good salary). In 1898 he moved up to the *Louisville Evening Post* and was present at the assassination of Kentucky Governor William Goebel. (He reported that the governor's last words were "Be brave and fearless and loyal to the great common people"; but in his autobiography he revealed that the governor, who had just eaten an oyster, said, "Doc, that was a damned bad oyster.") During another stint as managing editor for the Paducah paper (1901-1904), he got an exclusive interview with an alleged wife murderer who had fled from Chicago and been captured in a nearby town. After he received more than for $100 the story, he decided to try New York in August 1904, and after a year and a half at the *New York Sun* he moved to the *New York World,* where he began a humor column, "New York Through Funny Glasses." Though he continued with straight reporting, it was on the basis of his humor columns that by 1906 he was making $150 a week from the *World,* and more money from syndication. The first of his many humor books, *Cobb's Anatomy: A Guide to Humor,* was published in 1912.

Hart Crane in Cleveland, 1916

MARC CONNOLLY (1890-1980) went to the *Pittsburgh Sun* as a reporter in 1908. In 1914 he wrote the lyrics for Alfred Ward Birdsall's musical *The Lady on Luzon,* his first professional job for the theater. His second job in the theater, to write the libretto and lyrics for another musical, *The Amber Empress,* was to be his last for several years. When the play finally opened in New York two years later, it had been so extensively rewritten by others that Connolly could claim only the lyrics for two songs and the play's title. Connolly then went to work as a journalist and did not return to playwriting until he and George S. Kaufman collaborated on *Dulcy,* which opened on Broadway on 13 August 1921 with Lynn Fontanne as Dulcy Smith, a vapid middle-class housewife who excels at speaking in platitudes. The show ran for 246 performances and was included in *Best Plays of 1921-1922.*

GREGORY CORSO (1930-) left school at thirteen and lived in the streets of New York, supporting himself by theft and landing in prison for a three-year term when he was seventeen. Soon after his release in 1950, he met Allen Ginsberg in Greenwich Village and was soon associating with other writers of the Beat generation. In 1954, after a period of wandering around the country and working at marginal jobs, he went to Cambridge, Massachusetts, where he hung around Harvard University and spent much of his time reading and writing in the university library. In 1955 his one-act farce, *In This Hung-Up Age,* now considered one of the earliest statements of the Beat philosophy, was performed by the Harvard Dramatic Workshop. His first book, *The Vestal Lady on Brattle and Other Poems,* was published later that year.

HART CRANE (1899-1932) quit high school in Cleveland in late 1916 and went to New York to become a writer.

"The Hive," one of the poems he wrote after his arrival, appeared in the March 1917 issue of the *Pagan*, a Greenwich Village little magazine—an event that convinced Crane's mother, at least, that her son was meant to be a poet—and by the end of the year he had a poem accepted for publication in the better-known *Little Review*, edited by Margaret Anderson and Jane Heap. Supported by an allowance from home and continuing to publish poems, he began haunting the offices of both magazines, becoming an associate editor of the *Pagan* in April 1918 and a year later becoming the sole member of the *Little Review's* "advertising department." Selling ads on a commission basis, he hoped to earn $4,000 a year but, aside from some full-page ads that he sold to his father, president of the Crane Candy Company, he was largely unsuccessful. In fact the main benefits he derived from the job were free office space and stationery—and the opportunity to meet other writers. From late 1919 until spring 1923 Crane spent alternating periods of time for the most part in Cleveland and New York bowing to pressure to enter his father's business (and failing), trying to support himself at various jobs, including working briefly as a journalist and—somewhat more successfully—as a copywriter for ad agencies. Having written some of the poems he later included in his first book, *White Buildings* (1926), as early as 1919, he began in 1922 to write his ambitious long poem "For the Marriage of Faustus and Helen," a precursor of his major and still-longer poem *The Bridge* (1930), which he started to plan in early 1923 and worked on for the next seven years.

JOHN WILLIAM DE FOREST (1826-1906), prevented from going to Yale by typhoid fever, went to Syria at twenty, returned home and began to support himself by writing, first with *History of the Indians of Connecticut from the earliest known period to 1850* (1851), researched in the Yale library, and *Oriental Acquain-* *tance; Or, Letters from Syria* (1856), based on his Mideastern travels; then with *European Acquaintance* (1858), about his extensive travels in England, Germany, Switzerland, France and Italy in 1850-1855. When he returned to the United States, he began writing novels. His first, *Witching Times*, about the Salem witch trials, was serialized in *Putnam's Monthly Magazine* in 1856 and 1857 but not published as a book; his third, *Miss Ravenel's Conversion* (1867), which grew out of his experiences fighting for the Union in the Civil War, has been hailed as a milestone in the history of American fiction.

FLOYD DELL (1887-1969) dropped out of high school in Davenport, Iowa, in 1904. He worked in a candy factory and then for a job printer while distributing literature and doing odd jobs for the Socialist party. In 1905 he became a cub reporter in Davenport, Iowa, but two years later he lost his job in the Panic of 1907. The next year he was in Chicago, where he found work as a free-lance book reviewer. The biggest market for his reviews proved to be the *Chicago Evening Post's Friday Literary Review* (which first appeared on 5 March 1909), in part because the editor, Francis Hackett, liked Dell's style but also, in all likelihood, because he could turn out between thirty and a hundred brief reviews and one long review a week. After Hackett left the *Review*, Dell edited it from July 1911 until September 1913, when he left Chicago for Greenwich Village. His first book, *Women as World-Builders*, is a collection of feminist articles that had been published in the *Review*. His first—and best—novel, was *Moon-Calf* (1920), whose sensitive young hero's love affairs and socialist politics attracted the attention of the 1920s rebellious new generation (though in fact the period in which the "moon-calf" Felix Fay grows up is 1887-1908, the years of Dell's own youth).

PAUL LAURENCE DUNBAR (1872-1906)

Paul Lawrence Dunbar.

of local photographers. He left an errand boy's job with the first, L. C. Mundy, to become a photograph printer for A. C. Hopkins, who fired him for daydreaming and ruining too much expensive paper. He found more success with Abner B. Gardner, who taught him how to retouch negatives to remove warts, wrinkles, and blemishes. At seventeen he went to Boston, where he worked at writing and painting and supported himself meagerly with his printing and retouching skills, but by 1875 he was back in Utica working at his old job. Later that year he began work as a newspaper proofreader and quickly became a reporter for the *Utica Daily Observer,* which began publishing his short stories. He also became friends with a liberal Catholic priest, Edward A. Terry, who would be the model for Father Forbes in his best-known novel, *The Damnation of Theron Ware* (1896), in which a young, poorly educated, fundamentalist Methodist minister is confronted by the liberal religious views of a scholarly Catholic priest.

graduated from Central High School in Dayton, Ohio, the only black in his class, in 1891. Taking a job as an elevator operator, he began giving recitations of his poetry, having it published in newspapers and magazines within the next year. He paid in installments for the printing of his first book, *Oak and Ivy* (1893), and his next, *Majors and Minors* (1895), but a laudatory review of this volume by William Dean Howells, the "Dean of American Letters," established his literary reputation.

CHARLES HENRI FORD (1913-) having already had poems published in the *New Yorker* and elsewhere, dropped out of high school at sixteen and started the literary magazine *Blues: A Magazine of New Rhythms.*

HAROLD FREDERICK (1856-1898) graduated from the Advanced School in Utica, New York, in 1871, and worked at various odd jobs and then for a series

DASHIELL HAMMETT (1894-1961) quit Baltimore Polytechnic Institute after one semester of his freshman high-school year and worked at various jobs between 1909 and 1915, including office boy for the B & O Railroad and recorder of stock prices on a chalkboard in the firm of Poe and Davies. In 1915 he became an operative for the Baltimore office of the Pinkerton's National Detective Agency. With time out for service in the U. S. Army (24 June 1918-29 May 1919) at Camp Mead, Maryland, where he was first diagnosed as having tuberculosis and after a period of hospitalization for the disease (6 November 1920-15 May 1921), Hammett worked for Pinkerton's (often part-time because of his illness) in Baltimore (1915-June 1918, May 1919-May 1920), Spokane, Washington (May 1920-6 November 1920), San Francisco (June 1921-1 December 1921), a job in which he discovered not only the raw materials for his

I'm a two-fisted loafer. I can loaf longer and better than anybody I know. I did not acquire this genius. I was born with it. I quit school when I was thirteen because I wanted to loaf. I sold newspapers for a while, loafed, became a stevedore, loafed, worked in a machine shop, loafed, became a stock broker, loafed, went into the advertising business, loafed, tried hoboing in earnest, loafed, became a Pinkerton detective for seven years and went into the army.

I was a sergeant during the war, but—please get this straight—not in the war. The war and my service in the army were contemporary, that's all you can say about it. . . .

—Dashiell Hammett,
to an interviewer
for the New York
Evening Journal
(Summer 1934)

novels and short stories but also a method of observation that shaped the starkly realistic style in which he wrote them. In February 1922 he entered Munson's Business College, where he spent a year and a half apparently hoping to prepare for a career as a reporter, but his career took a different turn the following fall when the *Smart Set* accepted "The Parthian Shot," a one-hundred-word fictional anecdote, for the October 1922 issue. Within a year he had had twelve pieces published in five national magazines, including "From the Memoirs of a Private Detective," a non-fiction story in the March 1923 issue of *Smart Set*. His first hard-boiled detective story, which introduced the now-well-known operative the "Continental op," was "Arson Plus," published in the 1 October 1923 issue of *Black Mask* magazine.

JOEL CHANDLER HARRIS (1848-1908) became a printer's devil at thirteen for the weekly newspaper *Countryman*, published by Joseph Addison Turner at Turnwold Plantation near Eatonton, Georgia, and soon began smuggling his own paragraphs into the paper. A year later his poems, essays, and book reviews were appearing in the *Countryman*. As formative as this literary apprenticeship might have been, still more important was the time he spent listening to the folktales told by Turner's slaves, who later served as the models for the characters in the narrative frames of his Uncle Remus tales. By the time he invented this character in fall 1876 he was on the staff of the *Atlanta Constitution* and had developed a regional reputation as a newspaper humor writer. His first book, *Uncle Remus: His Songs and His Sayings* (1880), brought him international renown.

MOSS HART (1904-1961) worked in a fur vault in summer 1917 and that autumn, instead of entering the eighth grade, got a job as an office boy for the producer Augustus Pitou, Jr., whose six theater companies put on one-night shows all over the United States. Within six months he was Pitou's secretary. In autumn 1922, faced with finding a replacement for a play that had proved un-

As it turned out, I couldn't have contrived a better beginning in the theatre than to start as an office boy for Augustus Pitou. True, Mr. Pitou was not exactly a "Broadway" producer, but his was a theatrical office nonetheless, and it was in the New Amsterdam Theatre Building, smack among the great ones, to boot.

Augustus Pitou, Jr. (to give him his full name), and his father before him, was known as the "King of the One Night Stands." Mr. Pitou, Sr., had long since passed on, but he had left to Augustus Pitou, Jr., a stable of stars, a map of the United States, the Official Railway Guide, and the route sheets. . . . I doubt if the theatergoing public of New York had ever heard of [Pitou's stars] but to the residents of Fond du Lac and Eau Claire, Wisconsin, their annual one night stand was an event not to be missed.

—Moss Hart, Act One (1959)

popular, Pitou asked Hart to read and evaluate a pile of manuscripts that had been submitted to him, and Hart soon decided, "Why, I could write a better play than any of these myself." The next day he gave Pitou act one of *The Beloved Bandit,* listing the author as Robert Arnold Conrad. Pitou was enthusiastic and had Hart write to "Mr. Conrad" for the rest of the play, which turned out to be a resounding failure everywhere; Pitou lost $45,000, and Hart lost his job. His first successful play was *Once in a Lifetime* (1930), which he wrote with George S. Kaufman.

BRET HARTE (1836-1902) left school at thirteen to work in a law office and took a job a year later in a counting-house. In March 1854 he joined his mother and stepfather in Oakland, California, and later that year he left home, wandering around the state teaching school and panning for gold. Returning home in 1856, he announced that he was going to become a writer, and read the complete works of Charles Dickens while he worked for the summer in a local drugstore. After serving briefly as a tutor and Wells Fargo guard, he became an apprentice printer for the *Northern Californian* in 1857 and soon began reporting for the Humboldt County, California, paper as well. In early 1860, after the editor had gone away leaving Harte in charge of the paper, some of the county's whites surprised and massacred a nearby encampment of some sixty Indians, mostly women and children. Harte wrote an angry editorial and immediately discovered himself persona non grata with the locals. Though he seems not to have been physically endangered, within a month he had left for San Francisco, where he became a printer for the *Golden Era.* He also began contributing sketches to the literary magazine, and in December 1860 its pages contained "The Work on Red Mountain," a shorter draft of the story

Harte later published as "M'Liss," his first important piece of fiction.

ERNEST HEMINGWAY (1899-1961) started as a cub reporter for the *Kansas City Star* in October 1917–an experience that had an important influence on his literary style. His first known story, "Kerensky, the Fighting Flea"–a report on an office boy who moonlighted as a bantam-weight boxer–was published 16 December 1917.

He signed up as a Red Cross ambulance driver in spring 1918 and was sent to Italy. Wounded near Schio, Italy, on 8 July 1918, he spent the rest of the year in the American Red Cross Hospital in Milan.

After another year recovering from his wounds at home in Oak Park, Illinois, he was hired in January 1920 to spend five months as a companion to a disabled young man in Toronto. By February Hemingway was writing for the weekly edition of the *Toronto Star.* After spending the summer in upper Michigan and the fall looking for work, he took a job with the Chicago-based *Cooperative Commonwealth,* a magazine published by the Cooperative Society of America, in December 1920.

By September 1921 he had quit, and

Use short sentences. Use short first paragraphs. Use vigorous English. Be positive, not negative.

*   *   *

Eliminate every superfluous word. . . .

*   *   *

Avoid the use of adjectives, especially such extravagant ones as splendid, gorgeous, grand, magnificient, etc.

　　—Excerpted from the Kansas City Star's
　　style sheet, Hemingway's first writing text

Those were the best rules I ever learned for the business of writing. I've never forgotten them.

　　—Ernest Hemingway on the Star's *sheet,*
　　quoted in the Kansas City Times,
　　26 November 1940

in late November he and his new wife, Hadley, had sailed for Europe, where he would report on the Genoa economic conference and other events for the *Toronto Star*. They settled in Paris, where in January 1922 he set out to write one true sentence; by the end of May he had written six, marking the true beginning of his career as a fiction writer. His first, brief book, *Three Stories and Ten Poems*, was published in Paris in autumn 1923.

DUBOSE HEYWARD (1885-1940) quit school at fourteen to work in a Charleston hardware store. Stricken with polio at eighteen and no longer capable of handling heavy nail kegs and tools, he took a job as a cotton checker for a steamship company, gaining the insight into the lives of Charleston's black people that he later employed in his novel, *Porgy* (1925), better known in the opera version, *Porgy and Bess* (1935), on which he collaborated with George and Ira Gershwin.

E. W. HOWE (1853-1937), after his father–a Methodist minister and abolitionist–deserted the family in 1865 to run away with a widowed relative, began in 1866 to work as a tramp printer in Gallatin, Maysville, and St. Joseph, Missouri; Council Bluffs; Chicago; Omaha; Cheyenne; Salt Lake City; Falls City, Nebraska; Denver; and Golden, Colorado, where in 1873 he and a friend bought a newspaper, the *Golden Eagle* (before long Howe had become sole owner of the paper and renamed it the *Golden Globe)*. By 1877 he was back in Kansas and started the *Atchison Globe*. After his father visited him in 1882 he began thinking about his unhappy childhood and started writing his first novel, *The Story of a Country Town* (1883), for which he drew upon his own experiences.

WILLIAM DEAN HOWELLS (1837-1920) began setting type for the *Hamilton*

[Ohio] *Intelligencer*, edited by his father, in 1846. He left school in 1849, when his father bought the *Dayton Transcript,* and worked at printing and other jobs at that and subsequent family papers. His first publication was a poem in the 23 March 1852 issue of the *Ohio State Journal,* and he wrote more poetry and some fiction for the *Jefferson* [Ohio] *Sentinel,* which his father bought later that year. In 1857 he left home and his last job as a printer, going to Columbus, Ohio, where he became a journalist, writing for several Ohio papers. Though he is not remembered for his realistic novels, including *The Rise of Silas Lapham* (1885) and *A Hazard of New Fortunes* (1889), his first book was *Poems of Two Friends* (1860), which also includes poetry by his friend John J. Piatt.

Very soon I could set type very well, and at ten years and onward till journalism became my university, the printing-office was mainly my school.

–William Dean Howells,
Years of My Youth *(1916)*

LOUIS L'AMOUR (1908-) left school at fifteen and wandered around the world working at odd jobs that included circus roustabout, lumberjack, miner, and merchant seaman. He returned to live with his parents in Oklahoma City in the late 1930s and received more than 200 rejection slips before magazines began accepting his stories. His first book, *Smoke from this Altar* (1939), is a collection of poems. After serving in World War II, he began writing detective, adventure, and western stories for pulp magazines. He published his first novel, *Hopalong Cassidy and the Rustlers of West Fork,* under the pseudonym Tex Burns in 1951.

RING LARDNER (1885-1933) graduated from high school in 1901 and worked as an office boy and then a freight hustler before studying briefly at Armour Insti-

Kansas writers E. W. Howe and William Allen White, circa 1900

tute, Chicago, in 1902; rested (1903); and then worked in 1904-1905 as a bookkeeper and meter reader for the Niles Gas Company ("When I entered a cellar and saw a rat reading the meter ahead of me, I accepted his reading and went on to the next house.") He was hired as a reporter for the *South Bend Times* in 1905. By 1913 he was working for the *Chicago Tribune,* and on 7 March 1914 "A Busher's Letters Home," his first story narrated by the bragging, semi-literate baseball player Jack Keefe, appeared in the *Saturday Evening Post.* Lardner went on to produce three volumes of O'Keefe stories–including his second book, *You Know Me Al,* as well as a comic strip, drawn by Dick Dorgan.

JACK LONDON (1876-1916) finished grade school in 1889 and went to work full-time in a West Oakland, California, cannery putting pickles in jars for eighteen hours a day, at 10¢ an hour. He escaped at fifteen by borrowing $300, buying a sloop, and becoming "Prince of the Oyster Pirates," a raider of commercial oyster beds in San Francisco Bay. A year later he decided he would be safer on the side of the law and joined the California Fish Patrol. A few days before his seventeenth birthday, 12 January 1893, he signed up as a seaman on a sealing schooner and spent seven months at sea, visiting the seal-hunting grounds of the northwestern Pacific. His experiences not only provided the basis for his novel *The Sea-Wolf* (1904) but for his first publication, "Story of a Typhoon off the Coast of Japan," published in the 12 November 1893 issue of the *San Francisco Morning Call.*

ANITA LOOS (1893-1981) started out as a child actress in her father's amateur stock company, but eventually became bored with acting and wrote a script for a short film, which was accepted by the American Biograph Company in 1912. *The New York Hat,* directed by D. W. Griffith, was released in 1913 with Mary Pickford, Lionel Barrymore, and Dorothy and Lillian Gish in the lead roles. Loos later claimed to have written 105 movie scripts between 1912 and 1915, some in collaboration with producer John Emerson, whom she married in 1919. The two continued to write film scripts, as well as stage plays (*The Whole Town's Talking* [1923] and *The Fall of Eve* [1925]) and books (*How to Write Photoplays* [1920] and *Breaking into the Movies* [1912]). Loos's best-selling first novel, *"Gentlemen Prefer Blondes": The Illuminating Diary of a Professional Lady* (1925), was made into a stage play (1926) and a movie (1928).

RING LARDNER'S CHRONOLOGY FOR 1901-19??

1901 *Was graduated from the Niles High School.*
"And so young!" they said.
Accepted an office boy's portfolio with the Harvester Company in Chicago. Canned.
Served a prominent Chicago real-estate firm in the same capacity. Canned.
Was appointed third assistant freight hustler at the Michigan Central in Niles. Canned for putting a box of cheese in the through Jackson car, when common sense should have told me that it ought to go to Battle Creek.

1902 *"Studied" mechanical engineering at Armour Institute, Chicago. Passed in rhetoric. Decided not to become a mechanical engineer.*

1903 *Rested. Recovered from the strain which had wrought havoc with my nervous system.*

1904 *and Part of 1905 Became a bookkeeper for the Niles Gas Company.*

Part of 1905, 1906, and Part of 1907 Society reporter, court-house man, dramatic critic and sporting editor for the South Bend, Indiana, Times.

Part of 1907 Sports reporter for the Chicago Inter Ocean.

1908 *to 1912 Baseball writer on the Chicago Examiner, the Chicago Tribune, St. Louis Sporting News, Boston American, and copy reader on the Chicago American.*

1913 *Resting on the Chicago Tribune.*

1914 *Started writing for The Saturday Evening Post. Its circulation was then only a little over a million.*

19?? *Died intestate.*

—from "Who's Who—And Why," Saturday Evening Post, 28 April 1917

CHARLES MACARTHUR (1895-1956) left home in 1912, worked that summer for *Oak Leaves*, a newspaper in Oak Park, Illinois, and then took a job with the City Press, a Chicago news service. After service in Mexico with the Illinois militia (1916) and service in France during World War I, he found a job at the *Chicago Examiner*, moving on to the *Chicago Tribune* before going to New York in 1924 and working for the *New York American* until 1927, when he quit to devote full time to playwriting. His experience as a journalist lies behind the extraordinarily popular play *The Front Page* (1928), which he wrote with Ben Hecht.

HORACE MCCOY (1897-1955) left high school in 1913 and, over the next four years, worked as a mechanic, a traveling salesman, and a taxi driver. After service in World War I he worked as a reporter in Dallas, becoming sports editor for the *Dallas Journal* before leaving the paper in 1929. During the 1920s he also began writing short stories; his first published story, "Brass Buttons," appeared in the March 1927 issue of the Dallas-based *Holland's Magazine*. Many of the stories he wrote between 1927 and 1934

Jack London at nineteen

were published in the detective magazine *Black Mask* and feature the flying Texas Ranger Capt. Jerry Frost. After two years of supporting himself as a freelance writer and satisfying his urge for the spotlight by playing lead roles in the Dallas Little Theatre, in 1931 McCoy headed west where he managed to support himself by working as an extra and stand-in and by writing fiction and film scripts. His first novel, *They Shoot Horses, Don't They?*, was published in July 1935.

HERMAN MELVILLE (1819-1891) was withdrawn from Albany Academy after his father's death on 28 January 1832 and went to work at the New York State Bank. After spending most of 1834 working on his uncle Thomas Melville's farm in Pittsfield, Massachusetts, he returned to Albany in January 1835 to clerk in his brother Gansevoort's store and enter Albany Classical School. In fall 1837 he took a teaching position in Pittsfield,

and a year later entered Lansingburgh Academy to take a course in surveying and engineering. In June 1839 he sailed for Liverpool in the crew of the trader *St. Lawrence*. After this first sea voyage he decided to seek his fortune in the west, traveling as far as the headwaters of the Mississippi before visiting his Uncle Thomas in Galena, Illinois, and being told that the current business recession made it impossible for his uncle to help him financially. Back in New York by autumn 1840, he read Richard Henry Dana, Jr.'s recently published *Two Years Before the Mast* and decided to return to sea. In December he signed on as a seaman on the whaling ship *Acushnet*, which sailed for the Pacific on 3 January 1841. The following June he and a friend jumped ship in the Marquesas, planning to live at ease in what seemed to be a tropical South Seas paradise. Instead they were captured by the Typees, thought to be a man-eating tribe. Though they were prisoners, they were treated kindly. Melville's friend was allowed to go in search of medical help after Melville injured his leg and eventually ended up back in the United States. Melville was rescued by the Australian whaler *Lucy Ann* in August and signed on as a seaman. Because the captain was ill, the ship docked in Papecte, where Melville and another sailor left the crew and went to the island of Eimeo. After about two weeks as a beachcomber, Melville signed on with a third whaler, the *Charles and Henry* of Nantucket, which spent almost three months in the South Pacific, reaching the coast of South America before turning north and reaching Maui in April 1843. The next month Melville was paid his share of the voyage's profits and sailed to Honolulu, where he signed a one-year indenture to be a clerk and bookkeeper in a store. The captain of the *Acushnet* had reported Melville's desertion to the American consul in Honolulu, however, and, deciding it was unwise to remain there, Melville signed on as a seaman aboard the frigate *United States* in August, reaching Boston on 3 October 1844. Melville never went to sea again (except as a passenger). All his novels and stories of the sea–beginning with his most autobiographical novel, *Typee* (1846)–draw upon his voyages in 1839 and 1841-1844.

. . .a whale-ship was my Yale College and my Harvard.
—*Herman Melville*,
Moby-Dick *(1851)*

H. L. MENCKEN (1880-1956) graduated valedictorian from Baltimore Polytechnic Institute in 1896 and worked in his father's tobacco business until his father's death on 13 January 1899 freed him to enter journalism, as he had wanted. Hired by the *Baltimore Morning Herald* a few days later, he had his first story–a report on the theft of a horse, buggy, and some harness–published on 24 February 1899. By 1903 he was city editor and that same year he published his first book, *Ventures into Verse*.

CLIFFORD ODETS (1906-1963) dropped out of high school in 1923 and found a series of minor acting jobs, reaching Broadway in 1929, when he was hired as Spencer Tracy's understudy in *Conflict*, by Warren F. Lawrence. The next year he joined the Group Theatre in New York as an actor, but by 1933, frustrated because he had been given only a few minor roles, he began writing plays. The New York taxi strike on February 1934 helped convince him to join the Communist party (which he left eight months later) and inspired him to write *Waiting for Lefty*–his best-known and first-produced play–which opened in New York on 5 January 1935 and by July had been produced in at least thirty American cities.

JOHN O'HARA (1905-1970) had decided to become a Yale man by the time he started at Fordham Preparatory School

H. L. Mencken, 1904 (courtesy of the Mencken Room, Enoch Pratt Free Library)

in the Bronx, New York, in February 1920, but by the time he was kicked out of Fordham Prep in June 1921 for poor grades and out of the preparatory department of Keystone State Normal School for low grades and disciplinary reasons the next year, his father, Dr. Patrick O'Hara, decided that his wayward oldest son would have to work for a year before he would even consider sending him to Yale. After a year off at home on Pottsville, Pennsylvania, young O'Hara entered Niagara University Prep School in fall 1923, and the following June he was listed in the commencement program as class poet and valedictorian. After some last minute celebrating, he was not allowed to graduate with his class, and, again thinking that work would help his son to take life more seriously, Dr. O'Hara insisted he wait a year before attending Yale and, in the fall of 1924, found him a job with the *Pottsville Journal*. After Dr. O'Hara died intestate in March 1925, his family slipped from prosperity to genteel poverty, and his twenty-year-old son gave up on his dreams of mingling with the right set at Yale, though he regretted not going for the rest of his life.

THOMAS PAINE (1737-1809) was apprenticed to a staymaker in Thetford, England in 1753. After sailing on a privateer and working for a while as a staymaker, he went to work as customs officer in Lewes, only to be fired in 1772 after writing an article arguing that customs officers deserved higher wages. The next year, out of work and low on funds, he went to London, where he met Benjamin Franklin, who offered to help him find a job in Philadelphia. Paine arrived in that city in November 1774, went to work as an editor for the *Philadelphia Magazine*, and in January 1776 published *Common Sense*.

DOROTHY PARKER (1893-1967) graduated from Miss Dana's School in Morristown, New Jersey, in 1911. By 1913 she was working for *Vogue*, chiefly as a caption writer ("Brevity is the Soul of Lingerie," for example), and in 1916 she joined the staff of *Vanity Fair* as a writer of fashion items and drama criticism. In 1920 she was named chief drama critic, only to be fired later that year for writing negative reviews for the shows of three *Vanity Fair* backers (David Belasco, Charles Dillingham, and Florenz Ziegfeld). She went on to write acerbic reviews for *Ainslee's* (1920-1933), the *New Yorker* (1927-1931), and *Esquire* (1959-1962), and to have her poems and short stories published in scores of magazines. Her first book, *Men I'm Not Married To* (bound with friend Franklin Pierce Adams's *Women I'm Not Married To*), was published in 1922.

KATHERINE ANNE PORTER (1890-1980)— born Callie Russell Porter—was married at the age of sixteen in Lufkin, Texas, to John Henry Koontz, a twenty-year-old clerk for the Southern Railway Company. Though she later told some friends that she had eloped from a New Orleans convent and others that she was a star in a traveling theater company when a member of a New Orleans audience convinced her to marry him (both

This British political cartoon, published at the time of Thomas Paine's *Rights of Man* (1791-1792), refers to Paine's early career as a staymaker as it shows him lacing Britannia into an uncomfortable French corset (courtesy of the Gimbel Collection, American Philosophical Society)

versions were considerably embroidered over the years), she had completed the only year of private schooling her father could afford in 1905, as a day student at the Thomas School, a Methodist-oriented school in San Antonio, and had moved with her father and sister Gay to Victoria, Texas, where–in the manner of many daughters of proud but penurious families–she and her sister gave lessons in "music, physical culture and dramatic reading." Rather than eloping, she and Gay both married on 20 June 1906 in a double wedding performed by a Methodist minister. Porter left Koontz in February 1914 and went to Chicago, where she found work as an extra and bit player in silent films, but six months later– exhausted and discouraged–she left, going to live with Gay and her family in Louisiana and supporting herself by giving poetry readings and singing on the lyceum circuit. In June 1915 she divorced Koontz and took the name Katharine Anne Porter in memory of her grandmother (the basis for Porter's fictional Sophia Jane Rhea in "The Old Order"). A few months later Porter was diagnosed as having tuberculosis and spent from fall 1915 until spring 1917 in a series of Texas hospitals. After her discharge she found work as a journalist, first as a society columnist for the *Fort Worth Critic* and by September 1917 as a reporter for Denver's *Rocky Mountain News.* Over the next five years, which took her from Denver to Greenwich Village to Mexico City and back to Texas and New York, she worked at writing and placed a few short stories with magazines, but she later chose to ignore this apprentice work and to call "María Concepción," which appeared in the December 1924 issue of *Century* magazine, "my first short story." She was thirty-four years old. Her first collection of stories, *Flowering Judas,* appeared in 1930.

JOHN HOWARD PAYNE (1791-1852) left prep school in November 1808 and made his New York acting debut on 24 February 1809 as Young Norval in *Douglas,* a tragedy by John Home. After acting in plays up and down the Atlantic coastline, he sailed in January 1813 for England, where he found little work as an actor but had occasional successes as a playwright. He is now remembered mainly for "Home, Sweet Home!," the lyrics he wrote for his opera *Clari; or, the Maid of Milan,* which opened in London on 8 May 1823.

WILLIAM SIDNEY PORTER (1862-1910) went to work in his uncle's Greensboro, North Carolina, drug store at seventeen and passed the state licensing exam at nineteen. He left Greensboro in 1882 and went to Texas, where he worked on a cattle ranch, then as a bookkeeper, a drugstore clerk, and a draftsman, going to work as a teller in the First National Bank of Austin in early 1891. In March 1984, while still working at the bank, he began publishing a weekly humor newspaper, the *Rolling Stone,* writing most of the contents himself. The paper lasted a year, during which–to keep it going–Porter borrowed heavily from his father-in-law and friends and may have begun embezzling funds from the bank. Though there is some question about who was responsible for them, the shortages did exist and were quickly discovered. Porter, who may have been covering for someone, ended up in prison, where he began publishing short stories in periodicals using the now-famous pseudonym O. Henry to conceal his identity.

DAMON RUNYAN (1880-1946) was a full-time reporter for the *Pueblo* [Colorado] *Evening Press* by the time he was fifteen. (Two years later a printer's error changed his last name from Runyan to Runyon; he liked it and kept it.) After serving in the Philippines during the Spanish-American War, he took a series of newspaper jobs before being hired as a sports reporter for the *Denver Post* in 1905 and going on the next year to the more-established Denver paper, the *Rocky Mountain News.* He began to have his stories and poems published in national magazines, and in early 1911 he arrived in New York and convinced publisher Desmond Fitzgerald to bring out his first book, *The Tents of Trouble: Ballads of the Wanderbund and Other Verse* (1911).

WILLIAM SAROYAN (1908-1981) dropped out of school in Fresno before completing the eighth grade and delivered messages for the Postal Telegraph Company. In 1926 he moved with his family to San Francisco and worked as a clerk, telegrapher, and finally manager for the Postal Telegraph Company's San Francisco office. He published his short story, "The Daring Young Man on the Flying Trapeze," in the February 1934 issue of *Story* magazine and won immediate acclaim.

A group of sportswriters: Heywood Broun and Damon Runyon are fourth and fifth from left

WALT WHITMAN (1819-1892) went to work at eleven as an office boy for two prominent attorneys, James B. and Edward Clark; he then worked briefly in a doctor's office before summer 1831, when he started at the printing office of Samuel E. Clemens, editor of the *Long Island Patriot,* and began to contribute "sentimental bits" to the paper soon after he was hired. The next summer he left the paper to work for printer Erastus Worthington, and by autumn he was setting type for Brooklyn's most successful printer, Alden Spooner. After he had a few pieces published in the *New York Mirror,* Whitman looked for employment in Manhattan, but failing to find suitable employment, he went to live with his family in Hempstead, Long Island, in May 1836 and took the first of a series of teaching jobs in nearby towns. He quit teaching in spring 1838 and started his own weekly newspaper, *Long Islander,* in Huntington. When the paper failed in May 1839, he found a job in Jamaica, Queens, with the *Long Island Democrat,* whose editor had been impressed with some of his pieces for the *Long Islander* and reprinted some of them. By the following winter Whitman had returned to teaching, but in May 1841 he again sought employment in Manhattan, this time finding a job as a printer for Park Benjamin's weekly, *New World.* He also began to have his stories and poems published in a variety of newspapers and magazines and made such a reputation as a writer that in February 1842, less than a year after he arrived in Manhattan, he was named editor of the *New York Aurora.* By mid May he had been fired–either because the owners disliked the political opinions expressed in his editorials or because he never showed up at work before noon (he still managed to get the paper out on time). After a few weeks of unemployment, he became editor of the *Evening Tatler* only to find himself out of work the following fall, at which time he went back to work for Park Benjamin, who commissioned him to write a temperance novel for the *New World.* Whitman's first separately published work–actually a supplement to the November 1842 *New World,* rather than a book–was this novel, *Franklin Evans; or the Inebriate.*

JOHN GREENLEAF WHITTIER (1807-1892) left his family farm in 1829 to take the editorship of the *American Manufacturer,* a political weekly in Boston.

Two years later a Hartford, Connecticut, publisher brought out his first book, a collection of stories and poems called *Legends of New-England* (1831).

RICHARD WRIGHT (1908-1960) was valedictorian of the ninth-grade class of 1925 at Smith-Robinson School in Jackson, Mississippi, but the following fall he had to leave Lanier High School after only a few weeks and work to help support his family. Working at a local hotel and making extra money by bringing bootleg whiskey to the prostitutes who had rooms there, he gave so much of his earnings to his family that he despaired of ever saving enough money to escape from Jackson. Later in autumn 1925 he solved the problem by breaking into the storehouse at Jackson College, selling the canned fruit that he stole to various local restaurants, and hopping a train to Memphis with the profits. Working as a dishwasher at a drugstore and as an assistant and delivery boy at a local optical company, he saved enough money for his mother and brother to join him in early autumn 1927. Meanwhile he had begun his literary self-education, having persuaded a white fellow worker to lend him his library card so that he could check out books at the whites-only public library on the pretense that he was picking them up for a white man. (On his first visit he handed the librarian a note that he had written and signed with his coworker's name: "Dear Madam: Will you please let this nigger boy have some books by H. L. Mencken.") Especially inspired by the realistic fiction of Sinclair Lewis and Theodore Dreiser, he began writing but not submitting work for publication. In November 1927, fearing that, if he did not leave the South, he "would perish, either because of possible violence of others against me, or because of my possible violence against them," he left Memphis for Chicago, to be followed later by his mother and brother. Wright started out as a delivery boy for a delicatessen but soon took a job as a dishwasher at a cafeteria, where he worked off and on until February 1929. In 1928 he took a summer job at Chicago's central post office, and in March 1929 he began working there full-time; but he lost the job in spring 1930 because the stock-market crash of October 1929 caused the post office to cut back its staff. Though he hoped to find an editorial or reportorial position, his only journalistic success was the appearance of "Superstition," his first-published mature short story, in the April 1931 issue of *Abbott's Monthly Magazine,* which ceased publication that year and never paid him for his contribution, Before signing up with the Federal Writer's project in spring 1935, he worked intermittently at various low-paying jobs, becoming part of the Chicago left-wing literary circle that included Nelson Algren and Jack Conroy and becoming executive secretary of the Chicago John Reed Club in 1933. His first book, *Uncle Tom's Children: Four Novellas* (1938), was followed in 1940 by his best-known novel, *Native Son,* the first book by a black American to become a main selection of the Book-of-the-Month Club. For much of his fiction and nonfiction Wright drew on his own life. Most notably, *Black Boy* (1945), an autobiographical account of southern racism, is based on his life up to the time he left Memphis, while *Native Son* (1940) reflects his experiences on Chicago's South Side.

RICHARD YATES (1926-   ) graduated from prep school in 1944, served as a private in the infantry during World War II, and went to work as a rewrite man for UPI after the war. Following a job as a publicity writer for Remington Rand, he spent two years in Europe working at fiction writing and then returned to the United States, where he worked as a free-lance ghost writer until 1959. His first novel, *Revolutionary Road* (1961), won a National Book Award.

First Books—
Famous and Forgotten—
By Well-Known
American Writers

by MORRIS P. COLDEN

There is a strong sentimental element in literary history. One of the ways this feeling manifests itself is through an interest in the first books of famous authors: the books that in some cases launched careers but in most cases made no impression at the time of publication. Because many of these firsts were ephemeral or privately printed publications, they are rare and therefore now bring high prices from collectors. Edgar Allan Poe's *Tamerlane and Other Poems* (1827), a forty-page pamphlet attributed to "A Bostonian," survives in eleven copies. The last copy sold at auction in 1975 brought $123,000. Ernest Hemingway's *Three Stories and Ten Poems,* published in Paris in 1923 and limited to 300 copies, brings up to $6,000.

Some first books are of such rarity as to be known through only a single copy; and there are titles for which no copy has survived. Robert Frost had two copies of *Twilight* printed in 1894 and subsequently destroyed one of them. No copy of Vladimir Nabokov's first poetry pamphlet, printed in Russia in 1914, has been located; his second poetry pamphlet, *Stikhi* (1916), survives in only a few copies. Nathaniel Hawthorne was so embarrassed by *Fanshawe* (1828) that he later destroyed any copies he secured. Willa Cather subsidized publication of *April Twilights* (1903) and subsequently bought all the unsold copies, which she threw in a lake.

Because many first publications were collaborative efforts or editorial jobs or ghost-writing assignments, there is frequent disagreement about what really qualifies as an author's first book. John O'Hara's *Appointment in Samarra* (1934) was preceded that year by *Reminiscences from "Kungsholm" West Indies Cruise,* a booklet made up of the issues of the ship's paper, edited by O'Hara. F. Scott Fitzgerald's *This Side of Paradise* (1920) was preceded by the published librettos for three Princeton University Triangle Club shows, for which he wrote the lyrics. James Thurber's *Is Sex Necessary?* (1929)—written with E. B. White—was preceded by six published Ohio State University Scarlet Mask Club librettos for which Thurber wrote the books. Bibliographers argue about whether such publications should be regarded as first books—or whether the designation should be restricted to works entirely written by a single author.

Authorship is an egotistical endeavor, but there have been notable cases in which fledgling writers have tried their wings anonymously. Some no doubt hoped to be overwhelmed by the resulting fame. James Fenimore Cooper concealed his authorship of *Precaution* (1820) because he was not sure that writing fiction was a gentlemanly endeavor. Hawthorne published *Fanshawe* anonymously out of shyness or diffidence. Other anonymous maiden efforts range from William Hill Brown's *The Power of Sympathy* (1789) and Charles Brockden Brown's *Alcuin* (1798) to Sylvia Plath's *A Winter Ship* (1960).

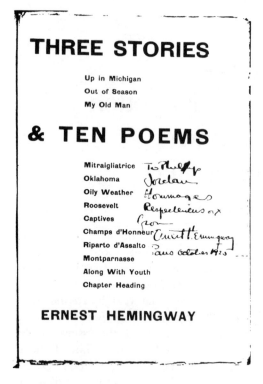

THREE STORIES

Up in Michigan
Out of Season
My Old Man

& TEN POEMS

Mitraigliatrice
Oklahoma
Oily Weather
Roosevelt
Captives
Champs d'Honneur
Riparto d'Assalto
Montparnasse
Along With Youth
Chapter Heading

ERNEST HEMINGWAY

Title page for Hemingway's first book

Authors who break into print early–apart from school publications–tend to be poets. Hilda Conkling published commercial volumes of verse at the ages of ten (*Poems by a Little Girl*, 1920) and twelve (*Shoes of the Wind*, 1922). Nathalia Crane published a book of poems, *The Janitor's Boy* (1924), when she was eleven. She won the competition for the best poem on Lindbergh's flight when she was fourteen with "The Wings of Lead," which concludes:

> We hear the clinking tambourine
>   of Miriam anew,
> We believe in every miracle since
>   Lindbergh flew the blue,
>
> The wonder of the long draw
>   when the bow-string is a
>   thread–
> The beauty of a courage that can
>   raise the wings of lead.

William Cullen Bryant's first book, *The*

Embargo, or Sketches of the Times; A Satire. By A Youth of Thirteen (1808), was published at the expense of the poet's proud father, who approved of this virulent attack on Jefferson's policies and morals.

First books are often financed by the writer or his family. Poe–or somebody–paid to have *Tamerlane* printed. Hawthorne spent $100 to have *Fanshawe* printed. Louisa May Alcott's *Flower Fables* (1855) was published at the expense of a friend appropriately named Miss Wealthy Stevens. Henry David Thoreau underwrote publication of *A Week on the Concord and Merrimack Rivers* (1849). When the book failed to sell, Thoreau observed, "I have now a library of nearly nine hundred volumes, over seven hundred of which I wrote myself." Edith Wharton's anonymous *Verses* (1878) was privately printed when she was sixteen. Stephen Crane paid for *Maggie* (1893). Edwin Arlington Robinson paid for *The Torrent and the Night Before* (1896). Eugene O'Neill's father put up the money for *Thirst* (1914). William Faulkner's *The Marble Faun* (1924) was a vanity press book. Adrienne Rich's father privately published her first two books when she was ten (*Ariadne, A Play in Three Acts and Poems*, 1939) and twelve (*Not I, But Death, A Play in One Act*, 1941). *Jim's Book* (1942) was privately published by James Merrill's family when he was sixteen. Karl Shapiro's *Poems* (1935) was privately printed when he was a relatively ripe twenty-two.

Other precocious writers have made it on their own. Frank Norris's *Yvernelle* (1892) was commercially published while he was a Berkeley undergraduate. James Gould Cozzens published "A Democratic School" in the *Atlantic Monthly* (March 1920) when he was sixteen; his first novel, *Confusion* (1924), was published when he was a Harvard sophomore. Truman Capote's "My Side of the Matter" appeared in *Story* magazine (May-June 1945) when he was seventeen; his first novel, *Other Voices, Other Rooms* (1948), appeared three years later. Stephen Vincent Benét's *Five Men and Pompey* (1915) appeared when he was a seventeen-year-old Yale freshman.

Young authors want to practice their trades; they publish whatever and whenever they can. Some commence as ghostwriters. Jimmy Breslin was the uncredited author of Jimmy Demaret's *My Partner Ben Hogan* (1954). Mary McCarthy collaborated on H. V. Kaltenborn's *Kaltenborn Edits the News* (1939) without title-page credit. Writers who combine academic careers with literature often start with textbooks. Irvin Faust's first book was *Entering Angel's World: A Student-Centered Casebook* (1963). John Gardner began by coediting *The Forms of Fiction* (1962) with Lennis Dunlap; it was followed by *The Complete Works of the Gawain-Poet in a Modern English Version with a Critical Introduction by John Gardner* (1965). Walker Percy's first separate publication was a philosophy monograph, *The Symbol as Need* (1954).

Wealthy Harry Crosby (he was J. P. Morgan's nephew) launched the Black Sun Press in 1928 to publish other writers as well as his own work. Another Paris-based imprint that served its owner's literary ambitions was Robert McAlmon's Contact Press, founded in 1922. McAlmon did not self-publish his first book, but his second and seven more bore the Contact imprint. The most famous Contact publication was Hemingway's *Three Stories and Ten Poems*.

First books may be bitter experiences. Theodore Dreiser's *Sister Carrie* (1900) was unenthusiastically handled by the publisher (because Mrs. Doubleday was shocked by it) and sold only 456 copies. Dreiser was so disappointed that he did not publish another book for eleven years. Edward Noyes Wescott wrote *David Harum* (1898) while dying of tuberculosis. The enormously popular novel was posthumously published. John Kennedy Toole's *A Confederacy of Dunces* (1980) appeared eleven years after the author committed suicide, presumably in despair over his inability to find a publisher.

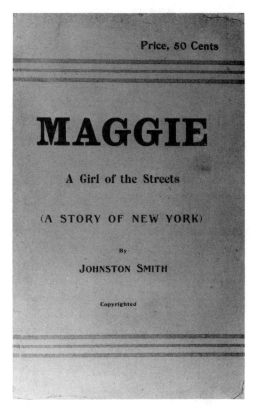

Cover for Stephen Crane's first book

There are baffling cases of authors who produce highly successful first books and quit: Margaret Mitchell's *Gone With the Wind* (1936), Harper Lee's *To Kill a Mockingbird* (1960), and Humphrey Cobb's *Paths of Glory* (1935). Ralph Ellison published *Invisible Man* in 1952; only two collections of his essays have subsequently appeared. Edith Summers Kelly published one book during her lifetime, *Weeds* (1923); it made little impression in its day but has since been hailed as a cornerstone of feminist literature. Her second novel, *The Devil's Hand*, was posthumously published in 1974. Henry Roth's proletarian novel *Call It Sleep* (1934) was his only book—except for a limited edition of a memoir published in 1979.

Some authors endure long apprenticeships, writing in obscurity. Others commence their careers with masterpieces—or, failing that, with first books that mark them as comers.

CLASSIC FIRSTS

Nelson Algren, *Somebody in Boots* (1935)

Sherwood Anderson, *Windy McPherson's Son* (1916)

James Baldwin, *Go Tell It on the Mountain* (1953)

Charles Brockden Brown, *Alcuin* (1798)

William Hill Brown, *The Power of Sympathy* (1789)

Edgar Rice Burroughs, *Tarzan of the Apes* (1914)

Truman Capote, *Other Voices, Other Rooms* (1948)

Raymond Chandler, *The Big Sleep* (1939)

Humphrey Cobb, *Paths of Glory* (1935)

Robert Coover, *The Origin of the Brunists* (1966)

Stephen Crane (as Johnston Smith), *Maggie: A Girl of the Streets* (1893)

E. E. Cummings, *The Enormous Room* (1922)

Richard Henry Dana, Jr., *Two Years Before the Mast* (1840)

J. P. Donleavy, *The Ginger Man* (1955)

Theodore Dreiser, *Sister Carrie* (1900)

T. S. Eliot, *Prufrock and Other Observations* (1917)

Ralph Ellison, *Invisible Man* (1952)

James T. Farrell, *Young Lonigan* (1932)

F. Scott Fitzgerald, *This Side of Paradise* (1920)

William Gaddis, *The Recognitions* (1955)

Dashiell Hammett, *Red Harvest* (1929)

Joel Chandler Harris, *Uncle Remus: His Songs and Sayings* (1881)

Joseph Heller, *Catch-22* (1961)

Ernest Hemingway, *Three Stories and Ten Poems* (1923)

O. Henry, *Cabbages and Kings* (1904)

George V. Higgins, *The Friends of Eddie Coyle* (1972)

E. W. Howe, *The Story of a Country Town* (1883)

James Jones, *From Here to Eternity* (1951)

Edith Summers Kelly, *Weeds* (1923)

Ken Kesey, *One Flew Over the Cuckoo's Nest* (1962)

Harper Lee, *To Kill a Mockingbird* (1960)

Norman Mailer, *The Naked and the Dead* (1948)

Bernard Malamud, *The Natural* (1952)

Wallace Markfield, *To An Early Grave* (1964)

Horace McCoy, *They Shoot Horses, Don't They?* (1935)

Carson McCullers, *The Heart Is a Lonely Hunter* (1940)

Herman Melville, *Typee* (1846)

Edna St. Vincent Millay, *Renascence* (1917)

Henry Miller, *Tropic of Cancer* (1934)

Margaret Mitchell, *Gone With the Wind* (1936)

Edgar Allan Poe, *Tamerlane and Other Poems* (1827)

Reynolds Price, *A Long and Happy Life* (1962)

Thomas Pynchon, *V.* (1965)

Edwin Arlington Robinson, *The Torrent and the Night Before* (1896)

Philip Roth, *Goodbye, Columbus* (1959)

J. D. Salinger, *The Catcher in the Rye* (1951)

Budd Schulberg, *What Makes Sammy Run?* (1941)

Gertrude Stein, *Three Lives* (1909)

Wallace Stevens, *Harmonium* (1923)

William Styron, *Lie Down in Darkness* (1951)

Henry David Thoreau, *A Week on the Concord and Merrimack Rivers* (1849)

Mark Twain, *The Celebrated Jumping Frog of Calaveras County* (1867)

Kurt Vonnegut, *Player Piano* (1952)

Edward Noyes Wescott, *David Harum* (1898)

Nathanael West, *The Dream Life of Balso Snell* (1931)

Richard Yates, *Revolutionary Road* (1961)

OTHER FIRST BOOKS OR PAMPHLETS

Louis Adamic, *Robinson Jeffers: A Portrait* (1929)

Franklin Pierce Adams (F.P.A.), *In Cupid's Court* (1902)

Conrad Aiken, *Earth Triumphant and Other Tales in Verse* (1914)

Louisa May Alcott, *Flower Fables* (1855)

Hervey Allen, *Ballads of the Border* (1916)

Louis Auchincloss (as Andrew Lee), *The Indifferent Children* (1947)

John Barth, *The Floating Opera* (1956)

Saul Bellow, *Dangling Man* (1944)

Stephen Vincent Benét, *Five Men and Pompey* (1915)

R. P. Blackmur, *Dirty Hands or The True Born Censor* (1932)

Van Wyck Brooks, *Verses By Two Undergraduates* (1905), with John Hall Wheelock

William S. Burroughs (as William Lee), *Junkie* (1953)

James M. Cain, *79th Division Headquarters Troop A Record* (1919), edited with Malcolm Gilbert

Willa Cather, *April Twilights* (1903)

Walter Van Tilburg Clark, *Christmas Comes to Hjalsen* (1930)

Hilda Conkling, *Poems by a Little Girl* (1920)

Jack Conroy, *The Disinherited* (1933)

James Fenimore Cooper, *Precaution* (1820)

Malcolm Cowley, *Racine* (1923)

James Gould Cozzens, *Confusion* (1924)

Nathalia Crane, *The Janitor's Boy* (1924)

Clarence Day, *The '96 Half-Way Book* (1915)

Peter DeVries, *But Who Makes the Bugler?* (1940)

James Dickey, *Poets of Today VII* (1960), with Paris Leary and Jon Swan

John Dos Passos, *One Man's Initiation–1917* (1920)

Finley Peter Dunne, *Mr. Dooley in Peace and War* (1898)

Edward Eggleston, *The Manual: A Practical Guide To Sunday Schoolwork* (1869)

Ralph Waldo Emerson, *Letter From the Rev. R. W. Emerson, to the Second Church and Society* (1832)

William Faulkner, *The Marble Faun* (1924)

Irvin Faust, *Entering Angel's World; A Student-Centered Casebook* (1963)

Robert Frost, *Twilight* (1894)

Erle Stanley Gardner, *The Case of the Velvet Claws* (1932)

John Gardner, *The Forms of Fiction* (1962), edited with Lennis Dunlap

Allen Ginsberg, *Siesta in Zbalba and Return* (1956)

Ellen Glasgow, *The Descendant* (1897)

James Norman Hall, *Kitchener's Mob* (1916)

John Hawkes (as J. C. B. Hawkes, Jr.), *Fiasco Hall* (1943)

Nathaniel Hawthorne, *Fanshawe* (1828)

Henry William Herbert, *The Brothers* (1835)

William Dean Howells, *Poems of Two Friends* (1860), with John J. Piatt

Ring Lardner, *Zanzibar* (1903), with Harry Schmidt

Sinclair Lewis (as Tom Graham), *Hike and the Aeroplane* (1912)

Vachel Lindsay, *The Tree of Laughing Bells* (1905)

Amy Lowell, *Dream Drops or Stories from Fairy Land by a Dreamer* (1887), with Katherine Bigelow Lawrence Lowell and Elizabeth Lowell

Robert Lowell, *The Land of Unlikeliness* (1944)

John P. Marquand, *The Prince and the Boatswain* (1915), with J. M. Morgan

Edgar Lee Masters, *A Book of Verses* (1898)

H. L. Mencken, *Ventures into Verse* (1903)

James Merrill, *Jim's Book* (1942)

Kenneth Millar, *The Dark Tunnel* (1944)

Anaïs Nin, *D. H. Lawrence An Unprofessional Study* (1932)

Frank Norris, *Yvernelle A Legend of Feudal France* (1892)

John O'Hara, *Reminiscences from "Kungsholm" West Indies Cruise* (1934)

Eugene O'Neill, *Thirst* (1914)

Walker Percy, *The Symbol as Need* (1954)

S. J. Perelman, *Dawn Ginsbergh's Revenge* (1929)

Sylvia Plath, *A Winter Ship* (1960)

Ezra Pound, *A Lume Spento* (1908)

Ellery Queen, *The Roman Hat Mystery* (1929)

Adrienne Rich, *Ariadne, A Play in Three Acts and Poems* (1939)

Conrad Richter, *Brothers of No Kin* (1924)

Henry Roth, *Call It Sleep* (1934)

Damon Runyon, *The Tents of Trouble* (1911)

Carl Sandburg (as Charles A. Sandburg), *In Reckless Ecstasy* (1904)

Karl Shapiro, *Poems* (1935)

Rex Stout, *How Like A God* (1929)

Jesse Stuart, *Harvest of Youth* (1930)

James Thurber, *Is Sex Necessary?* (1929), with E. B. White

John Kennedy Toole, *A Confederacy of Dunces* (1980)

John Updike, *The Carpentered Hen and Other Tame Creatures* (1958)

Robert Penn Warren, *John Brown* (1929)

Edith Wharton (as E. N. Jones), *Verses* (1878)

Walt Whitman, *Franklin Evans; Or, The Inebriate* (1842)

Tennessee Williams, *Battle of Angels* (1945)

Edmund Wilson, *The Undertaker's Garland* (1922), with John Peale Bishop

Thomas Wolfe, *The Crisis in Industry* (1919)

Cornell Woolrich, *Cover Charge* (1926)

FIRST BOOKS BY MINORS

Thomas Bailey Aldrich, *The Bells: A Collection of Chimes* (1855)–age nineteen. Preceded by a broadside poem, *Farewell!* published at ten.

Richard Harding Davis, *The Adventures of My Freshman* (1884)–age twenty.

Paul Leicester Ford, *Webster Genealogy* (1876)–age eleven; a pamphlet.

Philip Freneau, *The American Village* (1772)–age twenty. He also published *A Poem, On The Rising Glory of America,* a collaboration with Hugh Henry Brackenridge, in 1772.

Alexander Hamilton, *A Full Vindication of the Measures of Congress* (1774)–age nineteen; a pamphlet.

Amy Lowell, *Dream Drops* (1887)–age thirteen; written in collaboration with her mother and sister.

James Russell Lowell, *To the Class of '38, by their Ostracized Poet* (1938)–age nineteen; a broadside.

Cotton Mather, *A Poem Dedicated to the Memory of the Reverend and Excellent Mr. Urian Oakes* (1682)–age nineteen.

John Howard Payne, *Julia, Or the Wanderer; A Comedy* (1806)–age fifteen.

Theodore Roosevelt, *Notes on Some of the Birds of Oyster Bay, Long Island* (1879)–age twenty; a broadside. Preceded by *The Summer Birds of the Adirondacks in Franklin County, N.Y.* (1877), a pamphlet written in collaboration with H. D. Minot.

George Santayana, *Lines on Leaving the Bedford Street Schoolhouse* (1880)–age seventeen; a pamphlet.

Daniel Webster, *A Funeral Oration Occasioned by the Death of Ephraim Simonds* (1801)–age nineteen.

Writing Under Cover: American Literary Pseudonyms

by MORRIS P. COLDEN

Various circumstances prompt authors to use pseudonyms–ranging from modesty to the attempt to establish a brand name. Often the pseudonym will be abandoned after the writer's apprenticeship, but in some cases the nom de plume becomes better known than the actual name–as with Mark Twain and O. Henry.

In the eighteenth century many American writers imitated the British practice of writing journalism or essays under pen names. Most notably, Benjamin Franklin invented Poor Richard (Richard Saunders) as the putative author of almanacs and pithy sayings.

The group of nineteenth-century writers identified as the local colorists or vernacular humorists frequently created personas with amusing or outlandish names: Dan DeQuille (William Wright), Petroleum Vesuvius Nasby (David Ross Locke), Artemus Ward (Charles Farrar Browne), Josh Billings (Henry Wheeler Shaw), and Sut Lovingood (George Washington Harris). The most notable name to emerge from this school was, of course, Mark Twain. An earlier example of this tradition was Washington Irving–who was also Geoffrey Crayon, Diedrich Knickerbocker, Launcelot Langstaff, and Jonathan Oldstyle, Gent.

Pseudonyms are most frequently found on apprentice works (see First Books) for reasons that may include coyness or the desire to conceal a hack job. Upton Sinclair wrote dime novels about the army and navy as Lt. Frederick Garrison and Ensign Clyde Fitch. Sinclair Lewis's first book, *Hike and the Aeroplane*

(1912), a juvenile written to earn a fast buck, was credited to Tom Graham. A commercial job by Katherine Anne Porter, *My Chinese Marriage* (1921), was credited to M. T. F.

Stephen Crane signed his first book, *Maggie* (1893), Johnston Smith to conceal his authorship of a shocking novel. No publisher would risk taking it, so Crane paid to have it printed. He originally chose the pseudonym Johnson Smith because of its combination of ordinary names, but accepted the printer's error of Johnston Smith.

William Sidney Porter allegedly selected the pseudonym O. Henry to conceal the circumstance that he was writing in prison. It has become so familiar that it can be misspelled with impunity: it now frequently appears in print as O'Henry.

Willard Huntington Wright began writing the Philo Vance mysteries as therapy after a nervous collapse. He signed them S. S. Van Dine to distinguish them from his serious art criticism.

Edward Zane Carroll Judson was the prodigiously productive and popular Ned Buntline, writer of dime novels; his most famous character was Buffalo Bill, based on William F. Cody.

Louis Auchincloss published his first book, *The Indifferent Children* (1947), as Andrew Lee, presumably to separate his literary and legal careers. William S. Burroughs published his first novel, *Junkie* (1953) as William Lee, probably to conceal his own drug addiction. Vladimir Nabokov wrote his early Russian books as V. Sirin to distinguish them from his father's work. Nathan Weinstein tried out Nathaniel von Wallenstein Weinstein before deciding on Nathanael West.

Some authors have utilized multiple pseudonyms, usually as a consequence of their productivity. Frederick Faust, best known as Max Brand, published as Frank Austin, George Owen Baxter, Lee Bolt, Walter C. Butler, George Challis, Peter Dawson, Martin Dexter, Evin Evan, Evan Evans, John Frederick, Frederick Frost, David Manning, Dennis Manning, Peter Henry Morland, Hugh Owen, Nicholas Silber, Henry Uriel, and Peter Ward—as well as Frederick Faust. Ray Bradbury has also written as D. R. Banat, Edward Banks, Leonard Douglas, William Elliott, Don Reynolds, and Leonard Spaulding.

Prolific writers—especially in the mystery field—use multiple pseudonyms to differentiate series or types of books. Salvatore A. Lambino, who legally changed his name to Evan Hunter, writes the 87th Precinct novels as Ed McBain. He is also Curt Cannon, Hunt Collins, Ezra Hannon, and Richard Marston. Donald Westlake publishes hard-boiled fiction as Richard Stark. He has also written as Curt Clark, Tucker Coe, Timothy J. Culver, and J. Morgan Cunningham. Frederic Dannay and Manfred B. Lee were best known under the joint pseudonym Ellery Queen, but they also wrote the Drury Lane series as Barbaby Ross. Cornell Woolrich was also William Irish and George Hopley. Kenneth Millar published his first four novels under his own name but switched to John Macdonald for *The Moving Target* (1949) to signal a change in his material. After a complaint from John D. MacDonald (AKA John Wade Farrell, Robert Henry, John Lane, Scott O'Hara, Peter Reed, Henry Rieser), Millar's byline evolved from John Ross Macdonald to Ross Macdonald.

Juvenile series may be produced by squads of writers under house names (bylines shared by different writers). The popular nineteenth-century Peter Parley books were mostly written by Samuel G. Goodrich, but one of his hacks was Nathaniel Hawthorne. Nick Carter was probably first used by John Russell Coryell, but others wrote most of the 1,000 Nick Carter titles. Coryell made a career of writing under house names; he produced series books as Bertha M. Clay, Tyman Currio, Lillian R. Drayton, Julia Edwards, Geraldine Fleming, Margaret Grant, Barbara Howard, Harry Du-Bois Milman, Milton Quarterman, and Lucy May Russell. Maxwell Grant, the house by-line for the Shadow series, was variously Lester Dent, Bruce Elliot, Walter D. Gibson, Dennis Lynds, and Theodore Tinsley.

The king of the series writers was Edward L. Stratemeyer (1862-1930), who formed a syndicate to produce and market the juvenile series he developed. His creations included Nancy Drew, the Hardy Boys, Tom Swift, Bomba the Jungle Boy, the Bobbsey Twins, the Rover Boys, the Motor Boys—and others. Stratemeyer usually created the character and outlined the plot; then he wrote the book himself or turned it over to one of the house writers. Most of the series carried distinguishing house names. The Rover Boys books were credited to Arthur M. Winfield, the Bobbsey Twins books to Laura Lee Hope, and the Nancy Drews to Carolyn Keene. Stratemeyer's daughter, Harriet Stratemeyer Adams (1894-1982), took over the syndicate; she wrote most of the Nancy Drew mysteries and many of the Hardy Boys titles.

William Faulkner is a borderline case. He was born William Falkner and later adopted the original spelling of the family name. One F. Scott Fitzgerald story, "On An Ocean Wave," appeared in *Esquire* as by Paul Elgin because Fitzgerald was submitting more stories than the magazine could publish under his name. Eight of Dashiell Hammett's early magazine pieces were credited to Peter Collinson. (Peter Collins was a variant for John Doe.) As a cub reporter in the *Pottsville Journal* John O'Hara wrote a column signed Trewq (see typewriter keyboard), and he later wrote a radio column for the *New York Morning Telegraph* as Franey Delaney.

FAMOUS (AND FORGOTTEN) PSEUDONYMS

Forrest J. Ackermann: Dr. Acula, Sylvius Agricola, S. F. Balboa, Nick Beal, Jacques Deforest Erman, Laurajean Ermayne, Mirta Forsto, Coil Kepac, Allis Kerlay, Alden Lorraine, Katarin Markov Merritt, Seena Nader, Astrid Notte, Forry Rhodan, Spenser Strong, Vespertina Torgosi, Allis Villette, Claire Voyant, Hubert George Welles, Weaver Wright

Michael Avallone: Nick Carter, Priscilla Dalton, Mark Dane, Jean-Anne de Pre, Dora Highland, Steve Michaels, Dorothea Nile, Edwina Noone, Vance Stanton, Sidney Stuart, Max Walker

Ambrose Bierce: Dod Grile

John Dickson Carr: Carr Dickson, Carter Dickson, Roger Fairborn

Henry Carter: Frank Leslie

Charles Heber Clark: Max Adeler

William Cobbett: Peter Porcupine

Michel Guillaume Jean de Crèvecoeur: J. Hector St. John, A Farmer in Pennsylvania

Charles A. Davis: J. Downing, Major

Joseph Dennie: Colon

George Horatio Derby: John Phoenix and Squibob

John Dickinson: A Farmer in Pennsylvania

Joseph Rodman Drake and *Fitz-Greene Halleck:* Croaker and Croaker, Jun.

Corey Ford: John Riddell, June Triplett

Paul W. Ganley: Toby Duane

Erle Stanley Gardner: Kyle Corning, A. A. Fair, Charles M. Green, Carleton Kendrake, Charles J. Kenny, Robert Parr, Les Tillray

Elizabeth Meriwether Gilmer: Dorothy Dix

Irwin Granich: Michael Gold

Asa Greene: Elnathan Elmwood and George Fibbleton, Esq.

Thomas C. Halliburton: Sam Slick

Alexander Hamilton: Phocion, Pacificus

Henry Harland: Sidney Luska

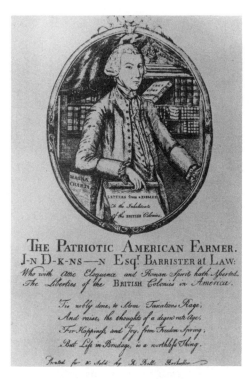

Tribute to John Dickinson printed in 1768, after he was revealed to be the author of *Letters from a Farmer in Pennsylvania* (1768), the most popular political pamphlet in the American colonies before the appearance of Thomas Paine's *Common Sense* in 1776.

Henry William Herbert: Frank Forester

Marietta Holley: Josiah Allen's Wife

Johnson Jones Hooper: Simon Suggs

Francis Hopkinson: Peter Grievous

Robert E. Howard: Patrick Ervin, Patrick Howard, John Taverel

Kin Hubbard: Abe Martin

L. Ron Hubbard: Elron, Tom Easterbrook, Michael Keith, Rene Lafayette, Legionnaire 14830, Ken Martin, John Seabrook, Kurt VonRachen

Helen Hunt Jackson: Saxe Holm

William Fitzgerald Jenkins: Murray Leinster

R. M. Johnston: Philemon Perch

LeRoi Jones: Imamu Amiri Baraka

Emily C. Judson: Fanny Forester

Philip Klass: William Tenn

Alfred Henry Lewis: Dan Quin

Charles B. Lewis: M. Quad

Miriam F. Leslie (Mrs. Frank Leslie): Frank Leslie

Paul Myron Anthony Linebarger: Cordwainer Smith

Sara Jane Lippincott: Grace Greenwood

H[oward] P[hillips] Lovecraft: Lawrence Appleton, Isaac Bickerstaff, Jr., John J. Jones, Humphrey Littlewit, Archibald Maynwaring, Henry Paget-Lowe, Ward Phillips, Richard Raleigh, Ames Dorrance Rersley, Edward Softly, Augustus T. Swift, Lewis Theobald, Jr., Albert Frederick Willie, Zoilus

James Russell Lowell: Hosea Biglow

James Madison: Helvidius

H. L. Mencken and *G. J. Nathan:* Major Owen Arthur James Hatteras

Bill Miller and *Robert Wade:* Wade Miller, Dale Wilmer, Whit Masterson, Will Daemer

Donald Grant Mitchell: Ik Marvel

Sarah Wentworth Morton: Philenia

Mary N. Murfree: Charles Egbert Craddock

Judith Sargent Murray: Constantia

Robert Henry Newell: Orpheus C. Kerr [office seeker]

C. F. M. Noland: Colonel Pete Whetstone

Jonathan Odell: Camillo Querno

Thomas Paine: Forester

William Gilbert Patten: Burt L. Standish

James Kirke Paulding: Launcelot Langstaff, Oliver Oldstyle, Hector Bull-Us

David Graham Phillips: John Graham

Elizabeth Waties Allston Pringle: Patience Pennington

Georgiana Ann Randolph: Craig Rice, Daphne Saunders, Michael Venning

Leo Rosten: Leonard Q. Ross

Samuel Seabury: A. W. Farmer [A Westchester Farmer]

Elizabeth Cochrane Seaman: Nelly Bly

Alice B. Sheldon: James Tiptree, Jr.

Charles Henry Smith: Bill Arp

Seba Smith: Major Jack Downing

Harry Clement Stubbs: Hal Clement

Mary Virginia Terhune: Marion Harland

William Tappan Thompson: Major Joseph Jones

Mortimer Neal Thomson: Q. K. Philander Doesticks, P. B.

Royall Tyler: Spondee

Boyd B. Upchurch: John Boyd

Gore Vidal: Edgar Box

Francesca Vinciguera: Frances Winwar

William Anthony Parker White: Anthony Boucher

Josiah Flint Willard: Josiah Flynt

Sara Payson Willis: Fanny Fern

John Joachim Zubly: Helvetius

Looking Backward: American Literary Title Sources

by JUDITH S. BAUGHMAN

The intention behind the title of a work will vary from author to author and from book to book. Some titles are meant to encapsulate the theme of the volume (*For Whom the Bell Tolls, All the King's Men*); some convey a mood (*Tender Is the Night, Home from the Hill*); some describe the principal figure (*The Titan, The Great Gatsby*); some focus upon a particular setting (*Winesburg, Ohio; Main Street*); some suggest the primary action (*The Caine Mutiny, Adventures of Huckleberry Finn*); some provide the central symbol (*The Catcher in the Rye, The Scarlet Letter*).

Many titles are drawn from other works (Shakespeare and the Bible are gold mines for titles, and William Butler Yeats may be the most "plunderable" of modern writers). For *Winner Take Nothing* Hemingway invented a title source, which he then "quoted" as an epigraph in mock-medieval style. There is not always an intimate connection between the title source and the new work; a phrase may be chosen for its sound, as was James Gould Cozzens's *The Last Adam*. But in certain cases the work that supplies the title phrase may also provide a key to the meanings of the novel; thus Keats's "Ode to a Nightingale" explicates Fitzgerald's *Tender Is the Night*.

James Agee, *Let Us Now Praise Famous Men*, photographs by Walker Evans (1941)

Let us now praise famous men, and our fathers that begat us.
    —Ecclesiasticus 30:24 (Apocrypha)

Maxwell Anderson, *Both Your Houses* (1933)

A plague o' both your houses!
They have made worms' meat of me.
    —Shakespeare, *Romeo and Juliet*, III, i

Maxwell Anderson, *Saturday's Children* (1927)

Monday's child is fair of face,
Tuesday's child is full of grace,
Wednesday's child is full of woe,
Thursday's child has far to go,
Friday's child is loving and giving,
Saturday's child has to work for its living,
But a child that's born on the Sabbath day

Is fair and wise and good and gay.
    —Anon., "Monday's Child Is Fair of Face" (nursery rhyme)

Louis Auchincloss (as Andrew Lee), *The Indifferent Children* (1947)

HAMLET: My excellent good friends! How dost thou, Guildenstern? Ah, Rosencrantz! Good lads, how do ye both?

ROSENCRANTZ: As the indifferent children of the earth.

GUILDENSTERN: Happy in that we are not over-happy.
    On Fortune's cap we are not the very button.

HAMLET: Nor the soles of her shoe?

ROSENCRANTZ: Neither, my lord.

HAMLET: Then you live about her waist, or in the middle of her favors?

GUILDENSTERN: Faith, her privates we.

HAMLET: In the secret parts of Fortune? O, most true! she is a strumpet.
    —Shakespeare, *Hamlet*, II, ii

Louis Auchincloss (photograph by Duane Michals)

James Baldwin, *Another Country* (1962)
BARABAS: I must needs say that I have been a great usurer.
FRIAR BARNARDINE: Thou hast committed. . .
BARABAS: Fornication? But that was in another country; and besides, the wench is dead.
> –Christopher Marlowe, *The Jew of Malta*, IV, i

Philip Barry, *Tomorrow and Tomorrow* (1931)
Tomorrow, and tomorrow, and tomorrow,
Creeps in this petty pace from day to day,
To the last syllable of recorded time;
And all our yesterdays have lighted fools
The way to dusty death.
> –Shakespeare, *Macbeth*, V, v

Philip Barry, *War in Heaven* (1938)
There was war in heaven: Michael and his angels fought against the dragon; and the dragon fought and his angels,
And prevailed not.
> –Revelation 12:7-8

Peter S. Beagle, *A Fine and Private Place* (1960)

The grave's a fine and private place,
But none, I think, do there embrace.
> –Andrew Marvell, "To His Coy Mistress"

S. N. Behrman, *Rain from Heaven* (1934)
The quality of mercy is not strained,
It droppeth as the gentle rain from heaven
Upon the place beneath: . . .
> –Shakespeare, *The Merchant of Venice*, IV, i

Saul Bellow, *Seize the Day* (1956)
Seize the day, put no trust in the morrow!
(Carpe diem, quam minimum credula postero.)
> –Horace, *Odes*, Book I, Ode xi

Stephen Vincent Benét, *The Beginning of Wisdom* (1921)
For the very true beginning of her [wisdom] is the desire of discipline; and the care of discipline is love.
> –Wisdom of Solomon 6:17 (Apocrypha)

Stephen Vincent Benét, *John Brown's Body* (1928)
John Brown's body lies a-moldering in the grave,

His soul is marching on.
>   —Thomas Brigham Bishop,
>   "John Brown's Body"

Ray Bradbury, *The Golden Apples of the Sun* (1953)
Though I am old with wandering
Through hollow lands and hilly lands,
I will find out where she has gone,
And kiss her lips and take her hands;
And walk among long dappled grass,
And pluck till time and times are done
The silver apples of the moon,
The golden apples of the sun.
>   —William Butler Yeats, "The Song
>   of the Wandering Aengus"

Pearl S. Buck, *A House Divided* (1935)
If a house be divided against itself, that house cannot stand.
>   —Mark 3:25
—Also quoted in Abraham Lincoln's speech, 16 June 1858, at the Republican State Convention, Springfield, Illinois

James Branch Cabell, *The King Was in his Counting House* (1938)
The king was in his countinghouse
Counting out his money;
The queen was in the parlor
Eating bread and honey;
The maid was in the garden
Hanging out the clothes,
Along came a blackbird,
And snipped off her nose.
>   —Anon., "Sing a Song of Six-
>   pence" (nursery rhyme)

James Gould Cozzens, *The Just and the Unjust* (1942)
That ye may be the children of your Father which is in heaven: for he maketh his sun to rise on the evil and the good, and sendeth rain on the just and on the unjust.
>   —Matthew 5:45

James Gould Cozzens, *The Last Adam* (1933)
The first man Adam was made a living soul; the last Adam was made a quickening spirit.
>   —I Corinthians 15:45

James Gould Cozzens, *Men and Brethren* (1936)
Therefore let all the house of Israel know assuredly, that God hath made that same Jesus, whom ye have crucified, both Lord and Christ.
Now when they heard this, they were pricked in their heart, and said unto Peter and to the rest of the apostles, Men and brethren, what shall we do?
>   —Acts 2:36-37

James Gould Cozzens, *The Son of Perdition* (1929)
Those that thou gavest me I have kept, and none of them is lost, but the son of perdition.
>   —John 17:12

August Derleth, *Still Small Voice* (1940)
And after the earthquake a fire; but the Lord was not in the fire; and after the fire a still small voice.
>   —I Kings 18:21

Bernard DeVoto, *Across the Wide Missouri* (1947)
Oh, Shenandoah, I long to hear you,
Way-hay, you rolling river!
Oh, Shenandoah, I long to hear you,
Ha-ha, we're bound away,
'Cross the wide Missouri.
>   —Anon., "Shenandoah" (shanty)

Bernard DeVoto, *The Crooked Mile* (1924)
There was a crooked man, and he went
    a crooked mile,
He found a crooked sixpence against a
    crooked stile;
He bought a crooked cat, which caught
    a crooked mouse,
And they all lived together in a little
    crooked house.
>   —Anon., "There Was a Crooked
>   Man" (nursery rhyme)

Peter DeVries, *Let Me Count the Ways* (1965)

How do I love thee? Let me count the
   ways.
I love thee to the depth and breadth
   and height
My soul can reach, when feeling out of
   sight
For the ends of Being and ideal Grace.
           —Elizabeth Barrett Browning,
            Sonnets from the Portuguese, no. 43

Joan Didion, *Slouching Towards Bethlehem* (1968)
And what rough beast, its hour come
   round at last,
Slouches towards Bethlehem to be
   born?
           —William Butler Yeats,
            "The Second Coming"

Theodore Dreiser, *The Hand of the Potter* (1919)
After a momentary silence spake
Some Vessel of a more ungainly Make;
"They sneer at me for leaning all awry:
What! did the Hand then of the Potter
   shake?"
         —Edward FitzGerald, *Rubáiyát of*
         Omar Khayyám

Nora Ephron, *Crazy Salad: Some Things About Women* (1970)
It's certain that fine women eat
A crazy salad with their meat
Whereby the Horn of Plenty is undone.
         —William Butler Yeats, "A
          Prayer for My Daughter"

William Faulkner, *Go Down, Moses and Other Stories* (1942)
Go down, Moses,
Way down in Egypt land,
Tell old Pharaoh,
Let my people go.
   —Anon., "Go Down, Moses"(spiritual)

William Faulkner, *Absalom! Absalom!* (1936)
. . . O my son Absalom, my son, my son
Absalom! would God I had died for
thee, O Absalom, my son, my son!
             —II Samuel 18:33

William Faulkner, *The Sound and the Fury* (1929)
It is a tale told by an idiot, full of
sound and fury, signifying nothing.
        —Shakespeare, *Macbeth*, V, 5

Edna Ferber, *No Room at the Inn* (1941)
And she brought forth her firstborn
son, and wrapped him in swaddling
clothes, and laid him in a manger; because there was no room for them in
the inn.
            —Luke 2:7

Dorothy Canfield Fisher, *The Bent Twig* (1915)
'Tis education forms the common mind:
Just as the twig is bent, the tree's
inclined.
        —Alexander Pope, "Epistle I,
        To Lord Cobham"

F. Scott Fitzgerald, *Tender Is the Night* (1934)
Already with thee! tender is the night,
  And haply the Queen-Moon is on her
    throne,
    Clustered around by all her starry
      Fays;
   —John Keats, "Ode to a Nightingale"

F. Scott Fitzgerald, *This Side of Paradise* (1920)
Well this side of Paradise! . . .
There's little comfort in the wise.
        —Rupert Brooke, "Tiare Tahiti"

Robert Frost, *A Boy's Will* (1913)
  And a verse of a Lapland song
  Is haunting my memory still:
  "A boy's will is the wind's will,
And the thoughts of youth are long,
  long thoughts."
        —Henry Wadsworth Longfellow,
        "My Lost Youth"

George Garrett, *Do, Lord, Remember Me* (1965)

Do, Lawd, remember me,
Do, Lawd, remember me,
When I'm in trouble,
Do, Lawd, remember me.
> —Anon., "Do, Lawd, Remember
> Me" (spiritual)

Ellen Glasgow, *Barren Ground* (1925)
Now would I give a thousand furlongs of sea for an acre of barren ground.
> —Shakespeare, *The Tempest*, I, i

Ellen Glasgow, *The Voice of the People* (1900)
The voice of the people is the voice of God. (Vox populi vox Dei.)
> —Alcuin, "Letter to
> Charlemagne"

Nancy Hale

A. B. Guthrie, Jr., *These Thousand Hills* (1956)
Every beast of the forest is mine, and the cattle upon a thousand hills.
> —Psalms 50:10

Nancy Hale, *Between the Dark and Daylight* (1943)
Between the dark and the daylight,
When the night is beginning to lower,
Comes a pause in the day's occupations,
That is known as the Children's Hour.
> —Henry Wadsworth Longfellow,
> "The Children's Hour"

Lorraine Hansberry, *A Raisin in the Sun* (1959)
What happens to a dream deferred?
  Does it dry up
  like a raisin in the sun? . . .
  Or does it explode?
> —Langston Hughes, "Harlem"

Mark Harris, *Bang the Drum Slowly . . .* (1956)
Oh, bang the drum slowly and
  play the fife lowly,

Play the Dead March as you carry
  me along;
Take me to the green valley, there
  lay the sod o'er me
For I'm a young cowboy and I
  know I've done wrong.
> —Anon., "The Cowboy's
> Lament" (song)

Lillian Hellman, *The Children's Hour* (1934)
(See Nancy Hale, *Between the Dark and the Daylight*)

Lillian Hellman, *The Little Foxes* (1939)
The little foxes, that spoil the vines.
> —The Song of Solomon 2:15

Ernest Hemingway, *For Whom the Bell Tolls* (1940)
Any man's death diminishes me because I am involved in mankind, and therefore never send to know for whom the bell tolls; it tolls for thee.
> —John Donne, "Meditation XVII"

Ernest Hemingway, *In Our Time* (1925)
Give peace in our time, O Lord.
—*The Book of Common Prayer*

Ernest Hemingway, *The Sun Also Rises* (1926)
The sun also ariseth, and the sun goeth down, and hasteth to his place where he arose.
—Ecclesiastes 1:5

Ernest Hemingway, *Winner Take Nothing* (1933)
Unlike all other forms of lutte or combat the conditions are that the winner shall take nothing; neither his ease, nor his pleasure, nor any notions of glory; nor, if he win far enough, shall there be any reward within himself.
—Unsigned epigraph by Hemingway

Robert Herrick, *The Web of Life* (1900)
The web of our life is of a mingled yarn, good and ill together.
—Shakespeare, *All's Well That Ends Well*, IV, iii

John Hersey, *Into the Valley* (1943)
Yea, though I walk through the valley of the shadow of death, I will fear no evil: for thou art with me; thy rod and thy staff they comfort me.
—Psalms 23:4

Chester Himes, *Cast the First Stone* (1952)
He that is without sin among you, let him first cast a stone at her.
—John 8:7

William Humphrey, *Home from the Hill* (1958)
Home is the sailor, home from sea,
    And the hunter home from the hill.
—Robert Louis Stevenson, "Requiem"

William Inge, *Splendor in the Grass* (1961)
Though nothing can bring back the hour
Of splendor in the grass, of glory in the flower.
—William Wordsworth, "Ode. Intimations of Immortality from Recollections of Early Childhood"

Henry James, *The Golden Bowl* (1904)
The almond tree shall flourish, and the grasshopper shall be a burden, and desire shall fail; because man goeth to his long home, and the mourners go about the streets:
Or ever the silver cord be loosed, or the golden bowl be broken, or the pitcher be broken at the fountain, or the wheel broken at the cistern.
Then shall the dust return to the earth as it was: and the spirit shall return unto God who gave it.
—Ecclesiastes 12:5-7

Henry James, *The Wings of the Dove* (1902)
For years fleet away with the wings of the dove.
—George Gordon, Lord Byron, "The First Kiss of Love"

Diane Johnson, *The Shadow Knows,* (1974)
Who knows what evil lurks in the hearts of men? The Shadow knows! (LAUGHS)
—*The Shadow* (Mutual Radio, 1936-   ): opening lines of the program

James Jones, *From Here to Eternity* (1951)
Gentlemen-rankers out on a spree,
Damned from here to Eternity,

God ha' mercy on such as we,
Ba! Yah! Bah!
                –Rudyard Kipling,
                "Gentlemen-Rankers"

James Jones, *Go to the Widow-Maker*,
(1967)
What is a woman that you forsake her,
And the hearth-fire and the home-acre,
To go with the old grey Widow-maker?
            –Rudyard Kipling, "Harp
                Song of the Dane Women"

James Jones, *Some Came Running*
(1958)
And when he was gone forth into the
way, there came one running, and
kneeled to him, and asked him, Good
Master, what shall I do that I may in-
herit eternal life? . . .

Then Jesus beholding him loved him,
and said unto him, One thing thou
lackest: go thy way, sell whatsoever thou
hast, and give to the poor, and thou
shalt have treasure in heaven: and
come, take up the cross, and follow me.

And he was sad at that saying, and
went away grieved: for he had great
possessions.
                –Mark 10:17-22

James Jones, *Whistle* (1978)
There was an almost standard remark
the night medic on duty would make to
the newly arrived patients at the hospital. He said, "If you want anything, just
whistle for it."
                –R. J. Blessing, *Memoirs*

Bounce, and dance; bounce, and
    dance;
        Jiggle on your strings.
    Whistle toward the graveyard.
Nobody knows who or what moves your
batten.
        You'll not find out.
                –French jingle translated
                by James Jones

Marjorie Kellogg, *Like the Lion's Tooth*
(1972)
Did he die or did she die?
Seemed to die or died they both?
God be with the times when I
Cared not a thraneen for what chanced
So that I had the limbs to try
Such a dance as there was danced–
Love is like the lion's tooth.
            –William Butler Yeats, "Crazy
                Jane Grown Old Looks at
                the Dancers"

Ken Kesey, *One Flew Over the Cuckoo's
Nest* (1962)
One flew east, one flew west,
One flew over the cuckoo's nest.
                –Anon., "One Flew East"
                (nursery rhyme)

Ken Kesey, *Sometimes a Great Notion*
(1964)
Sometimes I live in the country,
Sometimes I live in the town;
Sometimes I get a great notion
To jump into the river. . . an' drown.
            –Huddie Ledbetter and John Lomax,
                Good Night, Irene (popular song)

John Knowles, *A Separate Peace* (1959)
"You and me, we've made a separate
peace."
                –Ernest Hemingway, "A Very
                Short Story," *In Our Time*

Jack London, *The God of His Fathers &
Other Stories* (1901)
God of our fathers, known of old,
Lord of our far-flung battle line,
Beneath whose awful Hand we hold
Dominion over palm and pine–
Lord God of Hosts, be with us yet,

Lest we forget–lest we forget!
                —Rudyard Kipling,
                    "Recessional"

Good Lord, deliver us.
                —Anon., Cornish prayer

Norman Mailer, *The Armies of the Night* (1968)
And we are here as on a darkling plain
Swept with confused alarms of struggle and flight,
Where ignorant armies clash by night.
                —Matthew Arnold, "Dover Beach"

Arthur Miller, *Situation Normal* (1944)
SNAFU (Situation Normal All Fucked Up)
                —World War II army saying

Mary McCarthy, *Cast a Cold Eye* (1950)
On limestone quarried near the spot
By his command these words are cut:
    Cast a cold eye
    On life, on death.
    Horseman, pass by!
                —William Butler Yeats,
                    "Under Ben Bulben"

Margaret Mitchell, *Gone With the Wind* (1936)
I have forgot much, Cynara! gone with the wind,
Flung roses, roses riotously with the throng,
Dancing, to put thy pale, lost lilies out of mind;
                —Ernest Dowson, "Cynara"

Carson McCullers, *The Heart Is a Lonely Hunter* (1940)
My heart is a lonely hunter that hunts on a lonely hill.
                —Fiona Macleod (William Sharp),
                    "The Lonely Hunter"

Joyce Carol Oates, *With Shuddering Fall* (1964)
Into the breast that gives the rose
Shall I with shuddering fall.
                —George Meredith, "The Spirit of the Earth in Autumn"

Larry McMurtry, *Horseman, Pass By* (1961)
(See Mary McCarthy, *Cast a Cold Eye*)

Flannery O'Connor, *A Good Man Is Hard to Find* (1955)
A good man is hard to find,
You always get the other kind.
                —Eddie Green, "A Good Man Is Hard to Find" (popular song)

Larry McMurtry, *Leaving Cheyenne* (1963)
"My foot in the stirrup, my pony won't stand,
Good-bye, Old Paint, I'm a-leavin' Cheyenne."
                —Anon., "Good-bye Old Paint" (cowboy song)

Flannery O'Connor, *The Violent Bear It Away* (1960)
And from the days of John the Baptist until now, the kingdom of heaven suffereth violence, and the violent bear it away.
                —Matthew 11:12 (Douay Bible)

Terrence McNally, *And Things That Go Bump in the Night* (1966)
From ghoulies and ghosties and long-leggety beasties
And things that go bump in the night,

Clifford Odets, *Awake and Sing!* (1939)
Awake and sing.
                —Isaiah 26:19

Clifford Odets, *Clash by Night* (1942)
(See Norman Mailer, *The Armies of the Night*)

John O'Hara, *Appointment in Samarra* (1934)
I [Death] was astonished to see him in Baghdad, for I had an appointment with him tonight in Samarra.
    —W. Somerset Maugham,
     Sheppy, Act III

John O'Hara, *The Horse Knows the Way* (1964)
Over the river, and through the wood,
To grandfather's house we go;
 The horse knows the way
 To carry the sleigh,
Through the white and drifted snow.
   —Lydia Maria Child, "Thanks-
    giving Day"

John O'Hara, *A Rage to Live* (1949)
Wise wretch! with Pleasures too
 refin'd to please;
With too much spirit to be e'er at
 ease;
With too much Quickness ever to
 be taught;
With too much thinking to have a
 common Thought:
You purchase Pain with all that
 Joy can give,
And die of nothing but a Rage to
 live.
    —Alexander Pope, "Epistle
     to a Lady"

O. Henry (William Sydney Porter), *Cabbages and Kings* (1904)
"The time has come," the Walrus said,
"To talk of many things:
Of shoes–and ships–and sealing wax–
Of cabbages–and kings–
And why the sea is boiling hot–
And whether pigs have wings."
    —Lewis Carroll (Charles
     Lutwidge Dodgson), "The
     Walrus and the Carpenter"

Eugene O'Neill, *Ah, Wilderness!* (1933)
A Book of Verses underneath the
 Bough,
A Jug of Wine, a Loaf of Bread–and
 thou
Beside me singing in the Wilderness–
Oh, Wilderness were Paradise enou!
    —Edward FitzGerald,
     Rubáiyát of Omar Khayyám

Dorothy Parker, *Enough Rope* (1926)
Give a man enough rope and he'll hang himself.
      —Proverb

Go hang yourselves [critics] . . . you shall never want rope enough.
   —Francois Rabelais, "Author's
    Prologue," Book V, *Gargantua*
    and Pantagruel

S. J. Perelman, *Listen to the Mocking Bird* (1949)
Listen to the mockingbird, listen the
 mockingbird,
Still singing where the weeping willows
 wave.
    —Septimus Winner (Alice
     Hawthorne), "Listen to
     the Mockingbird"

Lee Pennington, *I Knew a Woman* (1977)
I knew a woman, lovely in her bones,
When small birds sighed, she would
 sigh back at them;
Ah, when she moved, she moved more
 ways than one:
The shapes a bright container can
 contain!
    —Theodore Roethke,
     "I Knew a Woman"

Katherine Anne Porter, *Pale Horse, Pale Rider: Three Short Novels* (1939)
And I looked, and behold a pale

horse: and his name that sat on him was Death, and Hell followed with him. And power was given unto them over the fourth part of the earth, to kill with sword, and with hunger, and with death, and with the beasts of the earth.

—Revelation 6:8

Marjorie Kinnan Rawlings, *Golden Apples* (1935)

(See Ray Bradbury, *The Golden Apples of the Sun*)

John Rechy, *City of Night* (1963)
The City is of Night; perchance of
   Death,
But certainly of Night.

—James Thomson, "The City of Dreadful Night"

O. E. Rölvaag, *Giants in the Earth* (1931)
There were giants in the earth in those days ... mighty men which were of old, men of renown.

—Genesis 6:4

Philip Roth, *When She Was Good* (1967)
There was a little girl
Who had a little curl
Right in the middle of her forehead;
And when she was good
She was very, very good,
But when she was bad she was horrid!

—Henry Wadsworth Longfellow, "There Was a Little Girl"

J. D. Salinger, *The Catcher in the Rye* (1951)
Gin a body meet a body
   Coming through the rye;
Gin a body kiss a body,
   Need a body cry?

—Anonymous Scottish ballad altered by Robert Burns, "Coming Through the Rye"

William Saroyan, *The Daring Young Man on the Flying Trapeze and Other Stories* (1934)
He flies through the air with the greatest of ease,
This daring young man on the flying trapeze;
His figure is handsome, all girls he can please,
And my love he purloined her away!

—George Leybourne, "The Man on the Flying Trapeze" (popular song)

William Saroyan, *My Heart's in the Highlands* (1939)
My heart's in the Highlands, my
   heart is not here,
My heart's in the Highlands
   a-chasing the deer;
A-chasing the wild deer, and following the roe,
My heart's in the Highlands wher
   ever I go.

—Robert Burns, "My Heart's in the Highlands"

Irwin Shaw, *Rich Man, Poor Man* (1970) and *Beggarman, Thief* (1977)
Tinker,
Tailor,
Soldier,
Sailor,
Rich man,
Poor man,
Beggarman,
Thief.

—Anon., "Rich Man, Poor Man" (nursery rhyme)

Irwin Shaw, *The Young Lions* (1948)
And say, what is thy mother? A lioness: she lay down among lions, she nourished her whelps among young lions.

—Ezekiel 19:2

The young lions roar after their prey, and seek their meat from God.

—Psalms 104:21

William Saroyan and his daughter, Lucy, 1955 (courtesy of the William Saroyan Collection, Clifton Waller Barrett Library, University of Virginia Library)

Robert Sherwood, *There Shall Be No Night* (1940)
There shall be no night there.
—Revelation 22:5

Max Shulman, *Barefoot Boy With Cheek* (1943)
Blessings on thee, little man,
Barefoot boy, with cheek of tan!
—John Greenleaf Whittier,
"The Barefoot Boy"

Max Shulman, *Rally Round the Flag, Boys!* (1957)
Yes, we'll rally round the flag, boys,
we'll rally once again,
Shouting the battle cry of Freedom.
—George Frederick Root,
"The Battle Cry of Freedom"

Neil Simon, *Come Blow Your Horn* (1961)

Little boy blue, come blow your horn,
The sheep's in the meadow, the cow's in
the corn;
But where is the boy who looks after
the sheep?
He's under the haystack fast asleep.
Will you wake him? No, not I,
For if I do, he'll be sure to cry.
—Anon., "Little Boy Blue"
(nursery rhyme)

Eileen Simpson, *Poets in their Youth: A Memoir* (1982)
We poets in our youth begin in
gladness;
But thereof comes in the end
despondency and madness.
—William Wordsworth, "Resolution and Independence"

Upton Sinclair, *One Clear Call* (1948)
Sunset and evening star,
And one clear call for me!
And may there be no moaning of the
bar,
When I put out to sea.
—Alfred Lord Tennyson,
"Crossing the Bar"

Upton Sinclair, *Wide Is the Gate* (1944)
Enter ye in at the strait gate: for wide
is the gate, and broad is the way, that
leadeth to destruction; and many there
be which go in thereat:
Because strait is the gate, and narrow
is the way, which leadeth unto life, and
few there be that find it.
—Matthew 7:13-14

C. W. Smith, *Thin Men of Haddam* (1973)
O thin men of Haddam
Why do you imagine golden birds?
Do you not see how the blackbird
Walks around the feet
Of the women about you?
—Wallace Stevens, "Thirteen Ways
of Looking at a Blackbird"

Wallace Stegner, *Fire and Ice* (1941)
Some say the world will end in fire,
Some say in ice.
>   –Robert Frost, "Fire and Ice"

And fire and ice within me fight
Beneath the suffocating night.
>   –A. E. Housman, *A Shropshire
>   Lad,* no. 30

Into the eternal darkness, into fire and
  into ice.
>   –Dante, *The Inferno,* III

Wallace Stegner, *On a Darkling Plain*
(1940)

(See Norman Mailer, *The Armies of the
Night*)

John Steinbeck, *East of Eden* (1952)
So he drove out the man; and he
placed at the east of the garden of Eden
Cherubims, and a flaming sword which
he turned every way, to keep the way of
the tree of life.
>   –Genesis 3:24

John Steinbeck, *The Grapes of Wrath*
(1939)
Mine eyes have seen the glory of the
  coming of the Lord;
He is trampling out the vintage where
  the grapes of wrath are stored.
>   –Julia Ward Howe,
>   "Battle Hymn of the Republic"

John Steinbeck, *In Dubious Battle*
(1936)
His utmost power with adverse power
  opposed
In dubious battle on the plains of
  Heaven,
And shook his throne.
>   –John Milton, *Paradise Lost*

John Steinbeck, *Of Mice and Men*
(1937)
The best-laid schemes o' mice an' men
  Gang aft a-gley,

An' lea'e us nought but grief an' pain,
  For promised joy.
>   –Robert Burns, "To a Mouse"

John Steinbeck, *The Winter of Our Dis-
content* (1961)
Now is the winter of our discontent
Made glorious summer by this sun of
  York.
>   –Shakespeare, *Richard III,* I, i

John Kennedy Toole, *A Confederacy of
Dunces* (1980)
When a true genius appears in the
world, you may know him by this sign,
that the dunces are all in confederacy
against him.
>   –Jonathan Swift, "Thoughts
>   on Various Subjects, Moral
>   and Diverting"

Robert Penn Warren, *All the King's
Men* (1946)
Humpty Dumpty sat on a wall,
Humpty Dumpty had a great fall;
All the king's horses
And all the king's men
Couldn't put Humpty Dumpty together
  again.
>   –Anon., "Humpty Dumpty"
>   (nursery rhyme)

Robert Penn Warren, *At Heaven's Gate*
(1943)
Hark! hark! the lark at heaven's gate
  sings.
>   –Shakespeare, *Cymbeline,* II, iii

Robert Penn Warren, *Band of Angels*
(1956)
I looked over Jordan, and what did I
  see?
Coming for to carry me home.
A band of angels coming after me,
Coming for to carry me home.
>   –Anon., "Swing Low, Sweet
>   Chariot" (spiritual)

Robert Penn Warren, *World Enough and Time* (1950)
Had we but world enough and time,
This coyness, lady, were no crime.
   —Andrew Marvell, "To His
    Coy Mistress"

Eudora Welty, *The Golden Apples* (1949)
(See Ray Bradbury, *The Golden Apples of the Sun*)

Edith Wharton, *The Fruit of the Tree* (1907)
Of Man's first disobedience, and the fruit
Of that forbidden tree whose mortal taste
Brought death into the world, and all our woe,
With loss of Eden.
   —John Milton, *Paradise Lost*

Edith Wharton, *The Glimpses of the Moon* (1922)
   What may this mean,
That thou, dead corse, again in complete steel
Revisit'st thus the glimpses of the moon,
Making night hideous; and we fools of nature
So horridly to shake our disposition
With thoughts beyond the reaches of our souls?
   —Shakespeare, *Hamlet*, I, iv

Edith Wharton, *The Gods Arrive* (1932)
   Heartily know,
   When half-gods go,
   The gods arrive.
   —Ralph Waldo Emerson,
    "Give All to Love"

E. B. White, *One Man's Meat* (1942)
One man's meat is another man's poison.
   —English proverb

What's one man's poison, signor,
Is another's meat or drink.
   —Beaumont and Fletcher,
    Love's Cure, II, ii

William Allen White, *The Old Order Changeth* (1910)
And slowly answered Arthur from the barge:
The old order changeth, yielding place to new;
And God fulfills himself in many ways,
Lest one good custom should corrupt the world.
   —Alfred Tennyson,
    "The Passing of Arthur"

Thornton Wilder, *The Ides of March* (1948)
The Ides of March have come.
   —Julius Caesar, *Caesar*, Section 63

Beware the Ides of March.
   —Shakespeare, *Julius Caesar*, I, ii

Thornton Wilder, *The Skin of Our Teeth* (1942)
. . . I am escaped with the skin of my teeth.
   —Job 19:20

John E. Williams, *Nothing But the Night* (1948)
In all the endless road you tread
There's nothing but the night.
   —A. E. Housman, *A Shropshire Lad,* no. 60

Lanford Wilson, *Balm in Gilead and Other Plays* (1965)
Is there no balm in Gilead; is there no physician there?
   —Jeremiah 8:22

Thomas Wolfe, *Look Homeward, Angel* (1929)

Look homeward angel now, and melt
  with ruth:
And, O ye dolphins, waft the hapless
  youth.

          –John Milton, "Lycidas"

Philip Wylie, *Generation of Vipers* (1942)

. . . O generation of vipers, who hath warned you to flee from the wrath to come?

          –Matthew 3:7

Philip Wylie, *Night unto Night* (1944)

The heavens declare the glory of God; and the firmament sheweth his handiwork.

Day unto day uttereth speech, and night unto night sheweth knowledge.

          –Psalms 19:1-2

Richard Yates, *A Special Providence* (1969)

Not a whit, we defy augury; there's a special providence in the fall of a sparrow.

          –Shakespeare, *Hamlet*, V, ii

Richard Yates, *Young Hearts Crying* (1984)

I heard their young hearts crying
Loveward above the glancing oar
And heard the prairie grasses sighing:
No more, return no more!

          –James Joyce, "Watching the
           Needleboats at San Sabba"

Stark Young, *So Red the Rose* (1934)

I sometimes think that never blows
  so red
The Rose as where some buried
  Caesar bled;

          –Edmund Fitzgerald,
           Rubáiyát of Omar Khayyam

"Without Whom . . . " :
Book Dedications

by MORRIS P. COLDEN

Many book dedications are formulaic. Thus: "To my wife [mother] without whose love and encouragement this book would never have been written." But there are certain dedication pages that reveal bits of literary history. Of particular interest are the dedications to other authors or literary associates. Perhaps the most famous pairing of American authors appears in the dedication of *Moby-Dick* (1851): "In token of my admiration for his genius, *This book is inscribed to NATHANIEL HAWTHORNE.*" Hawthorne did not reciprocate by dedicating a volume to Herman Melville. However, Hawthorne was capable of strong feelings of loyalty and gratitude, as evidenced by the dedication of *Our Old Home:* "To FRANKLIN PIERCE, *AS A SLIGHT MEMORIAL OF A COLLEGE FRIENDSHIP, PROLONGED THROUGH MANHOOD, AND RETAINING ALL ITS VITALITY IN OUR AUTUMNAL YEARS, This Volume is Inscribed By* Nathaniel Hawthorne." Hawthorne had written the campaign biography for the fourteenth president, and Pierce had rewarded him with the remunerative consulship at Liverpool. When *Our Old Home* was published in 1863 Pierce was in disrepute for his support of slavery; Hawthorne was warned that a dedication to Pierce would cost him readers and even cast doubt on his own commitment to the Union. Hawthorne was undeterred and compounded the crisis by inserting a preface addressed to Pierce, declaring, "For other men there may be a choice of paths—for you, but one; and it rests among my certainties that no man's loy-

alty is more steadfast, no man's hopes or apprehensions on behalf of our national existence more deeply heartfelt, or more closely intertwined with his possibilities of personal happiness, than those of *FRANKLIN PIERCE.*" The warnings were accurate: Hawthorne was denounced for loyalty to his friend.

College friendships are frequently celebrated in dedications. Booth Tarkington dedicated *Cherry* (1903) to his entire Princeton class: "To the diligent and industrious members of the class of 1893 at Nassau Hall; also to the idler spirits who wasted the Golden Hours of Youth in profitless playing of toss-the-ball; and even to those more dissolute ones who risked the tutor's detection at pitch-the-penny and carved their names on Adam's table,—in brief, to all of that happy class is dedicated this heroic tale of the days when Commencement came in September."

As would be expected, several of Mark Twain's dedications employ the exaggeration that characterizes his humor. In *Following the Equator* (1897): "This book is affectionately inscribed to my young friend Harry Rogers, with recognition of what he is, and apprehension of what he may become unless he forms himself a little more closely upon the model of The Author."

William Faulkner used the dedication of *Sartoris* (1929) to acknowledge a debt to an older author who had aided him during his apprenticeship: "To SHERWOOD ANDERSON *through whose kindness I was first published, with the belief that this book will give him no reason to regret*

Franklin Pierce, the friend to whom Nathaniel Hawthorne dedicated *Our Old Home* (courtesy of the New Hampshire Historical Society)

that fact." Faulkner's most eloquent dedication was to his family servant in *Go Down, Moses* (1942): "To MAMMY CAROLINE BARR Mississippi (1840-1940) who was born in slavery and who gave to my family a fidelity without stint or calculation of recompense and to my childhood an immeasurable devotion and love." Mammy Caroline has been identified as the inspiration for Dilsey in *The Sound and the Fury* (1929).

Eugene O'Neill dedicated his only comedy, *Ah, Wilderness!* (1933) to a critic: "To GEORGE JEAN NATHAN *who also, once upon a time, in peg-top trousers went the pace that kills along the road to ruin."*

James Branch Cabell usually wrote acrostic dedications for his books. *Jurgen* (1919) was dedicated to critic Burton Rascoe:

BEFORE each taradiddle,
Uncowed by sciolists,
Robuster persons twiddle

Tremendously big fists.

"Our gods are good," they tell us;
"Nor will our gods defer
Remission of rude fellows'
Ability to err."

So this, your JURGEN, travels
Content to compromise
Ordainments none unravels
Explicitly . . . and sighs.

The dedication page of E. E. Cummings's *No Thanks* (1935) lists the fourteen publishing houses that had rejected the book. Other authors have celebrated happier publishing experiences, as in J. D. Salinger's *Franny and Zooey* (1961): "As nearly as possible in the spirit of Matthew Salinger, age one, urging a luncheon companion to accept a cool lima bean, I urge my editor, mentor, and (heaven help him) closest friend, William Shawn, *genius domus* of *The New Yorker,* lover of the long shot, protector of the unprolific, defender of the hopelessly flamboyant, most unreasonably modest of born great artist-editors, to accept this pretty skimpy-looking book."

John O'Hara wrote more books than most major authors and therefore had more opportunities to dedicate them. The literary dedicatees of his volumes included Franklin P. Adams, Philip Barry, Robert Benchley ("The Best of Company"), *New Yorker* editors Wolcott Gibbs and William Maxwell, and Random House editor Albert Erskine. Ross Macdonald, another productive novelist, dedicated books to publisher Alfred A. Knopf, agents Ivan von Auw and Dorothy Olding, and writers Anthony Boucher, William Campbell Gault, and Eudora Welty.

Kurt Vonnegut recalled an old friendship in the dedication of *Jailbird* (1979): "For Benjamin D. Hitz, close friend of my youth, Best man at my wedding. Ben, you used to tell me about Wonderful books you had just read, and then I would imagine that I had read them too. You read nothing but the best, Ben, while I studied chemistry. Long time no see."

The dying James Jones, struggling to complete his trilogy, left a dedication for the posthumously published *Whistle* (1978): "This book is dedicated to every man who served in the US Armed Forces in World War II—whether he survived or not; whether he made a fortune serving or not; whether he fought or not; whether he did time or not; whether he went crazy or didn't."

The dedication of Robert Coover's *Gerald's Party* (1986) records a dream encounter with a fellow writer: "For John Hawkes, who, standing beside me in a dream one night long ago, long before we'd become friends, and remarking upon another author's romanticization of autumn, (there seemed to be hun-

dreds of them, actually, stooped-over, on the endless tree-lined streets before us), observed wistfully: 'It's so true, people still do that, you know, count the dead leaves. Ten, nine, eight, seven, six, five, three, four . . . .'"

Nelson Algren regarded dedications as fluid. He changed the dedicatees of *Chicago: City on the Make* from Carl Sandburg (1950) to Herman and Marilou Kogan (1961) to Joan Baez (1968); when the book was posthumously published in 1983 it was re-dedicated to Algren. *Never Come Morning* was originally dedicated to Algren's sister Bernice in 1942, then to Jean-Paul Sartre in 1958, and finally to agent Candida Donadio in 1963. *The Neon Wilderness* was originally published in 1947 with a dedication to his parents; in 1962 he re-dedicated it to Ruth Reinhardt.

A linking of great names in a masterpiece is T. S. Eliot's acknowledgment of another poet's editorial assistance with *The Waste Land* (1925): "For Ezra Pound *il miglior fabbro*" [the better craftsman].

Reciprocal dedications may indicate something more than a working relationship. In 1933 Dashiell Hammett suggested that his new girlfriend Lillian Hellman try her hand at dramatizing a true-crime story by William Roughead called "Closed Doors; or the Great Drumsheugh Case" about a girls' school in Edinburgh, Scotland, that was forced to close because the owners were rumored to be lesbians. She wrote *The Children's Hour,* her first play. It ran 691 performances on Broadway, earning the new playwright over $125,000. When *The Children's Hour* was published in 1934 by Knopf, it was dedicated "for Dashiell Hammett with thanks." That same year, Knopf also published Hammett's *The Thin Man,* featuring Nora Charles, modeled on Hellman. It was dedicated "To Lillian."

LITERARY FRIENDSHIPS: HAWTHORNE AND MELVILLE

After his copies of *Moby-Dick* (1851) ar-

Herman Melville, portrait by Asa W. Twitchell, circa 1847 (courtesy of the Berkshire Atheneum)

most recently, *The Scarlet Letter* (1850). About fifteen years Hawthorne's junior but with five novels already in print and his sixth–*Moby-Dick*–in progress that summer, Melville seemed at the moment to be rapidly ascending as a literary figure in terms of both popular appeal and critical reception–a position that changed drastically within the next few years. The duration of their close friendship extended roughly from the date of their first meeting to that of Hawthorne's move from Lenox, Massachusetts, to West Newton in November 1851, within a few weeks of his reading and praising *Moby-Dick*.

MELVILLE CONFIDES HIS DESPAIR
TO HAWTHORNE

I shall at last be worn out and perish . . . . What I feel most moved to write, that is banned,–it will not pay. Yet, altogether, write the other *way, I cannot.*
–Letter to Nathaniel
Hawthorne, June 1851

---

rived from the publisher, Herman Melville sent one to the man whose name appears on the dedication page, "In token of my admiration for his genius." When Nathaniel Hawthorne responded with an "exultation-breeding letter" of praise for his white whale, Melville immediately and gratefully replied: "Whence come you, Hawthorne? By what right do you drink from my flagon of life? And when I put it to my lips–lo, they are yours and not mine. I feel that the Godhead is broken up like the bread at the Supper, and that we are the pieces. Hence the infinite fraternity of feeling." Although Hawthorne's letter has not survived, Melville's exultant reply reveals the nature of its perceptive appreciation. In November 1851, when this exchange of letters occurred, the two men had known each other for only little more than a year.

They had met in the summer of 1850 when both were living in the Berkshires. By then Hawthorne had established a substantial reputation with the publication of several volumes of stories and

Their friendship began on 5 August 1850. In the company of Oliver Wendell Holmes, the Brahmin gentleman of letters; James T. Fields, Hawthorne's publisher; Evert Duyckinck, critic and editor of the New York *Literary World;* and others, Hawthorne and Melville made an excursion to Monument Mountain. The genial conversation that began then continued later, when they returned to the home of a friend in Stockbridge for a festive and "well-moistened" afternoon dinner. Featured in a discussion at the table were Holmes, who supported the notion of British cultural superiority, and Melville, who vigorously defended the Americans; Hawthorne characteristically listened and watched. Later in the afternoon the men in the party went on another excursion. By the end of August, Hawthorne and Melville had met on several occasions and visited each other.

Prior to the summer of 1850 Melville

had read at least some of Hawthorne's stories—and made occasional references to them in his own narratives. But it was not until mid July of that year, about two weeks before they met, when his aunt gave him a copy of Hawthorne's *Mosses from an Old Manse* (1846), that he drew from them the inspiration that nourished the friendship soon to follow and probably led to changes in the composition of *Moby-Dick*. Melville was so impressed with *Mosses from an Old Manse* that he wrote a penetrating, deeply personal "review," which Duyckinck published in the 17 and 24 August issues of the *Literary World*, just after the two authors met.

Entitled "Hawthorne and His *Mosses*," Melville's essay, written in the persona of "A Virginian Spending July in Vermont," conveys a clear sense of the dark themes that pervade Hawthorne's tales while not overlooking the subtle humor they contain:

> For spite of all the Indian-summer sunlight on the hither side of Hawthorne's soul, the other side—like the dark half of the physical sphere—is shrouded in a blackness, ten times black. But this darkness but gives more effect to the ever-moving dawn, that forever advances through it, and circumnavigates his world. Whether Hawthorne has simply availed himself of this mystical blackness as a means to the wondrous effects he makes it to produce in his lights and shades; or whether there really lurks in him, perhaps unknown to himself, a touch of Puritanic gloom,—this, I cannot altogether tell. Certain it is, however, that this great power of blackness in him derives its force from its appeals to that Calvinistic sense of Innate Depravity and Original Sin, from whose visitations, in some shape or other, no deeply thinking mind is always and wholly free.

Called the most adulatory review that one major American author has given another, Melville's essay employs language that has sexual connotations:

> To what infinite height of loving wonder and admiration I may yet be borne, when by repeatedly banqueting on these *Mosses* I shall have thoroughly incorporated their whole stuff into my being— that, I cannot tell. But already I feel that this Hawthorne has dropped germinous seeds into my soul. He expands and deepens down, the more I contemplate him; and further and further, shoots his strong New-England roots into the hot soil of my Southern soul.

Hawthorne's side of their friendship decidedly cooled following his move from Lenox. Several more letters were exchanged, and Melville visited Hawthorne in Concord. The distance that had come between them disturbed Melville greatly, but Hawthorne—often described as withdrawn and wraithlike—preferred to maintain it. Nevertheless, he never lost his respect for Melville as a profound, albeit melancholy, associate on an insatiable quest for faith. In late 1856, when Hawthorne was serving as American Consul in Liverpool, Melville stopped to visit him on his way to the Near East. Hawthorne wrote in his notebook that Melville "can neither believe, nor be comfortable in his unbelief; and he is too honest and courageous not to try to do one or the other. If he were a religious man, he would be one of the most truly religious and reverential; he has a very high and noble nature, and better worth immortality than most of us." The two men saw each other only once more after that visit—briefly and inconsequentially— when Melville stopped again in Liverpool and entered in his journal for 4 May 1857: "Saw Hawthorne." No reference to that meeting appears in

Hawthorne's notebook. But the feeling of intimacy endured in Melville, and when Hawthorne died in 1864, Melville's grief surfaced in his poem "Monody," which begins:

To have known him, to have loved
  him
    After loneness long;
And then to be estranged in life,
    And neither in the wrong;
And now for death to set his seal–
    Ease me, a little ease, my song!

–S. E. M.

Writing Close to Life: Romans à Clef

by MORRIS P. COLDEN

The *roman à clef* (novel with a key) is a work of fiction based on actual people, settings, or events. In most cases the material is disguised, but in others the sources are intentionally evident. The term requires qualification because all good fiction is drawn from reality. So is much bad fiction. What else do writers have to work with? They apply invention to observation and experience.

When Terry Southern praised Faulkner's "original characters" and deprecated Cozzens's "copied" characters, Cozzens noted: "Look, Stupid. It's a copy, all right. That's the whole point of writing fiction for grown-up readers. The copy is from life.... The whole point about created 'original' characters is that no one ever saw them. They're by definition strictly on paper, and the intelligent reader (as opposed to literary intellectuals making a cult of the abstract impressionistic) sees there's no reason to waste his reading time that way."

A roman à clef, then, is a work of fiction in which the dependence on the "real-life" sources goes beyond some invisible line of demarcation or in which the sources are so well known as to be generally recognizable. Indeed, such works often depend on reader recognition of the sources for their effect. That is, informed readers are supposed to penetrate the disguises. Many romans à clef can be read as the writer's revenge.

The most celebrated roman à clef in American literature is Ernest Hemingway's *The Sun Also Rises* (1926), based on an excursion to the fiesta of San Fermín at Pamplona, with a cast of identifiable characters:

Lady Duff Twysden, the model for Lady Brett Ashley in Ernest Hemingway's *The Sun Also Rises*

Robert Cohn–Harold Loeb
Lady Brett Ashley–Duff Twysden
Bill Gorton–Donald Ogden Stewart
Mike Campbell–Pat Guthrie
Braddocks–Ford Madox Ford
Pedro Romero–Niño de la Palma
Harvey Stone–Harold Stearns

After the novel was published, the wisecrack went around Paris that it should have been titled "Six Characters in Search of an Author–With A Gun Apiece."

Thomas Wolfe's fiction has been described as an extended roman à clef.

The Gant family in Altamont, Old Catawba, openly corresponds to the Wolfe family in Asheville, North Carolina. It was claimed that even the street addresses in the novel were unchanged.

Many writers have employed their hometowns as fictional settings; Sherwood Anderson's 1919 book, *Winesburg, Ohio* (Clyde, Ohio), is a prominent example. More interesting are the writers who have written cycles of novels about their native soil. William Faulkner's Jefferson in Yoknapatawpha County is Oxford, Lafayette County, Mississippi. John O'Hara's Gibbsville in Lantanengo County is Pottsville, Schuylkill County, Pennsylvania. These extended treatments are not so much romans à clef as attempts to create a fictional record of a way of life, to re-create a society. Faulkner described himself as "sole owner and proprietor" of Yoknapatawpha. O'Hara referred to Lantanengo as "my Pennsylvania protectorate."

Crimes provide a ready source for fiction. Poe's "The Mystery of Marie Roget" was based on the murder of Mary Rogers in New York. In Dreiser's *An American Tragedy* (1925) Clyde Griffiths was drawn from convicted murderer Chester Gillette. (Their initials are the same.) Dreiser also drew upon speculator Charles T. Yerkes for Frank A. Cowperwood in the trilogy consisting of *The Financier* (1912), *The Titan* (1914), and *The Stoic* (1947). O'Hara's *Butterfield 8* (1935) uses the unsolved murder of New York playgirl Starr Faithfull (her real name) as the basis for the death of his character Gloria Wandrous.

The most written-about criminal trial in American literature is the Sacco and Vanzetti case, in which two anarchists were executed in 1927 for a Massachusetts payroll robbery and murder. It inspired political writings, novels, drama, and verse—in which the men were thinly disguised or openly identified. Among the writers who responded to Sacco and Vanzetti were Upton Sinclair (*Boston* [1928]), Maxwell Anderson (*Winterset* [1935] and *Gods of the Lightning* [1928]), John Dos Passos (*U.S.A.* [1930-1936] and *Facing the Chair* [1927]), Edna St. Vincent Millay ("Justice Denied in Massachusetts" [1928]), James Thurber and Elliott Nugent (*The Male Animal* [1940]), Bernard DeVoto (*We Accept with Pleasure* [1934]), Ruth McKenney (*Jake Home* [1943]), Howard Fast (*The Passion of Sacco and Vanzetti* [1953]), and Katherine Anne Porter (*The Never-Ending Wrong* [1977]).

A contemporary by-blow of the roman à clef is the "non-fiction novel" in which undisguised material is handled with the techniques of fiction. Two huge best-sellers in this genre were Truman Capote's *In Cold Blood* (1965) and Norman Mailer's *The Executioner's Song* (1979) —both of which re-create murder cases and follow the criminals to their executions.

Authors have frequently been the subjects for other writers' romans à clef. Nathaniel Hawthorne's experiences at the Brook Farm community provided material for *The Blithedale Romance* (1852), in which Margaret Fuller is Zenobia and Hawthorne is Miles Coverdale. F. Scott Fitzgerald appears as Hunt Conroy in Wolfe's *You Can't Go Home Again* (1940) and as Manley Holliday in Budd Schulberg's *The Disenchanted* (1950), and Scott and Zelda Fitzgerald became David and Rilda Westlake in Carl Van Vechten's *Parties* (1930). Hemingway provided the model for Philippe in Fitzgerald's "Count of Darkness" stories, for Ahearn in Irwin Shaw's *The Young Lions* (1948), and for George Elbert Warner in Dos Passos's *Chosen Country* (1951) and *Century's Ebb* (1975). John Dos Passos was the partial model for Richard Gordon in Hemingway's *To Have and Have Not* (1937). As noted in the following catalogue, Jack Kerouac's characters provide a who's who of the Beat movement.

A Catalogue of Literary Clefs

Franklin Pierce Adams
Rutherford Hayes Adler, in Edna Ferber's *The Girls* (1921)

Nelson Algren
Lewis Brogan, in Simone de Beauvoir's *The Mandarins* (1954)

I've been in whorehouses all over the world and the women there always close the door, whether it's in Korea or India. But this woman flung open the door and called in the public and the press.
—Nelson Algren on The Mandarins

John Peale Bishop
Thomas Parke D'Invilliers, in F. Scott Fitzgerald's *This Side of Paradise* (1920)

Maxwell Bodenheim
Count Bruga, in Ben Hecht's *Count Bruga* (1926)

William S. and Joan Burroughs
Will and Mary Dennison, in Jack Kerouac's *The Town & the City* (1950)

William S. Burroughs
Wilson Holmes (Bull) Hubbard, in Jack Kerouac's *Vanity of Duluoz* (1968)

Neal Cassady
Cody Pomeroy, in Jack Kerouac's *The Dharma Bums* (1958), *Visions of Cody* (1972), *Book of Dreams* (1961), *Big Sur* (1962), and *Desolation Angels* (1965)
Dean Moriarity, in Kerouac's *On the Road* (1957)

Gregory Corso
Raphael Urso, in Jack Kerouac's *Book of Dreams* (1961) and *Desolation Angels* (1965)
Yuri Gligoric, in Kerouac's *The Dharma Bums* (1958)

Harry and Caresse Crosby
Anthony and Fontana Lister, in Kay Boyle's *My Next Bride* (1934)

Emily Dickinson
Alison Stanhope, in Susan Glaspell's *Alison's House* (1930)
Mercy Philbrick, in Helen Hunt Jackson's *Mercy Philbrick's Choice* (1876)

T. S. and Vivienne Eliot, the models for Jeremy Pratt Cibber and Adele Cibber in Richard Aldington's *Stepping Heavenward*

T. S. Eliot and Vivienne Eliot
Jeremy Pratt Cibber and Adele Cibber, in Richard Aldington's *Stepping Heavenward* (1931)

William Gaddis
Harold Sand, in Jack Kerouac's *The Subterraneans* (1958)

Allen Ginsberg

Carlo Marx, in Jack Kerouac's *On the Road* (1957)

Adam Moored, in Kerouac's *The Subterraneans* (1958)

Irwin Garden, in Kerouac's *Visions of Cody* (1972), *Book of Dreams* (1961), *Big Sur* (1962), *Desolation Angels* (1965), and *Vanity of Duluoz* (1968)

Leon Levinsky, in Kerouac's *The Town & the City* (1950)

Ben Hecht

Ben Helgrin, in Maxwell Bodenheim's *Ninth Avenue* (1926)

John Clellon Holmes

Balliol Mac Jones, in Jack Kerouac's *The Subterraneans* (1958)

James Watson, in Kerouac's *Book of Dreams* (1961)

Tom Wilson, in Kerouac's *Visions of Cody* (1972)

Randall Jarrell

Random Varnum, in Jack Kerouac's *Desolation Angels* (1965)

Philip Lamantia

Francis DaPavia, in Jack Kerouac's *The Dharma Bums* (1958)

Ring Lardner

Owl Eyes, in F. Scott Fitzgerald's *The Great Gatsby* (1925)

Abe North, in Fitzgerald's *Tender Is the Night* (1934)

Sinclair Lewis

Unnamed novelist, in Ernest Hemingway's *Across the River and Into the Trees* (1950)

Lloyd McHarg, in Thomas Wolfe's *You Can't Go Home Again* (1940)

Walter Lippmann

Felix Leitner, in Louis Auchincloss's *The House of the Prophet* (1980)

Horace Liveright

Jo Boshere, in Ben Hecht's *A Jew in Love* (1931)

Jack London

Gordon Blake, in Rose Wilder Lane's *He Was a Man* (1925)

Malcolm Lowry

Hamo, in Conrad Aiken's *A Heart for the Gods of Mexico* (1939) and *Ushant* (1952)

Norman Mailer

Harvey Marker, in Jack Kerouac's *Desolation Angels* (1965)

Michael McClure

Ike O'Shay, in Jack Kerouac's *The Dharma Bums* (1958)

Patrick McLear, in Kerouac's *Big Sur* (1962) and *Desolation Angels* (1965)

Edna St. Vincent Millay

Rita Cavanaugh, in Edmund Wilson's *I Thought of Daisy* (1929)

George Jean Nathan

Maury Noble, in F. Scott Fitzgerald's *The Beautiful and Damned* (1922)

Dorothy Parker

Julia Glenn, in George S. Kaufman and Moss Hart's *Merrily We Roll Along* (1934)

Maxwell Perkins

Foxhall Edwards, in Thomas Wolfe's *You Can't Go Home Again* (1940)

Ezra Pound

George Lowndes, in H. D.'s (Hilda Doolittle's) *HERmione* (1981)

Kenneth Rexroth

Reinhold Cocoethes, in Jack Kerouac's *The Dharma Bums* (1958)

Delmore Schwartz

Van Humboldt Fleisher, in Saul Bellow's *Humboldt's Gift* (1975)

Charles Scribner's Sons

James Rodney & Co., in Thomas Wolfe's *You Can't Go Home Again* (1940)

Chard Powers Smith

Hubert Elliot, in Ernest Hemingway's "Mr. and Mrs. Elliot" (1924)

Gary Snyder

Japhy Ryder, in Jack Kerouac's *The Dharma Bums* (1958)

Ernest Walsh

Martin Sheehan, in Kay Boyle's *Year Before Last* (1932)

Thomas Wolfe

Youngblood Hawke, in Herman Wouk's *Youngblood Hawke* (1962)

Alexander Woollcott

Sheridan Whiteside, in George S. Kaufman and Moss Hart's *The Man Who Came to Dinner* (1939)

Literary Cons: Hoaxes, Frauds, and Plagiarism in American Literature

by MORRIS P. COLDEN
and DAVID A. PLOTT

There is a long tradition of hoaxes and frauds in literature. Shakespeare has inspired a shelf of plays that pretend to be his work. The most celebrated faker in the annals of English literature was T. J. Wise who fabricated first editions of nineteenth-century English writers. The pamphlets he printed were the actual works of the writers, but they were not the earliest editions, as they claimed to be. Some of his productions are now worth more as fakes than they were when regarded as authentic.

There is a distinction between hoaxes and frauds. A hoax is usually intended as a joke on the credulous with the hoax to be revealed at some point. In a literary fraud there is an intention to get away with it and to profit in terms of money or reputation. False death reports have been a favorite subject for spoofs. Benjamin Franklin predicted the death of a rival almanac maker and then announced that the prediction had come true. Since the victim was in fact alive, the hoax was harmless, if macabre.

Franklin rewrote a story of Persian origin as a biblical parable and had it bound into his own Bible. He enjoyed reading it aloud to friends, pretending that it was from the Book of Genesis.

"The Sale of the Hessians" is generally attributed to Franklin. Originally published in French, it was part hoax and part political satire. Purportedly a letter from the Count de Schaumbergh to Baron Hohendorf, commander of the Hessian troops in America, it expresses indignation at the British use of German mercenaries in the Revolutionary War.

Edgar Allan Poe struggled to win attention in the competitive world of New York journalism. In 1844 he planted a spurious report in the *New York Sun* about a transatlantic balloon crossing from Wales to South Carolina in seventy-five hours. "The Great Balloon Hoax," as it was labeled, was soon exposed as a fiction. Poe's friend Richard Adams Locke announced in the *Sun* in 1835 the discovery of life on the moon. This "Moon Hoax" was widely believed; it anticipated Poe's story "The Unparalleled Adventures of One Hans Pfall" (1835), describing a balloon voyage to the moon. Later, in 1899, Poe was himself the subject of a hoax when Ambrose Bierce, Carroll Carrington, and Herman Scheffauer hatched the plan to publish Scheffauer's poem "The Sea of Serenity" as a lost Poe poem in the *San Francisco Examiner*. There was little public interest, however, and the hoax was a flop.

Some hoaxes have been so successful that the hoaxers had difficulty exposing them. In 1917 H. L. Mencken wrote an article in the *New York Evening Mail* celebrating the seventy-fifth anniversary of the introduction of the bathtub in America and providing a spurious history of its use. The material was accepted as accurate and entered the reference books. When Mencken revealed the hoax, it was too late. His imposture had become history.

FRANKLIN'S APOCRYPHA

1. And it came to pass after these Things, that Abraham sat in the Door of his Tent, about the going down of the Sun.

2. And behold a Man, bowed with Age, came from the Way of the Wilderness, leaning on a Staff.

3. And Abraham arose and met him, and said unto him, Turn in, I pray thee, and wash thy Feet, and tarry all Night, and thou shalt arise early on the Morrow, and go on thy Way.

4. And the Man said, Nay, for I will abide under this Tree.

5. But Abraham pressed him greatly; so he turned, and they went into the Tent; and Abraham baked unleavend Bread, and they did eat.

6. And when Abraham saw that the Man blessed not God, he said unto him, Wherefore dost thou not worship the most high God, Creator of Heaven and Earth?

7. And the Man answered and said, I do not worship the God thou speakest of; neither do I call upon his Name; for I have made to myself a God, which abideth alway in mine House, and provideth me with all Things.

8. And Abraham's Zeal was kindled against the Man; and he arose, and fell upon him, and drove him forth with Blows into the Wilderness.

9. And at Midnight God called unto Abraham, saying, Abraham, where is the Stranger?

10. And Abraham answered and said, Lord, he would not worship thee, neither would he call upon thy Name; therefore have I driven him out from before my Face into the Wilderness.

11. And God said, Have I born with him these hundred ninety and eight Years, and nourished him, and cloathed him, notwithstanding his Rebellion against me, and couldst not thou, that art thyself a Sinner, bear with him one Night?

12. And Abraham said, Let not the Anger of my Lord wax hot against his Servant. Lo, I have sinned; forgive me, I pray Thee:

13. And Abraham arose and went forth into the Wilderness, and sought diligently for the Man, and found him, and returned with him to his Tent; and when he had entreated him kindly, he sent him away on the Morrow with Gifts.

14. And God spake again unto Abraham, saying, For this thy Sin shall thy Seed be afflicted four Hundred Years in a strange Land:

15. But for thy Repentance will I deliver them; and they shall come forth with Power, and with Gladness of Heart, and with much Substance.

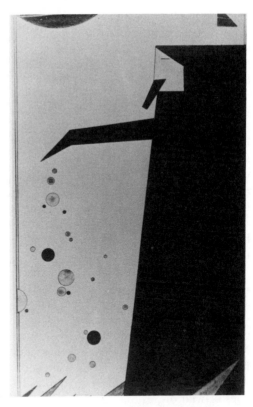

Arthur Davison Ficke's "portraits" of Spectrist poets Anne Knish (himself) and Emanuel Morgan (Witter Bynner) (courtesy of the Beinecke Rare Book and Manuscript Library, Yale University)

The line between hoax and fraud is not always clear. In 1969 writer Michael Grady assembled a team to write the ultimate sensational sex novel under the pseudonym Penelope Ashe. The project was intended as a form of protest against the randy best-sellers by Harold Robbins and Jacqueline Susann. The result was *Naked Came the Stranger,* which was energetically promoted and sold more than 100,000 copies in cloth. Even after the hoax was revealed, the novel continued to sell.

Publisher Mitchell Kennerley was involved in a famous hoax as well as a fraud. In 1916 poets Witter Bynner and Arthur Davison Ficke responded to the multiplying schools of modern poetry by creating "Spectrism" in which the two star poets were Anne Knish (Ficke) and Emanuel Morgan (Bynner). Their collected works were published as *Spec-*

tra by Kennerley. Bynner and Ficke reviewed their own book favorably, as did other respectable critics. When the spoof was admitted in 1918, critics retaliated by insisting that the *Spectra* poems were better than the serious verse by Ficke and Bynner.

In 1917 Kennerley published *Jap Herron: A Novel Written From the Ouija Board.* The "transcriber," Emily Grant Hutchings, claimed that the novel had been dictated to her by the spirit of Samuel Langhorne Clemens. *Jap Herron* is the story of an orphan boy who becomes a noble country newspaper publisher. It attracted little attention on publication and was withdrawn by Kennerley after Harper and Brothers, Mark Twain's publisher, sought an injunction to prevent sale of the novel.

The Reverend Samuel Andrew Peters fled to England during the American Revolution because his Tory sympathies had enraged his congregation in Hebron, Connecticut, and caused him considerable physical abuse. Gone, but not forgetting, Peters went on to write his *General History of Connecticut* (1781) during his stay in England. In it, Peters invented outright lies about his former homeland, describing laws which did not exist and giving detailed accounts of fictional events, such as a catastrophic invasion of caterpillars along the Connecticut River and an attack of giant bullfrogs in Windham. Peters deliberately confused fact with fiction so that his readers would swallow the whole thing as truth.

Maria Monk, author of *Awful Disclosures* (1855), was both a pathological liar and the perpetrator of one of nineteenth-century America's most notorious religious hoaxes. A sometime prostitute, Monk convinced a clergyman that she had been a novice at the Hôtel Dieu convent in Montreal. She invented fantastic tales of wild orgies that took place regularly and systematically at the nunnery. Her books were best-sellers, despite the evidence that they were entirely fraudulent. The works succeeded in fueling an anti-Catholicism that never needed help to bring it alive. She was eventually disgraced, jailed for pickpocketing, and died in prison.

In 1920 *The Story of Opal: The Story of an Understanding Heart*, purportedly the diary of Opal Whiteley between the ages of six and twenty-one, was published. The first reviews were laudatory but it was soon denounced as a fraud. There was no question that the book was Whiteley's work; nevertheless, it was revealed that the published volume was not her actual childhood diary but a later concoction. She also claimed that she was not really Opal Whiteley but the abandoned daughter of the French royal family. The book was rediscovered and republished in 1986 as *The Singing Creek Where the Willows Grow*.

Jerzy Kosinski is well known as a Polish-born author who writes in English (see Eccentric Writers). In a 1982

Cover for a late paperback reprint of Monk's so-called exposé

Village Voice article, "Jerzy Kosinski's Tainted Words," Geoffrey Stokes and Eliot Fremont-Smith charged that Kosinski hired people to rewrite or revise his work for him without credit. This article also alleged that Kosinski's best-known novel, *The Painted Bird* (1965), had been written in Polish and that he had attempted to hire a ghost translator. Moreover, it was suggested that the CIA had been involved in the publication and perhaps in the writing of Kosinski's first two nonfiction books, published under the pseudonym Joseph Novak. Kosinski denied all these allegations but declined to seek legal redress. His defenders have counterclaimed that Kosinski is the target of Communist libel, and that most of the charges against him originated in Poland.

Two of Lillian Hellman's nonfiction

books, *An Unfinished Woman* (1969) and *Pentimento* (1973), have been denounced as apocryphal. Martha Gellhorn—who was in Spain with Ernest Hemingway during the Spanish Civil War—insists that Hellman could not have been present at some of the Hemingway encounters described in the books and that Hellman lied about her self-glorifying activities during that war. Moreover, there are contradictions between *An Unfinished Woman* and *Pentimento*.

More damaging to Hellman's reputation are the revelations about the "Julia" material in *Pentimento*. According to Hellman, she was a close friend of Julia, an American medical student and member of the anti-Nazi underground movement in Vienna before the war. Hellman claims to have smuggled money to Julia, to have gone to London for her body after she was killed by the Nazis, and to have searched for Julia's child. Hellman declared in *Pentimento*, "I trust absolutely what I remember about Julia." In 1983 Dr. Muriel Gardiner published *Code Name: "Mary"* which revealed strong similarities between her own activities in prewar Vienna and those attributed to Julia. Dr. Gardiner was not killed by the Nazis. Though she did not know Hellman, who appropriated and fictionalized her life, she had once shared a house with Wolf Schwabacher, Hellman's lawyer. In " 'Julia' and other fictions by Lillian Hellman" (*Commentary*, June 1984), Samuel McCracken lists inconsistencies, improbabilities, and falsehoods in *Pentimento*, ranging from impossible dates and nonexistent trains to the absence of any record of Julia's death in London. Hellman declined to refute these charges, claiming that she was withholding proof of her veracity to protect Julia's family. Given the evidence, Martha Gellhorn's conclusion seems just: "In my specialized study of apocryphism, Miss Hellman ranks as sublime."

Plagiarism is a more serious matter than simple fraud because it involves the attempt to steal someone else's work. An early blatant case of American plagiarism involved *The Asylum; or, Alonzo and Melissa*, an 1811 Gothic novel by Isaac Mitchell; it was republished in the same year by Daniel Jackson as *Alonzo and Melissa; or, the Unfeeling Father*. In 1933 a young Englishman named Cecil Henderson copied Dashiell Hammett's *The Maltese Falcon* (1929) and submitted it to an English publisher with minor revisions. After the book was published as *Death in the Dark*, the plagiarism was immediately detected and it was withdrawn by publisher Lincoln Williams. Henderson explained that he had copied *The Maltese Falcon* for practice and had submitted it to a publisher "unthinkingly."

Prominent authors have been the targets of suits charging that their work was plagiarized from unpublished material that they had access to. Playwrights Sidney Howard (*They Knew What They Wanted*) and Eugene O'Neill (*Strange Interlude*), whose plays were produced by the Theatre Guild in 1924 and 1928 respectively, sustained their defenses against authors claiming to have submitted similar material to the Theatre Guild. In the O'Neill matter, the plaintiff, who wrote under the pen name Georges Lewys, charged that *Strange Interlude* was similar if not identical to her novel *The Temple of Pallas-Athena* (1924) in 450 words or idioms. The court held that an author cannot "claim a copyright on words in the dictionary, or usual English idioms, or on ideas."

In 1941 John Igual de Montijo filed suit claiming that Hemingway had plagiarized *For Whom the Bell Tolls* (1940) from his screenplay titled *Viva Madero*. Hemingway denied that he had been present at a 1939 gathering in Hollywood when Montijo read *Viva Madero* aloud. The suit was thrown out of court, but Hemingway was outraged by his $8,000 bill for legal fees.

Two James Joyce scholars, Joseph Campbell and Henry Morton Robinson, charged that Thornton Wilder plagiarized his play *The Skin of Our Teeth*

(1942) from *Finnegans Wake* (1939). Wilder did not respond, and the matter was forgotten—perhaps because it is so difficult to understand *Finnegans Wake*.

Theodore Dreiser and Dorothy Thompson visited Russia at the same time in 1927. Her book about the trip, *The New Russia* was published in September 1928; his *Dreiser Looks at Russia* appeared in November. Sinclair Lewis, Thompson's husband, was furious at the duplications of passages in the two books and charged that Dreiser had cribbed from Thompson's newspaper columns. (Similar accusations had been made against Dreiser's *An American Tragedy*, 1925.) Dreiser claimed that Thompson had cribbed her columns from her conversations with him and that they had both used the official handouts they had been given in Russia. Thompson's publisher Horace Liveright—who had been Dreiser's publisher—brought suit against Dreiser but dropped the case.

When Dreiser and Lewis were guests at a dinner in 1931 Lewis publicly denounced Dreiser as the "man who plagiarized 3,000 words from my wife's book." Dreiser retaliated by slapping Lewis's face twice.

Some plagiarism claims have been instigated by disgruntled writers against more successful authors who may have been careless in citing sources for research material. After publication of *The Big Money* (1936), John Dos Passos and his publisher were pestered by Frank B. Copley, who claimed the biographical sketch of Frederick W. Taylor in the novel was drawn from his *Frederick W. Taylor, Father of Scientific Management* (1923) without proper acknowledgment. Dos Passos considered this charge frivolous, and after an exchange of letters, Mr. Copley let the matter rest.

In 1978 John Gardner was accused in *Newsweek* and the *New York Times Book Review* of having plagiarized passages in *The Life and Times of Chaucer* (1977) from the work of other scholars. Gardner admitted to "borrowing passages,"

and to prevent further charges carefully acknowledged sources and influences in all his novels published after 1978.

Most plagiarism suits are dismissed or dropped. Strong cases are usually settled out of court. Three authors sued Alex Haley over his *Roots* (1976), which purported to be a nonfiction account of the author's family from the time of his great-great-great-great grandfather's enslavement. The claim by Margaret Walker Alexander that *Roots* infringed on the copyright of her novel *Jubilee* (1966) was rejected by a federal judge in 1978. That year Harold Courlander charged that substantial material in *Roots* had been taken from his 1967 novel *The African*. This suit was settled out of court; an undisclosed payment was made to Courlander and his publisher. The third suit was instituted by Emma Lee Paul who claimed that *Roots* drew upon her autobiographical book *The Bold Truth*, which had been submitted to Haley's publisher before *Roots* was published; this suit was dismissed.

In addition to plagiarism cases, charges of fraud were made by researchers who challenged the factual basis of *Roots*. Haley admitted that parts of his book were fictionalized, but defended it as "a symbolic history of a people."

THE CLIFFORD IRVING-HOWARD HUGHES AFFAIR

No literary hoax attracted more publicity than that of Clifford Irving's alleged biography of the reclusive billionaire Howard Hughes. All of the elements of the drama conspired to make it one of the most complex and devious frauds ever perpetrated on a major publisher: an engrossing, publicity-shy eccentric; a little-known author whose most recent work, *Fake!* (1968), was a biography of an internationally known art forger, Elmyr de Hory; the nation's largest publishing house, hungry for a best-seller; mysterious Swiss bank accounts; and a text so convincingly written that everyone–including the most skeptical experts–agreed it had to be authentic.

On 7 December 1971 McGraw-Hill and *Life* magazine jointly announced that on 7 March 1972 McGraw-Hill would publish what they claimed was the authentic autobiography of Howard Hughes–as told to Clifford Irving in a hundred hours of interviews conducted during secret meetings "throughout the Western Hemisphere"–with excerpts to appear earlier that year in *Life*. The publishing world was stunned. So were dozens of professional Hughes watchers who had all been thwarted in their own efforts to get at the mysterious Hughes, who had not granted an interview since 1958 and whose lawyers had countered every effort to uncover details of his life with vigorous legal obstacles.

It was only natural, then, that the McGraw-Hill announcement was greeted with skepticism. The announcement triggered a mad hunt for the truth by hundreds of journalists, dozens of publishing executives, and more than a few prosecutors. Was this really the work of Howard Hughes? The fact that Hughes himself did not come forward immediately to deny ever having met Irving only added fuel to the controversy. Frantic efforts by Hughes's lawyers to have publication of the book halted were rebuffed by McGraw-Hill and dismissed by the public. If the book was not authentic, they why did not Hughes deny it in public immediately? Why did he wait a full month–until the controversy had reached dramatic proportions–to say anything? Even the manner in which Hughes dismissed the book was bizarre. He held a conference call from his hotel in the Bahamas with seven journalists in Los Angeles–all of whom later agreed, that, based on the answers he gave to their "test questions," the man on the telephone was indeed Hughes–and told them, "I don't know Irving. I never saw him. I never even heard of him until a matter of days ago when this thing first came to my attention."

But the most difficult challenge was presented by the manuscript Irving had delivered to McGraw-Hill. Hughes watchers who read it agreed it was genuine. The details appeared to be true, and more important, the language in which Hughes spoke in the book rang true. In addition, McGraw-Hill held several other pieces of evidence that pointed to its authenticity. McGraw-Hill executives had letters that Irving claimed were written by Hughes checked by handwriting analysts who were widely acknowledged as among the world's best. They agreed the letters could have been written only by Hughes himself. As one of them put it, the chances were "one in a million" that the letters were forged. Most important, though, checks totaling at least $650,000 that had been made out to "H. R. Hughes" and given by McGraw-Hill to Irving for delivery had been signed and deposited to a Swiss bank account. In addition, lie detector tests conducted on Irving as well as a fingerprint analysis made of the alleged Hughes letters proved inconclusive; they could not be used to prove the book was a fraud.

The attention Irving devoted to every detail was so exacting that no one seemed able to prove the book was a fake. But when Hughes publicly denied ever having had anything to do with Irving, it was a only a matter of time before the carefully orchestrated fraud would end. Hughes had convinced enough people that the book was indeed a fake; all they had to do was prove it. Federal and state prosecutors, Swiss police, U.S. postal inspectors, private detectives hired by Hughes, and a hoard of journalists throughout the world began to pore over every detail of the Hughes-Irving affair.

Ironically, the Swiss banking system, known for its secrecy, provided one of the first clues. The "H. R. Hughes" who had deposited, then withdrawn, the money intended for Howard Hughes, turned out to be a certain "Helga R. Hughes"–who was quickly discovered to be Edith Irving, the hoaxer's wife.

Irving's elaborate descriptions of his dealings with Hughes—secret meetings in Mexico, Puerto Rico, the Bahamas, California, and Florida, in parked cars or hotel rooms—were checked, and odd details began to emerge. Irving had not always been where he claimed, and in certain cases, it was clear he could never have met with Hughes when he said he had. Nonetheless, investigators were unable to get at the central evidence supporting Irving. Handwriting analysts insisted the letters that Irving had given to McGraw-Hill were written by Hughes. And no one could dispute the fact that many of the details in the biography could have come from no one other than Hughes. Was Hughes himself involved in the affair? Had he granted the interviews to Irving and then, for unexplained reasons, decided alter to deny it?

The difficult missing link—the piece of evidence necessary to prove that Irving's book was a hoax—came from James Phelan, a free-lance reporter who had once collaborated with Noah Dietrich, a former Hughes aide, on a book about the billionaire. The book was never published, and the project had been abandoned. Phelan was under the impression that only a handful of persons had ever seen the manuscript, but, unknown to him, Irving had procured a copy, which provided a rich source of genuine anecdotes about Hughes.

Shocked by news that an unknown author had been granted the privilege of writing an authorized biography of Hughes, Phelan had set out to get to the bottom of the affair. He offered to examine the Irving manuscript for authenticity, but McGraw-Hill, already convinced it was the real thing, turned him down.

The Phelan material is what gave Irving's manuscript its appearance of truth. For example, Frank McCulloch, *Time* magazine's expert on Hughes and the last man to have interviewed the billionaire in person, was skeptical about the Irving manuscript until he was allowed to read it and came across details of his interview with Hughes. Since only he and Hughes were present at the interview, McCulloch assumed the information had to have come from Hughes. What he did not know was that Hughes had told Dietrich; Dietrich had told Phelan; and a friend of Dietrich's, Stanley Meyer, had given a copy of Phelan's manuscript to Irving. It was only when McGraw-Hill—besieged by too many disturbing revelations about Irving and the Swiss bank accounts—finally agreed to compare Phelan's manuscript with Irving's, that the publishing house conceded it had been duped.

Clifford Irving, his wife, Edith, and Richard Suskind, who had helped Irving research the book, were eventually convicted for their roles in the century's most elaborate publishing hoax. Irving was sentenced to two and a half years in prison. One of the most intriguing details to emerge from Irving's trial was the fact that he himself had forged the Hughes letters using a copy of a genuine Hughes letter that appeared in the 21 December 1970 issue of *Newsweek* magazine as his model.

The Profession of Authorship: Authors/Publishers/Editors/Agents

by MORRIS P. COLDEN

Authors' relationships with those who publish their work and manage their literary affairs can become intensely close or intensely bitter–in some cases both.

The great Boston house of Ticknor & Fields cultivated the atmosphere of a gentlemen's literary club and assembled the most distinguished group of American authors in the nineteenth century. The members of this club included most of the leading figures of the first American Renaissance: Nathaniel Hawthorne, Ralph Waldo Emerson, Henry David Thoreau, James Russell Lowell, Henry Wadsworth Longfellow, and Oliver Wendell Holmes. Partner James T. Fields exerted the force of his personality to acquire books and authors for his firm. During a visit to Hawthorne in 1849 Fields expressed eagerness to publish his next book. Hawthorne denied that he had anything on hand, but Fields insisted that there was a manuscript in the room. As Fields was leaving, Hawthorne handed him a manuscript, saying, "It is either very good or very bad–I don't know which." The work was a novelette Hawthorne planned to be included in a volume of "Old-time Legends"; but Fields persuaded him to enlarge it into *The Scarlet Letter* (1850).

Some publishers have placed the well-being of their authors before their self-interest. Thomas Niles of Roberts Brothers urged a reluctant Louisa May Alcott to write a juvenile book about girls. When *Little Women* was ready for publication in 1869 he advised her to take a royalty instead of a flat payment of $1,000. His advice made her financially secure. In 1870 her royalties amounted to $12,292.50–said to be more than any other American writer had received. Niles looked after her literary affairs for the rest of her life. Neither one ever married. After she died in 1888 he lost interest in his work.

The legendary Maxwell Perkins of Charles Scribner's Sons was America's most renowned literary editor, and he reputedly had more books dedicated to him by grateful authors than any other publishing figure. Among the writers he discovered or nurtured were F. Scott Fitzgerald, Ernest Hemingway, Ring Lardner, Thomas Wolfe, and James Jones. Perkins's relationship with Wolfe was the most complex, for he labored with Wolfe to prune and shape huge manuscripts into published novels. After generously acknowledging Perkins's aid in the dedication to *Of Time and the River* (1935)–

To
MAXWELL EVARTS PERKINS

A GREAT EDITOR AND A BRAVE AND HONEST MAN, WHO STUCK TO THE WRITER OF THIS BOOK THROUGH TIMES OF BITTER HOPELESSNESS AND DOUBT AND WOULD NOT LET HIM GIVE IN TO HIS OWN DESPAIR, A WORK TO BE KNOWN AS "OF TIME AND THE RIVER" IS DEDICATED WITH THE HOPE THAT ALL OF IT MAY BE IN SOME WAY WORTHY OF

THE LOYAL DEVOTION AND THE PATIENT CARE WHICH A DAUNTLESS AND UNSHAKEN FRIEND HAS GIVEN TO EACH PART OF IT, AND WITHOUT WHICH NONE OF IT COULD HAVE BEEN WRITTEN

—the acutely sensitive Wolfe was distressed by charges from Bernard DeVoto and other critics that he could not complete a book without Perkins and left Scribners. Wolfe, who died in 1938 before publishing another novel, named Perkins as his literary executor.

Two notable editorial stables were at Random House. Saxe Commins's authors included William Faulkner, Eugene O'Neill, and Sinclair Lewis. W. H. Auden observed: "Efficiency of mind and goodness of heart are rarely combined in equal measure, but in Saxe they were." The dedication page in Faulkner's *Big Woods* (1955) reads:

MEMO TO: Saxe Commins
FROM: Author
TO: Editor

We never always saw eye to eye
but we were always
looking at the same thing

Albert Erskine's Random House authors included Faulkner, John O'Hara, Robert Penn Warren, James Michener, and Eudora Welty. When Faulkner told Bennett Cerf, the cofounder of Random House, that Erskine was "the best book editor I know," Cerf asked if he had said that to Erskine. Faulkner replied, "No, I haven't. Bennett, when I've got a horse running good, I don't stop him to give him some sugar." Cerf, who relished the company of celebrities and became a television celebrity himself, had the ability to develop friendships with Random House authors, including O'Neill, Faulkner, Lewis, Gertrude Stein, and Truman Capote. He managed to keep the easily provoked John O'Hara in the Random House fold for twenty-three years. O'Hara dedicated *And Other Stories*

James T. Fields, Nathaniel Hawthorne, and William D. Ticknor, 1863
(photograph by J. W. Black)

(1968) "To BENNETT CERF, *an amiable man*." Despite O'Hara's unsuccessful attempts to quarrel with Cerf, he retained complete trust in his publisher's probity. O'Hara allowed his royalties to accumulate in an interest-free account at Random House, so that the publisher was making money on the author's money. At O'Hara's death the account stood at $1,005,401.28.

Cerf got along well with the redoubtable Gertrude Stein while admitting to her that he did not understand her writing. The dust jacket for *The Geographical History of America or the Relation of Human Nature to the Human Mind* (1936) carried a signed note by Cerf:

This space is usually reserved for a brief description of a book's contents. In this case, however, I must admit frankly that I do not know what Miss Stein is talking about. I do not even understand the title.

I admire Miss Stein tremendously, and I like to publish her books, although most of the time I

Albert Erskine, John O'Hara, and Bennet Cerf admiring O'Hara's Rolls-Royce Silver Shadow in the courtyard at Random House

do not know what she is driving at. That, Miss Stein tells me, is because I am dumb.

I note that one of my partners and I are characters in this latest work of Miss Stein's. Both of us wish that we knew what she was saying about us. Both of us hope, too, that her faithful followers will make more of this book than we are able to!

Although in the popular mind editors are thought of as discoverers of talent, in the twentieth century most books come through agents. However, one of the most famous discoveries was made by Harold S. Latham, editor-in-chief at Macmillan, when he followed up a lead and contacted Margaret Mitchell on a trip to Atlanta. After insisting that she had not written a novel, she turned the typescript over to him. Mitchell then wired Latham to return it, but he kept it and offered her a $500 advance to revise. (During revision the heroine's name was changed from Pansy to Scarlett.) After *Gone with the Wind* (1936) sold 25,000 copies, Macmillan voluntarily raised the royalty from 10% to 15%.

John Steinbeck and Pascal Covici enjoyed one of the closest author-editor relationships. Covici published *Tortilla Flat*

(1935), *In Dubious Battle* (1936), and *Of Mice and Men* (1937) under the Covici-Friede imprint. After his firm failed, Covici went to work as an editor at Viking Press, and Steinbeck insisted on going with him. Steinbeck's second book for Viking was *The Grapes of Wrath* (1939). During their thirty-year association Covici wrote Steinbeck hundreds of encouraging letters. *East of Eden* (1952) carried this dedication:

Dear Pat,

You came upon me carving some kind of little figure out of wood and you said, "Why don't you make something for me?"

I asked you what you wanted, and you said, "A box."

"What for?"

"To put things in."

"What things?"

"Whatever you have," you said.

Well, here's your box. Nearly everything I have is in it, and it is not full. Pain and excitement are in it, and feeling good or bad and evil thoughts and good thoughts— the pleasure of design and some despair and the indescribable joy of creation.

And on top of these are all the gratitude and love I have for you.

197

And still the box is not full.

JOHN

When Covici died in 1964, Steinbeck stated: "Pat Covici was much more than my friend. He was my editor. Only a writer can understand how a great editor is a father, mother, teacher, personal devil and personal god. For thirty years Pat was my collaborator and my conscience. He demanded of me more than I had and thereby caused me to be more than I should have been without him."

America's most flamboyant publisher was Horace Liveright of Boni and Liveright. After founding the firm with Albert Boni in 1917 to publish the Modern Library, Liveright gained control in 1918 by winning a coin flip. During the 1920s the offices resembled a speakeasy. Despite the nonstop party, his list included Eugene O'Neill, Ezra Pound, E. E. Cummings, Hart Crane, Conrad Aiken, Theodore Dreiser, Sherwood Anderson, Robinson Jeffers, and John Reed. Boni and Liveright published *The Waste Land* (1922), Faulkner's first two novels, and Hemingway's *In Our Time* (1925), and eventually boasted seven Nobel Prize winners. Liveright was committed to publishing unknown authors and controversial books.

Liveright was generous with advances at a time when they were not standard publishing practice. He made an allowance of $100 a week for five years to Anderson. Dreiser was provided with a drawing account of $4,000 for four years; yet when Dreiser learned that Boni and Liveright was entitled to share in the movie income for *An American Tragedy* (1925), he threw a cup of coffee in Liveright's face.

The firm was also an incubator for publishers, with Bennett Cerf (Random House), Richard Simon (Simon & Schuster) Edward Weeks, (the *Atlantic Monthly*), and Donald Friede (Covici-Friede) serving apprenticeships there. Cerf and Donald Klopfer bought the

Alfred A. Knopf

Modern Library from Liveright to launch Random House.

The death of Alfred A. Knopf in 1984 prompted John Hersey to pronounce him "the greatest publisher this country ever had." Knopf published sixteen Nobel Prize winners; his American authors included H. L. Mencken, Willa Cather, Wallace Stevens, Kahlil Gibran, John Updike, Dashiell Hammett, Raymond Chandler, James M. Cain, Ross Macdonald, John Hersey, Conrad Richter, and John Cheever. A princely figure, Knopf did not cultivate close relationships with his authors, whom he tended to regard as greedy people interfering in matters they knew nothing about. He once advised a writer: "If you ever have a book published, leave everything in your contract up to the publisher. Don't bother to read it. And whatever you do, don't have a lawyer read it. Once you do this, it becomes a horse trade between you and your publisher. Trust your publisher, and he can't fail to treat you generously."

Two authors who were exempt from his suspicion were Mencken and Cather.

Mitchell Kennerley

Mencken cited him as "the perfect publisher," and the two Teutons maintained a long friendship cemented by music and wine. Mencken became a director of the firm and willed half his stock to Knopf. Cather remained with Knopf for twenty-seven years, and he once remarked, "Sometimes I think I'd like to get rid of the whole list and keep reissuing Willa Cather." She never asked for an advance.

When Knopf decided to go skiing instead of meeting with Shirley Jackson, she stuck a pin in the leg of a wax image of her publisher. He broke his leg.

Certain magazine editors have assembled strong groups of regular contributors who became identified with that magazine. George Horace Lorimer made the *Saturday Evening Post* the repository for the best commercial fiction published in America during the 1920s. Harold Ross's stable at the *New Yorker* included James Thurber, S. J. Perelman, John O'Hara, E. B. White, Robert Benchley, Vladimir Nabokov, and John

Cheever. The most influential of the pulp or dime novel editors was Captain Joseph Shaw, who edited *Black Mask* between 1926 and 1936. Shaw is credited with having shaped the hard-boiled school of writing. Among his star contributors were Dashiell Hammett and Raymond Chandler.

For JOSEPH THOMPSON SHAW with affection and respect, and in memory of the time when we were trying to get murder away from the upper classes, the week-end house party and vicar's rose garden, and back to the people who are really good at it—
—Raymond Chandler, Dedication to
Five Murders *(1944)*

As the old, close relationships between authors and publishers were sacrificed to publishing as an impersonal business in the twentieth century, literary agents came to provide the personal attention authors formerly expected from their publishers. Harold Ober (whose clients included F. Scott Fitzgerald, William Faulkner, and J. D. Salinger) not only served as Fitzgerald's private banker—lending him money against unsold or unwritten stories—but he took Fitzgerald's daughter into his home and became her surrogate father. After Fitzgerald broke with Ober over the agent's refusal to make one more loan, he wrote to Maxwell Perkins—who lent him the money: "When Harold withdrew from the questionable honor of being my banker I felt completely numb financially and I suddenly wondered what money was and where it came from. There had always seemed a little more somewhere and now there wasn't."

Women have been among the most prominent agents, perhaps as the result of mother instinct. Carol Brandt, the wife and partner of Carl Brandt, head of the Brandt & Brandt agency, became the lover of client John P. Marquand. Bernice Baumgarten, also of Brandt & Brandt, married client James Gould Cozzens and largely supported him during the years before *By Love Possessed* (1957).

Despite the evidence of many enduring associations, author-publisher relationships are often stormy. Vachel Lindsay sent Christopher Morley to plead with publisher Mitchell Kennerley for unpaid book royalties. Kennerley—who was notoriously reluctant to pay his authors—declared, "He has disgusting table manners: he deserves no royalties."

Some authors perigrinate from publisher to publisher seeking love and understanding—or at least larger advances and bigger advertising budgets. Sinclair Lewis left Harcourt, Brace after winning the Nobel Prize because he felt that the publisher had failed to exploit the publicity value of the award. Norman Mailer has been published by Rinehart, Putnam, Dial, New American Library, Grosset & Dunlap, Simon & Schuster, and Little, Brown—which paid a one-million-dollar advance for his projected cycle of novels beginning with *Ancient Evenings* (1983).

Harper's president Thomas B. Wells objected to unflattering remarks in John Dos Passos's *1919* (1932) about J. P. Morgan, who had made the firm a crucial loan. Dos Passos refused to revise, and Harper's refused to publish. The novel, which was the second volume in the *U.S.A.* trilogy (1930-1936), was published by Harcourt, Brace. Wells explained his position to Dos Passos's editor, Eugene Saxton: "It is difficult to be a businessman and a gentleman at the same time.... But when the opportunity comes to be both, I think one ought to grasp it."

THE REWARDS OF AUTHORSHIP; OR, HOW TO MAKE $4.90 AN HOUR

Freud observed that writers write in order to win three things: money, fame, and the love of beautiful women. It is impossible to measure fame, and there are no available figures on the beautiful women (or handsome men) who have loved writers. But there are statistics on the wages of writing, the Economic Survey of American Authors, prepared by the Center for the Social Sciences of Columbia University for the Authors Guild Foundation, Inc. (Paul W. Kingston and Jonathan R. Cole, *The Wages of Writing*, 1986).

The first problem raised by such a survey is to determine who is a writer. The country is full of unpublished writers who nonetheless regard themselves as writers. This 1980 survey was restricted to 2,241 living Americans who had published at least one book. The results confirmed that writing is a feast-or-famine trade—with more famines than feasts. In 1979 the median authorial income from writing was $4,775 (the average annual salary for a major-league baseball player was $371,000 in 1986); and twenty-five percent earned less than $1,000 from writing. The median author earned $4.90 per hour from writing—or $1.55 more than the federal minimum wage. These discouraging numbers are alleviated by the circumstance that writing is often a part-time occupation. The median amount of time spent on writing or related work was twenty hours a week (20 x $4.90 = $98). Forty-six percent of the authors had a "regular" job in addition to writing. Of the job holders, approximately one-third were on college or university faculties. Since academics are rewarded for publishing with promotion, tenure, raises, and grants, for these writers the direct income from writing is far exceeded by the ancillary rewards.

On the upside, five percent of the authors earned more than $80,000 from writing in 1979. The best-remunerated writers were those who produced genre fiction (mysteries, romances, westerns, sci fi). Twenty percent of these writers had an income of at least $50,000 in 1979—which was three times the income of writers of adult nonfiction books. Of course, productivity is a determining factor in earning power, and genre writers are usually more fecund than those who produce "straight" fiction.

Since the financial rewards are meagre and uncertain, it is to be concluded that many writers find gratification in the literary life itself. That is where the expectation of fame and love comes in.

Thrown to the Wolves: Reviews and Reviewers

by JOSEPH MILLER

Many authors take reviews personally and react strongly to unfavorable notices. After critic Max Eastman commented on the "false hair on his chest" manner of *Death in the Afternoon* (1932), Ernest Hemingway encountered him in Maxwell Perkins's office at Scribners. A scuffle ensued, with both men claiming victory. Hemingway had earlier responded to Lee Wilson Dodd's review of *Men Without Women* (1927) with a poem published in the *Little Review*:

Sing a song of critics
pockets full of lye
four and twenty critics
hope that you will die
hope that you will peter out
hope that you will fail
so they can be the first one
be the first to hail
any happy weakening or sign of
    quick decay.
(All are very much alike, weariness
    too great,
sordid small catastrophes, stack the
    cards on fate,
very vulgar people, annals of the
    callous,
dope fiends, soldiers, prostitutes,
men without a gallus*)
If you do not like them lads
one thing you can do
stick them up your asses lads
My Valentine to you.

*. . . . . . [Hemingway's "note"]

The extremely touchy John O'Hara stopped writing for *The New Yorker* for a decade after the magazine published Brendan Gill's unreceptive review of *A Rage to Live* in 1949. Since *The New Yorker* was O'Hara's preferred short-story market, he also stopped writing stories. Irritated by Orville Prescott's reviews of his books in the *New York Times*, O'Hara arranged his publication dates for days when Prescott, the Monday-Wednesday-Friday reviewer, did not appear.

Four months after James Gould Cozzens's *By Love Possessed* (1957) was published to overwhelming praise, Dwight Macdonald attacked it in "By Cozzens Possessed," charging that the novel "falls below any reasonable literary criterion." Concerned that Cozzens might not read the *Commentary* article, Macdonald sent him a copy. If Macdonald's intention was to initiate an attention-getting public squabble, Cozzens did not take the bait. He wrote Macdonald a private letter:

The copy of COMMENTARY you marked for me finally reached me, thanks. To tell you the truth the 100-critic chorus, though not really driving me off my head the way it drove you off yours, had come to lack freshness, so I found your novel pronouncements a nice change. I see that you don't understand prose structure very well; that shades of meaning in words are, like irony, altogether lost on you; and that your imperceptiveness is, for an educated adult, quite remarkable. Which, I suppose, is why the stylistic claptrap, the crypto-sentimentality, and the just plain childishness in so many of the books you indicate you admire actually can seem to you better "art" than a Somerset

201

Maugham's lucid thinking and perfect writing. I'm afraid your infirmity here makes me unable to take your 'literary criticism' very seriously. You'd always, it seems safe to guess, be wrong. However, in the field of the philippic (sorry to send you to your dictionary again) I think you're gifted. I haven't in years had the pleasure of reading so refreshingly venomous an outburst. For that, at least, let me award you an earned A–and I'll bet all those little-mag. people are just *loving* you to death!

Yours,
James Gould Cozzens

P.S. I dropped Bill Shakespeare a line to tell him you say "virgin knot untied" won't do. No word from him yet; perhaps he's out of town.

Vladimir Nabokov and Edmund Wilson had once been friends, and Wilson helped him to launch his American career after the Russian-born Nabokov fled France in 1940. By the early 1960s the friendship was showing signs of wear. Perhaps Wilson resented the fame that had resulted from Nabokov's *Lolita* (1955) or perhaps Wilson actually believed that his command of Russian was superior to Nabokov's when he wrote "The Strange Case of Pushkin and Nabokov" for the *New York Review of Books* in 1965 charging errors in Nabokov's translation of *Eugene Onegin*. A series of testy exchanges ensued. Nabokov responded in the *NYRB* citing Wilson's Russian blunders. Wilson replied in the same journal admitting some of his errors but reiterating his claim that the translation was unsatisfactory. Then Nabokov changed the venue to the London *Encounter* in February 1966:

A number of earnest simpletons consider Mr. Wilson to be an authority in my field ("he misses few of Nabokov's lapses," as one hasty well-wisher puts it in a letter to The New York Review on August 26), and no doubt such delusions should not be tolerated; still, I am not sure that the necessity to defend my work from blunt jabs and incompetent blame would have been a sufficient incentive for me to discuss that article, had I not been moved to do so by the unusual, unbelievable, and highly entertaining opportunity that I am unexpectedly given by Mr. Wilson himself of refuting practically every item of criticism in his enormous piece. The mistakes and misstatements in it form an uninterrupted series so complete as to seem artistic in reverse, making one wonder if, perhaps, it had not been woven that way on purpose to be turned into something pertinent and coherent when reflected in a looking glass. I am unaware of any other such instance in the history of literature. It is a polemicist's dream come true, and one must be a poor sportsman to disdain what it offers.

Wilson responded in *Encounter* insisting that the translation was awkward. At this point poet Robert Lowell joined the fight in *Encounter*. Admitting that he knew no Russian, Lowell nonetheless characterized the translation as eccentric. Nabokov's restrained rejoinder was that it is hard to judge a translation if you do not know the language in which the work was written. The public quarrel ended at this point, but the rift never healed. The course of their relationship is charted in the *Nabokov-Wilson Letters, 1940-1971* (1979).

In 1983 *Esquire* invited some prominent writers to strike back at "their worst notices and their least favorite critics." John Barth observed that his form of revenge was "to *forget who it was*, say, who dismissed *The Sot-Weed Factor* and *Giles Goat-Boy* as 'mere inflated spoofs.' " John Updike cited reviews of *Of the Farm*

(1965) by John Aldridge, of *Pigeon Feathers* (1962) by Alfred Chester, and of *The Centaur* (1963) by Norman Podhoretz. "To find oneself assaulted like this in print is certainly a salubrious experience for a young writer, for in a world that does much to soften and muffle its basic dangers he is invited to consider whether he intends to go on existing or not. My decision, after an initial flash of uncertainty, was to go on existing, even if everything these shrewd and inimical voices said was true." Erica Jong selected the review of *Fear of Flying* (1973) in which she was called a "mammoth pudenda" by Paul Theroux. "Since Mr. Theroux had no personal acquaintance with the organ in question, I cannot help but wonder whether some anxieties about his own anatomy were at the root (as it were) of the review."

F. Scott Fitzgerald, who received his full share of imperceptive reviews, expressed the proper philosophy for an author in his introduction to the 1934 Modern Library edition of *The Great Gatsby*: "Your pride is all you have, and if you let it be tampered with by a man who has a dozen prides to tamper with before lunch, you are promising yourself a lot of disappointment that a hard-boiled professional has learned to spare himself."

AMERICA'S FIRST GREAT BOOK REVIEWER

In the years between 1835 and his death in 1849, Edgar Allan Poe established himself as one of the most formidable book reviewers of his time and ultimately as the most important critic in American literature before Henry James and W. D. Howells. His reviews stand in marked contrast to the benign literary essays that continued to be the norm for most of his century–the sort of criticism typified by James Russell Lowell's cozy volumes *My Study Windows* (1871) and *Among My Books* (1876). Poe lived in the rough-and-tumble world of literary journalism. His reviews were fierce, contentious, and uncompromising. He was at the center of several important literary battles, and while Poe's literary journalism is uneven and many of his furies misguided, he was always a vehement defender and promoter of an American literature that was genuinely literary, and not merely a commodity of salable paper and print. His two greatest campaigns were fought against the piratical and unfair treatment of American writers by American publishers, and against collusion between unscrupulous authors and publishers on the one hand and editors and reviewers who were susceptible to bribery or flattery on the other.

The first abuse was the result of the lack until 1891 of any international copyright agreement with England. Because the American copyright law in effect in Poe's time protected only works written by Americans, publishing firms in the United States were obliged to pay American authors, but not British authors. As a result, publishers who were more interested in money than in encouraging the development of a native literary culture preferred to publish English books. Toward American writers they often acted as mere printers, requiring a deposit against any publishing losses they might incur. An 1843 statement by a spokesman for Harper and Brothers might have been applied to the entire publishing business in America at that time: "Publishing for American authors forms but an inconsiderable part of their business. . . ." A further abuse against American writers was that the works they sold to magazines were pilfered by newspapers, almanacs, anthologies, annuals, gift books, and every other sort of reprint enterprise. Poe fought against these abuses, insisting that this sort of piracy injured "our national literature by repressing the efforts of our men of genius; for genius, as a general rule, is poor in worldly goods and cannot write for nothing."

Poe's second great battle was against the literary cliques of Boston and New

York. Of the American books that found their way into print the vast majority came from these two centers, where authors, reviewers, publishers, and editors, were nearly all friendly acquaintances who took an interest in promoting one another's efforts. Good and bad books were praised indiscriminately and in vague general terms, more in the spirit of advertising than serious literary criticism. Poe felt that such practices not only degraded the public taste for literature but also condemned outsiders, especially Southern and Western writers, to the "dreadful damnation of silent contempt," if they were not openly abused. "Now, men of genius," Poe wrote, "will not resort to these manoeuvres, because genius involves in its very essence a scorn of chicanery; and thus for a time quacks always get the advantage of them, both in respect of pecuniary profit and what appears to be public esteem." He berated critics who were venal or subject to influence: "It is . . . the duty of all whom circumstances have led into criticism–it is, at least, a duty from which *we* individually shall never shrink–to uphold the true dignity of genius, to combat its degradation, to plead for the exercise of its power. . . ."

In this frame of mind Poe set out to criticize with impartiality the books that came his way. His taste was far from flawless, but he did nonetheless rise, to a remarkable degree, above the prevailing provinciality in taste and ideas. He pointed out the weaknesses and faults of Longfellow, and he made open mockery of William Ellery Channing–two figures at the center of the Boston literary establishment. Poe made many enemies, and when he was safely dead they got their revenge by blackening his reputation with falsifications, many of which were never refuted until literary historians set the record straight nearly a hundred years later. In his "The Literati of New York City," a series of articles which he published in *Godey's Lady's Book* between May and October 1846, Poe reviewed the reviewers and contributors to the important New York periodicals one by one, giving a sketch of each of them, summarizing their prejudices and partialities, and judging their merits as writers. In spite of his venom and vituperation, it cannot be denied that Poe, more than any other figure in the early nineteenth century, served to elevate literary journalism to the status of literary criticism.

Like all the best critics, Poe was not only pragmatic but also sought to formulate general principles by which literary works could be judged. The failure of inadequate critics, Poe felt, was in their poverty of ideas about literature as much as in their personal pettiness. This poverty he sought to remedy in his three great essays on the theory of poetry: "The Philosophy of Composition" (1846), "The Rationale of Verse" (1848), and "The Poetic Principle" (1850). In these essays he emphasized the intellectual and technical aspects of writing as opposed to the divine afflatus of inspiration. He also sought to establish a theory of beauty as an ideal by which to measure literary achievement. Poe's theories of beauty had their greatest influence in France, where they were seminal in the development of nineteenth-century aestheticism and ultimately the movement of art for art's sake.

POE REVIEWS HIS COMPETITORS

On Longfellow's Ballads

"Much as we admire the genius of Mr. Longfellow, we are fully sensible of his many errors of affectation and imitation. His artistic skill is great, and his ideality high. But his conception of the aim of poesy is all wrong; and this we shall prove at some future day, to our own satisfaction, at least. His didactics are all out of place. He has written brilliant poems, by accident; that is to say, when permitting his genius to get the better of his conventional habit of thinking, a habit deduced from German study. We do not mean to say that a didactic moral may not be well made the undercurrent of a poetical thesis; but that it can never be well put so obtrusively forth, as in the majority of his compositions."

On William Cullen Bryant
"But although it may be said, in general, that Mr. Bryant's position is comparatively well settled, still for some time past there has been a growing tendency to underestimate him. The new licentious 'schools' of poetry–I do not now speak of the transcendentalists, who are the merest nobodies, fatiguing even themselves, but the Tennysonian and Barrettian schools–having, in their rashness of spirit, much in accordance with the whole spirit of the age, thrown into the shade necessarily all that seems akin to the conservatism of half a century ago, –the conventionalities, even the most justifiable *decora* of composition, are regarded, *per se*, with a suspicious eye. . . . How few are willing to admit the possibility of reconciling genius with artistic skill! Yet this reconciliation is not only possible, but an absolute necessity. . . . The greatest poems will not be written until this prejudice is annihilated; and I mean to express a very exalted opinion of Mr. Bryant when I say that his works in time to come will do much towards the annihilation."

On Lowell's A Fable for Critics
"The *Fable for Critics*, just issued, has not the name of its author on the title page; and but for some slight foreknowledge of the literary opinions, likes, dislikes, whims, prejudices, and crotchets of Mr. James Russell Lowell, we should have had much difficulty in attributing so very loose a brochure to him. The *Fable* is essentially 'loose' ill-conceived and feebly executed, as well in detail as in general. Some good hints and some sparking witticisms do not serve to compensate us for its rambling plot (if plot it can be called) and for the want of artistic finish so particularly noticeable throughout the work–especially in its versification. . . . Two thirds of the

William Cullen Bryant at age thirty, portrait by Samuel F. B. Morse (courtesy of the National Academy of Design, New York)

force of the *Dunciad*, may be referred to its exquisite finish; and had the *Fable for Critics* been (what it is *not*) the quintessence of the satiric spirit itself, it would, nevertheless, in so slovenly a form, have failed." [Poe's harsh criticism of *A Fable for Critics* could not have been totally impersonal, since the poem includes the following couplet: "There comes Poe, with his raven, like Barnaby Rudge, / Three fifths of him genius and two fifths sheer fudge."]

On Hawthorne's Twice-Told Tales
"He is peculiar and *not* original–unless in those detailed fancies and detached thoughts which his want of general originality will deprive of the appreciation due to them, in preventing them from ever reaching the public eye. He is infinitely too fond of allegory, and can never hope for popularity so long as he persists in it. This he will not do, for allegory is at war with the whole tone of his nature. . . . He has the purest style, the finest taste, the most available scholarship, the most delicate humor, the most touching pathos, the most radiant imagination, the most con-

James Russell Lowell

sured praise) the tales in the collection, which contains "by no means the best of Mr. Poe's productions that we have seen," and offered by way of summary his evaluation of his style: "The style of Mr. Poe is clear and forcible. . . . His style may be called, strictly, an earnest one. And this earnestness is one of its greatest charms. A writer must have the fullest belief in his statements, or must stimulate that belief perfectly, to produce an absorbing interest in the mind of his reader. That power of simulation can only be possessed by a man of high genius. It is the result of a peculiar combination of the mental faculties. It produces earnestness, minute, not profuse detail, and fidelity of description. It is possessed by Mr. Poe, in its full perfection."

summate ingenuity; and with these varied good qualities he has done *well* as a mystic. But is there any one of these qualities which should prevent his doing doubly as well in a career of honest, upright, sensible, prehensible, and comprehensible things? Let him mend his pen, get a bottle of visible ink, come out from the Old Manse, cut Mr. Alcott, hang (if possible) the editor of 'The Dial,' and throw out of the window to the pigs all his odd numbers of 'The North American Review.' "

POE REVIEWS HIS OWN TALES

Poe often and vehemently denounced the practice of anonymous reviewing because of its tendency to encourage pretenses of impartiality and to conceal attacks "most unfair–most despicable and cowardly." Yet Poe himself took advantage of the same anonymity in order to review his own *Tales* in the *Aristidean* (October 1845), repeating plagiarism charges against Longfellow–this time for stealing "all that was worth stealing" of Poe's "The Haunted Palace" for his own "Beleaguered City." Otherwise Poe simply criticized one by one (with mea-

LONGFELLOW REVIEWS HAWTHORNE

When in 1837 Nathaniel Hawthorne brought out his first commercially published book, *Twice-Told Tales*, he discreetly approached Henry Wadsworth Longfellow, a former classmate at Bowdoin College, with the suggestion that Longfellow notice it in public. Longfellow was not yet the enormously popular poet he was to become, but he was more successful and better known than Hawthorne and had recently taken up his position as Smith Professor of Modern Languages at Harvard. Since the two men had not met in twelve years, Hawthorne attempted in his letter to give Longfellow an idea of what his life had been like since leaving college. "I seldom venture abroad till after dark," he wrote. "By some witch-craft or other– for I really cannot assign any reasonable why and wherefore–I have been carried apart from the main current of life, and find it impossible to get back again. . . . For the last ten years, I have not lived, but only dreamed of living."

Longfellow's favorable review of the book in the July 1937 issue of the influential *North American Review* began, "When a new star rises in the heavens, people gaze after it for a season with the naked eye, and with such telescopes as they may find." In assessing the "magnitude" of Hawthorne's star and "its place in the heaven of poetry," he said, "To this little work we would say, 'Live ever, sweet, sweet book.' It comes from the hand of a man of genius." The rest of the review was devoted to praise of Hawthorne for his use of American subjects in his tales, and to a sketch of Hawthorne's personality: "A calm, thoughtful face seems to be looking at you from every page; with now a pleasant smile, and now a shade of sadness stealing over its features. Sometimes, though not often, it glares wildly at you, with a strange and painful expression." It seems that Longfellow had expected to find a sweet, smiling transcendentalist in Hawthorne, and not the reclusive, tormented Calvinist that he was. Hawthorne was delighted with the review and wrote to Longfellow: "I frankly own that I was not without hopes that you would do this kind office for the book; though I could not have anticipated how very kindly it would be done. Whether or not the public will agree to the praise which you bestow on me, there are at least five persons who think you the most sagacious critic on earth—viz., my mother and two sisters, my old maiden aunt, and finally, the sturdiest believer of the whole five, my own self."

A Private Letter Becomes a Rave Review

When Ralph Waldo Emerson received a complimentary copy of the first edition of Walt Whitman's anonymous *Leaves of Grass*, he read it and was "in raptures." Once he had discovered the author's identity and his whereabouts, he wrote the following letter:

Concord, Massachusetts
21 July 1855

Dear Sir,
   I am not blind to the worth of the wonderful gift of "Leaves of Grass." I find it the most extraordinary piece of wit & wisdom that America has yet contributed. I am very happy in reading it, as great power makes us happy. It meets the demand I am always making of what seemed the sterile and stingy Nature, as if too much handiwork or too much lymph in the temperament were making our western wits fat & mean.

   I give you joy of your free & brave thought. I have great joy in it. I find incomparable things said incomparably well, as they must be. I find the courage of *treatment*, which so delights us, & which large perceptions only can inspire.

   I greet you at the beginning of a great career, which yet must have had a long foreground somewhere, for such a start. I rubbed my eyes a little to see if this sunbeam were no illusion; but the solid sense of the book is a sober certainty. It has best merits, namely, of fortifying & encouraging.

   I did not know until I, last night, saw the book advertised in a newspaper, that I could trust the name as real & available for a Post-office. I wish to see my benefactor, & have felt much like striking my tasks, & visiting New York to pay you my respects.

                                        R. W. Emerson

"I supposed the letter was meant to be blazoned," Whitman said later, and blazon it he did. His friend Charles A. Dana, managing editor of Horace Greeley's *New York Tribune*, convinced Whitman, on the strength of his own supposed friendship with Emerson, that Emerson would not object to his printing the letter in the *Tribune*, which Dana did on 10 October. Then Whitman sent clippings of the *Tribune* piece to Longfellow and other celebrities, arranged to have the letter printed in *Life Illustrated*, and eventually printed it as a broadside, which he distributed to editors and critics.

This letter then became central to Whitman's plans to promote subsequent editions of his book, which included many poems that Emerson had never seen. In 1856 he reprinted the letter at the end of the second edition, together with an effusive letter of his own addressed to Emerson. One Boston paper called Whitman's publication of this private letter without Emerson's permission "the grossest violation of literary comity and courtesy that ever passed under our notice." "I am so non-polite," Whitman wrote to a friend in 1857, "so habitually wanting in my responses and ceremonies." To this his correspondent replied, "I think your judgment of yourself is rather severe"–if Emerson and his aggrieved friends had "expected *common* etiquette from you, after having read *Leaves of Grass*, they were sadly mistaken in your character."

Emerson, who was only annoyed to have his private letter printed in the newspapers and circulated as a broadside, was truly angry when he saw Whitman's second edition which not only reprinted his letter but also had "I greet you at the beginning of a great career–R. W. Emerson" stamped on the spine.

HENRY JAMES GIVES WHITMAN A BAD REVIEW

When Whitman published *Drum-Taps* in October 1865, William Dean Howells said that in point of decency, at any rate, *Drum-Taps* was an improvement over the "preponderant beastliness" of *Leaves of Grass*, but that so long as Whitman chose "to stop at mere consciousness, he cannot be called a true poet." An anonymous review in the 16 November issue of the *Nation* went further, dismissing *Drum-Taps* as "the effort of an essentially prosaic mind to lift itself, by a prolonged muscular effort, into poetry. . . . We find nothing but flashy limi-

WHITMAN REVIEWS HIS OWN BOOK

Whitman also attempted to promote *Leaves of Grass* by writing three anonymous reviews, which appeared around the end of 1855. "An American bard at last!" he announced in the *United States Review*, and in the *Brooklyn Daily Times* he wrote: "Politeness this man has none, and regulation he has none. A rude child of the people!–No limitation–No foreigner–but a growth and idiom of America." (He does not seem to have gone to great lengths to disguise his style.) And in the *American Phrenological Journal* Whitman cited Tennyson's poetry with admiring tolerance but predicted that his own might yet prove "the most glorious of triumphs, in the known history of literature."

tations of ideas. We find art, measure, grace, sense sneered at on almost every page, and nothing positive given us in their stead." The writer concluded his review by addressing the poet: "You must be *possessed*, and you must strive to possess your possession. If in your striving you break into divine eloquence, then you are a poet. If the idea which possesses you is the idea of your country's greatness, then you are a national poet; and not otherwise."

Thirty-eight years later, with a sense of "deep and damning disgrace," Henry James–who had since come to regard Whitman as the greatest American poet–confessed to having written this review, "in the gross impudence of youth." Edith Wharton, hearing James read "When Lilacs Last in the Dooryard Bloom'd" ("his voice filled the hushed room like an organ adagio"), found "a new proof of the way in which, above a certain level, the most divergent intelligences walk together like gods."

LEAVES OF GRASS
SOME CRITICAL ASSESSMENTS

Before Walt Whitman became enshrined as the Good Gray Poet he was widely condemned as the Bad Obscene Bard. Here are some of the outraged responses to *Leaves of Grass*:

The slop-bucket of Walt Whitman.

A belief in the preciousness of filth.

Entirely bestial.

Nastiness and animal insensibility to shame.

Noxious weeds.

Impious and obscene.

Disgusting burlesque.

Broken out of Bedlam.

Libidinousness and swell of self-applause.

Defilement.

Crazy outbreak of conceit and vulgarity.

Ithyphallic audacity.

Gross indecency.

Sunken sensualist.

Rotten garbage of licentious thoughts.

Roots like a pig.

Rowdy Knight Errant.

A poet whose indecencies stink in the nostrils.

Its liberty is the wildest license; its love the essence of the lower lust!

Priapus—worshipping obscenity.

Rant and rubbish.

Linguistic silliness.

Inhumanly insolent.

Apotheosis of Sweat.

Mouthings of a mountebank.

Venomously malignant.

Pretentious twaddle.

Degraded helot of literature.

His work, like a maniac's robe, bedizened with fluttering tags of a thousand colors.

Roaming, like a drunken satyr, with inflamed blood, through every field of lascivious thought.

Muck of abomination.

ROBINSON SETS THE RECORD STRAIGHT

A rebel against genteel nineteenth-century perceptions of the proper subject matter for poetry, Edwin Arlington Robinson published his first book at his own expense in 1896. Reviewers' responses to the starkly realistic poems in *The Torrent and the Night Before*–which contained several of his best poems, including "Luke Havergal" and "Credo"–were not entirely negative, but Robinson found one review particularly irritating. Writing for the February 1897 issue of the *Bookman*, Harry Thurston Peck called the book too somber and concluded that Robinson's "humour is of a grim sort, and the world is not beautiful to him, but a prison-house." The next month's issue of the *Bookman* published a letter from Robinson, who stated: "I am sorry that I have painted myself in such lugubrious colours. The world is not a prison house, but a kind of spiritual kindergarten, where millions of bewildered infants are trying to spell God with the wrong blocks."

–K.L.R.

JENNIFER LORN: "A BOOK IN SEVEN MILLION"

Among the most extravagantly over-praised American novels was Elinor Wylie's *Jennifer Lorn: A Sedate Extravaganza* (1923), which was greeted on publication with unbridled rapture by critics and fellow writers.

Wylie, who had some reputation as a poet, was best known in literary circles as a femme fatale. Born Elinor Hoyt, she married Philip Simmons Hichborn when she was twenty. Five years later she left him for Horace Wylie, a married man fifteen years her senior, and Hichborn eventually killed himself. After giving most of his fortune to his wife in exchange for a divorce, Wylie married Elinor in 1916, but in 1921 she left him, divorcing him and marrying

Edwin Arlington Robinson, 1896 (photograph in chiaroscuro by William E. Butler, courtesy of Special Collections, Colby College). Robinson commented about this photograph: "I have a look that might lead one to think that I had just eaten the lining out of my own coffin, but that is the fault of an uncomfortable feel somewhere in my spinal column."

ROBINSON AND FROST: "THE OLD-FASHIONED WAY TO BE NEW"

Both revolutionaries in regard to poetic subject matter, Edwin Arlington Robinson and Robert Frost continued to employ traditional poetic forms at a time when more and more poets were turning to free verse. They were, as Frost said of Robinson, "content with the old-fashioned way to be new." When reviewers asked why he refused to abandon rhyme and meter, Robinson responded, "I write badly enough as it is." Frost, an enthusiastic amateur tennis player, answered the same question by stating, "Writing free verse is like playing tennis without a net."

–K.L.R.

BAD REVIEWS IN THE 1930S FOR FROST AND STEVENS

critic William Rose Benét during the year in which the publication of *Jennifer Lorn* brought her to the height of her fame.

The irresistible heroine of *Jennifer Lorn* is a young English bride in late-eighteen-century India. The chorus of praise for the novel was deafening. Sinclair Lewis exclaimed, "At last a civilized American novel." James Branch Cabell wrote, "I wonder if there has ever been written a more distinguished first novel." Carl Van Vechten declared it the perfect book and organized a torchlight procession through the streets of Manhattan in its honor. To a friend he wrote, "Have you read *Jennifer Lorn*: I consider it one of the masterpieces of all time. Indeed, I don't think I ever read any book I liked better. . . perhaps the most authentic book in seven million. . . a book in seven million."

There is a curious parallel between the fame and fortunes of Robert Frost and Wallace Stevens, who were nearly contemporaries. While both wrote poems in their college years, neither produced a volume of poetry until early middle age. Frost was thirty-nine when he published *A Boy's Will* in England in 1913, and Stevens was forty-four when he brought out *Harmonium* in 1923.

Reviewing *A Boy's Will* for *Poetry* magazine, Ezra Pound admired in it the virtues and values he was promoting in his own imagist school–compression and clarity of expression: "This man has the good sense to speak naturally and to paint the thing, the thing as he sees it." Thus Frost, who was later regarded as a conservative poet, began his career as an innovator, clearing away the falsity and fustian of Victorian verse with his clear, dry "natural speech of New England." Edward Thomas, an English poet who was Frost's close friend, wrote of Frost's second volume, *North of Boston* (1914): "These poems are revolutionary because they lack the exaggeration of rhetoric." And Pound, again in *Poetry*, said, "Mr. Frost's work is . . . the work of a man who will make neither concessions nor pretenses. . . . His book is a contribution to American literature. . . ."

There was no popular success in store for Stevens's *Harmonium*. He calculated that his royalties for the first half of 1924 amounted to $6.70. Nonetheless, *Harmonium* did receive favorable notices in important places, most notably a perceptive review by Marianne Moore in the *Dial*, and over the next two years critics such as Paul Rosenfeld, Gorham Munson, and Llewelyn Powys published essays on Stevens's poetry. Nothing could be more remote from Frost's dry New England style than Stevens's dandified aestheticism; nevertheless, Stevens also represented a major tradition in modern American poetry, that stemming from the European symbolists.

What Stevens and Frost shared was a profound individualism. Frost spoke the language of Yankee puritanism and agrarian independence, in the voice of the "small-holder," the farmer who owns and works his land, holding out against all the corrupt values of urban industrialization. Stevens's individualism was that of the man of imagination, living ardently his own inner life. "Life is not people and scene but thought and feeling," he wrote in his "Adagia," and also, "The world is myself. Life is myself." Stevens, like Frost, was passionately a champion of personal freedom and spontaneity, and disdainful of ideologies, regimentation, and vulgar materialism.

All this skepticism and individualism did not sit well with the new breed of leftist critics in the 1930s, for the most part men much younger than Frost and Stevens. Both poets brought out new volumes of verse during the Depression: in 1935 Stevens's *Ideas of Order* and in 1936 Frost's *A Further Range*. These

Elinor Wylie (courtesy of the Beinecke Rare Book and Manuscript Library, Yale University)

books set the critics railing against everything they perceived as irrelevant to the current crisis in the world. Stanley Burnshaw, writing in the *New Masses*, called Stevens's volume "the record of a man who, having lost his footing, now scrambles to stand up and keep his balance." He called *Harmonium* "the kind of verse that people concerned with the murderous world collapse can hardly swallow today except in tiny doses" (although Burnshaw recognized that *Harmonium* had already begun to look like one of the classics of the 1920s, a decade that was definitely over). Further criticism came from Geoffrey Grigson, writing in *New Verse* under the title "The Stuffed Goldfinch." He found in *Ideas of Order* "less panache, periwinkle, cantilene, fewer melons and peacocks" than in *Harmonium*, "but still the finicking privateer, prosy Herrick, Klee without rhythm, observing nothing, single artificer of his own world of mannerism, mixer-up of chinoiserie. . . . Too much Wallace Stevens, too little everything else. . . . Decidedly, this charming Wallace Stevens is fixed in his 1923. He

Robert Frost and Wallace
Stevens, 1935 (courtesy of
The Henry E. Hunting-
ton Library and
Art Gallery)

is dated between the two realities of the past and the future; that means, he is an 'imagist' emanation of a *dies non* we do not remember and do not bother to recall."

Stevens answered these criticisms first by publishing an *apologia* on the dust jacket of the 1936 edition of *Ideas of Order*: "While it is inevitable that a poet should be concerned with [questions of political and social order], this book, although it reflects them, is primarily concerned with ideas of order of a different nature, as, for example, the dependence of the individual, confronting the elimination of established ideas, on the general sense of order. . . . The book is essentially a book of pure poetry. I believe that, in any society, the poet should be the exponent of the imagination of that society. *Ideas of Order* attempts to illustrate the role of the imagination in life, and particularly the role of the imagination in life at present. The more realistic life may be, the more it needs the stimulus of the imagination." Stevens did not leave the matter there. He seems to have been

seriously concerned with the true relationship of a private introspective poet and the world of politics and society, and seriously dismayed by the criticism of himself as an irrelevant aesthete. He set about immediately to write a sequence of five poems on this theme, each of them centered on the image of a statue standing in a public place, broadly representing art in a world of flux. Various characters appear in the poems, and each is defined by his particular relationship to the statue. The five poems, published as *Owl's Clover*, are among the weakest of Stevens's works, written as they are in long verse paragraphs, full of loose syntax and flaccid rhetoric.

Robert Frost's *A Further Range* came in for even severer criticism from the leftist critics. The attack had begun even before the book's publication when Newton Arvin reviewed Edwin Arlington Robinson's posthumously published *King Jasper*, for which Frost had written an introduction, in the 8 January 1936 issue of the *New Republic*. Criticizing Frost's praise of Robinson's refusal "to use poetry as a vehicle of grievances against the un-Utopian state," Arvin found in Frost's attitude "a cant of skepticism, a complacency of the pessimist." Arvin and other leftist critics were calling for a literature that would voice its support for revolutionary class struggle and speak up for the rights of the masses. When *A Further Range* came out the following June, these critics–led by Arvin–were prepared. Writing for the *Partisan Review*, Arvin asserted that Frost was not, as many had said, the voice of all New England but only that of "the New England of nasalized negations, monosyllabic uncertainties, and non-committal rejoinders." Rather than representing the New England that had given birth to the militant reformers of the nineteenth century, Frost was the "laureate" of "Yankee renunciation." Horace Gregory, in the *New Republic*, carried the attack still further, asserting that Frost was not the inheritor of the great New England tradition of Emerson and Whittier, because he refused "to carry an unwelcome load of social responsibility." When Frost did venture into political commentary in his poems, Gregory said, "his wisdom may be compared with that of Calvin Coolidge." R. P. Blackmur, in the *Nation*, wrote that Frost was "at heart, an easygoing versifier of all that comes to hand, and hence never lacks either a subject or the sense of its mastery"–not a true poet but a "bard," who promises escape, not confrontation. The harshest criticism came from the *New Masses*, where Rolfe Humphries, in a review titled "A Further Shrinking," wrote, "There is an aspect of Robert Frost which criticism can dismiss with objuration; when you call him a reactionary -------, or a counter-revolutionary --- -- - -----, you have, in essence, said it all."

Frost's reaction to such criticism was rage and anxiety. But he was not without his defenders, most notably Bernard DeVoto. In January 1938 DeVoto published "The Critics and Robert Frost" in *Saturday Review of Literature*. He began by thumping all of Frost's detractors, from Amy Lowell onward. He called Blackmur's assessment "one of the most idiotic reviews since the invention of movable type. The monkeys would have to tap typewriters throughout eternity to surpass it, and Mr. Blackmur may regard his immortality as achieved." Then DeVoto defended Frost against the attacks of the left-wing critics by asserting that he was "the only pure proletarian poet of our time. His is the only body of poetry of this age which originates in the experience of humble people, treated with the profound respect of identification, and used as the sole measure of the reality and value of experience." DeVoto also accused the critics of misconstruing Frost's comic mode: "Much of the impatience that one kind of critic feels for him comes from his antic willingness to make jokes about the verities. The pure literary thinker will permit truth no handmaiden but solemnity. . . . It is besides a traditional habit of Yankees to say less than they mean, to say it lightly, and to let any fool go uncorrected who therefore takes them for fools."

What effect did these negative reviews on the 1930s have upon the subsequent works of Frost and Stevens? For Frost, next to none. Rather than change his position, he expressed it more vigorously. As Louise Bogan summarized his later career: "the evidence increasingly showed, there would be no shocking confrontations, as in the later Yeats, and no profound spiritual insights, as in the case of Eliot. . . . If he consistently clung to the middle region of mild faith and to a middle tone–which ruled out the noble, 'lofty,' and transcendent manner–he did not slip back into any false romanticism of style or of attitude, and he continued to avoid the plaintive, the inflated, and the confused."

Wallace Stevens would seem, on the other hand, to have been profoundly affected by the challenge of the leftist critics. After writing *Owl's Clover* in an attempt to clarify his own position on the relationship of poetry and society, Stevens set out in his true stride. Beginning with *The Man with the Blue Guitar* (1937) all of Stevens's work was devoted to the meaning of poetry and its relation to life. Most of Stevens's chief ideas can be found in his only prose volume, *The Necessary Angel* (1951), which is subtitled "Essays on Reality and the Imagination." His *Notes toward a Supreme Fiction* (1942) is the central work among his long late poems, and that poem, together with all the rest of his late poetry, constitutes one of the most rigorous and extended defences of poetry in the English language.

Neither Frost's nor Stevens's reputations can be said to have suffered much as a result of the attacks of the 1930s. Frost, who had already been awarded the Pulitzer Prize for poetry twice before, won it again for *A Further Range* and yet again in 1943 for *A Witness Tree*. Fellowships, medals, and honorary degrees were showered upon him in his old age, including honorary degrees from Oxford and Cambridge Universities. Resolutions of the U.S. Senate on his seventy-fifth and eighty-fifth birthdays conferred upon him a kind of unofficial poet-laureateship, and he was invited to read a poem at the inauguration of President Kennedy in 1961. Stevens too was honored in his own time, and the great poetry he wrote in his old age ultimately ensured that he would be regarded as a major American poet, especially as the aesthetic poets' poet and defender of poetry.

Literary Patronage:
Theodore Roosevelt

by SANFORD E. MAROVITZ

Along with Thomas Jefferson and Woodrow Wilson, Theodore Roosevelt was among the most distinguished men of letters ever to have occupied the White House. Many of his volumes of history received great acclaim soon after publication. A member of the American Academy of Arts and Letters, he was the constant associate of the leading writers of his day; and, as President of the United States for most of the first decade of the present century, he was in a position of great influence over contemporary literary directions in this country. A voracious reader with an intense power of concentration, Roosevelt was aware of all current major American authors and many of the minor ones. His sense of propriety in letters was very strong, however, and he vigorously opposed the naturalistic themes, conflicts, and language that were becoming not only acceptable but laudable in some literary quarters.

He was deeply offended, for example, by the fictionalized exposés of David Graham Phillips and Upton Sinclair, who revealed respectively the corruption in American politics and the sordid effects of labor exploitation on the lower classes at the turn of the century. Although he did not deny that parts of what Sinclair described in *The Jungle* (1906) were true, he did not believe that the conditions in Chicago's meat-packing industry were indicative of American life as a whole, which he asserted was being maligned as fundamentally rotten. Thus he insisted that such fiction was not only ill-advised but downright un-American because it suggested that the social structure of the nation

Theodore Roosevelt on a round-up in Minnesota, 1885 (photograph by Ingersoll)

was already too far gone to be reformed and that destruction or revolution was its only corrective.

In holding this attitude Roosevelt was far from alone at the time. For the most part his interest in the American West and his political career coordinated with his social background among upper-class New York families to make it possible for him to become acquainted with many important editors and authors, including Henry Adams, Edith Wharton, Hamilton Wright Mabie, Richard Watson Gilder, Hamlin Garland, William Vaughn Moody, Richard Harding Davis, Finley Peter Dunne ("Mr.

215

Dooley"), and a great many others. It is no wonder that William Dean Howells, who supported Roosevelt's advocacy of a simplified manner of spelling in English, thought of him as a human dynamo. Among the multitude of authors with whom he associated and often dined, his relations with three of them—Owen Wister, Stephen Crane, and Edwin Arlington Robinson—are especially consequential, though the durations for each relationship varied from only a few months to the better part of a lifetime.

Owen Wister first saw Roosevelt in the boxing ring at Harvard in 1879, when he was a freshman and the future President was a junior. According to Wister's autobiographical account of their friendship, after the first encounter he and Roosevelt met nearly every day, and by the time Roosevelt graduated the following year, their relationship had solidified. In the mid 1880s it became advisable for both young men to travel west for their health. Intending to write at length in the West, Roosevelt moved to a ranch he had recently purchased in North Dakota; while writing his *Hunting Trips of a Ranchman* (1885) and his biography of artist Thomas Hart Benton (1887) as well as magazine articles at the ranch, he was losing his debilitating asthmatic condition and gaining considerable strength. His writing there and later largely reflects the attitude toward life that he displayed in the Badlands of Dakota, on the battlefield in Cuba, in New York politics, and in the Presidency: directness and virility with a strong injection of platitudinous morality in order to instruct a reading public that he believed needed to have true Americanism more clearly defined and exemplified for them.

With this kind of attitude Owen Wister and their mutual friend, Frederic Remington, the widely admired illustrator, were totally sympathetic. Wister entered details of his first trip to Wyoming and, afterward, to other western territories in journals from which

Owen Wister in costume for one of the many roles he played in Harvard theatricals, 1880 (courtesy of American Heritage Center, University of Wyoming, Laramie)

he later drew heavily in composing his western stories. His intention was to celebrate and save for posterity the West that was rapidly passing from existence, and Remington often provided the memorable illustrations for his texts. The novel for which Wister is best known today is *The Virginian* (1902), in which the anonymous hero is partly based on Theodore Roosevelt. It is a book that the President greatly admired when it appeared.

Roosevelt read Wister's stories as they were published in magazines during the 1890s and commented on them to the author. That Wister took his friend's criticism seriously enough to act upon it is evident from an incident that occurred after the publication of "Balaam and Pedro" in *Harper's Monthly* (January 1894). In that story he described a brutal scene in which a rancher becomes so enraged over the inability of his tired horse to travel well on the trail that he gouges out one of the animal's eyes with his thumb, an act that brings the righteous ire of the Virginian down upon him with "sledge-hammer blows of justice." Horrified by Balaam's viciousness, Roosevelt urged Wister to excise the description when he incorporated the story in his novel, and the author reluctantly did so. If the suggested revision thinned out the realism with which Wister intended to display life on the frontier—with its cruelty as well as its nobility—the change may well have assured a larger commercial success for *The Virginian* in that the more delicate segment of the marketplace would have been shocked by the episode in its original form.

By the time Roosevelt died in 1919, he had achieved nearly mythic stature for Wister, who kept on his desk long afterward a cartoon by J. N. Darling that was published the morning following Roosevelt's death. In this "great cartoon," Wister wrote, Roosevelt "is in cowboy dress, on his horse, headed for the Great Divide: but he is turning back for a last look at us, smiling, waving his hat. On his horse: the figure from other days; the Apparition, the crusader, bidding us farewell."

The year after he was appointed commissioner of the New York City Police in 1895, Roosevelt met Stephen Crane. Roosevelt had published the third volume of his *The Winning of the West* in 1894, and Crane had returned in mid 1896 from several months in the West and Southwest; there he had stored in his imagination material that he would employ in some of his best short fiction, including "The Blue Hotel," "The Bride Comes to Yellow Sky," and several tales and sketches set in Mexico. His initial association with Roosevelt seemed auspicious. Soon after the publication of *George's Mother* in 1896, Crane sent Roosevelt a signed copy, which drew an immediate letter of response from the police commissioner. The letter made it

clear that Roosevelt had already read *Maggie: A Girl of the Streets* (1893) and *The Red Badge of Courage* (1895). Perhaps he had not read *Maggie* very closely because in his letter he referred to the heroine as "Madge." *The Red Badge of Courage*, however, drew Roosevelt's praise; it was his favorite of Crane's books thus far, he said, though he obviously appreciated as well the new inscribed volume he had just received.

Crane's congenial relations with Roosevelt proved short lived. In August of the same year, Crane had a skirmish with the New York City Police at Madison Square Garden and wrote of it to Roosevelt. The commissioner responded politely, indicating that he intended to visit the Garden himself that evening to see how the police were operating. At the time that Roosevelt was appointed commissioner, the police force of the city was notoriously corrupt, and he was making an extensive effort to clean it up. In writing to Crane, he reminded the young author of the police officer's difficult role in New York City at the time, particularly in the area of Madison Square Garden, where crowds were often immense and unruly.

Although nothing further came of that incident, Crane again became involved in a controversy with the police later that year as he was commencing a series of articles on life near the bottom of the social ladder in New York City. He described a shocking scene that he witnessed at a police court in Greenwich Village on 14 September, and the following evening he arranged to interview two or three "chorus girls" in the Tenderloin district near Broadway. After the interview, as he was helping one of the girls onto a streetcar, a police detective arrested one of them for soliciting. Knowing that she was being falsely accused, Crane attempted to defend her, but she was charged and jailed overnight nevertheless. He was warned by the arresting detective and several other officers to forget about defending her in court because his reputation would be jeopardized, but when her case came to trial, he was there to assist her. He affirmed her innocence, however guilty of soliciting she may have been at other times, and called the arresting detective a liar. When he complained again to Roosevelt, his complaint was ignored, and the relationship between the two men ended with that incident.

The ramifications of Crane's "knight-errantry" in the Tenderloin district, however, were enduring. From late 1896 to the end of his short life, he was considered *persona non grata* by the New York City Police and harassed by them whenever he returned to the city. Evidently, Roosevelt never forgave Crane's outspoken and highly publicized censure of the police during his term as commissioner, for even when Crane praised him later as a commendable leader of troops in Cuba, Roosevelt said nothing to or about him. The commissioner's truth and Crane's truth were clearly incompatible when the subject in question was the seamy side of life in New York City.

But Roosevelt was neither a hypocrite nor a snob, and his moral views as a man of letters were no more demanding or precious than those of the conventional literary elite of his day, both inheritors of and participants in what George Santayana called "the genteel tradition." Roosevelt himself has been cited as being "in many ways [that tradition's] personification and voice," though in many others he represents the force, vigor, and drive of frontier America, as his Dakota days and his courage on Kettle Hill in the Spanish-American War suggest. If his literary insight was at times inhibited by his moral extremism and the propriety insisted upon by writers of the genteel tradition, he was nonetheless sensitive to good poetry—however much of its underlying substance he may have missed.

It was directly to this sensitivity that Edwin Arlington Robinson could attribute a stroke of good fortune. Just after the turn of the century, Robinson was broke, in poor health and spirits, and drinking heavily (partly as the result of seeking out the free lunches that came with the price of a drink in saloons at the time) when a friend found him a job working on the New York subway, then under construction. For nine months—from the late fall of 1903 to August 1904—he worked underground clocking the laborers as they came and went and tallying the supplies delivered to the tunnel entrances through the day. It was a cold, dark, depressing routine for which he received two dollars a day, but he had no alternative. When the section of tunnels where he worked was finished, he was laid off. By then, he already had three books published.

Robinson's second collection—*The Children of the Night* (1897)—came to Roosevelt's attention in early 1904, when his son Kermit, then at Groton, sent him a copy of the volume indicating that he had been strongly impressed by the poems. Campaigning for the elections that fall, Roosevelt is said to have read and reread the book as he traveled. Although he acknowledged that he did not understand everything in the poetry, he was affected by Robinson's power with words, and the following year he wrote a letter inviting the poet to the White House. Robinson declined because he felt that his clothes were too shabby, but his friends, recognizing the President's decided interest in the poems, advised Roosevelt of the poet's moneyless state and urged him to find a suitable position for the destitute writer. Roosevelt sought a government post that would enable Robinson to remain in or near the United States because he felt that an author away from his homeland loses his source of inspiration, and when a position in Canada became available, he offered it to the poet. But Robinson refused; the job took him too far away from New York, to which he had grown accustomed. Surprised by the rejection, Roosevelt asked Robinson more specifically and perhaps a little ironically what kind of work he was seeking, and eventually the President was able to place him in the Custom House on Wall Street as a "special agent of the Treasury" at an annual salary of two thousand dollars, quite a lift from that two-dollar-a-day wage in the subway a year earlier. Moreover, little work was expected of him in the job, which was more a sinecure than a responsible position—a point that Roosevelt made clear soon after Robinson had begun. In fact, the President was giving him leisure to write under salary, and once Robinson's conscience was assuaged, he spent only minimal time in the office. In 1909, when Roosevelt left the White House, Robinson was eased out of the Custom House under threat of having to work regular office hours if he stayed. Even with extended hours of freedom daily he had worked with little success at playwriting and published only a handful of poems in magazines during his four years as a Treasury agent.

Robinson remained grateful to Roosevelt not only for the job, which helped him to four years of financial security, but also for the President's efforts to advance his reputation. Robinson had never been able to place his work in the popular magazines, which provided poets with the opportunity of gaining a market for their books. Editors had been reluctant to accept Robinson's poems, and in consequence his first three books had achieved a very limited readership. However, Roosevelt influenced Scribners to bring out several of Robinson's poems in their monthly magazine and to republish the poet's *The Children of the Night*, no longer available because the original publisher had gone into bankruptcy. Still further, Roosevelt wrote a solid appreciation of Robinson's work. Published in the 12 August 1905 issue of the *Outlook* only two months after the poet slipped into his sinecure on Wall Street, Roosevelt's article brought more than favorable attention to his poems—it provoked the anger of professional critics who considered Robinson at best a minor poet unworthy of such publicity. But within the next decade the critical tide turned decidedly in Robinson's favor. As one of Robinson's chief biographers has stated, "An American President, patron of letters in the tradition of enlightened rulers, saved him at a critical moment."

Many of the authors with whom Roosevelt carried on enthusiastic discussions about their work and his own, in the White House and elsewhere, would have concurred with this tribute to the President; but Robinson's debt to him was unquestionably the greatest.

MARK TWAIN CATALOGUES "FENIMORE COOPER'S LITERARY OFFENCES."

Cooper's art has some defects. In one place in *Deerslayer,* and in the restricted space of two-thirds of a page, Cooper has scored 114 offences against literary art out of a possible 115. It breaks the record.

There are nineteen rules governing literary art in the domain of romantic fiction–some say twenty-two. In *Deerslayer* Cooper violated eighteen of them. These eighteen require:

1. That a tale shall accomplish something and arrive somewhere. But the *Deerslayer* tale accomplishes nothing and arrives in the air.

2. They require that the episodes of a tale shall be necessary parts of the tale, and shall help to develop it. But as the *Deerslayer* tale is not a tale, and accomplishes nothing and arrives nowhere, the episodes have no rightful place in the work, since there was nothing for them to develop.

3. They require that the personages in a tale shall be alive, except in the case of corpses, and that always the reader shall be able to tell the corpses from the others. But this detail has often been overlooked in the *Deerslayer* tale.

4. They require that the personages in a tale, both dead and alive, shall exhibit a sufficient excuse for being there. But this detail also has been overlooked in the *Deerslayer* tale.

5. They require that when the personages of a tale deal in coversation, the talk shall sound like human talk, and be talk such as human beings would be likely to talk in the given circumstances, and have a discoverable meaning, also a discoverable purpose, and a show of relevancy, and remain in the neighborhood of the subject in hand, and be interesting to the reader, and help out the tale, and stop when the people cannot think of anything more to say. But this requirement has been ignored from the beginning of the *Deerslayer* tale to the end of it.

6. They require that when the author describes the character of a personage in his tale, the conduct and conversation of that personage shall justify said description. But this law gets little or no attention in the *Deerslayer* tale, as Natty Bumppo's case will amply prove.

7. They require that when a personage talks like an illustrated, gilt-edged, tree-calf, hand-tooled, seven-dollar Friendship's Offering in the beginning of a paragraph, he shall not talk like a negro minstrel in the end of it. But this rule is flung down and danced upon in the *Deerslayer* tale.

8. They require that crass stupidities shall not be played upon the reader as "the craft of the woodsman, the delicate art of the forest," by either the author or the people in the tale. But this rule is persistently violated in the *Deerslayer* tale.

9. They require that the personages of a tale shall confine themselves to possibilities and let miracles alone; or, if they venture a miracle, the author must so plausibly set it forth as to make it look possible and reasonable. But these rules are not respected in the *Deerslayer* tale.

10. They require that the author shall make the reader feel a deep interest in the personages of his tale and in their fate; and that he shall make the reader love the good people in the tale and hate the bad ones. But the reader of the *Deerslayer* tale dislikes the good people in it, is indifferent to the others, and wishes they would all get drowned together.

11. They require that the characters in a tale shall be so clearly defined that the reader can tell beforehand what each will do in a given emergency. But in the *Deerslayer* tale this rule is vacated.

In addition to these large rules there are some little ones. These require that the author shall

12. *Say* what he is proposing to say, not merely come near it.

13. Use the right word, not its second cousin.

14. Eschew surplusage.

15. Not omit necessary details.

16. Avoid slovenliness of form.

17. Use good grammar.

18. Employ a simple and straightforward style.

Even these seven are coldly and persistently violated in the *Deerslayer* tale.

–*North American Review* (July 1895)

Literary Censorship
in America

by FELICE F. LEWIS

The history of literary censorship in America dates back to the Colonial period. For example, a statute enacted in Massachusetts Bay Colony in 1711, entitled "An Act against Intemperance, Immorality, and Profaneness, and for Reformation of Manners," prohibited the writing, printing, or publishing of filthy, obscene, or profane songs, pamphlets, or mock sermons.

Recorded instances of censorship in the colonies indicate that aside from publications critical of governmental policies and personnel, the printed matter banned consisted primarily of books and pamphlets considered blasphemous. At one time blasphemy, a charge leveled against any religious philosophy inconsistent with predominant local beliefs, was thought so heinous an offense as to warrant a death sentence in Maryland, Massachusetts, and Plymouth Colony.

No record has been found of an effort by colonial authorities to suppress material solely on the grounds that it had a tendency to arouse sexual desires, as would be the case after the founding of the Republic. One legal action did involve a somewhat erotic English novelette, Henry Neville's *The Isle of Pines*, which depicts the cohabitation of a man and four women shipwrecked on a desert island; Marmaduke Johnson, the Cambridge printer who was convicted and fined in 1668 for having the book on his premises, was charged with possessing unlicensed material in violation of the Massachusetts licensing law.

During the early years of the Repub-lic at least some erotic literature was evidently in circulation. An edition of *The Arabian Nights*, a book that censors would eventually try to suppress, was published by a Baltimore firm in 1794, and an almanac of that period featured a very frank ballad on bundling. Moreover, suggestive English novels published in the 1700s (some of which—for example, Daniel Defoe's *Moll Flanders* and *Roxana*—the U.S. Customs Bureau banned as late as the twentieth century) were no doubt customarily imported, as well as erotic classics. Yet for thirty-four years after the drafting of the Constitution in 1787 there were no state or federal antiobscenity laws. The first such statutes were adopted by Vermont in 1821, Connecticut in 1834, and Massachusetts in 1835.

In 1815 a Pennsylvania court ruled that a painting was obscene, relying on English common-law precedents. And in 1821 a novel, *Memoirs of a Woman of Pleasure*, met the same fate in Boston. The defendants in these two earliest obscenity cases of record in the United States were found guilty of intentionally contriving to corrupt the morals of young people and other citizens, and of creating in their minds "inordinate and lustful desires." *Memoirs of a Woman of Pleasure* (better known as *Fanny Hill*) was written by a Scotsman, John Cleland, around 1749. An Englishman was sentenced to the pillory for selling it a few years later, and for the next two centuries the story of Fanny's countless libidinous escapades, though told in relatively discreet language, was apparently so widely assumed to be obscene that dealers on both sides of the Atlantic seldom dared to stock it.

Despite the antiobscenity laws passed by various states, and by Congress beginning in 1842, few other prosecutions seem to have occurred (and none involving a fictional work) until Anthony Comstock, while working as a salesman in New York City, began his crusade against artifacts of every type that he considered immoral. He is credited with having written the comprehensive 1868 New York state antiobscenity statute that the Young Men's Christian Association sponsored. Immediately thereafter Comstock began having dealers in erotic literature arrested. By December of 1872, backed by the YMCA Committee for the Suppression of Vice, which he helped form, Comstock was in the nation's capitol lobbying for a bill to strengthen the previous federal prohibitions against the mailing of obscene publications. The so-called Comstock Act, signed by President Grant in 1873, has never been repealed. In addition, Comstock helped organize antivice groups in several northeastern cities, one being a predecessor of Boston's militant Watch and Ward Society, the instigator of the 1920s "Boston book massacre."

When Comstock was named Secretary of the New York Society for the Suppression of Vice he was himself authorized to make arrests, a power he used to punish and harass distributors of any products of which he disapproved—for instance, people who published contraceptive information and those who sold the "rubber goods" as well. The fiction he attacked consisted principally of books such as *Fanny Hill*, *The Lustful Turk*, and *A Night in a Moorish Harem*; yet he also attempted to suppress works long regarded as literary classics. In 1894 he opposed the sale of *Tom Jones*, *The Decameron*, *The Heptameron*, *Gargantua and Pantagruel*, and several other books that were among the assets of a bankrupt firm. The New York Supreme Court judge

Anthony Comstock

who decided the case (*In re Worthington*) firmly rejected Comstock's point of view, relying on what came to be known as the whole-book rule. While the judge conceded that "a seeker after the sensual and degrading parts of a narrative may find in all these works, as in those of other great authors, something to satisfy his pruriency," he noted that "to condemn a standard literary work, because of a few of its episodes, would compel the exclusion from circulation of a very large portion of the works of fiction of the most famous writers of the English language." Other courts, however, refused for decades to accept the whole-book rule.

By the turn of the century, literature written by distinguished contemporary foreign authors was being attacked. In 1890 Leo Tolstoy's *The Kreutzer Sonata*, a diatribe against licentious practices in Russia, was banned by postal authorities in New York City, but in Philadelphia it was ruled not obscene. In 1897 a charge brought by Comstock against the American publisher of *The Triumph of Death*, a complex psychological study by Gabriele d'Annunzio of an adulterous love affair, was rejected by a New York City court. And in 1905 George Bernard Shaw's play *Mrs. Warren's Profession*, which blames English social conditions of that day for the prevalence of prostitution, was closed after one performance in both New Haven and New York City, although the producer and others arrested on opening night in New York were eventually acquitted.

While up to this point American authors had seldom given censors a reason to find fault with their work, two American masterpieces of the 1850s were harshly criticized for many years—Nathaniel Hawthorne's *The Scarlet Letter* and Walt Whitman's *Leaves of Grass*. Whitman's celebration of sexuality was a decided deviation from the literary mores of the nineteenth century, as was the blunt language he used to convey his poetic vision of the divinity of human and animal life. In contrast, Hawthorne wrote with the utmost circumspection in relating the tragic consequences of a minister's adulterous transgression in a seventeenth-century Puritan community, yet *The Scarlet Letter* was also accused of fostering immorality. Neither book appears to have precipitated a legal action, but a new edition of *Leaves of Grass* was withdrawn by a Boston publisher in 1881 when he was threatened with prosecution.

In the 1890s a few Americans, emulating the naturalism of Émile Zola, began to write somewhat more frankly than had the vast majority of their predecessors. However, in order to have their fiction published they usually were forced to delete or modify expressions that violated the prevailing code of propriety. Such was the experience of Stephen Crane with *Maggie: A Girl of the Streets*. At first unable to find a publisher for the novel, Crane had it printed at his own expense in 1893, using a pseudonym. When Appleton agreed to pub-

Seal of the Society for the Suppression of Vice

lish it three years later, after *The Red Badge of Courage* had catapulted Crane into the ranks of leading modern authors, taboo words in the original version were reduced to *d—* and *h–ll* or were omitted.

The practice of cleansing literature of any unrefined terminology, which began in England well before Queen Victoria ascended the throne, was so common during her reign (1837-1901) that it is generally associated with the Victorian era. Works by eminent English writers of earlier periods, including Shakespeare's plays, were habitually expurgated before being republished in their homeland and in America. Thus at the dawn of the twentieth century reputable editors and publishers were long accustomed to observing the limits imposed by the "genteel" tradition and tended to think that prudence required them either to reject bolder manuscripts or to insist on revisions.

The first American work of fiction defended in court was apparently *Hagar Revelly*, a romance by Daniel Carson Goodman. It illustrates that in 1913 a relatively innocuous novel could lead to an obscenity judgment. Hagar's sensual experiences are described in a few lines, in guarded terms, without mention of the culminating act; and her character is compared unfavorably with that of her sister Thatah, a paragon of virtue who takes care of Hagar's illegitimate child and wins the man whom Hagar longed to marry. Two legal actions followed the book's publication by Mitchell Kennerley. A clerk who had sold a copy of it was convicted by a New York State court. More fortunate was Kennerley, against whom a federal charge was brought under the Comstock Act. Although he failed in his effort to have the indictment dismissed, the trial jury found that *Hagar Revelly* was not immoral.

Earlier, three of Theodore Dreiser's powerful naturalistic novels had appeared. His first, *Sister Carrie* (1900), was unorthodox despite the paucity of its sexual material, for Dreiser presented Carrie's waywardness sympathetically and as being no impediment to her achievement of fame and fortune. While not legally banned, the book was denounced as immoral by most reviewers and by Frank Doubleday, who was abroad when his firm contracted to publish it. Doubleday, after endeavoring unsuccessfully to persuade Dreiser to release the firm from its obligation, refused to advertise the work. Whether due to insufficient promotion (as Dreiser claimed) or the generally poor reviews, fewer than 500 copies of the Doubleday edition were sold. When *Sister Carrie* was republished by B. W. Dodge & Company seven years later, it was still castigated by a few critics but others praised it effusively, and it came close to being a best-seller.

Although Dreiser's subsequent novels were likewise criticized, he had been widely recognized as a leading American author before The *"Genius"* ran into censorship trouble. Several months after publishing it in 1915, the John Lane Company recalled all of the unsold volumes upon being notified by John Sum-

ner (successor to Comstock as the chief agent of the Society for the Suppression of Vice) that the book contained seventy-five lewd and seventeen profane passages. Over the next sixteen years Dreiser and his friends kept seeking a way to have the novel republished, even going so far as to confer with Sumner about the possibility of an expurgated edition. The problem could not be solved by deleting an occasional phrase, however, for in language no more frank than was usual Dreiser had drawn the picture of an artist who indulged his obsessive preoccupation with sexual gratification at every opportunity and who thought that his exceptional talent exempted him from conforming to ordinary standards of behavior. Finally, in 1923, Boni & Liveright brought out an unrevised edition of The *"Genius"*, and this time Sumner did not intervene.

Meanwhile Sumner, in January of 1920, had seized the plates and unsold copies of James Branch Cabell's *Jurgen* from the book's publisher, Robert M. McBride & Company. Cabell—a polished, recondite, antirealistic novelist—was at the height of his fame, and the pseudomythical *Jurgen* had been praised unstintingly when it appeared the previous year. Nevertheless, sale of the work was suspended for nearly three years, until the judge presiding at McBride's trial directed the jury to return a verdict of acquittal. Calling Cabell's style brilliant, the judge remarked: "The most that can be said against the book is that certain passages therein may be considered suggestive in a veiled and subtle way of immorality, but such suggestions are delicately conveyed and the whole atmosphere of the story is of such an unreal and supernatural nature that even these suggestions are free from the evils accompanying suggestiveness in more realistic works."

For Theodore Dreiser another tangle with antivice crusaders lay just ahead, over a novel containing very little sexual material and greeted by reviewers as a masterpiece—*An American Tragedy*. Pub-

John Sumner

cause it included Herbert Asbury's short story "Hatrack," about a small-town prostitute who took her Protestant clients to the Catholic cemetery and her Catholic clients to the Masonic burial grounds. Though the magistrate who heard the case found that Mencken had committed "no offense" in Boston, a Cambridge dealer was fined for selling the same publication.

Among the novels banned extralegally around that time were Ernest Hemingway's *The Sun Also Rises*, William Faulkner's *Mosquitos,* Sherwood Anderson's *Many Marriages* and *Dark Laughter,* Conrad Aiken's *Blue Voyage,* Upton Sinclair's *Oil!,* and John Dos Passos's *Manhattan Transfer.* When *An American Tragedy* received the same treatment, a partner in the firm of Boni & Liveright, Donald Friede, went to Boston in 1927 and sold a copy to a police lieutenant, confident that no court would rule against him, but Friede was mistaken. He was found guilty of selling obscene literature, and his conviction was unanimously upheld by the Supreme Judicial Court of Massachusetts. The judge who delivered the adverse opinion of Massachusetts's highest court maintained that suppression was justified because "even assuming real literary excellence, artistic worth and an impelling moral lesson in the story, there is nothing essential to the history of the life of its principal character that would be lost if these passages were omitted which the jury found were obscene, indecent and manifestly tending to corrupt the morals of youth." In future years other judges would also assert that a condemned work would have been equally as effective, if not more so, had the author excluded controversial material.

lished by Boni & Liveright in 1925, this work, a two-volume fictionalized version of an actual murder case, was informally banned in Boston. Censors in that city had developed a procedure which resulted in the suppression of literature throughout Massachusetts. Whenever a joint committee of booksellers and members of the Watch and Ward Society concluded that a publication might be legally obscene, the Board of Trade of the Boston Book Merchants relayed that information to its constituency. Dealers tended to heed the warning so scrupulously that legal actions were rare until publishers and other interested parties began to invite test cases in the late 1920s by themselves selling a proscribed book or literary journal on the streets of Boston. H. L. Mencken, for example, was arrested on the Boston Common in April 1926 for selling a copy of that month's issue of *American Mercury,* which had been banned in that city be-

Not in the least persuaded by such advice were a number of American authors who were on the verge of departing much more drastically than had Dreiser from Victorian literary mores. One was William Faulkner, whose sensational sixth novel *Sanctuary*

H. L. Mencken (center) after his arrest for selling a copy of the April 1926 copy of the *American Mercury* on Boston Common (courtesy of the Enoch Pratt Free Library, Baltimore, Maryland)

(1931) features incidences of rape and voyeurism as well as terms such as *whore* and *son of a bitch*. Another was James T. Farrell, who in *Young Lonigan* (1932) also used those and similar expressions and referred indirectly to masturbation and venereal disease. Surprisingly, for some fifteen years neither of these books was involved in litigation; but when Viking Press published *God's Little Acre* (1933), a tragi-comic depiction by Erskine Caldwell of a rural Southern family's primitive values and lifestyle in which risqué allusions abound, John Sumner immediately sued Viking and a clerk who had sold a copy of the novel. Although that suit was dismissed by a New York City magistrate on the grounds that the book had "no tendency to inspire its readers to behave like its characters," in 1950 the work was ruled obscene in Massachusetts.

The most famous literary case of the 1930s arose over a contemporary foreign novel, James Joyce's *Ulysses*. Before the work was published in book form, an excerpt that had appeared in the July-August 1920 issue of the *Little Review* was declared obscene by a New York state court in a suit brought by John Sumner against Margaret C. Anderson and Jane Heap, copublishers of the influential Greenwich Village journal, who had been publishing the novel in serial form. When *Ulysses* was published in Paris by Shakespeare & Company in 1922, the Bureau of Customs prohibited its admission into the United States. Joyce, unable to obtain an American copyright, could not stop the clandestine printing and sale of the book until Bennett Cerf of Random House came to his aid. Cerf arranged for copies to be imported, then contested the government's seizure of the novel. A federal trial without jury ensued in 1933 before Judge John M. Woolsey of the Southern District of New York. Judge Woolsey held that *Ulysses* was neither obscene nor pornographic. (He defined *obscene* as meaning a tendency "to stir the sex impulses or to lead to sexually impure and lustful thoughts," and *pornographic* as meaning "written for the purpose of exploiting obscenity.") He said, commenting on the novel's extraordinarily explicit erotic and emetic passages: "[Joyce's] attempt sincerely and honestly to realize his objective has required him incidentally to use certain words which are generally considered dirty words and has led at times to what many think is a too poignant preoccupation with sex in the thoughts of his characters. . . . Although [the book] contains . . . many words usually considered dirty, I have not found anything that I consider to be dirt for dirt's sake. Each word of the book contributes like a bit of mosaic to the detail of the picture which Joyce is seeking to construct for his readers." The Circuit Court of Appeals affirmed Judge Woolsey's decision by a two-to-one vote in 1934, evidently relying primarily on the whole-book rule. Judge Augustus Hand said for the court: "While in a few spots it is coarse, blasphemous and obscene, it does not, in our opinion, tend to promote lust. The erotic passages are submerged in the book as a whole and have little resultant effect."

The *Ulysses* decisions did not induce customs to lift its ban against the importation of certain novels, for example D. H. Lawrence's *Lady Chatterley's Lover* and Henry Miller's *Tropic of Cancer.* Nevertheless, for a decade or more American literature was rarely attacked successfully in court, perhaps because until the late 1940s it seldom contained language as frank as that in *Ulysses.* The record was mixed in Massachusetts. Lillian Hellman's 1934 play *The Children's Hour*, a study of lesbianism with no suggestive scenes or dialogue, was banned in Boston; Lillian Smith's *Strange Fruit*, a tragic story of miscegenation, was ruled obscene in 1945 by Massachusetts's highest court; and, as mentioned above, the same court found *God's Little Acre* obscene in 1950. On the other hand, cleared of obscenity charges in Massachusetts during that period were Erskine Caldwell's *Tragic Ground*, Kathleen Winsor's *Forever Amber*, and James M. Cain's *Serenade*. In Pennsylvania, a 1948 obscenity trial without jury ended in a judgment of not guilty for five book dealers charged with possessing and intending to sell Farrell's *Studs Lonigan* trilogy and *A World I Never Made*, Faulkner's *Sanctuary* and *The Wild Palms*, Caldwell's *God's Little Acre*, Calder Willingham's *End As a Man*, and Harold Robbins's *Never Love a Stranger.* In New York, Jim Tully's *Ladies in the Parlor* was declared obscene in 1935, but subsequently no literary work by an author of repute is known to have been legally banned until *Memoirs of Hecate County*, a collection of short stories by Edmund Wilson, was published by Doubleday & Company in 1946.

Edmund Wilson was one of the most esteemed literary and social critics in America, and *Memoirs of Hecate County* had received good to excellent reviews. Moreover, of the six stories in the volume only "The Princess with the Golden Hair" contained erotic material, but that story demonstrates that around the end of World War II American fiction was once more undergoing a metamorphosis. Wilson's protagonist, a young male writer, relates in diary form every detail of his intimacy with lower-class Anna and his concomitant pursuit of Imogen, the beautiful, pampered wife of a wealthy executive. While much of the work is devoted to observations about the differing lives and personalities of the two women, the anatomically forthright accounts of the unnamed protagonist's numerous acts of intercourse with Anna, and of his climactic seduction of Imogen, leave little to the reader's imagination.

Memoirs of Hecate County was held to be obscene in both New York and California. Doubleday persuaded the U. S. Supreme Court to review the New York case, arguing that the relevant state law was unconstitutional. After considering for the first time whether the Constitution's guarantees of freedom of speech and press protect literature alleged to be obscene, the Court handed down no opinion because the Justices were divided equally, four to four, on the merits of Doubleday's appeal. As a result, the conviction was allowed to stand.

Traditionally taboo four-letter words such as *fuck* and *shit* had begun appearing very occasionally in American literature, for instance in Farrell's *A World I Never Made* (1936) and Faulkner's *The Wild Palms* (1939). These and related biological terms were used much more extensively by Willingham in *End As a Man* (1947), but the work was cleared of obscenity charges in New York as well as in Pennsylvania; and a complaint against another novel of that period, which contained many previously uncommon sexual expressions, Charles O. Gorham's *The Gilded Hearse* (1948), was dismissed by a New York City magistrate. The courts decided in essence that each was a serious literary work whose theme made the unorthodox language acceptable.

Not until 1957 did the U.S. Supreme Court rule on the validity of statutes forbidding distribution to the general public of obscene products. However, as early as 1942 the Court indicated, in *Chaplinsky v. New Hampshire*, that its justices had always assumed obscenity was not protected by the First Amendment's provisions for freedom of speech and of the press. At issue in *Chaplinsky* was a law prohibiting "fighting" words, under which a man was convicted for calling a policeman "a God damned racketeer" and "a damned Fascist." Speaking for the court, which unanimously upheld the conviction, Justice Frank Murphy said: "There are certain well-defined and narrowly limited classes of speech, the prevention and punishment of which have never been thought to raise any Constitutional problem. These include the lewd and obscene, the profane, the libelous, and the insulting or 'fighting' words . . . ." That dictum was cited fifteen years later when the Supreme Court initially ruled, in *Roth v. United States* and a companion case, that obscenity is not within the area of constitutionally protected speech or press.

Prior to the landmark *Roth* case, the Supreme Court held in *Joseph Bursyn v. Wilson* (1952) that the Constitution does not permit censorship of a motion picture on the grounds that it is "sacrilegious." That decision, together with *Roth's* definition of obscenity as material appealing to "prurient interest," finally silenced assertions that sacrilege, blasphemy, and profanity were punishable under antiobscenity laws.

Another notable pre-*Roth* case, *Butler v. Michigan*, rose over a paperback edition of John Howard Griffin's first novel, *The Devil Rides Outside*. The publisher's district manager was tried and found guilty under a law which prohibited sale to the general public of books that tended to corrupt the morals of minors. The finding of the Supreme Court in February of 1957 was that the law violated the due process clause of the Fourteenth Amendment because, in the words of Justice Felix Frankfurter, such a measure would "reduce the adult population of Michigan to reading only what is fit for children."

In *Roth v. United States* the question before the Supreme Court was the constitutionality of the Comstock Act. The historic ruling, handed down on 24 June 1957, also applied to *People v. Alberts*, which raised the same issue with respect to a California criminal obscenity statute. In neither instance was the court asked to decide whether the publications that led to the conviction of the two defendants were in fact obscene. A majority of the justices, agreeing that "obscenity is not protected speech," sustained the laws; but in delivering the Court's opinion Justice William Brennan indicated that the First Amendment imposes limits on the restraint of obscenity: "All ideas having even the slightest redeeming social importance–unorthodox ideas, controversial ideas, even ideas hateful to the prevailing climate of opinion–have the full protection of the [First Amendment] guarantees, unless excludable because they encroach upon the limited area of more important interests . . . . The portrayal of sex, *e.g.*, in art, literature and scientific works, is not itself sufficient reason to deny material the constitutional protection of freedom of speech and press." Those comments proved as influential as the definition of obscenity in *Roth*: "whether to the average person, applying contemporary community standards, the dominant theme of the material taken as a whole appeals to prurient interest."

Shortly thereafter the San Francisco Municipal Court held that Allen Ginsberg's *Howl and Other Poems* had "some redeeming importance" and was not obscene. The *Roth* guidelines were also instrumental in allowing *Lady Chatterley's Lover* (privately printed in Italy in 1928) to emerge from its thirty years of suppression. Grove Press had released in 1959 the first unexpurgated edition of Lawrence's novel to be openly published in the United States or Great Britain. Mailed copies were seized by the Post Office Department, but litigation over the book ended with a 1960 U.S. Court of Appeals judgment in favor of Grove. The following year Grove published Henry Miller's *Tropic of Cancer*, which had been banned by Customs since its Paris debut twenty-seven years earlier. The battle to clear Miller's novel was likewise won, although more than sixty legal cases were initiated, in twenty-one states, before the U.S. Supreme Court reversed a Florida conviction by a five-to-four vote in 1964.

Of greater significance was the Supreme Court's holding with respect to John Cleland's *Memoirs of a Woman of Pleasure* (or *Fanny Hill*), which after being considered indecent for some 200 years was published by G. P. Putnam's Sons in 1963. Unlike most of the literature that had thus far survived attacks in federal and state courts, this work had previously received little or no critical attention. During the litigation that followed in New York, New Jersey, and Massachusetts, several prominent university professors testified that the novel had literary and historical value, but the Massachusetts Supreme Court upheld the Boston conviction, declaring that a book need not be completely worthless before it could be deemed obscene. That judgment was reversed by the U.S. Supreme Court in 1966 by a vote of six to three, at which time Justice Brennan enunciated new guidelines, saying that the control of obscenity required a showing that "(a) the dominant theme of the material taken as a whole appeals to a prurient interest in sex; (b) the material is patently offensive because it affronts contemporary community standards relating to the description or representation of sexual matters; and (c) the material is utterly without redeeming social value." While Justice Brennan's opinion was joined only by Chief Justice Warren and Justice Fortas, Justices Black and Douglas maintained, as they

had consistently in the past, that the First Amendment barred any suppression of literature on obscenity grounds; and Justice Stewart, whose position as formerly was that hard-core pornography alone could be banned, found that Cleland's novel did not meet his criterion of obscenity.

Three months later the Massachusetts Supreme Court cleared William Burroughs's *Naked Lunch*, concluding that the work could not be said to have no redeeming social importance. Thereafter, censorship actions involving books were directed primarily against cheaply printed paperback "pulps" dealing almost entirely with deviant sexual behavior and generally not copyrighted. The U. S. Supreme Court had declared fifty such novels obscene on the same day that it issued the *Fanny Hill* ruling, but subsequently the Court overturned every obscenity conviction it reviewed in which a book was at issue until 1973.

On 21 June 1973, a majority of the Justices specifically rejected the "utterly without redeeming social value" test and adopted new standards to be used in identifying sexual material unprotected by the First Amendment. All of the five cases decided that day (one of which involved a novel, *Suite 69*) were sent back to the lower courts for reconsideration in light of the revised guidelines. Chief Justice Burger announced the new criteria in *Miller v. California*, a case that arose over unsolicited advertisements: "The basic guidelines for the trier of fact must be: (a) whether 'the average person, applying contemporary community standards' would find the work, taken as a whole, appeals to the prurient interest [Roth]; (b) whether the work depicts or describes, in a patently offensive way, sexual conduct specifically defined by the applicable state law; and (c) whether the work, taken as a whole, lacks serious literary, artistic, political, or scientific value."

States immediately began to revise their laws to comport with *Miller*, but legal actions against disseminators of literature by authors of repute essentially ceased. Undiminished, however, were the extralegal campaigns against dealers selling books and magazines disapproved by various organizations such as the National Federation for Decency and the American Renewal Foundation. Those measures received support from the 1986 report of the Attorney General's Commission on Pornography, which devoted more than thirty pages to suggesting steps that citizens could take to discourage the marketing of sexual material, including publications not legally obscene.

Much of the recent effort of censors has been directed toward purging public-school libraries. In response, a number of suits opposing the banning of books by school authorities have been initiated, with mixed results, by parents, students, teachers, and organizations such as the American Civil Liberties Union. In 1982 the U.S. Supreme Court decided one case of that type, *Board of Education v. Pico*. Nine books had been removed from a high-school library and one from a junior-high-school library by the Board of Education of the Island Trees Union Free School District No. 26 in New York. The nine were *Slaughterhouse-Five*, by Kurt Vonnegut, Jr.; *The Naked Ape*, by Desmond Morris; *Down These Mean Streets*, by Piri Thomas; *Best Short Stories of Negro Writers*, edited by Langston Hughes; *Go Ask Alice*, anonymous; *Laughing Boy*, by Oliver La Farge; *Black Boy*, by Richard Wright; *A Hero Ain't Nothin' But a Sandwich*, by Alice Childress; and *Soul on Ice*, by Eldridge Cleaver. The book in the junior-high-school library was *A Reader for Writers*, edited by Jerome Archer. The issue before the Supreme Court was whether the Board of Education was entitled to a summary judgment in its favor without a trial, as a federal District Court had ruled, or whether there were questions about the board's reasons for removing the books which warranted a trial, as the Court of Appeals had decided in reversing the District Court. Although five members of the Supreme Court held that the case should be remanded for trial, only four of them acquiesced to the conclusion expressed in Justice Brennan's plurality opinion: that under the First Amendment "local school boards may not remove books from school library shelves simply because they dislike the ideas contained in those books and seek by their removal to 'prescribe what shall be orthodox in politics, nationalism, religion, or other matters of opinion.'" Significant also is the fact that Justice Brennan limited the scope of the decision by emphasizing that the plurality opinion did not extend to the acquisition of library books, or to textbooks or required reading material. Furthermore, he implied that the First Amendment does not prevent school authorities from banning works found to be pervasively vulgar or educationally unsuitable. In addition, all of the nine Justices indicated that the federal courts should not ordinarily intervene in the resolution of conflicts which arise in the daily operation of school systems. For these reasons, the outcome of pending and future disputes over censorship in the public schools remains very much in doubt.

Book Battles: Literary Feuds

by JAMES J. MARTINE
and MORRIS P. COLDEN

A literary movement has been defined as consisting of two writers who do not like each other. This wisecrack makes the point that authorial egos are fragile and that writers can be intensely competitive. Some writers enjoy quarreling. Others apparently see feuds as a means to attract publicity. Ambitious neophytes may attack prominent writers to draw attention to themselves. Young Hemingway tried to start a feud with H. L. Mencken by dedicating *The Torrents of Spring* (1925) to "H. L. MENCKEN AND S. STANWOOD MENCKEN IN ADMIRATION." Since S. Stanwood Menken (whether Hemingway deliberately misspelled his name is a mystery) was an antivice crusader, the pairing of names was intentionally incongruous. Hemingway may have been retaliating for an unreceptive review of *In Our Time* (1925) that had appeared in H. L. Mencken's *American Mercury*. But Mencken did not take the bait, and the feud was stillborn. Hemingway continued an active feuder, especially with reviewers.

Hemingway's principal target in *The Torrents of Spring* was Sherwood Anderson, for the book is an extended parody of Anderson's *Dark Laughter* (1925). Hemingway explained to Anderson—who had helped to get *In Our Time* published—that the ridicule was meant to help Anderson: "You see I feel that if among ourselves we have to pull our punches, if when a man like yourself who can write very great things writes something that seems to me, (who have never written anything great but am anyway a fellow craftsman) rotten, I ought to tell you so." Anderson made no public response, but he avoided Hemingway thereafter. Gertrude Stein was also satirized in *The Torrents of Spring*, which triggered a bitter feud. In *The Autobiography of Alice B. Toklas* (1933), Stein described Hemingway as a coward and stated that he had learned how to write by imitating her work. Hemingway retaliated in several places. In *Green Hills of Africa* (1935) he wrote that he had taught her how to write, and he included a parody of Stein's best-known line in *For Whom the Bell Tolls* (1940): "A rose is a rose is an onion. . . . An onion is an onion is an onion . . . a stone is a stein is a rock is a boulder is a pebble." Hemingway posthumously settled this score in *A Moveable Feast* (1964), in which Stein is ridiculed—along with F. Scott Fitzgerald, Ford Madox Ford, Ernest Walsh, John Dos Passos, and other targets of opportunity.

Edgar Allan Poe suffered from the neglect of his genius and engaged in many literary quarrels resulting from his harsh reviews of other writers, as well as attempts to publicize himself. The two motives were often indistinguishable. Obviously hoping to cause a literary sensation, Poe wrote "The Literati of New York City" for *Godey's Lady's Book* in 1846. In this survey of the literary scene he published comments that had been made to him in conversations with other writers. Many of the thirty-eight editors and writers mentioned by Poe were outraged by

231

his comments and by his ungentlemanly conduct. They counterattacked. Instead of advancing his career, the articles made him a literary outcast in New York. Poe counterattacked his detractors, especially Thomas Dunn English, whom he accused of plagiarism. English responded by publishing a notice in the *New York Evening Mirror* claiming that Poe had obtained money from him under false pretenses and accusing him of forgery: "He is not alone thoroughly unprincipled, base and depraved, but silly, vain and ignorant—not alone an assassin in morals, but a quack in literature." Poe sued the *Mirror*—but not English—for damages and was awarded $225.06.

James Fenimore Cooper was a landed gentleman with strong feelings about the respect due him. The Cooper family owned a piece of property on Lake Otsego known as Three Mile Point, which the citizenry of Cooperstown were accustomed to using as a picnic spot. When Cooper returned from an extended stay abroad in 1837, he closed it to the public. The townspeople protested and passed resolutions—including one calling for the removal of Cooper's books from the library. The local Whig newspapers attacked Democrat Cooper; he sued for damages and won.

Cooper then wrote the matter into his novel *Home as Found* (1838), in which Edward Effingham represents Cooper. The press began referring to Cooper and his family as the Effinghams, which he unaccountably regarded as an insult. Since *Home as Found* was critical of American society—Cooper believed in political, not social equality—the novel and its author were attacked as anti-American. Cooper sued everyone in sight, with mixed results.

Mark Twain mostly enjoyed his feuds and claimed to have compiled a list of people to hate in order to occupy himself on long train trips.

Bernard DeVoto's *The Literary Fallacy* (1944) attacked Sinclair Lewis, claiming that it was impossible to determine whether his characters are intended as caricatures. DeVoto, who had previously praised Lewis's fiction, blamed the influence of critic Van Wyck Brooks for the distortion of American life in fiction. Lewis replied in the *Saturday Review of Literature*: "I denounce Mr. Bernard DeVoto as a fool and a tedious and egotistical fool, as a liar and a pompous and boresome liar." The feud ended there, and Lewis later seconded DeVoto's nomination to the National Institute of Arts and Letters.

Lillian Hellman's reputation for carelessness with the truth involved her in acrimonious public quarrels. In 1980 Mary McCarthy called her "a dishonest writer" on a television talk show: "I once said in an interview that every word she writes is a lie, including 'and' and 'the.'" Literature watchers believed that the bad feeling between the writers went back to the Spanish Civil War in which Hellman supported the Stalinists and McCarthy sided with a more moderate faction. Hellman instituted a $2.25 million defamation suit against McCarthy but died before the case came to trial.

Norman Mailer took on most of the writers of his generation in an essay appearing in *Advertisements for Myself* (1959), "Evaluations—Quick and Expensive Comments on the Talent in the Room." Among those singled out for detraction were James Jones ("has sold out badly over the years"), William Styron ("not nearly as big as he ought to be"), Jack Kerouac ("lacks discipline, intelligence, honesty and a sense of the novel"), Saul Bellow ("I cannot take him seriously as a major novelist"), J. D. Salinger ("no more than the greatest mind ever to stay in prep school"), James Baldwin ("too charming a writer to be major"), and women writers. The objects of Mailer's criticism replied that the title of his book explained the purpose of his comments and that he was trying to boost his fame after two unsuccessful novels—*Barbary Shore* (1951) and *The Deer Park* (1955). *Advertisements*

NORMAN MAILER ON FEMALE WRITERS

No writer since Oscar Wilde—with the possible exception of Ernest Hemingway—has been as successful as Norman Mailer in manipulating the machinery of celebrity in his own favor. By now, the question of good, bad, or indifferent is not even raised when Mailer publishes a new book. He is unassailably famous, with a fame which, like a Juggernaut, tramples everything that is not swept out of its path. Accordingly, the following attack upon women writers may be regarded as advertisement for himself in his role as the Hercules of Male Chauvinism:

I have a terrible confession to make—I have nothing to say about any of the talented women who write today. Out of what is no doubt a fault in me, I do not seem able to read them. Indeed I doubt if there will be a really exciting woman writer until the first whore becomes a call girl and tells her tale. At the risk of making a dozen devoted enemies for life, I can only say that the sniffs I get from the ink of the women are always fey, old-hat, Quaintsy Goysy, tiny, too dykily psychotic, crippled, creepish, fashionable, frigid, outer-Baroque, *maquillé* in mannequin's whimsy, or else bright and stillborn.* Since I've never been able to read Virginia Woolf, and am sometimes willing to believe it can conceivably be my fault, this verdict may be taken fairly as the twisted tongue of a soured taste, at least by those readers who do not share with me the ground of departure—that a good novelist can do without everything but the remnant of his balls.

* *With a sorry reluctance to spoil the authority of this verdict, I have to admit that the early work of Mary McCarthy, Jean Stafford and Carson McCullers gave me pleasure.*

—from *Advertisements for Myself* (1959)

for Myself cost Mailer a flock of friends; but only one serious feud developed, with Gore Vidal, of whom he wrote: "At his worst he becomes his own jailer and is imprisoned in the excessive nuances of narcissistic explorations which do not go deep enough into himself, and so end as questions and postures."

Unlike other writers who had been attacked in print by Mailer, Vidal remained friends with him for a while. They had what amounted to a literary nonaggression pact. But by 1970 their friendship deteriorated. Vidal had taken up the causes of feminism and liberation for women long before it became

fashionable for other men to do so. Norman Mailer set forth his own particular view of sex and male relationships with women in *The Prisoner of Sex* (1971). Vidal thought Mailer's opinions of women were "fascistic," and most feminists had long identified Mailer as a regressive misogynist. On 22 July 1971 in the *New York Review of Books*, Vidal noted what he perceived to be a link from Henry Miller to Norman Mailer to mass murderer Charles Manson. When Vidal went on to say that Mailer considered women as objects to be poked, humiliated, and killed, Mailer was not the only one to think of it as a less than indirect allusion to a stabbing incident involving Mailer and his wife. Mailer was furious. Five months later the two confronted each other backstage prior to an appearance on Dick Cavett's television show. Mailer had been drinking heavily, and as he greeted Vidal he gave him a light slap on the face. Vidal slapped him back. Mailer responded by butting Vidal in the head with his own head. Once on the air, Mailer, quite drunk and clearly still smarting from what he had taken as a reference to his stabbing of his wife, called Vidal a liar and a hypocrite–in those words.

It was clear that Vidal and Mailer were not two people who could be invited to the same party. Yet–some five years later they both turned up at the home of Lally Weymouth, and the feud between the profeminist and the feminists' public enemy number one reignited. Vidal arrived unexpectedly, and Mailer accused him of looking like a "dirty old Jew." Vidal answered in kind with almost the same words. Mailer, as he had done with many before Vidal, invited him to step outside and fight. As an afterthought, Mailer suggested Vidal could bring along a male friend who had accompanied him to the party and Mailer would fight them both–with one arm tied behind his back. Vidal refused to respond. Mailer now suggested that he had a twelve-year-old son who could clobber both Vidal and his friend. Again, there was no response from Vidal. Finally, Mailer threw his drink in Vidal's face. The distraught hostess tried to intercede, but was interrupted by editor Clay Felker who restrained Weymouth saying, "Shut up–they're *making* your party!"

The animosity between the two became increasingly bitter, fueled by Dick Cavett who knew a good thing when he saw it. Cavett asked both authors back to his show on 2 January 1978 to describe the events at Weymouth's party. They declined to appear together so Cavett taped each for back-to-back but separate appearances. Vidal now for the

first time quite specifically raised the matter of the stabbing. When Mailer saw the taped segment with Vidal, he stormed out with the angry warning that he would seek legal redress for comments he deemed actionable. Cavett calmed him down, and Mailer finally taped his segment responding to Vidal point by point, rehashing his version of the fight at the party, and sadly stating that stabbing his wife was not something of which he was proud.

It would take years for things to calm down, but on 17 November 1985 the two men shared the stage of the Royale Theatre in New York City at a benefit for the writers organization P.E.N. The time had come for, if not rapprochement (Vidal had not changed his opinion of Mailer's view of women), then at least a truce. They had become, without either noticing it, the elder statesmen in the battle among the sexes.

Characters' names can cause trouble when people with the same names claim to have been injured by the fictional characters' behavior. Sinclair Lewis's *Babbitt* (1922) elicited damage claims from actual George Babbitts. Such suits are rarely successful, but occasionally the similarities are strong enough to make it necessary to change characters' names in subsequent editions. James T. Farrell's *Bernard Clare* (1946) became *Bernard Clayre* (1948) in England and then *Bernard Carr* (1960). The possibility of truly coincidental similarities between characters and actual people was responsible for the disclaimer that formerly appeared in many novels: "This book is a work of fiction. The characters are imaginary, and the resemblance to actual persons is accidental." Despite that statement in *From Here To Eternity* (1951), Scribners, New American Library, and Columbia Pictures were sued by Joseph A. Maggio who had served with James Jones in the army and claimed that he had been libeled by the character Angelo Maggio in the novel. Jones defended himself by explaining he had used the name after he was told

British actor William Charles Macready as Shakespeare's *Henry IV* and American actor Edwin Forrest as Spartacus in Robert Montgomery Bird's *The Gladiator*

that Maggio had been killed in battle and that there were no similarities between the actual and fictional Maggios. The jury brought in a verdict of acquittal.

THE ASTOR PLACE RIOT

Although American political independence began with the success of the Revolution, her cultural independence did not come until a good many years later, despite pleas and assertions by many of her most esteemed writers. The domination of American letters by British authors and of the American stage by British actors and dramatists, particularly Shakespeare, inevitably generated hostility among the proud, often arrogant, individualists of the expanding United States. Nowhere was this hostility more clear than in the famous Astor Place Riot of 1849, the calamitous result of a theatrical rivalry between the British William Charles Macready and the

American Edwin Forrest, both established Shakespearean actors of the day.

Though not by reputation a subtle actor, Macready profoundly identified with the characters he played, giving his performances a commanding sense of authenticity that appealed to a sophisticated audience. Forrest, in contrast, represented the "muscular school" of acting; he might be called an early-nineteenth-century Sylvester Stallone, attractive to Americans whose feelings of nationhood were characterized more by brute strength than rationality. Initially cordial, relations between the two vain actors and their intense rivalry—apparently instigated by Forrest—served as the spark that set off explosive forces among the chauvinistic American populace.

On 7 May three separate productions of *Macbeth* were performed before large audiences in New York City, with Macready, Forrest, and a third Shakespearean, Thomas Hamblin, in the title roles.

HEMINGWAY AND O'HARA

Hemingway's wisecracks about other writers have achieved the status of literary lore. John O'Hara's disappointment at having been unable to attend Yale was known to his friends. During the Spanish Civil War, correspondents Hemingway, Vincent Sheean, and James Lardner were counting their money; Hemingway remarked, "The thing for us to do is to pool our resources and send John O'Hara to Yale." This comment remained in the category of literary scuttlebutt until the target put it into print five years later. In a 1942 *Newsweek* column O'Hara reported the anecdote, commenting: "It's a mean little story, but (and?) it shows what my friends think of me."

Forrest and Hamblin had no problems with their performances that evening, but a large number of Anglophobic working-class people and hooligans—partly incited by Ned Buntline (E. Z. C. Judson)—author of the "Buffalo Bill" series two decades later—attended Macready's opening at the Opera House in Astor Place. They shouted, catcalled, and hissed at him throughout his performance, tossing eggs, vegetables, even chairs onto the stage, but Macready managed to see it through to the end. Bitter over the experience, he wanted to terminate his engagement immediately, but upon petition by nearly fifty New York notables—including Herman Melville and Washington Irving—he was persuaded to remain.

The climate was again volatile in the Opera House when Macready next performed there on the evening of 10 May. The audience was quiet during the first two scenes, but when Macready stepped on stage in scene three, the ruckus started anew; again the hooting, yelling, and hissing disrupted but did not stop the performance. Outside the theater a dense crowd of Anglophobes and Forrest supporters became violent. Police and militia, fully armed, attempted to restrain the mob, who pelted them with rocks and stones, with which they also broke theater windows. Shortly after the final curtain the mob became more forceful, and the militia opened fire. In the next few minutes twenty-two people were killed, and scores were injured.

Unaware of the riot outside until after the play had ended, Macready completed his performance, fully satisfied with the ovation he received from the thinned-out audience. Several of the "patriots" loitering outside waited for him to leave the theater, anxious to capture and kill him because so many of their fellows had been slain while protesting his appearance, but he was hidden in the theater until early in the morning, when he was spirited away in a carriage.

Although Macready had courageously stood fast in the midst of embarrassment and danger, and although little of the blame for the occurrence could be reasonably attributed to him, his reputation was injured because he was looked upon as a vain, headstrong British actor in the wrong place at the wrong time. Though he never appeared at the riot scene, Forrest's name was also somewhat besmirched. People felt that he could have pacified his rowdy supporters. Buntline was sentenced to a year in jail for his part in instigating the riot.

The mayhem and slaughter around the Opera House at Astor Place testify to the broad and occasionally fatal political dimensions of the Shakespearean theater in America during the last century. It was just short of sixteen years later that President Abraham Lincoln was assassinated by Shakespearean actor John Wilkes Booth while seated in Ford's Theater in Washington.

—S.E.M.

Eccentric Writers

by DAVID A. PLOTT

As people avoid someone afflicted with the itch, with jaundice, the fits, or insanity, so sensible men stay clear of a mad poet.

—*Horace*, The Art of Poetry

The notion that poets or writers are disproportionately represented among the eccentric or the simply mad has long been familiar. Plato would have nothing of their second-rate truths and illusions in his Republic; and Horace, himself a poet, saw a need to warn his readers that some writers might indeed be mad.

The inclination throughout history to view writers and their works with more than a little suspicion asserts itself with astonishing frequency—from the seventeenth-century closing of the theaters by the Puritans in England to the twentieth-century banning of books in American communities. Authors and their works have been repeatedly accused of undermining widely accepted social, religious, and political beliefs. Although classical and Renaissance writings sometimes suggested that the life of the mind attracted a fair share of degenerates and madmen, it was not until the romantic movement of the late-eighteenth and early-nineteenth centuries that the image of the writer as inspired, gifted, or touched began to take hold. And it is in the modern period that the portrait of the artist as eccentric has achieved something close to perfection. The following is a sampling of American writers whose behaviors contributed to keeping that perception of the writer alive in America.

A. BRONSON ALCOTT, TRANSCENDENTAL CASTLE BUILDER

In the nineteenth-century New England of Transcendentalists and other high-minded idealists, no one was more noted for his good-natured eccentricities than the philosopher Bronson Alcott (1799-1888). A sometime teacher (and an unorthodox one, at that), Alcott was an inveterate wanderer, incapable of making a living for himself and his family, but always able to depend on the generosity of friends who indulged his odd habit of living in a world less real than the one everyone else seemed forced to live in. He passed his life in blissful poverty, never quite capable of dealing with life on its own terms or of seeing the pathetic limits of his own intellectual powers. Indeed, his daughter Louisa May Alcott once described him as a "man up in a balloon, with his family and friends holding the ropes which confine him to earth, and trying to haul him down."

Born in Connecticut, the oldest of the New England Transcendentalists, Alcott was raised in a rural setting close to nature and its simple charms. A mark of his boyhood was his constant loneliness, the result of too few playmates his age, which forced him to take pleasure in his studies and in his relations with adults. Even in youth, he turned with intensity to his own thoughts for amusement.

The man who would grow up to be one of New England's most beloved—but also most ridiculed—philosophers began his career as a peddler of books. He liked selling books from door to door because it gave him a chance to meet new people and to strike up conversations. Friends would complain that once Alcott began talking, it was impossible to stop him—a fault which might have been excused if he had not been widely considered a deadly bore.

Although Alcott had a passion for words, he was not, unfortunately, a naturally gifted writer. His prose was either hopelessly impenetrable or embarrassingly obvious. He had a talent for stating the obvious, and when he was not stating the obvious, no one was quite sure what he was saying. (Emerson once described Alcott's writing style as "All stir and no go.") According to Odell Shepard, Alcott's biographer, Ellery Channing, composed a ninety-page, unpublished essay sometime around 1850, in which he caricatured Alcott and Henry David Thoreau as "Mr. Pseudo-Pistos" and "Moses Bucolics."

Alcott's eccentricities never offended anyone deeply. He was too good-natured. Even Channing, in his public pronouncements, was forced to acknowledge the man's charm and intellectual energy. But Alcott was exasperating in small ways. For example, so extreme was his aversion to killing any living thing that he would refuse to kill even the most nettlesome insects and rodents. When potato bugs threatened to destroy his vegetable garden, he collected them in a can and dumped them into the yard of a neighbor, with whom he had had a number of philosophical and political disputes.

Alcott theorized that it was possible to rid oneself of sin by adhering to a strict vegetarian diet, and he also believed that people with fair hair and blue eyes were innately good, whereas dark-eyed and black-haired individuals were probably evil.

Alcott's most enduring eccentricity, though, was his habit of seeing everything in abstract terms. Unlike his good friend, Thoreau, who moved with stunning skill from the abstract to the concrete, Alcott could never quite see things in concrete form. It was a fault he himself acknowledged on more than one occasion. He once tried to write about his children, but realized immediately that "ere I am aware I have left

the consideration of them as individuals and have merged their separate existences into the common life of the Spirit. I have left their terrestrial life, with the varied phenomena that typify its action, and am roaming at large over the domain of the celestial world. . . ."

The most famous example of Alcott's utter inability to deal with the terrestrial world is his involvement in a project to build a summer home for Ralph Waldo Emerson, who, seeing Alcott's poverty, had sought to help him financially by hiring him for the job. Bringing Thoreau into the project to lend Alcott some practical assistance, Emerson stood by while Alcott plunged into the venture. Despite Alcott's enthusiasm, he proved incapable of building anything but castles in the air. When the house—which Emerson's mother called "The Ruin"—was completed, it was uninhabitable. Neither rain nor insects could be kept out because Alcott had chosen what he considered an open design, something sure to please the mind, but not the body.

DELIA BACON, THE LADY WHO TOOK ON SHAKESPEARE

The enduring image of Delia Bacon (1811-1859) as an eccentric genius was assured in January 1856, when she published an article in *Putnam's* magazine arguing that Shakespeare's plays were written by seventeenth-century English philosopher Francis Bacon and a few of his friends. The Baconian theory, as it came to be known, still has its followers today among the lunatic fringes of academia, and her book on the subject, *The Philosophy of the Plays of Shakespeare Unfolded* (1857), remains a classic of historical criticism gone awry.

The biography of the woman who took on Shakespeare is a good deal less amusing than the theory that made her famous. The daughter of a minister who himself had a reputation as a misguided eccentric, Bacon's early years were marked by a number of incidents that may well have signaled trouble in

Delia Bacon, 1853

abrupt turnaround. In April of 1822 her foster parents evicted her from their home, alleging that she had become an uncontrollable liar. And, when her six-year-old brother was run over and killed by a stagecoach in July of the same year, her faith in a benevolent deity was all but extinguished.

Her lifelong interest in literature was stimulated by an older brother, Leonard, a student at Yale, with whom she read endlessly in Shakespeare and other giants of the English Renaissance. When she enrolled in a school run by Catherine and Mary Beecher (older sisters of Harriet Beecher Stowe), Bacon quickly earned a reputation as a passionate student of history and literature. Indeed, she was viewed with jealousy by at least one fellow student, Harriet Beecher, who remained a lifelong rival.

Soon after completing her studies, Bacon began her career as a writer. In 1831, at the age of twenty, she published her first book, *Tales of the Puritans*, a collection of short stories in which she transformed episodes of Puritan life into something resembling Gothic romances. In 1845 Bacon began to develop eccentricities. She locked herself up in a room at the Tontine Hotel in New Haven and began an intensive study of Shakespeare and the English Renaissance. Friends pleaded with her to spend more time outside of her room, arguing that it was unnatural not to come out even to eat her meals.

Bacon persisted in her isolation, until one day she joined her friends at a meal, only to find Alexander Mac-Whorter, a graduate in theology from Yale, staring at her from across the table. Ten years younger than Bacon, MacWhorter had heard of the eccentric who had launched into a study of Shakespeare and wanted to meet her. Bacon later found out about his interest, and rather than waiting to be introduced to him formally, she sent the young man a note asking him to come to her room. The move, unorthodox and even scandalous for a single lady in those days, indi-

the decades to come. Her father, the Reverend David Bacon, plunged the family into bankruptcy while Delia was still an infant. Convinced that a Utopian Western settlement was possible under his direction, he talked someone into giving him title to twenty-square miles of Ohio territory, where he promptly set up a community named Tallmadge. When the venture failed, leaving him penniless, he was forced to make a living as an itinerant pastor and was branded as a man who had succumbed ignominiously to the fantasies of an over-heated imagination.

When her father suddenly died, seven-year-old Delia was sent by her mother to live with friends in Hartford, Connecticut. Missing her mother and siblings desperately, she found consolation in religion when a revival swept the Connecticut Valley in 1821. It was obvious to her mother and to her foster parents, though, that her newfound religious fervor was unusually intense. Her letters reveal an unhealthy sense of sin in a child so young, and her mind seemed easily bent by the force of strong emotions. Ironically, Bacon soon experienced an

cates both her eccentric nature and her impatience with tradition.

The two struck up a relationship that had all of the outward appearances of a steamy affair. Talk spread, and despite warnings by Bacon's mother to "break with the young man at once," the relationship continued. When Bacon shared with MacWhorter her nascent theory that someone else had written Shakespeare's plays, MacWhorter was intrigued, and told her his own theories about the inadequacies of nineteenth-century biblical scholarship. The two seemed suited; for they indulged each other in intellectual eccentricities that would have been termed madness by everyone else. In 1846 Bacon began experiencing unbearable periods of nervous exhaustion–due in large part to her undaunting research into Shakespeare. She entered an asylum in Brattleboro, where she convinced MacWhorter to spend ten days with her. It was during their stay that MacWhorter confessed his love to her, and the two agreed to spend their lives together.

But Bacon began to hear mysterious rumors that MacWhorter was showing her passionate letters to him to his friends, making fun of her, and claiming to be indifferent to the older woman's affections. When it finally became clear to her that she was being taken for a fool, she fought back. With the help of her brother Leonard, she filed charges before a Connecticut clergymen's association, charging MacWhorter with "Calumny, Falsehood, and Disgraceful Conduct, as a man, a Christian, and especially as a candidate for the Christian ministry."

MacWhorter's two-week ecclesiastical trial, which began on 4 August 1847, provided ample gossip for New Haven and surrounding communities. Bacon's odd personality was given full airing before a merciless public, and despite her insistence that she had been taken in by MacWhorter's deceptive entreaties, the three-member panel split 2-1 in MacWhorter's favor. Catherine Beecher's 1850 book, *Truth Stranger than Fiction* (which aimed to vindicate Bacon), only added to Bacon's anguish by further publicizing the unhappy episode.

Bacon's biographer, Vivian Hopkins, suggests that the MacWhorter affair had an enduring impact on Bacon's volatile mind. Nonetheless, Bacon, who made a living teaching and lecturing, was unchecked in her pursuit of the "real" Shakespeare. She moved to Boston, where her lively intellect found an appreciative audience in such notable New England figures as Emerson. Bacon's introduction to Boston society came by the way of Hawthorne's sister-in-law, Elizabeth Peabody, who ran a bookstore Bacon one day visited. Bacon was thumbing through a copy of *The Scarlet Letter* (1850) when Peabody introduced herself as a relative of Hawthorne. Ironically, she handed Bacon a copy of *Truth Stranger than Fiction*, telling her the main character was a good deal saucier than Hester Prynne. Peabody was astonished, then delighted, when Bacon identified herself as the heroine of Beecher's book.

With letters of introduction from Emerson (who was intrigued by Bacon's theory of Shakespeare), Bacon soon set off for England to prove her theory that Shakespeare did not write the plays attributed to him. In a famous episode, she told a doubtful, but indulgent Thomas Carlyle, "much as I respect you, Mr. Carlyle, I must tell you that you do not know what is really in the *Plays* if you believe that booby wrote them." By 1856 she had convinced Hawthorne, who was then American consul in Liverpool, that her theory deserved credit, and that he should help her get her book published. Though Hawthorne was generous in providing help (which eventually got the book published), the author of *The Scarlet Letter* soon became convinced that Bacon was nearing madness.

In letters to Leonard Bacon, Hawthorne argued that her exhausting work on the book, as well as her obsession

Maxwell Bodenheim selling his poems in Washington Square, 1948 (courtesy of Wide World Photos)

with the theory, were edging her toward insanity. The final blow came with publication, as Hawthorne had predicted. Despite Hawthorne's preface, Bacon's eccentric theory was received with universal ridicule. The rejection of a theory she had spent her entire adult life developing devastated Bacon. She quickly slipped into periods of delusion, and on her return to the United States in April 1858, she was placed in Bloomingdale Asylum. On 2 September 1859–at the age of forty-eight–she died with her family gathered around her, a woman thwarted once in her love for a man, and once in her love for an idea.

MAXWELL BODENHEIM, "THE BOHEMIAN COUNT"

The literary reputation of Maxwell Bodenheim (1892-1954) is now so obscured by his reputation as a wild, self-destructive, sex-craved maniac among the literary set in Chicago and Greenwich Village that one forgets his considerable talents as a poet, novelist, and playwright.

Born into poverty in Hermanville, Mississippi, he died impoverished in the Bowery (see Death and Dying). Yet despite his determined neglect of his health, and his steady and tragic dissipation, his early days in Chicago and later in New York were marked by his good-natured stunts and his passionately eccentric personality.

After having been jailed for desertion from the army and discharged in 1911, he eventually settled in Chicago, where he met Ben Hecht, who was to become one of his closest friends. In 1923, Hecht described Bodenheim this way in the *Chicago Literary Times*: "Maxwell Bodenheim, in manner and appearance, is the ideal lunatic. He is bowlegged and has pale green eyes. While uttering the most brilliant lines to be heard in American conversation he bares his teeth, clucks weirdly with his tongue, and beats a tattoo with his right foot. He greets an adversary's replies with horrible parrot screams. Having finished an epigram of his own he is overcome with ear-splitting guffaws."

Bodenheim and Hecht often collaborated in playing tricks on other critics and the public. They feigned contempt for one another in the pages of the *Chicago Literary Times*, and on one occasion agreed to debate each other before a local literary club. The topic: "Resolved: That People Who Attend Literary Debates Are Imbeciles." Hecht stood before the audience, drank several glasses of water, and then uttered his only contribution to the evening: "The affirmation rests." Bodenheim turned the audience's puzzlement to anger when he took to the stage and responded, "You win." The two were reported forced to flee the angry crowd through a side exit.

Hecht made one of Bodenheim's hoaxes the subject of a novel, *Count Bruga* (1926). Well known for his contempt of the fashionable literary movements coming out of Europe, Bodenheim wrote what was alleged to be the manifesto of the "Monotheme school of poetry." It argued that poets should write on one theme only, which was to be assigned by a nonexistent European Count named Rene d'Or, the leader of the movement. Bodenheim disguised himself and played the role of the Count in Chicago.

Bodenheim became notorious for his sexual activity, which was viewed with humor in the early 1920s, but scorned at as it turned to tragedy later in the decade, when–for reasons that will never be clearly known–several of his female lovers attempted to kill themselves. Some of them succeeded. The sensational news accounts that resulted further damaged the writer's reputation. He spent most of the rest of his life living a vagrant's existence in New York, bumming drinks off of sympathetic listeners, gradually dissipating the enormous talent that produced ten volumes of poetry and fourteen novels.

HUGH HENRY BRACKENRIDGE, DISPENSER OF NAKED JUSTICE

The author of the massive prose satire *Modern Chivalry* (1792-1805), Hugh Henry Brackenridge (1748-1816), was not a man whose talents were limited to picaresque narratives. A graduate of Princeton, where his closest friends were Philip Freneau and James Madison, and author of patriotic plays, poems, and fiction during the Revolution, Brackenridge became active in politics after the war, settling in Pittsburgh and serving as a state legislator (1786-1788) and a Pennsylvania Supreme Court justice (1799-1816).

His behavior in court was reportedly eccentric. Even on the rough and ready frontier of western Pennsylvania, his dress was considered careless. His one suit of clothes was often disheveled, and he is reported to have shown up in court more than once unshaven, with his shirt open, and without stockings. He was often seen giving instructions to

the jury with his bare feet resting on the bar of justice. According to legend at least, he was once seen riding naked in the rain with his clothes folded under his saddle. When asked for an explanation, he is said to have replied, "the storm you know, would spoil the clothes, but it couldn't spoil me."

WILLIAM BYRD, THE FLOURISHING VIRGINIAN

The narratives of William Byrd (1674-1744) provide a vivid, detailed, and often sharply humorous portrait of backwoods America. He had the instincts of a reporter, filling his works with precise satiric observations. While he wrote one book, *A Discourse Concerning the Plague* (1721), that was published during his lifetime, and another, *The History of the Dividing Line* (1841), that he circulated in manuscript, most of his writings were meant solely for private consumption, and he invented his own secret shorthand in an attempt to insure that his diaries would remain that way. (Modern scholars have deciphered them.)

Even *A Discourse Concerning the Plague, With Some Preservatives Against It. By a Lover of Mankind*, the only book he had published in his lifetime, betrays his eccentricity, as well as his desire to enhance the earnings of Virginia tobacco planters (he owned one of the largest plantations). The discourse prescribes a variety of preventatives against the plague, including shooting guns out of windows and firing "pistols in our rooms." Tobacco, however, is the preventative Byrd defends most elaborately. To avoid the plague, he says, "We should provide ourselves with fresh, strong scented tobacco." He goes on to say: "We should hang bundles of it round our beds, and in the apartments where we most converse. If we have an aversion to smoking, it would be prudent to burn some leaves of Tobacco in our dining rooms lest we swallow the infection with our meat . . . take snuff plentifully . . . to secure the passages to our brain. . . . The pass to our stomachs should be also safely defended, by chewing this great *Antipoison*. In short, we should both abroad and at home, by night as well as by day, take care to have our sovereign antidote very near us; an antidote which seems designed by Providence as the strongest natural preservative against this great destroyer."

Byrd's diet was also eccentric. He believed that he could prolong his life by chewing ginseng root and eating only milk and boiled or fried meat. He also devised a vigorous routine of calisthenics. (He died at seventy.)

In his secret diaries he employed various invented euphemisms. Scholars believe that "I danced my dance"–a sentence that appears often–refers to his calisthenics. He was particularly inventive with euphemisms for sex: "I rogered my wife" appears with amazing frequency (he married twice and outlived both wives), and "rogered" a prodigious number of other women as well during his years as a bachelor. Byrd by no means limited his sexual activities to the indoors either. On one occasion he performed a "flourish" with a willing lady under the shrubbery in St. James Park in London.

Byrd chronicled his sexual exploits alongside his reports of his frequent devotional acts, giving the work a wonderfully complex, often inadvertently comic tone. In one well-known entry (for 30 July 1710), he wrote: "In the afternoon my wife and I had a little quarrel which I reconciled with a flourish. Then she read a sermon in Dr. Tillotson to me. It is to be observed that the flourish was performed on the billiard table."

At sixty-seven he reported his dalliance with a servant: "I rose about 6 and played the fool with Sarah, God forgive me. However, I prayed and had coffee."

SAMUEL CLEMENS,
THE IRREVERENT HUMORIST

Samuel Clemens (1835-1910) was an inveterate trickster and practical joker, whose passion for humor was inseparable from his sense of identity. An entire book could be filled with nothing but anecdotes about jokes he played on friends and enemies alike. Even in the dark moods to which he was incessantly prone, he was always on the lookout for ways to have fun at the expense of others.

Even when the occasion, such as a church service, called for at least some degree of reverence, Clemens could not resist the opportunity to poke fun. He once approached a minister who had just delivered a sermon and told him that he had enjoyed the sermon because it was so familiar to him; he had a book at home that contained every single word of it. The minister replied angrily that it was not possible. He said he had written the sermon himself and asked to see the book. The next day Clemens sent the minister an unabridged dictionary.

Clemens's second book, *The Innocents Abroad* (1869), had its origin in a collection of travel essays he wrote for a California newspaper while accompanying a group of Christians on a pilgrimage to the Holy Land. In order to get a berth on *The Quaker City*, the ship the group had chartered for the voyage, Clemens involved himself in a minor hoax. Along with Edward H. House, a correspondent for the *New York Tribune*, Clemens showed up slightly drunk at the Wall Street booking office for the voyage, which was sponsored by Henry Ward Beecher's Plymouth church in Brookland (Beecher himself, who was later to be dragged into court on charges of adultery, had an impeccable reputation for piety at the time). After an official told them there were no spaces left for the voyage, House introduced Clemens as a Baptist minister who had just arrived in town from San Francisco, after having recently spent time as a missionary in the Sandwich Islands. At this point Clemens spoke up, saying that his congregation had decided to send him on a trip to restore his health after his backbreaking missionary work. He asked if Beecher would be on board during the trip, and if Beecher would allow him occasionally to conduct religious services. The official, who later acknowledged that he had suspected the two men of being drunk, suddenly changed his mood, and said Clemens would be welcome aboard the ship. The next day, Clemens identified himself properly and signed up for the trip, to the enduring embarrassment and anger of the official.

Clemens was not above playing malicious practical jokes, especially when they gave him the opportunity to even a score with someone. Lilian Aldrich, wife of Thomas Bailey Aldrich, once insulted Clemens by refusing to serve him dinner because her husband had invited Clemens without telling her and because Clemens showed up eccentrically dressed in a sealskin coat, a hat with the fur turned out, yellowish-brown trousers and socks, gray coat and waistcoat, and a violet tie. Mrs. Aldrich, bred in New York high society and accustomed to the fine manners of Boston's elite, was scandalized. She was sure Clemens was drunk–though he apparently was not–and refused to serve him dinner. Years later, Clemens got back at her when the Aldriches visited the Clemenses at Nook Farm in Hartford.

First thing in the morning, Clemens knocked furiously at the Aldriches' door. When Thomas Aldrich appeared, Clemens complained loudly enough for Mrs. Aldrich to hear that his wife Olivia Clemens, who was in feeble health and six-months' pregnant, had been kept awake most of the night by obscene noises coming from the Aldriches' room. He explained that they were in a room just below the Aldriches' and had heard everything. "Do try to move more quietly," he said, "though Livy would rather suffer than have you give up your game on her account." The Aldriches were mortified. But when

they tried to apologize to Clemens's wife, they were told not only that Livy had not been kept awake, but that the Clemenses' room was in another wing of the house and that they could not have heard the Aldriches.

One of Clemens's most notorious jokes involved the distinguished New England writers John Greenleaf Whittier, Henry Wadsworth Longfellow, Oliver Wendell Holmes, and Ralph Waldo Emerson. What was meant in part, at least, to be a humorous poke at the New England literary establishment turned out to be one of the most painfully embarrassing moments in Clemens's ambiguous relationship to the Boston literary set.

Clemens had been invited to speak at Whittier's seventieth birthday party (17 December 1877), which was attended by almost everyone of any social distinction in Boston, including the butts of his joke. Instead of giving a straightforward tribute to Whittier, Clemens told a bogus story. He said that while traveling in the Far West recently, he stopped for the night at a miner's cabin in the Sierra foothills. When the miner answered the door, Clemens introduced himself as the famous Mark Twain. The man was dismayed, saying he had already played host to three unscrupulous literary men named Emerson, Holmes, and Longfellow–all no-good bums who had eaten all his food, drunk his best whiskey, cheated at cards, and then stolen his boots.

As Clemens continued telling the story, everyone who had gathered for Whittier's party listened in stunned silence–except for one guest who, according to William Dean Howells, indulged in "hysterical and blood-curdling laughter" (the ever-proper Howells refused to hand the man's name "down in infamy"). Then Clemens reached what he thought was a decent punch line. He said he told the miner that the three men were obviously imposters, to which the miner replied, "Ah! imposters, were they? Are *you*?" No one laughed at what

Emily Dickinson

trips to Philadelphia and Washington, D.C., Dickinson spent her entire life at her family's home in Amherst. Much of that time she spent alone in her bedroom, constructing out of her isolation a vivid, sensuous, but transcendental world in some 1,800 poems. Only seven of her poems were published in her lifetime, and those who read her work either in print or in manuscript were struck by its erratic style. The *Atlantic Monthly* reviewer of *Poems*, the first collection of her verse (published posthumously in 1890), spoke of Dickinson's want of grammar and her peculiar leaps of logic. He assured his readers that Dickinson's certain fate was oblivion.

Much Madness is divinest Sense—
To a discerning Eye—
Much Sense—the starkest Madness—
'Tis the Majority
In this, as All, prevail—
Assent—and you are sane—
Demur—you're straightway dangerous—
And handled with a Chain—
    —Emily Dickinson, Poem 435

---

they considered obvious bad taste. Clemens sat down and the next day apologized in writing. (Emerson, who by this time had become extremely forgetful, had already forgotten not only the whole dinner but also having ever met Clemens and was, Howells reported, "a good deal mystified" by Clemens's letter.) This story suggests the tension that ran beneath Clemens's practical jokes. They may have been in fun, but they also said something fierce and articulate about his real convictions.

EMILY DICKINSON, AMHERST'S RECLUSIVE LADY IN WHITE

Few other major American writers have been so often labeled eccentric as Emily Dickinson (1830-1886). Although her eccentricity may be somewhat exaggerated—much of her daily life consisted of little more than domestic chores—the profoundly personal style of her poetry has only added to her reputation for idiosyncrasy.

Aside from a year spent at Mount Holyoke Female Seminary (now Mount Holyoke College) in 1847-1848 and brief

For residents of Amherst, many of whom knew only vaguely that she wrote poetry, what was most striking about Dickinson was her behavior. She is reported to have dressed only in white and to have moved about like a serene ghost on those rare occasions when she left her room.

She was fascinated with children, sharing their flights of fancy and their detachment from the world of adults. She never married and never had a physical relationship with a man, and yet she was passionately in love with at least three men, two of whom were married. She wrote them dozens of letters, but always shied away from anything more than a relationship of words. Indeed, her letters and poems suggest an involvement with life that is the antithesis of the life she actually lived. She would frequently refuse to see guests whom she had invited to the house, or would consent to speak to them only from her upstairs bedroom with her door just slightly ajar. The erratic style of her letters to friends and neighbors left many of them puzzled, and some of them wrote back asking her to explain herself. She charged her letters with the same intensity as her poems, viewing language as something never to be released to the public (even to a public of one) without laborious refinement. As a result, even her brief conversations were described as epigrammatic and lapidary by friends.

The final eccentricity, of course, is the manner in which her poems have come down to us. After her death, her sister came upon dozens of neatly folded, carefully sewn fascicles, containing hundreds of poems, stacked in a camphor box. Dickinson was at once writer, editor, reader, and archivist of her own creation.

For all of her withdrawal from life, few American writers have left a record of a world as fully described or as vividly experienced as the one Dickinson created in her poetry.

JOSEPH FERDINAND GOULD, THE HISTORIAN WHO TALKED TO SEAGULLS

Educated at Harvard, where he graduated in 1911, Joseph Gould (1889-1957) was the author of "The Oral History of the World," a work he spent most of his adult life working on and boasting about.

Gould was one of the most colorful eccentrics to settle in Greenwich Village before World War I. He passed most of his life there, wandering in and out of bars, seeking an audience for his poems and literary theories, and generally letting everyone in sight know that he was Joe Gould: "I'm Joe Gould the poet. I'm Joe Gould the historian. I'm Joe Gould the wild Chippewa Indian dancer. And I'm Joe Gould, the greatest

authority in the world on the language of the seagull."

Gould's prolix and eccentric writing made him unpopular with publishers, although he did manage to see some of his work into print in his lifetime. "Civilization," a rambling essay published in *Dial* (1929), is reported to have influenced William Saroyan–so much so, that Saroyan later sought a meeting with Gould. Gould by this time resembled an emaciated but good-natured street bum, shabbily dressed, toothless, and smelling of alcohol.

Despite the testimony of people in the Village that Gould always carried around the notebooks in which he transcribed "The Oral History of the World," no text of the work has yet been found. We are left with little but vivid stories of one of Greenwich Village's most self-assured bohemians. He once boasted that his "Oral History" "will live as long as the English language."

JERZY KOSINSKI, THE WRITER AS SURVIVALIST

In Jerzy Kosinski's best-known novel, *The Painted Bird* (1965), there is an episode that aptly illustrates the predicament of the novelist himself: a peasant captures a raven, paints it in bright colors, and then releases it; but the bird is later torn apart by other birds–a grim metaphor of the cruelties of alienation.

Kosinski (1933-) has been described as a master survivor. He was six years old when the Nazis occupied Poland and was abandoned by the relatives with whom his parents left him for safekeeping. He wandered the Polish countryside, abused and beaten by peasants–some of whom once tortured him by throwing him into a dung pool, and the shock left him mute–a condition which lasted for five years. He arrived as a penniless immigrant in the United States at the age of twenty-four and took to stealing caviar and other goods from Polish stores in New York to feed himself while he worked on a Ph.D. and wrote.

It is difficult to determine the truth about Kosinski's life (see Frauds), but he claims to be on constant alert against communist kidnappers. His apartments have secret hiding places; he is usually armed; he carries false identity cards; his trench coat has twenty-three secret pockets; and his car is always stocked with food and weapons for a getaway.

JAMES RUSSELL LOWELL, THE BIZARRE BRAHMIN

The name of James Russell Lowell (1819-1891)–like those of Longfellow and Holmes–is intimately linked to the genteel tradition in nineteenth-century New England. Lowell's talents were prodigious, extending from poetry to journalism to education to social activism. *A Fable for Critics* (1848) reveals not only a marvelous sense of satire but also a gift for trenchant critical insights. Despite his immense learning, he achieved a homely native idiom in such works as *The Bigelow Papers* (1848; second series, 1867), and in poems such as "The Cathedral," he displayed an ability to draw poetry up to an engaging level of religious speculation.

Few readers of Lowell, though, are aware that he had a positively strange side. His image as the quintessential Boston Brahmin obscured his lapses into the bizarre. Novelist and critic William Dean Howells once dined at Lowell's, and when dinner was over the poet decided not to usher his guest out the front door. Instead, he insisted that the two climb over the wall in the backyard. The younger Howells made it over on the first try, but Lowell fell several times before finally tumbling unhurt at Howells's feet. "I commonly do that the first time," he told Howells.

Lowell, who once spent hours perched atop a lamppost crowing like a rooster, is also reported to have eaten–with a knife and fork–the flowers from the centerpiece at a Boston literary dinner. On another occasion he became the center of attention at a poets' meeting when he demonstrated how a horse moves by galloping about with his coattails in his hands. More than once he mistook a stranger for an old friend and swung him around in the street. As C. David Heymann has suggested, "Had he been any less accomplished a poet he would surely have been handcuffed and led off, never to be heard from or seen again."

CHARLES MACARTHUR, FRONT-PAGE WIT

Charles MacArthur (1895-1956), best known for the famous play, *The Front Page* (1928), and such films as *The Scoundrel* (1935), *Barbary Coast* (1935), and *Wuthering Heights* (1939)–all written with his friend Ben Hecht, was an inveterate practical joker. As a fledgling reporter for *Oak Leaves*, a suburban Chicago paper, in about 1915, he had a run-in with the Chief of Police, a Mr. Sweeney. Determined to get even, MacArthur telephoned Sweeney and identified himself as the editor in chief of the *Chicago Tribune*, the single most powerful man in the city. He accused Sweeney of unfairly holding a man in the city jail for rape. The man's name, MacArthur said, was Henry Wadsworth Longfellow. MacArthur explained that the man could not possibly be guilty of rape, as he was a good friend of the *Tribune* and, besides, he was a hermaphrodite.

After MacArthur threatened the chief with pillory in the pages of the *Tribune* if Longfellow were not released immediately, Sweeney was apparently cowed enough to spend the entire day telephoning stationhouses throughout the city trying to find Longfellow.

According to Ben Hecht, MacArthur, who was always a heavy drinker, rode in planes over Berlin during World War I dropping empty whiskey bottles on the German capitol. In fact, MacArthur was so notorious for his drinking that one of his fellow soldiers called him "the

Cotton Mather, 1727; mezzotint by Peter Pelham (courtesy of the Houghton Library, Harvard University)

Chemical War Service's chief weapon." There was a mock proposal to fly him over Berlin, holding him upside down and letting him breathe on the city.

As a reporter back in Chicago, MacArthur had the peculiar habit of playing poker with prisoners on death row. He allegedly was good enough at the game to win the condemned man's last penny before he was executed. Somehow he managed to strike up brief friendships with the prisoners–friendships that would invariably end at dawn. He once convinced a convicted murderer, Carl Otto Wanderer, to read an attack on MacArthur's newspaper editor from the gallows. Unfortunately, Wanderer's hands were tied at his sides for the hanging, and he was unable to honor the agreement.

Once when a gate attendant at a prizefight would not let MacArthur and Ring Lardner in to cover the event, the two men went drinking instead. Fortunately, in a restroom where they went to relieve themselves, they discovered that on each toilet was a button that said, simply, "press." MacArthur and Lardner set about dismantling the toilets in order to get the buttons. When they returned to the prizefight wearing the "press" buttons, the attendant let them in.

COTTON MATHER, THE QUINTESSENTIAL PURITAN

Cotton Mather (1663-1728) stands as a symbol of both the genius and the severity of late Puritanism in New England. His ecclesiastical history of New England, *Magnalia Christi Americana* (1702), is a monumental example of early American historical and biographical writing. But what alienated New Englanders who were already beginning to turn away from the harsher side of Puritanism at the close of the seventeenth century was Mather's uncompromising piety, his profound lack of a sense of humor. The man who vigorously defended the Salem witch trials in *The Wonders of the Invisible World* (1693) took everything seriously.

Mather's attitude toward his own urine is likely to strike modern readers as an excess of Puritan piety. He recorded in his diary that every excretory activity ought to be accompanied "with some holy thoughts of a repenting and an abased soul." He even formulated prayers to utter "when I am at any time obliged into the urinary discharges."

JOAQUIN MILLER, "THE BYRON OF OREGON"

Joaquin Miller (1837-1913), who published dozens of poems, plays, novels, and other writings in his lifetime, is a splendid example of how a moderate amount of talent combined with aggressively cultivated eccentricity can win a writer at least a small place in literary history.

Miller was a sensation in his own day for his outlandish costume and his deliberately outrageous behavior. A sometime lawyer and frontier poet, he left the West Coast in 1870 to live for a

Joaquin Miller in the 1870s (courtesy of the
Honnold Library for the
Claremont Colleges)

while in London, where he earned a
name for himself by dressing in outfits
that reflected the Englishmen's exaggerated notion of the Far West—buckskin
britches, boots, a sealskin greatcoat, and
an enormous sombrero. He once told
Edmund Gosse: "It helps sell the
poems, you know, and it tickles the
duchesses."

And sell them it did. Miller's London
reputation quickly spread to America,
where it managed to irritate two other
writers who claimed to speak for the Far
West: Mark Twain and Bret Harte.
When Twain attended a dinner in London for Ambrose Bierce, Miller, who
felt he was being ignored, swallowed a
fish whole to get attention.

Miller was not above inventing colorful stories about himself, which helped
sell his poems. He claimed to have been
born in "a covered wagon, pointed
west," and to have been rescued from
prison by an Indian sweetheart. He also
falsely claimed to have been with filibus-
ter William Walker in Nicaragua.

His best-known book, *Songs of the Sier-
ras* (1871), earned him instant success in
London, where he was called "the
Byron of Oregon." The comparison was
unfortunate, since it not only aggravated his inclination toward preposter-
ous histrionics but also confirmed his
earlier decision to abandon his wife, The-
resa Dyer ("Minnie Myrtle"), and their
two children. He told her, "Lord Byron
separated from his wife, and some of
my friends think I am a second Lord
Byron. Farewell." Miller was never quite
able to live down the conviction among
some people that he was merely an eccentric fraud: conviction that has only continued to grow since his death in 1913.

EZRA POUND'S
ADVERTISEMENTS FOR HIMSELF

Perhaps no figure has contributed in so
many different ways to the shaping of
modern literature as Ezra Pound
(1885-1972). Poet, critic, translator, and
befriender of struggling writers, Pound
had an impact on modern literature far
beyond the influence of his own poetry.

Indeed, throughout his life Pound devoted much of his energy to the services
of literature. He also, however, spent a
good deal of energy cultivating eccentricities, all of which succeeded in drawing
attention to himself. He wore a flowing
cape, topping off the visual effect with a
mane of ill-kempt hair, and a cane.
Ford Madox Ford reported having once
seen Pound, with his beard trimmed to
a sharp point, wearing pants made of
green billiard cloth, a pink coat, a blue
shirt, a large sombrero, and a blue ear-
ring. In addition to attracting attention
to himself through his dress, Pound was
not above unusual antics. During a dinner at which Pound decided that poet
William Butler Yeats was monopolizing
the conversation, Pound ate two red tu-
lips from the centerpiece to assure that
his presence that evening would not go
unnoticed.

A few years later Pound sought to call attention to himself in yet another way. After the traditional, and then well-known, poet Lascelles Abercrombie called on younger poets to abandon their poetic experiments and study Wordsworth, Pound wrote him a letter charging that "Stupidity carried beyond a certain point becomes a public menace," and challenged the older, mild-mannered poet to a duel. When Abercrombie heard that Pound was a good fencer, he was terrified, but then he realized that the man who was challenged had his choice of weapons and suggested that they should use the unsold copies of their own books. Pound, who was still virtually unknown outside his own avant-garde literary circle, realized that he would probably have a much larger supply of ammunition but that winning the duel because of it would not generate the sort of publicity he had had in mind. The duel never took place.

Years later, after Pound had gone to spend his remaining years in Italy, a young poet made a pilgrimage to see the now-great poet. As Donald Hall reports, Pound answered the door himself, startling the young man who managed to stutter, "How are you, Mr. Pound?" Pound responded with a single word: "Senile."

THOMAS PYNCHON, THE MAN AT THE END OF THE RAINBOW

Thomas Pynchon (1937-) may well be the most inventive novelist writing in America today, and he is certainly the most encyclopedic in the range of his cultural, historical, and scientific knowledge. From Oedipus Maas in *The Crying of Lot 49* (1966) to Tyrone Slothrop in *Gravity's Rainbow* (1973), the characters of Pynchon's novels have been gripping examples of the psychology of paranoia. At the same time, Pynchon himself has become legendary for avoiding public attention with such ingenuity that specula-

tion has emerged that the author himself is profoundly afflicted with the disorder that permeates his fiction. Speculation has been fueled by the long silence that has followed the publication of *Gravity's Rainbow*.

In "The Quest for Pynchon," a twelve-page essay published in *Mindful Pleasures: Essays on Thomas Pynchon* (1976), Mathew Winston, a professor at Columbia University, exhausts the limit of what is known about the man. Pynchon enrolled at Cornell University to study engineering physics but eventually took a degree in English. There are unconfirmed rumors that he was married briefly during his sophomore year, after which he joined the U.S. Navy. Winston says no information is available from this period of Pynchon's life. When Pynchon returned to Cornell, he once attended a party dressed as F. Scott Fitzgerald in his Princeton years. He also worked on the Cornell literary magazine, the *Cornell Writer*, and began writing short stories. Little is known of his life after graduation. He lived in Manhattan, Seattle (where he worked briefly for the Boeing Company), southern California, and Mexico.

Winston's effort to uncover Pynchon's background has met with curious resistance. The novelist has apparently asked the principal of his high school not to disclose anything about him. Pynchon's military records were destroyed when a records office in Saint Louis burned down, and his file at Cornell has mysteriously disappeared. In addition, friends from his Cornell years have steadfastly refused to reveal anything about the novelist.

Pynchon has granted no interviews and has not released any photographs of himself.

JEROME DAVID SALINGER, NEW HAMPSHIRE HERMIT

The author of *The Catcher in the Rye* (1951) resembles Thomas Pynchon in

J. D. Salinger, 1979 (photograph by Michael McDermott–Black Star)

his stubborn withdrawal from the world–his aversion to publicity of any kind and his ambivalent attitude even toward publishing. Despite the fact that his novel about a precocious and independent young boy, Holden Caulfield, is one of the most popular and widely read books of the past thirty-five years, J. D. Salinger (1919-) himself remains secluded in his home in Cornish, New Hampshire, resisting any efforts to learn more about him.

After the publication of *The Catcher in the Rye*, Salinger was so appalled by the instant fame and the "curiosity seekers" that came with it (although, ironically, he had struggled hard to succeed as a writer), that he moved to Cornish, where at first he had some contact with local high-school students. He even granted an interview to a Claremont, New Hampshire, high-school paper in November 1953, but he later suspected the paper of exploiting him and ceased to interact with the students. He built a fence around his property to keep the curious out.

Claiming to be writing constantly, he has published only one piece since 1963 ("Hapworth 16, 1924," in the *New Yorker*, 19 June 1965), and he now considers publication "a terrible invasion" of his privacy. In fact, the only interview Salinger has granted in recent years was to protest an unauthorized edition of his short stories, apparently published in Berkeley, California, and reported in the *New York Times*, 3 November 1974. The book was suppressed.

Salinger fought to assure his privacy again in November 1986 when he filed an injunction to prevent the publication by Random House of *J. D. Salinger: A Writing Life*, an unauthorized biography by Ian Hamilton, who in the course of his research discovered at least seventy Salinger letters donated by their recipients to libraries. At first Hamilton quoted from them substantially, but Salinger was able to block publication on the ground that the book violated copyright. Hamilton then paraphrased the letters' contents. Still unsatisfied, Salinger filed suit claiming that because he had copyrighted the letters, the information in them, as well as the exact words he had employed, could not be published without his permission. U.S. Federal Judge Pierre N. Laval disagreed, stating that only Salinger's "particular words or manner of expression" were protected by copyright. Despite his ruling in Hamilton's favor, Laval temporarily blocked the book's distribution so that Salinger's lawyers could have time to appeal his decision.

On 29 January 1987 in a landmark decision, the U.S. Court of Appeals for the Second District ruled against Hamilton and Random House. Judge Jon O. Newman, author of the decision, stated that the book's close paraphrases of the copyrighted letters had gone beyond the limits of the "fair use" provision of the copyright law. Random House filed a request that the court of appeals reconsider its decision and announced its intention to take the case to the U.S. Supreme Court if necessary.

WILLIAM SAROYAN, GAMBLING WITH IMMORTALITY

William Saroyan (1908-1981)–whose cheerful assertion that he was the greatest writer in the world rankled Ernest Hemingway–was given to compulsive gambling as well as bragging. Saroyan's gambling became so uncontrolled in the years after World War II that at one point in 1947, he owed $30,000–a large sum in those years. He was forced to give up all of his personal property to settle his debt; when it was all over, he and his wife were left with a suitcase apiece. Saroyan had allowed himself to get further and further into debt by assuring his wife that he would write better under such a psychological stimulus. In the end, however, he bitterly accused her of not having done enough to prevent him from gambling.

Saroyan also saved junk compulsively. Once, when his mother-in-law opened two enormous trunks he had asked her to keep for him temporarily, she discovered that they were filled with an odd assortment of worthless items–string, broken clocks, nails, and bits of hardware. Visitors to Saroyan's apartment late in his life were astonished at the clutter of odd magazines and receipts he insisted on keeping.

HENRY DAVID THOREAU, THE SOCIABLE RECLUSE

The author of *Walden* (1854), the book that set the prototype for the American author who renounces society for a life of isolated independence, Henry David Thoreau (1817-1862) spent much of his life wandering the countryside and sought in all his writings to cultivate the myth of the outsider, the vagrant, the eccentric living in the borders of respectability. His classic account of his sojourn on Walden Pond, in a cabin of his own making, is a masterpiece of radical individualism, providing brilliant commentary on the society he briefly withdrew from.

The peculiar problem with *Walden*, though, is that the heroic isolation, self-sufficiency, and independence it celebrates are largely fictional. Certainly his neighbors must have doubted his proficiency as a woodsman after he accidentally set fire to 300 acres of forest while trying to cook fish in a hollowed-out pine stump. In fact, Thoreau returned often to his mother's home, which was less than two miles away, and his mother and sister visited the cabin every Saturday to bring him fresh provisions. He dined frequently in the homes of such distinguished Concord residents as the Emersons and Alcotts, and rather than living in isolation, he had dozens of visitors. Indeed, the evidence suggests that Thoreau may never have been as closely in contact with the society he sought to condemn as when he claimed to withdraw from it.

Thoreau has secured a reputation today as an eccentric of a rather different order from the one his contemporaries found him to be. His self-important posturing in such works as *Walden*, alternately bellicose and charming, is redeemed by the sheer imagination Thoreau invests in his own eccentricity. He made of it an art, and the results are often unquestionably provocative. In the realm of literature, as perhaps also in life, he deserves to be called the eccentric's eccentric, for he saw in the deliberately antic the possibilities for transforming the ordinary.

JONES VERY, THE TRANSCENDENTALIST MESSIAH

A mystic poet whose friends included the circle of transcendentalists surrounding Ralph Waldo Emerson, Jones Very (1813-1880) wrote pious meditational sonnets that at their best reveal profound religious insight.

He was a brilliant student at Harvard, where one of his Bowdoin Prize essays eventually brought him to the attention of Emerson. After graduating in 1836, he began tutoring Greek at Har-

Jones Very, 1870 (courtesy of Essex Institute, Salem, Massachusetts)

vard and enrolled in the divinity school. He would apparently be seized by mystical experiences while teaching, which sometimes frightened his students. In autumn 1838 he left Harvard after an incident in which he gazed at his students with burning eyes and cried, "Flee to the mountains, for the end of all things is at hand." After he returned to his hometown of Salem, Massachusetts, and tried to convince people that he was the second incarnation of Jesus Christ, he ended up in McLean Hospital for the insane, where he spent about a month.

Very's claim that God dictated sonnets to him in visions is only one of the many strange assertions that led those around him to question his sanity, but he always managed to maintain the friendship and support of Emerson and others, despite his fanatic insistence that they adopt his religious positions. When Emerson was helping him to prepare his *Essays and Sonnets* (1839) for publication, Very vehemently objected to even the most minor alterations in his poems. Each sonnet should be left "exactly as it was done the first time," he explained, because "such was the will of God." "Cannot the spirit parse and spell?," asked the exasperated Emerson. Emerson later delighted in repeating this exchange for the amusement of his friends, but he considered Very "a treasure of a companion."

At the end of 1840 Very withdrew from literary life, secluding himself in Salem for his last forty years.

JOHN WHEELWRIGHT, THE BLUEBLOOD SOCIALIST

Poet John Wheelwright (1897-1940) was a Boston Blueblood, tracing his ancestry on both sides to some of New England's earliest settlers, including Massachusetts governor, John Brooks, and the Reverend John Wheelwright, one of the leaders of the Antinomian Rebellion (1636-1638). Despite his lifelong preference for upper-class acquaintances, he never stopped championing the proletariat. His sympathies were always with the underdog, and his poems reveal a clear socialist strain.

Reputedly the only person ever expelled from Harvard for misspelling a word (see Schooldays), Wheelwright was as well known in crusty Boston society for his strange antics as for his radical politics. Winfield Townley Scott has written that at a reception given in honor of Allen Tate, "Wheelwright made from one end to the other of the room a slow progress underneath the huge rug."

A FAMOUS LITERARY CONVERSATION THAT NEVER TOOK PLACE

Certain literary anecdotes are so good that they become literary history–whether or not they actually happened. Among the most widely cited of these defining anecdotes is this exchange between Hemingway and Fitzgerald:

Fitzgerald: The very rich are different from you and me.
Hemingway: Yes, they have more money.

This crushing rejoinder is supposed to contrast Fitzgerald's naiveté with Hemingway's pragmatism. But it never happened.

These are the facts. In "The Rich Boy" (1926) Fitzgerald wrote: "Let me tell you about the very rich. They are different from you and me." A decade later Hemingway wrote in "The Snows of Kilimanjaro" (1936): "He remembered poor Scott Fitzgerald and his romantic awe of them and how he had started a story once that began, 'The very rich are different from you and me.' And how someone had said to Scott, yes they have more money." This paper exchange is the source for the putative conversation that has become enshrined as history.

However, a similar exchange involved Hemingway and critic Mary Colum–in which Hemingway was the straight man. As attested to by Maxwell Perkins, who was present, Hemingway remarked that "I am getting to know the rich." Colum responded, "The only difference between the rich and other people is that the rich have more money." By writing this squelch into "Snows" with Fitzgerald as the dupe, Hemingway was able to shift the humiliation to Fitzgerald–who was not even there.

Writers Who Went To War And Wrote About It, From The Civil War To Vietnam

by KAREN L. ROOD

Like me to write you a little essay on The Importance of Subject? Well the reason you are so sore you missed the war is because war is the best subject of all. It groups the maximum of material and speeds up the action and brings out all sorts of stuff that normally you have to wait a lifetime to get.

—Ernest Hemingway, Letter to F. Scott Fitzgerald, 15 December 1925

AMERICAN CIVIL WAR

AMBROSE BIERCE (1842-1914) enlisted as a private for three-months' service in the Ninth Indiana Infantry on 19 April 1861 and fought under Gen. George McClellan in West Virginia at Philippi, Laurel Hill (where he rescued a wounded comrade under fire), Rich Mountain, and Carrick's Ford. Re-enlisting as a sergeant on 14 August 1861, he was promoted to sergeant-major on 5 September and took part in skirmishes at Greenbrier (3 October) and Buffalo Mountain (13 December) in West Virginia before the Ninth Infantry was sent to Tennessee in February 1862.

In April he fought at Shiloh, where the Ninth Infantry suffered heavy casualties and was commended for heroism. Commissioned a second lieutenant on 1 December, he rescued the commander of the Ninth Infantry from the field at the Battle of Stones River (near Murfreesboro, Tennessee) on 31 December. In March 1863 he was transferred to the headquarters of the brigade commander, Gen. William B. Hazen, who made him acting topographical officer, a position he held for the rest of the war.

He served at Chickamauga (September 1863) and Missionary Ridge (November 1863) and on 23 June 1864 was wounded in the head at Kennesaw Mountain. Returned to duty in late September, he designed and oversaw the construction of fortifications at Pulaski, Tennessee, in October, and fought at Franklin (November 1864) and Nashville (December 1864) before accompanying Gen. William Sherman on his March to the Sea. Discharged in late March or April 1865, he was brevetted major in 1867 in recognition of his distinguished service.

Bierce probably had more firsthand experience on Civil War battlefields than any other American poet or fiction writer, and in 1887 he noted, "To this

Lt. Ambrose Bierce

GEORGE WASHINGTON CABLE (1844-1925) joined Company J of the Fourth Mississippi Cavalry on 9 October 1863 and was slightly wounded in a skirmish at Port Gibson, Mississippi, the next day. He took part in numerous other skirmishes against Sherman's troops in January and February 1864. Suffering an arm wound on 29 February, he was assigned to the quartermaster's department on 10 March to recuperate. He fought again at Tupelo, Mississippi, on 14 July 1864 and clerked for various officers, including Gen. Nathan Bedford Forrest, for the duration of the war. The war and its aftermath figure in several of his novels: *Dr. Sevier* (1884), set in his native New Orleans before and during Union occupation; *John March, Southerner* (1895), a story of New South versus Old South in the Reconstruction era; *The Cavalier* (1901), a Civil War historical romance that draws on his cavalry experience; and *Kincaid's Battery* (1908), in which he attempted to recreate the huge commercial success of *The Cavalier* with a story about the artillery.

day I cannot look over a landscape without noting the advantages of the ground for attack or defense. . . . I never hear a rifle-shot without a thrill in my veins. I never catch the peculiar odor of gunpowder without having visions of the dead and dying." He was obsessed with his war experiences and wrote about them in nonfiction, poetry, and some twenty-five short stories—including "One of the Missing," "A Son of the Gods," "A Tough Tussle," "Chickamauga," "One Affair at Coulter's Notch," "An Occurrence at Owl Creek Bridge," and "Parker Adderson, Philosopher." Most of the stories were collected in the first and later enlarged editions of *Tales of Soldiers and Civilians* (1892, simultaneously published in England as *In the Midst of Life*) and *Can Such Things Be?* (1893). His war reminiscences are included in volume one of *The Collected Works of Ambrose Bierce* (1909), and his poetic reflections on the war appear in *Black Beetles in Amber* (1892).

JOHN ESTEN COOKE (1830-1886) enlisted as a private in the Confederate army's Howitzer Brigade, commanded by Gen. Nathan George, on 9 April 1861. He was given charge of a gun at the First Battle of Manassas (Bull Run) in July 1861 and received a lieutenant's commission in Gen. Jeb Stuart's cavalry on 21 April 1862. Eventually becoming a close friend of both Stuart and Gen. Stonewall Jackson, he was named inspector of horse artillery in April 1864 and served in that capacity until Lee's surrender at Appomattox (9 April 1865). He later drew upon his war experiences for two biographies: *The Life of Stonewall Jackson* (1863) and *A Life of Gen. Robert E. Lee* (1871); a collection of nonfiction sketches: *Wearing of the Gray* (1867); and several novels: *Surry of Eagle's Nest* (1866), *Fairfax* (1868), *Mohun* (1869), *Hilt to Hilt* (1869), and *Hammer and Rapier* (1870).

JOHN WILLIAM DE FOREST (1826-1906) organized a company to serve in the Twelfth Connecticut Volunteers (also known as the Charter Oak Regiment) in autumn 1861. After receiving a captain's commission on 1 January 1862, he served in the Louisiana campaign of early 1862 and the Shenandoah Valley campaign of autumn 1864 (for a total of forty-five days under fire). He was discharged because of ill health on 2 December 1864, but on 10 February 1865 he entered the Veteran Reserve Corps as a captain and spent the duration of the war in Washington, D.C., where he wrote *Miss Ravenel's Conversion from Secession to Loyalty* (1867), which Robert H. Woodward has identified as "The first war novel in either English or American literature to be written by an author who could describe battlefield scenes from firsthand." Though it was published about a year after John Esten Cooke's novel drawing on his experiences on the other side of the battle lines, *Surry of Eagle's Nest* (1866), De For-

est's novel was not only written first but it treated war in a strikingly original way. While Cooke incorporated his battle experiences into the sort of conventional historical romance that appealed to popular audiences, De Forest depicted the war realistically, describing battle as it would have been experienced by the participants, including soldiers who drank and swore and were more often concerned with their own advancement than with honor, duty, and loyalty to their cause. Cooke's novel sold well; De Forest's did not, but it is recognized today as a hallmark in the early history of realism in American fiction, and some scholars believe that it may have influenced the best-known novel about the Civil War, Stephen Crane's *The Red Badge of Courage* (1895).

After the war De Forest was promoted to major by brevet "for gallant and meritorious services during the war" (May 1866) and served with the Bureau of Refugees, Freedmen and Abandoned Lands in Greenville, South Carolina, from October 1866 until his discharge on 1 January 1868. He wrote about the division between North and South during the Reconstruction period in his 1881 novel, *The Bloody Chasm*, and around 1890 he assembled his notes, articles, and letters from the war and Reconstruction years into a narrative of his experiences. He was unable to find a publisher and they did not appear in print until the 1940s, when they were published as *A Volunteer's Adventures* (1946, edited by James H. Croushore) and *A Union Officer in the Reconstruction* (1948, edited by Croushore and David Morris Potter).

JOSEPH KIRKLAND (1830-1893) enlisted as a private in Company C of the Twelfth Illinois Volunteer Infantry on 25 April 1861 and was elected lieutenant. Rising to captain and named aide-de-camp to Gen. George McClellan in August, he went with the general-in-chief of the Union Army to Washington,

D.C., where he spent much time with John Hay and John Nicolay, secretaries to President Lincoln, and renewed his acquaintance with Lincoln, whom he had met through his involvement in Illinois Republican politics.

Finally tired of inactivity, he requested and received a transfer to the staff of Gen. Fitz-John Porter, commander of the Fifth Army Corps, and participated in the siege of Yorktown, Virginia, during the Peninsular Campaign (April-May 1862). After taking part in the battles at Malvern Hill and Hanover Court House that summer, he was brevetted major and then hospitalized for jaundice, rejoining Porter's staff in time for the defeat of Lee at Antietam (September 1862).

In November Porter was relieved of command to face court-martial for disobeying orders and thus costing the Union the Second Battle of Bull Run (Manassas, August 1862), which had taken place while Kirkland was in the hospital. Kirkland then volunteered to serve as aide to Gen. Daniel Butterfield and had his horse shot from under him during the Union defeat at Fredericksburg in December. In January, however, when Porter was cashiered and dismissed from the army, Kirkland, even though he had not been with Porter at Bull Run, was, along with the rest of Porter's staff, reduced one grade in rank, and promptly resigned from the army. His novel *The Captain of Company K* (1891) is based on his war experiences.

Sidney Lanier (courtesy of Johns Hopkins University)

casionally under artillery fire but saw little action. While guarding the beaches in March, they saw the battle of the two great ironclad ships, the Union *Monitor* and the Confederate *Merrimack*. After more inaction in North Carolina and back in Virginia, the company fought in the seven days of battles around Richmond (26 June-2 July 1862).

Later in July Lanier and his brother,

Whenever it shall become the rule that the man who causes a war shall be its first victim, war will be at an end.
> *—Joseph Kirkland, The Captain of Company K (1891)*

SIDNEY LANIER (1842-1881) enlisted as a private in the Macon Volunteers in July 1861 and was stationed near Norfolk, Virginia, where his company was oc-

---

His army stands in battle-line arrayed:
His couriers fly: all's done: now God decide!
—And not till then saw he the Other Side
> *Or would accept the shade.*

Thou land whose sun is gone, thy stars remain!
Still shine the words that miniature his deeds.
O thrice-beloved, where'er thy great heart bleeds,
> *Solace hast thou for pain!*
> *—from Sidney Lanier, "The Dying Words of Stonewall Jackson" (1865)*

Clifford, transferred to the Mounted Signal Corps, where they were attached to the staff of Major-Gen. S. G. French. Though their duties included scouting Union troop movements and were sometimes dangerous, they also had much free time. After a furlough home in spring 1863, however, they saw action at Chancellorsville (May), where the death of Stonewall Jackson inspired the poet to write one of his few war poems, "The Dying Words of Stonewall Jackson" (which alludes to Jackson's last words: "Order A. P. Hill to prepare for battle. Tell Major Hawks to advance the Commissary train. Let us cross the river and rest in the shade"). He was then assigned to scouting near the mouth of the James River, where his detachment again skirmished with Union troops, and in August 1864 the Lanier brothers were sent to Wilmington, North Carolina, and assigned to serve as signal officers on blockade runners. On 2 November Sidney's ship managed to get through the Union blockade of the harbor, but it was captured fourteen hours later. Lanier spent four months in Union war prisons, most of the time at Point Lookout, Maryland. By February 1865 he was suffering from severe tuberculosis. He was smuggled out of the prison after his guards were bribed and made his way home for a long convalescence. His war experiences figure in book two of his only novel, *Tiger-Lilies* (1867), which he began in 1863 and completed after the war.

MARY N. MURFREE (1850-1922), who wrote under the pseudonym Charles Egbert Craddock, lived and attended school in occupied Nashville, Tennessee, and her family's home in Murfreesboro was destroyed during the Battle of Stones River (December 1862). She later used her war experiences in two of her novels: *Where the Battle was Fought* (1884), set at her family's Murfreesboro house, and *The Storm Centre* (1905).

THOMAS NELSON PAGE (1853-1922)

spent his childhood at Oakland, the family plantation in Hanover County, Virginia–"within sound of the guns of battles in three great campaigns in which not less than three hundred thousand men fell," Page wrote in the introduction to the Plantation Edition of his writings (1906-1912). Speaking of himself in the third person, he added, "During his boyhood and youth the recollection of the great Civil War was the most vital thing within his knowledge." Page drew on these memories for short stories collected in *In Ole Virginia* (1887), *Among the Camps* (1891), and *The Burial of the Guns and Other Stories* (1894); and a novel, *Two Little Confeder-*

Hit wuz jes' like hail; an' we wen' down de slope (I long wid de res') an' up de hill right to'ds de cannons, an' de fire wuz so strong dyar (dey hed a whole rigiment o' infintrys layin' down dyar onder de cannons) our lines sort o' broke an' stop; de cun'l was kilt, an' I b'lieve dey wuz jes' 'bout to bre'k all to pieces, when Marsh Chan rid up an' cotch hol' de fleg an' hollers, "Foller me!" an' rid strainin' up de hill 'mong de cannons. I seen 'im when he went, de sorrel four good lengths ahead o' ev'y urr hoss, jes' like he use' to be in a fox-hunt, an' de whole rigiment right arfter 'im. Yo' ain' nuver hear thunder! Furst thing I knowed, de roan roll' head over heels an' flung me up 'g'inst de bank, like yo' chuck a nubbin over 'g'inst de foot o' de corn pile. An dat's what kep' me from bein' kilt, I 'spects. . . . 'Twan' mo'n a minit, de sorrel come gallupin' back wid his mane flying', an' de rein hangin' down on one side to his knee. "Dyar!" says I, "fo' Gord! I specks dey done kill Marsh Chan, an' I promised to tek care on him."

I jumped up an' run over de bank, an' dyar, wid a whole lot o' dead men, an' some not dead yit, onder one o'de guns wid de fleg still in he han', an' a bullet right th'oo he body lay Marse Chan.
—from Thomas Nelson Page, "Marse Chan,"
In Ole Virginia *(1887)*

---

ates (1888). He also wrote a biography, *Robert E. Lee: The Southerner* (1909; revised as *Robert E. Lee: Man and Soldier*, 1911).

Page's sentimental fiction about a romanticized Old South was extremely popular in the late nineteenth and early twentieth centuries. Even Abolitionist Thomas Wentworth Higginson, who had commanded a black regiment during the war, is said to have wept over the death of the Confederate soldier and slave owner, as described by his faithful slave in Page's "Marse Chan" (collected in *In Ole Virginia*).

HENRY TIMROD (1828-1867) served in a militia troop raised to defend the coastline around Beaufort, South Carolina (July-September 1861), and enlisted as a private in the Thirtieth South Carolina Regiment of the Confederate army (February 1862). Aware that Timrod was tubercular, the commander, Col. Lawrence M. Keitt, appointed the poet regimental clerk. In April 1862 Timrod took a three-month leave of absence to serve as a war correspondent for the *Charleston Mercury* and covered the action during the Confederate retreat from Shiloh. Officially discharged because of ill health on 15 December 1862, he reenlisted in July 1863. He had served only one day before he was afflicted with a severe lung hemmorhage and allowed to withdraw his enlistment. The ode he wrote to be sung at the Confederate memorial service in Charleston's Magnolia Cemetery on 16 June 1866 is probably the best-known Southern poem to come out of the Civil War. A revised version was published in the *Charleston Courier* two days later and collected in *The Poems of Henry Timrod* (1873), which also includes other poems—such as "Ethnogenesis," "The Cotton Boll," "A Cry to Arms," "Carolina," "Charleston," "Christmas," and "Spring"–inspired by the war and events surrounding it.

Lt. Albion W. Tourgée (courtesy of the Chatauqua County Historical Society)

Sleep sweetly in your humble graves
Sleep martyrs of a fallen cause!–
Though yet no marble column craves
The pilgrim here to pause.

Stoop angels hither from the skies!
There is no holier spot of ground
Than where defeated valor lies
By mourning beauty crowned.

–from Henry Timrod, "Confederate Memorial Ode" (1866)

ALBION W. TOURGEE (1838-1905) joined the Twenty-seventh New York Volunteer Infantry on March 1861, during his junior year at the University of Rochester. Elected sergeant, he was soon severely reprimanded for leading a protest against army food (but his actions brought the desired results). After surviving the Union defeat at the First Battle of Bull Run (Manassas, July 1861), he was struck in the back by the wheel of a gun carriage and paralyzed from the waist down.

Discharged from the army, he gradually recovered over the next year and graduated from the University of Rochester. On 11 July 1862 he enlisted as a lieutenant in the 105th Ohio Volunteer Infantry and in October fought at Perryville, Arkansas, where he was slightly wounded in the hip. Captured by Confederate troops at Murfreesboro (January 1863), he spent four months in captivity before being freed in a prisoner exchange. He joined his regiment in time for the march on Chattanooga and fought in the Battle of Chickamauga (September). After reinjuring his back, he left the army on 6 December 1863. Moving south after the war, he became a well-known carpetbagger during the Reconstruction period. He drew on his war years for three of his novels—*Toinette* (1874), *Figs and Thistles* (1879), and *Hot Plowshares* (1883)—and wrote a history of the 105th, *The Story of a Thousand* (1896).

WALT WHITMAN (1819-1892) went to Virginia in December 1862 to see his brother George, who had been slightly wounded at the Battle of Fredericksburg. Strongly affected by what he saw while visiting hospitals in search of his brother (whom he finally found recovered and back on the battlefield), he decided to go to Washington, D.C., where until November 1863 he worked mornings as a copyist in the army paymaster's office and spent his afternoons nursing the wounded in nearby military hospitals. Back in Washington the next month, he returned to visiting the wounded. He recorded his experiences

Walt Whitman, 1865, photograph by Mathew Brady (courtesy of the Oscar Lion Collection, Rare Book Division, New York Public Library, Astor, Lenox and Tilden Foundations)

and emotions during the war in *Drum-Taps* (1865) and *Sequel to Drum-Taps* (1865), which also includes his well-known eulogies for Abraham Lincoln, "O Captain! My Captain!" and "When Lilacs Last in the Dooryard Bloom'd."

Bearing the bandages, water and sponge,
Straight and swift to my wounded I go,
Where they lie on the ground after the battle
  brought in,
Where their priceless blood reddens the grass
  on the ground,
Or to the rows of the hospital tent, or under
  the roof'd hospital,
To the long rows of cots up and down each
  side I return,
To each and all one after another I draw
  near, not one do I miss,
An attendant follows holding a tray, he car-
  ries a refuse pail,
Soon to be filled with clotted rags and blood,
  emptied, and filled again.
  —from Walt Whitman, "The
  Wound-Dresser," Drum-Taps, (1865)

▲▲

THE CURIOUS CASE OF STEPHEN CRANE

By far the best-known novel about the Civil War, *The Red Badge of Courage* (1895) is so vividly realistic that more than one reader has come away from the book convinced that its author, Stephen Crane, who was born in 1871, must surely have fought in the Civil War. Even veterans of the war were sure that they had fought with Crane. One in particular, Col. John L. Burleigh, swore, after reading Crane's novel, that he "was with Crane at Antietam." After the April 1896 issue of the *Book Buyer* reproduced a handwritten note in which Crane stated, "I have never been in a battle . . . ," another reader decided that there was only one possible explanation for Crane's having written such a realistic book. According to R. W. Stallman, the unnamed Crane fan told the *Book Buyer* "that the soul of some great soldier had gone into Stephen Crane at his birth, and that this theory of reincarnation explained how the author who had never seen battle was able to write descriptions in the guise of a seer's authority and compel his reader to accept his statement without question."

Though Crane was not the first writer to write realistic fiction about the Civil War, his book was the first nonromantic novel about the war to be popular. The American public was unprepared in 1867 to accept De Forest's realistic depictions of a war just ended. Crane's novel came at the end of a long vogue for Civil War memoirs and sentimental novels that presented the war in the light of patriotism, heroism, and romance, and in fact the public was tiring of such books. Crane had read some of the memoirs himself and wondered "that *some* of these fellows don't tell how they *felt* in those scraps!" When he interviewed veterans themselves, he found that they could not remember much

War correspondent Stephen Crane in Athens, 1897 (courtesy of the Stephen Crane Collection [#5505], Clifton Waller Barrett Library, University of Virginia Library)

about their actual battlefield experiences. Tolstoy's *Sebastopol* (1855) and Kipling's *The Light that Failed* (1890) provided useful models for the depiction of battle, but finally Crane was thrown back on his own imagination, his own sense of human nature, for the psychological dimension that makes his book so realistic.

Though *The Red Badge of Courage* was well reviewed on both sides of the Atlantic, it was initially more popular in England and some American readers found the book unpatriotic, including one, Gen. A. C. McClurg, who considered the novel a vicious attack on the American fighting man and called it the product of a "diseased imagination."

Such criticism was overwhelmed by praise, and Crane, who had never even viewed a battle from a distance, became a famous war novelist, with editors clamoring for more war stories. He complied with the Civil War stories collected in *The Little Regiment* (1896).

In November 1896 Crane set out to see war for the first time, to cover Cuba's revolt against Spain for Irving Bacheller's newspaper syndicate. He never got to Cuba on that trip. Instead the *Commodore*, the ship that he had boarded in Florida, sank, and he spent thirty hours in a dinghy with the ship's captain, the cook, and an ill-fated oiler, who drowned as the four men were washed ashore from their capsized boat at Daytona Beach on 3 January 1897. Crane began writing one of his finest short stories, "The Open Boat," almost immediately, finishing it some time in February. He then began searching unsuccessfully for another way to get to Cuba before deciding in March to go instead to cover the war that was about to break out between Greece and Turkey for the *New York Journal*. Stopping first in London, he signed on as a correspondent for the *Westminster Gazette* as well, and he arrived in Athens on 7 April. Joining him there was Cora Stewart, owner of a Jacksonville nightclub/brothel called the Hotel de Dream (a pun on the name of the previous owner, Ethel Dreme), with whom he had fallen in love. Determined to follow him to Greece, she convinced the *New York Journal* to hire her as their first and only female war correspondent, signing her dispatches Imogene Carter. Though her estranged husband's refusal to grant her a divorce prevented her from marrying Crane, they later told people that they had married in Athens. Ten days after Crane's arrival there Turkey declared war on Greece, and on 5 May 1897 at Velestino he saw men in battle

for the first time. He had gone to Greece to see if his *Red Badge* "is not all right" and discovered that it was. Following the Greek retreat south, he reached Athens a few days after the armistice was signed on 20 May. He later drew on his Greek experiences for "Death and the Child," collected with other short stories in *The Open Boat* (1898), and a novel, *Active Service* (1899).

By the time *The Open Boat* was published in April 1898 Crane was headed once again for Cuba, this time to cover the Spanish-American War for the *New York World*. For the first month he was based in Key West covering the naval blockade of Cuba with other correspondents on the *Triton* and the *Three Friends*. He went ashore at Guantánamo after the marine landing on 10 June 1898. A few days later he was impressed by the marine signalmen at Cuzco, who stood in full view under enemy fire sending semaphore messages to a gunboat. "Marines Signaling Under Fire," his story about them for the *World* (1 July 1898), is often called one of the best dispatches of the Spanish-American War.

In late June he was at San Juan to cover the famous charge of Theodore Roosevelt and the Rough Riders, but by early July he became ill with what was eventually diagnosed as malaria and was back in New York by mid July. When he got there he was fired by the *World*, whose management considered him disloyal, in part because he had filed a report with the *New York Journal* for a fellow correspondent who had been wounded.

Crane immediately took a job with the *Journal* and, still ill, went to cover the campaign in Puerto Rico. He had time to file only three dispatches before the war ended on 12 August. His short stories about the war in Cuba were published as *Wounds in the Rain*. His war poems appeared in *War Is Kind* (1899).

WORLD WAR I

HERVEY ALLEN (1889-1949) had already served in an infantry unit of the Pennsylvania National Guard in 1916 on the Mexican border (where he turned out his first book, *Ballads of the Border*, that same year) and was recalled to active duty in 1917 when the United States entered World War I. He was wounded and gassed at Fismette, on the Vesle River, in August 1918. He drew on his war experiences for his well-known war ballad "The Blindman," for a nonfiction account of his war years, *Toward the Flame* (1926), and for two works of fiction, *It Was Like This: Two Stories of the Great War* (1940).

Then we pulled out the men that were smothered in the dirt; some were cut in pieces by the shell fragments and came apart when we pulled them out of the bank. Lieutenant Quinn, a Pittsburgh boy, who had just got his commission a week before, was so mixed with the two men who had lain nearest to him that I do not know yet whether we got things just right.

—Hervey Allen, Toward the
Flame *(1926)*

GERTRUDE ATHERTON (1857-1948) went to Paris in 1916 to "study the war work of the French women" aboard a ship that was nearly hit by a torpedo in the Garonne River. She visited wounded soldiers in hospitals in Paris and in numerous sections of the war zone and wrote a pamphlet, *Life in the War Zone* (1916), as publicity for a drive to raise money for better food for the wounded. In her novel *The White Morning* (1918) she fancifully created an uprising of German women who take over the government and end the war.

WILLIAM ROSE BENÉT (1886-1950) volunteered for service in the Aviation Section of the U.S. Army Signal Corps in 1918 and, despite his poor eyesight, was given flight instruction and commis-

sioned a second lieutenant. He served out the war in ground service at posts in Florida and Texas. He drew on his war years for his long, semi-autobiographical poem *The Dust Which Is God* (1941), which won the Pulitzer Prize for Poetry in 1942.

JOHN PEALE BISHOP (1892-1944) entered the U.S. Army ROTC on 27 August 1917 at Fort Benjamin Harrison, Indiana, and was commissioned a first lieutenant in the infantry on 27 November 1917. He served at division headquarters at Camp Zachary Taylor, Kentucky, from 15 December 1917 until 30 May 1918, when he was sent to Camp Sherman, Ohio, where he served until 15 August 1918. On 11 September he sailed for France. Commanding Prisoner of War Escort Company No. 257 in the Meuse, he supervised German POWs who were repairing roads and digging up corpses from battlefields–the basis for his short story "Resurrection," which he and Edmund Wilson included in the 1922 collection of their poems, stories, and a play on the subject of death, *The Undertaker's Garland*. After spending two weeks on leave in England in August 1919, Bishop returned to the United States on 27 October 1919 and was discharged on the thirtieth.

JAMES BOYD (1888-1944) was commissioned a second lieutenant in the U.S. Army Ambulance Service on 28 August 1917, and on 1 July 1918 he arrived in Genoa, where he commanded Ambulance Service Section 520, attached to the 332d Infantry Regiment. He was transferred to France on 28 August 1918 and took part in the Saint-Mihiel operation and the Meuse-Argonne offensive (September-November 1918), where the ambulance drivers worked in twenty-four-hour shifts. On 2 July 1919 he was honorably discharged and later drew on his war experiences when he was writing book two of his novel *Roll River* (1935) and less directly, perhaps,

Archer saw first a knitted sweater, still intact but soppy from the putrefaction beneath it. A clayey brown rag was over the face. The taut wire pulled again, sharply; something broke near the throat and a greenish blue substance, like a fowl's ordure, crumbled and fell over the sweater.

"What the hell? Give me that pick."

An arm was embedded in the earth at one side. The pick tore into the soft flesh and the aperture showed a horrid pink; something was left behind in the hard clay. The cadaver began to lift itself from the grave. The jointless head fell back, thickening the greenish ooze on the neck; the uneven arms spread out with each jerk of the wire, hunching their slimy sleeves. In the space where the thighs divide a glinting puddle of muck had seeped through the breeches cloth. The legs trailed woodenly.

The cadaver bent backward over the brink of the pit and dragged heavily on the ground. . . .

Disgust clutched at Archer's sides. It was horrible that this putrescent thing sprawling on the ground should have been a few months before a boy, fine with youth, warm and strong. He had thought of death in battle as something clean and swift in its anguish. He had thought it a desirable thing that life should go out violently when the blood was at its full and the body unspent. He had never dreaded death, only manglement and disease and the slow dissolution of time. But here the body was not utterly dead; it had acquired a new life in its very putrefaction. It would go on for a long time yet, still younger than the earth in which it was hidden, not utterly dead as the dust and stones are dead.

—John Peale Bishop,
"Resurrection"(1922)

---

for his historical novels *Drums* (1925), *Marching On* (1927), and *Long Hunt* (1931).

THOMAS BOYD (1898-1935) enlisted in the U. S. Marine Corps on 14 May 1917

and, after basic training at Parris Island, South Carolina, he was attached to the Sixth Regiment, stationed in Quantico, Virginia, in August. Sent to France with the Second Division of the American Expeditionary Force, he fought near Verdun in March, and at Belleau Wood, Soissons, and St. Mihiel before being gassed at Blanc Mont on 6 October 1918. He was awarded the Croix de Guerre and honorably discharged in July 1919. His first novel, *Through the Wheat* (1923), was highly praised for its realisitic depiction of the war and compared to Stephen Crane's *The Red Badge of Courage*. A later novel, *In Time of Peace* (1935), charts the difficult adjustment to civilian life of the first novel's marine-sergeant hero. Boyd also published a collection of short stories about the war, *Points of Honor* (1925).

WILLIAM EDWARD CAMPBELL (1893-1954), who used the pen name William March, enlisted as a private in the U. S. Marine Corps on 25 July 1917 and rose to the rank of sergeant by the time he was honorably discharged in August 1919. Arriving in France on 24 February 1918, he joined the Second Division near Les Esparges, southeast of Verdun. On 9 June, at Belleau Wood, he was wounded in the head and left shoulder. Returning to the front on 29 June, he fought at Soissons in mid July and in the Argonne offensive (Ocotober 1918) at Blanc Mont, where he distinguished himself by leaving shelter while under fire to rescue wounded men from the field and by helping to drive back Germans attempting to capture the first-aid station. Awarded the Distinguished Service Cross, the Navy Cross, and the Croix de Guerre with palm for "extraordinary heroism in action," he was engaged in heavy fighting along the Meuse when the Armistice was declared on 11 November 1918. After serving with the Army of Occupation in Germany, he was sent by the marines to study at the University of Toulouse (March-July 1919). He later used the letters he had written to his sister from France as the basis for his first novel, *Company K* (1933).

MALCOLM COWLEY (1898-   ) left Harvard in early 1917, during his sophomore year, and went to Paris with the intention of becoming an ambulance driver, but he was told that there was an oversupply of ambulance drivers and was assigned to drive munitions trucks for the French army instead. As he wrote in *Exile's Return* (1934; revised 1951), "the ambulance corps and the French military transport were college extension courses for a generation of writers." Among other lessons, the war taught them "courage, extravagance, fatalism," and it "created in young men a thirst for abstract danger, not suffered for a cause but courted for itself. . . . It revivified the subjects that had seemed forbidden because they were soiled by many hands and robbed of meaning: danger made it possible to write once more about love, adventure, death." Cowley returned to the United States in fall 1917 and entered the U. S. Army. The war ended before he could be sent abroad. His war experiences inform many of the poems in *Blue Juniata* (1929), and he touches on them in *Exile's Return*, his groundbreaking study of his literary generation.

HARRY CROSBY (1898-1929) signed up for the American Field Service Ambulance Corps before he finished his last year at St. Mark's School in Southborough, Massachusetts, and not long after graduation, he sailed for France (6 July 1917). He was assigned to Section Seventy-one, which was sent in late July to the Somme sector of the front. On 8 August he carried a wounded man in his ambulance for the first time. At the end of the month the United States Army took over the American Field Service ambulance units and gave the volunteers the option of returning home or enlisting in the army as privates. Crosby enlisted in September and

in late October he was reassigned to Section Twenty-nine, which was sent to the front at Verdun. On 11 November, he wrote home, "we carried more wounded for the length of time we worked (from 7 A.M. til 4 P.M.) than have ever been carried by any American Field Service section." (The number is said to have been 265, of which perhaps one out of three died before reaching the hospital.) As he was driving through enemy shelling on the twenty-second, a shell burst ten yards away from his ambulance, which was totally destroyed (as he described the incident in one of the letters published in his *War Letters*, 1932), "There was a deafening explosion and then flying rocks, eclats, mud, everything in sight shot past us." Crosby, who had dived to the floor of the ambulance, was miraculously unharmed but this narrow escape was the beginning of an obsession with death that marks all his poetry, and Verdun became the setting for a recurring nightmare that he wrote down again and again in his diaries—a forever barren landscape in which everyone was dead or mortally wounded, and all innocence destroyed. Until his suicide on 10 December 1929, he celebrated 22 November as his "death day." He continued to serve and on 23-25 August 1918, at the Battle of the Orme, his section carried 2,000 wounded soldiers and was cited for "disdaining danger, without regard for fatigue" and "carrying on without pause . . . in violently bombarded zones." Crosby himself was cited on another occasion as "always demonstrating elan and courage." After the Armistice on 11 November 1918, his section was not immediately discharged. He was still in France when he cabled his parents with boyish enthusiasm: "Saturday, March 1, 1919. Won oh Boy!!!!!!! THE CROIX DE GUERRE. Thank God."

All Crosby's books of poetry (1925-1930) were published in limited editions by his Paris-based Black Sun Press, which also published his diaries as *Shadows of the Sun* (3 volumes,

Harry Crosby (center) and friends wearing their Croix de Guerre

1928-1930). Crosby was not a good poet, and by the late 1920s he was most emphatically a madman; yet for his contemporary Malcolm Cowley, writing in *Exile's Return* (1934; revised 1951), Crosby was a sort of extreme symbol of their generation. Though others have questioned the applicability of Crosby's experience to an understanding of the far better writers to come out of World War I, Crosby's life holds a continuing fascination (as evidenced by Edward Germain's 1977 edition of the diaries and Geoffrey Wolff's 1976 biography). Harry Crosby will be remembered not for his poetry, but for his brief, war-scarred life.

E. E. CUMMINGS (1894-1962) signed up with the Norton-Harjes Ambulance Service on 7 April 1917 and sailed for France on the twenty-eighth, arriving in Bordeaux ten days later. His unit entrained for Paris, but only Cummings and his friend Slater Brown, whom he had met aboard ship, reached that destination. The rest of their unit got off at the wrong stop. Having been in a separate car from the others, they had not seen the others get off the train and,

finding themselves alone in Paris, they made their way to the Norton-Harjes headquarters to report their presence. Officials somehow lost track of them, however, and they spent five weeks entertaining the women of Paris and otherwise amusing themselves before they were assigned to Section Sanitaire 21 in the small village of Germaine. Arriving on 13 June, they quickly began to rebel against the regimentation of military life and became bored as the inactive unit moved about from Nesle, to Noyon, to Jussy, to Chevincourt, and by late August to Assevillier. They made a game of trying to outwit the military censors (early on Cummings wrote to his parents that he was in "a place hardly *germain* to my malcontent"). He and Brown did not get along with the other men in their unit, who were mostly Midwesterners and considered Cummings and Brown "effete Easterners and probably fairies," Brown recalled later, because of their New England accents. They were also disliked by their superior officer, who frequently criticized their lack of military discipline. To show their distaste for their fellow Americans, Cummings and Brown, who—unlike the

Pvt. E. E. Cummings on leave from Camp Devens, 1918 (courtesy of the Houghton Library, Harvard University)

others—spoke good French, spent most of the time with the French cooks and mechanics in their unit. They also fraternized with the French enlisted men in nearby military units, where they heard the then-well-kept secret about the French army mutiny after General Nivelle's defeat in the Aisne campaign. When they repeated the story, voiced their pacifist views, and generally demon-

strated their disdain for their superiors in their own unit, they came under suspicion. Cummings did not help matters by starting to write his letters in French, which his commanding officer did not understand. Then, hoping to get out of the ambulance service by joining the French military, Cummings and Brown wrote a letter volunteering for the Lafayette Escadrille but stating that they did not want to kill Germans. The letter aroused the suspicions of French censors, who were further enraged by letters home in which Brown repeated many of the stories he had heard from French troops and said that "the French soldiers are all despondent and none of them believe that Germany will be defeated."

On 23 September 1917 Cummings and Brown were arrested as suspected spies and confined in a large cathedral-like room at the Dépôt de Triage in La Ferté–Maché. Cummings's imprisonment, which he found more enjoyable than his stint in the ambulance service, is the basis for his first book, *The Enormous Room* (1921), a sort of modern *Pilgrim's Progress* in which Brown is "B." and Cummings himself is "C."

Cummings was released in December 1917 and sent back to the United States (Brown got out a month later). By May 1918, however, his draft board had placed him in Class 1—"Subject to call for service"—and in July he was drafted into the United States Army. Sent for infantry training to Camp Devens, Massachusetts, he remained there as a private (refusing an opportunity to attend a training school for officers and NCO's) until his discharge on 17 January 1919. His attitude toward the war and his brief service in the army is reflected in poems such as "my sweet old etcetera" in *is 5* (1926) and "i sing of Olaf . . . " in *Viva* (1931).

JOHN DOS PASSOS (1896-1970) volunteered for the Norton-Harjes Ambulance Corps in March 1917. Though he wanted "to see what the war was like,"

John Dos Passos (second from left) at the official attachment of three American Red Cross ambulance sections to the Italian army, Milan, 13 December 1917

i sing of Olaf glad and big
whose warmest heart recoiled at war:
a conscientious object-or

. . . though all kinds of officers
(a yearning nation's blueeyed pride)
their passive prey did did and curse
until for wear their clarion
voices and boots were much the worse,
and egged the firstclassprivates on
his rectum wickedly to tease
by means of skilfully applied
bayonets roasted hot with heat-Olaf (upon
what were
once knees)
does almost ceaselessly repeat
"there is some shit I will not eat"
> —from E. E. Cummings,
> *"i sing of Olaf . . . "*

he was a pacifist and had "a horror of serving in the army"–a distinct possibility after the United States entered the war in April and instituted the draft. While he was waiting to be inducted into the ambulance corps, he attended meetings protesting American involvement in the war ("In the spring of 1917 some people caught socialism the way others caught the flu," he wrote later). Before he could get too deeply involved in politics, however, he was called in May to report to automotive-training school for ambulance drivers, and, after he successfully completed the course (even though he was so myopic that he could not read even the top letter on the eye chart and, before he got to the school, had never driven any type of motor vehicle in his life), he sailed for France on 20 June 1917.

After arriving in Paris in early July and attending a training camp at Sandricourt, north of Paris, he was assigned, along with his Harvard friend Robert Hillyer, to Section Sanitaire 60, which in August was sent to Bar-le-duc, near Verdun, where the Allies were preparing for a major offensive. On 15 August 1917, the night before they were sent to the front, Dos Passos and Hillyer agreed to collaborate on an antiwar novel, writing alternate chapters. Hillyer later abandoned the project, but Dos Passos's chapters–after he revised the manuscript six times–became his first novel, *One Man's Initiation–1917*, published in 1920. The life of its main character, Martin Howe, in prep school, at Harvard, in New York, and during the war is based on Dos Passos's own experiences up to the time he returned to the United States in August 1918.

At the "devilish hot section" of the front where they were sent on 16 August 1917, the members of Dos Passos's section worked shifts of up to seventy hours for the next week, and Dos Passos grew more and more bitter about the war. He had already written to a friend about the mutinies that had swept the demoralized French army that spring (incidents the French government was trying to keep secret) and suggested surreptitiously (to avoid alerting the censors) that revolution was the answer. Now he wrote, "The war is utter damn nonsense–a vast cancer fed by lies and self-seeking malignity on the part of those who don't do the fighting." (Though he preached revolution, Dos Passos's only act of rebellion was a protest against army food, which earned him and seven others a brief stay in the stockade.)

The war is utter damn nonsense–a vast cancer fed by lies and self seeking malignity on the part of those who don't do the fighting.

Of all the things in this world a government is the thing least worth fighting for.

None of the poor devils whose mangled dirty bodies I take to the hospital in my ambulance really give a damn about any of the aims of this ridiculous affair–They fight because they are too cowardly & too unimaginative not to see which way they ought to turn their guns–

–John Dos Passos, Letter to
Rumsey Marvin, 23 August 1917

After the army took over the Norton-Harjes Ambulance Corps, Dos Passos, rather than enlisting in the army and remaining with his section in France, joined the American Red Cross ambulance service and was sent to Italy, leaving Paris with a convoy of ambulances in mid November and reaching Milan in early December. Serving in Dolo and Bassano, he continued to work on the book that became *One Man's Initiation*, and his letters were attracting the attention of the censors. On 20 July he was expelled from Italy and put on a train to Paris with instructions to report to his superiors there.

Meanwhile his draft board had been looking for him (they had never recorded the information that he was in the ambulance service, and he had not gotten their notices because he was overseas). In Paris he was given the choice of returning to the United States to report voluntarily to the draft board or being deported. Choosing to return voluntarily, he sailed for New York on 10 August and once there convinced his draft board that he had not been intentionally delinquent. He was inducted into the U.S. Army Medical Corps on 26 September 1918, and, after basic training at Camp Crane in Allentown, Pennyslvania, he shipped out for France on 11 November amid rumors that the war was over (Germany did, in fact, sign the Armistice that day). With little to do in peace-time France, Dos Passos's ambulance section found itself spending a lot of time drilling. In March 1919 Dos Passos was among a group of men assigned to study at the Sorbonne. Still a private, he was discharged in France in 1919. His 1921 novel *Three Soldiers*–in which John Andrews is, in many ways, Dos Passos himself–draws on his army experience. The war also figures in *1919* (1932), the second novel in Dos Passos's *U.S.A.* trilogy.

WILLIAM FAULKNER (1897-1962), having been rejected for training in the Aviation Section of the U. S. Army Signal

Cadet William Faulkner in the uniform of a Royal Flying Corps officer

Corps as too short and too light (he was 5'5 1/2" tall), managed to pass himself off as an Englishman (though the charade may not have been absolutely necessary) and enlisted in the Canadian division of the RAF on 14 June 1918. He began aviation training in Toronto on 10 July 1918, but the war ended before he completed the course, and on 4 January 1919 he was "Discharged in consequence of being Surplus to R.A.F. requirements." Faulkner later said that to celebrate the Armistice he "took up a rotary-motored spad with a crock of bourbon in the cockpit, gave diligent attention to both, and executed some reasonably adroit chandelles, an Immelman or two, and part of what could easily have turned out to be a nearly perfect loop." The loop was not completed, he went on, because "a hangar got in the way and I flew through the roof and ended up hanging in the rafters." The story, which grew more elaborate over the year, seems to have been pure fabrication. Faulkner biographer Joseph Blotner found no evidence that Faulkner's RAF flight training ever got

beyond the preliminary classroom stage. Faulkner later drew on his RAF experiences and those of his fellow cadets for his first novel, *Soldiers' Pay* (1926), about a gravely wounded returned veteran.

Donald Mahon's homecoming, poor fellow, was hardly a nine days' wonder even. Curious, kindly neighbors came in—men who stood or sat jovially respectable, cheerful: solid business men interested in the war only as a by-product of the rise and fall of Mr. Wilson, and interested in that only as a matter of dollars and cents, while their wives chatted about clothes to each other across Mahon's scarred, oblivious brow; a few of the rector's more casual acquaintances democratically uncravated, hushing their tobacco into a bulged cheek, diffidently but firmly refusing to surrender their hats; girls that he had known, had danced with or courted of summer nights, come now to look once upon his face, and then quickly aside in hushed nausea, not coming any more unless his face happened to be hidden on the first visit (upon which they finally found opportunity to see it); boys come to go away fretted because he wouldn't tell any war stories. . . .
—*William Faulkner,* Soldiers' Pay *(1926)*

DOROTHY CANFIELD FISHER (1879-1958) sailed for France with her two children, Sally and John, in August 1916, following her husband John Fisher, who had gone over as an ambulance driver the previous spring. Almost immediately she became involved in organizing the printing and distribution of Braille books for the war blind in Paris. In June 1917 she joined her husband at a training camp for American ambulance drivers at Crouy in the war zone, and she took charge of procuring and preparing the camp's food. When the camp closed in October, she returned to Paris, where Sally became ill with typhus. Taking both children to Guethary, in Basque country, for Sally's convalescence, she helped to establish a home for refugee children. They were forced by circumstances of the war to remain in Basque country until October 1918, when they were finally able to go to Versailles. They sailed for America in spring 1919. Fisher later drew on her wartime experiences in France for three books of short stories–*Home Fires in France* (1918), *The Day of Glory* (1919), and *Basque People* (1931)–and for part of her semiautobiographical novel *The Deepening Stream* (1930).

F. SCOTT FITZGERALD (1896-1940) was commissioned a second lieutenant in the U. S. Army Infantry on 26 October 1917, and in November he reported for training at Fort Leavenworth, Kansas, where the captain in charge of his platoon was Dwight D. Eisenhower (Fitzgerald failed to impress him). Expecting to be killed in battle, he began writing a novel to serve as his memorial. As Fitzgerald recalled later, "Every evening, concealing my pad behind Small Problems for Infantry, I wrote paragraph after paragraph on a somewhat edited history of me and my imagination." He was eventually discovered and prevented from working on his novel during study period, but by writing during his free time–from 1 P.M. to midnight on Saturdays and 6 A.M. to 6 P.M. on Sundays–he managed to finish it in about three months. (The novel, which he called "The Romantic Egoist," was rejected by Scribners in August 1918, but after much revision it became *This Side of Paradise*, which Scribners published in 1920.)

After a leave from the army in February 1918 (he spent the time at Princeton, finishing "The Romantic Egoist"), Fitzgerald reported on 15 March to Camp Zachary Taylor, near Louisville, Kentucky, where he joined the Forty-fifth Infantry Regiment and served for several weeks as aide to the regimental-school commander. The Forty-fifth was transferred to Camp Gordon, Georgia, in April, and in June it was combined

with the Sixty-seventh Infantry Regiment at Camp Sheridan, near Montgomery, Alabama. Though he was promoted to first lieutenant there and was credited with preventing men from drowning during an exercise on the Talapoosa River, Fitzgerald never impressed his superiors as a leader of men. The most notable event of his time at Camp Sheridan was his meeting Zelda Sayre, with whom he fell in love on 7 September 1918 (he wrote the exact date in the *Ledger* he kept) and married on 30 March 1920–four days after

---

"This western-front business couldn't be done again, not for a long time. The young men think they could do it but they couldn't. They could fight the first Marne again but not this. This took religion and years of plenty and tremendous sureties and the exact relation that existed between the classes. The Russians and Italians weren't any good on this front. You had to have a whole-souled sentimental equipment going back further than you could remember. You had to remember Christmas, and postcards of the Crown Prince and his fiancee, and little cafes in Valence and beer gardens in Under den Linden and weddings at the mairie, and going to the Derby, and your grandfather's whiskers."

"General Grant invented this kind of battle at Petersburg in sixty-five."

"No, he didn't–he just invented mass butchery. This kind of battle was invented by Lewis Carroll and Jules Verne and whoever wrote Undine, and country deacons bowling and marraines in Marseilles and girls seduced in the back lanes of Wurtemburg and Westphalia. Why, this was a love battle–there was a century of middle-class love spent here. This was the last love battle."

"You want to hand over this battle to D. H. Lawrence," said Abe.

"All my beautiful lovely safe world blew itself up here with a great gust of high explosive love," Dick mourned persistently.

–F. Scott Fitzgerald,
Tender Is the Night *(1934)*

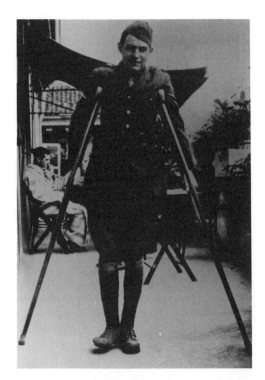

Ernest Hemingway at the American Red Cross Hospital in Milan, September 1918 (courtesy of the John F. Kennedy Library)

the publication of *This Side of Paradise*.

Fitzgerald's regiment was shipped north to Camp Mills, on Long Island on 26 October 1918, in preparation for embarkation to France, but the war was already winding down and in November the regiment was ordered back to Camp Sheridan. AWOL in New York when the train left, Fitzgerald convinced an engineer at Penn Station that he had an urgent message for Woodrow Wilson, and, when his regiment arrived in Washington, D.C., he was waiting for them beside the track with two girls and a bottle of liquor.

Back at Camp Sheridan he was made aide-de-camp to Gen. J. A. Ryan, who failed to see any humor in finding Fitzgerald in bed during an inspection tour and ordered his aide to take riding lessons after Fitzgerald fell off his horse during a parade.

Discharged early (in February 1919) because the army found him expend-

able, Fitzgerald regretted for the rest of his life that he had not fought in the war that had so marked his generation and so radically reshaped his world (a change he described most eloquently in *Tender is the Night*, 1934). Some of his wartime experiences stateside took fictional form in *The Beautiful and Damned* (1922); see also his 1936 short story, "I Didn't Get Over," collected in *Afternoon of an Author* (1957).

ERNEST HEMINGWAY (1899-1961) signed up as an American Red Cross ambulance driver and sailed for Europe on 21 May 1918. In early June he was posted to Milan, where on his first day of duty he was sent to the site of a munitions-factory explosion and put to work gathering bodies and parts of bodies (most of them women's) from the surrounding fields–an experience he described much later in his nonfiction book about bullfighting, *Death in the Afternoon* (1932). A few days later he was assigned to ARC Section Four at Schio, in the foothills of the Dolomites, and later that month he was sent to set up an emergency canteen at Fossalta in the Piave river valley. On 8 July 1918, shortly after midnight in a forward listening post, he was wounded in both legs by schrapnel. Hemingway picked up another wounded man and, while he was staggering toward the command post, was hit in the right knee by machine-gun fire. He continued another 100 yards to the post and collapsed–the first American wounded in Italy.

Spending the rest of the year in the American Red Cross Hospital in Milan, Hemingway met Agnes von Kurowsky, the nurse who served as the model for Catherine Barkley in *A Farewell to Arms* (1929). Promoted to first lieutenant and awarded the Croce de Guerra, Hemingway sailed for home in January 1919, reaching New York on the twenty-first. When the ship docked, he was interviewed by a *New York Sun* reporter, who decided that the 227 scars on Hemingway's legs showed he had taken

Arriving where the munitions plant had been, . . . we were ordered to search the immediate vicinity and surrounding fields for bodies. We found and carried to an improvised mortuary a good number of these and, I must admit, frankly, the shock it was to find that these dead were women rather than men. In those days women had not yet commenced to wear their hair cut short, . . . and the most disturbing thing, perhaps because it was the most unaccustomed, was the presence and, even more disturbing, the occasional absence of this long hair. I remember that after we had searched quite thoroughly for the complete dead we collected fragments. Many of these were detached from a heavy, barbed-wire fence. . . . We agreed too that the picking up of the fragments had been an extraordinary business, it being amazing that the human body should be blown into pieces which exploded along no anatomical lines, but rather divided as capriciously as the fragmentation in the burst of a high explosive shell.

—Ernest Hemingway, Death in the Afternoon *(1932)*

Through the other noise I heard a cough, then came the chuh-chuh-chuh—then there was a flash, as when a blast-furnace door is swung open, and a roar that started white and went red and on and on in a rushing wind. I tried to breathe but my breath would not come and I felt myself rush bodily out of myself and out and out and out and all the time bodily in the wind. I went out swiftly, all of myself, and I knew I was dead and that it had all been a mistake to think you just died. Then I floated, and instead of going on I felt myself slide back. I breathed and I was back.

—Ernest Hemingway, A Farewell to Arms *(1929)*

more punishment than "any other man, in or out of uniform," who had "defied the shrapnel of the Central Powers" (Hemingway had embellished his war record, claiming to have fought with the

Arditti near Mount Grappa in October and early November). Though Hemingway made fullest use of his World War I experiences in his 1929 novel, *A Farewell to Arms,* he first drew on them for two of the ten short prose vignettes in the little book his friend William Bird printed in Paris in 1924, *in our time,* and for "Soldier's Home" and "Big Two-Hearted River," two of the twelve short stories he added to the vignettes for *In Our Time* (1925), published by Boni & Liveright in New York. Like "Soldier's Home" and "Big Two-Hearted River," Hemingway's first novel, *The Sun Also Rises* (1926), focuses on the lingering effects of the war on a wounded veteran.

I was an awful dope when I went to the last war. I can remember just thinking that we were the home team and the Austrians were the visiting team.

—Ernest Hemingway, letter to Maxwell Perkins, 30 May 1942

JOYCE KILMER (1886-1918), having already published "Trees"—the poem that would earn him national recognition—in the August 1913 issue of *Poetry* magazine, enlisted in the Seventh Regiment of the National Guard in 1917, three weeks after the United States entered World War I, and then, hoping to reach the battlefield sooner, he transferred as a private to the 165th Infantry, previously the "Fighting Sixty-ninth" of New York, a unit in the famous Rainbow Division. (As Christopher Morley later wrote in his memorial tribute to Kilmer, "the poet must go where the greatest songs are singing.") After training at Camp Mills, Long Island, he was sent to France, where he wrote a few war poems, collected after his death in volume one of *Joyce Kilmer* (1918), edited by Robert Cortes Holliday. At first he worked at record-keeping in the adjutant's office, and later he was attached to the regimental intelligence section,

Sgt. Joyce Kilmer, May 1918

where he rose to the rank of sergeant, but he finally managed to secure a front-line assignment. As friends later recalled, "He would always be doing more than his orders called for. . . ," and he "had a romantic love of death in battle." On 28 July 1918 at Ourcq Kilmer, having discovered that his battalion would not go into battle first, volunteered and was allowed to serve with the lead battalion. Early in the five-day battle for the hills above Ourcq, he discovered that there were machine-gun nests ahead in the woods and led a patrol to establish their location.

On 30 July 1918 he was found dead with a bullet in his head and was posthumously awarded the Croix de Guerre. His unfinished history of his regiment, which he had started in France, was published in *Father Duffy's Story* (1919), by his friend Francis P. Duffy. While a Kilmer cult had grown up during the poet's lifetime, it was not until his mother, Annie Kilburn Kilmer, set "Trees" to music and included it in her

Whimsical Whimsies (1927) that the poem became popular with—and much parodied by—millions of Americans.

CHARLES MACARTHUR (1895-1956) served in France with Battery F of the famous Rainbow Division, fighting at Cantigny, Chateau-Thierry, and the Argonne. He wrote about his experiences as an enlisted man in *A Bug's Eye View of the War* (1919).

JOHN MONK SAUNDERS (1897-1940) was trained as a pilot at the U. S. Military Aeronautics Department at Berkeley in 1917 and was commissioned a second lieutenant in the U. S. Army Air Corps. His experiences as a pilot in World War I served him well in Hollywood, where he earned his first major screen credit for *Wings* (1927), a film about World War I aces. He also wrote the screenplay for *The Last Flight* (1931), the film version of his novel about a wounded veteran and his friends in Paris and Portugal, *Single Lady* (1931), a sort of "cleaned up" imitation of Hemingway's *The Sun Also Rises* (1926). *Single Lady* appealed to moviegoers and to the readers of *Liberty* magazine, where it was serialized as "Nikki and Her War Birds" before book publication, but the Broadway-musical version, *Nikki* (1931), was a flop.

ALAN SEEGER (1888-1916), who even in his lifetime had the satisfaction of seeing himself called the American Rupert Brooke, enlisted in the French Foreign Legion in August 1914, determined to fight gloriously for the country in which he had lived for two happy years. After preliminary training in Rouen, he was assigned to Batallion C of the Deuxième Régiment Etranger and by 23 October he was at the front near Reims, where he began a long period of six days in the trenches followed by three days rest in nearby villages or woods—see his poem "The Aisne (1914-15)." During that summer his regiment was moved around from sector to sector, and in

Alan Seeger

late September they fought at Champagne—see "Champagne, 1914-15." After Champagne the regiment did not return to the front until May 1916, when they were quartered in a chateau called Bellinglise (about which Seeger wrote a sonnet) when they were not serving in the trenches. For Decoration Day, 30 May 1916, Seeger was invited to write "Ode in Memory of the American Volunteers Fallen for France." He was supposed to read it in front of the statue of Lafayette and Washington in Paris, but in typical military fashion, his permission for leave came too late.

On 4 July 1916 his unit was ordered to drive the Germans from the village of Belloy-en-Santerre. The attack was successful, but Seeger, who had been in the first wave of attacks, was killed by machine-gun fire. He was posthumously awarded the Croix de Guerre and the Medaille Militaire. His war poems, including his famous "I Have a Rendezvous with Death," were published in his *Poems* (1916), in which British dramatist William Archer's introduction confidently proclaimed, "Of all the poets who have died young, none has died so

happily." Though Seeger's poems about the glory of war—like Brooke's—were later overshadowed by the antiwar writing that came out of the war, his poems achieved immediate popularity, not only on the home front but in the trenches. Now overshadowed by Cummings, Dos Passos, and Hemingway, he lives on in French memories. During the 1970s a street in Biarritz was renamed for him.

Yet sought they neither recompense nor
  praise,
Nor to be mentioned in another breath
Than their blue coated comrades whose great
  days
It was their pride to share—ay, share even to
  the death!
Nay, rather, France, to you they rendered
  thanks
(Seeing they came for honor, not for gain),
Who, opening to them your glorious ranks,
Gave them the grand occasion to excel,
That chance to live the life most free from
  slain
And that rare privilege of dying well.
  —from Alan Seeger, "Ode in Memory
   of the American Volunteers
   Fallen for France" (1916)

ELLIOTT WHITE SPRINGS (1896-1959) entered the Aviation Section of the U. S. Army Signal Corps as a private in May 1917 and attended the U. S. School of Military Aeronautics in Princeton, New Jersey, from 5 July to 25 August 1917. He was promoted to sergeant and sailed in September 1917 to England, where he entered the First School of Military Aeronautics in October. He went on to the School of Aerial Fighting in Ayr, Scotland, in January 1918. Commissioned a first lieutenant on 19 March 1918, he was attached to the Eighty-fifth Squadron of the Royal Fighting Corps, stationed at Hounslow, England. In June 1918 he participated in bombing raids on Zeebrugge and Bruges and was slightly injured when his plane was shot down. After a hospital stay in St. Omer, France, he became a flight commander in the 148th American Aero Squadron, attached to the Royal Air Force, in July 1918. On 22 August 1918 he was promoted to captain and rated military aviator.

In October 1918, when he was awarded the British Distinguished Flying Cross, the citation mentioned "numerous engagements" in which Springs had performed heroically, singled out two engagements, on 3 and 22 August 1918, for special mention, and concluded, "This officer has at all times shown the greatest determination and courage and his work as Flight Commander in this Squadron has been marked by rare combination of cool judgment and most aggressive fighting tactics." He was also awarded a Distinguished Service Cross for his actions over Bapaume, France, on 22 August 1918.

He returned to the United States in February 1919 and was discharged on the fifteenth. Official records credited him with destroying eleven German planes and ranked him third among living American aces.

After the war, Springs employed his firsthand knowledge of the war to write aviation fiction, including *War Birds* (1926; which was purported to be the "Diary of an Unknown Aviator"), *Nocturne Militaire* (1927), *Leave Me with a Smile* (1928), *Above the Bright Blue Sky* (1928), and *War Birds and Lady Birds* (1931). His greatest success came later—with his Spring Maid sheet ads.

LAURENCE STALLINGS (1894-1969) enlisted in the U. S. Marine Corps as a second lieutenant in October 1917, underwent basic training at Parris Island, South Carolina, and went to France with the Second Division, Forty-seventh Company, in the Third Battalion of the Fifth Marines. After fighting at Chateau-Thierry, he was wounded on the last day of battle at Belleau Wood

Capt. Laurence Stallings (courtesy of the New York Public Library at Lincoln Center, Astor, Lenox and Tilden Foundations)

(26 June 1918), while leading his men in a grenade attack on a German machine-gun nest. Shot in his right leg by a bullet that tore off the kneecap, he threw his grenade as he fell and destroyed the nest. (While he persuaded army surgeons not to cut off his leg, amputation was necessary after he reinjured it in 1922.) Awarded the Croix de Guerre and a Silver Star, Stallings spent eight months in a French hospital before returning to the United States in February 1919. He spent another month in a Brooklyn navy hospital and retired, as a captain, in June 1920. He used his war experiences in a novel, *Plumes* (1924), the story of a disillusioned young war hero; *What Price Glory?* (1924), the powerful antiwar play he wrote with Maxwell Anderson; and in short stories. Ernest Hemingway included one of them, "Vale of Tears" (1931), in his anthology *Men at War* (1942), but the others—"The Big Parade" (*New Republic*, 17 September 1924), "Esprit de Corps" (*Scribners*, August 1928), "Turn Out the Guard" (*Satur-*

day *Evening Post*, 13 October 1928), and "Return to the Woods" (*Colliers*, 5 March 1942)–have never been collected in a book.

He also wrote two nonfiction books about the war, *The First World War: A Pictorial History* (1933) and *The Doughboys* (1963).

GERTRUDE STEIN (1874-1946) and ALICE B. TOKLAS (1877-1967) were visiting philosopher Alfred North Whitehead in England when England declared war on Germany on 4 August 1914, and they were unable to return to their home in Paris until October. In spring 1915 they went to Majorca, but the following spring, concerned about the plight of their adopted country, they returned to France and joined the American Fund for French Wounded. In early 1917 Stein learned to drive, bought a Ford, which she christened "Aunt Pauline" ("Auntie" for short) after her aunt Pauline Stein, and had it converted to a truck for use in delivering supplies for the wounded. In April they went to Perpignan, in southwestern France, to work for the American Fund, and in the autumn, after they had been recalled to Paris, they were sent to open a supply depot in Nimes, where they remained until shortly after the Armistice, on 11 November 1918. Then, because Stein spoke excellent German, they were sent to start a civilian relief operation in Alsace and served there until the following spring. Despite Stein's idiosyncratic driving (for example, she never learned to use reverse gear, a fact that made parking tricky and necessitated some driving in circles), Stein and Toklas made a valuable contribution to the war effort, even selling their last Matisse, the once-controversial *La Femme au Chapeau*, to buy supplies needed for their relief work in Alsace. connaissance Francaise in 1922. Stein wrote about her World War I experiences in *The Autobiography of Alice B. Toklas* (1933), *Everybody's Autobiography* (1937), *Wars I Have Seen* (1945), and war

We had a few adventures, we were caught in the snow and I was sure we were on the wrong road and wanted to turn back. Wrong or right, said Gertrude Stein, we are going on. She could not back the car very successfully and indeed I may say even to this day when she can drive any kind of car anywhere she still does not back a car very well. She goes forward admirably, she does not go backwards successfully. The only violent discussions that we have had in connection with her driving a car have been on the subject of backing.

Soon we came to the battle-fields and the lines of trenches of both sides. To any one who did not see it as it was then it is impossible to imagine it. It was not terrifying it was strange. We were used to ruined houses and even ruined towns but this was different. It was a landscape. And it belonged to no country.

I remember hearing a french nurse once say and the only thing she did say of the front was, c'est un paysage passionant, an absorbing landscape. And that was what it was as we saw it. It was strange. Camouflage, huts, everything was there. It was wet and dark and there were a few people, one did not know whether they were chinamen or europeans.

—Gertrude Stein, The Autobiography
of Alice B. Toklas *(1933)*

Really the composition of this war, 1914-1918, was not the composition of all previous wars, the composition was not a composition in which there was one man in the centre surrounded by a lot of other men but a composition that had neither a beginning nor an end, a composition of which one corner was as important as another corner, in fact the composition of cubism.

—Gertrude Stein, Picasso *(1938)*

Stein and Toklas each received the French government's Medaille de la Re-

Staff of the American Fund for the French Wounded, circa 1917: Standing in the second row are Alice B. Toklas (far left) and Gertrude Stein (far right) (courtesy of the Beinecke Rare Book and Manuscript Library, Yale University)

poems including "Work Again," "Decorations," "Won," and "Accents in Alsace," collected in *Bee Time Vine and Other Pieces 1914-1937* (1955) and *Geography and Plays* (1922). Toklas wrote about their experiences in *What Is Remembered* (1963).

EUNICE TIETJENS (1884-1944), poet and assistant editor of *Poetry: A Magazine of Verse*, convinced the managing editor of the *Chicago Daily News* to send her to Paris as that newspaper's first female war correspondent and sailed for France in October 1917. Though she had been assigned to write human-interest stories about life in wartime Paris, she soon began covering the war zone as well, visiting the small towns at the front on trips that lasted from a few days to several weeks and once going into the frontline trenches. The *Chicago Daily News* ordered Tietjens home in October 1918, but she volunteered for service with the Red Cross and remained in France until January 1919. Tietjens wrote about her wartime experiences in her autobiography, *The World at My Shoulder* (1938), and drew on them for poems such as "Mud," "Song for a Blind Man Who Could Not Go to War," and "Deserted Battlefield," collected in her 1919 book, *Body and Raiment*.

EDITH WHARTON (1862-1937) was living in Paris when Germany declared war on France on 3 August 1914, and within two weeks she had thrown herself into relief efforts. Her first project was necessitated by the patriotic and charitable activities of well-to-do women like herself. Because these ladies of fashion had begun making clothing for the troops with such fervor, local seamstresses were out of work. Wharton established a workroom that eventually employed as many as a hundred women at once and used her social connections in France and the United States to get large orders for their work.

Near the end of 1914, after the Battle of the Marne in September and the fighting around Ypres in October had forced thousands of civilians from their homes, Wharton undertook a more ambitious project than the workroom, founding the American Hostels for Refugees, which for the remainder of the war provided free medical care, free or inexpensive housing and clothing, and food and fuel at a nominal fee. After one year of operation, the hostels had assisted 9,330 refugees, served 235,000 meals, distributed 48,000 garments, given medical attention to 7,700 individuals, and placed 3,400 people in jobs. Much more than just a figurehead who lent her name to the fund-raising efforts of others, Wharton served as chief administrator and major fund raiser for the American Hostels, earning admiration for her hard work and considerable organizational skills.

She also visited the front, taking supplies to field hospitals, and saw the fighting first hand. She reported on trips to battle zones during the first half of 1915 in articles for *Scribner's* magazine and New York newspapers, which were collected in *Fighting France: From Dunkerque to Belfort* (1915). Meanwhile, in April, she started the Children of Flanders Rescue Committee, which became almost as large-scale an operation as the American Hostels. To raise funds for both organizations she solicited writings from her many literary friends for *The Book of the Homeless* (1915), which was published in New York and London.

In spring 1916 Wharton helped to found a treatment program for the many French soldiers who had contracted tuberculosis in the trenches. The International Red Cross took over this project a year and a half later, but by then Wharton had become aware of the need for similar facilities for civilians, and she opened four convalescent homes for them. At about the same time she raised $100,000 for Red Cross ambulances.

In April 1916 President Raymond Poincare of France made her a Chevalier of the Legion of Honor, even though the government had decided not to give awards to civilians and foreigners until the war was over. (In 1918 she received Belgium's Medal of Queen Elizabeth, and the next year King Albert of Belgium named her Chevalier of the Order of Leopold.)

Wharton later dealt with the war in two novels, *The Marne* (1918) and *A Son at the Front* (1923). Both were dedicated to Ronald Simmons, a young American friend of Wharton's who was a casualty of the war and the model for Boyleston in *A Son at the Front.*

BRAND WHITLOCK (1869-1934) was appointed American minister to Belgium on 1 January 1914 and served throughout World War I, working to mitigate the effects of the German occupation. He tried without success to save Edith Cavell, a Red Cross nurse accused of helping Allied prisoners of war to escape, from a German firing squad. In 1917 he followed the Belgian government into French exile. His post was raised to an ambassadorship on 29 September 1919, and he served until 1921. His memoir of his war was published as *Belgium: A Personal Narrative* (1919).

You will find no tales of heroism here. We were neither of us ever in much danger of getting killed ourselves. But to any one not elevated in a pulpit or barricaded behind an editorial desk the overpowering presence of death, that stood darkly in every heart, seemed to rob the very sun of its splendor and make the stars stab him like knives. No matter how rich men's minds had been or how full of joy and life, they were all turned now without release to the business of bringing death. The very quartermaster who matched suits was preparing shrouds for men to die in; the very worker in the hospital who patched up the gas and shell wounds was only getting men in shape to die and to inflict death. The air of the whole world seemed poisoned with decay; one could escape it nowhere; one choked in the very autumn clearness and the winds of spring, which were tainted now with the foulness of those seven million dead.

    —Edmund Wilson, Preface
    to The Undertaker's Garland *(1922)*

EDMUND WILSON (1895-1972) attended the military training camp in Plattsburg, New York, in August and September 1916 and entered the U. S. Army as a private in May 1917. He was assigned to the Medical Corps and was stationed at Base Hospital Unit Thirty-six in Detroit until November 1917, when he sailed for France. First stationed at Vittel in

Vosges, he was promoted to sergeant in October 1918 and served as an interpreter in the Intelligence Corps at Chaumont, France, until May 1919, when he returned to the United States. He was discharged in July 1919. Wilson drew on his Medical Corps experiences to describe the death of a young enlisted man from pneumonia in "The Death of a Soldier," published in *The Undertaker's Garland* (1922), by Wilson and John Peale Bishop.

SPANISH CIVIL WAR

Alvah Bessie in Spain, 1939

ALVAH BESSIE (1904-1985) is now best known as one of the Hollywood Ten, who were imprisoned and blacklisted for refusing, in 1947, to cooperate with the House Un-American Activities Committee investigation into the influence of the Communist party in the movie industry. His political activism began in the 1930s, when he joined the Communist party, and in 1938 he enlisted in the Abraham Lincoln Brigade of the Spanish Republican Army. Becoming a sergeant-adjutant, Bessie was awarded a Dombrowski Medal by the Polish Veterans of the International Brigades in 1946. He returned to the United States in 1939 and wrote about his experiences in *Men in Battle*, an autobiographical book published later that year. In 1952 he edited *The Heart of Spain*, an anthology of writings about the war. His largely autobiographical novel, *The Un-Americans* (1957), draws on both his war experiences in Spain and his difficulties with HUAC. In the 1960s he collaborated on the screenplay for and appeared in a Spanish film, *España otra vez* ("Spain Again"), about the reactions of an American doctor who fought for the Republican Army in Spain and returns thirty years later. Released in 1968, the film received an award from Spain's National Syndicate of Entertainment and was Spain's official Academy Award entry for Best Foreign Film. Though the film was never released in the United States, Bessie's 1975 book, *Spain Again*, includes portions of the screenplay as well as Bessie's own reactions to returning to Spain thirty years after he fought there.

JOHN DOS PASSOS (1896-1970) arrived in Spain as a correspondent for *Fortune* magazine on 4 April 1937. Three days later, in Valencia, he learned of the disappearance of his friend and translator José Robles, a professor at Johns Hopkins University who had been in Spain when the war broke out and had remained to serve the Republican government, first as a cultural attaché with the war ministry and then as interpreter to the ranking Soviet military adviser Gen. Ian Antonovich Berzin (known as Goriev in Spain). As Dos Passos eventually learned, Robles had been executed, probably, he concluded "because Russian secret agents felt that Robles knew too much about relations between the Spanish war ministry and the Kremlin and was not, from their point of view, politically reliable." By the time Robles's death was confirmed, Dos Passos was in Madrid, where he had planned to work with Ernest Hemingway and Dutch filmmaker Joris Ivens on filming *The Spanish Earth* (1937), a pro-Republican documentary film designed to educate the American public about the war. He lost interest in the project because of his quest for information about Robles and because he disagreed with Hemingway about the contents of the film, and the final results can be largely attributed to Hemingway. Although he went with Hemingway and Ivens into the battle zone for filming several times, Dos Passos felt not only that Hemingway was unwisely endangering the crew but that the film ought to place less emphasis on the battlefield and more on the new government's social reforms. His friendship with Hemingway was seriously damaged by their disagreement over the issues surrounding Robles's death. Determined to see the Republican government and their Soviet allies as the "good guys" in the fight against fascism–the forces of Gen. Francisco Franco attempting to overthrow Spain's elected government with the aid of Hitler and Mussolini–Hemingway argued that Robles had been executed because he must have been guilty of treason, a statement that enraged Dos Passos, who not only believed in his friend's innocence but was willing to recognize that Stalin's decision to aid the Spanish Republicans could be less than altruistic. Leaving Spain after about a month, Dos Passos later collected four essays on life in Barcelona, Pozorubio, Fuenteduena, and San Pol de Mar in a small book, *The Villages Are the Heart of Spain* (1938); these essays along with his earlier writings about Spain appear in *Journeys Between Wars* (1938). Dos Passos's first novel after the Spanish Civil War, *Adventures of a Young Man* (1939), features Glenn Spotswood, an idealistic party worker who becomes disillusioned with Communism and dies while fighting for the Republicans in Spain.

MARTHA GELLHORN (1908-) was in Spain as a correspondent for *Collier's Weekly* for the first time from mid March to May 1937. Staying in Madrid's Hotel Florida at a time when the city was under bombardment, she saw the fighting firsthand, often visiting the front with future husband Ernest Hemingway, who was working on his film *The Spanish Earth*. (In July 1937 she arranged, through her friend Eleanor Roosevelt, for Hemingway to show the film at the White House.)

Back in Spain from September 1937 until January 1938 she and Hemingway, along with Herbert Matthews, were the first American correspondents to reach Belchite after it had been retaken by the Republican Army in September, and in October they–along with Sefton Delmer, another journalist–were shot at by Franco's forces as they were on the way to the Brunete front. Hemingway was to remember and praise Gellhorn's courage for years to come. (She also visited the wounded in the military hospitals, and later wrote: "male reporters steered clear of all places where war was shown in ruined bodies. This is a statement not a criticism.")

Having begun what would prove to be a distinguished career as a war correspondent, Gellhorn returned to Spain again in 1938. Her experiences in Spain formed the background for some of the short stories collected in *The Heart of Another* (1941) and *The Honeyed Peace* (1953). Her "On Apocryphism" in the spring 1981 issue of the *Paris Review* was intended as a corrective to Lillian Hellman's misrepresentations of her activities in Spain during the war.

ERNEST HEMINGWAY (1899-1961) signed on with the North American Newspaper Alliance (NANA) as an "anti-war correspondent" in January 1937, and the next month he joined John Dos Passos, Archibald MacLeish, and Lillian Hellman on the board of Contemporary Historians, the group organized to produce *The Spanish Earth* (1937).

Reaching Spain on 16 March and arriving in Madrid on the twentieth he checked into the Hotel Florida, which served as a sort of home base for American correspondents, including–at various times–Martha Gellhorn (later to become his third wife), Josephine Herbst, Lillian Hellman, and Dos Passos. His work on *The Spanish Earth* brought him into close contact with Republican troops on and off the battlefield (including American volunteers), and he stored up observations that became the basis for his novel of the Spanish war, *For Whom the Bell Tolls* (1940). Robert Jordan may be based in part on Robert Hale Merriman, an officer and hero of the Abraham Lincoln Brigade who was killed in 1938.

Hemingway left Spain after forty-five days, arriving in Paris on 9 May, and on 8 July he and Gellhorn showed the film at the White House (the script was published in 1938). In early September he was back in Spain for the Republican's victory at Belchite, but despite their success there, the Republican army was faltering; Franco held two-thirds of the country and was expected to take Madrid, the original Republican capital, but shelling of the city was lighter than it had been on his previous visit. During a lull in the fighting, in August and September, he wrote *The Fifth Column*, a three-act play based on his experiences

there. Dorothy Bridges, the female correspondent in the play, bears a strong resemblance to Martha Gellhorn, while Philip Rawlings is much more part of the political scene than Hemingway. It was produced on Broadway in 1940 and published in *The Fifth Column and the First Forty-Nine Stories* (1939).

Hemingway left Spain at the end of the year, but–thoroughly absorbed with the Republican cause–he returned to Spain in March 1938 to follow the Republican Army retreat until mid May, when he returned to the United States still asserting that they could win. He made a final brief visit to Spain in November, by which time he had accepted the Republicans' eventual loss. (The war ended the following spring.)

Hemingway used his Spanish war experiences in not only a novel and a play but also in short stories, including "The Denunciation," "The Butterfly and the Tank," "Nobody Ever Dies," "Night Before Battle," and "Under the Ridge."

JOSEPHINE HERBST (1892-1969) arrived in Madrid in March 1937, a few days after Ernest Hemingway, who threw his arms around her as she walked into the lobby of the Hotel Florida, dragging her knapsack and coated with "white dust from shells exploding in the streets." Remaining until June, she saw the end of the "squalid internecine brawl in Barcelona," where for five days, beginning on 3 May, members of the Popular Front coalition that held a majority in the Spanish Republican government turned away from fighting Franco and fought among themselves, suppressing the anarchists and Trotskyites in their ranks. Even before this event, on her visits to the front and in her conversations with political insiders, Herbst had discovered that the issues were far from black and white, and she wrote very little about the war at that time–in part because she found it impossible to voice the unequivocal support of the Spanish Republic that her fellow leftist writers wanted to hear.

Langston Hughes, Mikhail Koltzov, Ernest Hemingway, and Cuban poet Nicolás Guillén in Madrid, 1937. Koltzov was the model for Karkov in Hemingway's *For Whom the Bell Tolls* (courtesy of the Beinecke Rare Book and Manuscript Library, Yale University).

Written much later, her memoir "The Starched Blue Sky of Spain" (*Noble Savage*, March 1960) is valuable for its objectivity in its presentation of conditions in the International Brigades, the complex politics underlying the war, and life among the American correspondents in besieged Madrid. Her account of Dos Passos and Hemingway's argument over the fate of José Robles is particularly revealing and generally more sympathetic to Dos Passos.

WILLIAM HERRICK (1915-   ) fought in the Abraham Lincoln Brigade in 1936 and 1937 and was severely wounded at the front near Madrid. He came away from the war still sympathetic to the Republic but disillusioned by the machinations of their Soviet allies; both attitudes are reflected in his 1969 novel about the war, *Hermanos!*

LANGSTON HUGHES (1902-1963) went to Spain as a correspondent for the *Baltimore Afro-American*, the *Cleveland Call and Post*, and the *Cleveland Globe* to cover the black Americans who were fighting in the International Brigades of the Spanish Republican Army. He arrived late in July 1937 and, after stops in Barcelona and Valencia, spent most of the next five months in and around beseiged Madrid. Traveling with mili-

tary convoys and visiting the front lines during battle, he barely escaped injury from artillery fire, hand-grenade fragments, and sniper fire, and one of his elbows was nicked by a dum-dum bullet. "Several times in Spain I thought I might not live long," he wrote later; but at the time he wrote to a friend that "it's a thrilling and poetic place to be." Having written the long, militant poem "Song of Spain" before he left the United States, Hughes wrote several more poems about the war–"Air Raid: Barcelona," "Moonlight in Valencia: Civil War," "Madrid-1937," "Letter from Spain Addressed to Alabama," "A Postcard from Spain Addressed to Alabama"–between his arrival in Spain and his departure in December 1937.

"Give Franco a hood and he would be a member of the Ku Klux Klan."
    –Langston Hughes,
    Dispatch to the Baltimore
    Afro-American, *18 December 1937*

ELLIOT PAUL (1891-1958) went to live in the small town of Santa Eulalia on Ibiza, the smallest island of the Balearics, off the coast of Spain in 1931. He escaped from the island in 1936, on the day before Franco's Italian allies reached the town and established a fascist government. Paul's *The Life and Death of a Spanish Town* (1937) celebrates prewar life in which the community's growing politicization and the advent of war politicization and the advent of war brought an end to that way of life.

WORLD WAR II AND KOREA

ROBERT ANDERSON (1917-   ) was an intelligence officer in the U.S. Navy from 1942 to 1946, serving on the *Alaska,* and was awarded a Bronze Star. His play *Come Marching Home* (1945), about a returned war hero, won the Army-Navy Playwriting Contest in 1945.

THOMAS BERGER (1924-   ) served with the U.S. Army in Europe from 1943 to 1946. His 1958 novel, *Crazy in Berlin*, deals with the experiences of a young soldier in postwar Berlin, and the sequel, *Reinhart in Love* (1962), follows the same character's life after his return to the United States.

VANCE BOURJAILY (1922-   ) entered the American Field Service in 1942 and served as an ambulance driver in Italy for two years, until a case of severe jaundice forced him to return to the United States, where he was drafted into the U. S. Army in 1944. Assigned to an infantry regiment in the 398th Division, he was stationed in Hawaii and Occupied Japan before his discharge in January 1946. He later drew on his war experiences for two novels, *The End of My Life* (1947) and *Confessions of a Spent Youth* (1960).

JOHN HORNE BURNS (1916-1953) entered the U.S. Army Infantry as a private in January 1942 and rose to the rank of second lieutenant by the end of the war. Serving as a mail censor with military intelligence, he was stationed in North Africa and then Italy–the setting for his first novel, *The Gallery* (1947), which reviewers at that time praised as one of the best novels to come out of World War II. Burns drew upon his own war experiences for his ironic portrait of Major Motes, the pompous mail censor, who finally realizes, "The whole war is obscene." Burns's second novel, *Lucifer with a Book* (1949), which deals with a returned veteran's inability to adapt to the hypocrisy of life as a teacher at a Northeastern prep school, is a fictionalized account of Burns's own postwar experiences while teaching at the Loomis School.

EVAN S. CONNELL, JR. (1924-   ) entered the U.S. Navy as an aviation cadet, earned his wings on V-E Day, and served as a flight instructor until his discharge. His 1960 novel, *The Patriot*, draws on his experiences as an aviation cadet. Though there are surface similarities between Connell and the main character, Melvin Isaacs, another character, Patrick Coles, probably bears a closer resemblance to his creator.

JAMES GOULD COZZENS (1903-1978) reported to U.S. Army Air Force officers' training school at the Greenbriar Hotel in Miami Beach, Florida, on 1 August 1943. Six weeks later he was commissioned a first lieutenant and assigned to the Training Literature Section of the Training Aids Directorate (TAD) at Gravelly Point in Washington, D.C., where he wrote manuals and special reports. In November 1942 TAD was transferred to Orlando, Florida, the setting for his World War II novel, *Guard of Honor*, published in 1948. (He also met

Maj. James Gould Cozzens at the Office of Information Services, Pentagon Building (courtesy of Jo H. Chamberlain)

models for the air-force characters in that novel.)

Cozzens was relocated with TAD to New York in May 1943, and, after he was promoted to captain in August, he began collaborating with William Vogel on "The Air Force Training Program," an article that appeared in the February 1944 issue of *Fortune* magazine. While he was working on the article, he visited training facilities throughout the country: when his plane was landing at Selman Field in Louisiana, it nearly collided with another plane (an experience that formed the basis for a key scene in *Guard of Honor*).

In October 1943 Cozzens was reassigned to the Office of Special Projects of the Office of Special Information at the Pentagon. His duties included writing speeches and statements for the air-force brass, conducting press briefings, and—after his promotion to major in August 1944—preparing memos on everything going on in all Pentagon air-force departments and in the combat zones (thus gaining access to virtually any classified material he wanted to see and becoming one of the best-informed men in the air force). One of his memos was a report on the attempt of black officers at Freeman Field, Indiana, to force their way into the whites-only officers'

club—an incident that provided the crisis for *Guard of Honor*. Cozzens was discharged on 18 October 1945. He used his wartime experiences most directly in *Guard of Honor*, but he also drew on them for parts of his last novel, *Morning Noon and Night* (1968). Cozzen's air-force diaries and Pentagon memos for the years 1943-1945 were published in 1984 as *A Time of War*.

OSSIE DAVIS (1917-) served in the U.S. Army from 1942 to 1945. Sent to Liberia as a surgical technician, he was later transferred to Special Services, where he wrote and staged his first play, an army show called *Goldbrickers of 1944*.

JAMES DICKEY (1923- interviewing) enlisted in the U.S. Army Air Corps in 1942 and served as a pilot with the 418th Fighter Squadron in the South Pacific, where he flew more than one hundred missions, during which time fellow pilots were captured and tortured, some killed, by the Japanese.

He describes his novel *Alnilam* (1987) as deriving "from general experiences many members of my generation underwent in the air war of 1941-1946." Yet, he adds, "scenes . . . incidents and physi-

James Dickey

correspondent for *Life* magazine. Visiting some twenty islands, he was aboard a battleship in the convoy that began the assault on Iwo Jima in January 1945. He entered Manila with the Sixth Army on 5 February, just after the first American troops had reached the city and remained there during the three-week-long battle that followed, interviewing many of the newly released American prisoners of war and writing to friends that published reports of Japanese atrocities were actually understated. In early March he went to Leyte, where he interviewed Gen. Douglas MacArthur, and by April 1945 he was back in San Francisco. His essays about the war, which include some of his pieces for *Life*, were published as *Tour of Duty* (1946), a book notable for its attempt to depict the soldier's state of mind. Edmund Wilson called it "probably the best thing Dos Passos has written since he finished *U.S.A.*"

From mid October to mid December 1945 Dos Passos covered the Nuremburg Trials for *Life*.

cal details" only come from his experiences as a combat pilot.

Awarded an Air Medal, Dickey was recalled to service during the Korean War and served as a training officer. He had begun writing poems–often dealing with his World War II experience–in 1947, and these war poems were included in his first four collections: *Into the Stone and Other Poems* (in *Poets of Today VII*, edited by John Hall Wheelock, 1960), *Drowning with Others* (1962), *Helmets* (1964), and *Buckdancer's Choice* (1965). One of his best-known war poems is "The Performance," which appeared in his first collection.

JOHN DOS PASSOS (1896-1970) went to England as a delegate to the International P.E.N. Congress on 5 September 1941 and toured England for six weeks as a guest of the British Ministry of Information, writing two long articles for *Harper's*, "England in the Great Lull" (February 1942) and "Some Glasgow People" (April 1942). In December 1944 he left for the South Pacific as a navy war

WILLIAM EASTLAKE (1917-) enlisted as a private in the U.S. Army Infantry in 1942 and was wounded in the Battle of the Bulge (December 1944). Awarded a Bronze Star, he had been promoted to staff sergeant by the time he was discharged in 1946. He drew on his experiences for his 1965 novel, *Castle Keep*.

RICHARD EBERHART (1904-) received a commission as a lieutenant in the U.S. Naval Reserve on 10 August 1942 and became a gunnery instructor, first in Hollywood, Florida, where he was sent in October 1942. The following May he was transferred to Dam Neck, Virginia, where he helped to write the *Free Gunner's Hand Book*, a pocket-sized manual, in summer 1943. In November 1944, just after his promotion to lieutenant commander, he became "fourth in command and Training Officer" at the naval air station in Wildwood, New Jer-

Lt. Richard Eberhart (USN) flying one of the kites he used in his work as an aerial-gunnery instructor in Virginia Beach, Virginia (courtesy of the Richard Eberhart Collection, Bake Library, Dartmouth College)

sey. The week before the war ended he was transferred to the naval air station in Alameda, California; he was discharged in June 1946.

While he was in the navy, Eberhart edited, with Selden Rodman, *War and the Poet: An Anthology of Poetry Expressing Man's Attitudes to War from Ancient Times to the Present* (1945). His war poems include "Dam Neck, Virginia," "World War," and "The Fury of Aerial Bombardment" in *Poems New and Selected* (1945); "An Airman Considers His Power," "At the End of War," and "A Ceremony by the Sea" in *Burr Oaks* (1947); and "Brotherhood of Man," first collected in *Selected Poems* (1951).

HOWARD FAST (1914-) was a member of the overseas staff of the U.S. Office of War Information from 1942 to 1944, and in 1944-1945 he covered the China-India-Burma Theater as a war correspondent attached to a special unit of the Signal Corps. In 1945 he became a foreign correspondent for *Esquire* and *Coronet*. His 1959 novel, *The Winston Affair*, is set in the Far East during World War II and deals with the court-martial of an American soldier who has been accused of murdering a British soldier.

MARTHA GELLHORN (1908-) served as a war correspondent for *Collier's* throughout World War II. She spent fall and winter 1939 covering the war in Finland. In early 1941–after her marriage to Ernest Hemingway on 21 November 1940–she was assigned to cover the war in the Far East for *Collier's*, and Hemingway signed on to report on the war there for *PM*. Arriving in Hong Kong in February, they went to Mainland China and Burma. Hemingway left for home in mid April, but Gellhorn traveled to Jakarta, in Java, returning to the United States in June. In mid July 1942 she left on a six-week fact-finding cruise in the Caribbean, and in October 1943 she left for London, traveling via Lisbon. On D-Day (6 June 1944) she crossed the English Channel on a hospital ship and managed to get ashore to cover the action before returning to London. She spent the rest of the war in Italy, France, and Germany, often under fire and close to the front lines. After the war (and her divorce from Hemingway in December 1945) she went to Java in 1946 to cover the fighting for Indonesian independence. She was later a war correspondent for the *Guardian* (London) in Vietnam (1966) and Israel (1967).

Gellhorn began drawing from her experiences for her fiction before the war ended. Her 1940 novel, *A Stricken Field*, deals with the experiences of a female correspondent in Prague in 1938-1939, between the Munich Pact and the Czechoslovakian Anschluss. Some of the stories and sketches in *The Heart of Another* (1941) focus on people in France and Finland during the early years of World

The *Adakian* staff: Dashiell Hammett is standing at the rear, fourth from the right

War II. After the war, she wrote *The Wine of Astonishment* (1948), a combat novel set during the period when the prospects for Allied victory were the bleakest. Though it received mixed reviews, the novel was praised for its realistic depiction of military life in wartime. *The Honeyed Peace* (1953) also contains stories that deal with either military life during the war or the effects of the war on its survivors.

DASHIELL HAMMETT (1894-1961) was allowed to reenlist in the U.S. Army, as a private, on 17 September 1942, even though he had had intermittent periods of illness from tuberculosis since his service stateside during World War I (24 June 1918-29 May 1919), and even though he was under surveillance by the FBI because of his activities on behalf of liberal and Communist causes. A week later he reported to a U.S. Army Signal Corps training regiment at Fort Monmouth, New Jersey, where he was given a desk job writing lectures and lesson plans and was promoted to corporal on 18 May 1943. By the following

month the army had become concerned about his politics, and on 29 June 1943 he was transferred to Company A, Twelfth Battalion, at Camp Shenango, Pennsylvania, where the army planned to keep soldiers considered subversive under a sort of house arrest until the end of the war. A week later the plan was overruled by the president. Hammett eventually ended up in the Fourteenth Signal Service Company and was assigned to Adak, a barren island in the Aleutian Chain, about 800 miles from the Alaskan mainland. On Adak, where he arrived on 8 September 1943, he was assigned to orientation services, which included starting a camp newspaper, the *Adakian*; the first issue appeared on 19 January 1944. (Another staff member was Bernard Kalb, now an NBC news correspondent.) Hammett edited and wrote for the *Adakian* without inserting his own political views, and he provided the introduction for *Wind Blown and Dripping* (1945), a collection of editorial cartoons that had appeared in the paper.

With Robert Colodny, Hammett was also assigned to write *The Battle of the*

Aleutians (1944), an illustrated booklet about military operations in the islands from June 1942 to August 1943 that was given to troops in the chain.

As another part of his job, Hammett lectured throughout the Aleutians in 1944, speaking to troops on subjects such as the progress of the war on other fronts, their part in the war effort, and events at home.

He was promoted to sergeant on 20 August 1944, and in spring 1945 he began making notes for a novel about a veteran's return home after the war, but he abandoned work on it after his transfer on 14 April to Fort Richardson in Anchorage, Alaska. Promoted to master sergeant (tec 3) on 27 June, he was honorably discharged on 6 September 1945. He took up work on his novel again after the war but gave it up in 1952 or 1953, after completing about 12,500 words. The completed fragment was published as "Tulip" in *The Big Knockover* (1966), a collection of his stories edited by Lillian Hellman.

Hammett was a celebrity in the Aleutians and even counted his commanding general among his fans—a fact that allowed him to display a certain amount of disrespect for authority. Once, when a chaplain called to complain about the *Adakian*'s printing the words "God damn," Hammett told him God was lucky to have gotten his name in the paper at all, and that if he wanted to pursue the matter he could talk to the general. Another time Hammett lay on a table reading throughout a major's inspection of the paper, telling the visitor, "If you have a complaint, major, take it up with the general." It turned out the major had really come to get Hammett's autograph.

MARION HARGROVE (1919-) was inducted into the U.S. Army on 18 July 1941 and was sent for basic training to Fort Bragg, North Carolina, where he was classified as a semiskilled cook. Having worked for the *Charlotte News* before he was drafted, he began writing a column, "In the Army Now," for the paper. Maxwell Anderson, who came to Fort Bragg to do background research for his play *The Eve of St. Mark* (Hargrove is thought to be the model for Francis Marion in the play), took some of Hargrove's columns to Henry Holt and Company, which published them as *See Here, Private Hargrove*, on 23 July 1942. Shortly before that date, Hargrove was transferred to New York to work as a staff writer for *Yank* magazine. Before he was discharged with the rank of sergeant in 1945, he traveled around the world as a feature editor for *Yank*. He later drew on his army experiences for a novel, *The Girl He Left Behind; Or, All Quiet in the Third Platoon* (1956).

MARK HARRIS (1922-) was drafted into the U.S. Army in January 1943 and spent two months at antiaircraft training in Virginia before he was sent to radio-operators' school in Athens, Georgia. In May 1943 he was sent to study engineering at Clemson University, and the following November he was shipped out to Camp Wheeler, near Macon, Georgia. On 12 February 1944–having become increasingly appalled by southern segregation practices in particular and army life in general–he went AWOL. He left behind a letter for his captain, in which he complained (as he remembered later) "that we were violating the ideals set forth in the Declaration of Independence, in the Constitution, and in all other documents we presumably revered. . . . I could not sustain my composure (I said, probably not that well) when confronted every day with expressions of racism in an army presumably dedicated to a war against Nazism." Asserting that the United States was involved in "a phoney war," he went on to state his "unwillingness further to serve the cause of the United States until the conditions noted above were corrected."

His captain was unimpressed, and Harris was apprehended four days later. On 21 February he was returned to Camp Wheeler and placed in a ward for nonviolent soldiers suspected of being "psychoneurotic." On 7 April 1944 he was honorably discharged for reasons of "poor health."

In his novel *Trumpet to the World* (1946) Harris based the wartime experiences of the main character, a well-educated black man, on his own, and he later returned to the subject in a still-more autobiographical novel, *Something About a Soldier* (1957). In his autobiography, *Best Father Ever Invented* (1976), he treats his wartime exploits from the perspective of thirty years.

JOHN HAWKES (1925-) drove an American Field Service ambulance in France and Germany in 1944-1945. His experiences in Occupied Germany form the background for his novel *The Cannibal* (1949), probably the most avant-garde work of American fiction to come out of the war.

THOMAS HEGGEN (1919-1949) enlisted in the U.S. Navy in December 1941 and spent a year as an ensign aboard ship in the Atlantic before being sent to the Pacific, where he served as an officer on a variety of ships for the next three years. He was released from active duty in October 1945 with the rank of lieutenant.

Although he had taken part in the campaigns at Guam, Peleliu, Iwo Jima, and Okinawa as an officer aboard an assault transport, when he began writing a novel about his war experiences soon after his return to civilian life, Heggen drew not upon his time in combat but upon his life aboard a navy cargo ship in the Pacific far from the battle zones. *Mister Roberts* (1946), which was praised for its "portrayal of the Navy as it usually is," was an immediate best-seller. The dramatic version, which Heggen wrote with Joshua Logan, was a smash hit when it opened on Broadway in February 1948 with Henry Fonda in the title role, and the 1955 movie version repeated the play's success.

JOSEPH HELLER (1923-) entered the U.S. Army Air Corps in 1942 and was sent to Corsica in May 1944 as a replacement in a combat group of the Twelfth Air Force. He flew sixty missions as a wing bombardier in a B-25 bomber. Heller later described his early missions—bombing railroad and highway bridges in Italy—as relatively short and safe. His squadron did not lose a plane until 3 June, and he first saw a plane shot down in flames on 3 August over Avignon. He enjoyed his first few months as a gunner, he said, "until my 37th mission," the second to Avignon, on 15 August. After another gunner in his plane was wounded, Heller remembered, "a co-pilot went a little berserk at the controls and I came to the startling realization—Good God! they're trying to kill me too! And after that it wasn't much fun."

This central event in Heller's combat experience lies behind the death of Snowden in Heller's first novel, *Catch-22* (1961), a central moment for Yossarian as well. Yet, although Heller kept a diary on Corsica and although there are other similarities between Heller's and Yossarian's experiences, *Catch-22* is not for the most part autobiographical, and it is more a satire on institutional bureaucracy in general than a depiction of military life in wartime.

Though *Catch-22* is now one of the most widely read novels to come out of World War II, it received mixed reviews when it was first published and was not a best-seller in the United States (though it was in England). In the 1960s the novel's sales grew in proportion to the protest against the Vietnam War, and after the movie version was released in 1970, its sales skyrocketed. Heller's "*Catch-22* Revisited," published in the April 1967 issue of *Holiday*, mingles memories of his combat experiences with a report on his return visit to the scenes of those events.

ERNEST HEMINGWAY (1899-1961) left the United States to cover the war in the Far East for the New York newspa-

A SECOND-HAND WAR STORY

Though Paul Gallico (1897-1976) served in the U.S. Navy during World War I and made a tour of London, Paris, Berlin, Prague, Vienna, and Rome for *Cosmopolitan* magazine just after the signing of the Munich pact in September 1938, he spent the early years of World War II in the United States. He was living in San Francisco during the British evacuation of Dunkirk in late May and early June 1940, and for the background of his best-known and extremely popular novelette *The Snow Goose* (1941), he drew on two *Saturday Evening Post* articles about the evacuation, his experiences while living in England during the 1930s, and his knowledge of sailing.

Gallico did eventually see the war firsthand. In 1944 *Cosmopolitan* sent him back to Europe as a war correspondent and European editor for the magazine.

per *PM* in February 1941, visiting Hong Kong, mainland China, and Burma before leaving for home in May. In 1942 he edited and wrote the introductions for *Men at War: The Best War Stories of All Time*, an anthology that he hoped would in some way aid the war effort. In May of that year he recruited a loosely organized group to gather information about Nazi agents in Cuba, which he then passed on to the U.S. Embassy in Cuba. He also equipped his fishing boat, the *Pilar*, as a Q-boat and with a crew of eight began cruising the Caribbean in June looking for German submarines. Hemingway drew on this experience for his posthumously published novel *Islands in the Stream* (1970), but unlike the protagonist of his book

he never encountered the enemy at sea.

In May 1944, having received an assignment to report on the Royal Air Force for *Collier's* magazine, Hemingway went to England, and on 6 June he observed the D-Day invasion at Omaha Beach from the deck of a landing craft. He got to France in July and followed the Allied forces to Paris, where leading a group of French resistance fighters, he "liberated" the bar at the Hotel Ritz on 25 August. By November he was with Allied forces in western Germany, and in December he covered the Battle of the Bulge in Luxembourg. He returned to the United States in March 1945. Two of the officers with whom he had become friends during his months with the Allied forces, Col. Charles Trueman (Buck) Lanham and Col. Charles Sweeney, served as models—along with Hemingway's vision of the soldier he would have been himself—for Col. Richard Cantwell in his 1950 novel, *Across the River and Into the Trees*. On 13 July 1947, at the recommendation of Gen. Raymond O. Barton, Hemingway received a Bronze Star for "meritorious service" as a war correspondent. According to the citation, "he displayed a broad familiarity with modern military science, interpreting and evaluating the campaigns and operations of friendly and enemy forces, circulating freely under fire in combat areas in order to obtain an accurate picture of conditions."

JOHN HERSEY (1914-) worked for Time, Inc., from 1937 to 1945, covering the war in China in 1939 and in the South Pacific in 1942. His first book, *Men on Bataan* (1942), is a nonfiction account of the fall of Bataan in April 1942. On 8-9 October 1942 he accompanied troops during the third Battle of Matanikau River on Guadalcanal and was later cited by the Secretary of the Navy for his helping to remove wounded men from the field under fire. A second nonfiction book, *Into the Valley* (1943), deals with his Guadalcanal experience. Critics praised its depiction of the life of the ordinary GIs and have compared it to Stephen Crane's war fiction.

Assigned to the Mediterranean Theater in 1943, Hersey covered the Sicilian invasion that summer and drew on his experiences there for his first novel, *A Bell for Adano* (1944), which was awarded a Pulitzer Prize in 1945. In 1944-1945 he covered Moscow and visited the sites of Nazi atrocities in Warsaw and Tallinn. His novel *The Wall* (1950) is a fictionalized presentation of the plight of the Jews in the Warsaw Ghetto from November 1939 to May 1943.

In September 1945 he went to Japan to cover China and Japan for *Life* and the *New Yorker*. His best-known book, *Hiroshima* (1946), grew out of his interviews with survivors of the atomic bombing of Hiroshima. The book's immediate and widespread impact was enhanced by Hersey's ability to employ novelistic techniques in the service of journalism, forcing the reader to view the bombing through the eyes of six survivors.

Hersey's 1959 World War II novel, *The War Lover*, is set in the cockpit of a plane during a bombing raid on Germany, and, as its title suggests, it examines the complex psychological traits that make some men love war.

MAC HYMAN (1923-1963) entered the U.S. Army Air Corps in spring 1943, and the next year he was commissioned a second lieutenant in photo-navigation. Based on Guam, he flew twenty-three missions, on which he navigated a B-29 reconnaissance plane to a target that had either been bombed or was about to be bombed—and photographed the site. On the day after the atomic bombing of Hiroshima, Hyman took the first photographs of the devastated city. Released from the air force in late 1945, he reenlisted for two years in November 1949, and, during this tour of duty, he began to employ his World War II experiences in the novel that eventually became *No Time for Sergeants* (1954), a bestseller that was adapted as a successful stage play (1955) and movie (1958).

RANDALL JARRELL (1914-1965) enlisted as a private in the U.S. Army Air Corps in 1942 and was sent to Sheppard Field in Wichita Falls, Texas, for aviation training. After washing out of flight school, he was posted in April 1943 to Chanute Field in Rantoul, Illinois, where he studied to be a link-trainer instructor and a celestial navigator. From November 1943 until his discharge in early 1946 he operated a celestial-navigation tower at Davis-Monthan Field in Tucson, Arizona. He drew on his wartime experiences for poems such as "2nd Air Force," "A Pilot from the Carrier," "Siegfried," "Eighth Air Force," "Lines," "Absent with Official Leave," and (perhaps his best-known poem) "The Death of the Ball-Turret Gunner"–published in *Little Friend, Little Friend* (1945) and *Losses* (1948).

JAMES JONES (1921-1977) enlisted in the U.S. Army in November 1939, and was sent to Fort Slocum, New York. By early 1940 he was at Hickham Field, near Honolulu, Hawaii, and temporarily assigned to the military police. He had transferred to the infantry by August and had been assigned to F Company, Second Battalion, in the Twenty-seventh Infantry ("Wolfhound") Regiment, which was stationed at Schofield Barracks. He was soon serving as company clerk and taking courses at the University of Hawaii. He continued to spend his free time–when he could afford it–in the Hotel Street area of Honolulu. In his *Viet Journal* (1974) he remembered it as "a swarming hive of bars, street vendors, tattoo parlors, shooting galleries, photo galleries, market shops, fruit and vegetable shops, and hooker joints occupying the rooms upstairs and the labeled hotels ... the bottomless receptacle of our dreams and frustrations, and of our money." On 7 December 1941 he was eating breakfast before

Pfc. Randall Jarrell at
Chanute Field, June 1943
(courtesy of Mary Jarrell)

going on guard duty, when he heard explosions coming from Wheeler Field, but he did not realize what was happening until the Japanese planes flew overhead. By then he and the other soldiers in the mess hall had run outside "with a sudden sense of awe that we were seeing and acting in a genuine moment of history." Jones spent the morning running messages for Regimental Headquarters, and that evening his company was taken to Makapuu Head, where they built and manned five pillboxes. His experiences in the peacetime army, up to and including Pearl Harbor, went into *From Here to Eternity* (1951), the first novel in his World War II trilogy. A shorter novel, *The Pistol* (1958), draws on his Pearl Harbor Day and Makapuu beach experiences.

In September the unit was called back to Schofield Barracks for combat training, and in November the Wolfhound Regiment began shipping out for Guadalcanal. Jones's troopship sailed on 6 December 1942, and he went ashore with F Company on or about 1 January 1943.

F Company went into battle on 11 Jan-

uary. Early in the action Jones was surprised by an obviously starving Japanese soldier, who attacked him with a bayonet. Jones disarmed the man and killed him. On the twelfth day Jones was hit in the head by fragments from a mortar shell. The wound was superficial, and he spent a week in the hospital, returning to F Company for the assault of Kokumbona village on 23 January. F Company is fictionalized as Charlie Company in *The Thin Red Line* (1962), the second novel in the trilogy, which covers the company's actions on Guadalcanal.

After a brief rest period, the regiment was shipped to New Georgia, another of the Solomon Islands. Jones, however, had a bad ankle, which he could walk on only with difficulty, and he was sent to hospitals at Efate, in the New Hebrides, and Aukland, New Zealand, before he was shipped home on the hospital ship *Matsonia*, arriving in May. He was sent first to Letterman General Hospital in Memphis, where he had an operation on his ankle. Jones's experiences from the time he boarded the hospital ship to his discharge on 6 July 1944 are fictionalized and distributed among several characters in *Whistle* (1978), the uncompleted third novel of the trilogy, which begins on a hospital ship much like the *Matsonia*.

After his discharge, Jones completed and revised *From Here to Eternity*. His second novel, *Some Came Running* (1958), is the story of a soldier who returns home and starts writing a novel. It, like the first two novels of the trilogy, was adapted as a film. He later wrote the text for *WW II* (1975) an illustrated history of the war, which includes much information about his own experiences.

MACKINLAY KANTOR (1904-1977) served as a war correspondent with the Royal Air Force in 1943 and then entered the U.S. Army Air Corps and flew eleven missions as a gunner in 1945. He was a war correspondent with the U.S. Air Force in Korea in 1950 and became a technical consultant for the air force in 1951. His 1943 novel, *Happy Land*, deals with the death of a young sailor in the Pacific during World War II; his long poem, *Glory for Me* (1945), which focuses on the problems of returned veterans, was the basis for the successful movie *The Best Years of Our Lives* (1946). For his 1951 novel, *Don't Touch Me*, Kantor drew on his experiences in Korea.

NORMAN MAILER (1923-) was drafted into the U.S. Army and sent to Fort Bragg, North Carolina, for basic training in late March 1944. As a college graduate, he was offered the opportunity to become an officer, but–already planning to write the great World War II novel–he chose to be a private because he thought his chances of seeing combat would be greater. Assigned to the intelligence section of the 112th Armored Cavalry Regiment, Mailer was sent to Leyte in the Philippines toward the end of General MacArthur's successful campaign to recapture the islands and just after Admiral Halsey's fleet had effectively crushed the Japanese navy. Mailer was sent to Luzon and assigned to type reports at combat-team headquarters. After he proved himself an incompetent typist he was placed, not in a combat unit, but in another desk job, where he interpreted aerial photographs. Disappointed though he was at the time, Mailer later said that his assignment gave him a "general's-eye view" of the war, as well as time to study military strategy and tactics by reading *Infantry Journal*.

Finally requesting a transfer to front-line duty, Mailer received an assignment to an Intelligence and Reconnaissance (I&R) unit and joined a platoon similar to the I & R platoon in *The Naked and the Dead* (1948). Mailer served as a rifleman during his division's move toward Manila, but his actual combat experience was limited to "a couple of firefights and skirmishes." From other members of the platoon he heard about an event that had taken place before he had joined them: their three-day patrol in enemy territory, which Mailer used as the basis for the trek to Mount Anaka in *The Naked and the Dead*. He also met another aspiring novelist, Francis Irby Gwaltney (whose war novel, *The Day the Century Ended*, was published in 1955). According to Gwaltney, Mailer "was a brave soldier but not a good one" because he was too nearsighted to "hit anything with a rifle" and wore glasses only for reading. "It's a miracle Mailer lived through the war," Gwaltney concluded.

V-J Day (14 August 1945) cut short Mailer's combat career, and he was sent to Tatiyama Naval Base in Occupied Japan, where he became a cook and was promoted to sergeant fourth grade. (According to Gwaltney, Mailer cooked as well as he shot a rifle.) After an altercation with his top sergeant and a further argument with his captain over it, Mailer found himself once again a private ("That," he said later, "was when the keel was laid for *The Naked and the Dead*.") He was discharged on 2 May 1946, and by June he had started work on *The Naked and the Dead*. When

Gwaltney was asked later how much of the novel's detail he recognized, he answered, "I recognized *all* of it. Some characters, he didn't even bother to change their names."

Though Mailer had not planned to write an antiwar novel, *The Naked and the Dead* quickly became one as he looked back over his experience with army brass, and reviewers were quick not only to recognize the book's importance but also to compare it to such great antiwar novels of World War I as John Dos Passos's *Three Soldiers* and Ernest Hemingway's *A Farewell to Arms*. Mailer's publisher, Stanley Rinehart, had set the tone for such enthusiasm when he had written some of the dust-jacket copy, in which he stated in part: "Twenty-seven years ago I was fortunate enough to be associated with the publication of John Dos Passos's *Three Soldiers*. In no year since have I felt the same surge of excitement for a war novel–not until the manuscript for Norman Mailer's *The Naked and the Dead* was readied for publication."

JAMES MICHENER (1907-) volunteered for service in the U.S. Navy in 1942. After attending officers' training school and taking a course to prepare for aircraft-carrier service in the Mediterranean, he was sent first to write reports in Washington, D.C., and then to the South Pacific.

Beginning as a troubleshooter for aviation maintenance in the Solomons, Michener visited at least fifty islands. Later he was given flight duty and made naval historian for the area from New Guinea to Tahiti, writing histories of shore operations at Bora Bora and Tongatabu, before he was discharged with the rank of lieutenant commander in 1945.

People he knew while stationed on the island of Espiritu Santo became the denizens of Bali-Hai in his collection of interrelated short stories, *Tales of the South Pacific* (1947). Though the book won a Pulitzer Prize, it has never been a best-seller; yet Michener's success as a writer was insured when it was adapted as the hit musical *South Pacific*, which opened on Broadway on 7 April 1949 and ran for 1,925 performances. For years afterward he advised aspiring writers, "Make sure Rodgers and Hammerstein read your first book."

During the Korean War Michener was a war correspondent and spent eight days on an aircraft carrier studying the operation of jet-fighter planes to gather background material for his novel *The Bridges at Toko-Ri* (1953).

ARTHUR MILLER (1915-) toured army camps in 1944 doing background research for the film version of Ernie Pyle's *Story of G. I. Joe* (1945). The journal he kept during the tour, published as *Situation Normal* (1945), records ordinary soldiers' accounts of their experiences in combat.

JOHN PATRICK (1906-) was an American Field Service ambulance driver in Egypt, Syria, and Southeast Asia from 1941 to 1944. On a troopship back to the United States he wrote a play, *The Hasty Heart* (1945), about his experiences while he was being treated for malaria in a British field hospital in Assam, Burma. Because wartime censors were confiscating and checking anything written on shipboard, he convinced a friend to smuggle the manuscript through customs in his concertina. The play was Patrick's first Broadway success, running for 241 performances. He later topped that success with another World War II play, *The Teahouse of the August Moon* (1953), adapted from Vern Sneider's novel about the American occupation of Okinawa, which ran for 1,027 performances on Broadway. He also wrote the screenplay for the popular 1956 film and a 1962 television production. When he attempted to capitalize on the continuing popularity of *The Teahouse of the August Moon* with a 1970 musical version, *Lovely Ladies, Kind Gentleman*, the play was a flop. Patrick also wrote the screenplay for the 1958 film version of *Some Came Running*, James Jones's novel about a veteran returned from World War II.

MARIO PUZO (1920-) served in the U. S. Army during World War II and, after his discharge, he worked for the army in Germany for two years after the war ended. His first novel, *The Dark Arena* (1955), focuses on the life of a veteran who is a civilian employee at an air base near Bremen, in Occupied Germany.

J. D. SALINGER (1919-) who was first classified 1-B by the Selective Service due to what he called a slight cardiac condition, was reclassified 1-A and drafted into the U. S. Army in 1942. By September he was attending a Signal Corps school for officers, first sergeants, and instructors. He went on to grade papers for aviation cadets (probably at a ground school in Nashville, Tennessee) and to write publicity releases for the Air Service Command in Dayton, Ohio, before he was reassigned to the Counter-Intelligence Corps in late 1943 and sent for training to Tiverton, Devonshire (a place that resembles the setting for his short story "For Esme–With Love and Squalor").

On D-Day he landed on Utah Beach with the Fourth Division five hours after the initial assault. He remained with the division as a special-security agent through five campaigns, interrogating civilians and POWs in an attempt to find Gestapo agents. He met Ernest Hemingway, who was in Europe as a war correspondent and showed some of his stories to the older writer. According to legend at least, he was disgusted when Hemingway shot off a chicken's head to demonstrate the efficiency of a German luger, but their relationship seems to have remained friendly. On 27 July 1946, while he was serving in Occupied Germany, Salinger wrote Hemingway an extremely friendly letter in which he explained that he was temporarily in a Nu-

Karl Shapiro in New Guinea, 1944

remberg hospital only because he was looking for a nurse like Catherine Barkley in *A Farewell to Arms*. Yet he later took several opportunities to attack Hemingway in print. In *The Catcher in the Rye* (1951), for example, Holden Caulfield calls Catherine's lover, Frederic Henry, "a phoney."

In addition to "For Esme–With Love and Squalor" and other short stories in *Nine Stories* (1953), in which he deals indirectly with his war experiences, Salinger also wrote stories about the war that were published in magazines during and just after World War II. He has never allowed these stories to be collected (though they appeared in a pirated–and suppressed–collection in 1974), but Salinger fans have tracked them down in back issues of the magazines at libraries. Before rushing to the library to read the following stories, the reader should bear in mind that Salinger did not want them republished for a reason–with one or two possible exceptions, they are not as good as his other short stories: "The Hang of It," *Collier's*

(12 July 1941); "Personal Notes of an Infantryman," *Collier's* (12 December 1942); "Soft Boiled Sergeant," *Saturday Evening Post* (15 April 1944); "The Last Day of the Last Furlough," *Saturday Evening Post* (15 July 1944); "Once a Week Won't Kill You," *Story* (November-December 1944); "A Boy in France," *Saturday Evening Post* (31 March 1945); "This Sandwich Has No Mayonnaise," *Esquire* (October 1945); "A Girl I Knew," *Good Housekeeping* (February 1948).

KARL SHAPIRO (1913-) was drafted into the U.S. Army in March 1941 and served in the Medical Corps as a company clerk in Australia and New Guinea, privately publishing some of his war poems in the *The Place of Love* (1942), while he was still in Australia.

By the time he was discharged in June 1946, Shapiro had had two volumes of poetry, *Person, Place and Thing* (1942) and *V-Letter and Other Poems* (1944), published in the United States and had won a Pulitzer Prize for the second of these books. Shapiro had mailed most of the contents of that book from the South Pacific to Evalyn Katz, his fiancée and literary agent, in V-letters—mail that was censored, then microfilmed and shipped to the United States, where it was printed in smaller format and posted to the recipient. In fact, Shapiro was nearly court-martialed for arguing with an army censor over his poem "Communist." "The censor," he said, "wanted me to explain it and I couldn't."

IRWIN SHAW (1913-) enlisted in the U.S. Army as a private in June 1942 and served with a Signal Corps camera crew in Africa and Europe, reaching Normandy two weeks after D-Day and helping to photograph battles for various French towns.

In his memoir *Paris! Paris!* (1977) he describes his arrival in the French capital on liberation day, 25 August 1944. While photographing the final action from the roof of the Comédie Française, he and his compatriots were caught in sniper fire. They escaped and made their way to the Chambre des Députés, where some non-English-speaking Germans tried to surrender to Shaw's friend—also a private—who did not speak German and offered—in Yiddish—to take their pictures instead. Shaw had been promoted to warrant officer by the time he was discharged in October 1945 and began work on *The Young Lions* (1948).

LAURENCE STALLINGS (1894-1968) was recalled to active service in the U.S. Marine Corps on 2 April 1942 and was stationed at the Pentagon. Although he had only one leg, he also spent time in Africa, Europe, and England—ostensibly as a public-relations adviser and interviewer checking on complaints of the troops (some friends believed he was engaged in intelligence work). He retired as a lieutenant-colonel on 27 June 1943 and wrote the unpublished play *The Streets Are Guarded* (produced in 1944), about a Marine hero in World War II.

GERTRUDE STEIN (1874-1946) and ALICE B. TOLKAS (1877-1967) remained in France during World War II, despite the warnings of friends, who at the beginning of the war urged them to exit the country while they were still able to do so. Leaving most of Stein's valuable art collection in Paris, they settled in the south of France, first at Bilignin and after February 1943 in Culoz.

They had to cope with food and clothing shortages, but they faced graver possibilities than meager rations. As Jews living under the puppet Vichy government of Marshall Henri Pétain they could have been sent to a concentration camp at any time, but they were protected both by a friend with connections in the Vichy government and by the local people, including the officials in Culoz who purposely left their names off all the lists required by the Germans. Even when a German major and his orderly and then a group of Italians were quartered in their house in August and September 1943 their Jewish-American identity remained undetected. American troops reached Culoz on 1 September 1944, and in mid December Stein and Toklas returned to Paris, where they found Stein's art collection largely intact.

Stein wrote about her experiences during the first year of the war in "The Winner Loses, A Picture of Occupied France," an article that appeared in the November 1940 issue of *Atlantic Monthly*, and she devoted much of her time during the war years to two projects: *Wars I Have Seen* (1945), a book about her life in France during both World Wars, and "Mrs. Reynolds," a short novel about a woman in France during World War II (published in *Mrs. Reynolds and Five Earlier Novelettes*, 1952). Toklas wrote about their war years in *What Is Remembered* (1963).

WILLIAM STYRON (1925-) transferred from Davidson College to Duke University as a member of a U.S. Marine Corps V-12 unit in 1943 and served for a time during World War II as a marine guard in a navy prison. As a member of the U.S. Marine Corps Reserve, he was recalled to active duty as a first lieutenant during the Korean War and in 1950 was sent to Camp Lejeune, North Carolina, where he went on a forced march similar to the one described in his novelette *The Long March* (1952). He was released from active duty in 1951. In the late 1960s Styron began another novel drawing on his experiences in the marines, but he abandoned work on "The Way of the Warrior" before he had completed it (an excerpt, "Marriott, the Marine," appeared in the September 1971 issue of *Esquire*). He turned instead to work on a play, *In the Clap Shack* (1973), set in the urological ward of a hospital on a southern marine base in 1943.

GORE VIDAL (1925-) joined the U.S. Army Enlisted Reserve Corps on 30 July 1943 and was sent to study engineer-

ing at Virginia Military Institute. He spent more time writing fiction than studying, and after one semester he was made a private in the U.S. Army Air Corps and sent to Peterson Field, Colorado. After he passed a maritime-navigation exam, he was made a maritime warrant officer, junior grade, in the U.S. Army Transportation Corps on 24 October 1944. He was sent to Umnak, one of the Aleutian Islands, where he served as first mate on Freight Ship 35 in the Alaskan Harbor Craft Detachment. While still in Alaska, he began writing a novel about his experiences there, which was published as *Williwaw* in spring 1946. On 9 March 1945, after the harsh climate had brought on an attack of rheumatoid arthritis, he was sent to a hospital in Fort Richardson, Alabama, and then to another hospital in Van Nuys, California. Work on his novel continued but was slowed by arthritis in his writing hand. He finished the book after he was assigned to limited duty at Camp Gordon Johnson, Florida.

After the end of the war, in October 1945 while Vidal was stationed at Mitchell Field, New York, he began writing another novel instead of writing the Mitchell Field history he was supposed to be working on. He had finished *In a Yellow Wood* (1947), the story of a returned veteran, by the time he was separated from the army on 15 February 1946. He also drew on his wartime experiences for part of a third novel, *The City and the Pillar* (1948).

KURT VONNEGUT (1922-) entered the U. S. Army in March 1943 during his junior year at Cornell University and was trained in mechanical engineering at the Carnegie Institute of Technology and the University of Tennessee. He went overseas in 1944 and was taken prisoner during the Battle of Bulge in Luxembourg that December. Sent to Dresden, he–like Billy Pilgrim and his fellow POWs in *Slaughterhouse-Five* (1969)–was put to work with other prisoners of war making a dietary supplement for pregnant women. Vonnegut and the other POWs survived the surprise fire bombings of Dresden by British and American planes on 13-14 February 1945 because–again as in *Slaughterhouse-Five*–they were locked up at night in a meat-storage cellar under the slaughterhouse. After Dresden had been almost totally destroyed by fire, Vonnegut was among the POWs set to work digging through the ruins of the city for corpses. When Soviet troops reached Dresden in April 1945, Vonnegut was freed, returned to the United States, and awarded a Purple Heart. Though he planned for years to write a book about Dresden and though his war experiences inform *Player Piano* (1952), *Mother Night* (1962), and *God Bless You, Mr. Rosewater* (1965), he did not deal with Dresden directly in his fiction until *Slaughterhouse-Five* (1969).

JOHN A. WILLIAMS (1925-) joined the U.S. Navy on 8 April 1943 and was one of the first blacks to be admitted to the hospital corps. After training as a corps-

...there is nothing intelligent to say about a massacre. Everybody is supposed to be dead, to never say anything or want anything ever again. Everything is supposed to be very quiet after a massacre, and it always is, except for the birds.

And what do the birds say? All there is to say about a massacre, things like "Poo-tee-weet?"

I have told my sons that they are not under any circumstances to take part in massacres, and that the news of massacres of enemies is not to fill them with satisfaction or glee.

I have also told them not to work for companies which make massacre machinery, and to express contempt for people who think we need machinery like that.

     –Kurt Vonnegut,
     Slaughterhouse-Five *(1969)*

man at the segregated Great Lakes Naval Base, he was sent overseas in 1944 and served in New Calendonia, New Hebrides, the Solomons, the Marshalls, the Palau group, and the Marianas. Having been brought up in an intergrated neighborhood in Syracuse, New York, Williams experienced blatant racism for the first time in the navy. Discharged on 4 January 1946, he twice tried unsuccessfully to write autobiographical war novels–in the early 1950s and in the 1960s. A fragment of the first appears as "Navy Black" in *Beyond the Angry Black* (1966), an anthology edited by Williams. He achieved success, when he broadened his perspective for *Captain Blackman* (1972), a novel that traces the experiences of black American soldiers from the Revolution through the Vietnam War. He approached his war experiences more directly in the title essay in his *This Is My Country Too* (1965).

WIRT WILLIAMS (1921-) served in the U.S. Navy aboard a destroyer

Kurt Vonnegut

I saw white Marines and black sailors line up for a race riot on Guam. A Chamorro girl told me she had been warned to stay away from black men because they had tails. My parents wrote asking me what was being cut out of my letters; I had endless conferences with the censors and refused to stop writing home and saying the Navy was rotten. I have a pitted face from the dry shaves I got in the Marine brig. I traveled up and down the islands of the Pacific because black hospital corpsmen were not wanted aboard ship, and I wound up with a land force. A white Texan on a dark night in the New Hebrides was a minute away from shooting me. A white Mississippian who had been there and who had dissuaded the Texan told me, "Williams, you ain't like them other niggers." When I told him he was wrong, he laughed. "You crazy," he said. "They ain't."
—John A. Williams,
This Is My Country Too *(1965)*

(1942-1944) and on a landing ship (1944-1946), leaving active duty with the rank of lieutenant commander in the reserves. His 1951 novel, *The Enemy*, is set on a destroyer searching the Atlantic for German submarines.

HERMAN WOUK (1915-) served in the U. S. Navy from 1942 to 1946, rising to the rank of lieutenant and receiving four campaign stars and a Presidential Unit Citation. His experiences aboard two destroyer-minesweepers, the U.S.S.

Zane and the U.S.S. *Southard*, form the background for his 1951 novel, *The Caine Mutiny*, which is otherwise not autobiographical. The novel won a Pulitzer Prize in 1952; Wouk adapted its court-martial sequence into a two-act play, *The Caine Mutiny Court Martial* (1954); and Humphrey Bogart won an Oscar for his starring role in the 1954 film version of the novel. More recently Wouk viewed the war from a global perspective in two novels, *The Winds of War* (1971) and *War and Remembrance* (1978).

The massacre of the European Jews by the German government in the 1940s is perhaps the most staggering event in human history. The world has yet to come to grips with it. In my sixteen-year labor on The Winds of War *and* War and Remembrance, *my aim was only to show the thing as it happened, in a frame of global war. Historians, artists, thinkers, and politicians will be grappling with this gigantic horror for centuries, and meantime the main task is to insure that it's never forgotten.*
—Herman Wouk,
Interview with Jean W. Ross,
Contemporary Authors
New Revised Series 6

RICHARD YATES (1926-) enlisted as a private in the U. S. Army Infantry in 1944 and served until 1946, later drawing on his experiences for his 1969 novel, *A Special Providence*.

FACT IMITATES FICTION: STEINBECK AND THE WAR EFFORT

Though John Steinbeck did eventually go into battle as a war correspondent during World War II, his major literary contribution to the war effort, *The Moon Is Down*, was written before he went overseas, on assignment for the For-

eign Information Service, a group of writers brought together by Robert E. Sherwood to write works that would counter the Germans' pro-Nazi propaganda.

After talking to refugees from

German-occupied countries at the F.I.S. offices in Washington, Steinbeck set out in October 1941 to write a play about the occupation of a town of freedom-loving, democratic people by the army of a totalitarian state. The first draft, which was set in the United States, was turned down by the F.I.S. because they were afraid that Steinbeck's warning—less than a month before Pearl Harbor—that the United States was not impregnable might be interpreted, Steinbeck remembered later, as "an admission that we might be defeated."

Steinbeck changed the locale to an unidentified European country and then wrote a novel version, which was published in March 1942 and aroused controversy that was heightened when the play version opened on Broadway the next month. *The Moon Is Down* celebrates resistance to and eventual victory over repression, but Steinbeck was criticized for making the invading army seem too human and for being unrealistic about what individuals could do to defeat a superior force of heavily armed and disciplined invaders.

While *The Moon Is Down* was unpopular on the homefront, it was extremely popular in occupied countries, where members of resistance movements found it inspirational. Steinbeck felt justified by their response to his book: "The little book was smuggled into the occupied countries. It was copied, mimeographed, printed on hand presses in cellars, and I have seen a copy laboriously hand written on scrap paper and tied together with twine. The Germans did not consider it unrealistic optimism. They made it a capital crime to possess it. . . ." In November 1946 Steinbeck was awarded Norway's King Haakon's Liberty Cross for writing *The Moon Is Down*, and while he was in Norway he was often asked by former resistance people how he had found out about their anti-German activities at a time when they were being kept secret. According to his biographer Jackson J. Benson, Steinbeck explained that he had no inside information, that "I guessed. I just put myself in your place and thought what I would do."

Steinbeck also wrote *Bombs Away: The Story of a Bomber Team* (1942) for the U.S. Army Air Corps before serving abroad as a war correspondent for the *New York Herald Tribune* from early June to late September 1943. He went first to England and then, in August, to North Africa, where he was assigned to help cover the invasion of Italy. He spent much of the invasion with a special-operations unit that was assigned to engage in diversionary tactics that would confuse the enemy about where the main invasion was taking place. Steinbeck went along and actually fought with the men on many of their night-time raids (some of which he could not write about because they were secret). The last five dispatches collected in *Once There Was a War* (1958), report their taking of Ventonene, an important German radar station. (The unnamed "commodore" in those reports is Lt. Douglas Fairbanks, Jr., who led the raid and earned a Silver Star for his bravery under fire.)

VIETNAM WAR

ROBERT A. ANDERSON (1944-   ) served in the U.S. Marine Corps (1966-1969), earning a Purple Heart and later drawing on his experiences for *Cooks and Bakers: A Novel of the Vietnam War* (1982).

WILLIAM C. ANDERSON (1920-), U.S. Air Force (1941-1964), retired as a lieutenant colonel after earning a Distinguished Flying Cross, an Air Medal with two clusters, a Commendation Medal, a Presidential Citation, a Berlin Airlift Ribbon, a European Theater Ribbon with five battle stars, and a Humanitarian Medal. His novel *The Gooney Bird* (1968) deals with the war in Vietnam.

ASA BABER (1936-) was a marine stationed in Southeast Asia in 1961. In *The Land of a Million Elephants* (1970), which was first serialized in *Playboy* (February-April 1970), he presents a fictional view of American military advisers (and other Western statesmen-diplomats-spies) unsuccessfully confronting an ancient and peace-loving Eastern culture in "Chanda" (Laos).

JOHN BALABAN (1943-) was an instructor at the University of Can Tho in 1967-1968 and field representative in South Vietnam for the Committee of Responsibility to Save War-Injured Children in 1968-1969. He returned to Vietnam in 1971 to collect the oral folk poems of Vietnamese farmers (his translations appeared in 1980 as *Ca Dao Vietnam*). His experiences in Vietnam are reflected in three volumes of poetry—*Vietnam Poems* (1970), *After Our War* (1974), and *Blue Mountain* (1982)—and a novel, *Coming Down Again* (1985).

JAN BARRY (1943-), a weapons and radio specialist in the U. S. Army (1962-1965), spent 1962-1963 in Vietnam with the Eighteenth Aviation Company of the U.S. Army support group. He collected his war poems in *Veteran's Day* (1983) and *War Baby* (1984), and he helped to edit three Vietnam War poetry anthologies: *Winning Hearts and Minds* (1972), *Demilitarized Zones* (1976), and *Peace Is Our Profession* (1981).

R. L. BARTH (1947-), in the U.S. Marine Corps from 1966 to 1969, served in Vietnam (1968-1969) with E Company, First Reconnaissance Battalion and collected his war poems in *Forced-Marching to the Styx: Vietnam War Poems* (1983).

ROBERT BAUSCH (1945-), who served in the U.S. Air Force (1965-1969), became a sergeant and was stationed in Illinois as an instructor in survival tactics. His novel about military service during the Vietnam War era, *On the Way Home*, was published in 1982.

DAVID CHAPMAN BERRY (1942-) was in the U.S. Army Medical Service Corps (1966-1969) and served in Vietnam in 1967-1968. He drew on his experiences for *Saigon Cemetery* (1972), a collection of poetry, and *G. R. Point*, a play.

JOSIAH BUNTING (1939-), U.S. Army Infantry, was a plans officer in Vietnam. His novel *The Lionheads* (1972) is set there in early 1968.

ROBERT OLEN BUTLER (1945-) learned Vietnamese in a U.S. Army training course and spent five months of 1971 with military intelligence near Saigon before he became interpreter for the U.S. Foreign Service Officer who worked with the mayor of Saigon. Though each of the novels in his Vietnam War trilogy—*The Alleys of Eden* (1981), *Sun Dogs* (1982), and *On Distant Ground* (1985)—focuses on different characters, the three books are unified by the fact that these men have briefly served together in a counterintelligence unit operating in and around Saigon toward the end of the war.

PHILIP CAPUTO (1941-), U.S. Marine Corps, landed at Da Nang in March 1965 with the first American ground-combat unit sent to Indo-China and served in Vietnam for sixteen months. He was mustered out in 1967 and went to work for the *Chicago Tribune*, which assigned him to cover the fall of Saigon. His first book, *A Rumor of War*, is a nonfiction account of his experiences as marine and journalist in Vietnam. *Del Corso's Gallery,* his 1983 novel, is the story of a photojournalist covering the fighting from Vietnam to Lebanon.

MICHAEL CASEY (1947-), U.S. Army, 1968-1970, served in Vietnam and collected his war poems in *Obscenities* (1972).

JOHN CASSIDY (1922-), who spent more than twenty years (1951-1973) as CIA operations officer and associate, serving in Latin America, Vietnam, and Spain, set his novel *A Station in the Delta* (1979) in Vietnam during the Tet offensive.

CHARLES COLLINGWOOD (1917-1985), chief foreign correspondent for CBS (1964-1975), covered Vietnam. His novel *The Defector* (1970) is about a reporter who helps a North Vietnamese official defect.

JAMES CRUMLEY (1939-) was in the U.S. Army from 1958 to 1961 and served in Southeast Asia. His novel *One to Count Cadence* (1969), set in the Philippines and Vietnam, depicts the earliest major combat involving American soldiers.

GEORGE DAVIS (1939-) served in the U.S. Air Force (1961-1968), spending 1967-1968 as a navigator in the seventieth Air Refueling Squadron in Thailand and receiving an Air Medal before his discharge as a captain. He drew on his war experiences for his first novel, *Coming Home* (1971).

JOHN M. DEL VECCHIO (1947-), U.S. Army (1969-1972), served in Vietnam as a combat correspondent attached to the 101st Airborne and earned a Bronze Star. In his first book, *The 13th Valley* (1982), he drew on his reports, letters, and diaries for a combat novel set in Vietnam during the early 1970s.

JEROME DOOLITTLE (1933-) worked

for the U.S. Information Agency in Laos (1969-1970) and in 1982 produced *The Bombing Officer,* a novel about a military man whose job is approving bombing targets.

CHARLES DURDEN (?-) went to Vietnam as a reporter. His novel *No Bugles, No Drums* (1976) is set in Vietnam during 1968-1969.

WILLIAM EASTLAKE (1917-) was a Vietnam correspondent for the *Nation* in 1968. His satiric antiwar novel, *The Bamboo Bed* (1969), is set in Vietnam during the late 1960s. Some of the poetry and prose in his *A Child's Garden of Verses for the Revolution* (1970) is also related to the war.

WILLIAM D. EHRHART (1948-), who entered the U.S. Marine Corps in 1966, served in Vietnam as Assistant Intelligence Chief with the First Battalion of the First Marines in 1967-1968 and was discharged in 1969. He has collected his war poems in *A Generation of Peace* (1975), *The Awkward Silence* (1980), *The Samisdat Poems* (1980), *Matters of the Heart* (1981), *The Outer Bank and Other Poems* (1984), and *To Those Who Have Gone Home Tired;* written two prose works about the war, *Vietnam-Perkasie* (1983) and *Marking Time* (1986); edited an anthology of Vietnam War poetry, *Carrying the Darkness* (1985); and helped to edit another such collection, *Demilitarized Zones* (1976).

ROBERT ELEGANT (1928-), who was a correspondent for *Newsweek* in Hong Kong (1958-1961) and chief of the *Los Angeles Times* Hong Kong bureau (1965-1969), set his suspense novel *A Kind of Treason* (1966) in Vietnam.

STEPHEN FLEMING (?-) served in Vietnam with the First Air Cavalry, U.S. Army, in 1966-1967 and drew on his experiences there for a novel, *The Exile of Sergeant Nen* (1986), the story of a Vietnamese paratrooper who fought the

French and the Americans and ends up in the United States working as a waiter in a restaurant owned by a corrupt South Vietnamese general.

BRYAN ALEC FLOYD (1940-), U.S. Marine Corps (1966-1968), served in Vietnam and collected his war poems in *The Long War Dead: An Epiphany* (1976).

DANIEL FORD (1931-)`visited Vietnam in 1964 on a grant to write a series of articles for the *Nation*. His novel *Incident at Muc Wa* (1967) is about the failure of a Special Forces operation during the early to mid 1960s.

JACK FULLER (?-) was a front-line reporter for *Stars and Stripes* in Vietnam. His first novel, *Fragment* (1984), begins with the main character's arrival there in August 1968.

RONALD J. GLASSER (1940-), a doctor in the U.S. Army Medical Corps during the late 1960s, was stationed at the evacuation hospital at Camp Zama in Japan. He wrote about the year he spent treating soldiers wounded in Vietnam in *365 Days* (1971) and drew on some of the experiences covered in this memoir for a novel, *Another War, Another Peace* (1985).

AMLIN GRAY (1946-) was drafted in 1966 and, as a conscientious objector, was trained for alternative service as a medic. Sent to Vietnam in 1967, he was stationed near the front until his discharge in 1968. His two-man Vietnam play, *How I Got That Story*, won an Obie Award in 1981.

JAY GROEN (?-) and DAVID GROEN (?-), brothers who are both veterans of the Vietnam War, wrote *Huey* (1984), a novel whose protagonist–like David Groen–is a helicopter pilot serving a one-year tour of duty in Vietnam.

WINSTON GROOM (1943-), who became a captain during his service in the U.S. Army (1965-1967), served in Viet-

nam and set his 1978 novel *Better Times than These* in Vietnam's Ia Drang Valley during 1966-1967. He also deals with the war in his 1986 novel *Forrest Gump*, and in 1983 he collaborated with Duncan Spencer on *Conversations with the Enemy*, the story of PFC Robert Garwood, a marine who was taken prisoner by the North Vietnamese and court-martialed for collaboration with the enemy on his return to the United States.

DAVID HALBERSTAM (1939-) was Vietnam correspondent for the *New York Times* in 1962-1963 and won a Pulitzer Prize for his reporting in 1963. He also wrote about the war in a nonfiction book, *The Making of a Quagmire* (1965), and a novel, *One Very Hot Day* (1968), set during one day in late 1962 (the battle at the novel's climax resembles the defeat of the South Vietnamese at Ap Bac in December 1962, significant as one of the early battles in which Americans were killed).

JOE HALDEMAN (1943-) spent part of his hitch in the U.S. Army (1967-1969) as a combat engineer in Vietnam, where he was wounded and earned a Purple Heart as well as other medals. He drew on his war experiences for two novels, *War Year* (1972) and *The Forever War* (1974), and short stories collected in *Infinite Dreams* (1978); he also edited the anthology *Study War No More* (1977).

GUSTAVE HASFORD (1947-), who became a corporal during his service in the U.S. Marine Corps (1966-1968), was a combat correspondent in Vietnam with Task Force X-Ray of the First Marine Division. His novel *The Short-Timers* (1979), set during the Tet offensive in January 1968, was the basis for Stanley Kubrick's film *Full Metal Jacket* (1987), for which Kubrick, Hasford, and Michael Herr wrote the screenplay.

BO HATHAWAY (1942-), U.S. Army, Special Forces (1964-1967), served in Vietnam, becoming a sergeant and earning a Bronze Star. His novel *A World of Hurt* (1981), set in 1964, is the story of two draftees who volunteer for the Special Forces and are sent to a base near Nha Trang.

LARRY HEINEMANN (1944-), U.S. Army Infantry (1966-1968), fought in Vietnam, becoming a sergeant and earning a Combat Infantryman's Badge. His novel *Close Quarters* (1977) focuses on the experiences of a young enlisted man who spends 1967 in Vietnam. His 1986 novel *Paco's Story*, about a wounded soldier's return to an insensitive community, won a National Book Award.

DAVID HUDDLE (1942-), a military intelligence specialist in the U.S. Army (1964-1967), spent 1966-1967 in Vietnam. He collected his short stories about the war in *A Dream with No Stump Roots in It* (1975) and his war poems in *Paper Boy* (1979).

WILLIAM TURNER HUGGETT (?-) served in Vietnam as an infantry combat officer and pacification adviser in the U.S. Marine Corps. His novel *Body Count* (1973) is set in Vietnam during spring and summer 1968.

WARD JUST (1935-), *Washington Post* Saigon correspondent in 1965-1967, has written about the war in two nonfiction books, *To What End* (1968) and *Military Men* (1970); in short stories collected in *The Congressman Who Loved Flaubert and Other Stories* (1973) and *Honor, Power, Riches, Fame and the Love of Women*; and in three novels, *Stringer* (1974), *In the City of Fear* (1982), and *The American Blues* (1984).

BERNARD KALB (1932-) was a news correspondent in Southeast Asia for fifteen years beginning in the mid 1950s, first for the *New York Times* and then for CBS. *The Last Ambassador* (1981), a novel he wrote with his brother and fellow journalist Marvin Kalb, is set in Vietnam during the period immediately preceding the fall of Saigon on 30 April 1975.

RON KOVIC (1946-) entered the U.S. Marine Corps in 1964 and served in Vietnam, where on 29 January 1968 a bullet entered his right shoulder, passed through a lung, and severed his spinal cord, leaving him permanently paralyzed below the middle of his chest. He followed up his powerful, best-selling memoir, *Born on the Fourth of July* (1976), with *Around the World in Eight Days* (1984), a novel about a Vietnam veteran's attempts to confront his war experiences.

WENDY WILDER LARSEN (?-) spent 1970-1971 with her journalist husband in Saigon, where she met Tran Thi Nga, the bookkeeper in his office. After the two women were reunited in the United States in 1975, they told their stories in a verse novel, *Shallow Graves* (1986), an English-language version of the *troyen*, a Vietnamese form.

MCAVOY LAYNE (1943-), a U.S. Marine Corps infantryman in Vietnam (1966-1967), wrote *How Audie Murphy Died in Vietnam* (1973), a sequence of lyric poems, or "poetic novel," that tells the story of a marine battle hero who becomes a prisoner of war during the 1966-1967 period of the war.

LOYD LITTLE (1940-), a U.S. Army medic who was staff sergeant in the Fifth Special Forces Group, served in Vietnam and Laos in 1964-1965, and earned a Combat Medical Badge and an Army Commendation Medal. His first novel, *Parthian Shot* (1975), which won an Ernest Hemingway Foundation Award, is set in Vietnam during 1964. His second novel, *In the Village of the Man* (1978), is set in Laos.

JOE MAGGIO (1938-), who served in the U.S. Marine Corps (1959-1961) and the U.S. Army (1961-1966), ran gunboats in the Mekong Delta during the early years of the war. In 1965 and 1966 he also served as an agent for the CIA in Cuba, Laos, and Vietnam. He was back in Vietnam in 1968-1969 as a correspondent for *Mainland Journal* and a free-lance stringer for *Tropic Magazine*, UPI, AP, and Reuters. His novel *Company Man* (1972) is about CIA mercenaries in Vietnam.

STEVE MASON (?-) served as a U.S. Army infantryman in Vietnam and collected his war poems in *Johnny's Song: Poetry of a Vietnam Veteran* (1986).

TOM MAYER (1943-) went to Vietnam as a journalist on a Guggenheim Fellowship (1966) and later collected his short stories about the war in *The Weary Falcon* (1971).

GERALD MCCARTHY (1947-), who served with the U.S. Marine Corps in Vietnam (1966-1967), published his war poetry in *War Story* (1977).

WALTER MCDONALD (1934-), a U.S. Air Force pilot and instructor (1959-1971), spent 1969-1970 in Vietnam and later gathered his war poems in *Caliban in Blue and Other Poems* (1976) and *Burning the Fence* (1981).

GENE D. MOORE (1919-), who was drafted into the U.S. Army as a private in 1941 and retired as a colonel in 1968, served in Vietnam. His Vietnam War novel *The Killing at Ngo Tho* (1967) was published while he was still there.

ROBIN MOORE (1925-), a civilian, trained with the Green Berets and went into combat with them in Vietnam. His first, and best-known, novel about the war, *The Green Berets* (1965), is set in the Vietnam highlands during 1964. He has since written or helped to write four more Vietnam War novels: *The Country Team* (1967), *Court Martial* (1971) with Henry Rothblatt, *The Khaki Mafia* (1971) with June Collins, and *Search and Destroy* (1978).

Tim O'Brien

TIM O'BRIEN (1946-) entered the U.S. Army in 1968 and served with the 198th Infantry until his discharge as a sergeant in March 1970. He spent all of 1969 in Vietnam, receiving a Purple Heart after he was wounded at My Lai. He calls his first book, *If I Die in a Combat Zone, Box Me Up and Ship Me Home* (1973), a war memoir because–though he made up most of the dialogue–its events are his actual war experiences. His first novel, *Northern Lights* (1975), deals with a Vietnam veteran's return home; his second, *Going after Cacciato* (1978), which won a National Book Award, is set mostly in Vietnam at roughly the time he served there and has been favorably compared to Hemingway's war fiction and to Heller's *Catch-22*.

PERRY OLDHAM (1943-), who served in the U.S. Air Force (1966-1970), spent 1969-1970 in Vietnam and collected his war poems in *Vinh Long* (1976).

BASIL T. PAQUET (1944-), a U.S. Army medic (1966-1968), served in Vietnam during 1967-1968. He has helped to edit two volumes of Vietnam War writing–*Winning Hearts and Minds* (1972), a poetry anthology, and *Free Fire*

Zone (1973), a short-story anthology–both of which contain his work.

WILLIAM PELFREY (1947-) served in Vietnam during 1969 as a corporal in the U.S. Army's Fourth Infantry Division, earning a Bronze Star, a Vietnamese Cross of Gallantry, and a Combat Infantryman's Badge. His first novel, *The Big V* (1972), set in Vietnam during the late 1960s, was nominated for a National Book Award.

DONALD PFARRER (1934-), U.S. Navy (1957-1960, 1965-1966), served in Vietnam, becoming a lieutenant and receiving a Bronze Star, a Purple Heart, and a South Vietnamese Cross of Gallantry. His novel *Neverlight* (1982) is about a naval officer in Vietnam.

MICHAEL ROBERT PICK (1947-) served in Vietnam and collected his war poems in *Childhood, Namhood, Manhood: The Writings of Michael Robert Pick, a Vietnam Veteran* (1982).

JOHN CLARK PRATT (1932-), who retired from the U.S. Air Force as a lieutenant colonel in 1974, spent 1969-1970 as a fighter pilot stationed in Laos. When the air force information office read his *The Laotian Fragments* (1974), which he describes as "a hyper-realistic documentary novel set during late 1969 and early 1970," they labeled the book top secret and took ten months to clear the novel's "facts" for publication as fiction. Pratt has also compiled a collection of " 'factual' and 'fictional' perspectives" on the war, *Vietnam Voices: Perspectives on the War Years, 1941-1982* (1984), and his "Bibliographic Commentary: 'From the Fiction, Some Truths,' " was published in *"Reading the Wind": The Literature of the Vietnam War* (1987) by Timothy J. Lomperis.

NICHOLAS PROFFITT (1943-), a sergeant in a U.S. Army ceremonial unit, went to Vietnam as a correspondent and drew on his experiences there for

David Rabe (copyright 1985
Thomas Victor)

two novels, *Gardens of Stone* (1983) and *Embassy House* (1986).

DAVID RABE (1940-) served in the U.S. Army from January 1965 until his discharge as a specialist fourth class in January 1967. He spent the last eleven months of his tour of duty working with a field-hospital support group in Vietnam. Out of his army experiences grew three critically acclaimed plays: *Sticks and Bones* and *The Basic Training of Pavlo Hummel*, each of which opened in New York in 1971 and ran for more than 350 performances, and *Streamers*, which premiered at New York's Lincoln Center in April 1976 and ran for 478 performances.

ROB RIGGAN (1943-) served in the U.S. Army Medical Corps (1968-1971), spending part of his tour of duty in Vietnam. His first novel, *Free Fire Zone* (1984), is about a medic in Vietnam.

KELLY ROLLINS [pseud.] (1924-), a career officer in the U.S. Air Force

(1943-1945, 1948-1973), retired as a colonel and drew on his Vietnam War experiences for a novel, *Fighter Pilots* (1981).

LARRY ROTTMANN (1942-), a U.S. Army infantryman (1966-1969), served in Vietnam in 1967-1968. His novel *American Eagle* (1977) is about a Navajo Vietnam War veteran. He has also helped to edit two Vietnam War anthologies: *Winning Hearts and Minds* (1972, poetry) and *Free Fire Zone* (1973, short stories).

JONATHAN RUBIN (?-), a Special Forces sergeant in Vietnam (1962-1964), set his novel *The Barking Deer* (1974) in Buon Yon, a Montagnard village of strategic value to both an American Special Forces detachment and the Vietcong. Set in 1964, the novel exhibits an appreciation for the Montagnard way of life and empathy for soldiers on both sides.

DICK SHEA (?-) was a U.S. Navy lieutenant stationed at Da Nang in March 1965, when the landing of the first two battalions of U.S. Marines there marked the American escalation of the war. His impressionistic novel *Vietnam Simply* (1967) is one of the earliest works of antiwar fiction by an American military man.

JAMES PARK SLOAN (1944-), U.S. Army (1964-1967), served as a paratrooper in Vietnam, becoming a sergeant and earning an Army Commendation Medal and a Vietnamese Medal of Honor. His military experience lies behind his first novel, *War Games* (1971).

STEVEN P. SMITH (1943-), U.S. Army (1964-1967), spent 1965-1966 in Vietnam as a specialist fourth class in the First Air Cavalry, earning fourteen Air Medals and an Army Commendation Medal. His first novel, *American Boys* (1975), is set in Vietnam during the mid 1960s.

SCOTT C. S. STONE (1932-), U.S.

Navy (1951-1954), served in Korea. As a member of the U.S. Army Reserve, he was on active duty in 1960-1962 and served in Vietnam. His first novel, *The Coasts of War* (1966), is about an American naval officer advising a Vietnamese junk force during the early 1960s. His 1980 novel *Spies* is set in Laos and Vietnam.

THOMAS TAYLOR (1934-) was commissioned a second lieutenant in the U.S. Army in 1960 and was discharged as a major in 1968, having served in Germany, Greece, Saudi Arabia, Panama, and Vietnam and having earned a Silver Star, a Bronze Star with "v" device and oak leaf cluster, an Air Medal, a Purple Heart, an Army Commendation Medal, and a Vietnamese Cross of Gallantry. His novels *A-18* (1967) and *A Piece of This Country* (1970) both deal with the Special Forces in Vietnam during 1964.

JAMES TROWBRIDGE [pseud.] (?-) was an intelligence officer in Vietnam. His novel *Easy Victories* (1973) is about intelligence operations in Vietnam before and during the 1968 Tet offensive.

ROBERT VAUGHAN (1937-), U.S. Army (1955-1973), was a helicopter pilot in Korea, Germany, and Vietnam. He has written three Vietnam War novels: *Brandywine's War* (1971) with Monroe Lynch; *The Valkyrie Mandate* (1974), set in Saigon in 1963; and *The Quick and the Dead* (1984).

PATRICIA WALSH (1942-) was a U.S. Foreign Service nurse-anesthetist in Vietnam (1967-1968) and was injured in Da Nang during the 1968 Tet offensive. Her novel *Forever the Sad Heart* (1982) is about a Vietnam War nurse.

JAMES WEBB (1946-), U.S. Marine Corps (1968-1972), went into heavy combat with I Corps in Vietnam, leaving the corps as a captain, with a Navy Cross, a Silver Star, two Bronze Stars, a National

Stephen Wright (photograph© Jerry Bauer)

Achievement Medal, and two Purple Hearts. His first novel, *Fields of Fire* (1978), is about marines fighting in Vietnam during the late 1960s. Two later novels, *A Sense of Honor* (1981) and *A Country Such as This* (1983), deal with the war less directly.

BRUCE WEIGL (1949-), U.S. Army communications specialist (1967-1970), served in Vietnam with the First Air Cavalry (1967-1968) and earned a Bronze Star. He included his war poems in *A Romance* (1979) and *The Monkey Wars* (1985).

WILLIAM WILSON (?-), whose novel *The LBJ Brigade* (1966) was one of the earliest antiwar novels to come out of the Vietnam conflict, is known only by his publisher's blurb on the book's dust jacket: "A young American soldier's shocking story of warfare in Vietnam." His publisher refused to release any more information about his identity.

TOBIAS WOLFF (1945-), U.S. Army (1964-1968), served with the Special Forces in Vietnam, becoming a first lieutenant. His short stories about the war were published as *In the Garden of North American Martyrs*. *The Barracks Thief* (1984), a novel about three paratroopers who will soon be sent to Vietnam, won a Faulkner Prize.

STEPHEN WRIGHT (1946-) served from December 1969 to November 1970 as a military intelligence officer. His first novel, *Meditations in Green* (1983), which alternated hard-hitting descriptions of the war with an account of a military intelligence officer's difficulty in adjusting to life as a civilian, won a Maxwell Perkins Award.

Away from the Writing Table: Politics, Sex, and Other Vices in the Lives of American Writers

by JAMES J. MARTINE

On 28 May 1934, having read *Tender Is the Night* soon after the novel's publication, Ernest Hemingway wrote to F. Scott Fitzgerald: "Forget your personal tragedy.... You see, Bo, you're not a tragic character. Neither am I. All we are is writers and what we should do is write." What writers should do is write. That is what by definition makes writers writers. Not all writers could have or would have taken Hemingway's advice; a good number of them were involved in politics and a variety of other vices. As H. L. Mencken once advised James T. Farrell, the three traps for a writer are alcohol, women, and politics.

POLITICS

Throughout American history politicians have written books. Some write them to impress the intellectuals, their peers, and their constituencies, to enhance their reputations, or to set the record straight. *Profiles in Courage* (1956) by then Senator John F. Kennedy, Richard Nixon's *Six Crises* (1962), and Hubert Humphrey's *The Education of a Public Man* (1976) are only a few examples of this sort of book. Other politicians—from William Bradford, the second governor of Plymouth Colony, and John Winthrop, the first governor of the Massachusetts Bay Colony, to Theodore Roosevelt and Woodrow Wilson—wrote histories. Benjamin Franklin and Thomas Jefferson are nearly as well known for their literary contributions as for their roles in the birth of this nation. The United States, however, as yet really has no great tradition of those who have combined careers in politics

and imaginative writing as, for instance, the French have. It has been pointed out that there probably is no twentieth-century American equivalent of André Malraux.

Of particular interest is the way in which politics touch the lives of Americans who are by definition writers–those whose careers and vocations are in their particular art form and who earn their bread with their pen or typewriter or word processor. Equally interesting may be the way in which writers inform the political process with their vision and insight.

While it is clear that the lives of novelists and poets are not unaffected by politics, some writers have been more directly affected by, and involved in, the political process than others. Philip Freneau, now best remembered as the author of poems such as "The Wild Honey Suckle" and "To a Caty-Did," was known as the "Poet of the Revolution" for his propagandistic satires and patriotic prose and poetry. In 1791 he founded the *National Gazette,* which during its three years of existence was supported by James Madison and Thomas Jefferson (who said the *Gazette* prevented the nation from "galloping fast into monarchy") while it was denounced by Alexander Hamilton and George Washington (who called the poet "that rascal Freneau"). During those same years he served as a U.S. State Department translator, a position to which Jefferson had appointed him.

The involvement of literary figures in active politics does not insure the rule of reason or intellectual moderation; on occasion, passions have reigned. William Cullen Bryant is now remembered as the gentle author of "Thanatopsis," a poem read by generations of school children. During his lifetime, he was equally well known as a newspaper editor, one of the leading citizens of New York. Writing poetry was only recreation for him, and during his nearly fifty years as editor of the *New York Evening Post* (1829-1878) his influence was clearly felt in the politics of the city, the state, and the nation. Bryant, a lawyer, had earlier entered political life as justice of the peace and town clerk in Great Barrington, Massachusetts, but it was in New York City that he gained public recognition as a supporter of liberal political causes. He endorsed government control over currency and was a strong advocate of the abolition of slavery, becoming one of the founding members of the national Republican party in 1856.

Beginning in 1830, there was a political struggle among New York newspapers. Bryant, who supported President Andrew Jackson, charged that "the most outrageous possible insult had been offered" to him in the form of "a significant word spelt with four letters [liar]" by Col. William L. Stone of the *Commercial Advertiser,* who supported Henry Clay. At eight o'clock on the morning of 20 April 1831, Bryant caught up with the rival editor on Broadway, produced a cowhide whip, and proceeded to strike Stone on the shoulders. Stone reciprocated by hitting Bryant with his cane. The fight raged until three passersby pulled the whip from the hands of the author of such meditative poems as "To the Fringed Gentian" and "The Yellow Violet."

The next day Bryant apologized in the *Post* for having "taken the law into my own hands," but this was not the only time that politics cast Bryant adrift in turbulent waters. Dr. William Holland, editor of an earlier *New York Times,* was so offended by Bryant's sarcasm and wit in political and editorial quarrels that in 1838 he sent Bryant a formal challenge to a duel. Bryant made light of the affair and Holland did not pursue the matter. This sensitive poet was a forceful influence upon the politics of this country during the nineteenth century.

Another abolitionist, John Greenleaf Whittier, author of the enormously popular poem *Snow-Bound* (1866), also considered politics, not poetry, his life's work. Encouraged by his lifelong friend William Lloyd Garrison, editor of the foremost abolitionist journal, the *Liberator,* Whittier wrote significant antislavery works including *Justice and Expediency* (1833), which led to his election as a delegate to the National Anti-Slavery Convention held in December 1833 in Philadelphia. In 1835 he was elected to the Massachusetts legislature and served one term. The antislavery cause was not universally popular, and in September of that year he was threatened by a mob while on a lecture tour in Concord, New Hampshire, fleeing a round of bullets. Ill health and the political climate in 1842 kept him from securing one of the Massachusetts seats in the U.S. Congress. This mild Quaker poet who played a major role in the movement for the abolition of slavery throughout the 1840s and 1850s never quite felt truly comfortable wedding politics to poetics. He once confided to a friend: "I have been compelled again to plunge into the political whirlpool; for I have found that my political reputation is more influential than my poetical: so I try to make myself a man of the world—and the public are deceived, but I am not. They do not see that I have thrown the rough armor of rude and turbulent controversy over a keenly sensitive bosom—a heart of softer and gentler emotions than I dare expose."

Even those great nineteenth-century authors who could not properly be termed literary politicians or political *litterateurs* were touched by politics. Nathaniel Hawthorne, who had held positions in the Boston Custom House (1839-1841) and the Salem Custom House (1846-1849), was appointed in 1853 as the U.S. Consul at Liverpool by President Franklin Pierce who had been Hawthorne's schoolmate at Bowdoin College and for whom Hawthorne had written a campaign biography (see "Without Whom . . . "). Hawthorne, in his turn, confided to his *English Notebooks* (1941) that he felt very awkward about his ineffectual attempt to get a consular appointment from Pierce for his friend Herman Melville, who would eventually, in 1866, begin a nineteen-year tenure as Inspector of Customs for the Port of New York.

One of America's great poets, Walt Whitman, who began as a printer's devil and typesetter, became editor of the *Brooklyn Daily Eagle* in 1846 only to be forced to resign in January 1848 because of his activities on behalf of the Free Soil party. He then established and edited a Free Soil paper, the *Brooklyn Freeman,* which lasted one year. As editor of the *Brooklyn Daily Times* (1857-1859), he continued to lead a bohemian life until the shattering onset of the Civil War (see Writers Who Went to War). In January 1865 he obtained a clerkship in the Department of the Interior, but the new Secretary of the Interior, James Harlan, discharged him on 20 June 1865, apparently because Whitman was the author of *Leaves of Grass,* which some critics took to be a dirty

Stencil used by Nathaniel Hawthorne when he was Surveyor in the Salem Custom House (collection of C. E. Frazer Clark, Jr.)

book. W. D. O'Connor wrote *The Good Gray Poet* (1866) in defense of Whitman's "obscenity," and friends obtained a position for Whitman in the Attorney General's office in October 1866. A stroke on 23 January 1873 forced Whitman to leave Washington.

Two other writer-diplomats of the nineteenth century were poet James Russell Lowell and prolific novelist-playwright William Dean Howells. Lowell served as Minister to Spain from 1877 to 1880 and Minister to England from 1880 to 1885. Howells, who later served as editor in chief of the *Atlantic Monthly* (1871-1881), was one of the most influential forces in American literature, but his life was not free of practical politics. When he was twenty-three years old he wrote the campaign biography of Abraham Lincoln, who began his first term of office on 4 March 1861. That year Howells was appointed U.S. Consul to Venice, a position he held until 1865, when Lincoln was assassinated.

As America entered the twentieth century, more and more writers were not only joining Mark Twain and Henry James to trade in their pens for an invention by Christopher Sholes called the typewriter but also actively seeking political office. In 1905 Jack London ran for mayor of Oakland, California, as a Socialist, and while his campaign got wide national notice, he could not muster a total of 500 votes in his hometown.

One of the best-known political battles of the twentieth century was Upton Sinclair's EPIC campaign. Sinclair–a passionate reformer, an ardent pacifist, and the apotheosis of the benevolent spirit of pre-World-War-I American socialism–wrote many novels about specific political situations, and his main concerns were politics and economics. After the publication of *The Jungle* (1906), a novel about the horrible conditions in the Chicago stockyards and meat-packing industry, he came to national celebrity. American literary critics have sneered at his literary efforts, but the fact remains that his fiction brought about important reforms–including the passage of the Pure Food and Drug Act in 1906.

A lifelong "co-opper," Sinclair spent the money realized from *The Jungle* to found a co-operative Socialist venture, Helicon Home Colony, in a building that had formerly been a private school on the Palisades across the Hudson River from upper Manhattan. For a brief time in autumn 1906 the Helicon Hall charboy who tended the furnace, swept out the rooms and staircases, and cleaned the fish pond was Sinclair Lewis. Helicon Hall came to an abrupt and spectacular conclusion at four o'clock on a Sunday morning in March 1907 when the place burned to the ground. Sinclair moved to California in about 1914.

It is a critical commonplace to point to Sinclair's involvement in electoral politics as the principal cause of his decline as a novelist. He was nominated twice as a Socialist candidate for Congress and twice as a Socialist candidate for governor of California; he once ran as a Socialist candidate for the U.S. Senate. It was in 1934 during the depths of the Depression, that he made his best-known run for office. Enrolling in the Democratic party, he announced himself as a candidate for governor of the state of Califor-

Upton Sinclair during his 1934 campaign for the governorship of California (courtesy of the Lilly Library, Indiana University)

nia. The lifelong Socialist in Sinclair rationalized that, after all, his great-grandfather, Commodore Arthur Sinclair had been one of the founders of the Democratic party. At that time, 509,000 people were on the relief rolls in Los Angeles County, and Sinclair dreamed of a series of self-help co-operatives across the state. The rest of his platform included a graduated income tax, old-age pensions, and a tax on land held idle for speculation. Taking as his slogan "End Poverty in California" (EPIC), he published pamphlets titled *I, Governor of California And How I Ended Poverty* (1933) and *EPIC Answers How to End Poverty in California* (1934). In the first pamphlet, Sinclair wrote as though he had already been elected, and he wrote so convincingly that he almost began to believe that he had already won the election: but the often ideal world of art is a long way from the mundane and practical world of politics. Since he received no money at all from Democratic party funds, the sale of 435,000 pamphlets at a quarter a copy financed his EPIC campaign. The primary campaign lasted ten months and Sinclair defeated seven other Democratic party candidates including the favorite of the regular Democratic machine, political journalist George Creel. Sinclair tallied 436,000 votes, Creel 228,000. Sinclair's total was larger than all other seven put together; he was the Democratic party's candidate for governor and the legally chosen head of the party. His run for governor, like Helicon Hall, came to an unhappy end. The EPIC campaign was a grass-roots movement, amateurish and chaotic even in Sinclair's own recollection of it. With no help from the regular Democratic machine, Sinclair ran up against the Republican machine, which spent an estimated ten million dollars, much of it to attack the writer using what he had written in his books to vilify him. The Hearst newspapers and the motion-picture industry played leading roles in mounting a campaign remarkable for its viciousness. Sinclair received thirty-seven percent of the vote, while his Republican opponent, Frank Merriam, got a little over forty-nine percent of the tabulation, with the remainder going to the Progressive candidate, Raymond L. Haight.

A serious Socialist, Sinclair was a devout enemy of communism through the years when many American liberals were being converted to it, and, though he continued his attempts at reform, he confined his campaigns to his books and avoided the public arena. As he had concluded from his EPIC experience, he had "written too many books to be a politician."

Most people, asked to identify the most political of American writers, would probably name one or all three of the troika whose work was associated with the 1930s—John Steinbeck, John Dos Passos, and James T. Farrell. While the politics of Steinbeck and Dos Passos

began well left of center, their positions became increasingly more conservative as they grew older. Steinbeck, who was a dedicated spokesman for the oppressed people in this country in the 1930s, became a staunch supporter of Lyndon Johnson and his policies in Southeast Asia in the 1960s. On 28 May 1966 Steinbeck wrote to his friend Lyndon Johnson, a man he called "the Boss," to thank him for receiving him and his son. He expressed his gratitude to the President for explaining to Steinbeck's son his responsibility as a young man in uniform and the efficacy of Johnson's policies in Vietnam. Steinbeck had a personal, almost protective relationship with the President. As a confidant of presidents and ambassadors, Steinbeck revealed a political stance that would not have been expected of the Steinbeck in the 1930s. All three writers, however, must be recorded by history as men concerned with the plight of disenfranchised and excluded members of the American society and who saw political activism and government action as means of redress for social inequities.

In 1937 John Dos Passos made a political decision that had a devastating impact on his literary reputation. While in Spain with Ernest Hemingway to write a script for a documentary film about the Spanish Civil War (see Writers Who Went to War), Dos Passos argued bitterly with Hemingway and announced that he was returning home to denounce the Communists, who, he felt, were showing their true tyrannical nature in Spain. Hemingway warned that the critics would bury him. Dos Passos did as he threatened, attacking the Communists in a series of magazine articles that shocked and disappointed those party members who had considered him their most promising spokesman. The retaliation was sure. Taking as the occasion for their attacks the 1938 publication of the one-volume edition of Dos Passos's *U.S.A.* trilogy (*The 42nd Parallel*, 1930; *1919*, 1932; and *The Big*

Money, 1936), Communist reviewer Mike Gold, who had announced in 1933, after publication of *1919*, that Dos Passos had surpassed the achievement of James Joyce and that "Dos Passos belongs to the marvelous future" now stated unequivocally, while reviewing the trilogy as a whole, that Dos Passos had always been full of "merde" and that he hated communism because "organically he seems to hate the human race."

Granville Hicks, an editor at *New Masses*, concurred, for the most part. In 1932, he declared "we now have an American writer capable of giving us the America we know." But in 1938, he confessed that he was wrong: "When *1919* appeared, I believed that Dos Passos had established his position as the most talented of American novelists–a position he still holds. As early as 1934, however, I was distressed by his failure to shake off habits of mind that I had thought–quite erroneously as it turns out–were dissolving under the influence of contact with the revolutionary movement." He concluded: "If he follows the path he is now on, his claims to greatness are already laid before us and later critics will only have to fill in the details of another story of genius half-fulfilled." Hicks's prediction came to pass. After 1938, Dos Passos was treated by most critics as a writer past his prime.

Not all writers believed in the magical panaceas of government intervention or reform. Although Ernest Hemingway involved himself in large causes on the international stage–the Spanish civil war and both world wars (see Writers Who Went to War)–his interest seems to have been more in tactics and combat than in socio-economic or philosophical matters. In 1932 Hemingway wrote to Dos Passos that he could not be a Communist because "I hate tyranny and, I suppose, government. . . . I can't stand any bloody government, I suppose." This statement may be Hemingway's most straightforward artic-

ulation of his political theory, which is evident in his 1933 short story "The Gambler, the Nun, and the Radio," where Mr. Frazer thinks that a belief in any new form of government is one of the opiates of the people and says, "What you wanted was the minimum of government, always less government." This statement makes Hemingway not so much an anarchist as a follower in the tradition of Thomas Paine, Thomas Jefferson, and Henry David Thoreau, who believed that the government is best which governs least.

If writing too many books does, as Sinclair suggested, disqualify an author from being a politician, it scarcely can be seen as an impediment to the desire to hold public office. Howard Fast is one of America's most prolific writers, having published more than seventy novels, the best known of which may be his controversial *Spartacus* (1951) which uses the great slave revolt of 71 B.C. as a metaphor for the struggle of oppressed people. Fast–who joined the American Communist party in 1943, at a time when most American intellectuals were abandoning communism–found time in 1952 to mount an unsuccessful campaign for the U.S. Congress on the American Labor party ticket.

Another prolific American writer, popular with the reading public but generally held in low esteem by academic critics, is James Michener. From the *Tales of the South Pacific* (1948) through *Hawaii* (1959) to *Texas* (1986), Michener has produced a string of best-selling "big" novels, often adapted into motion pictures. His sagas of Texas, Poland, and outer space have become synonymous with best-sellers and big bucks. Yet all his celebrity and financial support could not prevent his defeat when he stood as Democratic candidate for Congress in Bucks County, Pennsylvania, in 1962.

The game of politics, serious and speculative, is not without its moments of humor. Consider the tries for public office by Gore Vidal, William F. Buckley, and Norman Mailer, whose running mate was Pulitzer Prize-winning *New York Daily News* columnist, Jimmy Breslin, the author of several well-received novels.

An admiring critic has characterized Gore Vidal as a detoured politician, and by birth and background he was immersed in a milieu of politics. The grandson of the powerful populist U.S. Senator from Oklahoma, Thomas Gore, Vidal was raised in his grandfather's house near Washington, D.C. While he began as a conventional Democrat, who is said to have basked in the warming glow of the Kennedy Camelot, he broke with the family and began to write articles blasting the Kennedys. Becoming an unconventional Democrat, the novelist was nominated in 1960 as the Democratic candidate for the congressional seat in New York State's 29th District, which has always been firmly Republican. Though he is witty and articulate and though he conducted a vigorous campaign, gaining almost 20,000 votes more than the presidential candidate John F. Kennedy in that district, Vidal lost the election by some 25,000 votes. That might have been the end of Vidal's pursuit of political office, but in 1982 he launched a brief and mildly amusing campaign in California for the U.S. Senate. While Vidal has never held public office—and since he now lives much of the year in a villa in Ravello, Italy, he may never—he has been a continual gadfly whose sardonic wit has made him effectively the perpetual leader of the opposition to whomever the incumbents might be. One of Vidal's two consuming interests has been the political *mise en scene*. His fourth book, *The Season of Comfort* (1949), is about a political family; and three of his plays, *The Best Man* (1960), *Weekend* (1968), and *An Evening with Richard Nixon* (1972) are about politics, politicians, and political candidacy. His later novels *Washington, D.C.* (1967), *Burr* (1973), and *1876* (1976) underscore this preoccupation.

Two authors who had major run-ins— intellectual, near-physical, and fully physical conflicts—with Vidal have also sought public office. One was the *National Review* editor William F. Buckley, Jr., syndicated columnist and author of best-selling espionage novels. In 1965, Buckley got no more than ten percent of the vote in his campaign to become mayor of New York City, but he gathered enough grist for his mill to grind out a book on that campaign, *The Unmaking of a Mayor* (1966). Buckley's conservative politics scarcely suited the taste of Vidal, and vice versa of course, and the two sparred often orally and in print—but always at long range until the explosive 1968 Democratic convention in Chicago. With only ABC commentator Howard K. Smith between them and with a national television audience looking on, Vidal called Buckley a "crypto-Nazi," which prompted Buckley to respond by calling Vidal a "queer." He then insisted that Vidal stop calling him a crypto-Nazi or "I'll sock you in your goddamn face."

If there were one person with whom Vidal seemed to have a cosmic destiny, it would be another man who ran for mayor of New York City, Vidal's sometime friend Norman Mailer (see Book Battles). In *Advertisements for Myself* (1959), Mailer wrote: "Like many another vain, empty, and bullying body of our time, I have been running for President these last ten years in the privacy of my mind, and it occurs to me that I am less close now than when I began." In the early 1960s Mailer geared up for a run at the mayoralty of New York City, but his candidacy was brought to an abrupt halt when the writer was incarcerated in New York's Bellevue Hospital for stabbing his second wife. In 1969, however, with running mate Jimmy Breslin by his side (Breslin ran for city council president), Mailer won the hearts of many New Yorkers with his eccentric views such as the secession of New York City from the state to form a fifty-first state and a campaign slogan of "No More Bullshit." He finished fourth

VACHEL LINDSAY AND SARA TEASDALE

When poets Vachel Lindsay and Sara Teasdale began to exchange letters in the summer of 1913, each was on the verge of achieving national recognition. Lindsay had already published "General William Booth Enters Heaven" in the 1913 issue of *Poetry* magazine, and the American poetry world was buzzing over the originality and vigor of the work. Publisher Mitchell Kennerley was about to publish Lindsay's first trade volume, *General William Booth Enters into Heaven and Other Poems* (1913), and Teasdale had published two books, *Sonnets to Duse and Other Poems* (1907) and *Helen of Troy and Other Poems* (1911), the first at her family's expense and the second with only slight acclaim. In 1913 she was writing many of the poems included in *Rivers to the Sea* (1915), which won her extensive recognition. As a result, her publisher, Macmillan, announced a willingness to bring out another volume of her verse as soon as it was ready.

During the early months of the relationship, letters were the only means of communication between the two poets. They did not meet for the first time until February 1914, when Lindsay, "devastated with anticipation," made an overnight visit to St. Louis to see the woman who had inspired his verses for nearly a year. Lindsay's letters to Teasdale, 245 of which are at Yale, are a remarkable record of his ability to fall in love at a distance with his own imaginative creation. In fall 1913, while he was working on "The Congo," he was also writing to Teasdale two and three times a week. Her responses to this "Niagara of ink," as Lindsay called his letters, are open to conjecture, as Lindsay burned her letters (at her request) in August 1914,

when she rejected him and married shoe manufacturer Ernst Filsinger.

The volume of the Lindsay/Teasdale correspondence is understandable, as the two had much more in common than poetry. Each was the youngest of several children and still living at home with ailing, elderly parents; each had a strong religious background; and each thought of love in highly romantic, essentially nonphysical terms. Soon after beginning their correspondence, each began to rely on the other for critical comments on new verses, as well as for advice on how to live happily with officious parents. The very real difference between them–and perhaps the most important reason for Teasdale's decision not to marry her fellow poet–was money: the Teasdales were reasonably affluent, and their daughter was used to a refined life-style. The Lindsays, on the other hand, struggled financially, and Lindsay, contemptuous of money, was ill-prepared for–and uninterested in–all things practical. Lindsay, moreover, considered himself the poet of Springfield, Illinois, and the Middle West. Teasdale was bored to distraction by the Middle West. St. Louis was intolerable, and the idea of moving to Lindsay's parochial Springfield was impossible. She preferred New York, and New York, for Lindsay, was "a gigantic spider's nest."

By the time of their first meeting, Lindsay was writing lengthy letters (eight to twenty pages) and was already three-quarters in love. Teasdale was more than a little puzzled by his expressions of ardor. Without having met her correspondent, she had already been termed "a rare bird" and "a prize package," and she had been invited to Springfield to meet his parents. When she apparently inquired about his intentions, Lindsay enigmatically replied: "It really amounts to a mania with me–getting letters–and writing them–if I have a minute–and just the *right* person– is equally a pleasure. . . . A nice girl to write to is a grand thing" (24 November 1913). Teasdale soon learned that Lindsay needed a woman to inspire his creative work and that his recent loss of his girlfriend had been traumatic, not only emotionally but also creatively. By late 1913, still without having met him, she had become one of his "inspiration girls," as the family called Lindsay's many female friends.

The relationship largely continued at long distance, and Lindsay's imagination became increasingly active. He asked for a lock of her hair and wrote about the "saucy gold circle of fairyland silk" (in "On Suddenly Receiving a Curl Long Refused"). He wrote new poems for her almost daily, reflecting on her eyes, her letters, her writing pen, and her white silk shawl (which she wore at their first meeting). He named her "Saraphim," "golden queen," "Polly Ann," and "Gloriana." When she objected, he asked if she would prefer to be called "Jezebel Semiramis Priscilla Mather." Teasdale was not only amused but also responsive. Her concept of love was romantic in nature, and Lindsay seemed to be Sir Walter Raleigh and Sir Galahad wrapped into one. She went so far as to invite him to New York for the month of July 1914, where, properly chaperoned, they walked, visited friends, and courted. She assisted in organizing his second commercially published collection, *The Congo and Other Poems* (1914), and the majority of the poems in the volume are for her or reflect her critical appraisals. Although she refused to accept his ring, she purchased a friendship bracelet for him.

At the end of July 1914, Lindsay left New York for Springfield, and Ernst Filsinger was given his turn to court. Teasdale had decided that her unrequited love for poet John Hall Wheelock was hopeless and that, approaching thirty, she must marry. She was determined to choose between Lindsay and Filsinger. By the end of August 1914, the choice was Filsinger, and a despairing Lindsay was forced to struggle to complete "the best song of my days," his grand statement of his love for her, "The Chinese Nightingale," finally finished in the fall 1914.

In the next few years, Teasdale wrote her best works. Her *Love Songs* (1917) won the first Columbia University poetry prize (1918), the precursor of the Pulitzer Prize for Poetry. Lindsay dedicated his *Chinese Nightingale and Other Poems* (1917) and his *Collected Poems* (1923, revised 1925) to "Sara Teasdale. Poet." The two poets continued as friends, and when Lindsay married in May 1925, Teasdale sent her "white silk shawl" to Elizabeth Conner, Lindsay's bride.

After the initial euphoria of marriage, both suffered the tragedy of marital disillusionment. Teasdale's marriage ended in divorce; Lindsay's separation and possible divorce loomed imminent at the time of his suicide, by drinking Lysol (5 December 1931). Teasdale's elegy "Deep in the Ages," which quotes "The Chinese Nightingale," was written for her former suitor. Less than fourteen months later (30 January 1933), Teasdale herself was discovered dead in her bath from an overdose of sedatives.

–D. C.

MACLEISH IN GOVERNMENT

Urged by Supreme Court Justice Felix Frankfurter and President Franklin Delano Roosevelt, Archibald MacLeish accepted the president's nomination as Librarian of the Congress. Opposed by some as "a fellow-traveller of the Communist party" and by others as not a professional librarian, MacLeish was nevertheless confirmed by the Senate (63-8) and assumed the position in October 1939. Early in his tenure he began the process of reorganizing the library and won budget increases from Congress to begin a union catalogue, to build a folksong archive, to develop an interlibrary loan and photocopying system, and to improve the salaries of the underpaid librarians. Later during his five-year tenure he enlarged the collections and added departments in order to bring into being his vision of the library as "a people's library of reference" rather than a library solely for members of the Congress.

During World War II, MacLeish was to hold positions as the Director of the Office of Facts and Figures (1941-1942), Assistant Director of the Office of War Information (1942-1943), and Assistant Secretary of State for Cultural Relations (1944-1945). The Office of Facts and Figures was created by FDR to provide the American people with a coherent and detailed picture of the defense and foreign policies of the Roosevelt administration. MacLeish served without pay and reported directly to the President. After the United States entered the war the OFF was eliminated and replaced by the Office of War Information under the direction of Elmer Davis. The purpose of the OWI, quite similar to that of the OFF, was to provide as much accurate information about the war effort as was possible to the American people. MacLeish served as assistant director until 30 January 1943, when he resigned because of policy disputes.

On 4 December 1944, President Roosevelt nominated MacLeish to serve as Assistant Secretary of State for Public and Cultural Relations. Before the Senate Foreign Relations Committee MacLeish articulated his view of the job: to direct U.S. information policies in the United States and abroad and to oversee cultural exchanges in such areas as science, technology, art, and literature. In this office MacLeish argued repeatedly for improved understanding through communication and he endorsed the United Nations concept that would eventually be UNESCO. When Harry S. Truman assumed the presidency, MacLeish resigned his position in the State Department and was appointed shortly thereafter as chairman of the United States delegation to draw up final plans for the UN's education, scientific, and cultural programs. Over the next two years (1946-1947) MacLeish argued powerfully and persuasively for U.S. support of UNESCO. He thought that through the "preservation, increase, and dissemination of men's knowledge of themselves, their world, and each other" peace was possible. He saw UNESCO as an important step in reaching that goal.

–V. H. J.

Norman Mailer and Jimmy Breslin during their 1969 Democratic primary campaign in New York City (courtesy of AP/Wide World Photos)

among five candidates in the Democratic primary election.

It is as a writer that Mailer has seriously addressed the politics of the day. In 1960, he covered the Democratic convention for *Esquire,* and his article "Superman Comes to the Supermarket" characterized John F. Kennedy as "the Existential Hero." It was Mailer, in *Miami and the Siege of Chicago* (1968), who first dubbed Richard M. Nixon as the apotheosis of the mediocre.

What is consistent in these half dozen tales of twentieth-century authors' seeking office is a record of frustration and futility. None was ever elected.

SEX

Ernest Hemingway once claimed that he had had every woman he ever wanted—which is quite an impressive boast, until one notices the essential ambiguity in that statement. Hemingway was married four times, was involved in the standard youthful sexual escapades, and had a writer's imagination. Before readers see too much sexual autobiography in

Hemingway's novels—or in any other writer's work—they should remember Somerset Maugham's observation that any novel is what happened, plus what might have happened, plus what never happened.

Hemingway's writings indicate that among the things this quintessential man's man abhorred were homosexuals and homosexual behavior. His fiction scorns them; and there are tales of the macho writer going out of his way to punch an obvious homosexual. This behavior, while excessive, would place him in the mainstream of a long-standing American aversion. However, Hemingway's image as a champion of straight sex has been modified by the posthumously published *Garden of Eden* (1986), in which the autobiographical hero engages in sexual role-switching games with his wife.

Historically this nation has always been at least circumspect, and frequently homophobic, when dealing with homosexuals and homosexuality. There are records from the early seventeenth century of a ship's master, Richard Cornish, being hanged for alleged homosexual activity; in *Of Plimmouth Plantation*

William Bradford, writing on the events of 1642, was distressed that "even sodomy and buggery (things fearful to name) have broke forth in this land oftener than once." On Manhattan Island in 1646, Jan Creoli was executed for his homosexuality by being choked to death and then "burned to ashes." The death penalty was prescribed in early seventeenth-century New England for male homosexuality, and church canonists regularly insisted that lesbian acts merited capital punishment. Nor did more liberal thinkers do much to mitigate the severity of these censures. Thomas Jefferson was among those who in their revision of Virginia law in autumn 1776, recommended that rather than the death penalty "Sodomy with a man or woman shall be punished, if a man, by castration." Homophobia continued into the twentieth century. Gardner Jackson, who in 1915 was a student at Amherst College, later recalled the antipathy that Robert Frost, then a faculty member at the college, manifested toward faculty member, Stark Young, a poet, author of the well-received novel *So Red the Rose* (1934), and influential drama critic for the *New York Times.* Young's great popularity with undergraduates as well as his homosexuality may have triggered Frost's resentment, and Jackson recalled that Frost was "almost obsessed with a preoccupation to paw over Stark Young's eroticism and interest in erotic literature."

Until very recently biographers have been far from candid and especially circumspect in handling the matter of homosexuality in the lives of their subjects. Gay Wilson Allen, author of a major biography of Walt Whitman (1955, revised 1967) is careful to use the word, "homoerotic" rather than "homosexual" in describing the poet because, Allen believed, the latter word suggested, perversion. As late as 1971, Patricia Meyerowitz, in describing Gertrude Stein's relationship with Alice B. Toklas, insisted that emotional attachments existed between the two, and that they "made a home for themselves," but denied that they were lesbians. As a matter of fact, Stein and Toklas had nearly a husband-and-wife relationship. Their life together was almost conventional except for the fact that they both happened to be women. Many academic biographers are reluctant to include material of an explicitly sexual nature, even heterosexual. Do we conclude after reading the 1,846 pages (and 269 pages of notes) of Joseph Blotner's *Faulkner: A Biography* (1974), that the biographer did not know that Faulkner and Meta Carpenter were lovers? Of course not. The biographer is discreet. Leon Edel, in his five-volume comprehensive biography of Henry James, (1955-1972), approaches the writer's sexuality psychoanalytically but leaves his sexual activity, or lack thereof, open-ended. Arguments still rage among James scholars as to whether he was homosexual, heterosexual, or asexual.

With the recent gay-liberation movement scholars have been more overt in their discussions of writers' sexuality. The reader may be cautious in accepting what his own eyes have not seen, but the list of writers now generally accepted as homosexual includes Walt Whitman, W. H. Auden, Tennessee Williams, Gertrude Stein, Willa Cather, Allen Ginsberg, James Baldwin, and Truman Capote.

Walt Whitman is counted among this nation's best poets. His poetry is powerful, all-encompassing, forceful, gentle, rambunctious, blatant, and subtle. In 1855 Whitman wrote:

Through me forbidden voices,
Voices of sexes and lusts, voices veil'd
    and I remove the veil,
Voices indecent by me clarified and
    transfigur'd.
I do not press my fingers across my
    mouth,
    I keep as delicate around the
    bowels as around the head
    and heart,

Copulation is no more rank to me
    than death is.

Whitman insisted that he believed in the flesh and the appetites. He felt that seeing, hearing, and feeling are miracles, and his youthful poetry expressed this enthusiasm. Some of Whitman's friends and all of his critics were troubled when the so-called "Calamus" poems first appeared in the third edition (1860) of *Leaves of Grass*. The calamus is a species of plant, the sweet flag, which appears in myth and literature as a symbol for male relationships. His "Children of Adam" poems are warmly sensual and homoerotic. "Once I Pass'd Through a Populous City," contains the lines: "I remember only a woman I casually met there who detain'd me for love of me,/Day by day and night by night we were together–all else has long been forgotten by me, / I remember I say only that woman who passionately clung to me. . . ." An early manuscript of this poem shows the word "man" deleted and "woman" substituted. Whitman knew about homophobia. Yet one wonders about the delicacy and disguise in this poem when even a poem as well-known as "Crossing Brooklyn Ferry," which was published as "Sun-Down Poem" in the second edition (1856) of *Leaves of Grass* contains: "I am he who knew what it was to be evil / . . . Was call'd by my nighest name by clear loud voices of young men as they saw me approaching or passing, / Felt their arms on my neck as I stood, or the negligent leaning of their flesh against me as I sat, / Saw many I loved in the street . . . yet never told them a word. . . ." It is not only Whitman's poetry that is often homosexually suggestive. When Whitman included in his two notebook diaries of 1862-1863 the names of young men with whom he had slept, the poet meant "slept with" in the same way most people use the term–as a euphemism for sexual relations.

It is one of the ironies of American history that Horatio Alger, Jr., whose name has entered our language as a symbol and a synonym for the rags-to-riches tale of a boy's rise through ambition and hard work, was a minister who was separated from his church, the First Unitarian Church of Brewster, Massachusetts, in 1866 for homosexual activity allegedly involving two boys in his parish. His novels and stories achieved huge popular appeal. Perhaps 20,000,000 copies of his books have been sold.

Two great defenders of freedom of sexual choice were Emma Goldman and Gore Vidal. Goldman, anarchist activist, feminist, agitator, and author of *The Social Significance of the Modern Drama* (1914), in the early decades of the twentieth century spoke out and wrote articles on the unjust treatment of homosexuals. Vidal believes in the innate bisexuality of all people. To Vidal, one chooses to be heterosexual or homosexual or to move back and forth between the two. He insists that the experiences of most people demonstrate that it was possible to have a mature sexual relationship with a man on one day and a mature sexual relationship with a woman on the next day. On the third day, he suggests, if everything goes well it would be possible to have that mature sexual relationship with both together, although Vidal concludes by advising that one would have to be in good physical condition for this sort of regimen.

Sex and politics are the main subject of Vidal's essays, and many of his novels and plays deal with politics or homosexuality. His third novel, *The City and the Pillar,* written when he was twenty-one, achieved instant notoriety; it was a shocking book to be published for a popular audience in 1948, not merely because its subject matter was homosexuality but because Vidal purposely created as a protagonist Jim Willard, an ordinary, all-American, lower-middle class, athletic young man, who is presented as a perfectly normal person, different only in his sexual preference. In this work Vidal attempted to demonstrate the "dead-on normality" of homosexuality,

Tennessee Williams and Gore Vidal (courtesy of the Harry Ransom Humanities Research Center, University of Texas at Austin)

yet the book ends with Willard's hysterically strangling to death his boyhood friend, his imagined perfect lover. This flawed ending and the inability to reconcile it with the attempt to show the "naturalness" of homosexual relations was greeted with suspicion by reviewers and, although Vidal would later revise the novel's conclusion, brought the writer an early questionable fame. His novel *Myra Breckenridge* (1968), an attack on accepted sexual norms and an assault on the myths of a machismo American culture, was better received. *Two Sisters* (1970) and *Myron* (1970) made it clear that Gore Vidal would be the champion of sexuality; hetero-, homo-, and bi-, as Norman Mailer was the heir to Ernest Hemingway's crown as the masculine heavyweight champion of American literature. It seemed inevitable that the two would clash (see Book Battles). The predominant sexual preference in this nation is still hetero-.

There are extraordinary stories about George S. Kaufman, coauthor of *Of*

Thee I Sing (1932), *You Can't Take It With You* (1936), and *The Man Who Came To Dinner* (1939). Since his was an "open" marriage, Kaufman, who had a charge account at the brothel of the renowned Polly Adler, maintained a separate apartment for his assignations. His friends called this brilliant wit a male nymphomaniac, and the American press dubbed him public lover number one. Kaufman's reputation may have been exacerbated, or enhanced (depending on one's view), by his involvement with movie star Mary Astor and the publication of "sensational" portions of her diary in the press. Astor's husband had been granted an uncontested divorce in 1935. When the actress later entered a suit for custody of their child, the motion-picture industry was in an uproar at the prospect of Astor's candid and detailed diary appearing in print. The press published portions of what Astor later insisted was a forged version loaded with amorous details and containing a "box score" of many big names in the business. The few pages of the authentic diary which came into the possession of the newspapers were a romantic and sentimental account of Astor's relationship with Kaufman, which had begun in New York City well before her divorce and continued in Palm Springs and Hollywood. While he was in Hollywood working on the screenplay for the Marx Brothers' *A Night at the Opera,* Kaufman resumed his affair with Astor until he was confronted by her irate husband. The playwright fled Hollywood.

Kaufman, who was always careful that his relationships with women were conducted with discretion, suddenly found himself in the national headlines. From mid July to mid August 1936 a daily volume of scandal would flow from the Superior Court, where Mary Astor was countersuing to set aside the divorce and to gain an annulment and custody of her child. On 17 August 1936, *Time* magazine cast Kaufman as "Mary Astor's No. 1 partner-in-sin." Using diary entries for support, New York newspapers had Kaufman leading the field of "top ten" lovers by several lengths. Kaufman, who had returned to Hollywood to collaborate on a project with Moss Hart, was called as a witness by lawyers representing Astor's husband. After Kaufman failed to appear in court, a bench warrant was issued for his arrest. There followed a comic scene in which sheriff's deputies chased Kaufman through front doors, out back doors, and onto a yacht bound for Catalina. The deputies continued their hot pursuit by plane. Finally, hidden on a stretcher covered with blankets, his face covered by bandages, Kaufman escaped Hollywood on a train bound for New York, where the tabloid headlines welcomed him as "Public Lover No. 1."

Of course Kaufman was not the only American writer with a prodigious libidinal reputation. Jack London's friends called him "The Stallion," and a biographer identified him as a sexual anarchist. Sex for some writers could be a strangely complicated matter. William

Seabrook reputedly enjoyed tying up beautiful naked women, binding them to beds or pillars, sometimes suspending them overhead from the ceiling—although it was reported he paid them well, he never had sex with them.

"The all-embracing Dr. Franklin" does not refer only to Benjamin Franklin's many intellectual concerns. He was quite a lady's man, a fact that was somewhat obscured by nineteenth-century editors. Some of his exploits, such as his effort to seduce a friend's mistress in London, are recorded in his *Autobiography.* He also had an illegitimate son, by Deborah Read, whom he came to consider his common-law wife until her death in 1774. During the Revolution, while he was in France, he wrote and printed on his own press a series of playful "bagatelles," some of which were seductive essays addressed to French ladies. These works, along with his earlier defense of illegitimacy in "The Speech of Polly Baker" and his "Advice on the Choice of a Mistress," present a side of Franklin that is seldom revealed to schoolchildren.

While some authors, like some people, enjoyed casual, even anonymous sex, many more preferred the state of bliss associated with marriage. And so they married–and married–and married.

At the top of the list of much-married authors is Robert Nathan, author of *Portrait of Jennie* (1940) and more than fifty other books of poetry and prose, who waltzed down the aisle a lucky seven times. Norman Mailer's record of six wives (including one common-law) just nips out a man he much admired, Henry Miller, whose marriage to Hiroko Tokuda in 1967 came fifty years after his first wedding, to Beatrice Sylvas Wickens in 1917.

While Hemingway did not have much enthusiasm for politics, he was a self-proclaimed expert on love, marriage, drinking, and sex. Writing about sex in "Fathers and Sons," Hemingway advised "all the equipment you will ever

George S. Kaufman and Moss Hart (courtesy of the Billy Rose Theatre Collection, New York Public Library at Lincoln Center, Astor, Lenox and Tilden Foundations)

have is provided and each man learns all there is for him to know about it without advice."

Some writers get poor notices as lovers, and others get rave reviews. Meta Carpenter, who became William Faulkner's paramour while he was writing screenplays in Hollywood in 1932, confides in her book about Faulkner, *A Loving Gentleman* (1976), published fourteen years after the writer's death, that he would cover their bed with gardenia and jasmine petals and that Faulkner was "ravenous, carnal and female-intoxicated in the act of love." He wrote poems for her such as:

Meta
Bill
Meta
Who soft keeps for him his love's
long girl's body sweet to fuck.
Bill.

His letters referred to her as "my April and May cunt . . ." and "my sweet-assed gal."

Two weeks before his twenty-first birthday, Thomas Wolfe wrote a covenant with God in which he swore to "hereby abjure the mental and carnal fleshpots–beasts which have well-nigh

MUCH-MARRIED AUTHORS OR, "GET ME TO THE CHURCH FOUR TIMES"	
Author	Times Wed
Robert Nathan	7
Norman Mailer	6
Henry Miller	5
Mary McCarthy	4
Sherwood Anderson	4
Erskine Caldwell	4
Ernest Hemingway	4

destroyed" him. Wolfe did not succeed much. The series of thirty-five pocket notebooks he kept from 1926 until just before his death in 1938 is one of the most interesting and amazing records in the American literary-sexual canon. Wolfe's appetites were ravenous, and his cataloguing of them is candid and brilliant. He was a giant of a man, and his passions were worthy of his stature. He lived deeply, intensely, and vividly, and he was compelled to keep lists. In 1930-1931, for example, he listed by name thirteen women with whom he had had sexual relations in sixteen months. Wolfe's fondness for lists continued in 1934, when he completed a list of women with whom he had had sex in the United States and the states in which they were born. Nor were American women the only ones to impress the writer. On a trip to Europe in 1935, he was a great patron of brothels. Although Wolfe was drinking heavily, he kept a careful account of his sojourn in Paris, where he "went to swell whorehouse but departed after haggling over price–then to whorehouse Rue du Moulins–lay with big blonde."

Thomas Wolfe was a bachelor, and the great love of his life was Aline Bernstein, a married woman nineteen years his senior with whom he had a stormy on-again, off-again liaison. Wolfe's relationship with and treatment of Mrs. Bernstein was by turns passionate and profound, selfish and reprehensible. His remarks about her could be scurrilous, and drafts of some of his letters to her contain passages of brutal anti-Semitism. Yet she remained perhaps the one true experience of love in his life, certainly the one that meant the most to him.

A man who had more than one true experience of love–many more–was Henry Miller, and he wrote about his love life in detail. Miller's passions were raging and consuming, and his is a remarkable case in American literature. He is one of this country's best writers, yet his works will not be found in most college curricula–nor have excerpts from his work found their way into literature anthologies. Perhaps it is true that Henry Miller is for audiences mature enough to get beyond the steamiest scenes and pornographic passages in *Tropic of Cancer* (1934) or *Tropic of Capricorn* (1936) to the mind of their creator, a mind consumed by a quest for meaning in what appears to be a chaotic universe, a mind devoted to art, music, and

Henry Miller

poetry, and fixed on a commitment to his fellowman. There is an excess of enthusiasm, a passionate desire to embrace people and to show them love. Quite the reverse of being immoral, Miller is a moralist. Moreover, he loved to laugh and to have his readers engage his comic vision of life with him.

Both his *Tropics* are filled with passages describing coitus–on hardwood floors, in rowboats and telephone booths, on a crowded subway, standing up in vestibules, during piano lessons, and on a cinder-path embankment about to be sprayed by a shower of hot sparks from a train passing on the railroad tracks beside it. Henry Miller wrote about himself. The reader of his best works wonders how far the writer stretches the reader's willingness to suspend disbelief, how far Miller stretches reality–only to discover that the greatness of his work lies precisely in the access that Miller has allowed the reader to his fantasies. Did it *really* happen, just as it is described? That is a question to ask about journalism, not literature.

OTHER VICES

On 19 August 1935, Hemingway wrote to Ivan Kashkin: ... "Don't you drink?... I have drunk since I was fifteen and few things have given me more pleasure.... What else can change your ideas and make them run on a different plane like whisky? ... The only time it isn't good for you is when you write or when you fight.... Modern life, too, is often a mechanical oppression and liquor is the only mechanical relief."

When Mencken cautioned writers against alcohol, he might have added drugs to his list of vices. A random listing of American writers who were known to use drugs would have to begin with Edgar Allan Poe, though it is necessary to shatter the romantic myth of "the reveller upon opium." There is no evidence that Poe used drugs habitually. The persona of the "lost drunkard or the irreclaimable eater of opium" was a character he created, not Poe himself. He may have been a part-time madman, and he may have been better than a part-time drunkard, but a junkie he was not. The story that Poe was under the influence of drugs when he was found semiconscious on the streets of Baltimore on 3 October 1849, four days before his death, is a hoax. He *was* found nearly unconscious, dirty, dressed in outsized clothing that was not his own, and very near death, but there is no clear evidence to support the story that he had taken any drugs.

Perhaps no other thing so clearly illustrates Poe's innocence when it came to drugs as the single demonstrable instance of his drug use. In November 1845 Poe was rejected as a suitor for the hand of Sarah Helen Whitman, a widow six years his senior, because her family was dismayed by Poe's drinking. Poe purchased two ounces of laudanum in Provi-

Edgar Allan Poe (photograph by S. W. Hartshorne, Providence, Rhode Island; courtesy of Brown University Library)

dence, Rhode Island, and proceeded to Boston, where he wrote a letter to Mrs. Annie Richmond (whom he had earlier begged to leave her husband and come with him), swallowed half of the drug in a "suicide attempt," and headed for the post office to mail the letter. Before he could reach his destination, Poe was caught on the street by spasms of vomiting. He had not been aware that the amount of opium in an ounce of laudanum, directly ingested, would be rejected by the stomach before the drug could have any effect. *Effect* may have been what Poe had in mind–visions perhaps of Annie Richmond (Poe wanted Mrs. Whitman, but he wanted Mrs. Richmond even more) rushing to his side. The reality was something quite different–passersby stopping to stare at Poe, who had suddenly bent over, retching into the gutter.

Some writers, even great ones, used controlled drugs such as sedatives and barbiturates to ease psychological, spiritual, and even physical pain. When William Faulkner, for example, needed to dry out after a spell of his alcoholism, or to gain relief from the back pain caused by five broken vertebrae in various stages of natural splinting, he prescribed for himself a remedy of Seconal washed down by a half dozen or so beers. He also found that this combination helped to prevent sleepless nights.

There are, obviously, writers given to the recreational or sportive use of depressants, antidepressants, and hallucinogens. Norman Mailer was formerly a user of marijuana, Seconal, Miltown, Demerol, and Benzedrine, and the last part of *The Deer Park* (1955) was written under the influence of mescaline. Mailer's "secret weapon" was the heavy use of marijuana, and his writings about it contributed to the development of the vast drug subculture in the late 1960s. Friends remember that Mailer's aggression was aggravated by the use of marijuana.

Allen Ginsberg, one of the leading poets of the Beat Generation, and once informally designated press secretary to Mailer during his abortive first "campaign" for mayor, attained notoriety in the mass media as spokesperson for hallucinogenic and addictive drugs, peyote, and lysergic acid (LSD-25). Chanting and reading his poems to the accompaniment of a three-piece jazz group, Ginsberg toured college campuses, espousing his predilection for "apolitical mystic communism," homosexual romance, and marijuana-high meditation. Where Ginsberg went, controversy followed, including faddish "riots" at Princeton and the University of Pennsylvania. College students loved to throw beer, sometimes still in glasses, bottles, or pitchers, at Ginsberg.

William S. Burroughs, best known as the author of *Naked Lunch* (1959), was introduced to the use of morphine and its derivatives by a Times Square hustler before the end of World War II. For the next fifteen years, he was a steady drug user; the availability of drugs and efforts to keep out of trouble with authorities shaped where Burroughs lived. When trouble with the New York City law enforcement authorities occurred in 1946, he moved to Texas. In 1948 Burroughs attempted to straighten out his life by entering the drug rehabilitation center in Lexington, Kentucky. When he returned to Texas, he was already back on drugs. Burroughs was so troubled by Texas police that he moved to Louisiana. After his home there was raided by police in 1949, he moved to Mexico to avoid prosecution for illegal possession of drugs and firearms. Burroughs found firearms, and he had little trouble acquiring drugs, in Mexico. On the night of 7 September 1951, the author accidentally killed his wife, reportedly while attempting to shoot a glass off her head. Burroughs denied this version of the shooting. Eventually Mexican police let the matter drop, but he left the country. After a trip to North Africa, Burroughs went off to the South American jungle in search of the legendary hallucinogen, Yage. His novel *Junkie* (1953) describes his jailings on drug charges.

Ken Kesey, one of the leaders of the LSD revolution on the West Coast, used drugs in an attempt to find new forms of artistic expression. He had been introduced to the serious use of drugs, particularly LSD, while acting as a paid volunteer for government-sponsored drug experiments conducted at a veterans' hospital in Menlo Park, California. Kesey drew upon both his experience with drugs and his hospital work in the composition of *One Flew Over the Cuckoo's Nest* (1962). Some of the book was written during his night shifts at the hospital, and, according to the author, some parts were written while he was under the influence of peyote. In 1963, Kesey moved to La Honda, fifteen miles from Palo Alto, and his mountain home there became the gathering place for a band of his friends who were dubbed The Merry Pranksters, a group devoted

Neal Cassady and Ken Kesey (shirtless at center) with the Merry Pranksters (photograph by Ted Streslinsky)

to day-glo paint, rock-and-roll music, and drug use. At La Honda, he completed his novel *Sometimes a Great Notion* (1964). Two years later Kesey was arrested for possession of marijuana.

The leading voice of the Beat Generation, Jack Kerouac, described the devastating effects of his long-term alcoholism in *Big Sur* (1962) and *Satori in Paris* (1966), which cover the years 1960 to 1965. Kerouac's life-style as much as his writing put a generation on the road to drugs, sex, alcohol, jazz, and fast automobiles. In the late 1950s there was scarcely a coffee house in any major American city in which his name was not spoken with reverence. Some of his greatest fans had even read his books. Kerouac died an alcohol-related death in 1969, still bitter about the indifferent critical reception of his works and his inability to be accepted into the pantheon of serious and important writers. Kerouac wrote one of his best-selling novels, *The Subterraneans* (1958), in three stimulated nights on benzedrine. The story of his love affair with a black woman, it received little serious critical attention and was purchased by some who did not read it but carried it about with them to set before them, not on *coffee tables* but on coffee-*house* tables.

Benzedrine, mescaline, marijuana, morphine, opium, peyote, Seconal, Dem-erol, Miltown, and LSD stock an impressive medicine cabinet. But, as this country is told so often by a variety of groups from MADD and SADD to those defending the rights of the cannabis culture, America's drug of choice is, and always has been, alcohol.

Teachers of courses in American literature at the university level often threaten to teach a course in great American alcoholics, only to discover that they already are. If one were to take all the works by alcoholics out of American literature, it would be tantamount to taking works by consumptives and homosexuals out of British literature; there would not be much left. Heavy drinking will not make one a great writer; yet even the most cursory student of America's national literature may ask why so many great American writers, including four of the seven who have won the Nobel Prize for literature, were alcoholics or reformed alcoholics. The roll is instructive:

Maxwell Bodenheim
Truman Capote
Raymond Chandler
John Cheever
Hart Crane
William Faulkner
F. Scott Fitzgerald
Dashiell Hammett

Ernest Hemingway
Jack Kerouac
Ring Lardner
Sinclair Lewis
Jack London
Edna St. Vincent Millay
John O'Hara
Eugene O'Neill
Dorothy Parker
Edgar Allan Poe
William Sydney Porter (O. Henry)
James Whitcomb Riley
Edwin Arlington Robinson
William Seabrook
George Sterling
Tennessee Williams
Thomas Wolfe

There is nothing funny about alcoholics or alcoholism. It is the case, however, that drinkers, novice or experienced, on occasion do things that are instructive, informative, and even entertaining. Obviously, the amount of alcohol that individual writers consumed varied at different times in their lives. Almost all of them at one time or another attempted to go on the wagon.

Sinclair Lewis could polish off a quart of brandy a day. Jack London reached and passed the quart-of-whisky-a-day mark. John O'Hara's drinking reached a bottle a day at its peak. William Faulkner could consume a bottle of Jack Daniel's a day, and on at least one occasion drank a full case of bourbon in less than a week.

Edgar Allan Poe and F. Scott Fitzgerald led perhaps two of the most tragic lives in American literature, and not just because Poe was dead at age forty and Fitzgerald at forty-four. Both were profoundly affected by the illnesses (of very different kinds) of their wives. Both went on the wagon; both fell off. Poe joined the Sons of Temperance on 27 August 1849 but forgot his teetotal vows in the final weeks before his death in 7 October of that same year. Fitzgerald, who was trying to pay off his debts, had to stay sober, or try to, to hold a position in Hollywood as a screenwriter in

the late 1930s. His fall from the wagon got him run out of Hanover, New Hampshire, where he had been sent by Walter Wanger to collaborate with Budd Schulberg on a film about the Dartmouth Winter Carnival, and is recorded in Schulberg's novel *The Disenchanted* (1950). Both Poe and Fitzgerald were poor drinkers who should never have tasted a drop.

Poe had a very low tolerance for alcohol. One glass of wine would go to his head and little more than that got him drunk. Apologists suggest that Poe did not consume great quantities of alcohol and got drunk infrequently. Scholars who are familiar with the alcoholic as a type recognize the pattern in his life. How much is too much varies from writer to writer, but alcohol was dangerous for Poe, and even a little bit was too much for him. After the death of his wife, Virginia Clemm Poe, in 1847 at the age of twenty-four, Poe drank too much. He might remain horribly drunk for three weeks at a time, only to end up reciting *Eureka* (1848) for the edification of the patrons of taprooms. His courtship of Sarah Whitman was doomed by the fact that before he showed up at her home five days before Christmas 1848 to make final preparations for their wedding, Poe and some friends had caroused all over Providence, Rhode Island. When he finally got to the Whitman home, he was noticeably drunk.

Fitzgerald, who also had a low tolerance for alcohol, has ironically become, in popular mythology at least, the archsymbol of the alcoholic Jazz Age. The Roaring Twenties seem typified in the images of Scott and Zelda Fitzgerald, both intoxicated, jumping into the fountain at the Plaza Hotel in Manhattan or riding on the tops of taxis. Fitzgerald's life is matched by the Janus-faced coin of the decades of the 1920s and 1930s. The drunken "good times" were balanced by hangovers, arrests for public intoxication, hands that shook so badly Fitzgerald could not light a cigarette, hospitalization, and a half-hearted attempt at suicide. The story of the early rise and abrupt fall of his literary reputation, as well as his personal fortunes, is an apt emblem of those two decades. As the celebrations of the 1920s ended, Fitzgerald's life during the 1930s encompassed enough pathos, irony, and agony to make his biography one of the saddest records of an American literary life since Poe's.

Ernest Hemingway found it hard to think of Fitzgerald as a drunkard since he was affected by such small quantities of alcohol. The master tough guy thought of himself as a two-fisted drinker and, compared to Fitzgerald, Hemingway had a hollow leg. He could hold his booze, and there was a lot of it to hold. When drinking, he could be arrogant, offensive, abusive, and nasty. He might set off a barroom brawl in Key West or seek out a bare knuckle fight in the Bahamas–although it has been pointed out that he usually fought older and smaller men. Then again Hemingway would get into altercations–with Max Eastman, Wallace Stevens, and others–while sober. With years of drinking, however, would come hypertension, mild diabetes mellitus, and an enlarged liver. Yet Hemingway could be a warm and amusing drunk–generous with friends. He may still hold (–or may not; such things are fragile) the world's record for consuming the most double daiquiris at a single sitting–sixteen.

Raymond Chandler was a periodic drunk. One of the things that drove him to drink was writing movies. When Paramount needed the screenplay for *The Blue Dahlia* in a rush, Chandler insisted that he could write it only when drunk. He required Paramount to provide around-the-clock secretaries, nurses, and limousines standing by to run errands and deliver his pages to the studio. The assignment was completed on time and won Chandler a 1946 Academy Award nomination for the best original screenplay.

Faulkner was of a family and a South-ern male tradition, in which the consumption of alcohol was expected. Both his father and grandfather were heavy drinkers, and as a young boy Faulkner was permitted to finish off the remains of his grandfather's toddies. In the mid 1920s, he worked for a bootlegger running a launch from New Orleans down the Industrial Canal into the Gulf where he would pick up raw alcohol. He said that "civilization began with distillation," and "there is no such thing as bad whisky. There's just some whiskies better than others." In Hollywood, he had bouts in which he matched phenomenal drinkers such as Frederick Faust (author of *Destry Rides Again* under the pen name Max Brand) glass for glass, Faulkner's bourbon against Faust's dark rum. Faulkner's capacity for consuming alcohol was legendary. There was, to be sure, a lifelong series of drying-out sessions, but the writer had tremendous recuperative powers.

As with most drinkers, there was a light side and a dark side to his alcohol consumption. Once, in Hollywood, Faulkner "went on the wagon," that is, he abstained from drinking bourbon. His version of abstinence included having seven or eight bottles of beer before 7:30 A.M., and then drinking nothing the rest of the day. Concerned about keeping his employment while he had been drinking heavily, he hired a man in a black suit to walk two or three feet behind him with a small black bag containing a bottle of bourbon, which he presented to Faulkner upon request. The man in the black suit turned out to be a nurse hired by Faulkner for the weekend to see that he got to work on Monday. Faulkner's daughter Jill has told the story of the day of her sixteenth birthday when she asked that he not get drunk. Faulkner's response was that "nobody remembers Shakespeare's daughter."

Another Nobel Prize winner who was unable to control his drinking was the first American to win the prize for literature, Sinclair Lewis. He would sleep for long periods in his clothes or fall asleep in the middle of lunch or a conversation and awake suddenly refreshed. He could write for several days and nights in a row without sleep. On occasion, he would go on benders, drinking for thirty-six hours with very little sleep. These sprees would be followed by a trip to Bill Brown's Training Camp, well known for the speedy if temporary rehabilitation of drunkards. Moreover, Lewis had a reputation as a nuisance drunk. He was known to drink all day and in the evening attend a posh dinner party, where he would leap up and walk behind the chairs of the other guests and heap abuse on the gathered company. He would then collapse and be put to bed. On one occasion in 1932, when he was refused admittance to a nice New York City bar because he was intoxicated, he sat outside on the street curb and said, "What's the use of winning the Nobel Prize if it doesn't even get you into speakeasies?"

One of the most tragic stories of alcoholic dissipation is that of Maxwell Bodenheim, author of *Replenishing Jessica* (1925) and *Naked on Roller Skates* (1930). By 1935, he was forced to live on relief, and throughout the 1940s his life was an alcoholic chaos. After his second wife died in 1950, Bodenheim married a much younger woman, Ruth Fagan, with whom he lived in the most squalid conditions and sold his poems to strangers in Greenwich Village often in return for drinks. During a drinking bout on 6 or 7 February 1954, Bodenheim was shot and killed by a friend who then stabbed Ruth to death (see Finales).

Not all drinking adventures end tragically. When Samuel Clemens (Mark Twain) was a reporter in Virginia City, Nevada, he and Charles Farrar Browne (Artemus Ward) held a Christmas Eve drinking spree that ended with the two of them walking arm-in-arm over a string of roof tops. The police might have shot them as burglars had not Twain's editor, Joe Goodman, stepped in and identified the inebriated pair.

For every Sinclair Lewis there is an Upton Sinclair. Sinclair was a total teetotaler, perhaps because his father, a salesman for a liquor company, and three of his uncles fell victim to the wares the father purveyed. His father died in delirium tremens in a public hospital. The only alcohol to pass Sinclair's lips was an occasional Sunday sip from the communion cup. To him, the best champagne tasted like apple juice. Sinclair's long correspondence with H. L. Mencken was punctuated by a series of disagreements political and otherwise, but at base, they argued over the pernicious effects, or benefits, of alcohol. Mencken's attacks upon prohibition, his defense (and appreciation) of wine and distilled spirits (not to mention good German beers) grated upon the abstemious Sinclair. He dubbed Mencken "the champion of the American saloon" and wondered what other contributions the brilliant mind of Mencken might have made had it not been so occupied by the trivia of brands, vintages, and lagers. Mencken, for his part, believed that Sinclair was too preoccupied with the dangers of the products of the vintners', brewers', and distillers' arts.

Sinclair's preoccupation led him to write *The Cup of Fury* (1956), the thesis of which is that great writers are great not because of alcohol, but in spite of it. He recounts the downward spiral of Ambrose Bierce, "an eminent tankard man"; Jack London's alcoholism; and Stephen Crane's steady drinking. Sinclair describes the deterioration of novelist-playwright Susan Glaspell's relation with her husband George Cram Cook, because of his heavy drinking, a story Glaspell herself had told thirty years before in *The Road to the Temple* (1926). Also portrayed are the last years in the life of William Sydney Porter, who had to be watched, helped to sober up, and forced to sit down and work. Sinclair concludes by recommending *Asylum* (1935) and *No Hiding Place* (1942) by William Seabrook, which describe that author's confinement for alcoholism.

The Cup of Fury is perhaps the most strident temperance work worth reading since Walt Whitman published his first book, *Franklin Evans; or, The Inebriate: A Tale of the Times*, in 1842. In Sinclair's book, no one who becomes immersed in the cup of fury ever escapes, but not every American writer lost the battle with John Barleycorn. Two of American literature's best writers were heavy drinkers who successfully quit. John O'Hara and Eugene O'Neill overcame what the Irish call "a good man's failing." Both began drinking early in their lives, not with particularly salubrious results.

During his less than nine months at Princeton in 1906-1907, O'Neill was noted as a drinker, having on one occasion drained a full bottle of absinthe in a single evening (with some bizarre results). The culmination came when, faced with suspension, he dropped out of school (see Schooldays). In the years after he left Princeton, O'Neill drank steadily. In 1910 he sailed for South America as a seaman and ended up in Buenos Aires, where it became evident that he was actually trying to drink himself to death. On his return to New York City in June 1911, he took a room above a saloon and drank steadily with his friends and other sailors. He had no job; his chief associates were derelicts, drunks, and prostitutes, and the main interest of his life was alcohol. It was finally O'Neill's commitment to playwriting and his dedication to the cause of American drama that slowed his drinking. Even after the success of his initial plays and the first of four eventual Pulitzer prizes in 1920, O'Neill still drank heavily at times. In November of 1923, O'Neill took his weekend house guests Hart Crane and Malcolm Cowley into the cellar of his house in Ridgefield, Connecticut, where there were three fifty-gallon casks of homemade hard cider. Cowley went to bed after midnight leaving O'Neill and Crane drawing pitchers of the cider. They continued drinking through the next day. Then O'Neill vanished. His frantic wife went to New York City in search of him and found him a week later in the back room of one of his old haunts, the Hell Hole, where he had drunk himself into a coma. On New Year's Day 1925 O'Neill quit drinking. He was thirty-seven years old, and, aside from an occasional bottle of ale with his dinner, although he lived to be sixty-five, he never drank again.

O'Neill came from a family of heavy drinkers; John O'Hara's father was a teetotaler. O'Hara was "regarded as a difficult drinker at a time when inebriety was a national pastime." During the 1920s he lost a position as a reporter for the *New York Herald Tribune* and a job with RKO Studios in New York because he showed up too drunk to work and missed an average of one day a week when he was too hung over to work. O'Hara's heavy drinking, which continued through the 1940s, often turned him into a profane and violent drunk. In 1953 O'Hara's stomach lining was perforated by an ulcer, and he hemorrhaged severely. Warned by physicians that any more drinking would kill him, he thought he might go on the wagon—"at least for a year." There was another event, however, that intervened. On 9 January 1954 O'Hara's beloved second wife, Belle, died. That night he poured a bottle of whisky down the kitchen sink and, though he lived until 1970, he never again took a drink.

What in the nineteenth century Nathaniel Hawthorne called "the Good Creature," in "My Kinsman, Major Molineux," would become in the twentieth century what Hemingway called "the giant killer," in both "The Short Happy Life of Francis Macomber" and "The Gambler, The Nun, and The Radio." Norman Mailer, the *enfant terrible* of American letters and heir apparent to Hemingway's heavyweight crown of American literature, says that you know you have had enough to drink when a "carelessly lit match sent you up in flames."

Finales:
How American Writers Died; Where They're Buried; Epitaphs and Last Words

by RONALD BAUGHMAN

The subject of death has elicited from writers responses ranging from the eloquent to the banal, from the lofty to the commonplace, from the truly poignant to the blatantly sentimental. Authors, particularly poets, have searched for the exact adjective to describe death: it has been viewed as "fearful" and "dusty" (Shakespeare), "beauteous" (Vaughan), "eloquent, just, and mighty" (Raleigh), "easeful" (Keats), "Sane and sacred" (Whitman), and "a maggoty minus and dumb" (E. E. Cummings). Moreover, death frequently assumes human parts: an "icy hand" (Shirley), "an earthly cold hand" (Shakespeare), a "dull cold ear" (Gray), "arms of cool-enfolding" (Whitman), "desultory feet" (Rossetti), "ribs" (Milton), and "jaws" (Tennyson).

Located in a multitude of sites–in a "dark vale" (Sir Owen Seamen), in "dens and shades" (Milton), "in the valley of the shadow" (the Bible)–death, which should "be not proud" (Donne), appears in many guises: as "the enemy" (Virginia Woolf), "a slave's freedom" (Nikki Giovanni), "the least of all evils" (Bacon), an "untimely frost" (Burns), a "slumber" (Shelley), "the poor man's friend" (Edward FitzGerald), and the "stroke of a lover's pinch" (Shakespeare). Furthermore, death bears a "pale flag" (Shakespeare), rides a "pale horse" (the Bible), has "an imperishable wing" (Rossetti), casts a "shadow at the door" (Edmund Blunden), "hath so many doors" (Beaumarchais), "opens unknown doors" (Masefield), and appears in "ranks" (Thomas Moore).

The descriptions that follow–of the deaths of writers, their final resting places, their last words–attempt to capture the variety of experience and response as individual men and women confront their own mortality. Yet a line from James Dickey's "For the Last Wolverine"–"Lord, let me die, but not die out"– provides a fitting epitaph for all these writers: though they had to die, their work lives on.

DEATH BY NATURAL CAUSES

In this section are sketches of the final days of writers who died from natural causes. Information about their burial sites, epitaphs, last words, and/or deathbed works is also included. Whether unusually dramatic or quietly ordinary, details of the deaths of these authors often reveal much about their characters and lives. But, as Theodore Roosevelt wrote in a 12 March 1900 letter, "Death is always and under all circumstances a tragedy, for if it is not, then it means the life itself has become one."

LOUISA MAY ALCOTT
(29 November 1832-6 March 1888)

Burial Site: Sleepy Hollow Cemetery, Concord, Massachusetts

In 1888 Alcott's health declined dramatically, requiring that she live in a rest home, Dunreath Place in Roxbury, Massachusetts. On Sunday, 4 March 1888, she left the home to attend her seriously ill father, Bronson Alcott, who passed away during her visit. The journey to her father's bedside and his death took their toll on her, and she wrote, "Shall I ever find the time to die?" Two days later she did die, without family members to comfort her, at Dunreath Place. Father and daughter were buried in the family plot during a single funeral service. Louisa May was interred at the foot of her parents' graves near two of her sisters who had served as models for Beth and Meg in her novel *Little Women* (1868-1869). Her grave is decorated each year for her services as a civil war nurse.

NELSON ALGREN
(28 March 1909-9 May 1981)

Burial Site: Oakland Cemetery, Sag Harbor, Long Island, New York

A writer who consistently shunned the literary establishment and whose characters were primarily outcasts from society, Algren was nonetheless pleased to be elected late in his life to the American Academy and Institute of Art and Letters. Kurt Vonnegut, Jr., and Peter Matthiessen had planned a celebration at Algren's home in Sag Harbor in honor of his induction. When Algren had severe chest pains and his doctor insisted that he go to a hospital, the novelist refused, saying, "I can't, they're throwing a party for me." Before the party, his body was found on the bathroom floor of his house by a friend,

Roy Finer, a New York City homicide detective.

At the time of his death, Algren was working on *The Devil's Stocking*, his first novel in twenty-five years and a work that had stirred only perfunctory interest from potential publishers. Moreover, he had left Chicago, the city in which he had spent most of his life and which appears prominently in his fiction. About Chicago, he had said, "Never did a writer do more for a city and never did a city repay him more meagerly. I'd been fed up with Chicago for years before I left. I was treated like a nonperson there. I never got invited to speak at the local universities, never got included on TV talk panels. I would have liked that kind of attention."

Novelist Irwin Shaw made an Algren-like statement when he heard of his friend's death: "It's not so bad. He'd just won a big award and he was about to mix drinks at a party. Now he won't have to wash the glasses."

CHARLES BROCKDEN BROWN
(17 January 1771-22 February 1810)

Burial Site: Friends Burial Ground, Philadelphia, Pennsylvania

During his last three years, Brown's life was marked by tragedy, notably the deaths of his sister Elizabeth, of his brother Joseph, and of his father-in-law. His own health was also declining rapidly. While on a journey through New Jersey, he was wracked by coughing attacks. He returned home to Philadelphia on 10 November 1809 and was confined to bed, clearly in the final stages of advanced tuberculosis. A sea voyage was planned, but he died before he could undertake the journey. At his death he was editor of the semiannual *American Register, or General Repository of History, Politics, and Science*, which he had founded in 1806, and was preparing a two-volume "System of General Geography," a statistical, topographical, and descriptive survey of the earth.

RAYMOND CHANDLER
(23 July 1888-26 March 1959)

Burial Site: Mount Hope Cemetery, San Diego, California

Outwardly a charming and witty man, Chandler was often inwardly reclusive and sad. He frequently relied on alcohol to bolster his wit as well as to relieve his sadness. His wife, Pearl Eugenie Hurlbert, whom he called Cissy, was seventeen years his senior; he adored her although he endured insensitive comments about their age difference. When Cissy died at the age of eighty-four on 12 December 1954, Chandler was consumed with grief; he tried to shoot himself with a pistol in February 1955, and he had to be hospitalized for alcoholism and suicidal depression.

In April Chandler traveled to England. There he enjoyed a celebrity status he had never received in America. He was invited almost daily to lunches and to dinner parties, which at first were a healthy tonic for him. Soon, however, the social demands became tiring. The following September he returned to New York, where he continued to drink heavily and again had to be hospitalized for exhaustion and severe malnutrition as the result of his drinking.

When in 1959 he proposed marriage to Helga Greene and she accepted, Chandler's prospects improved. He intended to work on a new Philip Marlowe novel, and Greene convinced him to travel from California to New York to accept the presidency of the Mystery Writers of America. They had intended to go on to England, but Chandler returned to his home in La Jolla alone and again drank excessively. On 23 March 1959 he was taken to La Jolla Convalescent Hospital with pneumonia. His condition worsened rapidly and he was rushed to the Scripps Clinic, where he died at 3:50 in the afternoon on 26 March.

STEPHEN CRANE
(1 November 1871-5 June 1900)

Burial Site: Evergreen Cemetery, Hillside, New Jersey
Epitaph: Stephen Crane–Poet–Author–1871-1900

While Crane was living at Brede Place in Sussex, England, his tuberculosis was complicated by malaria contracted when he was a war correspondent in Cuba in 1898. Taken to a sanitarium in Badenweiler, Germany, he gave deathbed instructions to a friend, Robert Barr, for the completion of *The O'Ruddy*; Barr promised to finish the work according to the author's intentions. It was also to Barr on 5 June 1900 that Crane uttered his final words: "Robert–when you come to the hedge–that we must all go over–it isn't so bad. You feel sleepy–you don't care. Just a little dreamy anxiety–which world you're really in–that's all." Crane's body was taken to a London mortuary for a week of viewing. In mid-June, Cora Crane, his common-law wife, and Helen Crane, his niece, accompanied his remains to New York and then to Hillside, New Jersey.

Cora tried to provide endings for some of Crane's unfinished stories, such as "The Man from Duluth" and "The Squire's Madness." In 1902 she made arrangements for the publication of *Last Words*, a collection of short pieces from Crane's papers. Barr finished *The O'Ruddy* and the work appeared in 1903.

EMILY DICKINSON
(19 December 1830-15 May 1886)

Burial Site: The family plot in West Cemetery, Amherst, Massachusetts
Epitaph: Called Back

Throughout much of her adult life, Dickinson was dominated by fear–of people, of God, of life, and of death. After 1862 she dressed only in white, a color associated with bridal purity and with death, and from 1865 on she remained for the most part in her upstairs room. When visitors came to see her, she often hid behind a screen or listened from an adjoining room to their conversation with other household members.

One of Dickinson's persistent themes in her 1,775 poems was the presence of death, personified usually as a male caller: "Because I could not stop for Death–/He kindly stopped for me–/The Carriage held but just Ourselves–/And immortality." In 1884, while sitting up with a dying relative in her brother's home, she suffered a chill leading to three later attacks that she labeled "revenge of the nerves." Her doctor diagnosed her illness as "nervous prostration," though later scholars have determined that she may have suffered from Bright's disease, a kidney ailment which reduced her energy over the last year and one-half of her life and which led to her death on 15 May 1886. In January 1885, she had received a gift of Hugh Conway's novel *Called Back*, the title of which haunted her and which supplied her epitaph.

Nearly two-thirds of Dickinson's poems, which she stitched together in packets and placed in a camphorwood chest, were written in a seven-year period, but only eight of these works were published during her lifetime. Col. Thomas Wentworth Higginson and Dr. Josiah T. Holland recognized her poetic talents, but both advised her to keep her works to herself because, as Holland declared, they were "not suitable for publication." Only her friend Helen Hunt Jackson encouraged her to publish her poetry; yet when Dickinson submitted verse for an anthology Mrs. Jackson was compiling, both Holland and Mrs. Jackson changed the poet's wording without consulting her. These alterations so upset Dickinson that she never again released her poetry to publishers. After Dickinson's death, her sister, Lavinia, burned many of the poet's papers, as she had requested. But when Lavinia discovered the large cache of poems in the camphorwood chest as well as in other repositories throughout the poet's room, she decided not to destroy them. Instead, she resolved to have these works published, a project that was begun on 12 November 1890,

when the first volume of Dickinson's poetry, edited by Higginson and Mabel Loomis Todd, appeared. The first complete edition, *The Poems of Emily Dickinson*, three volumes edited by Thomas H. Johnson, was published in 1955.

HILDA DOOLITTLE (H. D.)
(10 September 1886-28 September 1961)
Burial Site: The family plot, Nisky Hill Cemetery, Bethlehem, Pennsylvania
Epitaph (from her poem "Epitaph"):

Hilda Doolittle Aldington
Sept. 10, 1886-Sept. 28, 1961
So You May Say
Greek Flower; Greek Ecstasy
Reclaims Forever

One Who Died
Intricate Song's Lost Measure.

A variety of illnesses plagued Doolittle throughout her life. Nonetheless, she resolutely continued writing poetry and became one of the central figures in the Imagist movement. In 1956 she slipped on a highly polished wooden floor and broke her hip, an injury from which she never fully recovered. Five years later she suffered a stroke that made her speech nearly incomprehensible. Doolittle died at her home near Zurich, Switzerland, with her long-time friend Bryher (Winifred Ellerman) at her side. Earlier that same day she had received an advance copy of her final long poem, *Helen in Egypt* (1961).

THEODORE DREISER
(27 August 1871-28 December 1945)
Burial Site: Forest Lawn Memorial Park, Glendale, California
Epitaph:

Oh space!
Change!
Toward which we run so gladly
Or from which we retreat in terror
Yet that promises to bear us in itself
Forever.
Oh, what is this that knows
The road I came?

On 21 December 1945, Dreiser told a

Theodore Dreiser's
gravestone

friend that he felt as if he were "the lone-liest man in the world," but he perse-vered in his writing, finishing all but the last two chapters of his novel *The Stoic* at 5:00 A.M. on 27 December. On the morning of the 28th, he awoke at 3:00 A.M. and told Helen, his wife, that he had an intense pain. He then collapsed. He rested in bed throughout the day; his doctor and a clergyman looked in on him. Finally, he asked his wife to kiss him and died of a heart attack at 6:50 P.M.

Throughout his life, Dreiser had cam-paigned against the tyranny of capital-ists who, he believed, oppressed the poor. He had applied for membership in the Communist party, which denied his request, and in his will he directed Helen to leave part of his $100,000 es-tate to a Negro orphanage of her choos-ing. Although Dreiser hated displays of affluence, Helen, for unknown reasons, decided that he should be buried in California's Forest Lawn, one of Ameri-ca's symbols of opulence. He was buried elaborately in Lot 1132 of the Whisper-ing Pines section, quite close to the grave of cowboy actor Tom Mix. The fu-neral had to be postponed for a few days, however, because of a gravedig-gers' strike—a touch that Dreiser might have applauded.

When told that the novelist had died, town officials in his native Terre Haute,

Indiana—who generally regarded him as an immoral and un-American writer—indicated that he would soon be forgot-ten, unlike his brother Paul, who had written the music for the state song "On the Banks of the Wabash" and for whom a bronze plaque had been erected. That Theodore Dreiser had written the lyrics for the same song did not modify the citizens' opinion of him, and no memorial yet honors the novel-ist in his hometown. Among Dreiser's posthumous publications are *The Bul-wark* (1946) and *The Stoic* (1947). His epi-taph is drawn from his poem "The Road I Came."

RALPH WALDO EMERSON
(25 May 1803-27 April 1882)

Burial Site: Sleepy Hollow Cemetery, Con-cord, Massachusetts
Epitaph:

The passive Master lent his hand
To the vast soul that o'er him
planned.

Throughout his life Emerson main-tained a philosophical optimism that did not leave him until, perhaps, his final months. Within his family he had borne several painful deaths: of his brother Charles (1835), of his beloved first wife, Ellen (1845), and, possibly most devastat-ing of all, of his five-year-old son, Waldo (1842), for whom he had written this epitaph: "The hyacinthine boy for whom Morn well might break and April bloom." Despite his bereavements, Emerson could say, "I grieve that grief can teach me nothing."

Yet his friends and admirers grieved as they witnessed his physical and mental decline during his final months. He became confused about ordinary events and could not remember people with whom he had been intimate. Henry Wadsworth Longfellow's death and funeral in March 1882 upset him, but a few weeks later, when his son Edward read Longfellow's "The Midnight Ride of Paul Revere" aloud to his father, Emerson did not recall who the author was or that he had heard the poem before. He died at 9 P.M. on 27 April 1882. Emerson's epitaph comes from his poem "The Problem."

Gravestone for F. Scott and Zelda Fitzgerald

WILLIAM FAULKNER
(25 September 1896-6 July 1962)

Burial Site: St. Peter's Cemetery, Oxford, Mississippi
Epitaph: Beloved go with God

During June 1962 reviews of Faulkner's recently published novel *The Reivers* began to appear, but they were not as positive as he had hoped. In the early morning hours of Sunday, 17 June, he saddled one of his favorite horses, Stonewall, and went riding by himself. The horse was easily startled, and on this ride he threw Faulkner, who landed hard on his back and could not at first get up. When the riderless Stonewall appeared at the house, family members began a search and ultimately found the novelist struggling to walk along Old Taylor Road. Faulkner's back injury persisted, and he repeated a familiar routine of drinking heavily to relieve his suffering. On 5 July he checked into Wright's Sanitarium in Byhalia, Mississippi. A few moments past 1:30 A.M. on 6 July, Faulkner suddenly sat up in bed and then fell back after suffering a coronary occlusion. He was dead within an hour.

Out of respect to its most famous citi-zen, Oxford closed the shops around its town square–the setting for the final scene of *The Sound and the Fury* (1929)–during the funeral services on 8 July. Faulkner's epitaph, which was selected by his brother John, comes from "My Epitaph," the last poem in William Faulkner's verse collection *A Green Bough* (1933). The writer lies with four generations of his family in a plot marked "Falkner."

F. SCOTT FITZGERALD
(24 September 1896-21 December 1941)

Burial Site: Saint Mary's Church Cemetery, Rockville, Maryland
Epitaph: So we beat on, boats against the current, borne back ceaselessly into the past.

While his wife, Zelda, alternated between stays in Highland, a mental hospital in Asheville, North Carolina, and her home in Montgomery, Alabama, Fitzgerald lived during 1939 and 1940 in Hollywood, working on screenplays and the novel that was to be his last major work, *The Last Tycoon* (1941). There he became romantically involved with Sheilah Graham, a gossip columnist. In late November 1940, Fitzgerald experienced a fainting sensation at Schwab's drugstore. He had suffered a heart attack and was confined to bed, where he devised a writing board that allowed him to work a few hours each day.

On 20 December Fitzgerald worked on the seventeenth episode of his novel and then went to dinner and a movie premiere with Sheilah Graham. Leaving the theater, he experienced another dizzy spell and had to be helped to his car. The following day, while resting after lunch in a easy chair, he made notes in a copy of the *Princeton Alumni Weekly* about the football team. He suddenly leapt to his feet, lurched for the mantelpiece, and fell dead.

Fitzgerald had wished to be buried in a family plot at Saint Mary's Church, Rockville, Maryland, but the bishop of the Baltimore diocese would not give his permission since Fitzgerald had not been a practicing Roman Catholic at his death. Instead, the novelist was interred at the Rockville Union Cemetery.

After her husband's death, Zelda Fitzgerald spent much of her time with her family in Montgomery but returned during periods of acute depression to Highlands. On 10 March 1948 the hospital building in which she slept caught fire, killing her along with eight other patients. She was buried beside her husband in Union Cemetery. In 1975, F. Scott and Zelda Fitzgerald were reinterred at Saint Mary's at the request of the church, fulfilling the novelist's wishes. The epitaph on their gravemarker, selected by their daughter Scottie, is the last line of *The Great Gatsby* (1925).

ROBERT FROST

(26 March 1874-29 January 1963)

Burial Site: Old Bennington Cemetery, Bennington, Vermont
Epitaph: I had a lover's quarrel with the world

In December 1962 Frost had operations for cancer of the prostate and of the bladder. Then in late December and early January he suffered three pulmonary embolisms. While he was recovering from his second embolism, he learned that he had won America's most prestigious award for poetry, the Bollingen Prize, news that greatly improved his spirits. Following his third embolism on 7 January 1963, Frost could not have visitors, but he started to write a sequel to his 1962 Christmas poem, "The Prophets Really Prophesy as Mystics, The Commentators Merely by Statistics." Blood clots reached his lungs on the night of 28 January; he soon lost consciousness and died about 2 o'clock the next morning. A private memorial service was held on 31 January, followed by a large public ceremony on 17 February. In June 1963 the poet's ashes were buried in the Frost family plot at the Old Bennington Cemetery. Frost's epitaph is drawn from his poem "The Lesson for Today" (1942), the final lines of which read:

> And were an epitaph to be my story
> I'd have a short one ready for my
> own.
> I would have written of me on my
> stone:
> I had a lover's quarrel with the world.

ZANE GREY

(31 January 1872-23 October 1939)

Burial Site: Altadena, California
A record-holding deep-sea fisherman, Grey traveled extensively on fishing expeditions and installed a weighted exercise device in his home to help him keep in shape for the sport. After a morning workout with this apparatus, he suffered a fatal heart attack. His death received worldwide attention, for he had become one of the world's most successful authors, with sales of his books exceeding twenty-seven million copies in his lifetime.

DASHIELL HAMMETT

(27 May 1894-10 January 1961)

Burial Site: Arlington National Cemetery, Arlington, Virginia

Hammett—who early in his career was an agent for the Pinkerton's Detective Agency and who later, during the McCarthy era, was vilified as a left-wing political activist—served a six-month jail term in 1951 for contempt of court after refusing to answer questions about the Civil Rights Congress bail fund, for which he had acted as chairman. Following his release from federal prison, he sometimes lived in a small gatehouse attached to a friend's estate in Katonah, New York, and on other occasions resided with playwright Lillian Hellman on Martha's Vineyard. Poverty-stricken and ill, he started but then abandoned a novel he called "Tulip" (the unfinished work was later published in the Hellman-edited collection *The Big Knockover* [1966]). Dying from lung cancer in a New York City hospital, Hammett, who had been in the army during both world wars, was granted his request to be buried in Arlington National Cemetery.

NATHANIEL HAWTHORNE
(4 July 1804-19 May 1864)

Burial Site: Sleepy Hollow Cemetery, Concord, Massachusetts

After his return from Italy in 1860, Hawthorne appeared physically robust, but his health declined rapidly for inexplicable reasons, and he steadfastly refused to see doctors. While on a journey with former president Franklin Pierce, Hawthorne's illness forced him to be confined to bed in a hotel, the Pemigewasset House in Plymouth, New Hampshire. As if fulfilling his persistent literary theme of human isolation, he died among strangers, except for Pierce. Before his death, Hawthorne had been at work on four romances: "The Ancestral Footstep" and "Dr. Grimshawe's Secret" (two variations on the same story); "Septimus Felton"; and "The Dolliver Romance." A copy of "The Dolliver Romance" was carried on his coffin to his grave. "The Dolliver Romance" was serialized in the *Atlantic Monthly* in 1864 and 1871 and then published in book form in 1876. "Septimius Felton" appeared in 1872, and Hawthorne's son, Julian, edited and published "Dr. Grimshawe's Secret" in 1883.

HENRY JAMES
(15 April 1843-28 February 1916)

Burial Site: City of Cambridge Cemetery, Cambridge, Massachusetts
Epitaph:

> Henry James O. M.
> Novelist—Citizen
> of Two Countries
> Interpreter of his
> Generation on both
> Sides of the Sea

During the summer of 1915 James became a British citizen after having lived in England for forty years. He decided to change his citizenship because he wanted easy access to his home, Lamb House in Rye, an area that was declared off limits to aliens when World War I broke out. After becoming a British subject, James fell ill, and in October, while staying at Lamb House, he suffered heart irregularities. On 2 December, at his London apartment in the Carlyle Mansions, he had a stroke. Reporting on the experience to a friend, he claimed that his first thoughts were, "So it has come at last—the Distinguished Thing." His maid later declared that she had heard him say, "It's the beast in the jungle, and it's sprung."

Confined to his bed in London, James became more and more an invalid. Friends in England, including Prime Minister Herbert Asquith, drafted a petition to give him the Order of Merit, an honor that was announced on 1 January 1916. Telegrams from all over the world arrived at his apartment, as did well-wishers. When the King's representative presented the award to him, James said to his maid, "Turn off the light so as to spare my blushes."

During his final months, James's bed

was placed near a window so that he could view the Thames below. He enjoyed watching the boats pass but in his confusion sometimes thought that he too was on a ship bound for foreign cities. Calling often for paper and pen, he passed his hand over the page as if writing, and he frequently dictated letters to his secretary, who recorded his sometimes confused communications. At one point he adopted the persona of Napoleon Bonaparte and repeated with near perfect accuracy two of the general's letters.

On 24 February 1916 James lapsed into unconsciousness after a night of terrifying dreams, and on the afternoon of the 28th he died. Because arrangements could not be made for Westminster Abbey, his funeral was held in Chelsea Old Church, and his body was cremated at Golders Green. James's sister-in-law, the widow of William James, smuggled his ashes through British Customs, since she was fearful that war restrictions might not allow for such cargo to travel out of the country. She took the writer's ashes to America, where they were buried beside the graves of his mother and sister.

JAMES JONES
(6 November 1921-9 May 1977)

Burial Site: Sagaponack, New York

After being hospitalized in Southampton, New York, for congestive heart failure aggravated by bronchitis, Jones used a tape recorder to dictate parts of his final book, *Whistle*. He managed to finish all but the last three and one-half chapters of the planned thirty-four-chapter novel. After Jones died, his friend Willie Morris completed the book, following an outline and Jones's carefully recorded instructions. *Whistle* was published on 22 February 1978.

Jones had once requested that his body be cremated and that his ashes be scattered off the coast of Florida. However, his friends and neighbors Irwin Shaw and Peter Matthiessen secured permission to have his ashes interred in the old cemetery bounded by Sag Main Street and Montauk Highway, near Jones's home in Sagaponack, New York.

JACK KEROUAC
(12 March 1922-21 October 1969)

Burial Site: The family plot of his third wife, Stella Sampas Kerouac, Edson Cemetery, Lowell, Massachusetts
Epitaph: He honored life

A life of restless wandering, difficult relationships, and heavy drinking and drug use took its toll on Kerouac. On Monday, 20 October 1969, as he was carrying his notebook, an open can of tuna, and a glass of whiskey to his chair in front of the television set, Kerouac began hemorrhaging internally. His liver had failed, and his chest and throat were filling with blood. He underwent surgery in a St. Petersburgh, Florida, hospital but died eighteen hours later without recovering consciousness. Two of Kerouac's books, *Pic* (1971) and *Visions of Cody* (1972), were posthumously published.

SINCLAIR LEWIS
(7 February 1895-10 January 1951)

Burial Site: Greenwood Cemetery, Sauk Centre, Minnesota

While living in Italy, Lewis experienced an attack of delirium tremens and was rushed by ambulance to the Clinica Electra on the outskirts of Rome. While resting in bed on 10 January 1951, he turned to the window and saw the dawn breaking. "There, the sun," he said, and died soon afterward.

Lewis's ashes were returned to his hometown in Minnesota, although no one knew the writer's intentions in that regard; he had left instructions in his will, but various officials would not allow Lewis's companion, Alexander Manson, to read the document. Sauk Centre, the town that Lewis had bitterly satirized as Gopher Prairie in *Main Street,* was a possibly uncomfortable resting place for him. Lewis had written a warm remembrance of the town for his high-school class's fiftieth anniversary, but he had never forgotten how he had been ridiculed and rejected as a young boy and adult in the town. Yet when he died, the town fathers eulogized him, renamed for him the street where his family home had stood, and established an annual celebration in his honor.

When the urn with the novelist's ashes arrived in Sauk Centre, it was placed in a First National Bank vault until funeral arrangements could be made. On the day of the burial, according to Lewis's biographer Mark Schorer, a two-foot square hole was axed out of the frozen Minnesota earth. The writer's brother, Dr. Claude Lewis, decided, however, that the urn should not be interred but instead should be kept in the public library as a lasting memorial. At the gravesite, Dr. Lewis knelt, unsealed the container, and poured its contents into the earth. The day was bitterly cold and windy, and gusts of wind blew some of the ashes across the landscape. One witness was heard to say, "Red Lewis scattered over eighty acres of Stearns County."

ROBERT LOWELL
(1 March 1917-12 September 1977)

Burial Site: Dunbarton, New Hampshire

After spending two weeks in Dublin, Ireland, where he visited his estranged third wife, Caroline Blackwood Lowell, their six-year-old son, and Mrs. Lowell's daughter, Lowell flew back to New York City. At Kennedy Airport he took a taxi to the Manhattan apartment of his second wife, novelist Elizabeth Hardwick, from whom he had been divorced in the early 1970s. While in the taxi Lowell suffered a massive heart attack. Arriving at Hardwick's apartment house, the driver unsuccessfully attempted to revive his passenger and then drove to the nearby Roosevelt Hospital, where Lowell was pronounced dead on arrival.

Earlier in September Lowell's final collection of poems, *Day by Day*, had been

published, and on 19 January 1978, this volume was named winner of the National Book Critics Circle Award for poetry.

CARSON MCCULLERS
(19 February 1917-29 September 1967)

Burial Site: Oak Hill Cemetery, Nyack, New York

Beginning with her senior year in high school, when she was stricken with rheumatic fever, McCullers led a life of physical and emotional suffering. She endured many serious illnesses: a cancerous right breast that had to be removed, bouts of acute depression and failed suicide attempts, shattered legs and arms, and crippling strokes, one of which virtually paralyzed her left arm for the last twenty years of her life. Her marital experience proved to be a source of both joy and pain for her; three years after she and Reeves McCullers married on 20 September 1937, they separated and eventually divorced, only to remarry and then separate again. This pattern of unity and estrangement continued until Reeves McCullers committed suicide in a Paris hotel on 19 November 1953. On 15 August 1967, Carson McCullers suffered a massive brain hemorrhage and remained comatose for forty-seven days, dying without regaining full consciousness on 29 September in the Nyack Hospital. She was buried the day after filming began on the movie version of her acclaimed novel *The Heart is a Lonely Hunter* (1940).

FRANK NORRIS
(5 March 1870-25 October 1902)

Burial Site: Mountain View Cemetery, Oakland, California

Soon after they were married, Norris and his wife planned a European voyage, which had to be canceled when Mrs. Norris suddenly became ill with appendicitis. After she was released from the hospital, Norris himself experienced abdominal pain. Identifying his discomfort as indigestion, Norris failed to seek immediate medical help. He died at the age of thirty-two of peritonitis caused by a perforated appendix.

Norris's novel *The Pit* ran in the *Saturday Evening Post* from 20 September 1902 to 21 January 1903, but only six installments had appeared before he died. The book was published posthumously on 15 January 1903.

CLIFFORD ODETS
(18 July 1906-14 August 1963)

Burial Site: Forest Lawn Memorial Park, Glendale, California

Like some intellectuals of the time, Odets became during the 1930s a member of the Communist party, and, like Dashiell Hammett, he was called to testify about his leftist politics before the House Un-American Activities Committee in the early 1950s. That he was buried in Forest Lawn, the epitome of capitalistic grandeur, seems highly ironic.

While he was dying of cancer, Odets was preparing a musical version of his play *Golden Boy* (1937), which, after William Gibson completed the scripting, was produced in 1964. In addition, convinced that television was a vehicle for reaching an enormous audience, he was working on *The Richard Boone Show*, a television drama series that debuted after Odets's death.

JOHN O'HARA
(31 January 1905-11 April 1970)

Burial Site: Princeton Cemetery, Princeton, New Jersey
Epitaph:
> Better
> Than Anyone Else
> He Told the Truth
> About his Time
> He Was
> A Professional
> He Wrote
> Honestly and Well.

On the night of 10 April 1970, while working on a sequel to *The Ewings*, a novel he had completed in February of

John O'Hara's gravestone

that year, O'Hara experienced pain in his left arm and chest. He left his typewriter after composing this sentence, his last, on typescript page 74: "Edna had not suspected him, and now his affair with Alicia was a thing of the past." O'Hara told his wife that he was going to bed, and she checked on him through the night and next morning. At 1:30 P.M., she found him dead.

O'Hara's epitaph was selected by his wife from his own self-assessment during a 1961 interview. Among his posthumously published works are *The Ewings* (1972), *The Time Element* (1972), and *Good Samaritan* (1974). O'Hara's complete study—his desk, lamps, books, and papers—was given to and reconstructed in the Pennsylvania State University Library in 1974.

THOMAS PAINE
(29 January 1737-8 June 1809)

Burial Site: None

As the author of *Common Sense* (1776) and *The American Crisis* (1776-1783), Paine was one of the most important voices of the American Revolution. He had been declared a traitor to his native England, had served a prison sentence in France, and, finally, had been denied American citizenship because of his controversial views. He died in poverty in a New York City lodging house after many clergymen had denounced his views and after repeated assassination attempts had been made on him. The only mourners present during his burial on his New Rochelle, New York, farm were a French woman and her two small sons, a Quaker watchmaker, and two black gravediggers.

Yet, even in death, Paine found no rest. An eccentric English pamphleteer, William Cobbett, exhumed Paine's body in 1819 and took the remains to England, planning an elaborate memorial for Paine that never materialized. Cobbett bequeathed Paine's body to his son in 1835; but when the younger Cobbett declared bankruptcy, the remains were seized by the courts and then lost forever.

In 1839 a monument was erected to Paine in New Rochelle. It bears this inscription:

"The world is my country;
To do good my religion."
Thomas Paine
Author of
Common Sense

Born in England, January 29, 1737
Died in New York City, June 8, 1809
"The palaces of kings are built upon the ruins of the bowers of Paradise."

—Common Sense

JOHN REED
(22 October 1887-17 October 1920)

Burial Site: The Kremlin Wall, Moscow, Russia

Born into a well-to-do family in Portland, Oregon, Reed graduated from Harvard. He wrote poetry and served

as a reporter for the *American Magazine* in 1911 and two years later for the *Masses*. Reed's growing interest in social problems of the working class had led to his work on the *Masses* and to his friendship with Lincoln Steffens, a prominent American Socialist.

While covering events of World War I, Reed observed and supported the October Revolution in Russia, but when he returned to the United States, his radical views were attacked and he was jailed. Becoming estranged from the Socialist movement in this country, he established the American Communist party in 1919, directed its newspaper *The Voice of Labor,* and wrote an American Communist manifesto. When he attempted to return to the United States after a second journey to Russia, he was denied admission; going back to Russia, he lived and worked there until he was stricken with typhus and died shortly before his thirty-third birthday.

The Russians, who considered Reed's book *Ten Days That Shook the World* (1919) one of the best analyses of their revolution, gave him a hero's funeral. Guarded by fourteen Red Army soldiers, his body lay in state for a week in Moscow's Labor Temple. Reed is the only American whom the Soviets have granted the honor of burial in the Kremlin Wall.

THEODORE ROETHKE
(25 May 1908-1 August 1963)

Burial Site: The family plot, Oakwood Cemetery, Saginaw, Michigan

Throughout his life Roethke experienced manic-depressive states that often made his personality and behavior wildly eccentric. Physically, he was imposing. Although he was overweight, he was an excellent dancer, an enthusiastic tennis player, and a fine swimmer. Perhaps his general athleticism explains why friends relaxing beside a backyard swimming pool were unconcerned when he dived into the water. A few minutes later they discovered him floating face down in the pool, dead of a heart attack.

DELMORE SCHWARTZ
(8 December 1913-11 July 1966)

Burial Site: Cedar Park Cemetery, Paramus, New Jersey

While carrying out his garbage, Schwartz suffered a fatal heart attack in a hallway of his run-down Times Square hotel. His final ten years had been filled with paranoia, anxiety, loneliness, and despair. After a *New York Times* reporter recognized Schwartz's name during a routine check of morgue listings, the *Times* on 14 July 1966 presented a long obituary along with a photograph of the poet. That afternoon, Schwartz's aunt, who had been notified by family friends, came to assume responsibility for the body. Many of Schwartz's papers were recovered only through a chance meeting in a bar between critic Dwight Macdonald's son and the owner of a moving company that had stored the material.

JOHN STEINBECK
(27 February 1902-20 December 1968)

Burial Site: His ashes were scattered into Whaler's Bay from Point Lobos, California, on the day before Christmas

As a correspondent for *Newsday*, Steinbeck reported on the Vietnam War, and he traveled extensively throughout the Far East. His only injury occurred in Hong Kong as he helped a Chinese man push a hand truck loaded with beer. His gesture of goodwill seriously damaged one of his spinal discs. On 8 October 1967, difficulties with his back caused him to be hospitalized, and on 23 October he underwent nearly five hours of surgery for the ruptured disc. While convalescing at home in Sag Harbor, New York, in July 1968, he suffered a stroke and later a series of heart failures. His health steadily declined until on 20 December he went into a coma. Rousing at one point, he said, "I seemed to hear the sound of distant drums." He then murmured, "Maybe it's just Shirley [a family friend] playing the bagpipes." He died soon after these remarks.

HENRY DAVID THOREAU
(12 July 1817-6 May 1862)

Burial Site: Sleepy Hollow Cemetery, Concord, Massachusetts

On a bitterly cold 3 December 1860, Thoreau caught a bad cold while studying tree-growth patterns in Inches' Woods in Boxboro, Massachusetts. His cold worsened and eventually was the cause of his death nearly eighteen months later. In the spring of 1861, his doctor recommended that he seek a warmer climate to relieve what was now severe bronchitis. Instead, Thoreau traveled to the Middle West after learning about the supposedly therapeutic value of Minnesota's dry air. On 10 May 1861, along with Horace Mann, Jr., the seventeen-year-old son of the well-known educational reformer, Thoreau set out for an intended three-month stay in the Minnesota countryside. After less than two months, however, Thoreau's health deteriorated so rapidly that the two returned to Concord.

Back in his own home, Thoreau continued to work as industriously as he was able, lecturing and writing, although he was now fully aware that he would never recover. In the spring of 1862 relatives and friends visited frequently while Thoreau lay dying. Visitors invariably commented on his cheerfulness. They also discussed with him his thoughts about his mortality. Parker Pillsbury, an antislavery orator, asked him about his attitude toward the next life, to which Thoreau replied, "One world at a time." When Edmund Hosmer, a Concord farmer, pointed out the arrival of an early robin, Thoreau said, "Yes. This is a beautiful world; but I shall see a fairer." Thoreau's Aunt Louisa Dunbar asked him if he had made his peace with God; to which Thoreau replied, "I did not know we had ever quarreled, Aunt." His only discernible last words were "Moose" and "Indian." Thoreau was buried in the New Burying Ground in Concord, and then later interred in the Sleepy Hollow Cemetery.

There is a flower known to botanists, one of the same genus with our summer plant called "Life Everlasting," a Gnaphalium *like that, which grows on the most inaccessible cliffs of the Tyrolese mountains, where the chamois dare hardly venture, and which the hunter, tempted by its beauty, and by his love, (for it is immensely valued by the Swiss maidens,) climbs the cliffs to gather, and is sometimes found dead at the foot, with the flower in his hand. It is called by botanists the* Gnaphalium leontopodium, *but by the Swiss,* Edelweisse, *which signifies,* Noble Purity. *Thoreau seemed to me living in the hope to gather this plant, which belonged to him of right. The scale on which his studies proceeded was so large as to require longevity, and we were the less prepared for his sudden disappearance. The country knows not yet, or in the least part, how great a son it has lost. It seems an injury that he should leave in the midst his broken task, which none else can finish,—a kind of indignity to so noble a soul, that it should depart out of nature before yet he has been really shown to his peers for what he is. But he, at least, is content. His soul was made for the noblest society; he had in a short life exhausted the capabilities of this world; wherever there is knowledge, wherever there is virtue, wherever there is beauty, he will find a home.*

—*from Emerson's graveside eulogy to Thoreau*

WALT WHITMAN
(31 May 1819-26 March 1892)

Burial Site: Harleigh Cemetery, Camden, New Jersey

During the spring of 1887, Whitman suffered his second stroke in four years. At the time he was at work on *November Boughs*, which contained "A Backward Glance O'er Travel'd Roads," a summary of his literary theories. Since early 1887 Horace Traubel had visited Whit-

Death mask of Walt Whitman, by Thomas Eakins and Samuel Murray (courtesy of the Houghton Library, Harvard University)

man two and three times a day. In addition to assisting the poet with the publication of *November Boughs* (1888) and *Good-Bye, My Fancy* (1891), a collection of poetry and prose pieces, Traubel recorded nearly every word Whitman uttered during his last thirty-nine months. Again with help from Traubel, the poet prepared what is now known as the deathbed edition of *Leaves of Grass* (1892).

On 17 December 1891 Whitman was ordered to bed because of a severe chill. Death seemed imminent and funeral plans were made, but the poet rallied and survived until the following March. In his final days he expressed a longing for death, which came on 26 March at approximately 6:40 in the evening. Whitman was buried in a Quincy granite mausoleum based on William Blake's drawing for *The Gates of Paradise*, a monument that the American poet had specifically requested.

WILLIAM CARLOS WILLIAMS
(17 September 1883-4 March 1963)

Burial Site: Hillside Cemetery, Lyndhurst, New Jersey

Toward the end of his life, Williams suffered a series of cerebral hemorrhages that eventually left him unable to read, write, or talk. He tried to type messages, but this task proved difficult, for his memory was so impaired that he often could not remember how to spell words or how to finish sentences. In perhaps his last note to anyone, he wrote to his longtime friend and publisher James Laughlin, "You have been very faithful, it is deeply appreciated. I wish I could write as I could formerly."

Williams posthumously received the Pulitzer Prize for *Pictures from Brueghel and Other Poems* in April 1963, and in May 1963 he was awarded the Gold Medal of the National Institute of Arts and Letters.

THOMAS WOLFE
(3 October 1900-15 September 1938)

Burial Site: Riverside Cemetery, Asheville, North Carolina
Epitaph: Tom / son / W. O. and Julia E. / Wolfe / A Beloved American Author / Oct. 3 1900-Sept. 15, 1938 / The Last voyage, the longest, the best / –Look Homeward, Angel / Death bent to touch his chosen son with / Mercy, love, and pity, and put the seal / Of honor on him when he died./–The Web and The Rock

While touring the Pacific Northwest in June 1938, Wolfe joined two men, one a newspaper man and the other an executive for the Oregon State Motor Association, in a publicity effort to encourage tourism in national parks. They determined to travel to twelve parks in fourteen days; they succeeded in visiting eleven in thirteen days. Their journey was exhausting. On 5 July, Wolfe decided to travel to Vancouver by coastal steamer. While he was on board, a passenger who appeared to be suffering from influenza shared a flask of whiskey with the novelist. On Saturday, 9 July, Wolfe became sick with a bad cold that turned into pneumonia; he was hospitalized with a temperature of 105 degrees that remained at that level for three days.

Two months later, X-rays detected a spot on his lungs, and in September he underwent surgery for tuberculosis at Johns Hopkins Hospital. Doctors later decided that during some point in his early years, Wolfe had contracted tuberculosis but that he had cured himself. His attack of pneumonia–with its beginnings in the shared whiskey bottle infected with influenza–reopened the t.b. lesions, sending the bacteria into his bloodstream and eventually into his brain. On Tuesday, 13 September 1938, Wolfe went into a comma; he died two days later at 6:30 A.M. of tuberculosis of the brain. A special coffin had to be built to accommodate his six-foot six-inch body.

In 1932, Wolfe had started a novel that dramatized the lives of characters on a train journey home. The working title for the book was *K-19*, designating the train number. Wolfe's editor, Maxwell Perkins, convinced Wolfe to abandon the project in favor of other writing. Six years later, family members placed Wolfe's coffin on a Baltimore train bound for Asheville. When the train left the station, Edward Aswell of *Harper's* noted that a sign in one of the train windows had the Pullman designation "K-19" printed on it.

The most famous symbol in Wolfe's work is the angel that appears in the title of his first novel, *Look Homeward, Angel* (1929), and that is a recurring figure throughout the book. The angel, which suggests the creative visions of protagonist Eugene Gant and of his father, evolves into a death image when associated with Eugene's dying brother, Ben. The angel figure is based on actual monuments that Wolfe's gregarious, hard-drinking father worked on in his tombstone cutting shop. The elder Wolfe ordered the structures from Italy and then carved names and dates in their bases. Many people have assumed that Thomas Wolfe's grave is marked by one of the angel monuments, but it is not. One such angel does exist in a cemetery in Hendersonville, North Carolina, however.

RICHARD WRIGHT
(4 September 1908-28 November 1960)

Burial Site: Père Lachaise Cemetery, Paris, France

Best known as the author of the novel *Native Son* (1940) and the memoir *Black Boy* (1945), Wright became an expatriate in Paris following World War II. Because of his involvements with the Communist party when he was younger,

he often believed that he was being pursued by the FBI and CIA. In November 1960 symptoms of grippe and a fever forced Wright to seek treatment at the Clinique Chirurgicale Eugène Gibez in Paris. Physicians at the clinic pronounced him cured, and during his last night there, Wright rested easily, satisfied that he would soon be back to work. However, as he reached up to turn out the light over his head, he suddenly died. The writer's long-held suspicions of American enemies and the unexpectedness of his death have fueled speculation by Constance Webb, his biographer, that he may have been the victim of foul play. Wright's body was cremated, along with a copy of *Black Boy*, and his ashes were deposited in creche #4596 at Père Lachaise Cemetery.

ACCIDENTAL DEATHS, MURDERS, SUICIDES, WAR CASUALTIES

The discussions of these writers' final days attempt to provide a measure of explanation for their deaths, although causes are often not completely discernible, particularly in the cases of those who chose to end their own lives. Many of these writers died at the pinnacles of their literary careers, a fact which makes their deaths seem even more inexplicable. Perhaps the Polish novelist Henryk Sienkiewicz provided the most appropriate comment, especially for self-inflicted deaths, when he declared, "To whom life is heavy, the earth will be light."

SHERWOOD ANDERSON
(13 September 1876-8 March 1941)

Burial Site: Roundhill Cemetery, Marion, Virginia

In February 1941 *Reader's Digest* employed Anderson to write a series of sketches about ordinary people of South America. While on a ship bound for the area, Anderson and his wife ate hors d'oeuvres. Soon after eating, he was stricken with severe abdominal pains and taken to a hospital in Colon, Panama, where he died eight days later of abdominal congestion and peritonitis, presumably from having swallowed a

toothpick. In the Ohio town where Anderson had operated a factory before becoming a writer, the *Elyria Chronicle-Telegram* announced his death in this headline: "Sherwood Anderson, Former Elyria Manufacturer, Dies."

JOHN BERRYMAN
(25 October 1914-7 January 1972)

Burial Site: Resurrection Cemetery, Mendota Heights, St. Paul, Minnesota

Berryman was constantly haunted by the suicide of his father, John Allyn Smith, on 26 June 1926. Five years later, when he was a seventeen-year-old student at South Kent School in Connecticut, Berryman himself attempted suicide after being bullied by classmates; and, although he believed that his afflictions enhanced his creativity, he was compelled to seek treatment for alcoholism and for psychological problems throughout his adult life.

On Friday, 7 January 1972, Berryman told his wife, Kathleen Donahue Berryman, that he intended to clean his office at the University of Minnesota–adding, "You won't have to worry about me any more." He went to the Washington Avenue Bridge over the Mississippi River, and at approximately 9:30 A.M. walked to the west end of the bridge, climbed the railing on the north side, and jumped, falling nearly one hundred feet to the embankment below. Police identified him by his name printed on the bow of his glasses and by a blank check in his billfold.

Berryman was given a Roman Catholic funeral at St. Francis Cabrini Church, where he had been attending Mass. Before he died he had been at work on a novel and a book of poems. His collection of poetry, *Delusions, Etc.*, was published in 1972, and his novel, *Recovery*, and a volume of essays and stories, *The Freedom of the Poet*, appeared in 1973.

AMBROSE BIERCE
(24 June 1841-1913?)

Burial Site: Unknown

Associated with a group of writers, including George Sterling, who viewed suicide as part of the artist's role, Bierce frequently promised that he would take his own life before he was seventy years old. In December 1913 he traveled to Texas and perhaps to the Grand Canyon. He was last known to have been in Chihuahua, Mexico, on the day after Christmas 1913, and indicated in a Christmas letter that he intended to go further south. He then disappeared somewhere in the Mexican desert. Rumors about his cause of death have persisted. One view held that financial ruin drove him to suicide. Another, more persistent speculation maintained that Bierce had joined Pancho Villa's army in the border war between Mexico and the United States and that the writer had been killed in battle. Yet another view held that he had died at the hands of Mexican bandits.

MAXWELL BODENHEIM
(6 May 1892-6 or 7 February 1954)

Burial Site: Cedar Park Cemetery, Oradell, New Jersey

A once-promising poet, playwright, and novelist, Bodenheim became during the 1940s an alcoholic skid-row bum, begging for money for drink and food and selling his poems in the streets. In 1951 he met Ruth Fagan, an attractive woman in her thirties who also had a history of mental illness; as a young girl she had set fire to her parents' home. Bodenheim and Fagan, who may have married, lived together in one cheap hotel after another.

In 1953 a third skid-row bum, Harold Weinberg, joined them, forming a precarious triangle. Weinberg, twenty-five, had been discharged from the army for mental problems and had a history of arrests. He was sexually attracted to Fagan, who was alternately drawn to and repelled by him. The trio frequently quarreled, and at one point Weinberg severely cut Bodenheim's arm with a knife; yet they remained together. On the night or early morning of 6 or 7 February 1954, following a drunken argument, Weinberg shot Bodenheim in the heart and then, struggling with Fagan, stabbed her to death with a hunting knife. After his arrest and conviction, Weinberg was confined to a hospital for the criminally insane.

WILLIAM CULLEN BRYANT
(3 November 1794-12 June 1878)

Burial Site: Roslyn Cemetery, Long Island, New York

Bryant had been suffering from a bad

cold and had confided to a minister friend that he felt extremely lonely, tired, and ill. While walking up the stone steps fronting the home of writer and Civil War general James Grant Wilson, the eighty-three-year-old Bryant became faint and fell backward, hitting his head against the steps. Refusing medical help, he insisted that he be taken home. Yet when he stood before his own front door, he inquired, "Whose house is this? What street is this?"

According to his attending physician, Bryant had suffered a severe concussion that ordinarily would have killed its victim. Bryant remained in bed but suffered hemorrhaging that left him semiconscious and unable to speak. He died in his sleep on 12 June 1878 at 5:30 A.M.

JOHN HORNE BURNS
(7 October 1916-11 August 1953)

Burial Site: Holyhood Cemetery, Brookline, Massachusetts

Although his biographer, John Mitzel, denies them, rumors have persisted that Burns's death was a suicide. While the novelist was living in Leghorn, Italy, his volatile homosexual relationship with an Italian doctor ended abruptly. Burns went sailing, suffered a severe sunburn, fell into a coma, and died about six hours later from a cerebral hemorrhage. He was buried in Florence, Italy, a city he loved. However, his parents, with whom he had strained relationships, insisted that he be buried at home with Roman Catholic rites, and in late August 1953 his body was disinterred and shipped to Boston.

HART CRANE
(21 July 1899-27 April 1932)

Burial Site: None

During the last year of his life, with funds from a Guggenheim Fellowship, Crane lived in Taxco, Mexico, in a community of artists. Although he continued to write, he was often in trouble with authorities for public drunkenness and homosexual encounters with young Indian boys. When Peggy Cowley–separated from her husband, literary critic Malcolm Cowley–arrived in Taxco, she and Crane became romantically involved. Crane was exuberant about his presumably first heterosexual affair, but their relationship proved to be a stormy one. Nonetheless, Crane and Mrs. Cowley planned to return to New York City to marry.

Before they left Mexico, the poet drank heavily and threatened suicide. While two of Mrs. Cowley's friends visited, Crane repeatedly announced that he would drink iodine, although the women easily prevented him from doing so. On another occasion, he had to have his stomach pumped to remove Mercurochrome. Despite these episodes, Crane worked on a review of Phelps Putnam's *The Five Seasons* for *Poetry*, and he began one of his best poems, "The Broken Tower."

Crane was often violent, provoking fights and smashing anything he could, and these drunken scenes usually were followed by desperate searches for homosexual assignations. His guilt after these encounters often drove him to further drunkenness and further sexual excesses. While aboard the *Orizba* bound for New York, for example, he was beaten by ship hands whom he had tried to seduce.

On the morning of 27 April, Crane became extremely upset with Mrs. Cowley. While other passengers on the ship watched, he tried to climb the railing but was pulled back by a steward and locked in his cabin, where he drank heavily. Before noon, Crane escaped from his cabin and went to Mrs. Cowley's room; he was dressed in his pajamas and a coat. Peggy Cowley urged him to put on proper clothes, but he replied, "I'm not going to make it, dear. I'm utterly disgraced." When she persisted with requests that he ready himself for lunch, he replied, "All right, dear. Goodbye." Those were Crane's last known words. He kissed Mrs. Cowley and then left her cabin. A few moments before noon, he threw off his coat, climbed the railing, and jumped overboard 275 miles north of Havana. Although four lifeboats were lowered and remained in the area for two hours, Crane was not seen again.

HARRY CROSBY
(4 June 1898-10 December 1929)

Burial Site: His wife, Caresse, took Crosby's ashes with her to Europe, where they were lost.

During the last eight years of his life, Crosby frequently voiced a fascination with death, particularly with taking his own life. While a member of the American Ambulance Corps in World War I, Crosby had been known for his daredevil willingness to confront danger, and after the war he continued his zeal for the dangerous.

This sense of daring, friends of his suggested, may have led to the murder-suicide pact he entered into with one of his mistresses, Josephine Rotch Bigelow. The day before their deaths, Mrs. Bigelow had given Crosby a poem that concluded "Death is *our* marriage." On Tuesday, 10 December 1929, Crosby and Bigelow went to the apartment of Stanley Mortimer, a friend of theirs, in the New York Hotel des Artistes. There they removed their shoes and stretched out on a bed. Crosby placed the barrel of a .25 caliber Belgian pistol to Mrs. Bigelow's left temple and fired, killing her instantly. Evidence indicated that Crosby held her in his arms and then, two hours after her death, put the pistol to his own forehead and shot himself.

FREDERICK FAUST (MAX BRAND)
(29 May 1892-11 May 1944)

Burial Site: Nettuno-Anzio American Cemetery, Italy

The creator of the Dr. Kildare and Tom Mix novels, which evolved into highly popular movie, radio, and television productions, Faust became a widely read and successful writer. Orphaned at thirteen, he achieved lavish financial success that went well beyond his expectations; yet he did not manage money well and was often pressed to pay outstanding debts. He owned a villa in Florence, Italy, cruised the islands of Greece, suffered bouts of alcoholism, and engaged in many love affairs. While a screenwriter in Hollywood, Faust worked with such writers as William Faulkner, Ayn Rand, and Dalton Trumbo. When the United States entered World War II, Faust used his influence to become a war correspondent, sending his dispatches to the North American Newspaper Alliance, which directed his reports primarily to *Harper's Magazine*.

Assigned to the 88th Infantry Division, the 351st Second Battalion, "E" Company, Second Platoon, Faust volunteered to be in the first assault wave on 11 May 1944 in the battle of Santa Maria Infante north of Naples, Italy. Nearly fifty-two years old and plagued with a serious heart condition, Faust was nonetheless determined to record the young soldiers' initial reactions to combat by being with them as they landed. When military superiors worried about his refusal to bear arms in battle, Faust agreed to carry a club made for him from an olive branch, the irony of which was not lost on the soldiers with him. During the heavy exchange of artillery between the Allied and the Axis forces, the writer was wounded in the chest by a shell fragment. Twice he refused medical assistance, insisting that others were more severely wounded than he. When the corpsmen checked on him a third time, he was dead. The night he died, his wife, Dorothy, awoke from a dream in which her husband called to her twice. The next morning she told her family about the dream and later that day heard the radio news report announcing her husband's death. Faust was initially interred at the divisional cemetery at Carano, Italy, but later was buried at the Nettuno-Anzio American Cemetery.

The grave of Philip Freneau

PHILIP FRENEAU
(2 January 1752-19 December 1832)

Burial Site: His ancestral home near Mount Pleasant, New Jersey

"The Poet of the Revolution" and a radical democrat, Freneau was hired in 1791 by Thomas Jefferson to edit the *National Gazette*. When the *Gazette* ceased publication in 1793, he returned to his family's small farm outside Freehold, New Jersey, where he eked out a meager living by farming and editing two short-lived weekly newspapers, and from 1802 to 1807 by serving in the merchant marine. After quitting the sea, he walked nearly every day to Freehold, where he spent his time either in the library or, more often, in the Davis-Lippincott Store, which was primarily a tavern. He had applied for a pension of $35 a year, but he did not live long enough to enjoy this sum that went finally to his wife and children.

On 18 December, after having drunk a large quantity of wine, Freneau started home from the tavern. Caught

in a sudden blizzard, he froze to death and was not found until the next morning. At Freneau's grave site was erected a monument bearing a long inscription entitled "Poet's Grave."

JOHN GARDNER
(21 July 1933-14 September 1982)

Burial Site: Grandview Cemetery, Batavia, New York

During his forty-nine years, Gardner produced eleven books–novels, verse narratives, and literary criticism. Four days before he was to marry for the third time, Gardner rode his Honda 750 motorcycle north on Route 92 through Oakland Township in Susquehanna County, Pennsylvania. At about 2:30 in the afternoon, he crashed two miles from his rural home and died en route to the Barnes Kasson Hospital in Susquehanna. At the time of his death, he was serving as director of the creative writing program at the State University of New York at Binghamton.

THOMAS HEGGEN
(23 December 1919-18 May 1949)

Burial Site: Lakewood Cemetery, Minneapolis, Minnesota

Heggen's only novel, *Mister Roberts* (1946), won immediate critical and popular acclaim. It was adapted by Joshua Logan for a long-running Broadway production and later became a popular movie. The success of *Mister Roberts* earned Heggen considerable financial rewards. However, the extent of his initial achievement overwhelmed him; he was stricken with debilitating fear that he could not surpass *Mister Roberts* in his next work. Associating with a circle of artistic people in New York City, he drank heavily and squandered money and time. He underwent psychiatric treatment in hope of overcoming his writer's block and relied heavily on a variety of pills to help him sleep as well as to lessen his daytime anxieties. On the evening of 18 May, Heggen took an overdose of barbituates and, at approx-

Memorial bust of Ernest Hemingway, near Ketchum, Idaho

mately 9:30, drowned in his bathtub.

ERNEST HEMINGWAY
(21 July 1899-2 July 1961)

Burial Site: Ketchum, Idaho

Two years before his suicide, Hemingway's physical and mental health declined rapidly. In November 1960 his wife, Mary, decided that he needed extensive medical care and had him admitted to the Mayo Clinic in Rochester, Minnesota, where he was diagnosed as having diabetes, hypertension, and severe depression. In December and January he underwent a series of electroshock treatments for his depression, treatments that improved his spirits but diminished his memory.

Because of his treatments Hemingway was unable to accept an invitation to the inaugural ceremonies of President John F. Kennedy; yet he was delighted to have been asked. In February, when in-

vited to write a sentence in a presentation volume for the president, Hemingway agonized all day over the task but could not complete it.

In early April 1961 Mary Hemingway severely sprained her foot in a fall. Her accident intensified Hemingway's despair, and he had to be forcibly restrained from shooting himself. He was returned to the Mayo Clinic and given another series of shock treatments. He was released too early, Mary Hemingway felt, but the couple returned to their home in Ketchum, Idaho, on Friday, 30 June 1961. The next evening they went to dinner with friends. On Sunday, 2 July, Hemingway woke early, unlocked the gunrack, loaded a double-barreled Boss shotgun, and walked to his front foyer. He placed the gun butt on the floor and the barrels above his eyebrows and pulled the trigger.

Funeral services for Hemingway were held on 5 July in Hailey, Idaho, with his burial in Ketchum. A large, flat gravestone bearing his name and dates of birth and death was placed over his grave. A memorial bust, which was erected outside Ketchum on a bluff overlooking Trail Creek, was inscribed with words Hemingway had written and had read at the funeral of his sportsman friend Gene Van Guilder:

BEST OF ALL HE LOVED THE FALL
THE LEAVES YELLOW ON THE COTTONWOODS
LEAVES FLOATING ON THE TROUT STREAMS
AND ABOVE THE HILLS
THE HIGH BLUE WINDLESS SKIES
NOW HE WILL BE A PART OF THEM FOREVER.
– Ernest Hemingway–Idaho–1939

In 1928 Hemingway's mother had sent him a chocolate cake and the .32 caliber revolver with which his father had shot himself in the head that same year. Hemingway's sister, Ursula, killed herself in 1966, as did his brother, Leicester, in 1982.

ROBERT HOWARD
(22 January 1906-11 June 1936)

Burial Site: The Howard family plot, Greenleaf Cemetery, Brownwood, Texas
Epitaph: Howard / Robert E. / Author and Poet / 1906-1936 / They were lovely and pleasant in their lives / and in their death they were not divided.

Howard's father was a family doctor who practiced in small West Texas towns. Because Dr. Howard was often absent from home, Robert Howard became deeply attached to his mother, who read poetry and mythic stories to him. Howard was a physically weak child, and his early boyhood was plagued by beatings from schoolmates. In his teenage years, however, he pursued a regimen of body-building and soon became a powerful six-foot-tall, two-hundred-pound man. He molded himself into an actual version of the literary figure he was to create in his novels, Conan the Barbarian.

When on 11 June 1936 Howard's comatose mother was diagnosed as terminally ill, the novelist parked his car in his driveway, sat for a while in the driver's seat, and then fatally shot himself in the head. His mother died the next day.

SIDNEY HOWARD
(26 June 1891-23 August 1939)

Burial Site: The cemetery on Church Road, Tyringham, Massachusetts
After achieving financial success through his plays, Howard fulfilled his dream in 1935 of owning and operating a five-hundred-acre dairy farm in Tyringham, Massachusetts. Four years later, while working on his adaptation of Carl Van Doren's biography of Benjamin Franklin, Howard put his writing aside to harrow a nearby field. He cranked the tractor to start it, but the vehicle had been left in gear. It lurched forward, crushing him against the garage wall.

RANDALL JARRELL
(6 May 1914-15 October 1965)

Burial Site: His ashes were buried in New Garden Cemetery, Greensboro, North Carolina, near the campus of Guilford College
Epitaph: Randall Jarrell / Poet / Teacher / Beloved Husband / 1914-1965

Whether Jarrell's death was an accident or suicide is still being debated; current opinion, however, leans toward suicide. In January 1965 Jarrell slashed his left wrist and had to be hospitalized at North Carolina Memorial Hospital. In May 1965 he returned to the same hospital for treatment of manic depression. He resumed his teaching duties that fall at the University of North Carolina in Greensboro but on 10 October reentered North Carolina Memorial for further psychiatric care. His wrist wounds were also treated in October 1965 at the Hand Rehabilitation Center in Chapel Hill.

On the evening of 15 October Jarrell decided to take a walk. He headed south, facing oncoming traffic, along U.S. 15-501, a heavily used but poorly lighted highway. A few moments before 7:30 P.M. Jarrell was struck by a car. The driver, who was going approximately forty-five miles per hour, reported that the man walking beside the road seemed to hurl himself into the side of the car. Jarrell's skull was fractured, and he died less than five minutes after being struck.

VACHEL LINDSAY
(10 December 1879-5 December 1931)

Burial Site: Oak Ridge Cemetery, Springfield, Illinois
Best known for *General William Booth Enters into Heaven and Other Poems* (1913) and *The Congo and Other Poems* (1914), Lindsay spent much of his career on walking tours of the United States, during which he performed his rhythmic poetry in what he called "the higher vaudeville." In 1925 he married Elizabeth Conner, a high-school teacher whom he had met in Spokane, Washing-

ton. During this decade, however, Lindsay's waning popularity and increasing marital difficulties resulted in serious emotional problems for the poet. On 5 December 1931 these psychological strains reached their zenith, and he prepared an elaborate suicide ceremony for himself. In the middle of his dining-room table, he arranged a pillow and blanket, two lighted candles, and a circle of photographs of his wife and children. Lying inside this display of artifacts from his life, Lindsay drank a bottle of Lysol and died. He is buried near Lincoln's tomb.

ROSS LOCKRIDGE
(25 April 1914-6 March 1948)

Burial Site: Rose Hill Cemetery, Bloomington, Indiana

Lockridge began his only novel, *Raintree County*, in 1938 but abandoned it in 1939. In 1941 he returned to his manuscript and later sent it to Houghton Mifflin. Editors there were so impressed with the work that they awarded Lockridge their prize for best first novel—with the stipulation he revise large sections of his huge, five-volume work. While the novel was still unpublished, Metro-Goldwyn-Mayer named it the winner of a $150,000 prize in a contest designed to obtain new movie scripts. The studio, however, insisted on further substantial revisions before it would award the prize money. Soon afterward, the Book-of-the-Month Club chose Lockridge's work as a club selection provided he edit the novel according to BOMC specifications. Although he strongly objected to each of these demands, Lockridge acquiesced in order to gain publication and the promised rewards for his labor. He wrote and rewrote *Raintree County* and in the course of his effort suffered emotionally and physically. He underwent electroshock treatments for depression, but refused to endure the prescribed number of treatments because of his fear of them. Furthermore, his family counseled him

that hard physical exercise and continued work on his novel would more effectively resolve his difficulties. When the actual publication of the book occurred on 4 January 1947, Lockridge was too exhausted to take much pleasure in the event. Two months later he locked himself in the garage of his new home, turned on the motor of his new Kaiser, and died of asphyxiation.

JACK LONDON
(12 January 1876-22 November 1916)

Burial Site: His ashes were placed beneath a large boulder on his homesite, Beauty Ranch, near Glen Ellen, California

During his later years in California, London numbered among his friends the Piedmont writers—Ambrose Bierce, George Sterling, Joaquin Miller, and others—who advocated suicide. London's final six years were filled with anxiety about the waning reputation of his novels and about money. Increasingly he felt betrayed by friends, business associates, and nature itself. He planted thousands of eucalyptus trees and grapevines on his ranch in hopes of earning an income independent from his writing, but these crops failed. He built a large stone home, Wolf House, that was gutted by fire. On 22 November 1916, at the age of forty, he took an overdose of a prescribed medicine intended to help him sleep. Although his death certificate declared that he had died of uremic poisoning, he was more likely a suicide. London's second wife, Charmian Kittredge London, built on their ranch a second stone home, House of Happy Walls, which has become a repository for London memorabilia.

F. O. MATTHIESSEN
(9 February 1902-21 March 1950)

Burial Site: Springfield, Massachusetts

The literary critic taught at Harvard University for much of his academic career. While traveling on an ocean liner to Europe in the mid 1920s, he met the painter Russell Chaney; the two had a long but sometimes stormy homosexual relationship. In 1938 Matthiessen suffered a severe depression that included haunting suicidal visions of his jumping out of a window. When Cheney died in 1945, Matthiessen became intensely lonely and fearful about his future. Concerned friends frequently monitored his health and whereabouts, but on 31 March he checked into the Manger Hotel by the North Station in Boston and jumped from a twelfth-floor window.

On the desk in Matthiessen's hotel room were found his Yale Skull and Bones pin, his apartment keys, two three-by-five-inch notecards upon which he had written his last words, and letters to friends he had written sometime earlier. His suicide note read:

> I have taken this room in order to do what I have to do. My will is to be found on my desk in my apartment at 87 Pinckney St., Boston. Here are the keys. Please notify Harvard University—where I have been a professor.
>
> I am exhausted. I have been subject to so many severe depressions during the past few years that I can no longer believe that I can continue to be of use to my profession and my friends. I hope that my friends will be able to believe that I still love them in spite of this desperate act.
>
> F. O. Matthiessen

On the reverse side of one of the notecards, Matthiessen had written:

> I should like to be buried beside my mother in the cemetery at Springfield, Mass. My sister . . . will know about this.
>   *but not until morning*
> Please notify, Kenneth B. Murdock, . . .and Jonathan Ogden Bulkley . . . who will notify my other
>   *but not until morning*
> Yale friends . . . I would like them to

go to my apartment and to see that the letters on the desk are mailed.

How much the state of the world has to do with my state of mind I do not know. But as a Christian and a socialist believing in international peace, I find myself terribly oppressed by the present tensions[.]

MARGARET MITCHELL
(8 November 1900-16 August 1949)

Burial Site: Oakland Cemetery, Atlanta, Georgia

On 11 August 1949, Mitchell and her husband, John Marsh, drove to a movie theater at the northeast corner of Thirteenth and Peachtree Streets, Atlanta. Mitchell parked the car on the east side of Peachtree and started across the busy road with John at about 8:20 P.M. When the couple were more than halfway across, an automobile driven by an off-duty taxi driver, traveling too fast and momentarily hidden by a curve, bore down on them. Margaret Mitchell retreated, but the car skidded and veered toward her, striking her as she neared the curb she had just left. She was rushed to Grady Hospital but never regained consciousness, dying at 11:59 A.M. five days later. Her accident had created worldwide concern; telephone calls and written messages arrived from around the world, including a call from President Harry S. Truman. Her funeral was conducted at the Protestant Episcopal Cathedral, and she was buried beside her father, her mother, and a brother who had died in infancy.

FRANK O'HARA
(27 June 1926-25 July 1966)

Burial Site: Green River Cemetery, Amagansett, Long Island, New York

O'Hara was a member of a community of artists known as The New York School, which included such figures as poet John Ashbery and painters Jackson Pollock and Mark Rothko. On Saturday, 23 July 1966, O'Hara and a friend, J. J.

Mitchell, were house guests of another friend on Water Island, Fire Island, New York. That evening, O'Hara and Mitchell went to a bar-discotheque, the Fire Island Pines. At 2:00 A.M., deciding to return to their friend's home, the two boarded a beach taxi, a covered jeep, along with several other passengers. Moments later, the beach buggy damaged a rear wheel, and a replacement jeep was called for. The headlights of the stalled vehicle momentarily blinded the driver of the second jeep, and O'Hara, who stepped out in front of the fast-moving vehicle, was struck in the abdomen. He was taken to Bayview General Hospital in Mastic Beach where he underwent surgery, but died on the evening of 25 July of traumatic internal abdominal injury. At the time of his death, O'Hara was at work on a Jackson Pollock retrospective.

DAVID GRAHAM PHILLIPS
(31 October 1867-24 January 1911)

Burial Site: Kensico Cemetery, Valhalla, New York
Epitaph: On an Ionic cross are the words: "Forgive them Father, for they know not what they do."

Labeled by a reviewer in the *Bookman* "the most distinguished American novelist of his time," Phillips enjoyed critical and popular acclaim. He lived with his sister, Carolyn, throughout his adult life in a New York City apartment across from Gramercy Park.

Beginning in the summer of 1910, Phillips received a series of threatening letters from Fitzhugh Coyle Goldsborough, a man who believed that Phillips had slandered his sister in his novel *The Fashionable Adventures of Joshua Craig* (1909). Although Phillips ignored these letters, Goldsborough's convictions intensified. He rented a front room at the Rand School of Social Science on Nineteenth Street in order to watch Phillips's activities.

On Monday, 23 January, Phillips ate his breakfast at noon, as was his custom, after correcting proofs for his forthcoming novel, *Susan Lenox: Her Fall and Rise*. He then took a long walk—also his custom—stopping at the Princeton Club, which was located at the corner of Gramercy Park and Lexington Avenue. At 1:30 P.M., Goldsborough shot Phillips six times and then shot and killed himself. Phillips was rushed to Bellevue Hospital, where he remained alive until approximately eleven o'clock the next evening. Before he died, Phillips said, "I could have won against two bullets but not against six."

SYLVIA PLATH
(27 October 1932-11 February 1963)

Burial Site: Heptonstall Churchyard, Yorkshire, England
Since she was not the son her autocratic father had always wanted and since he had died after a long illness when she was eight years old, Plath suffered at an early age some of the unresolvable emotional conflicts that were to haunt her life and that led to suicide attempts and psychiatric treatment. For Plath, as for Anne Sexton, her poetry was at least in part a vehicle for gaining control over her emotional conflicts.

On 16 June 1956 she married the British poet Ted Hughes, with whom she had a daughter and a son. Later she and Hughes separated, and Plath moved to London with her two small children in December 1962. She felt that her fortunes had improved, however. She was living in an apartment house where William Butler Yeats had once stayed; her autobiographical novel *The Bell Jar* had appeared on 14 January 1963; and the BBC wanted to do a series of interviews with her. Also, she was continuing work on her *Ariel* poems. Yet on 11 February 1963 Plath blew out the pilot light on her gas oven, placed her head in the oven, and died of asphyxiation. She was thirty years old.

ANNE SEXTON
(9 November 1928-4 October 1974)

Burial Site: In her former husband's family plot, Forest Hills, Jamaica Plain, Massachusetts

Epitaph: Sexton's gravemarker, inscribed with her name and dates and with those of her father-in-law and sister-in-law, lies flat on the ground at the foot of a large, coffin-shaped monument bearing the name Sexton.

In 1954, a year after the birth of her first daughter, Sexton was hospitalized for suicidal tendencies, a pattern that was repeated in 1956, a year after the birth of her second daughter. Following her hospitalization, a psychiatrist suggested that she write poetry as a therapeutic aid, a suggestion that launched her literary career. She made repeated attempts at suicide, however, and at the height of her fame as a poet, when she was not quite forty-six years old, succeeded in killing herself.

On 4 October 1974 she invited her close friend, poet Maxine Kumin, to lunch at her home on Black Oak Drive in Weston, Massachusetts. Their lunch was pleasant, with Sexton giving no indication of what was to happen. After Kumin bade her goodbye, Sexton locked herself in her garage, sat in the front seat of her red Mercury, turned on the motor, and died of carbon-monoxide poisoning. She frequently had requested that her epitaph read "Rats Live on No Evil Star," a palindrome that she had found years earlier on the side of a barn in Ireland and that she had used as a title for one of her poems; the rat figure had also appeared as an emblem for the writer's self in other poems. Either family members or cemetery officials, however, blocked her request.

GEORGE STERLING
(1 December 1869-17 November 1926)

Burial Site: Sterling's ashes are in a six-by-nine-inch slot in a wall of the Chapel of Memorials, Oakland, California

Sterling's Carmel, California, home became the informal headquarters for the Piedmont writers, proponents of suicide as a means of, Sterling wrote, "leaving the world in a good temper when one selected the hour of one's going." A member of the group, the poet Nora May French, tried to give her lover, the novelist James Hopper, a poisoned sandwich, but she dropped it on the floor, where a pet dog ate it and immediately expired. Hopper, who apparently did not share French's enthusiasm for death, instantly left her, and French used Sterling's home to take her own life.

In 1926 H. L. Mencken notified Sterling that he would visit en route to the 17 November banquet of the Bohemian Club. Sterling, who was elated by the news, made elaborate preparations. When Mencken's arrival was unexpectedly delayed, Sterling and a friend drank much of the vintage wine purchased for the occasion. His binge caused Sterling a severe ulcer reaction and a debilitating three-day headache, which forced him to give up his role as toastmaster of the banquet. Instead of directing the club's festivities that evening, Sterling stayed in his room in the Bohemian Club and drank the contents of a vial of cyanide of potassium that he always carried with him.

SARA TEASDALE
(8 August 1884-29 January 1933)

Burial Site: Bellefontaine Cemetery, St. Louis, Missouri

Throughout her life, Teasdale's physical fragility inspired those who loved her to treat her with special consideration, beginning with her wealthy parents and extending later to three men whom she loved: John Hall Wheelock, Vachel Lindsay, and Ernest Filsinger. On 19 December 1914 she married Filsinger, a highly successful international businessman who made and sold shoes and who had a genuine interest in the arts, especially Teasdale's poetry. Teasdale and Filsinger were quite happy during their first five years together; but later

Filsinger's business dealings forced him to leave his wife alone for long periods of time. After the death of her father in 1921 and her mother in 1924, Teasdale grew deeply depressed. In 1926 she fell in love with a college student, Margaret Conklin, who had written to her about her poetry. They began living together in 1927, and in 1929 Teasdale divorced her husband. On 5 December 1931, after learning of Lindsay's suicide, Teasdale again became distraught. On 29 January 1933 she took an overdose of sleeping pills and was found dead in her bathtub.

NATHANAEL WEST
(17 October 1903-22 December 1940)

Burial Site: Mount Zion Cemetery, Maspeth, Queens, New York

In April 1940 West had married twenty-seven-year-old Eileen McKenney, model for the central character in Ruth McKenney's *My Sister Eileen* (1938), a collection of short stories later made into a popular stage play and movie. The couple were returning to Los Angeles from a hunting weekend in Mexico when they were killed in an automobile accident on a rain-slickened road in Imperial County, California. West ran a stop sign and crashed into another car. Eileen McKenney West died in the ambulance on the way to the hospital, and Nathaniel West died shortly after arriving at the hospital. Both had suffered skull fractures. West's casket, which also contained his wife's ashes, was buried in Mount Zion Cemetery in Queens.

THOMAS LANIER
(TENNESSEE) WILLIAMS
(26 March 1911-25 February 1983)

Burial Site: Calvary Cemetery, St. Louis, Missouri

Along with Eugene O'Neill, Williams, who wrote such works as *The Glass Menagerie* (1945) and *A Streetcar Named Desire* (1947), is considered to be one of America's two greatest playwrights. Williams lived a tempestuous life marked by alcohol, drugs, and homosexual encounters. In the last three years of his life, his health, always a major concern, declined rapidly. In his two-room suite in New York's Elysee Hotel, Williams choked to death on a plastic cap of the sort found on eyedrops or nasal spray, according to the coroner's report. Williams had often spoken of "cashing in," but his brother, Dakin, dismissed suicide as a possible cause of death. He is buried next to his mother, "Miss Edwina," who was the probable model for Amanda Wingfield in *The Glass Menagerie*.

MORE FINAL RESTING PLACES

The longer entries in this section describe notable monuments, epitaphs, or funeral plans, while the shorter ones provide information about where an author is buried and, in some cases, what appears on his or her gravemarker.

HENRY ADAMS
(16 February 1838-27 March 1918)

Burial Site: Rock Creek Cemetery, Washington, D.C.

After his wife, Marian, committed suicide, Adams enlisted sculptor Augustus Saint-Gaudens to design a memorial to her. Saint-Gaudens created a hooded, heavily cloaked figure that came to be known as *Grief*. When the statue was erected in Rock Creek Cemetery, a public outcry arose, for many observers felt that the figure was unchristian. The controversy surrounding the monument drew large crowds, thereby undermining the writer's intention of providing his wife a peaceful final resting place. According to his wishes, Adams was buried next to Mrs. Adams in an unmarked grave.

HORATIO ALGER, JR.
(13 January 1832-18 July 1899)

Burial Site: Glenwood Cemetery, South Natick, Massachusetts

MAXWELL ANDERSON
(15 December 1888-28 February 1959)

Burial Site: Fernhill Cemetery, Hartsdale, New York

ROBERT BENCHLEY
(15 September 1889-21 November 1945)

Burial Site: Prospect Hill Cemetery, Nantucket, Massachusetts

Benchley died in New York City of a cerebral hemorrhage. His family intended to take his cremated remains in a small bronze box to Nantucket, but when they arrived at Prospect Hill Cemetery they discovered that the box was empty. Officials at the crematorium had failed to place the humorist's ashes inside. Instead of being shocked and displeased, Benchley's wife stated, "You know, I can hear him laughing now."

ANNE BRADSTREET
(circa 1612-16 September 1672)

Burial Site: First Burial Ground, North Andover, Massachusetts

LOUIS BROMFIELD
(27 December 1896-18 March 1956)

Burial Site: Malabar Farm State Park, Lucas, Ohio

PEARL S. BUCK
(26 June 1892-6 March 1973)

Burial Site: Green Hills Farm, Perkasie, Pennsylvania
Epitaph: The Chinese calligraphy on her tombstone represents her first name: "Precious Gem."

WILLA CATHER
(7 December 1876-24 April 1947)

Burial Site: Old Burying Ground, Jeffrey Center, New Hampshire
Epitaph: (from her novel *My Antonia*): ... that is happiness; to be dissolved into something complete and great.

SAMUEL LANGHORNE CLEMENS (MARK TWAIN)
(30 November 1835-21 April 1910)

Burial Site: Woodlawn Cemetery, Elmira, New York

During his final years, Clemens endured many difficulties. Several of his financial investments proved unsound, and he was forced in 1895 to undertake an arduous world lecture tour to recoup his losses. While he was on his tour, his daughter Susy died of meningitis. During the next several years, Clemens's wife became an invalid and then died in 1904, his daughter Jean developed incurable epilepsy, and as his own health and creative powers diminished, the writer was often incapacitated by melancholy. In the midst of his personal gloom, he started the novel *The Mysterious Stranger*, begun in 1898 but not completed until much later and posthumously published in 1916.

Clemens's remark upon reading his own premature obituary–"The reports of my death are highly exaggerated"–is well known. Also familiar is his prophesy concerning his connection with Halley's Comet. The comet had appeared in the year of the writer's birth, 1835, and was expected again in 1910. Twain wrote, "It will be the greatest disappointment of my life if I don't go out with Halley's Comet. The Almighty has said, no doubt: 'Now here are two unaccountable freaks; they came in together, they must go out together.'" The novelist's gravemarker in Elmira reads:

Samuel Langhorne Clemens
Mark Twain
Nov. 30, 1835-Apr. 21, 1910

Clemens's daughter Clara erected a monument at the family home, Quarry Farm in Elmira. The memorial bears reliefs of her father and her husband, pianist Ossip Gabrilowitsch, with an inscription on the base:

> Death is the starlit strip
> Between the companionship
> Of yesterday and the reunion
> of tomorrow
> To the loving memory of
> My father and my husband
> C. C. G.   1937

And in Hannibal, Missouri, Clemens's childhood friend, best remembered for the literary character she inspired, is buried beneath this inscription: "Laura H. Frazer/'Becky Thatcher'/1837-1928"

JAMES FENIMORE COOPER
(15 September 1789-14 September 1851)

Burial Site: Christ Churchyard, Cooperstown, New York

ADELAIDE CRAPSEY
(9 September 1878-8 October 1914)

Burial Site: Her ashes, contained in an urn donated by her Vassar classmates, are at Mount Hope Cemetery, Rochester, New York

E. E. CUMMINGS
(14 October 1894-3 September 1962)

Burial Site: Forest Hills Cemetery, Boston, Massachusetts

CLARENCE DAY
(18 November 1874-28 December 1935)

Burial Site: Woodlawn Cemetery, Bronx, New York

PAUL LAURENCE DUNBAR
(27 June 1872-9 February 1906)

Burial Site: Woodland Cemetery, Dayton, Ohio
Epitaph:
Lay me down beneaf de willers in de grass

Whah de branch'll go a singin' as it pass.
An' w'en I's a-layin' low,
I kin hyeah it as it go
Singin', "Sleep, my honey, tek you' res' at las'."

Dunbar, a black poet who wrote some of his poems in Negro dialect, died from tuberculosis as he recited the Twenty-third Psalm. His mother had his body placed in a vault until spring, when he was buried beside a pool near a road. His epitaph is drawn from his poem "A Death Song" and Dunbar's mother later planted a willow tree next to his grave to reflect the landscape described in that poem. A boulder of granite with a bronze plaque was placed at the grave site in 1909.

WILLIAM DUNLAP
(19 February 1766-28 September 1839)

Burial Site: St. Peter's Church, Perth Amboy, New Jersey
Epitaph: Father of the American
Drama
Author, Poet, Writer
of 31 Plays
A Great Painter
His Paintings Hang in New York
Metropolitan Museum of Art
In the Capital, Washington
and in the Galleries
New England to the Midwest

ELLEN GLASGOW
(22 April 1874-21 November 1945)

Burial Site: Hollywood Cemetery, Richmond, Virginia
Epitaph: Tomorrow to fresh Woods, and Pastures New.
Before she died, Glasgow gave extensive instructions for her interment. She so hated her father that she demanded to be buried as far as possible from his grave. In contrast, she felt great affection for her two dogs, Jeremy, a Sealyham, and Billy, a French poodle. When they passed away she commemorated them in long obituaries for the local

newspaper and had them interred in her garden. Upon her death, according to her directions, the dogs were exhumed and placed with her in her coffin. Her epitaph is drawn from John Milton's "Lycidas."

PAUL GOODMAN
(9 September 1911-2 August 1972)

Burial Site: Stratford Center Cemetery, Stratford, New Hampshire

EDGAR A. GUEST
(21 August 1881-5 August 1959)

Burial Site: Woodlawn Cemetery, Detroit, Michigan

EDWARD EVERETT HALE
(3 April 1822-10 June 1909)

Burial Site: Forest Hills Cemetery, Boston, Massachusetts

LORRAINE HANSBERRY
(19 May 1930-2 January 1965)

Burial Site: Beth El Cemetery, Croton-on-Hudson, New York

MOSS HART
(24 October 1904-20 December 1961)

Burial Site: Ferncliff Cemetery, Hartsdale, New York

DUBOSE HEYWARD
(31 August 1885-16 July 1940)

Burial Site: St. Philip's Churchyard, Charleston, South Carolina

OLIVER WENDELL HOLMES, SR.
(29 August 1809-7 October 1894)

Burial Site: Mount Auburn Cemetery, Cambridge, Massachusetts

WASHINGTON IRVING
(3 April 1783-28 November 1859)

Burial Site: Sleepy Hollow Cemetery, North Tarrytown, New York

FRANCIS SCOTT KEY
(1 August 1779-11 January 1843)

Burial Site: Mount Olivet Cemetery, Frederick, Maryland

JOYCE KILMER
(6 December 1886-30 July 1918)

Burial Site: Oise-Aisne American Cemetery, Seringes-Sur-Nesles, France
(See Writers Who Went to War)
In 1986, to commemorate the centennial of Kilmer's birth, a ten-foot white oak tree was planted on the Rutgers University campus. It replaces the white oak that is said to have inspired Kilmer to write "Trees." That two-hundred-year-old tree had died twenty-five years before and was removed by tree surgeons.

OLIVER LA FARGE
(19 December 1901-2 August 1963)

Burial Site: National Cemetery, Sante Fe, New Mexico

MEYER LEVIN
(7 October 1905-9 July 1981)

Burial Site: Jerusalem

HENRY WADSWORTH LONGFELLOW
(27 February 1807-24 March 1882)

Burial Site: Mount Auburn Cemetery, Cambridge, Massachusetts

AMY LOWELL
(9 February 1874-1 May 1925)

Burial Site: Mount Auburn Cemetery, Cambridge, Massachusetts

JAMES RUSSELL LOWELL
(22 February 1819-12 August 1891)

Burial Site: Mount Auburn Cemetery, Cambridge, Massachusetts

CLAUDE MCKAY
(15 September 1890-May 1948)

Burial Site: Calvary Cemetery, Woodside, Queens, New York

JOHN P. MARQUAND
(10 November 1893-16 June 1960)

Burial Site: Sawyer's Hill Burying Ground, Newburyport, Massachusetts

EDGAR LEE MASTERS
(25 August 1868-5 March 1950)

Burial Site: Petersburg Oakland Cemetery, Petersburg, Illinois

COTTON MATHER
(12 February 1663-13 February 1728)

Burial Site: Copps' Hill Cemetery, Boston, Massachusetts

NATHANIEL MATHER
(1667-17 October 1688)

Burial Site: Charter Street Cemetery, Salem, Massachusetts
Epitaph: An Aged Person
That Had Seen But
Nineteen Winters
in the World

A son of Increase Mather and a brother of Cotton Mather, Nathaniel Mather died at age nineteen after publishing two almanacs. At sixteen he had graduated from Harvard College, where his father was president. In his brother's work *Magnalia Christi Americana* (1702), Nathaniel Mather was characterized in a biographical sketch entitled "Early Piety Exemplified."

HERMAN MELVILLE
(1 August 1819-28 September 1891)

Burial Site: Woodlawn Cemetery, The Bronx, New York; his tombstone bears carvings of an unrolled scroll, a quill pen, and a vine.

H. L. MENCKEN
(12 September 1880-29 January 1956)

Burial Site: Loudon Park Cemetery, Baltimore, Maryland
Epitaph: Mencken composed at least two epitaphs for himself, neither of which was used. To James T. Farrell he wrote, "Remember me to my friends, tell them

Herman Melville's gravestone

I'm a hell of a mess." In the December 1921 *Smart Set* he declared, "If, after I depart this vale, you ever remember me and have thought to please my ghost, forgive some sinner and wink your eye at some homely girl."

GRACE METALIOUS
(8 September 1924-25 February 1964)

Burial Site: Smith Meeting House Cemetery, Gilmantown, New Hampshire
After the publication of Metalious's sensational best-seller *Peyton Place* (1956), the townspeople of Gilmantown and the novelist quarreled bitterly about her fictional representation of them in the book. Metalious willed her body to the Dartmouth Medical School, but when her family objected, the medical school refused the donation. The New Hampshire Supreme Court then ruled that Metalious's burial should take place in the town where she had not been welcome and where she did not wish to remain.

KENNETH MILLAR
(ROSS MACDONALD)
(13 December 1915-11 July 1983)

Burial Site: His ashes were scattered in the Santa Barbara, California, channel, where, as he wrote in a 1973 letter to Julian Symons, "in the destructive element immersed, I have spent the best hours of my best days."

CINCINNATUS HINER–OR HEINE–
MILLER (JOAQUIN MILLER)
(8 September 1837-17 February 1913)

Burial Site: The Heights, his estate near Oakland, California

At his home north of Oakland, the eccentric poet built a masonry edifice–ten feet square and eight feet high–from 620 granite boulders set in concrete. He clearly intended the monument to himself to last forever. Three steps on the east side led to a hollow cavity near the top, and it was here that Miller wanted his body to be cremated. Oakland authorities, however, ruled that he have this service performed in the city. Thus, when Miller died, his friends deposited his Oakland-prepared ashes in the monument's cavity and then lit the crematorium fire.

CLEMENT CLARKE MOORE
(15 July 1779-10 July 1863)

Burial Site: Trinity Cemetery, New York City, New York

Carolers sing at Moore's graveside each Christmas Eve

MARIANNE MOORE
(15 November 1887-5 February 1972)

Burial Site: Evergreen Cemetery, Gettysburg, Pennsylvania

CHRISTOPHER MORLEY
(5 May 1890-28 March 1957)

Burial Site: Roslyn Cemetery, Roslyn, New York

OGDEN NASH
(19 August 1902-19 May 1971)

Burial Site: Little River Cemetery, North Hampton, New Hampshire

FLANNERY O'CONNOR
(12 August 1925-3 August 1964)

Burial Site: Memory Hill Cemetery, Milledgeville, Georgia

EUGENE O'NEILL
(16 October 1888-27 November 1953)

Burial Site: Forest Hills Cemetery, Boston, Massachusetts

MAXWELL PERKINS
(20 September 1884-17 June 1947)

Burial Site: Lakeview Cemetery, New Canaan, Connecticut

EDGAR ALLAN POE
(19 January 1809-7 October 1849)

Burial Site: Westminster Presbyterian Churchyard, Baltimore, Maryland

Poe died under mysterious circumstances. He may have been the victim of political thugs who drugged him and forced him to vote illegally in one polling place after another. The semiconscious writer was found outside a Baltimore tavern-polling site and was taken to a hospital, where he died several days later without regaining sufficient consciousness to explain what had occurred.

Poe's first burial site, which was in the rear of Baltimore's Westminster Presbyterian Churchyard, bears a marker topped by a stone relief of a raven and inscribed with the poet's most famous line, "Quoth the Raven nevermore." The marker also explains that in November 1875, Poe, his wife, and his mother-in-law were reinterred under a monument erected to him near the front of the churchyard. This monument, which was funded through gifts by school children, features a bronze cast of the writer's face.

WILLIAM SYDNEY PORTER
(O. HENRY)
(11 September 1862-5 June 1910)

Burial Site: Riverside Cemetery, Asheville, North Carolina

SOLOMON RABINOWITZ
(SHOLOM ALEICHEM)
(18 February 1859-13 May 1916)

Burial Site: Mount Neboh Cemetery, Glendale, New York

Because Aleichem had triskadekaphobia, an intense fear of the number 13, none of his manuscripts contained a page 13. Fittingly then, although he died on 13 May 1916, his gravemarker bears the inscription "May 12a, 1916."

AYN RAND
(2 February 1905-6 March 1982)

Burial Site: Kensico Cemetery, Valhalla, New York

QUENTIN REYNOLDS
(11 April 1902-17 March 1965)

Burial Site: Holy Cross Cemetery, Brooklyn, New York

JAMES WHITCOMB RILEY
(7 October 1849-22 July 1916)

Burial Site: Crown Hill Cemetery, Indianapolis, Indiana

EDWIN ARLINGTON ROBINSON
(22 December 1869-6 April 1935)

Burial Site: Gardiner Cemetery, Gardner, Maine

DAMON RUNYON
(4 October 1884-10 December 1946)

Burial Site: Manhattan

A prolific journalist and sports columnist, Runyon was best known for his amusing stories of the New York City underworld. His most famous collection was *Guys and Dolls* (1931), which inspired the successful 1950 musical play. Runyon left written instructions for the disposal of his remains: "I desire that my body be cremated and my ashes scattered over the island of Manhattan, the place that I truly loved and that was good to me." His final request was carried out by his long-time friend, flying ace Captain Eddie Rickenbacker. Walter Winchell raised large sums of money for the Damon Runyon Memorial Cancer Fund.

CARL SANDBURG
(6 January 1898-22 July 1967)

Burial Site: Carl Sandburg Birthplace, Galesburg, Illinois
Epitaph: For it could be a place to come and remember

While he was alive, Sandburg created an unusual reminder of his own heritage. In the backyard of his birthplace, he mixed soils from places he had lived with soils from his parents' Swedish birthplaces. Remembrance Rock, a red granite boulder erected by townspeople in Galesburg, rests upon earth taken from four historic locations: the Argonne (honoring American sacrifice during the World War I battle); Gettysburg; Valley Forge; and Plymouth Rock. Sandburg requested that his ashes be mixed with these soils. The boulder's name is taken from the title of his only novel, which was published in 1948; the novel also provides the line that serves as Sandburg's epitaph.

ALAN SEEGER
(22 June 1888-4 July 1916)

Burial Site: On the battlefield of Belloy-en-Santerre, France
(See Writers Who Went to War)

GERTRUDE STEIN
(3 February 1874-27 July 1946)

Burial Site: Père Lachaise Cemetery, Paris

WALLACE STEVENS
(2 October 1879-2 August 1955)

Burial Site: Cedar Hill Cemetery, Hartford, Connecticut

HARRIET BEECHER STOWE
(14 June 1811-1 July 1896)

Burial Site: Andover Chapel Cemetery, Phillips Academy, Andover, Massachusetts

JACQUELINE SUSANN
(20 August 1921-21 September 1974)

The tomb of James
Whitcomb Riley

Burial Site: Her family retained her ashes

BOOTH TARKINGTON
(29 July 1869-19 May 1946)

Burial Site: Crown Hill Cemetery, Indianapolis, Indiana

JAMES THURBER
(8 December 1894-2 November 1961)

Burial Site: Green Lawn Cemetery, Columbus, Ohio

HENRY TIMROD
(8 December 1829-6 October 1867)

Burial Site: Trinity Episcopal Cathedral Churchyard, Columbia, South Carolina

ALICE B. TOKLAS
(30 April 1877-7 March 1967)

Burial Site: Père Lachaise Cemetery, Paris
Toklas shares the tomb of her long-time companion Gertrude Stein. Her name and dates are on the reverse side of Stein's stone.

MARK VAN DOREN
(13 June 1894-10 December 1972)

Burial Site: Cornwall Hollow Cemetery, Cornwall, Connecticut

CARL VAN VECHTEN
(17 June 1880-21 December 1964)

Burial Site: His ashes were scattered in Shakespeare Garden, Central Park, New York City, New York

NOAH WEBSTER
(16 October 1758-28 May 1843)

Burial Site: Grove Street Cemetery, New Haven, Connecticut

EDITH WHARTON
(24 January 1862-11 August 1937)

Burial Site: Versailles

JOHN GREENLEAF WHITTIER
(17 December 1807-7 September 1892)

Burial Site: Union Cemetery, Amesbury, Massachusetts

THORNTON WILDER
(17 April 1897-7 December 1975)

Burial Site: Mount Carmel Cemetery, Hamden, Connecticut

EDMUND WILSON
(8 May 1895-12 June 1972)

Burial Site: Pleasant Hill Cemetery, Wellfleet, Massachusetts
Epitaph: A line in Hebrew that translates as "Be strong, be strong, and we shall strengthen one another."

MORE LAST WORDS

Since writers are masters of language, special significance is often attached to their final words. The material assembled here records, in some cases, the actual last words, written or spoken, of a dying author, and, in other cases, statements uttered or written by an author during his or her final days.

HENRY ADAMS
(16 February 1838-27 March 1919)

Adams said to his secretary, "Dear child, keep me alive."

LOUISA MAY ALCOTT
(29 November 1832-6 March 1888)

"It is meningitis?"

ROBERT BENCHLEY
(15 September 1889-21 November 1945)

During his final illness, Benchley read a book titled *Am I Thinking?* On its title page he wrote, "No. And supposing you were?"

ANDREW BRADFORD
(1686-24 November 1742)

The printer of the first American book with a two-color title page (see First Things First), Bradford said, "Oh Lord, forgive the errata!"

(BRIAN) DONN BYRNE
(20 November 1889-18 June 1928)

The novelist, who died in an automobile accident, said before leaving on his outing: "I think I'll go for a drive before dinner. Anyone come along?"

ALICE CARY
(26 April 1820-12 February 1871)

This Ohio writer of hymns and poems said, "I want to go away."

JOHN JAY CHAPMAN
(2 March 1862-4 November 1933)

Chapman, known primarily as a literary critic, said, "I want to take it away. I want to take it away."

SAMUEL CLEMENS (MARK TWAIN)
(30 November 1835-21 April 1910)

In a note written just before he died, Clemens stated, "Death, the only immortal, who treats us all alike, whose peace and whose refuge are for all. The soiled and the pure, the rich and the poor, the loved and the unloved." To his daughter Clara, Twain spoke his last worlds: "Good-bye. If we meet..."

FRANCIS MARION CRAWFORD
(2 August 1854-9 April 1909)

A writer of romantic and historical novels, Crawford said, "I love to see the reflection of the sun on the bookcase."

E. E. CUMMINGS
(14 October 1894-3 September 1962)

Warned by his wife that he should stop chopping wood on such a hot day, the poet replied, "I'm going to stop now, but I'm going to sharpen the axe before I put it up, dear."

FREDERICK DOUGLASS
(1817?-20 February 1895)

"Why, what does this mean?"

TIMOTHY DWIGHT
(14 May 1752-11 January 1817)

Stitching the cover to his essays on divine revelation, Dwight said, "There, I have done. Oh, what triumphant truth!"

JONATHAN EDWARDS
(5 October 1703-22 March 1758)

The Puritan divine said, "Trust in God and you need not fear."

RALPH WALDO EMERSON
(25 May 1803-27 April 1882)

Emerson said to Bronson Alcott, "Good-bye, my friend."

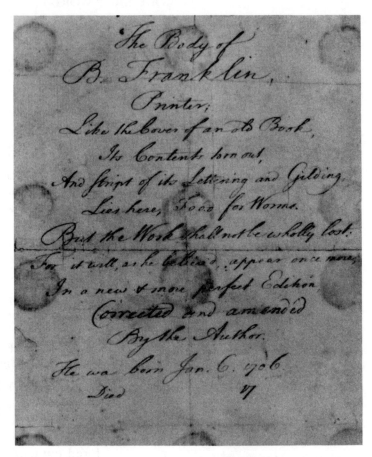

Benjamin Franklin's unused epitaph (courtesy of the Benjamin Franklin Collection, Yale University Library)

BENJAMIN FRANKLIN
(17 January 1706-17 April 1790)

Accounts of Franklin's final words vary. One source claims that he responded to his attendant's request that he change his position in bed with the words: "A dying man can do nothing easy." Another report has him replying to a friend's assurance that he would get well, "I hope not." When he was a young printer, Franklin composed for himself an epitaph—which does not appear on his tombstone but is worth noting:

The Body
of
Benjamin Franklin, Printer
Like the cover of an old book,
Its contents torn out,
And stripped of its lettering
and gilding,
Lies food for worms:
Yet the work itself shall not be lost,
for it will (as he believed) appear once
more,
In a new
And more beautiful edition,
Corrected and amended
by
The Author.

HORACE GREELEY
(3 February 1811–29 November 1872)

"It is done."

JOEL CHANDLER HARRIS
(9 December 1848-3 July 1908)

The creator of the Uncle Remus stories said, "I am about the extent of a tenth of a gnat's eyebrow better."

LAFCADIO HEARN
(27 June 1850-26 September 1904)

Known for his writings about Japan, Hearn said, "Ah–because of sickness."

JULIA WARD HOWE
(27 May 1819-17 October 1910)

The composer of "The Battle Hymn of the Republic" said, "God will help me . . . I am so tired."

WILLIAM DEAN HOWELLS
(1 March 1837-11 May 1920)

Howells died soon after writing about his friendship with Henry James: "Our walks by day were only in one direction and in one region. We were always going to Fresh Pond, in those days a wandering space of woods and water where people skated in winter and boated in summer."

ELBERT HUBBARD
(19 June 1856-7 May 1915)

Hubbard, who went down with the *Lusitania*, reportedly said to a friend, "Well, Jack, they have got us. They are a damned sight worse than I ever thought they were."

WASHINGTON IRVING
(3 April 1783-28 November 1859)

"Well, I must arrange my pillow for another weary night! When will this end?"

HENRY JAMES, SR.
(3 June 1811-18 December 1882)

"I stick by Almighty God–He alone *is*, all else is death. Don't call this dying: I am just entering upon life."

WILLIAM JAMES
(11 January 1842-26 August 1910)

"It's so good to get home."

GEORGE S. KAUFMAN
(16 November 1889-2 June 1961)

The playwright said, "I am not afraid any more."

JACK LONDON
(12 January 1876-22 November 1916)

In a telegram to his daughter London wrote, "I leave California Wednesday following. Daddy."

HENRY WADSWORTH LONGFELLOW
(27 February 1807-24 March 1882)

When his sister arrived from Portland, Maine, Longfellow said, "Now I know that I must be very ill, since you have been sent for."

COTTON MATHER
(12 February 1663-13 February 1728)

The Puritan writer exclaimed, "Is this dying? Is this all? Is this all that I feared, when I prayed against a hard death? O! I can bear this! I can bear it! I can bear it!...I'm going where all tears will be wiped from my eyes."

INCREASE MATHER
(21 June 1639-23 August 1723)

His son Cotton Mather said to him, "This day thou shalt be in Paradise. Do you believe it, Sir, and rejoice in the views and hopes for it?" Increase Mather responded, "I do! I do! I do!"

RICHARD MATHER
(1596-22 April 1669)

Father of Increase Mather and grandfather of Cotton Mather, Richard Mather answered a question about how he felt with the words: "Far from well, yet better than my iniquities deserve."

WILLIAMS HOLMES MCGUFFEY
(23 September 1800-4 May 1873)

Known for his *McGuffey's Readers*, this educator said, "Oh, that I might once more speak to my dear boys! But Thy will be done."

O. O. MCINTYRE
(18 February 1884-14 February 1938)

Newspaper columnist McIntyre said to his wife, "Snooks, will you please turn this way? I like to look at your face."

HERMAN MELVILLE
(1 August 1819-28 September 1891)

Alluding to a character in his novelette *Billy Budd*, Melville allegedly said, "God bless Captain Vere."

EDNA ST. VINCENT MILLAY
(22 February 1892-19 October 1950)

Preparing to go to bed, Millay wrote the following note to her maid: "Dear Lena, The iron is too high. Don't put it on where it says 'Linen' or it will scorch the linen. Try it on 'Rayon' and then perhaps on 'Woolen.' And Lena, be careful not to burn your fingers when you shift it from one heat to another. It is 5:30 and I have been working all night. I am going to bed. Good morning."

SILAS WEIR MITCHELL
(15 February 1829-4 January 1914)

As he lay dying this author-surgeon recalled a Civil War battlefield operation: "That leg must come off. Save the leg—lose the life."

EUGENE O'NEILL
(16 October 1888-27 November 1953)

While bedridden with pneumonia and a high fever, O'Neill could hardly talk. During a three-day bout of fever that at times reached as high as 104 degrees, he shouted, "Born in a hotel room—and God damn it—died in a hotel room!" He then went into a coma from which he never regained consciousness.

DOROTHY PARKER
(22 August 1893-7 June 1967)

A few days before her death, Parker wrote to her friend Beatrice Ames, "I want you to tell me the truth. Did Ernest [Hemingway] really like me?" Earlier, when asked to compose her own epitaph, she suggested, "Excuse my dust."

EDGAR ALLAN POE
(19 January 1809-7 October 1849)

Poe was in a semiconscious state before he died and may not have been able to speak. According to one source, however, the writer said, "My best friend would be the man who would blow my brains out with a pistol," while another account has him saying, "Lord help my poor soul."

WILLIAM SYDNEY PORTER
(O. HENRY)
(11 September 1862-5 June 19 10)

"Turn up the lights. I don't want to go home in the dark."

FREDERIC REMINGTON
(4 October 1861-26 December 1909)

When told that an operation for appendicitis was necessary, the Western artist and writer said, "Cut her loose, Doc."

KENNETH REXROTH
(22 December 1905-6 June 1982)

While dying, the poet recalled his father's last words: "He said he was dying of fast women, slow horses, crooked cards, and straight whiskey."

WILLIAM SAROYAN
(31 August 1908-18 May 1981)

In a statement to the Associated Press, Saroyan wrote five days before he died, "Everybody has got to die, but I have always believed an exception would be made in my case. Now what?"

HENRY WHEELER SHAW
(JOSH BILLINGS)
(21 April 1818-14 October 1885)

Billings, who died in a Monterey hotel while on a lecture tour, said, "My doctors East ordered rest of brain, but you can see I do not have to work my brain for a simple lecture—it comes spontaneously."

GERTRUDE STEIN
(3 February 1874-27 July 1946)

Duncan Sutherland reports that before she died, Stein asked, "What is the answer?" When no answer was forthcoming, she laughed and said, "In that case, what is the question?"

HARRIET BEECHER STOWE
(14 June 1811–1 July 1896)

As she lay dying, Stowe turned to her nurse and said, "I have had such a beautiful dream. I love you."

BAYARD TAYLOR
(11 June 1825-19 December 1878)

The journalist, poet, and novelist uttered these final words: "I want . . . oh, you know! What I mean . . . the stuff of life."

JAMES THURBER
(8 December 1894-2 November 1961)

As he lay in a semiconscious state, Thurber mumbled, "God bless...God damn."

HENRY TIMROD
(8 December 1829-6 October 1867)

Conflicting reports exist about the poet's last words. One source indicates that Timrod said, "I'm shot if I don't think I'm dying." A more poetic version, however, is provided by a biographer of the "Laureate of the Confederacy." Timrod, according to this source, said to his sister, Emily Goodwin: "And *this* is Death! It appears like two tides–two tides advancing and retreating. Now the power of Death recedes; but wait, it will advance again triumphant!" He recited Milton's "Death Rides Triumphant" and then a passage from one of his own poems: "Somewhere on this earthly planet, / *In the dust of flowers to be* / In the dew-drop and the sunshine / Waits a solemn hour to me." His sister replied that the hour had now arrived for him.

HORACE TRAUBEL
(19 December 1858-8 September 1919)

The writer who stayed by Walt Whitman's side during the elder man's dying hours and recorded nearly everything the poet uttered in his final three years and three months said, in his own dying moments, "I am tired, damned tired."

GEN. LEW WALLACE
(19 April 1827-15 February 1905)

The author of *Ben Hur* said to his wife, "We meet in Heaven."

BOOKER T. WASHINGTON
(5 April 1856-14 November 1915)

The black educator and author said, "Take me home. I was born in the South, I have lived and labored in the South, and I wish to die and be buried in the South."

DANIEL WEBSTER
(18 January 1782-24 October 1852)

One account of Webster's final words has him saying, "I still live...poetry." Yet, another source asserts that his last words were, "Well, children, doctor, I trust on this occasion I have said nothing unworthy of Daniel Webster. Life, life! Death, death! How curious it is."

NOAH WEBSTER
(16 October 1758-28 May 1843)

The lexicographer, educator, and author declared on his deathbed: "I have struggled with many difficulties. Some I have been able to overcome, and by some I have been overcome. I have made mistakes, but I love my country, and have labored for the youth of my country, and I trust no precept of mine has taught my dear youth to sin."

WALT WHITMAN
(31 May 1819-26 March 1892)

To an attendant, as the poet tried to have his pillow arranged for greater comfort, Whitman said, "Shift, Warry."

JOHN GREENLEAF WHITTIER
(17 December 1809-7 September 1892)

His niece asked if he knew who she was, to which the poet replied, "I have known thee all the time."

THOMAS WOLFE
(3 October 1900-15 September 1938)

Calling to his sister, the novelist said, "All right, Mabel, I am coming."

ALEXANDER WOOLLCOTT
(19 January 1897-23 January 1943)

When he was in the hospital prior to his death, Woollcott dismissed a visitor with these remarks: "I have no need of your God damned sympathy. I only wish to be entertained by some of your grosser reminiscences."

ELINOR WYLIE
(7 September 1885-16 December 1928)

When offered a glass of water, the poet replied, "Oh, is that all it is?"

THEY DIED OLD AND THEY DIED YOUNG

This section provides a list of American writers who were eighty years or older when they died and a list of authors who were thirty-nine or younger when they died.

THEY DIED OLD

John G. Neihardt 92
Harriet Tubman 92
Irving Bacheller 91
Abraham Cahan 91
Sarah Josepha Hale 91
Julia Ward Howe 91
Meredith Nicholson 91
George Bancroft 90
Djuna Barnes 90
Katherine Anne Porter 90
Helen Hooven Santmyer 90
Upton Sinclair 90
Anna Katharine Green 89
Archibald MacLeish 89
Carl Sandburg 89
Ruth Sawyer 89
Alice B. Toklas 89
Laura Ingalls Wilder 89
Bronson Alcott 88
George Barnard 88
Robert Frost 88
Anita Loos 88
Edwin Markham 88
Paul Green 87
Edward Everett Hale 87
Ezra Pound 87

Margaret Anderson 86
Janet Flanner 86
Donald Mitchell 86
E. B. White 86
Caroline Gordon 85
Oliver Wendell Holmes, Sr. 85
Donald Ogden Stewart 85
George R. Stewart 85
Harriet Beecher Stowe 85
Margaret Wilson 85
Conrad Aiken 84
Benjamin Franklin 84
Clement Clark Moore 84
Edward Streeter 84
T. S. Stribling 84
Edward Taylor 84
Carl Van Vechten 84
Noah Webster 84
John Greenleaf Whittier 84
William Cullen Bryant 83
Hugo Gernsback 83
William Dean Howells 83
Marianne Moore 83
Frank Sullivan 83
Floyd Dell 82
Mary Roberts Rinehart 82
Allen Tate 82
Margaret Ayer Barnes 81

Thorton W. Burgess 81
Edgar Lee Masters 81
John Trumbull 81
Jessamyn West 81
Stark Young 81
Henry Adams 80
S. N. Behrman 80
Pearl S. Buck 80
Philip Freneau 80
Julia Peterkin 80

THEY DIED YOUNG

Nathaniel Mather 19
Stephen Crane 29
Thomas Heggen 30
Robert Howard 30
Sylvia Plath 30
Harry Crosby 31
Phillis Wheatley 31
Hart Crane 32

Joyce Kilmer 32
Frank Norris 32
Alan Seeger 32
Wallace Thurman 32
John Kennedy Toole 32
Paul Laurence Dunbar 33
Ross Lockridge 33
John Reed 33
Lorraine Hansberry 35
Thomas Boyd 36
John Horne Burns 36
Adelaide Crapsey 36
Paul Leicester Ford 37
Henry Timrod 37
Nathanael West 37
Thomas Wolfe 37
Charles Brockden Brown 39
Grace Metalious 39
Flannery O'Connor 39

Vanity Fair magazine invited celebrities of the 1920s to provide their own epitaphs. The participants included some of the celebrated writers of the greatest era of American wit.

SHERWOOD ANDERSON
GOOD NIGHT,
'TWAS FUN ENOUGH, AND LIFE WAS DEAR
I TRIED TO GET MY WISH.
I DID NOT WANT TO DIE–
BEFORE THEY PUT ME HERE.

HERE LIES
ZONA GALE
I'M IN THE SUN, THE MOON, THE SKY
I'M NIMBLY PERCHING ON THE BOUGH,
I'M EVERYWHERE AT ONCE, BUT I
AM MUCH TOO MODEST TO TELL HOW.

HERE LIES
GEORGE S. KAUFMAN
"OVER MY DEAD BODY!"

HERE LIES
THE BODY OF RING LARDNER.
WHAT OF IT?

Bibliography

BASIC REFERENCE BOOKS FOR THE STUDY OF AMERICAN LITERATURE

Blanck, Jacob, and Michael Winship, comps. *Bibliography of American Literature,* 7 volumes to date. New Haven: Yale University Press. Describes the first printings of books by selected American authors who died before 1930.

Bruccoli, Matthew J., Richard Layman, and others, eds. *First Printings of American Authors,* 5 volumes. Detroit: Bruccoli Clark/Gale Research, 1977-1987. Supplements *Bibliography of American Literature.*

Contemporary Authors Bibliographical Series, 2 volumes to date. Detroit: Gale Research, 1986- . Bibliographical essays on selected American authors.

Gale Information Guide Library. Literary Series, 42 volumes to date. American Studies Series, 14 volumes to date. Detroit: Gale Research. Annotated bibliographies of American literature topics.

Nilon, Charles H. *Bibliography of Bibliographies in American Literature.* New York: Bowker, 1970.

Pittsburgh Series in Bibliography, 20 volumes to date. Pittsburgh: University of Pittsburgh Press. Each volume is a primary descriptive bibliography for an American author.

Rees, Robert A., and Earl W. Harbert, eds. *Fifteen American Writers Before 1900,* revised edition. Madison: University of Wisconsin Press, 1984. Bibliographical essays on John Adams, Bryant, Cooper, Stephen Crane, Dickinson, Edwards, Franklin, Holmes, Howells, Irving, Longfellow, James Russell Lowell, Norris, Taylor, Whittier.

Reference Guides to Literature, 42 volumes to date. Boston: Twayne. Includes secondary bibliographies for American authors.

Robbins, J. Albert, ed. *American Literary Manuscripts: A Checklist,* second edition. Athens: University of Georgia Press, 1977. Locates library manuscript holdings.

Scarecrow Author Bibliographies, 77 volumes to date. Metuchen, N.J.: Scarecrow. Includes primary and secondary bibliographies for American authors.

Tanselle, G. Thomas. *Guide to the Study of the United States Imprints,* 2 volumes. Cambridge: Harvard University Press, 1971.

Woodress, James, ed. *Eight American Authors: A Review of Research and Criticism,* revised edition. New York: Norton, 1971. Bibliographical essays on Clemens, Emerson, Hawthorne, James, Melville, Poe, Thoreau, Whitman.

Woodress and others, eds. *American Literary Scholarship: An Annual.* Durham: Duke University Press, 1965- . Bibliographical essays.

HISTORIES

Ehrlich, Eugene, and Gorton Carroth. *The Oxford Illustrated Literary Guide to the United States.* New York & Oxford: Oxford University Press, 1982.

Hoffman, Daniel, ed. *Harvard Guide to Contemporary American Writing.* Cambridge: Harvard University Press, 1979.

Horton, Rod W., and Herbert W. Edwards. *Backgrounds of American Liter-*

ary Thought, third edition. New York: Appleton-Century-Crofts, 1974.

Lehmann-Haupt, Hellmut, and others. *The Book in America,* second edition. New York: Bowker, 1961.

Mott, Frank Luther. *A History of American Magazines,* 5 volumes. Cambridge: Harvard University Press, 1957. Covers 1741-1930.

Spiller, Robert E., and others, eds. *Literary History of the United States,* fourth edition, revised, 2 volumes. New York: Macmillan, 1974. Volume 2 is a bibliography. Outdated, but still the standard work.

Tebbel, John. *A History of Book Publishing in the United States,* 4 volumes. New York: Bowker, 1972-1981.

Wilson, Edmund, ed. *The Shock of Recognition: The Development of Literature in the United States Recorded by the Men Who Made It,* 2 volumes. Garden City: Doubleday, 1955.

GUIDES, DIRECTORIES, HANDBOOKS

Basler, Roy P., and others, eds. *A Guide to the Study of the United States of America.* Washington, D.C.: Library of Congress, 1960.

Ghodes, Clarence, and Sanford E. Marovitz, *Bibliographical Guide to the Study of the Literature of the U.S.A.,* fifth edition. Durham: Duke University Press, 1984.

Hart, James O. *The Oxford Companion to American Literature,* fifth edition. New York: Oxford University Press, 1982.

Herzberg, Max J., and others. *The Reader's Encyclopedia of American Literature.* New York: Crowell, 1962.

Holman, C. Hugh. *A Handbook to Literature.* Indianapolis: Bobbs-Merrill, 1980. Dictionary of terms.

Hubbard, Linda, ed. *Publishers Directory,* 2 volumes. Detroit: Gale Research, 1987.

Johnson, Thomas H. *The Oxford Companion to American History.* New York: Oxford University Press, 1966.

Jones, Howard Mumford and Richard M. Ludwig. *Guide to American Litera-*

ture and Its Backgrounds Since 1890, fourth edition. Cambridge: Harvard University Press, 1972.

Kolb, Harold H., Jr. *A Field Guide to the Study of American Literature.* Charlottesville: University of Virginia Press, 1976.

Literary Market Place. New York: Bowker. Annual directory of American book publishing.

Ludwig, Richard M., and Clifford A. Nault, Jr., eds. *Annals of American Literature, 1602-1983.* New York: Oxford University Press, 1986.

BIOGRAPHICAL SOURCES

Burke, W. J., and Will D. Howe. *American Authors and Books: 1640 to the Present Day,* revised by Irving Weiss. New York: Crown, 1972.

Contemporary Authors, 120 volumes to date. Detroit: Gale, 1962- . Bio-bibliographical entries for world authors, but with concentration on Americans.

Dictionary of Literary Biography, 75 volumes to date. Detroit: Bruccoli Clark/ Gale Research, 1978- . Most volumes deal with American authors. Biographical-critical entries; each volume covers a genre and period. *Yearbooks* since 1980. Also *Concise Dictionary of Literary Biography,* 1987- .

Kunitz, Stanley J., and Howard Haycraft. *American Authors, 1600- 1900.* New York: Wilson, 1938.

Kunitz and Haycraft. *Twentieth Century Authors.* New York: Wilson, 1942. *Supplement,* 1955.

Millet, Fred B. *Contemporary American Authors: A Critical Survey and 219 Bio-bibliographies.* New York: Harcourt, Brace, 1940.

Warfel, Harry R. *American Novelists of Today.* New York: American Book Company, 1951.

CRITICAL SERIES

Cross Currents, 97 volumes to date. Carbondale: Southern Illinois University

Press. Most of the volumes are critical studies of American authors.

Minnesota Pamphlets, 65 volumes to date. Minneapolis: University of Minnesota Press. Critical monographs on individual authors.

Twayne United States Authors Series, 505 volumes to date. Boston: Twayne. Critical studies of individual authors; uneven.

Twentieth Century Interpretations. Englewood Cliffs, N.J.: Prentice-Hall. Collections of articles on individual works.

Twentieth Century Views. Englewood Cliffs, N.J.: Prentice-Hall. Collections of critical articles on individual authors.

Understanding Contemporary American Literature, 8 volumes to date. Columbia: University of South Carolina Press. Critical studies of individual authors.

COLONIAL AND EARLY AMERICAN

Elliott, Emory, ed. *Dictionary of Literary Biography 24: American Colonial Writers, 1606-1734.* Detroit: Bruccoli Clark/Gale Research, 1984.

Elliott, ed. *Dictionary of Literary Biography 31: American Colonial Writers, 1735-1781.* Detroit: Bruccoli Clark/Gale Research, 1984.

Elliott, ed. *Dictionary of Literary Biography 37: American Writers of the Early Republic.* Detroit: Bruccoli Clark/Gale Research 1985.

Emerson, Everett. *Puritanism in America.* Boston. Twayne/Hall, 1977.

Emerson, ed. *Major Writers of Early American Literature.* Madison: University of Wisconsin Press, 1972. Bibliographical essays.

Miller, Perry. *The New England Mind: From Colony to Province.* Cambridge: Harvard University Press, 1953.

Miller. *The New England Mind: The Seventeenth Century.* New York: Macmillan, 1939.

AMERICAN RENAISSANCE (ROMANTICISM)

Matthiesson, F. O. *American Renaissance: Art and Expression in the Age of Emerson and Whitman.* New York: Oxford University Press, 1941.

Miller, Perry. *The Raven and the Whale: The War of Words and Wits in the Era of Poe and Melville.* New York: Harcourt, Brace, 1956.

Myerson, Joel, ed. *Dictionary of Literary Biography 1: The American Renaissance in New England.* Detroit: Bruccoli Clark/Gale Research, 1978.

Myerson, ed. *Dictionary of Literary Biography 3: Antebellum Writers in New York and the South.* Detroit: Bruccoli Clark/Gale Research, 1979.

Myerson, ed. *The Transcendentalists: A Review of Research and Criticism.* New York: Modern Language Association of America, 1984. Bibliographical essays.

REALISM AND NATURALISM

Berthoff, Warner. *The Ferment of Realism: American Literature, 1884-1919.* New York: Free Press, 1965.

Martin, Jay. *Harvests of Change: American Literature, 1865-1914.* Englewood Cliffs, N.J.: Prentice-Hall, 1967.

Pizer, Donald, and Earl N. Harbert, eds. *Dictionary of Literary Biography 12: American Realists and Naturalists.* Detroit: Bruccoli Clark/Gale Research, 1982.

MODERN AND CONTEMPORARY (TWENTIETH CENTURY)

Bryer, Jackson R., ed. *Sixteen Modern American Authors: A Survey of Research and Criticism.* Durham: Duke University Press, 1973. Bibliographical essays on Sherwood Anderson, Cather, Hart Crane, Dreiser, Eliot, Faulkner, Fitzgerald, Frost, Hemingway, O'Neill, Pound, Robinson, Steinbeck, Stevens, William Carlos Williams, Wolfe.

Hassan, Ihab. *Contemporary American Literature.* New York: Ungar, 1973.

Hoffman, Frederick J. *The Twenties: American Writing in the Postwar Decade,* revised edition. New York: Macmillan, 1962.

Thorp, Willard. *American Writing in the Twentieth Century.* Cambridge: Harvard University Press, 1960.

REGIONAL LITERATURE (THE SOUTH)

Bain, Robert, Joseph M. Flora, and Louis D. Rubin, Jr., eds. *Southern Writers: A Biographical Dictionary.* Baton Rouge & London: Louisiana State University Press, 1979.

Jay B. Hubbell, *The South in American Literature, 1607-1900.* Durham: Duke University Press, 1954.

Rubin, Louis D., Jr., ed. *A Bibliographical Guide to the Study of Southern Literature.* Baton Rouge: Louisiana State University Press, 1969.

Rubin and others, eds. *The History of Southern Literature.* Baton Rouge: Louisiana State University Press, 1985.

REGIONAL LITERATURE (THE WEST)

Erisman, Fred, and Richard W. Etulain, eds. *Fifty Western Writers: A Bio-Bibliographical Sourcebook.* Westport, Conn. & London: Greenwood, 1982.

Etulain, Richard W. *A Bibliographical Guide to the Study of Western Literature.* Lincoln & London: University of Nebraska Press, 1982.

Lamar, Howard R., ed. *The Reader's Encyclopedia of the American West.* New York: Crowell, 1977.

A Literary History of the American West. Fort Worth: Texas Christian University Press, 1986.

Smith, Dwight L., ed. *The American and Canadian West: A Bibliography.* Santa Barbara & Oxford: ABC-Clio, 1979.

Vinson, James, and D. L. Kirkpatrick, eds. *Twentieth-Century Western Writers.* Detroit: Gale Research, 1982. Critical essays and bio-bibliographical data for 300 writers.

REGIONAL LITERATURE (THE MIDWEST)

Nemanic, Gerald, ed. *A Bibliographical*

Guide to Midwestern Literature. Iowa City: University of Iowa Press, 1981.

NOVEL

Cowie, Alexander. *The Rise of the American Novel.* New York: American Book Company, 1951.

Helterman, Jeffrey, and Richard Layman, eds. *Dictionary of Literary Biography 2: American Novelists Since World War II,* First Series. Detroit: Bruccoli Clark/Gale Research, 1978;

Karl, Frederick R. *American Fictions, 1940-1980: A Comprehensive History and Critical Evaluation.* New York: Harper & Row, 1983.

Kibler, James E., ed. *Dictionary of Literary Biography 6: American Novelists Since World War II,* Second Series. Detroit: Bruccoli Clark/Gale Research, 1980.

Martine, James J., ed. *Dictionary of Literary Biography 9: American Novelists, 1910-1945,* 3 volumes. Detroit: Bruccoli Clark/Gale Research, 1981.

Tanner, Tony. *City of Words: American Fiction, 1950-1970.* Harper & Row, 1971.

DRAMA

Bordman, Gerald. *The Oxford Companion to the American Theatre.* New York: Oxford University Press, 1984.

King, Kimball. *Ten Modern American Playwrights: A Bibliography.* New York: Garland, 1981. Covers Albee, Baraka, Bullins, Gelber, Kopit, Mamet, Rabe, Shepard, Simon, Wilson.

MacNicholas, John, ed. *Dictionary of Literary Biography 7: Twentieth-Century American Dramatists,* 2 volumes. Detroit: Bruccoli Clark/Gale Research, 1981.

Quinn, Arthur Hobson. *A History of the American Drama from the Civil War to the Present Day,* revised edition. New York: Appleton-Century-Crofts, 1936.

Weales, Gerald. *American Drama Since World War II.* New York: Harcourt, Brace & World, 1962.

Weingarten, Joseph A. *Modern American*

Playwrights, 1918-1945: A Bibliography, 2 volumes. New York, 1946-1947.

POETRY

Greiner, Donald J., ed. *Dictionary of Literary Biography 5: American Poets Since World War II,* 2 volumes. Detroit: Bruccoli Clark/Gale Research, 1980.

Kuntz, Joseph M., and Nancy C. Martinez, *Poetry Explication: A Checklist of Interpretation Since 1925 of British and American Poems Past and Present.* Boston: G. K. Hall, 1980.

Malkoff, Karl. *Crowell's Handbook of Contemporary American Poetry.* New York: Crowell, 1973.

Perkins, David. *A History of Modern Poetry from the 1890's to the High Modernist Mode.* Cambridge: Harvard University Press, 1976.

Quartermain, Peter, ed. *Dictionary of Literary Biography 45: American Poets 1880-1945,* First Series. Detroit: Bruccoli Clark/Research, 1986; *DLB 48,* Second Series, 1986; *DLB 54,* Third Series, 1987.

Stauffer, Donald Barlow. *A Short History of American Poetry.* New York: Dutton, 1974.

SHORT STORY

Current-Gárcia, Eugene, ed. *The American Short Story Before 1850: A Critical History.* Boston: Twayne, 1985.

Stevick, Philip, ed. *The American Short Story, 1900-1945: A Critical History.* Boston: Twayne, 1984.

Weaver, Gordon, ed. *The American Short Story, 1945-1980: A Critical History.* Boston: Twayne, 1983.

CHILDREN'S LITERATURE

Carpenter, Humphrey, and Mari Prichard, eds. *The Oxford Companion to Children's Literature.* New York: Oxford University Press, 1984. Covers world authors.

Cech, John, ed. *Dictionary of Literary Biography 22: American Writers for Children, 1900-1960.* Detroit: Bruccoli Clark/Gale Research, 1983.

Estes, Glenn E., ed. *Dictionary of Literary Biography 42: American Writers for Children Before 1900.* Detroit: Bruccoli Clark/Gale Research, 1985.

Estes, ed. *Dictionary of Literary Biography 52: American Writers for Children After 1960.* Detroit: Bruccoli Clark/Gale Research, 1986.

Something About the Author, 47 volumes to date. Detroit: Gale Research, 1971. Biographical entries for contemporary writers and illustrators of children's books.

SCIENCE FICTION

Barron, Neil, ed. *Anatomy of Wonder: Science Fiction.* New York: Bowker, 1981.

Bleiler, E. F., ed. *Science Fiction Writers: Critical Studies of the Major Authors from the Early Nineteenth Century to the Present Day.* New York: Scribners, 1982.

Cowart, David, and Thomas L. Wymer, eds. *Dictionary of Literary Biography 8: Twentieth-Century American Science-Fiction Writers,* 2 volumes. Detroit: Bruccoli Clark/Gale Research, 1981.

Reginald, R. *Science Fiction and Fantasy Literature: A Checklist, 1700-1974 with Contemporary Science Fiction Authors II,* 2 volumes. Detroit: Gale Research, 1979.

Searles, Baird, and others. *A Reader's Guide to Science Fiction.* New York: Facts on File, 1979.

MYSTERY AND DETECTIVE FICTION

Albert, Walter. *Detective and Mystery Fiction: An International Bibliography of Secondary Sources.* Madison, Ind.: Brownstone Books, 1985.

Hubin, Allen. *Crime Fiction, 1749-1980: A Comprehensive Bibliography.* New York & London: Garland, 1984.

FOLKLORE

Brunvand, Jan Harold. *The Study of Amer-*

ican *Folklore: An Introduction*, revised edition. New York: Norton, 1978.

Dorson, Richard M. *American Folklore*, revised edition. Chicago: University of Chicago Press, 1977.

HUMOR

Blair, Walter, and Hamlin Hill. *America's Humor: From Poor Richard to Doonesbury*. New York: Oxford University Press, 1978.

Rourke, Constance. *American Humor: A Study of the National Character*. New York: Harcourt Brace, 1931.

Trachtenberg, Stanley. *Dictionary of Literary Biography II: American Humorists, 1800-1950*, 2 volumes. Detroit: Bruccoli Clark/Gale Research, 1982.

WOMEN WRITERS

Duke, Maurice, Jackson R. Bryer, and M. Thomas Inge. *American Women Writers: Bibliographical Essays*. Westport, Conn. & London: Greenwood, 1983.

Mainiero, Lina, ed. *American Women Writers*,4 volumes. New York: Ungar, 1970-1982.

White, Barbara A. *American Women Writers: An Annotated Bibliography of Criticism*. New York & London: Garland, 1977.

BLACK LITERATUTE

Matthews, Geraldene O., comp. *Black American Writers, 1773-1949: A Bibliography and Union List*. Boston: G. K. Hall, 1975.

Matthews and others, comps. *Black American Writers*. Boston: G. K. Hall, 1975.

Davis, Thadious M., and Trudier Harris, eds. *Dictionary of Literary Biography 33: Afro-American Fiction Writers After 1955*. Detroit: Bruccoli Clark/Gale Research, 1984.

Davis and Harris, eds. *Dictionary of Literary Biography 38: Afro-American Writers After 1955: Dramatists and Prose Writers*. Detroit: Bruccoli Clark/Gale Research, 1985.

Gayle, Addison, *The Way of the New World: The Black Novel in America*. Garden City: Anchor/Doubleday, 1976.

Harris, Trudier, and Thadious M. Davis, eds. *Dictionary of Literary Biography 41: Afro-American Poets Since 1955*, 2 volumes. Detroit: Bruccoli Clark/Gale Research, 1985.

Harris and Davis, eds. *Dictionary of Literary Biography 50: Afro-American Writers Before the Harlem Renaissance*. Detroit: Bruccoli Clark/Gale Research, 1986.

Harris and Davis, eds. *Dictionary of Literary Biography 51: Harlem Renaissance-1940*. Detroit: Bruccoli Clark/Gale Research, 1986.

Hill, Errol, ed. *The Theater of Black Americans*, 2 volumes. Englewood Cliffs, N.J.: Prentice-Hall, 1980.

Redmond, Eugene B. *Drumvoices: The Mission of Afro-American Poetry, A Critical History*. Garden City: Anchor/Doubleday, 1976.

Sherman, Joan R. *Invisible Poets: Afro-Americans of the Nineteenth Century*. Urbana: University of Illinois Press, 1974.

Whitlow, Roger. *Black American Literature: A Critical History with a 1520-Title Bibliography of Works Written By and About Black Americans*, revised edition. Chicago: Nelson-Hall, 1976.

AMERICAN JEWISH WRITERS

Guttmann, Allen. *The Jewish Writer in America: Assimilation and the Crisis of Identity*. New York: Oxford University Press, 1971.

Nadel, Ira Bruce. *Jewish Writers in North America*. Detroit: Gale Research, 1981.

Walden, Daniel, ed. *Dictionary of Literary Biography 28: Twentieth-Century American-Jewish Fiction Writers*. Detroit: Bruccoli Clark/Gale Research, 1984.

NATIVE AMERICAN LITERATURE

Colonnese, Tom,and Louis Owens. *American Indian Novelists: An Annotated Critical Bibliography*. New York & London: Garland, 1985.

Littlefield, Daniel F., Jr., and James W.

Parins, eds. *A Bibliography of Native American Writers, 1772-1924.* Metuchen, N.J.: Scarecrow, 1981.

Marken, Jack W., comp. *The American Indian Language and Literature.* Arlington Heights, Ill.: AHM, Publishing Corp., 1978. Bibliography.

CHICANO LITERATURE

Cabello-Argandona, Roberto. *The Chicana: A Comprehensive Bibliographical Study.* Los Angeles: University of California, 1976.

Martinez, Julio A., and Francisco A. Lioneli, eds. *Chicano Literature.* (Westport, Conn.: Greenwood, 1984).

BOOK COLLECTING

American Book-Prices Current, 100 volumes to date. Various publishers, 1895- .

Boutell, H. S. *First Editions of Today and How to Tell Them,* fourth edition. Berkeley: Peacock, 1965.

McGrath, Daniel F., ed. *Bookman's Price Index: An Annual Guide to the Values of Rare and Other Out-of-Print Books.* 31 volumes to date. Detroit: Gale Research, 1964- .

OTHER TOPICS

Mencken, H. L. *The American Language.* New York: Knopf, 1936. *Supplements,* 1945 and 1948.

Rood, Karen Lane, ed. *Dictionary of Literary Biography 4: American Writers in Paris, 1920-1939.* Detroit: Bruccoli Clark/Gale Research, 1980.

SOURCES

In addition to the basic reference books listed on pp. 377-383 the following sources were used in compiling this book:

Ackroyd, Peter. *T. S. Eliot: A Life.* New York: Simon & Schuster, 1984.

Adams, J. Donald. *Copey of Harvard: A Biography of Charles Townsend Copeland.* Boston: Houghton Mifflin, 1960.

Aichinger, Peter. *The American Soldier in Fiction, 1880-1963: A History of Attitudes Toward Warfare and the Established Military.* Ames: Iowa State University Press, 1975.

Allen, Gay Wilson. *The Solitary Singer: A Critical Biography of Walt Whitman,* revised edition. New York: New York University Press, 1967.

Allen. *William James: A Biography.* New York: Viking, 1967.

Arbeiter, Jean, and Linda D. Cirino. *Permanent Addresses: A Guide to the Resting Places of Famous Americans.* New York: Evans, 1983.

Atkinson, Brooks, ed. *College in a Yard: Minutes By Thirty-Nine Harvard Men.* Cambridge: Harvard University Press, 1957.

Atlas, James. *Delmore Schwartz: The Life of an American Poet.* New York: Farrar, Straus & Giroux, 1977.

Axelrad, Jacob. *Philip Freneau: Champion of Democracy.* Austin & London: University of Texas Press, 1967.

Axelrod, Steven Gould. *Robert Lowell: Life and Art.* Princeton: Princeton University Press, 1978.

Baker, Carlos. *Ernest Hemingway: A Life Story.* New York: Scribners, 1969.

Barzun, Jacques, and Wendell Hartig Taylor. *A Catalogue of Crime,* second impression corrected. New York, Evanston, San Francisco & London: Harper & Row, 1971.

Beidler, Philip D. *American Literature and the Experience of Vietnam.* Athens: University of Georgia Press, 1982.

Benchley, Nathaniel. *Robert Benchley: A*

Biography. New York, Toronto & London: McGraw-Hill, 1955.

Benedict, Stewart, ed. *The Literary Guide to the United States.* New York: Facts on File, 1981.

Benson, Frederick R. *Writers in Arms: The Literary Impact of the Spanish Civil War.* New York: New York University Press/London: University of London Press, 1967.

Benson, Jackson J. *The True Adventures of John Steinbeck, Writer: A Biography.* New York: Viking, 1984.

Bernstein, Burton: *Thurber: A Biography.* New York: Dodd, Mead, 1975.

Berry, Faith. *Langston Hughes: Before and Beyond Harlem.* Westport, Conn.: Lawrence Hill, 1983.

Bevilacqua, Winifred Farrant. *Josephine Herbst.* Boston: Twayne, 1985.

Blackburn, William, ed. *Love, Boy: The Letters of Mac Hyman.* Baton Rouge: Louisiana State University Press, 1969.

Blotner, Joseph. *Faulkner: A Biography,* 2 volumes. New York: Random House, 1974; corrected, one-volume edition, 1984.

Brenman-Gibson, Margaret. *Clifford Odets: American Playwright.* New York: Atheneum, 1982.

Brown, Charles H. *William Cullen Bryant.* New York: Scribners, 1971.

Brown, Maurice F. *Estranging Dawn: The Life and Works of William Vaughn Moody.* Carbondale & Edwardsville: Southern Illinois University Press / London & Amsterdam: Feffer & Simons, 1973.

Bruccoli, Matthew J. *James Gould Cozzens: A Life Apart.* San Diego, New York & London: Harcourt Brace Jovanovich, 1983.

Bruccoli. *The O'Hara Concern: A Biography of John O'Hara.* New York: Random House, 1975.

Bruccoli. *Some Sort of Epic Grandeur: The Life of F. Scott Fitzgerald.* New York & London: Harcourt Brace Jovanovich, 1981.

Carr, Virginia Spencer. *Dos Passos: A*

Life. Garden City: Doubleday, 1984.

Carr. *The Heart Is a Lonely Hunter: A Biography of Carson McCullers.* Garden City: Doubleday, 1975.

Charters, Ann. *Kerouac: A Biography.* San Francisco: Straight Arrow Books, 1973.

Clareson, Thomas D. *Science Fiction in America, 1870s-1930s: An Annotated Bibliography of Primary Sources.* Westport, Conn. & London: Greenwood Press, 1984.

Clark, Tom. *The World of Damon Runyon.* New York: Harper & Row, 1978.

Coffin, Margaret M. *Death in Early America.* Nashville: Nelson, 1976.

Colvert, James B. *Stephen Crane.* San Diego, New York & London: Harcourt Brace Jovanovich, 1984.

Conversations with Writers, volume 1. Detroit: Gale Research, 1977.

Costa, Richard Hauer. *Edmund Wilson: Our Neighbor from Talcottville.* Syracuse: Syracuse University Press, 1980.

Cowan, Louise. *The Fugitive Group: A Literary History.* Baton Rouge: Louisiana State University Press, 1959.

Cox, J. Randolph. "More Mystery For a Dime: Street & Smith and the First Pulp Detective Magazine." *Clues: A Journal of Detection,* 2 (Fall/Winter 1981): 52-59.

Day, A. Grove. *James A. Michener* (New York: Twayne, 1964).

Donald, David Herbert. *Look Homeward: A Life of Thomas Wolfe.* Boston & Toronto: Little, Brown, 1987.

Donohue, H. E. F. *Conversations with Nelson Algren.* New York: Hill & Wang, 1964.

Duberman, Martin. *Black Mountain: An Exploration in Community.* New York: Dutton, 1972.

Easton, Robert. *Max Brand: The Big "Westerner."* Norman: University of Oklahoma Press, 1970.

Edel, Leon. *Henry James: The Untried Years, 1843-1870.* Philadelphia & New York: Lippincott, 1953. *Henry James: The Conquest of London, 1870-1881.* Philadelphia & New York: Lippincott, 1962. *Henry James: The Middle Years,*

1882-1895. Philadelphia & New York: Lippincott, 1962. *Henry James: The Treacherous Years, 1895-1901*. Philadelphia & New York: Lippincott, 1969. *Henry James: The Master, 1901-1916*. Philadelphia & New York: Lippincott, 1972.

Elliott, Emory. *Revolutionary Writers: Literature and Authority in the New Republic, 1725-1810*. New York & Oxford: Oxford University Press, 1982.

Engel, Bernard F. *Richard Eberhart*. New York: Twayne, 1971.

Fabre, Michel. *The Unfinished Quest of Richard Wright*, translated by Isabel Barzon. New York: Morrow, 1973.

Farr, Finis. *Margaret Mitchell of Atlanta: The Author of Gone With the Wind*. New York: Morrow, 1965.

Fatout, Paul. *Ambrose Bierce: The Devil's Lexicographer*. Norman: University of Oklahoma Press, 1951.

Franchere, Hoyt C. *Edwin Arlington Robinson*. New York: Twayne, 1968.

French, Warren. *J. D. Salinger*. New York: Twayne, 1963; revised, 1976.

Gallico, Paul. *Confessions of a Story Writer*. New York: Knopf, 1946.

Garrett, George. *James Jones*. San Diego, New York & London: Harcourt Brace Jovanovich, 1984.

Gauss, Christian. "Edmund Wilson: The Campus and the Nassau 'Lit'." *Princeton University Library Chronicle*, 5 (February 1944): 41-50.

Gelb, Arthur and Barbara. *O'Neill*. New York: Harper, 1962.

Gelb, Barbara. "Catching Joseph Heller." *New York Times Magazine*, 4 March 1979, pp. 14-16, 42-55.

Gelb, Barbara. *So Short a Time: A Biography of John Reed and Louise Bryant*. New York: Norton, 1973.

Giles, James R. *Irwin Shaw*. Boston: Twayne, 1983.

Gill, Brendan. *Here at the New Yorker*. New York: Random House, 1975.

Gittleman, Edwin. *Jones Very: The Effective Years, 1833-1840*. New York & London: Columbia University Press, 1967.

Green, Jonathon, comp. *Famous Last Words*. New York, London & Tokyo: Omnibus Press, 1979.

Gross, Miriam, ed. *The World of Raymond Chandler*. London: Weidenfeld & Nicolson, 1977.

Gruber, Frank. *Zane Grey: A Biography*. New York & Cleveland: World, 1970.

Gruen, John. *The Party's Over Now: Reminiscences of the Fifties—New York's Artists, Writers, Musicians, and Their Friends*. New York: Viking, 1972.

Guest, Barbara. *Herself Defined: The Poet H. D. and Her World*. Garden City: Doubleday, 1984.

Haffenden, John. *The Life of John Berryman*. Boston, London, Melbourne & Henley: Routledge & Kegan Paul, 1982.

Hagedorn, Hermann. *Edwin Arlington Robinson: A Biography*. New York: Macmillan, 1938.

Hall, Donald. *Marianne Moore: The Cage and the Animal*. New York: Pegasus, 1970.

Hall. *The Oxford Book of American Literary Anecdotes*. Oxford University Press, 1981.

Hamilton, Ian. *Robert Lowell: A Biography*. New York: Random House, 1982.

Haraszti, Zoltán. *The Enigma of the Bay Psalm Book*. Chicago: University of Chicago Press, 1956.

Harding, Walter. *The Days of Henry Thoreau*. New York: Knopf, 1966.

Harris, Leon. *Upton Sinclair: American Rebel*. New York: Crowell, 1975.

Harris, Mark. *Best Father Ever Invented: The Autobiography of Mark Harris*. New York: Dial Press, 1976.

Harris, Theodore F. *Pearl Buck: A Biography*, 2 volumes. New York: John Day, 1969, 1971.

Harrison, Gilbert A. *The Enthusiast: A Life of Thornton Wilder*. New Haven & New York: Ticknor & Fields, 1983.

Hartwell, David G. Preface to *A Voyage to the Moon*, by George Tucker. Boston: Gregg Press, 1975, pp. vii-ix.

Havens, Daniel F. *The Columbian Muse of Comedy. The Development of a Native Tradition in Early American Social Come-*

dy, 1787-1845. Carbondale & Edwardsville: Southern Illinois University Press, 1973.

Hedrick, Joan D. *Solitary Comrade: Jack London and His Work*. Chapel Hill: University of North Carolina Press, 1982.

Henson, Clyde E. *Joseph Kirkland* (New York: Twayne, 1962).

Hewett, David. "The Mark Hofmann Story." *Maine Antique Digest*, 14 (June 1986): 26A-31A; (July 1986): 1C-5C.

Heymann, C. David. *American Aristocracy: The Lives and Times of James Russell, Amy, and Robert Lowell*. New York: Dodd, Mead, 1980.

Heymann. *Ezra Pound: The Last Rower*. New York: Viking, 1976.

Holliday, Robert Cortes. Memoir in *Joyce Kilmer*, edited by Holliday. New York: Doran, 1918, I:17-101.

Hoopes, James. *Van Wyck Brooks: In Search of American Culture*. Amherst: University of Massachusetts Press, 1977.

Howe, Irving. *Sherwood Anderson*. New York: Sloane, 1951.

Howells, William Dean. *Years of My Youth*. New York & London: Harper, 1916.

Howgate, George W. *George Santayana*. Philadelphia: University of Pennsylvania Press/London: Oxford University Press, 1938.

Jantz, Harold S. *The First Century of New England Verse*. 1943; republished, New York: Russell & Russell, 1962.

Jarrell, Mary, ed. *Randall Jarrell's Letters*. Boston: Houghton Mifflin, 1985.

Karlinsky, Simon, ed. *Nabokov-Wilson Letters, 1940-1971*. New York: Harper & Row, 1979.

Kennedy, Richard S. *Dreams in the Mirror: A Biography of E. E. Cummings*. New York: Liveright, 1980.

Killorin, Joseph, ed. *Selected Letters of Conrad Aiken*. New Haven & London: Yale University Press, 1978.

Kingston, Paul W., and Jonathan R. Cole. *The Wages of Writing*. New York: Columbia University Press, 1986.

Kippax, John R. *Churchyard Literature: A Choice Collection of American Epitaphs, With Remarks on Monumental Inscriptions and the Obsequies of Various Nations*. Chicago: S. C. Griggs, 1877.

Klein, Holger, ed. *The First World War in Fiction: A Collection of Critical Essays* (New York: Harper & Row, 1977).

Kraft, Stephanie. *No Castles on Main Street: American Authors and Their Homes*. Chicago, New York & San Francisco: Rand McNally, 1979.

Layman, Richard. *Shadow Man: The Life of Dashiell Hammett*. New York: Harcourt Brace Jovanovich, 1981.

Le Comte, Edward S., comp. *Dictionary of Last Words*. New York: Philosophical Library, 1955.

Lee, Lawrence, and Barry Gifford. *Saroyan: A Biography*. New York: Harper & Row, 1984.

Leggett, John. *Ross and Tom: Two American Tragedies*. New York: Simon & Schuster, 1974.

Levine, George, and David Leverenz, eds. *Mindful Pleasures: Essays on Thomas Pynchon*. Boston: Little, Brown, 1976.

Lewis, R. W. B. *Edith Wharton: A Biography*. New York, Evanston, San Francisco & London: Harper & Row, 1975.

Leyda Jay. *The Melville Log: A Documentary Life of Herman Melville, 1819-1891*, 2 volumes. New York: Harcourt, Brace, 1951; enlarged, New York: Gordian Press, 1969.

Littlefield, George Emery. *Early Boston Booksellers 1642-1711*. 1900; reprinted, New York: Burt Franklin, 1969.

Littlefield. *The Early Massachusetts Press 1938-1711*. 1907; reprinted, New York: Burt Franklin, 1969.

Lomperis, Timothy J. *"Reading the Wind": The Literature of the Vietnam War, An Interpretive Critique*, with a bibliographic commentary by John Clark Pratt. Durham: Duke University Press, 1987.

Lowell, Robert. "John Ransom's Conversation." *Sewanee Review*, 56 (Summer 1948): 374-377.

Lowell. "Visiting the Tates." *Sewanee Re-*

view, 67 (October-December 1959): 557-559.

MacShane, Frank. *Into Eternity: The Life of James Jones, American Writer*. Boston: Houghton Mifflin, 1985.

MacShane. *The Life of Raymond Chandler*. New York: Dutton, 1976.

Maloff, Saul. "Iowa Writers' Workshop: The Time, the Space, The Quiet." *New York Times Book Review*, 29 November 1981, pp. 13, 40-41.

Marambaud, Pierre. *William Byrd of Westover, 1674-1744*. Charlottesville: University Press of Virginia, 1971.

Marcosson, Isaac F. *David Graham Phillips and His Times*. New York: Dodd, Mead, 1932.

Marion, John Francis. *Famous and Curious Cemeteries*. New York: Crown, 1977.

Margolies, Edward, and David Bakish. *Afro-American Fiction, 1853-1976*. Detroit: Gale Research, 1979.

Mariani, Paul. *William Carlos Williams: A New World Naked*. New York, St. Louis, San Francisco, Toronto, Sydney, London, Mexico & Hamburg: McGraw-Hill, 1981.

Martin, Jay. *Always Merry and Bright: The Life of Henry Miller*. Santa Barbara: Capra, 1978.

Martin. *Nathanael West: The Art of His Life*. New York: Farrar, Straus & Giroux, 1970.

Marvin, Frederic Rowland, comp. *The Last Words (Real and Traditional) of Distinguished Men and Women*. Troy, N.Y.: C. A. Brewster, 1900.

McDowell, Edwin. "Gallery Said to Possess First American Imprint." *New York Times*, 2 November 1985, p. 13.

McMurtrie, Douglas C. *The Book: The Story of Printing & Bookmaking*. New York: Covici Friede, 1937.

Mellow, James R. *Charmed Circle: Gertrude Stein & Company*. New York & Washington: Praeger, 1974.

Mellow. *Nathaniel Hawthorne in His Times*. Boston: Houghton Mifflin, 1980.

Meserole, Harrison T., ed. *Seventeenth-Century American Poetry*. New York: New York University Press, 1968.

Meserve, Walter J. *An Emerging Entertainment: The Drama of the American People to 1828*. Bloomington & London: Indiana University Press, 1977.

Meserve. *An Outline History of American Drama*. Totowa, N.J.: Littlefield, Adams, 1965.

Meyers, Jeffrey. "The Death of Randall Jarrell." *Virginia Quarterly Review*, 58 (Summer 1982): 450-467.

Mills, Hilary. *Mailer: A Biography*. New York: Empire Books, 1982.

Mitchell, Alix. "A Roomful of Writers." *Arts & Sciences Report* (Syracuse University), 1, no. 3 (January 1985): 2-3.

Mitzel, John. *John Horne Burns: An Appreciative Biography*. Dorchester, Mass.: Manifest Destiny Books, 1974.

Moore, Jack B. *Maxwell Bodenheim*. New York: Twayne, 1970.

Morison, Samuel Eliot. *The Intellectual Life of Colonial New England*, revised edition. New York: New York University Press, 1956.

Mott, Frank Luther. *American Journalism: A History of Newspapers in the United States Through 250 Years, 1690 to 1940*. New York: Macmillan, 1941.

Muste, John M. *Say That We Saw Spain Die: Literary Consequences of the Spanish Civil War*. Seattle & London: University of Washington Press, 1966.

Nance, William L. *The Worlds of Truman Capote*. New York: Stein & Day, 1970.

Nicosia, Gerald. *Memory Babe: A Critical Biography of Jack Kerouac*, edited by Fred Jordan. New York: Grove Press, 1983.

Noel, Joseph. *Footloose in Arcadia: A Personal Record of Jack London, George Sterling, Ambrose Bierce*. New York: Carrick & Evans, 1940.

Nolan, William F. *The Black Mask Boys: Masters in the Hard-Boiled School of Detective Fiction*. New York: Morrow, 1985.

Nolan. *The Ray Bradbury Companion: A Life and Career History, Photolog, and Comprehensive Checklist of Writings, With Facsimiles From Ray Bradbury's Un-*

published and Uncollected Work in all Media. Detroit: Gale Research, 1975.

O'Connor, Richard. *Ambrose Bierce: A Biography*. Boston & Toronto: Little, Brown, 1967.

Olsen, Otto H. *Carpetbagger's Crusade: The Life of Albion Winegar Tourgée* (Baltimore: Johns Hopkins University Press, 1965).

Oswald, John Clyde. *Printing in the Americas*. 1937; reprinted, New York: Hacker Art Books, 1968.

Parks, Edd Winfield. *Henry Timrod*. New York: Twayne, 1964.

Plimpton, George, ed. *Writers at Work: The Paris Review Interviews*, 1-5. New York: Viking, 1958-1981.

Pratt, Fletcher. Foreword to *Ralph 124C 41+*, by Hugo Gernsback. New York: Fell, 1950, pp. 19-24.

Princeton in the World War. Princeton: Office of the Secretary, Princeton University, 1932.

Publishers Weekly staff, and the Book Division, R. R. Bowker Company. *Publishers Weekly Yearbook: News, Analyses, & Trends in the Book Industry*. New York & London: Bowker, 1983. *The Book Publishing Annual: Highlights, Analyses & Trends*. New York & London: Bowker, 1984-1985.

Quinn, Arthur Hobson. *Edgar Allan Poe: A Critical Biography*. New York: Appleton-Century, 1941.

Rampersad, Arnold. *The Life of Langston Hughes. Volume I: 1902-1941, I, Too, Sing America*. New York & Oxford: Oxford University Press, 1986.

Richardson, Joan. *Wallace Stevens: The Early Years, 1879-1923*. New York: Morrow, 1986.

Ringe, Donald A. *Charles Brockden Brown*. New York: Twayne, 1966.

Reino, Joseph. *Karl Shapiro*. Boston: Twayne, 1981.

Roache, Joel. *Richard Eberhart: The Progress of an American Poet*. New York: Oxford University Press, 1971.

Rusk, Ralph L. *The Life of Ralph Waldo Emerson*. New York: Scribners, 1949.

Saroyan, Aram. *William Saroyan*. San Diego: Harcourt Brace Jovanovich, 1983.

Saxton, Martha. *Louisa May: A Modern Biography of Louisa May Alcott*. Boston: Houghton Mifflin, 1977.

Scherman, David E., and Rosemarie Redlich. *Literary America: A Chronicle of American Writers from 1607-1952*. New York: Dodd, Mead, 1952.

Schnick, Frank L. *The Paperbound Book in America: The History of Paperbacks and Their European Background*. New York: Bowker, 1958.

Schorer, Mark. *Sinclair Lewis: An American Life*. New York, Toronto & London: McGraw-Hill, 1961.

Schreuders, Piet. *Paperbacks, U.S.A.: A Graphic History, 1939-1959*, translated by Josh Pachter. San Diego: Blue Dolphin Enterprises, 1981.

Seager, Allen. *The Glass House: The Life of Theodore Roethke*. New York: McGraw-Hill, 1968.

Sewall, Richard B. *Emily Dickinson*, 2 volumes. New York: Farrar, Straus & Giroux, 1974.

Sifakis, Carl. *American Eccentrics*. New York: Facts on File, 1984.

Silverman, Kenneth. *The Life and Times of Cotton Mather*. New York, Cambridge, Philadelphia, San Francisco, London, Mexico City, São Paulo & Sydney: Harper & Row, 1984.

Silverman, ed. *Colonial American Poetry*. New York & London: Hafner, 1968.

Simmonds, Roy S. *The Two Worlds of William March*. University: University of Alabama Press, 1984.

Sinclair, Andrew. *Jack: A Biography of Jack London*. New York: Harper & Row, 1977.

Smith, Susan Sutton, ed. *The Complete Poems and Collected Letters of Adelaide Crapsey*. Albany: State University of New York Press, 1977.

Spearman, Walter, with the assistance of Samuel Selden. *The Carolina Playmakers: The First Fifty Years*. Chapel Hill: University of North Carolina Press, 1970.

Spindler, Elizabeth Carroll. *John Peale Bishop: A Biography*. Morgantown:

West Virginia University Library, 1980.

Spoto, Donald. *The Kindness of Strangers: The Life of Tennessee Williams*. Boston: Little, Brown, 1985.

Squires, Radcliffe. *Allen Tate: A Literary Biography*. New York: Pegasus, 1971.

Stallman, R. W. *Stephen Crane: A Biography*. New York: Braziller, 1968.

Steinbrunner, Chris, Otto Penzler, Marvin Lachman, and Charles Shibuk, eds. *Encyclopedia of Mystery and Detection*. New York, St. Louis & San Francisco: McGraw-Hill, 1976.

Steiner, Nancy Hunter. *A Closer Look at Ariel: A Memoir of Sylvia Plath*. New York: Harper's Magazine Press, 1973.

Stevens, Holly. *Souvenirs and Prophecies: The Young Wallace Stevens*. New York: Knopf, 1977.

Stock, Noel. *The Life of Ezra Pound*. New York: Pantheon, 1970.

Stowell, Marion Barber. *Early American Almanacs: The Colonial Weekday Bible*. New York: Burt Franklin, 1977.

Sweezy, Paul M., and Leo Huberman, eds. *F. O. Matthiessen (1902-1950): A Collective Portrait*. New York: Schuman, 1950.

Teichmann, Howard. *Smart Aleck: The Wit, World, and Life of Alexander Woollcott*, New York: Morrow, 1976.

Thomas, Isaiah. *The History of Printing in America, with a Biography of Printers*, 2 volumes, revised and enlarged edition. Albany: Printed by J. Munsell, 1874.

Thompson, Lawrance. *Robert Frost: The Early Years, 1874-1915*. New York, Chicago & San Francisco: Holt, Rinehart & Winston, 1966. *Robert Frost: The Years of Triumph, 1915-1938*. New York, Chicago & San Francisco: Holt, Rinehart & Winston, 1970. Thompson and R. H. Winnick, *Robert Frost: The Later Years*. New York: Holt, Rinehart & Winston, 1976.

Thompson. *Young Longfellow (1807-1843)* New York: Macmillan, 1938.

Toledano, Ben C., Peter Taylor, and George Garrett. *The Fugitives, The Agrarians, And Other Twentieth-Century Southern Writers*. Charlottesville: Alderman Library, University of Virginia, 1985.

Trilling, Diana. "Lionel Trilling: A Jew at Columbia," appendix to Lionel Trilling, *Speaking of Literature and Society*, edited by Diana Trilling. New York & London: Harcourt Brace Jovanovich, 1980, pp. 411-429.

Turner, Arlin. *George W. Cable: A Biography*. Baton Rouge: Louisiana State University Press, 1969.

Tytell, John. *Naked Angels: The Lives & Literature of the Beat Generation*. New York, St. Louis, San Francisco, London, Düsseldorf, Mexico, Toronto & Sydney: McGraw-Hill, 1976.

Unterecker, John. *Voyager: A Life of Hart Crane*. New York: Farrar, Straus & Giroux, 1969.

Van Doren, Carl. *Benjamin Franklin*. New York: Viking, 1938.

Van Doren, Carl. *Three Worlds*. New York & London: Harper, 1936.

Van Doren, Mark. *The Autobiography of Mark Van Doren*. New York: Harcourt, Brace, 1958.

Wagenknecht, Edward. *William Dean Howells: The Friendly Eye*. New York: Oxford University Press, 1969.

Walker, Franklin. *San Francisco's Literary Frontier*. New York: Knopf, 1939.

Wallis, Charles L. *Stories on Stone: A Book of American Epitaphs*. New York: Oxford University Press, 1954.

Walsh, Jeffrey. *American War Literature: 1914 to Vietnam*. London: Macmillan, 1982.

Washington, Ida H. *Dorothy Canfield Fisher: A Biography*. Shelburne, Vt.: New England Press, 1982.

Weales, Gerald. *Clifford Odets, Playwright*. New York: Pegasus, 1971.

White, Ray Lewis, ed. *The Achievement of Sherwood Anderson: Essays in Criticism*. Chapel Hill: University of North Carolina Press, 1966.

Wilburs, Stephen. *The Iowa Writers' Workshop: Origins, Emergence, & Growth*. Iowa City: University of Iowa Press, 1980.

Wilson, Edmund. *A Prelude: Landscapes,*

Characters and Conversations from the Earlier Years of My Life. New York: Farrar, Straus & Giroux, 1967.

Winship, George Parker. *The Cambridge Press 1638-1692*. Philadelphia: University of Pennsylvania Press, 1945.

Winterich, John T. *Early American Books & Printing*. 1935; reprinted, Detroit: Gale Research, 1974.

Wolff, Geoffrey. *Black Sun: The Brief Transit and Violent Eclipse of Harry Crosby*. New York: Random House, 1976.

Woodress, James. *Booth Tarkington: Gentleman from Indiana*. Philadelphia & New York: Lippincott, 1955.

Wylder, Jean. "Flannery O'Connor: A Reminiscence and Some Letters." *North American Review*, 255 (Spring 1970): 58-65.

Young, Thomas Daniel. *Gentleman in a Dustcoat: A Biography of John Crowe Ransom*. Baton Rouge: Louisiana State University Press, 1976.

Index